Encyclopedia
of
Candlestick Charts

Founded in 1807, John Wiley & Sons is the oldest independent publishing company in the United States. With offices in North America, Europe, Australia, and Asia, Wiley is globally committed to developing and marketing print and electronic products and services for our customers' professional and personal knowledge and understanding.

The Wiley Trading series features books by traders who have survived the market's ever-changing temperament and have prospered—some by reinventing systems, others by getting back to basics. Whether a novice trader, professional, or somewhere in-between, these books will provide the advice and strategies needed to prosper today and well into the future.

For a list of available titles, visit our web site at www.WileyFinance.com.

Encyclopedia
of
Candlestick Charts

Thomas N. Bulkowski

WILEY

John Wiley & Sons, Inc.

Published by John Wiley & Sons, Inc., Hoboken, New Jersey
Published simultaneously in Canada.

For general information on our other products and services or for technical support, please contact our Customer Care Department within the United States at (800) 762-2974, outside the United States at (317) 572-3993 or fax (317) 572-4002.

Wiley also publishes its books in a variety of electronic formats. Some content that appears in print may not be available in electronic formats. For more information about Wiley products, visit our web site at www.wiley.com.

Library of Congress Cataloging-in-Publication Data

Bulkowski, Thomas N., 1957–
    Encyclopedia of candlestick charts / Thomas N. Bulkowski.
        p. cm. – (Wiley trading series)
    Includes index.
    ISBN 978-0-470-18201-7 (cloth)
    1. Stocks—Charts, diagrams, etc.   2. Commodity futures—Charts, diagrams, etc.
3. Investment analysis.   I. Title.
    HG4638.B84   2008
    332.63'2042—dc22

                                                                2007040692

Printed in the United States of America.

10 9 8 7 6 5 4 3 2 1

*Twenty years ago, **Susan Blackburn** came to my aid after a car accident. She helped smooth the runway that would be my future. She is a priceless treasure, a dear friend.*

*Six years ago, **Barbara Rockefeller** was the wind beneath my wings, carrying me aloft. An incalculable amount of my publishing success I owe to her.*

These two women are the engines that have kept my airplane moving forward, and to them I dedicate this book.

Contents

Preface

Let me tell you a story. Over a decade ago, I was playing with a stock market program I wrote and decided to see if I could get candlesticks to display. I knew it was possible, because the company that wrote the charting module said so. They just didn't tell me how to do it. I read the manual written by someone for whom English was a second language and then struggled with programming the darn thing for countless hours with no success. I gave up.

Several years later, I tried again. This time I stumbled upon the right combination of elements to get the charting module to work. I drew my first candlestick.

The excitement I felt was not like riding the world's fastest roller coaster but more like learning that the stock you purchased yesterday will be taken over for a 40% premium. I scared my dog with a little cheering, which was followed by a warm fuzzy feeling that pervaded my body.

It took less than an hour for me to fall in love with candles.

I used my charting discovery and incorporated it into another program called Patternz that recognizes all of the candles in this book and provides performance tips. It's available free at my web site: ThePatternSite.com.

In helping a friend analyze the stock market, I would send the candle tips Patternz provides and added my own two cents. "This is a bearish engulfing candle, so that means price is likely to close lower tomorrow," I wrote in an e-mail. The stock turned into a fireworks display as it exploded upward. This happened not just once but practically every time I tried depending on candles to help determine future performance.

The more I used candles, the more I grew to distrust them. They just didn't work as advertised. "Here's a hanging man with overhead resistance set up by a rising window with prior minor highs and lows blocking price movement. That means price will go down in the coming days." The stock became a moon shot.

I had already read half a dozen candle books and pored over Internet sites to develop my Patternz program. The sources I checked couldn't even agree on candlestick configuration. Take an inverted hammer. One Internet site said, "The upper shadow should be *at least* two times the length of the body." Another site said, "The upper shadow is *no more than* two times as long as the body." Is a shooting star a single candle line or two? The answer depends on which source you check. I found a spelling error for one candle pattern duplicated letter for letter on at least two other web sites.

I decided to do my own research to find out how candles worked, and the result is this book. I didn't write this book for the money. I didn't write it to achieve fame or glory. I wrote it because I need this information to trade better. Candlesticks can help you do that, but only if you know what to look for, learn how they work, and understand the trading setups that bring out the best performance. This book covers all that and more.

If you've ever felt frustrated with candlestick performance or just want to learn how they behave, then this book is for you. No other book covers all of the candlesticks and includes statistical performance data for both bull and bear markets in an easy-to-understand format, as this one does.

Whether you're a novice trader or an experienced hedge fund manager, you can profit from this book. For a quick sample, read Chapter 1, "Findings." There I discuss the many discoveries I uncovered along the way. That chapter alone is worth more to your bank account than the cost of this book.

Use this book as a reference work. Don't try to read it from cover to cover. In the writing and publishing process, I'll have to do that several times, so I know what I'm talking about. I've taken liberties to keep the text lively, just in case.

Most candle chapters follow the same format, so once you become accustomed to the layout, everything will become familiar. A "Glossary and Methodology" chapter at the end of the book explains each table entry in detail and defines terms. Back there you'll also find a visual index with little pictures of all the candles to make recognition easier.

Here's a brief snapshot of the good stuff I cover for over 100 candle patterns:

- Identification guidelines describe what to look for.
- General statistics include performance over time and where performance is best in the yearly price range.
- Height statistics explore the performance of tall versus short candles, tall or short shadows, and a measure rule to help set price targets.
- Additional statistics look at volume trend, average volume, and breakout volume.
- The reversal rates table covers three methods of confirmation to detect reversals, the likely breakout direction based on the existing price trend, and where reversals or continuations are most likely to appear in the yearly price range.

- Performance indicators describe which of three entry methods give the best trading signals, how a 50-day moving average can help improve performance, and whether the position of the closing price indicates better performance.
- All statistics cover both bull and bear markets using more than 4.7 million candle lines in the research.

The tested performance of a surprising number of candles is opposite popular belief. Many candlesticks perform little better than randomly. Others are so rare that you may see only one in a lifetime—if you are lucky. But don't take my word for it. Do your own research and form your own conclusions. That's the real way to learn about candlesticks. Or you can save yourself the work and just buy this book.

THOMAS N. BULKOWSKI
June 2007

Acknowledgments

Thanks to:

James Bulkowski for listening to me complain about redoing the first 50 chapters;

Tom Helget for assistance when I struggled with technical issues;

Ronda Palm for encouraging words and unbounded enthusiasm; and

The Wiley workers: Mary Daniello and Pamela van Giessen.

Good eggs, all.

Encyclopedia
of
Candlestick Charts

Introduction

The candlestick trade I'm about to describe made me enough money to pay for three months of living expenses. That's not bad for an hour's work! In a moment, I'll outline the trading setup so you can tailor it to your liking.

On May 16, 2007, I went shopping for a stock to buy and found one in the diversified chemicals aisle of the market. What caught my eye first was a consolidation pattern called a descending triangle. Figure I.1 shows the chart pattern in May. Descending triangles have a flat bottom and a downward-sloping top. They break out downward 64% of the time, but upward breakouts can post spectacular results. I was looking for an upward breakout.

The next pattern I noticed was the Big W. A tall left side (C to A) leads to a reversal pattern, such as the Eve & Eve double bottom AB. Eve bottoms are wide, rounded turns, unlike Adam bottoms, which are narrow, often pointed—a single spike or two wide. Eve can have spikes like that shown at B, but the spikes are shorter and more numerous than what you see on Adam. The Eve & Eve double bottom is one of the more powerful and successful chart patterns. The theory behind a Big W is that the right side will mimic the left and price will climb after that.

The pattern that sealed the deal was the morning doji star candlestick. That candle pattern ended the day that price closed above the top of the descending triangle. My research said that the morning doji star is a highly reliable candle formation. Combined with additional analysis I did on the company, both fundamental and technical, the stock was a buy only if it gapped open higher. Why? Because the next day the company was holding a conference call before the market opened to discuss earnings. A higher open would mean the market liked its story.

The news reports the night before the meeting said that net profit was 53 cents versus 61 cents during the year-ago quarter even as revenue climbed by 30%. Just 1% of the revenue gain was from higher internal sales, though. Most was from acquisitions or currency translation. Analyst estimates ranged from $0.52 to $0.58, so earnings came in at the low end. All of this sounded bearish to me, but the technicals were shouting, "Buy!"

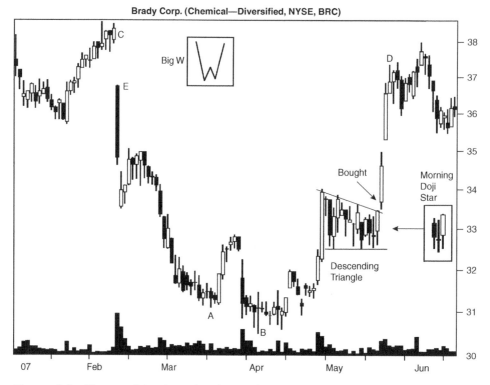

Figure I.1 The combination of a descending triangle, Big W, and morning doji star set up a profitable trade.

My candle research says that opening gap confirmation from a morning doji star results in the best performance. That means trading with the trend as soon as possible.

The next day, I watched the stock open and price took off. In the first minute, it shot from the prior close of 33.46 to 34. That left a tall white candle on the chart. Again, my research and knowledge of candles said that the body of a tall candle is often a support zone. So, I placed a buy order halfway down the body, at 33.78.

Sure enough, price turned down and nailed my buy order, filling most of it before moving up again. I had trouble fitting through the door because the smile on my face was so wide. Five minutes later, the remainder of the order filled.

By day's end, the stock had recovered and closed higher by 1.16. The next day a brokerage firm upgraded the stock and price moved higher still, this time up another 1.93. The following day price coasted upward 33 cents (D).

Exit time. Why? This is one of those situations where you get a feeling that it's time to leave, so I started my analysis. The height of the candle lines was diminishing, suggesting a trend change. The Commodity Channel Index (CCI, with default settings of 20 bars for the lookback and 5 for the DCCI line—dual

CCI, a smoothing of the CCI), an indicator, was rounding over and looked as if the next day would produce a sell signal. In other words, upward price momentum was slowing. I didn't want to hang around and give back my profits.

The falling window from C to E I thought added to overhead resistance, but my research said that happens only 25% of the time. The candle pattern at D also resembled a shooting star, with a tall upper shadow and small body after an upward price trend. This one wasn't perfect, because the body was too tall in relation to the height of the upper shadow. If you have no idea what an upper shadow and a body are, don't worry about it. I'll explain them later.

The day after D, I vowed that if the stock opened lower, I would sell. I thought of selling it all at the open but the futures market suggested a higher open for equities, so I decided to wait and see.

Volume was thin in the stock but it opened lower, just as I expected. I timed the exit as best as I could and got out just before price plummeted. By the day's close, however, the stock had gained it all back and then some. The candle that printed on the chart was a hanging man. Despite their reputation as a reversal, they act as a continuation pattern 59% of the time. That suggested more upside. But it doesn't matter because I don't own the stock anymore.

If you want to replicate this trading setup, look for:

- *Good industry relative strength.* If the stocks in the industry are doing well, then the chances improve that this stock will do well, too.
- *Better than expected earnings.* Only price can tell you how much the market likes the results, so watch the stock after the announcement of earnings. If price gaps upward, buy immediately or wait for a retracement and then buy.
- *A reason to buy the stock from a technical or fundamental perspective.* Even if price does not explode higher at the open, it should do well in the coming weeks based on your analysis.

I used an upward breakout from a descending triangle with a morning doji star inside a Big W pattern. The combination worked well but will be almost impossible to duplicate.

What Are Candlesticks?

Let's talk about candlesticks, starting at the beginning so everyone comes up to speed at the same time. I'll be brief because most people know what candle charts are. Figure I.2 shows two examples of candlesticks. The *line* (a single price bar) on the left is a white candle. This one shows the relative positions of the open, high, low, and close. Notice that the closing price is higher than the

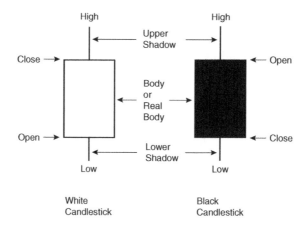

Figure I.2 White and black candlestick lines.

opening price. When that occurs, the body is white. On the right, the candle is black because price closed below the open. The upper shadow is hair growing from the top of the candle, and the lower shadow is a single leg dangling from the bottom of the candle. It may help to think of shadows as wicks.

Candles don't need either an upper or a lower shadow. They don't need a body, either (such as when the open and close are the same). The key concept to remember is that a black candle shows a close *below* the open and a white candle shows a close *above* the open. A black candle does *not* show price closing lower than the previous day, nor does a white candle show a higher close than the day before.

With this candle definition, you can have a stream of white candles in a declining price trend, and black candles forming a rising price trend. I've seen both situations, too.

That's all there is to candle configuration. Multiple candle lines along with variations in shadow and body length make up the many candle patterns.

The Data

I wrote a computer program to recognize all of the candlestick patterns in this book. With nearly five million candle lines to explore for *each* of over 100 candle patterns, doing it manually was not an option.

I created what I call the *standard database*, a collection of data that doesn't change in size. It contains the 500 stocks of the S&P 500 index for 10 years covering both bull and bear markets. From the standard database I derive the frequency rank and prorate the number of times a particular candlestick pattern is found to determine whether it appears more often in bull or bear markets. Details of the database are in the "Glossary and Methodology" section at the back of the book.

If I find too few candles in the standard database, then I use up to three more databases, one containing archived stocks I no longer follow, one that is a five-year/500-stock database, and one that is the current database I use for trading. Together they comprise almost five million candle lines (price bars). I removed any duplicated candles between databases, and all four contain split-adjusted, clean data.

The Price Trend

Many candles have a defined price trend that leads to the start of the candle pattern. For example, a hanging man appears in an upward price trend, and a hammer appears in a downtrend.

How do you determine the trend? I use a 10-day exponential moving average as a starting point and season it with special rules to allow price trends of a day or two to override the result. The method is a bit complicated but it works well. It is, however, not perfect, but the large sample size I use helps compensate.

Candle Performance

How do you measure candle performance? Since candlestick patterns often lead to short-term moves, I used the closest minor high or low (swing high or swing low), depending on the breakout direction, to gauge performance. The straight-line move often isn't a long one, but it serves as a good proxy of what you can expect. The statistics in this book should be used to compare results from candle to candle, not as benchmarks of how well you will do trading candles.

Candles Post Breakout

How do you determine if a candle acts as a reversal or a continuation pattern? I tested three methods and checked the results visually using hundreds of candles. I chose the best method. Two were variations of an exponential moving average (the price trend) compared to the closing price over time. They were not as accurate or as simple as just looking for the breakout to determine reversal or continuation, success or failure.

An upward breakout occurs when price closes above the top (highest high) of the candle. A downward breakout occurs when price closes below the bottom (lowest low) of the candle. Marry the breakout direction with the price trend leading to the candle and you get either a reversal or a continuation of the prior trend. This is the same method I used with chart patterns. It's simple, it's repeatable, and it's a method everyone can agree with just by looking at the price trend surrounding a candle.

But there's a problem. Take a dragonfly doji as an example. The candle looks like the letter T with the close at the top of the candle. You would expect price to break out upward sooner than downward just because of where price closes in the candle.

First, the big surprise with such candlesticks is that price does *not* break out upward the next day. In one test I ran on 20,000 dragonfly doji patterns, it took an average of *four* days to break out upward in a bull market. Downward breakouts in a bear market took exactly the same time, four days, to make the journey. Yes, the position of the closing price *does* influence whether a candle acts as a reversal or a continuation, but not to the extent many believe.

Second, if a candle is supposed to act as a reversal, then price should reverse direction, regardless of where it closes in the candle. That's almost by definition. If you placed a stop-loss order a penny below a candle in a downtrend that failed to reverse, you'd be stopped out. So price should reverse quickly or it's useless as a reversal indicator.

To be fair, I'm not that stringent. I wait for price to *close* either above the top or below the bottom of the candle before I determine whether it's a reversal or a continuation. A hanging man, for example, takes an average of three days to prove it's a reversal.

Finally, I checked the statistical results, visually, with the candles themselves and found that the method agrees with how I would categorize each candlestick pattern. In other words, if the statistics said the candle acted as a reversal, then it did. If the stats said the candle acted as a continuation, then it did. I used my eyes and counted the results, then compared the results to the stats. Both agree.

Why am I making such a big deal about this? Because 31% of the candles in this book fail. That is, they don't work as advertised, and many work little better than random chance. There are exceptions, of course, and those are the candles you should rely on. That's why I wrote this book—to find those gems hidden on the floor of the exchange.

Results of Others

Other candlestick researchers may find different results than the ones presented here. Many factors can contribute to this, including pattern recognition methodology, data used for testing, time period studied, and rules for measuring performance.

I am reminded of the tests researchers do on drugs. Does aspirin reduce the occurrence of heart attacks? Out of 50 studies, for example, some will conclude that it does, some will say it doesn't, and some may decide that it works only for women. However, the preponderance of results one way or the other will tilt the scale to a conclusion. I offer the information in this book as just one more test to add to the pile. Your results may vary.

Don't Write This Book

I read a book that used nearly six pages to justify why writing an encyclopedia like this one is a bad idea. The primary argument was that candles don't work alone but in groups. That sounds wonderful, but my response is this: Imagine five blind men. You ask each blind man how to get to the nearest grocery store in a neighborhood that he's never visited. "I don't know," come the replies, one after another. Then you put the five men together in an empty room and—eureka!—do they magically discover how to get to the grocery store? I don't think so. If candles don't work alone, then it's unlikely they'll work together.

Now, imagine one of the men can see. The sighted man, working alone, looks out a window and sees the grocery store down the road. Put him together with the others and they can hatch a plan to get there. In other words, finding a candlestick that works alone might help the performance of other candlesticks, too. After all, many candles become part of other, more complicated, candle patterns.

Suppose that you start not with 5 men but with 103, the same number as candlestick patterns in this book. You don't know how many can see, but you assume there are some. So you test each one, and when you're done, you separate the blind folks from those who need reading glasses from those with perfect vision. Some might suffer from night blindness, so the quirks of each are important and you make note of them.

Wouldn't you like to avoid spending time learning about reversal candles that fail to reverse more often than not? Wouldn't you like to avoid candles that perform randomly or near randomly and concentrate on proven winners?

That's what this candlestick encyclopedia is all about. It's about finding the candles that can make you money whether you rely on them standing alone or in combinations with other candles. It's about making money. And if you choose not to buy this book and learn the secrets it reveals, that's okay. I'll be the one using a transporter to beam up a pound of $50 bills, and you'll be the one gripping an empty wallet or purse, wondering where your money went.

Knowledge is power. Knowledge is money.

1

Findings

Arguably, you are reading the most important chapter because it discusses the discoveries I made about candles while researching this book. You may already know some of them, but the others are new. I'll refer to many of them in later chapters.

A Number of Candles Do Not Work as Expected

This is the big surprise for candle lovers. A candle that functions as a reversal of an upward trend should cause price to drop. Thus, a close above the top of the preceding candle would be a failure because price climbed instead of fell, whereas a close below the previous low would be a success. Similarly, a continuation candle should have price break out in the same direction as it entered. If price rose into the candle, for example, it should break out upward; a downward breakout would be a failure. How many of the 103 candles I looked at passed or failed according to this method?

> Passed: 69%
> Failed: 31%

If you listen closely, you may hear the half-glass-full people screaming. Yes, 69% of the candles worked, so let's discuss additional tests. If I say that a success rate of less than 60% is considered just random, then how many candles worked at least 60% of the time? There are 412 different combinations of 103 candles that acted as reversals or continuations in bull and bear markets. Of the 412, only 100 candles qualified, so the answer is 24%.

If I filter the group by using a frequency rank of 51 or better, then just 10% qualify. The 51 rank is about midway in the list of 103 candles. As a reference, the candle with rank 51 appeared 1,973 times out of 1,204,083 candle lines in 500 stocks over 10 years, including bull and bear markets. In other words, just 10% of candles work at least 60% of the time and occur frequently enough to be found.

If I raise the bar to a 66% success rate (meaning the candle should work as expected in two of three trades) and keep the frequency rank the same, then only 6% qualify. That means just 6% of the candles I consider to be investment grade.

Please remember that this applies only to stocks and not futures, exchange-traded funds, or other security types, so the results could change dramatically.

The following lists the investment grade candles:

Above the stomach

Belt hold, bearish and bullish

Deliberation

Doji star, bearish

Engulfing, bearish

Last engulfing bottom and top

Three outside up and down

Two black gapping candles

Rising and falling windows

These are the candle patterns in which price reverses or continues in the anticipated direction frequently, but it does not indicate how far price trends after that. For a more detailed description of performance over time, see Chapter 2, Statistics Summary.

An Unusually Tall Candle Often Has a Minor High or Minor Low Occurring within One Day of It

I looked at tens of thousands of candles to prove this, and the study details are on my web site, ThePatternSite.com.

Figure 1.1 shows examples of unusually tall candles highlighted by up arrows. A minor high or low occurs within a day of each of them (before or after) except for A and B. Out of 11 signals in this figure, the method got 9 of them right, a success rate of 82% (which is unusually good).

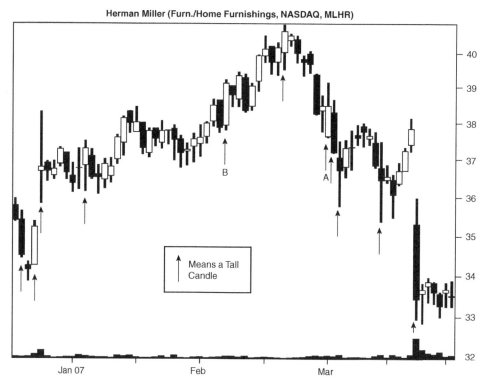

Herman Miller (Furn./Home Furnishings, NASDAQ, MLHR)

Figure 1.1   The up arrows highlight candles taller than average. A minor high or minor low occurs within plus or minus one day of most of the tall candles.

Follow these steps to use the results.

1. The tall candle must be above the highs of two and three days ago (for uptrends) or below the lows of two and three days ago (for down-trends).
2. Find the average high-low height of the prior 22 trading days (a calendar month), not including the current candle.
3. Multiply the average height by 146%. If the current candle height is above the result, then you have an unusually tall candle.

Expect a peak within a day from unusually tall candles 67% of the time during an uptrend and a valley within a day 72% of the time in a downtrend. Additional peaks or valleys can occur after that, so the minor high or low need not be wide or lasting. However, if you have a desire to buy a stock after a tall candle, consider waiting. The chances are that price will reverse and you should be able to buy at a better price.

The Best Performance Comes from Candles with Breakouts within a Third of the Yearly Low

This is true regardless of bull or bear markets, up or down breakouts. The percentages of chart patterns with breakouts within a third of the designated range that showed the best performance are:

Highest third: 5%
Middle third: 11%
Lowest third: 84%

I discovered another trend during chart pattern research that is similar. Here is where breakouts from the best-performing chart patterns with upward breakouts reside in the yearly price range:

Highest third: 27%
Middle third: 32%
Lowest third: 41%

For downward breakouts from chart patterns, the performance list is:

Highest third: 20%
Middle third: 25%
Lowest third: 55%

The results confirm that you should not short stocks making new highs but, rather, concentrate on those making new lows.

Gaps Don't Work Well as Support or Resistance Zones

Read the chapters on windows (both rising and falling) if you don't believe me. I looked for minor highs or minor lows in a price gap and found that most often price just shoots through the gap without stopping. Here are the results:

Gaps in an uptrend (rising window): Price finds overhead resistance within the gap only 20% of the time in a bull market and 16% of the time in a bear market.

Gaps in a downtrend (falling window): Price finds underlying support within the gap only 25% of the time in a bull market and 33% of the time in a bear market.

Reversals Occur Most Often Near Price Extremes

I split the yearly price range into thirds and then mapped those patterns with reversals onto the yearly price range (based on the breakout price). I found that those within a third of the yearly high acted as reversals most often, followed closely by those within a third of the yearly low. Here are the results:

Highest third: 45%
Middle third: 12%
Lowest third: 43%

I would like to say that if you see a candle that usually acts as a reversal in the middle of the yearly price range you should ignore it—chances are price will not reverse, and if it does it probably won't be a lasting move. However, I'm not sure that's correct.

For continuations, here is where they appear most often, based on the location of the breakout price:

Highest third: 42%
Middle third: 10%
Lowest third: 48%

For reference, this is where all candle types (whether signaling a reversal, a continuation, or indecision) appear within the yearly price range. Some candles are neither a reversal nor a continuation, like a high wave, spinning top, or doji.

Highest third: 63%
Middle third: 9%
Lowest third: 28%

Opening Gap Confirmation Gives the Best Entry Signal

I tested three confirmation methods: closing price, candle color, and opening gap. See Glossary and Methodology, Table 6, for definitions of the three methods. Here is how often each confirmation method worked:

Closing price confirmation: 5%
Candle color confirmation: 13%
Opening gap confirmation: 82%

Candles with Breakouts below the 50-Day Moving Average Give the Best Performance

I tore apart my computer software at least three times checking to see if I had made a mistake on this one. I found that when the breakout from a candle is below the 50-trading-day moving average, performance is better than if the breakout is above the moving average. Here is how often each resulted in better performance:

> Above the moving average: 14%
>
> Below the moving average: 86%

Candles with Long Bodies Sometimes Show Support or Resistance

I looked at candle bodies (i.e., between the open and close, not the high-low price range) that were twice as tall as the one-month (22 trading days) average for the three years ending May 28, 2007, in 453 stocks. I found that minor highs or lows stop (i.e., show evidence of support or resistance) somewhere within the 41,301 tall candles 39% of the time. Candle color didn't show any performance difference (both show support or resistance 39% of the time).

Then I split the candle height into 10% divisions, did a frequency distribution of the results, and found that minor highs and minor lows stopped evenly across the candle. In other words, *the middle of a tall candle showed no greater likelihood of exhibiting support or resistance than anywhere else in a tall candle.*

A second study increased the candle height to four times the average and lengthened the time studied to 15 years. Few stocks actually covered the entire range. I found 25,285 tall candles that showed support or resistance 66% of the time. White candles showed support or resistance 65% of the time and black candles showed support or resistance 67% of the time. The results were evenly distributed across the entire candle height, meaning the middle of the candle was *not* shown to have price stop there more often than any other part of the candle.

Let me also say that the taller a candle becomes, the higher the number of minor highs and lows that will appear within its body. That's why the hit rate increases from 39% to 66% for very tall candles. Imagine that a candle covers the entire price range, from yearly low to yearly high. It would include every minor low or high and consequently show a 100% success rate. Thus, I'm not sure that a tall candle is any more effective at showing support or resistance than any other candle.

Having said that, I have used tall candle support or resistance in my trading. For example, the trade I mentioned in the Introduction used a

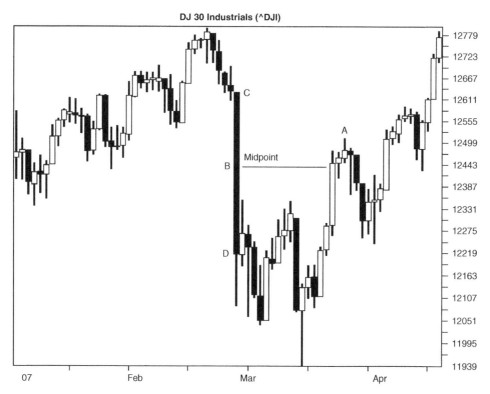

Figure 1.2 Price finds overhead resistance midway up a tall black candle.

tall-bodied candle at the open. I cut the body price range in half and used it as a buy price. The stock dropped to the midpoint and most of the order filled before price climbed again.

As an example, look at Figure 1.2. I received a call from a broker when the Dow Jones Industrial Average plummeted 416 points in one session. I told him that on the way back up, the index would likely pause midway up the tall black candle. Point B shows the midpoint of body CD. Point A is where price paused. It's not exactly at the midpoint, but it's close. Since I made that prediction, I've completed the analysis of tall candles, and it indicates that my prediction (of price stopping midway along the candle) was just a lucky guess.

Tall Candles Outperform Short Ones

This is the single best predictor of performance for both candles and chart patterns. It's worth the time to select candles taller than the median height. What is the median height? You'll have to refer to the individual chapter for the actual percentage because it varies slightly from candle to candle. I found it by taking the height of all of the candles of a particular type, dividing by the breakout price, and then finding the median. Candles with height/breakout price percentages greater than the median are tall candles. Here is how often tall or short candles performed better:

> Tall: 96%
> Short: 4%

Candles with Tall Shadows Get Better Performance

Candles with taller upper or lower shadows tend to perform better than do those with short shadows, regardless of the breakout direction or market condition (bull or bear). The following lists how often this worked:

> Tall upper shadows: 87%
> Short upper shadows: 13%
> Tall lower shadows: 88%
> Short lower shadows: 12%

Trade Bullish Candles in a Rising Primary Trend

If a reversal candle requires that the price trend leading to it is downward, then look for a downward retracement within an upward trend. Figure 1.3 shows an example of a morning doji star when the secondary trend is downward for a few days leading to the start of the candle formation. However, the underlying primary trend is upward.

After an upward breakout, the new trend joins the existing current and off it goes. You are much more likely to make a profit if the breakout joins the existing upward price trend than if the primary trend is downward and you expect a reversal to create a lasting trend change. That scenario *does* happen, but it's rare. This scenario is what I call the rise-retrace setup. Price retraces downward a portion of the prior up move before continuing the climb.

If price closes below the lowest low in the candle pattern, then close out a long trade. That situation represents a downward breakout and price is apt to continue moving lower.

Trade Bearish Candles in a Falling Primary Trend

This is the opposite situation of the prior tip. In this case, the best method to trade a bearish candle is when price is already tumbling. Price retraces a

Figure 1.3 A morning doji star appears in a downward price trend (secondary) when the primary trend is upward.

portion of the down move and then the bearish reversal candle appears. Once price breaks out downward, then it's off to the races.

What you don't want to do is depend on a bearish reversal candle in a primary uptrend to act as a trend reversal. It might, but the odds of a lasting decline are slim. Should price break out upward (i.e., it closes above the highest high in the preceding candle pattern), then close out your short position.

Avoid going long when the primary trend is downward. In that situation, you are trying to swim against the current; it's possible to do well, but it's unlikely. Upward breakouts tend to be short-lived in this scenario. If the primary trend is downward, then either remain in cash or go short. If you do find yourself in this situation, then exit a long trade if price closes below the lowest low in the preceding candle formation (a downward breakout).

Figure 1.4 shows this situation. Both the primary and secondary trends are downward when the morning doji star appears. Price reverses the trend but surfaces at A before being swept away by the downward-rushing current. If you traded this candle *perfectly* you would have made a dollar a share.

Abaxis Inc. (Medical Supplies, NASDAQ, ABAX)

Morning Doji Star

Secondary Trend

A

Primary Trend

Figure 1.4 Both the primary and secondary trends are downward, leading to a short reversal.

Candle Volume Is a Poor Predictor of Performance Except for Breakout Volume

I've never been a big fan of volume. I looked at volume four ways: the volume trend leading to the candle, the trend during the candle, the average during the candle, and breakout volume. I threw out the volume trend leading to the start of the candle because it didn't work well and made no sense anyway. What remained explores the relationship of volume inside the candle and during the breakout.

How often did candles perform better with a rising or falling volume trend?

Rising: 48%

Falling: 52%

How often did candles perform better if they had above- or below-average volume?

Above-average: 58%

Average or below-average: 42%

How often did heavy or light breakout volume lead to better performance?

Heavy breakout volume: 91%
Light breakout volume: 9%

Reversals Perform Better than Continuations

This is counterintuitive. You would expect price that resume trending after a candle pattern to perform better than those candles that reverse the trend. But what if the existing trend is getting old and feeling tired, whereas a reversal is young, vibrant, and ready to start a new day? The following shows how often reversals or continuations led to better performance:

Reversals: 59%
Continuations: 41%

Most Candlestick Patterns Perform Better in a Bear Market, Regardless of the Breakout Direction

I can understand good performance of candles with downward breakouts in a bear market. They are going with the flow, riding a downward current in a falling market. But what about upward breakouts? Upward breakouts in a bear market often perform better than do those in a bull market! The only explanation I can think of is that the sample counts are fewer for bear markets (because of a shorter measurement period) and that has led to bogus results. That would make sense in a few isolated cases, but not all the time. Here is how often candles in different market conditions perform better:

Bear market: 96%
Bull market: 4%

Price Has to Have Something to Reverse

If the move leading to a candle is short, then don't expect a large move after the breakout. In other words, reversals work only if there is a *trend* to reverse. Price won't move far if it's mired in a congestion zone.

More Candles Appear within a Third of the Yearly High than Elsewhere in the Yearly Trading Range

You will find candles sprinkled throughout the yearly price range, but more will appear with breakouts within a third of the yearly high than in the other two thirds. Here is where the candle breakout resides in the yearly price range:

Highest third: 63%
Middle third: 9%
Lowest third: 28%

Where Price Closes in the Last Candle Line of the Pattern Helps Determine Performance

I split the candle line into thirds (except for candles like a gravestone doji where the close is expected to be pegged at one end) and looked at performance. Here is where the closing price resides for the best performance:

Highest third: 28%
Middle third: 32%
Lowest third: 40%

2

Statistics Summary

The following pages show the top-performing candles. Candles with fewer than about 100 samples out of the 4.7 million studied mean you may never see them in the stock market. However, they may appear more often in other security types. Ties were not allowed. If a tie occurred, then I looked at the prior measurement period to break the tie. For example, both the bearish abandoned baby and downside Tasuki gap showed price climbing by 4.16% after 10 days in a bull market. To break the tie, I used the 5-day bull market/upward breakout measure (the abandoned baby won).

Overall Rank

The following list shows candle patterns ranked by performance in bull and bear markets over one, three, five, and ten days after the candle ends. I summed the performance results (after multiplying downward breakout results by −1) and sorted them. The number after the candle is the performance sum.

The theory behind the list is that the best-performing candle patterns will post good numbers in bull and bear markets and over time.

1. Three-line strike, bearish: 67.38%
2. Three-line strike, bullish: 65.23%
3. Three black crows: 59.83%
4. Evening star: 55.85%
5. Upside Tasuki gap: 54.44%
6. Hammer, inverted: 51.73%

7. Matching low: 50.00%
8. Abandoned baby, bullish: 49.73%
9. Two black gapping candles: 49.64%
10. Breakaway, bearish: 49.24%
11. Morning star: 49.05%
12. Piercing: 48.37%
13. Stick sandwich: 48.20%
14. Thrusting: 48.10%
15. Meeting lines, bearish: 48.07%

The three-line strike patterns and the bearish breakaway had fewer than about 100 samples.

A falling window is a gap, and we are really measuring the price performance surrounding the gap, not the gap itself. If included in the list, a falling window would rank seventh, at 50.44%.

Reversals: Bull Market

The top 15 best candles acting as reversals in bull markets are (based on how often price reverses, shown as a percentage):

1. Three stars in the South: 86%
2. Three-line strike, bearish: 84%
3. Three white soldiers: 82%
4. Identical three crows: 79%
5. Engulfing, bearish: 79%
6. Morning star: 78%
7. Three black crows: 78%
8. Morning doji star: 76%
9. Three outside up: 75%
10. Evening star: 72%
11. Belt hold, bullish: 71%
12. Evening doji star: 71%
13. Abandoned baby, bullish: 70%
14. Abandoned baby, bearish: 69%
15. Three outside down: 69%

The first two patterns had fewer than about 100 samples.

Continuations: Bull Market

The top 15 best candles acting as continuations in bull markets are (based on how often price continues, shown as a percentage):

1. Mat hold: 78%
2. Deliberation: 77%
3. Concealing baby swallow: 75%
4. Rising three methods: 74%
5. Separating lines, bullish: 72%
6. Falling three methods: 71%
7. Doji star, bearish: 69%
8. Last engulfing top: 68%
9. Two black gapping candles: 68%
10. Side-by-side white lines, bullish: 66%
11. Hammer, inverted: 65%
12. Last engulfing bottom: 65%
13. Advance block: 64%
14. Doji star, bullish: 64%
15. Separating lines, bearish: 63%

The mat hold, concealing baby swallow, and rising and falling three methods patterns had fewer than about 100 samples.

I do not consider the rising and falling window patterns in the list because they are gaps and the percentages associated with the candle patterns do not measure the gaps, but rather the performance of the candle lines on either side of the gaps. If you include them in the list, the rising window would rank fourth, at 75%, and the falling window would rank 11th, at 67%.

Reversals: Bear Market

The top 15 best candles acting as reversals in bear markets are (based on how often price reverses, shown as a percentage):

1. Three stars in the South: 100%
2. Breakaway, bearish: 89%
3. Three white soldiers: 84%
4. Three-line strike, bullish: 83%
5. Engulfing, bearish: 82%

6. Three black crows: 79%
7. Three-line strike, bearish: 77%
8. Three outside up: 74%
9. Upside gap three methods: 72%
10. Identical three crows: 72%
11. Evening star: 72%
12. Breakaway, bullish: 71%
13. Morning doji star: 71%
14. Belt hold, bullish: 71%
15. Evening doji star: 71%

The three stars in the South, the breakaway (both bearish and bullish), and the three-line strike (both bullish and bearish) patterns had fewer than about 100 samples.

Continuations: Bear Market

The top 15 best candles acting as continuations in bear markets are (based on how often price continues, shown as a percentage):

1. Kicking, bearish: 80%
2. Rising three methods: 79%
3. Separating lines, bearish: 76%
4. Deliberation: 75%
5. 13 new price lines: 74%
6. Doji star, bullish: 70%
7. Two black gapping candles: 69%
8. Separating lines, bullish: 69%
9. Doji star, bearish: 67%
10. Last engulfing bottom: 67%
11. Hammer, inverted: 67%
12. Last engulfing top: 67%
13. Mat hold: 67%
14. Falling three methods: 67%
15. In neck: 65%

The bearish kicking, three methods (both rising and falling), 13 new price lines, and mat hold patterns had fewer than about 100 samples.

I do not consider the falling and rising window patterns in the list because they are gaps, and the percentages associated with the candle patterns do not measure the gaps but, rather, the performance of the candle lines on either side of the gaps. If you include them in the list, the falling window would rank sixth, at 73%, and the rising window would rank seventh, at 72%.

Performance after 10 Days: Bull Market/Up Breakouts

The top 15 candles sorted by average rise in a bull market 10 days after the candle ended are:

1. Doji star, collapsing: 7.32%
2. Three black crows: 6.95%
3. Breakaway, bearish: 6.66%
4. Concealing baby swallow: 5.92%
5. Identical three crows: 5.67%
6. Evening star: 5.37%
7. Long day, black: 5.11%
8. Doji star, bullish: 5.10%
9. Hammer, inverted: 5.03%
10. Separating lines, bearish: 4.93%
11. Upside gap three methods: 4.92%
12. Three outside down: 4.84%
13. Two black gapping candles: 4.83%
14. Evening doji star: 4.79%
15. Stick sandwich: 4.69%

The collapsing doji star, bearish breakaway, and concealing baby swallow patterns had fewer than about 100 samples.

A falling window is a gap, and we are really measuring the price performance surrounding the gap, not the gap itself. If included in the list, a falling window would rank fourth, at 5.93%.

Performance after 10 Days: Bear Market/Up Breakouts

The top 15 candles sorted by average rise in a bear market 10 days after the candle ended are:

1. Three-line strike, bullish: 16.91%
2. Three black crows: 13.31%

3. Identical three crows: 10.03%
4. Evening star: 8.77%
5. Separating lines, bearish: 8.36%
6. On neck: 8.32%
7. Side-by-side white lines, bearish: 7.86%
8. Hammer, inverted: 7.74%
9. Three-line strike, bearish: 7.53%
10. Stick sandwich: 7.43%
11. Meeting lines, bearish: 7.16%
12. Matching low: 7.15%
13. Ladder bottom: 6.76%
14. Two black gapping candles: 6.45%
15. In neck: 6.34%

The bullish three-line strike had fewer than about 100 samples.

A falling window is a gap, and we are really measuring the price performance surrounding the gap, not the gap itself. If included in the list, a falling window would rank eighth, at 7.84%.

Performance after 10 Days: Bull Market/Down Breakouts

The top 15 candles sorted by average decline in a bull market 10 days after the candle ended are:

1. Three-line strike, bearish: 8.81%
2. Mat hold: 7.21%
3. Concealing baby swallow: 7.10%
4. Three white soldiers: 6.41%
5. Abandoned baby, bullish: 6.04%
6. Deliberation: 5.24%
7. Rising three methods: 5.10%
8. Downside gap three methods: 4.97%
9. Breakaway, bearish: 4.71%
10. Three outside up: 4.50%
11. Morning star: 4.23%
12. Three-line strike, bullish: 4.23%

13. Doji star, bearish: 4.09%
14. Separating lines, bullish: 3.95%
15. Long day, white: 3.91%

The three-line strike (both bearish and bullish), mat hold, concealing baby swallow, and bearish breakaway had fewer than about 100 samples.

A rising window is a gap, and we are really measuring the price performance surrounding the gap, not the gap itself. If included in the list, a rising window would rank 11th, at 4.49%.

Performance after 10 Days: Bear Market/Down Breakouts

The top 15 candles sorted by average decline in a bear market 10 days after the candle ended are:

1. Abandoned baby, bullish: 10.31%
2. Upside Tasuki gap: 9.20%
3. Morning star: 8.53%
4. Separating lines, bullish: 8.05%
5. Three white soldiers: 7.66%
6. Three outside up: 7.14%
7. Ladder bottom: 7.07%
8. Three inside up: 7.00%
9. Mat hold: 6.89%
10. Three-line strike, bearish: 6.82%
11. Deliberation: 6.72%
12. Piercing: 6.57%
13. Engulfing, bullish: 6.31%
14. Morning doji star: 6.25%
15. Long day, white: 6.21%

The mat hold and bearish three-line strike patterns had fewer than about 100 samples.

A rising window is a gap, and we are really measuring the price performance surrounding the gap, not the gap itself. If included in the list, a rising window would rank fifth, at 7.74%.

3

8 New Price Lines

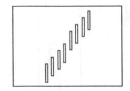

Behavior and Rank

Theoretical: Bearish reversal.

Actual bull market: Bullish continuation 53% of the time (ranking 37).

Actual bear market: Bearish reversal 50% of the time (ranking 44).

Frequency: 52nd out of 103.

Overall performance over time: 90th out of 103.

When you consider that price has to make eight consecutively higher highs, you would think that this candle pattern would be rare. It's not. More accurately, it's not as rare as many other candle patterns.

The pattern demonstrates rampant bullish enthusiasm as price climbs to a new high each day. Most, but not all, of the candles in the pattern will be white, reinforcing the bullish buying spree powering the stock higher. As all good things must come to an end, so it is with this candle pattern. But if you think the uptrend will end after eight new highs, you are in for a surprise. That magic number works 48% of the time. In the remainder of the cases, price continues upward.

The performance rank is in the lower reaches of the list—90 out of 103, where 1 is best. The good news is that you will see this candle pattern fairly often because it has a frequency rank of 52 out of 103 (with 1 being most common).

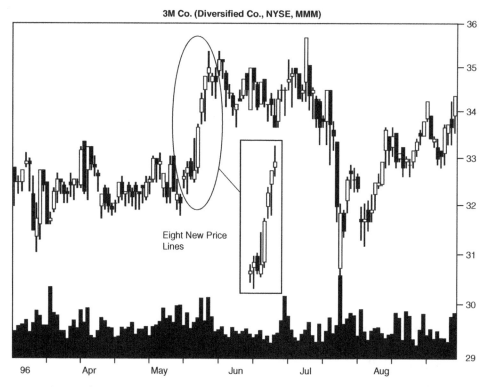

3M Co. (Diversified Co., NYSE, MMM)

Eight New Price Lines

Figure 3.1 Eight consecutive higher highs accurately signal that the trend will change from up to down.

Identification Guidelines

Figure 3.1 shows a good example of the eight new price lines candle pattern. In this example, the price trend begins in a congestion zone where the stock has been range-bound since March. Then price gaps up, leaving a mixture of black and white candles near the start before blazing upward in a stream of white candles. The pattern reminds me of the model rockets I used to launch as a kid. Price takes off in a cloud of smoke and flame and then detonates after candle eight.

Table 3.1 lists identification guidelines for the eight new price lines candlestick formation. Look for a series of eight consecutively higher highs (each

Table 3.1
Identification Guidelines

Characteristic	Discussion
Number of candle lines	Eight.
Configuration	Each day should make a higher high, but the candles can be black or white.

Table 3.2
General Statistics

Description	Bull Market, Up Breakout	Bear Market, Up Breakout	Bull Market, Down Breakout	Bear Market, Down Breakout
Number found	1,881	333	1,671	339
Reversal (R), continuation (C) performance	5.88% C	5.92% C	−6.33% R	−8.29% R
Standard & Poor's 500 change	0.98%	0.26%	−0.80%	−2.17%
Candle end to breakout (median, days)	3	2	3	3
Candle end to trend end (median, days)	6	6	8	8
Number of breakouts near the 12-month low (L), middle (M), or high (H)	L 113, M 326, H 1,280	L 39, M 84, H 208	L 354, M 454, H 726	L 106, M 124, H 105
Percentage move for each 12-month period	L 7.94%, M 5.25%, H 5.94%	L 10.35%, M 5.33%, H 5.63%	L −6.79%, M −5.89%, H −6.48%	L −11.22%, M −6.81%, H −7.61%
Candle end + 1 day	0.82%	1.18%	−1.25%	−1.50%
Candle end + 3 days	1.28%	1.48%	−2.12%	−2.81%
Candle end + 5 days	1.56%	1.58%	−2.53%	−3.24%
Candle end + 10 days	2.14%	1.32%	−2.01%	−3.41%
10-day performance rank	77	88	64	62

shadow is above the prior one). I did not allow any exceptions (a lower high in the series, for example) when I searched for candles that qualified.

Statistics

Table 3.2 shows general statistics. Waiting for price to close below the low of the candle pattern is unrealistic as a breakout signal. Instead, I used a close either above the pattern's high (upward breakout) or below the low of the pattern's last candle line to signal a downward breakout.

Also, I disallowed any pattern forming inside another one. For example, if 10 new highs appeared, I allowed only one eight new price lines pattern to be logged instead of three (three sets of eight new price lines, each separated at the start by a day).

Number found. As the table shows, this pattern occurs frequently. In fact, I found 4,224 of them, the majority of them coming from a bull market.

Reversal or continuation performance. If you tally the reversals and continuations, you find that price lines act as continuations slightly more often than reversals. However, reversals perform better than continuations do.

Upward breakout numbers are nearly the same. This pattern performs best after a downward breakout in a bear market—price drops more than 8%.

S&P performance. I measured performance by the change in the index from the day the candle breaks out to the swing high or low date (depending on the breakout direction). Between those dates, the index can move in any direction, as the numbers show.

Candle end to breakout. Regardless of the market conditions and breakout direction, it takes price an average of two to three days to close either above the highest high or below the last candle line's low. This suggests you have time to assess the situation before making any trading decisions.

Candle end to trend end. The median time to the trend end is between six and eight days. Downward breakouts take a bit longer. This makes sense when you consider that the price current is upward, so trying to swim against the current would take longer.

Yearly position, performance. Most of the 8 new price lines formations appear within a third of the yearly high. The lone exception is bear market/down breakouts. Those are slightly more numerous in the middle of the yearly price range. However, the best performance comes from those near the yearly low.

Performance over time. Eight new price lines formations are not as robust as one would hope. In two cases (bear market/up breakouts and bull market/down breakouts), price falters during days 5 to 10. The percentage moves over time are not exciting, either. A good move would be triple the results shown in the table.

Based on the sum of the performance over the four measurement periods (one, three, five, and ten trading days) when compared to other candles, the table shows the performance rank. The candle performs best after downward breakouts but it's still dismal.

Table 3.3 shows height statistics.

Candle height. Tall patterns perform substantially better than do short ones. To use this, measure the height of the price lines pattern from highest high to lowest low price and divide by the breakout price. For upward breakouts, the breakout price is the highest high in the candle pattern. For downward breakouts, use the last candle line's low in the pattern as the breakout price. Then compare the result with the median in Table 3.3. Tall price lines will have a value higher than the median.

For example, suppose Stan sees eight new price lines with a high of 76 and a low of 65. Is the pattern short or tall in a bull market with an upward breakout? The height is 76 − 65, or 11, so the measure would be 11/76, or 14.4%. That's a tall candle.

Table 3.3
Height Statistics

Description	Bull Market, Up Breakout	Bear Market, Up Breakout	Bull Market, Down Breakout	Bear Market, Down Breakout
Median candle height as a percentage of breakout price	10.07%	12.59%	11.96%	16.22%
Short candle, performance	4.34%	4.25%	−4.74%	−6.38%
Tall candle, performance	8.08%	7.77%	−8.59%	−10.57%
Percentage meeting price target (measure rule)	81%	83%	92%	92%
Median upper shadow as a percentage of breakout price	0.46%	0.51%	0.73%	1.05%
Short upper shadow, performance	5.03%	5.46%	−5.20%	−7.64%
Tall upper shadow, performance	6.85%	6.47%	−7.60%	−8.99%
Median lower shadow as a percentage of breakout price	0.37%	0.51%	0.38%	0.62%
Short lower shadow, performance	5.49%	5.81%	−5.87%	−8.00%
Tall lower shadow, performance	6.28%	6.03%	−6.87%	−8.57%

Measure rule. I changed the usual measure rule for this pattern because it is so tall. Measure the height from lowest low to highest high in the candle pattern. For upward breakouts, divide the height by 6. For downward breakouts, divide by 3. Then add it to (for upward breakouts) or subtract it from (for downward breakouts) the candle's highest high. The result is the target price. The Sample Trade section gives an example.

Shadows. The table's results pertain to the last candle line in the pattern. To determine whether the shadow is short or tall, compute the height of the shadow and divide by the breakout price. Compare the result to the median in the table. Tall shadows have a percentage higher than the median.

Tall upper or lower shadows perform better than candles with short shadows in all categories.

Table 3.4 shows volume statistics.

Candle volume trend. A rising volume trend within the candle pattern results in the best postbreakout performance except for bear market/up breakouts. That category does better with a falling volume trend.

Average candle volume. Heavy candle volume means better performance across the board except in a bear market after a downward breakout.

Breakout volume. Similarly, heavy breakout-day volume means better performance except in a bear market after a downward breakout.

Table 3.4
Volume Statistics

Description	Bull Market, Up Breakout	Bear Market, Up Breakout	Bull Market, Down Breakout	Bear Market, Down Breakout
Rising candle volume, performance	6.23%	5.74%	−6.57%	−8.66%
Falling candle volume, performance	5.33%	6.17%	−5.93%	−7.73%
Above-average candle volume, performance	5.98%	5.97%	−6.40%	−7.83%
Below-average candle volume, performance	5.76%	5.85%	−6.27%	−8.83%
Heavy breakout volume, performance	6.64%	6.43%	−6.83%	−8.27%
Light breakout volume, performance	4.94%	5.22%	−5.88%	−8.30%

Trading Tactics

If an unusually tall candle appears as the last day in the eight new price lines candlestick pattern, then the chance of a reversal is 67%. This is based on research I conducted using data from October 1999 to February 2007 (bull and bear markets) covering over 58,600 candles lines in an uptrend. I found that when the last candle was taller than the prior 22 trading days (one month), price made a minor high within a day (one day before to one day after the tall candle) 67% of the time. The same tall candle scenario worked for minor lows, but performance improved: 72% form a minor low within a day of the tall candle.

Watch for a Fibonacci retracement: Price often retraces between 38% and 62% of the eight new price lines formation's rise. Multiply the height of the candle pattern (or, more accurately, the height of the uptrend encompassing the eight new price lines candles) by 38% and subtract it from the eight new price lines high price to get the first potential reversal point. Multiply the height by 62% and subtract it from the high to get the potential bottom reversal point. I depend on the 62% boundary most often. If price drops below that level, then chances are price will continue lower.

Figure 3.2 shows the eight new price lines pattern appearing in a strong uptrend. The breakout is upward, and price continues higher for another month before topping out. You will see this behavior often, but only for straight-line runs. If the breakout is downward, it will likely be shallow (but there is no guarantee).

If the eight new price lines formation starts from a downturn, forming a V shape, then expect price to reverse soon after the price lines end. Figure 3.3 shows this V-shaped setup.

Figure 3.2 A strong price uptrend leads to an upward breakout and continuation of the trend for another month.

I split trading tactics into two basic studies, one concerning reversal rates and the other concerning performance. Of the two, reversal rates are more important because it is better to trade in the direction of the trend and let price run as far as it can.

Table 3.5 gives tips on finding the trend direction.

Confirmation reversal rates. Closing price confirmation gives the best indication of a reversal. That means waiting for price to close lower the day after the eight new price lines formation ends before taking a position. The high reversal numbers mean that price closes below the last candle line in the series, not below the pattern's low price eight bars back.

Reversal, continuation rates. This measure shows how often the candle pattern works as a reversal based on price closing above the pattern's high or below the low of the last candle line in the pattern. In a bull market, price continues higher 53% of the time. In a bear market, performance is random.

Yearly range reversals. Sorting the reversals into where they occur in the yearly price trend shows that most appear within a third of the yearly low. Continuations appear most often within a third of the yearly high.

Table 3.6 shows performance indicators that can give hints as to how your stock will behave after the breakout from a candle pattern.

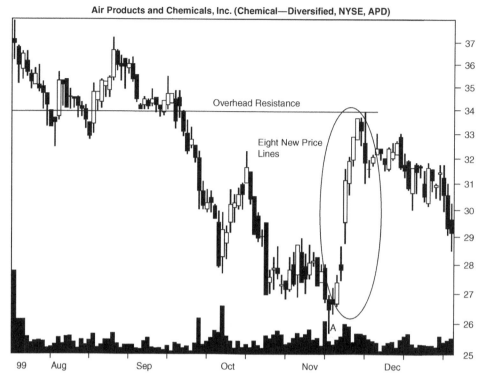

Figure 3.3   A V-shaped turn at point A coupled with overhead resistance suggested price would reverse after the candle ended.

Confirmation, performance. To help detect a reversal, trade only if a black candle appears the day after the eight new price lines formation ends in a bull market. For bear markets, the best confirmation method is to wait for the next day's opening price. If price gaps down, then expect a reversal. The difference between the confirmation methods is slight, so it really doesn't matter which method you use if you are hunting for a reversal.

Table 3.5
Reversal Rates

Description	Bull Market	Bear Market
Closing price confirmation reversal rate	73%	77%
Candle color confirmation reversal rate	71%	72%
Opening gap confirmation reversal rate	56%	56%
Reversal rate: trend up, breakout down	47%	50%
Continuation rate: trend up, breakout up	53%	50%
Percentage of reversals (R)/ continuations (C) for each 12-month low (L), middle (M), or high (H)	L 76% R/24% C, M 58% R/42% C, H 36% R/64% C	L 73% R/27% C, M 60% R/40% C, H 34% R/66% C

Table 3.6
Performance Indicators

Description	Bull Market, Up Breakout	Bear Market, Up Breakout	Bull Market, Down Breakout	Bear Market, Down Breakout
Closing price confirmation, performance	N/A	N/A	−6.38%	−8.37%
Candle color confirmation, performance	N/A	N/A	−6.44%	−8.27%
Opening gap confirmation, performance	N/A	N/A	−6.42%	−8.47%
Breakout above 50-day moving average, performance	5.88%	5.92%	−7.25%	−8.75%
Breakout below 50-day moving average, performance	5.89%	6.02%	−5.90%	−8.16%
Last candle: close in highest third, performance	5.84%	5.79%	−5.83%	−7.59%
Last candle: close in middle third, performance	5.75%	6.33%	−5.68%	−8.10%
Last candle: close in lowest third, performance	8.21%	5.99%	−7.27%	−9.36%

N/A means not applicable.
*Fewer than 30 samples.

Moving average. Most types of candlestick patterns will show better performance from candles that are below the 50-trading-day moving average. With this candle pattern, that applies to upward breakouts only, and the performance numbers are close. Downward breakouts show better performance if the breakout is above the moving average.

Closing position. A close in the lowest third of the last candle line gives the best performance in all cases except for bear market/up breakouts. Those perform better if the breakout is in the middle third of the candle line.

Sample Trade

Figure 3.3 shows this chapter's sample trade. Price begins trending down in an uneven decline. I am tempted to call it a downward staircase, but if your mom tried descending it, she'd likely twist her ankle . . . or worse.

Price bottomed at point A and then reversed. The reversal was startling in its strength. Price didn't just move higher; it went ballistic, retracing ground that took over a month to cover—in just eight days. Then price encountered a wall: overhead resistance.

The last candle in the eight new price lines formation turned black. The next day was also a black candle, and it, too, made a higher high but closed lower. The tall black candle confirmed a downward breakout. Price eased lower, bottoming at 28 and change in December.

Let's run through some numbers. Since we know the breakout is downward, what would be the price target using the measure rule? The candle height is the highest high minus the lowest low, or $33.69 - 26.31 = 7.38$. Thus, the target would be $33.69 - (7.38/3)$, or 31.23. Price meets or exceeds the target 92% of the time. By the way, since the breakout was downward, I divided the height by 3, as called for by the measure rule. If the breakout were upward, I would divide by 6, not 3, and add it to the highest price in the price lines. Price reaches the target the day after the eight new price lines candle formation ends.

Is the candle tall? The height is 7.38 and the downward breakout price is 32.50—that's the lowest price on the last bar of the price lines pattern. The measure is 7.38/32.50, or 22.7%. That is higher than the median shown in Table 3.3, so the candle is tall.

This price lines pattern is an example of how price reverses after a V-shaped entry. Contrast Figure 3.3 with Figure 3.2. In Figure 3.2, price trends upward in a near straight-line run. In Figure 3.3, price trends downward, leading to the start of the eight price lines' higher highs and forming a V shape when the downtrend reverses.

Price sometimes continues higher in situations like that shown in Figure 3.3, but with overhead resistance forming a ceiling, the top of the candle is a good time to take profits.

For Best Performance

The following list offers tips and observations to help choose candles that perform well. Consult the associated table for more information.

- Use the identification guidelines to help select the pattern—Table 3.1.
- Candles within a third of the yearly low perform best—Table 3.2.
- Select tall candles—Table 3.3.
- Use the measure rule to predict a price target. Divide the height by 3 or 6 before applying it to the breakout price. See discussion and Table 3.3.
- Candles with tall upper and lower shadows outperform—Table 3.3.
- Volume gives performance clues—Table 3.4.
- Tall candles signal minor highs or lows between 67% and 72% of the time—Trading Tactics discussion.
- Watch for a Fibonacci retracement of 38% to 62% of the prior uptrend—Trading Tactics discussion.

- A downturn forming a V shape may lead to a downward reversal—Trading Tactics discussion.
- Patterns within a third of the yearly low tend to act as reversals most often, whereas continuations appear within a third of the yearly high—Table 3.5.
- Candle color works best to confirm a reversal in a bull market, whereas opening gap confirmation works best in a bear market—Table 3.6.

4

10 New Price Lines

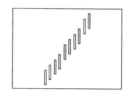

Behavior and Rank

Theoretical: Bearish reversal.

Actual bull market: Bearish reversal 51% of the time (ranking 50).

Actual bear market: Bullish continuation 54% of the time (ranking 40).

Frequency: 69th out of 103.

Overall performance over time: 100th out of 103.

Ten new price lines act as a continuation (49% of the time) almost as often as a reversal (51%). If the candle pattern worked perfectly as a reversal, then there would not be 12 and 13 new price lines candlestick patterns, but there are. Buying demand will push price higher until selling pressure forces it down. Gluing 8, 10, 12, or 13 consecutively higher highs together should not change the result, but you never know unless you take a closer look.

I thought the preceding candlestick pattern (eight new price lines) had a lousy overall rank, but this one drains a bit more from the pool with a rank of 100 out of 103, where 1 is best. The rank is based on performance over one, three, five, and ten days following the candle pattern end compared to other candle patterns.

Identification Guidelines

Figure 4.1 shows what 10 new price lines look like. This example starts from a congestion area of loose price movement during April and then forms the candle pattern in a straight-line run upward. A straight uphill run is common

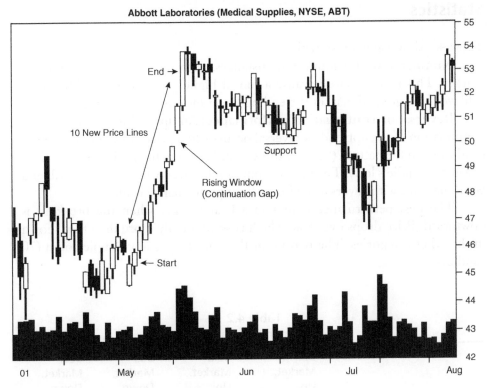

Abbott Laboratories (Medical Supplies, NYSE, ABT)

Figure 4.1   Ten new price lines form a straight-line run and price reverses near the end of the candlestick formation.

for 10 new price lines. Toward the end of this example, price gaps upward, forming a continuation gap called a rising window in candle terms. Three days later, the string of higher highs comes to an end. Price begins retracing the climb and finds support at the price of the rising window, as shown. Price eventually digs through the support layer and tumbles.

Ten new price lines are rare, but rarer still is a description of the candlestick formation. Table 4.1 shows the guidelines I used to locate the candle.

When searching for new price lines, look for 10 consecutively higher highs. That means each day's shadow is above the high of the prior day, but the candles can be black or white. Candle color is not important, nor is the size of the body.

Table 4.1
Identification Guidelines

Characteristic	Discussion
Number of candle lines	Ten.
Configuration	Ten consecutively higher highs.

Statistics

Table 4.2 shows general statistics.

Number found. I found 901 instances, with most coming from a bull market. This makes sense because a run of higher highs is more difficult to achieve if the general market is trending lower (as during a bear market).

Reversal or continuation performance. An upward breakout means a continuation of the uptrend. A reversal occurs when price closes below the last candle line in the pattern (because this candle is too tall to require price to close below the candle's low). The pattern splits almost evenly between reversals and continuations, with reversals taking a slight performance lead.

The best performance comes in a bear market when the breakout is downward. Price drops over 8%, which is substantially more than that shown in the other categories. The reason for that may be the low sample count (70 candles).

Table 4.2
General Statistics

Description	Bull Market, Up Breakout	Bear Market, Up Breakout	Bull Market, Down Breakout	Bear Market, Down Breakout
Number found	366	81	384	70
Reversal (R), continuation (C) performance	5.04% C	5.00% C	−5.26% R	−8.32% R
Standard & Poor's 500 change	1.01%	−0.64%	−0.68%	−2.67%
Candle end to breakout (median, days)	2	2	3	3
Candle end to trend end (median, days)	6	5	7	9
Number of breakouts near the 12-month low (L), middle (M), or high (H)	L 22, M 52, H 270	L 8, M 22, H 51	L 61, M 106, H 189	L 27, M 26, H 17
Percentage move for each 12-month period	L 6.58%, M 4.41%, H 5.12%	L 8.06%, M 4.66%, H 4.81%	L −5.27%, M −5.02%, H −5.28%	L −8.12%, M −8.77%, H −7.80%
Candle end + 1 day	0.86%	0.78%	−1.10%	−1.47%
Candle end + 3 days	1.08%	1.81%	−1.57%	−1.95%
Candle end + 5 days	0.96%	0.85%	−1.74%	−2.33%
Candle end + 10 days	1.84%	0.82%	−1.17%	−1.95%
10-day performance rank	92	92	90	83

S&P performance. The table shows how the S&P 500 index performed over the same dates as the candlestick formation. In three categories, the S&P dropped. That result is unusual because price in the candlestick trends higher and I would expect the general market to have a hand in that performance. The results suggest that company or industry factors play a larger role than the general market. Consider looking for the reason why price is moving up. If other companies in the industry are also doing well, then that bolsters the thinking that price may continue the uptrend after the candle pattern ends.

Candle end to breakout. It takes two or three days for price to break out. Downward breakouts take a day longer than upward breakouts, presumably because they are swimming against the primary upward price trend.

Candle end to trend end. It takes longer to reach the end of the trend for downward breakouts, based on the median time.

Yearly position, performance. Most of the time, the candle pattern has the breakout within a third of the yearly high. The exception comes from bear market/down breakouts, which appear more often near the yearly low. Upward breakouts show the best performance near the yearly low. Downward breakouts are mixed.

Performance over time. The performance over time is some of the worst I have seen. There's little consistency from period to period and column to column. A robust performer would show increasing numbers over time and in every category. The numbers suggest that after the candle ends, price meanders sideways. The rank reflects this dismal performance, with the best ranking being 83 for bear market/down breakouts.

Table 4.3 shows height statistics.

Candle height. Tall candles outperform short ones. To determine whether the candle is short or tall, compute its height from highest high to lowest low price in the candle pattern and divide by the breakout price. If the result is higher than the median, then you have a tall candle; otherwise it's short.

For example, say a candle has a high price of 49 and a low of 41. The height would be 49 − 41, or 8, so the measure in a bull market with an upward breakout would be 8/49, or 16%. That's a tall candle. Downward breakouts would use the low price in the last candle line as the divisor.

Measure rule. Use the measure rule to help predict how far price will rise or fall. Measure the candle height from highest high to lowest low in the candle pattern. For upward breakouts, divide the height by 6 and add it to the highest high. For downward breakouts, divide it by 3 and subtract it from the highest high. The result is the price target. Downward breakouts tend to hit the target more often than do upward breakouts.

What are the price targets for the 49/41 candle? The upward target would be (8/6) + 49, or 50.33. Downward breakouts would be 49 − (8/3), or 46.33. For a closer, more accurate target, multiply the height ratio (8/6 or 8/3 in

Table 4.3
Height Statistics

Description	Bull Market, Up Breakout	Bear Market, Up Breakout	Bull Market, Down Breakout	Bear Market, Down Breakout
Median candle height as a percentage of breakout price	10.82%	14.50%	13.70%	16.05%
Short candle, performance	3.67%	4.14%	−3.96%	−7.40%
Tall candle, performance	6.88%	6.14%	−7.20%	−9.34%
Percentage meeting price target (measure rule)	73%	74%	85%	93%
Median upper shadow as a percentage of breakout price	0.39%	0.58%	0.63%	0.65%
Short upper shadow, performance	4.23%	5.02%	−4.82%	−7.11%
Tall upper shadow, performance	5.93%	4.98%	−5.78%	−9.64%
Median lower shadow as a percentage of breakout price	0.39%	0.50%	0.36%	0.30%
Short lower shadow, performance	4.74%	5.05%	−4.61%	−8.02%
Tall lower shadow, performance	5.36%	4.95%	−5.96%	−8.61%

this example) by the appropriate percentage meeting the price target from Table 4.3.

Shadows. The results in Table 4.3 pertain to the last candle line in the pattern. To determine whether the shadow is short or tall, compute the height of the shadow and divide by the breakout price. Compare the result to the median in the table. Tall shadows have a percentage higher than the median.

Tall upper or lower shadows perform better in all conditions except for bear market/up breakouts.

Table 4.4 shows volume statistics.

Candle volume trend. A rising volume trend during the candle pattern results in the best postbreakout performance except for the low-sample-count bear market/up breakout.

Average candle volume. Candle volume is a measure of the average candle volume in the candlestick formation compared to the average over the prior month. Heavy candle volume suggests better performance after the breakout except in a bear market from candles with downward breakouts. In those cases, candles with light volume perform better.

Breakout volume. In all cases, candles with heavy breakout volume perform better than do those with light breakout volume.

Table 4.4
Volume Statistics

Description	Bull Market, Up Breakout	Bear Market, Up Breakout	Bull Market, Down Breakout	Bear Market, Down Breakout
Rising candle volume, performance	5.23%	4.83%	−5.52%	−8.66%
Falling candle volume, performance	4.76%	5.35%*	−4.77%	−7.71%*
Above-average candle volume, performance	5.57%	5.05%	−5.75%	−8.28%
Below-average candle volume, performance	4.26%	4.94%	−4.67%	−8.36%
Heavy breakout volume, performance	5.75%	5.03%	−6.06%	−9.41%
Light breakout volume, performance	4.15%	4.95%	−4.62%	−7.36%

*Fewer than 30 samples.

Trading Tactics

Look for overhead resistance that would cause the upward price trend to reverse. This would include rising or falling windows (gaps); minor highs and lows; round numbers (10, 20, 30); congestion areas; fundamental factors (like the release of poor earnings by another company in the same industry); and so on.

If an unusually tall candle appears as the last candle line in the candlestick, then the chance of a reversal is 67%. This is based on research I conducted using data from October 1999 to February 2007 (bull and bear markets) covering over 58,600 tall candles in an uptrend. I found that when the last candle was taller than the prior 22 trading days (one month), price made a minor high within a day (one day before to one day after the tall candle) 67% of the time. The same tall candle scenario worked for minor lows, too, but performance improved: 72% form a minor low within a day of the tall candle.

In many cases that I looked at, price retraced just over a third (38%) of the prior rise before resuming the uptrend. Many of you will know this as a Fibonacci retracement. Measure the height of the trend surrounding the 10 new price lines and multiply by 38%, 50%, and 62% to get the three most common retracement values. Add the three results to the lowest price to get possible turning prices.

For example, if the price trend has a high price of 55 and a low of 45, the height is 10. The three retracement values would be 10 × 38%, or 3.80; 10 × 50%, or 5; and 10 × 62%, or 6.20. Add the values to the low to get the three turning points of 48.80, 50, and 51.20.

Table 4.5
Reversal Rates

Description	Bull Market	Bear Market
Closing price confirmation reversal rate	78%	75%
Candle color confirmation reversal rate	77%	71%
Opening gap confirmation reversal rate	60%	51%
Reversal rate: trend up, breakout down	51%	46%
Continuation rate: trend up, breakout up	49%	54%
Percentage of reversals (R)/ continuations (C) for each 12-month low (L), middle (M), or high (H)	L 73% R/27% C, M 67% R/33% C, H 41% R/59% C	L* 77% R/22% C, M* 54% R/46% C, H* 25% R/75% C

*Fewer than 30 samples.

Before we get to the numbers, the last trading tactic is that when sharp turns in the price action occur, the 10 new price lines are more likely to end in a reversal. I'll explore this in the sample trade.

I split trading tactics into two basic studies, one concerning reversal rates and the other concerning performance. Of the two, reversal rates are more important, because it's better to trade in the direction of the trend and let price run as far as it can.

Table 4.5 gives tips to find the trend direction.

Confirmation reversal rates. If you are searching for a reversal from this candle pattern, the closing price the day after the candle ends can help. It correctly predicts a reversal between 75% and 78% of the time. A reversal is when price closes below the low of the last candle line, not the lowest low in the candle pattern (because it's often so tall).

Reversal, continuation rates. In a bull market, price breaks out upward slightly more often than downward. In a bear market, the results reverse, with continuations occurring more frequently.

Yearly range reversals. Reversals occur most often within a third of the yearly low. Continuations occur more often near the yearly high.

Table 4.6 shows performance indicators that can give hints as to how your stock will behave after the breakout from a candle pattern.

Confirmation, performance. If price continues trending upward, then there is nothing to do but hold on. However, if price reverses, then which confirmation method is best at issuing a trading signal? In a bull market, opening gap confirmation works best. That means waiting to trade only if price gaps open lower the next day.

In a bear market, candle color works best. That means waiting for a black candle to appear the next day before trading.

Table 4.6
Performance Indicators

Description	Bull Market, Up Breakout	Bear Market, Up Breakout	Bull Market, Down Breakout	Bear Market, Down Breakout
Closing price confirmation, performance	N/A	N/A	−5.30%	−8.20%
Candle color confirmation, performance	N/A	N/A	−5.24%	−8.22%
Opening gap confirmation, performance	N/A	N/A	−5.94%	−7.45%
Breakout above 50-day moving average, performance	5.05%	5.06%	−5.60%	−6.02%*
Breakout below 50-day moving average, performance	4.66%*	3.84%*	−5.17%	−8.57%
Last candle: close in highest third, performance	4.55%	4.65%	−5.33%	−8.65%*
Last candle: close in middle third, performance	4.79%	5.77%	−4.88%	−7.67%*
Last candle: close in lowest third, performance	6.88%	4.02%*	−5.46%	−8.36%*

N/A means not applicable.
*Fewer than 30 samples.

Moving average. Candles with breakouts above the 50-trading-day moving average result in the best performance in all categories except for bear market/down breakouts.

Closing position. Where the candle closes in the last line of the candle shows no consistent trend to help determine performance.

Sample Trade

Instead of discussing a sample trade, I thought it would be worthwhile to show you three versions of the candlestick that I found. Figure 4.2 shows the first variety.

In this example, price formed a peak in May 2002 and then declined substantially. During the recovery from this decline, there was a string of higher highs, forming the 10 new price lines pattern. The top of this candle pattern peaked near the same price as the old high. Those familiar with chart patterns will recognize this as a double top. The key to this example is to recognize that price often climbs to the site of an old high before reversing.

Figure 4.3 shows the next scenario. Price moves horizontally, or nearly so, trading in a narrow range. After breaking out from this flat base, price

Figure 4.2 Price reaches the site of significant overhead resistance and reverses.

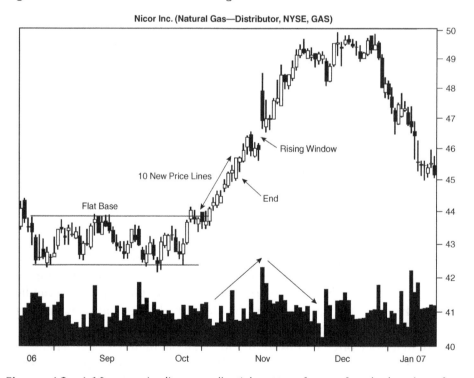

Figure 4.3 A 10 new price lines candlestick pattern forms after the breakout from a flat base.

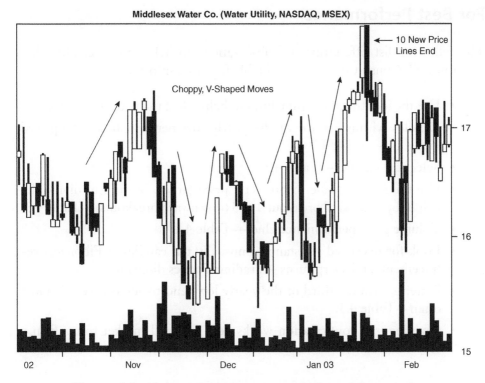

Figure 4.4   V-shaped price moves suggest a quick reversal.

begins trending. In this example, it forms a 10 new price lines candlestick. The breakout from this flat base or congestion area is powerful enough that price continues moving up, even after the 10 new price lines candlestick formation ends.

In this example, the height of the 10 new price lines is about 2 points and the trend after the candlestick ends is over 3 points—a powerful move indeed. These types of flat bases usually lead to explosive rallies, so they are worth searching for.

Watch volume, shown along the bottom of the chart. Notice that volume trends upward during the candlestick formation and peaks when price gaps higher (forming a rising window). Then, volume trends lower even as price continues higher. With volume decreasing, it's only a matter of time before the trend changes (but it may just change from up to sideways).

Figure 4.4 shows price moving up and reversing, moving down and reversing, in class 5 rapids few rafters would want to tackle. I have noticed that these sharp V moves often lead to quick price reversals.

In this example, price forms 10 new price lines but reverses as soon as the candle formation completes. You might also want to watch the angle at which price moves up in the candle pattern. Given that the rise in 10 new price lines is usually steep, climbs above 60 degrees are more likely to reverse than are climbs at 45 degrees or less.

For Best Performance

The following list offers tips and observations to help choose candles that perform well. Consult the associated table for more information.

- Use the identification guidelines to help select the pattern—Table 4.1.
- Candles within a third of the yearly low perform best for upward breakouts—Table 4.2.
- Select tall candles—Table 4.3.
- Use the measure rule to predict a price target. Be sure to divide the height by 6 (upward breakouts) or 3 (downward breakouts)—Table 4.3.
- Volume gives performance clues—Table 4.4.
- Look for overhead resistance, unusually tall candles, a Fibonacci retracement, and sharp turns—Trading Tactics discussion.
- Patterns within a third of the yearly low tend to act as reversals most often—Table 4.5.
- Opening gap confirmation works best in a bull market to confirm a reversal—Table 4.6.

5

12 New Price Lines

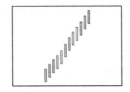

Behavior and Rank

Theoretical: Bearish reversal.

Actual bull market: Bullish continuation 51% of the time (ranking 46).

Actual bear market: Bullish continuation 61% of the time (ranking 22).

Frequency: 87th out of 103.

Overall performance over time: 99th out of 103.

Twelve new price lines occur more often than I expected until you consider that I searched for it in over 4.7 million candle lines. I uncovered 192. When you separate them into bull and bear markets, up and down breakouts, many of the statistics are subject to change, so interpret them with care.

This candlestick pattern is a study in buying demand that pushes price up for 12 consecutive days. It reminds me of a snowball tumbling downhill, collecting more snow as it goes, growing bigger, but eventually it will hit the valley floor and roll to a stop.

Price moving up must stop sometime, but saying it will stop after 12 days is unwise, and the statistics agree. Price might or might not make another higher high tomorrow or the day after. Look at the 8 or 10 new price lines candlestick. The thinking there is that price *had* to reverse after a string of 8 or 10 consecutively higher highs, but it didn't. And there is a 13 new price lines candle pattern, too. Why not 14 or 15? Maybe a 14 new price lines pattern is really two sevens glued together with one down day. The point is that reversals cannot be pinned to how many consecutively higher highs appear. However, you never know unless you take a look, and that is what this chapter is all about.

Twelve new price lines act as a bullish continuation pattern between 51% (bull market) and 61% (bear market) of the time. Whether the candlestick acts as a reversal or not is often determined not by the candlestick itself, but by other factors, such as industry trends, market trends, and overhead resistance.

The continuation rate of 61% is quite good, ranking 22nd out of 103, where 1 is best. However, when you look at the overall performance rank, not only do clouds gather, but it's a hurricane. The rank is 99 out of 103 where 1 is best, and it is based on the performance of price over the 10 days after the candle pattern ends compared to the other candle patterns.

Identification Guidelines

Identification of 12 new price lines is easy, and Figure 5.1 shows an example. Price moves in a trading range for most of April and then starts trending upward. After 12 consecutive new highs, one would expect price to retrace at least a portion of the up move, and it does, but for just two days. After that, price wobbles up and down then goes horizontal until June before gapping

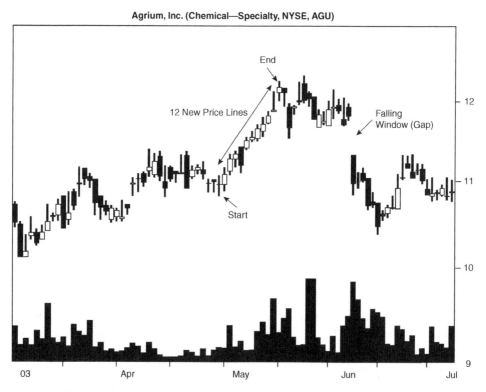

Figure 5.1 Twelve new price lines leave an area of congestion in a straight-line run and end with a trend reversal.

Table 5.1
Identification Guidelines

Characteristic	Discussion
Number of candle lines	Twelve.
Configuration	Twelve consecutively higher highs.

lower (falling window). The stock drops below the launch price (start) before finding solid ground just below 11.

Table 5.1 shows the identification guidelines of the 12 new price lines candlestick pattern. Look for 12 consecutively higher highs. The candles can be any color just as long as the upper shadow is above the prior candle's upper shadow. I did not allow any exceptions to this rule.

Statistics

Table 5.2 shows general statistics.

Number found. I uncovered 192 instances of this candlestick pattern, with most coming from a bull market.

Reversal or continuation performance. Usually we see bear markets showing better performance than bull markets, but it's mixed with this candle pattern.

S&P performance. Only in candles with upward breakouts in a bull market did the S&P 500 register a positive move over the same time period. I find that odd, since you would expect the general market to do well in a bull market. However, if the breakout is downward from 12 new price lines, the reason may be market weakness (a declining S&P 500).

Candle end to breakout. It takes three or four days for price to close above the top of the highest shadow, or close below the last candle line's low price.

Candle end to trend end. It takes between six and eight days to reach the trend end. Those patterns that follow the market trend (upward breakouts in a bull market and downward breakouts in a bear market) take less time than do those moving against the market current.

Yearly position, performance. Most of these candle patterns have breakouts within a third of the yearly high. Upward breakouts show the best performance within a third of the yearly low, while downward breakouts do best near the yearly high.

Performance over time. The performance of the candlestick pattern over time leaves much to be desired. Performance actually goes negative in the bear market/up breakout column. The results suggest that once price tops out, it tends to meander, not rising or falling much during the next two weeks

Table 5.2
General Statistics

Description	Bull Market, Up Breakout	Bear Market, Up Breakout	Bull Market, Down Breakout	Bear Market, Down Breakout
Number found	81	20	78	13
Reversal (R), continuation (C) performance	4.97% C	4.32% C	−4.88% R	−5.55% R
Standard & Poor's 500 change	0.99%	−0.62%	−0.44%	−3.17%
Candle end to breakout (median, days)	3	3	3	4
Candle end to trend end (median, days)	6	8	7	6
Number of breakouts near the 12-month low (L), middle (M), or high (H)	L 5, M 10, H 63	L 3, M 7, H 10	L 16, M 23, H 32	L 1, M 4, H 8
Percentage move for each 12-month period	L 6.23%, M 4.39%, H 5.07%	L 9.93%, M 4.20%, H 3.25%	L −4.32%, M −4.32%, H −5.68%	L −2.34%, M −3.79%, H −7.30%
Candle end + 1 day	0.67%	1.13%	−0.71%	−1.17%
Candle end + 3 days	1.20%	1.16%	−2.15%	−3.06%
Candle end + 5 days	1.17%	−0.10%	−1.84%	−2.42%
Candle end + 10 days	2.07%	1.65%	−1.11%	−1.42%
10-day performance rank	82	80	91	90

(10 trading days). The performance rank confirms the awful performance. The best rank of 80 (where 1 is best) appears in bear market/up breakouts.

Table 5.3 shows height statistics.

Candle height. Tall candles outperform short ones. To determine whether the candle is short or tall, compute its height from highest high to lowest low price in the candle pattern and divide by the breakout price. If the result is higher than the median, then you have a tall candle; otherwise it's short. For downward breakouts, use the low price from the last line in the candle as the breakout price, not the lowest low in the candle pattern.

For example, if Pamela sees 12 new price lines with a high of 69 and a low of 60, is the candle short or tall? The height is 69 − 60, or 9, so the measure would be 9/69, or 13%. Assuming an upward breakout in a bull market, the candle is tall. For downward breakouts with the last candle low at 68, the measure would be 9/68, or 13%. The candle would be short in a bull market.

Measure rule. Use the measure rule to help predict how far price will rise or fall. Compute the candle height from highest high to lowest low in the candle pattern. For upward breakouts, divide the height by 6 and add it to the

Table 5.3
Height Statistics

Description	Bull Market, Up Breakout	Bear Market, Up Breakout*	Bull Market, Down Breakout	Bear Market, Down Breakout*
Median candle height as a percentage of breakout price	12.69%	16.01%	14.36%	21.10%
Short candle, performance	3.69%	3.65%	−4.27%	−4.49%
Tall candle, performance	6.95%	5.09%	−5.74%	−6.71%
Percentage meeting price target (measure rule)	70%	70%	74%	85%
Median upper shadow as a percentage of breakout price	0.46%	0.54%	0.77%	1.27%
Short upper shadow, performance	3.48%	4.21%	−4.09%	−3.80%
Tall upper shadow, performance	6.43%	4.43%	−5.67%	−8.72%
Median lower shadow as a percentage of breakout price	0.30%	0.41%	0.32%	0.50%
Short lower shadow, performance	3.92%	4.00%	−4.89%	−4.46%
Tall lower shadow, performance	6.77%	4.69%	−4.86%	−7.63%

*Fewer than 30 samples.

highest high. For downward breakouts, divide the height by 3 and subtract it from the highest high. The result is the price target. Downward breakouts tend to hit the target more often than do upward breakouts.

What are Pamela's price targets for her candle? The upward target would be (9/6) + 69, or 70.5 and the downward target would be 69 − (9/3), or 66. You can multiply the height ratio (9/6 or 9/3) by the percentage meeting price target listed in the table to get a more accurate price target.

Shadows. The results in Table 5.3 pertain to the last candle line in the pattern. To determine whether the shadow is short or tall, compute the height of the shadow and divide by the breakout price. Compare the result to the median in the table. Tall shadows have a percentage higher than the median.

Upper shadow performance. Tall upper shadows work better than short ones.

Lower shadow performance. Tall lower shadows also work best in all cases except for bull market/down breakouts, but even there the numbers are close.

Table 5.4 shows volume statistics.

Candle volume trend. Candle formations with a rising volume trend tend to outperform those with a falling trend. The exception comes from candles in a bull market with upward breakouts.

Table 5.4
Volume Statistics

Description	Bull Market, Up Breakout	Bear Market, Up Breakout*	Bull Market, Down Breakout	Bear Market, Down Breakout*
Rising candle volume, performance	3.76%	4.76%	−4.91%	−6.49%
Falling candle volume, performance	6.01%	3.35%	−4.81%*	−0.73%
Above-average candle volume, performance	4.98%	3.79%	−5.69%	−5.52%
Below-average candle volume, performance	4.96%	5.62%	−3.77%*	−5.64%
Heavy breakout volume, performance	5.12%	3.56%	−6.18%	−6.83%
Light breakout volume, performance	4.85%	6.03%	−3.55%	−3.89%

*Fewer than 30 samples.

Average candle volume. Below-average candle volume shows better postbreakout performance in bear markets, and above-average volume works better with upward breakouts.

Breakout volume. Heavy breakout volume helps performance in all cases but one (bear market, up breakouts).

Trading Tactics

If a thick layer of overhead resistance appears, then expect price to reverse and move lower. That is not always the case, but it's the safer bet.

Figure 5.2 shows an example of what happens when 12 new price lines run into overhead resistance. The candle pattern leaves a congestion area and pushes its way higher. Twelve candles later, the pattern ends but price continues rising. When the stock nears the price level of the peaks in March and April, the uptrend stops. A trendline connecting the two prior peaks highlights the overhead resistance. Price cannot push through this layer, so it drops, slowly at first like a climber struggling to maintain his grip on the rock face. When exhaustion overcomes his will to survive, he plummets just as price does in the picture, bouncing off an overhanging ledge along the way.

Researching the candle pattern, I found that after it ends, price often retraces less than 38%. If the retracement exceeds this, then the likelihood is that price will make an extended move down. This is a generality, of course, so search for underlying support that would stop a downward move.

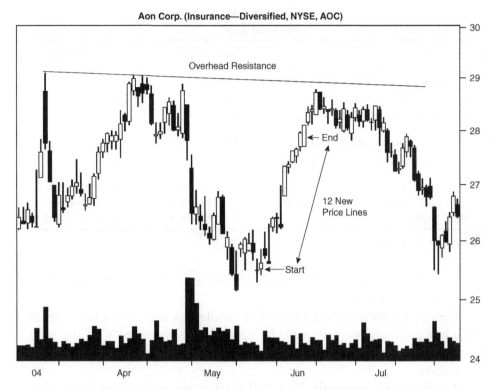

Figure 5.2 Overhead resistance halts the advance.

I also found during my study of this candle pattern that when the last candle in the pattern is substantially taller than the average candle, it suggests price will reverse.

Measure the high-low range of the candle line (a single price bar) and compare it to the average high-low range of the prior 22 trading days (i.e., find the height of each candle line over the prior month, not including the tall candle, and then average the result). If the tall candle is taller than 146% of the average, then the chance of price reversing within +/− 1 day is 67%. By *reversing* I mean that price is likely to form a minor high.

The same applies to the formation of a minor low—only tall candles show reversals within a day 72% of the time. My web site at ThePatternSite.com gives details on the study and performance.

I split trading tactics into two basic studies, one concerning reversal rates and the other concerning performance. Of the two, reversal rates are more important, because it's better to trade in the direction of the trend and let price run as far as it can.

Table 5.5 gives tips to find the trend direction.

Confirmation reversal rates. To help detect a reversal, wait for price to close lower a day after the candle formation ends. Of course, this only brings price closer to a downward breakout, which would confirm a reversal. The big

Table 5.5
Reversal Rates

Description	Bull Market	Bear Market*
Closing price confirmation reversal rate	72%	60%
Candle color confirmation reversal rate	69%	53%
Opening gap confirmation reversal rate	61%	43%
Reversal rate: trend up, breakout down	49%	39%
Continuation rate: trend up, breakout up	51%	61%
Percentage of reversals (R)/continuations (C) for each 12-month low (L), middle (M), or high (H)	L 76% R/24% C, M 70% R/30% C, H 34% R/66% C	L 25% R/75% C, M 36% R/64% C, H 44% R/56% C

*Fewer than 30 samples.

surprise here is that the success rate of this method isn't higher—60% (bear market) to 72% (bull market).

Reversal, continuation rates. The candlestick shines in a bear market where it acts as a continuation of the upward price trend 61% of the time. I would expect the opposite: price to reverse the uptrend more often in a bear market.

Yearly range reversals. In a bull market, reversals occur most often within a third of the yearly low. In a bear market, the results flip, with continuations happening most often near the yearly low.

Table 5.6 shows performance indicators that can give hints as to how your stock will behave after the breakout from this candle pattern.

Confirmation, performance. To signal a reversal, the best performance comes from waiting for price to gap open lower the day after the candle pattern ends (bull market). In a bear market, waiting for a black candle the next day works better.

Moving average. A breakout above the moving average works better in all cases except for bear market/up breakouts.

Closing position. Where price closes shows no consistent trend across the board.

Sample Trade

Figure 5.3 shows an example of 12 new price lines. Combining chart patterns with candlesticks, Pamela sees a symmetrical triangle form as a reversal of the downtrend from the June peak. Price forms a doji (see inset), a signal of equilibrium, on its way to the breakout. When price opens higher the next day, that's the buy signal she is looking for. She receives a fill of 27.80, a penny above the opening price.

Table 5.6
Performance Indicators

Description	Bull Market, Up Breakout	Bear Market, Up Breakout*	Bull Market, Down Breakout	Bear Market, Down Breakout*
Closing price confirmation, performance	N/A	N/A	−5.04%	−5.39%
Candle color confirmation, performance	N/A	N/A	−5.36%	−6.66%
Opening gap confirmation, performance	N/A	N/A	−5.44%	−6.39%
Breakout above 50-day moving average, performance	4.99%	4.29%	−6.17%*	−10.54%
Breakout below 50-day moving average, performance	2.86%*	5.01%	−4.53%	−5.12%
Last candle: close in highest third, performance	3.27%	5.18%	−4.09%*	−4.53%
Last candle: close in middle third, performance	7.09%*	3.65%	−4.45%*	−7.17%
Last candle: close in lowest third, performance	5.54%*	3.46%	−5.62%	−6.05%

N/A means not applicable.
*Fewer than 30 samples.

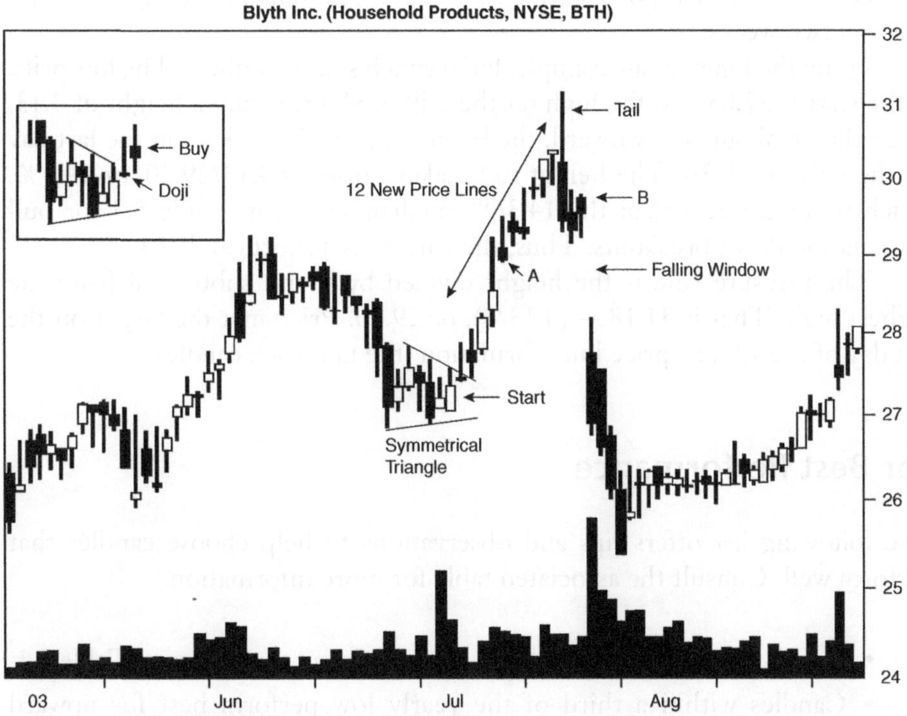

Figure 5.3 A tall candle with a long upper shadow on the last day of the 12 new price lines suggested the uptrend was over.

If the trade goes bad, a stop placed below the bottom of the symmetrical triangle would work well. The upside target is the old high at 29, a round number and site of overhead resistance (the June peak).

Each day she monitors the trade. The shooting star (this one has a tiny lower shadow, which is unusual but okay) that forms at A warns that the uptrend may be over. Since the shooting star appears at the target price of 29, she prepares to sell when the market opens.

The next day, she checks the stock and it has opened higher, so she decides to hold on. That's the right choice in this case because price continues moving up. As price climbs, eight new price lines turns into 10 and then 12. But the candle bodies shrink (the two large white candles below A grow smaller at A and even smaller three candles later—a doji) and that warns that the uptrend is losing steam.

On day 12, the candle has a tall upper shadow—a spike or tail—and that warns of a trend change. The tall candle itself suggests a price reversal (see Trading Tactics discussion), so she thinks the trend is over.

A trendline (not shown) drawn along the bottoms of the 12 new price lines candle pattern from the start upward would find that the last candle line pierces the trendline and price closes below it. That is another potential sell signal.

The next day, a black candle appears and it makes a lower close, confirming the sell signal. That night, she places a market order to sell the stock at the market open, shown as point B. She exits at 29.75, and makes nearly $2 a share in about two weeks.

Using the figure as an example, let's crunch some numbers. The low price at the start is 27.05 and the high (at the tail) is 31.18, giving a height of 4.13. Since the breakout is downward, the breakout price is the low on the last day (at the tail), or 29.30. The height to breakout price is 4.13/29.30, or 14.1%, which is slightly less than the 14.36% median shown in Table 5.3 for bull markets and down breakouts. Thus, the pattern is a short candlestick.

The measure rule is the height divided by 3 and subtracted from the highest high. That is 31.18 − (4.13/3), or 29.80. Price met the target on the last day of the 12 new price lines formation (the tall black candle).

For Best Performance

The following list offers tips and observations to help choose candles that perform well. Consult the associated table for more information.

- Use the identification guidelines to help select the pattern—Table 5.1.
- Candles within a third of the yearly low perform best for upward breakouts—Table 5.2.
- Select tall candles—Table 5.3.

- Use the measure rule to predict a price target but be sure to divide the height by 6 (upward breakouts) or 3 (downward breakouts)—Table 5.3.

- Candles with tall upper shadows outperform—Table 5.3.

- Volume gives performance clues—Table 5.4.

- Look for overhead resistance, a Fibonacci retracement, and a tall candle line at the end of the pattern—Trading Tactics discussion.

- The candle breaks out upward most often, especially in a bear market—Table 5.5.

- Patterns within a third of the yearly low tend to act as reversals most often in a bull market—Table 5.5.

- Opening gap confirmation works best in a bull market—Table 5.6.

6

13 New Price Lines

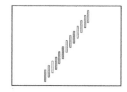

Behavior and Rank

Theoretical: Bearish reversal.

Actual bull market: Bearish reversal 57% of the time (ranking 36).

Actual bear market: Bullish continuation 74% of the time (ranking 5).

Frequency: 90th out of 103.

Overall performance over time: 95th out of 103.

Thirteen new price lines is the last of a series of similar candlestick patterns that began with eight new price lines. All appear as a rising price trend, and all have consecutively higher highs. Just because a trend has 13 new highs does not mean the uptrend is over.

This candle pattern is a study in upward price momentum and buying enthusiasm. Each day, players step up and push price higher, but the rise has to end sometime. What happens then? In an informal review of 47 candlestick patterns, 24 continued higher, 12 moved horizontally, and 11 trended down in the coming months. This suggests that the bullish enthusiasm is only sidelined, not lost, and holding on is often the best choice for additional gains.

As a continuation pattern in a bear market, the candlestick ranks near the top of the list: 5 out of 103 where 1 is first place (best). In a bull market, the pattern acts as a reversal more often, 57% of the time, ranking 36. The problem with this is that a well-performing candle should show the same behavior regardless of market conditions (bull or bear). If you know about system development and testing, then the bear market could be the out-of-sample test and we get a different answer (a continuation versus a reversal).

Turning to performance, the candle is awful, with an overall rank of 95 out of 103. That's okay because you won't find it often in a price series. The frequency rank is 90.

Identification Guidelines

Figure 6.1 shows an example of 13 new price lines and typical price behavior after it ends. Price launches upward from a rising window, helping to push price above the prior minor high in mid-October (point A). Once price pierces overhead resistance, it continues moving up in a strong incline, each day ending with a high price above the prior day. Thirteen candle lines later, the candlestick pattern ends but the uptrend does not. Price forms a tall white candle, which to many is bullish, but to me it warns of the approach of a minor high (based on research into tall candle lines). That's what happens. Price forms a bearish harami candlestick and then eases lower for the next two weeks or so before resuming the uptrend.

Notice that the slope of the rise after the 13 new price lines candle is nearly the same as that before the candle pattern. This happens from time to time, but more often you will see price move horizontally for months before

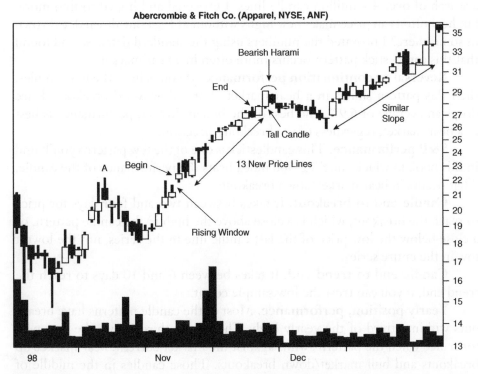

Figure 6.1 Price makes a strong move up during the 13 new price lines candle formation, goes horizontal, and then the rise continues.

Table 6.1
Identification Guidelines

Characteristic	Discussion
Number of candle lines	Thirteen.
Configuration	Thirteen consecutively higher highs.

the rise resumes, or if price continues up after a short pause, it does so at a shallower slope.

Table 6.1 shows what to look for in the 13 new price lines candle pattern, but there is not much to tell. Look for 13 candle lines, each with an upper shadow above the prior one. That means 13 consecutively higher highs. After that, price is supposed to reverse, but often continues higher. The statistics describe this and other behavior.

Statistics

Table 6.2 shows general statistics for the candlestick pattern, but I found few samples, so the numbers are likely to change, perhaps dramatically.

Number found. I located only 95 instances of this candlestick pattern in a search of over 4.7 million candle lines. I expected and hoped to find more, but how often can price make new highs without at least one down day thrown in somewhere? I prorated the numbers using the standard database and found that this candlestick pattern occurs more often in a bear market.

Reversal or continuation performance. If you believe the few samples, then this pattern shines in a bear market after a downward breakout. Price drops an average of 6.9%, the best of the bunch. In fact, performance is best in a bear market, regardless of the breakout direction.

S&P performance. This candlestick is one of the few patterns you'll find in this book in which the S&P 500 index beats the performance of the candle. That occurs in bear market/down breakouts.

Candle end to breakout. It takes between two and four days for price to reach the breakout, which is a close above the high in the candle pattern, or a close below the low price of the last candle line in the series, not the lowest low in the entire series.

Candle end to trend end. It takes between 6 and 10 days to reach the trend end, if you can trust the low sample count.

Yearly position, performance. Most of the candle patterns have breakouts within a third of the yearly high. The lowest third shows the best performance when the pattern swims against the market current: bear market/up breakouts and bull market/down breakouts. Those candles in the middle of the yearly trading range do better with the market current: bull market/up breakouts and bear market/down breakouts.

Table 6.2
General Statistics

Description	Bull Market, Up Breakout	Bear Market, Up Breakout	Bull Market, Down Breakout	Bear Market, Down Breakout
Number found	33	14	43	5
Reversal (R), continuation (C) performance	4.88% C	4.92% C	−4.24% R	−6.90% R
Standard & Poor's 500 change	1.22%	−0.88%	−0.89%	−8.22%
Candle end to breakout (median, days)	3	4	4	2
Candle end to trend end (median, days)	6	10	7	8
Number of breakouts near the 12-month low (L), middle (M), or high (H)	L 1, M 2, H 29	L 1, M 6, H 7	L 12, M 11, H 18	L 2, M 2, H 1
Percentage move for each 12-month period	L 1.46%, M 5.86%, H 4.91%	L 28.78%, M 4.43%, H 3.59%	L −4.54%, M −4.02%, H −4.43%	L −5.32%, M −8.50%, H −7.49%
Candle end + 1 day	0.79%	0.77%	−0.60%	−1.82%
Candle end + 3 days	1.28%	0.63%	−1.49%	−3.46%
Candle end + 5 days	1.73%	0.65%	−2.02%	−2.16%
Candle end + 10 days	2.52%	2.87%	−0.65%	−4.38%
10-day performance rank	69	57	101	42

Performance over time. This candle is a weak performer over time, as the numbers show. What do I mean by that? In a robust candle, performance should increase over time and in each category. With this candle, performance weakens in three out of four categories over the two-week span (10 trading days). The performance rank confirms this assessment, with the best rank, 42, coming from bear market/down breakouts. The percentage change after 10 days is not impressive.

Table 6.3 shows height statistics.

Candle height. Tall candles outperform. To use this finding, measure the height of the candlestick from lowest low to highest high price and then divide by the breakout price (for upward breakouts use the highest high; for downward breakouts use the low from the last candle line—price bar—in the pattern). If the result is greater than that listed in the table for the breakout direction and market condition, then you have a tall candle.

For example, Pete sees 13 new price lines with a high of 43 and a low of 37. Is the candle short or tall? The height is 43 − 37, or 6, so the measure

Table 6.3
Height Statistics*

Description	Bull Market, Up Breakout	Bear Market, Up Breakout	Bull Market, Down Breakout	Bear Market, Down Breakout
Median candle height as a percentage of breakout price	12.36%	13.50%	18.14%	14.48%
Short candle, performance	4.15%	3.17%	−3.25%	−7.54%
Tall candle, performance	5.83%	7.15%	−6.08%	−6.12%
Percentage meeting price target (measure rule)	76%	79%	60%	80%
Median upper shadow as a percentage of breakout price	0.38%	0.52%	0.81%	0.97%
Short upper shadow, performance	4.61%	4.26%	−4.20%	−7.69%
Tall upper shadow, performance	5.13%	5.80%	−4.29%	−4.94%
Median lower shadow as a percentage of breakout price	0.33%	0.37%	0.51%	0.18%
Short lower shadow, performance	3.69%	4.97%	−3.56%	−5.65%
Tall lower shadow, performance	5.80%	4.86%	−5.26%	−8.40%

*Fewer than 30 samples.

would be 6/43, or 14%. For an upward breakout in a bull market, the candle is tall.

Measure rule. Use the measure rule to help predict how far price will rise or fall. Compute the height of the candle and divide it by 6 for upward breakouts or 3 for downward breakouts, multiply it by the appropriate percentage shown in the table, and then apply it to the highest high.

What are the price targets for Pete's candle? Assume the last candle line has a low of 42 in a bull market. The upward target would be (6/6 × 76%) + 43, or 43.76. The downward target would be 43 − (6/3 × 60%), or 41.80.

Shadows. The table's results pertain to the last candle line in the pattern. To determine whether the shadow is short or tall, compute the height of the shadow and divide by the breakout price (the highest high for upward breakouts or the low price in the last candle line). Compare the result to the median in the table. Tall shadows have a percentage higher than the median.

Upper shadow performance. Candles with tall upper shadows work best in all cases except bear market/down breakouts.

Lower shadow performance. Tall lower shadows also work better than short ones in all cases except bear market/up breakouts.

Table 6.4 shows volume statistics, but the samples are few, so any conclusions may be unreliable.

Table 6.4
Volume Statistics*

Description	Bull Market, Up Breakout	Bear Market, Up Breakout	Bull Market, Down Breakout	Bear Market, Down Breakout
Rising candle volume, performance	5.07%	5.46%	−4.71%	−7.07%
Falling candle volume, performance	4.74%	2.86%	−3.53%	−6.44%
Above-average candle volume, performance	4.52%	4.73%	−4.55%	−7.00%
Below-average candle volume, performance	5.25%	5.19%	−3.75%	−6.79%
Heavy breakout volume, performance	5.00%	3.29%	−4.72%	−7.00%
Light breakout volume, performance	4.78%	7.24%	−3.75%	−6.79%

*Fewer than 30 samples.

Candle volume trend. Candles with a rising volume trend perform better than do those with falling volume.

Average candle volume. Candles with below-average volume compared to the one-month average tend to perform better after an upward breakout. Above-average candle volume does better than light volume for downward breakouts.

Breakout volume. Heavy breakout-day volume helps propel price farther in all market conditions and breakout directions except for upward breakouts in bear markets. Those do best after a light volume breakout—that is, if you can trust the low sample count results.

Trading Tactics

If an abundance of overhead resistance exists, then the end of 13 new price lines is more likely to see a reversal than a continuation of the uptrend.

Many times, price will retrace only a small amount before resuming the uptrend. If the retracement extends more than 38% of the prior up move, then expect the downtrend to continue.

Research has shown that a candle taller than 146% of the average height of the past 22 trading days means price is likely to form a minor high about 67% of the time. Thus, if a tall candle appears at or after the 13 new price lines candlestick, then expect a trend reversal. The reversal may not last long, however, depending on the strength of the company, industry, and general market.

The sample trade in Chapter 4, which discussed 10 new price lines, shows three varieties of price action. It's worth reviewing them because 13 new price lines show similar shapes.

Table 6.5
Reversal Rates*

Description	Bull Market	Bear Market
Closing price confirmation reversal rate	77%	56%
Candle color confirmation reversal rate	73%	57%
Opening gap confirmation reversal rate	72%	36%
Reversal rate: trend up, breakout down	57%	26%
Continuation rate: trend up, breakout up	43%	74%
Percentage of reversals (R)/ continuations (C) for each 12-month low (L), middle (M), or high (H)	L 92% R/8% C, M 85% R/15% C, H 38% R/62% C	L 67% R/33% C, M 25% R/75% C, H 12% R/88% C

*Fewer than 30 samples.

When price moves horizontally for a few months before the start of the 13 new price lines, it often continues moving up well after the end of the candlestick pattern. If price is already trending upward at the start of the 13 candlesticks, then a reversal is more likely. Finally, if price is choppy or V-shaped before the candle pattern, then a reversal is also more likely.

I split trading tactics into two basic studies, one concerning reversal rates and the other concerning performance. Of the two, reversal rates are more important, because it's better to trade in the direction of the trend and let price run as far as it can.

Table 6.5 gives tips to find the trend direction.

Confirmation reversal rates. If you are trying to determine whether a reversal will occur in a bull market, wait for price to close lower a day after the 13 candlestick ends. If that happens, a reversal follows 77% of the time.

In a bear market, candle color works better. That means waiting for a black candle to appear a day later before trading.

A reversal means that price closes below the breakout price and the breakout price is the low of the last candle line in the 13-candle series. Thus, if you wait for a lower close the next day, it should be comparatively easy for price to close below the low and post a reversal. Whether the reversal is a lasting one is anyone's guess.

Reversal, continuation rates. In a bull market, the candlestick acts as a reversal more often than a continuation. In a bear market, the results flip with continuations occurring more often. That means bull markets show downward breakouts and bear markets show upward breakouts more often. That is exactly the reverse of what common sense dictates, which would be an upward breakout in a bull market and a downward breakout in a bear market. Perhaps the low sample count has something to do with the results. Or we could just blame global warming. I do that elsewhere in this book a few times.

Table 6.6
Performance Indicators*

Description	Bull Market, Up Breakout	Bear Market, Up Breakout	Bull Market, Down Breakout	Bear Market, Down Breakout
Closing price confirmation, performance	N/A	N/A	−5.07%	−6.32%
Candle color confirmation, performance	N/A	N/A	−5.45%	−5.95%
Opening gap confirmation, performance	N/A	N/A	−5.04%	−5.65%
Breakout above 50-day moving average, performance	4.94%	4.92%	−11.31%	0.00%
Breakout below 50-day moving average, performance	1.46%	0.00%	−4.16%	−6.90%
Last candle: close in highest third, performance	3.77%	5.76%	−4.46%	−7.00%
Last candle: close in middle third, performance	5.87%	4.04%	−3.99%	−8.50%
Last candle: close in lowest third, performance	7.75%	0.00%	−4.23%	−3.39%

N/A means not applicable.
*Fewer than 30 samples.

Yearly range reversals. Reversals occur most often within a third of the yearly low. Continuations occur when the breakout is near the yearly high.

Table 6.6 shows performance indicators that can give hints as to how your stock will behave after the breakout from a candle pattern.

Confirmation, performance. The best performance comes after a black candle confirms a downward move the day after the 13-candle series ends (bull market). Shorting the stock then would give the best performance, but the difference between the other confirmation types is small.

In a bear market, a lower close the day after the candle pattern ends results in the best postbreakout performance.

Moving average. Candles with breakouts above the 50-trading-day moving average work better than do those below the average except for bear market/down breakout. The results are unreliable due to the low sample count.

Closing position. Where price closes in the last candle of the 13 new price lines pattern shows no consistent trend.

Sample Trade

Figure 6.2 shows the sample trade for this chapter. As a swing trader, Pete likes to jump into a trade as soon as price leaves a congestion area. When a tall white candle bursts out of congestion (the area circled in the figure), his buy order is triggered automatically and filled at 25 (the top of the area).

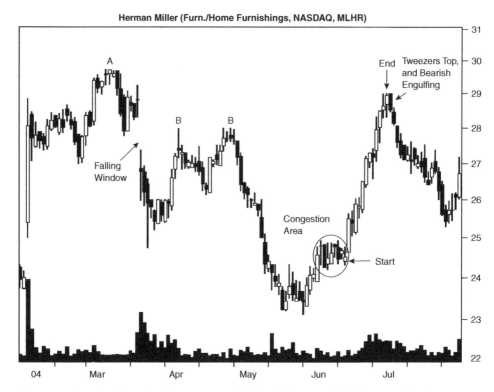

Figure 6.2   Overhead resistance coupled with the end of 13 new price lines suggests a trend change.

As sometimes happens, one new high leads to another, which leads to another. The stock climbs to the price of overhead resistance shown at B, set up by the two peaks in April and the falling window before that. Pete is sure that price is going to reverse there, but guess what: It doesn't, even after 10 consecutively higher highs—a 10 new price lines candlestick pattern.

Price continues making higher highs three more times, the last one by only a penny. The stock is approaching the old high at A, another resistance zone. After day 13, price forms a black candle and closes lower without making a new high. A close below the low of the last candle in the 13 new price lines series a day later confirms a downward breakout, leaving behind a tweezers top disguised as a bearish engulfing pattern. Facing overhead resistance and with price now moving down, Pete decides to get out. He sells the stock at 28 for a 3-point gain in about two weeks.

For Best Performance

The following list offers tips and observations to help choose candles that perform well. Consult the associated table for more information.

- Use the identification guidelines to help select the pattern—Table 6.1.
- Pick candles with breakouts in the middle third of the yearly price range and following the market trend—Table 6.2.
- Select tall candles—Table 6.3.
- Use the measure rule to predict a price target but be sure to divide the height by 6 (upward breakouts) or 3 (downward breakouts)—Table 6.3.
- Volume gives performance clues—Table 6.4.
- Trading Tactics discussion offers a variety of scenarios.
- The candle breaks out upward most often in a bear market—Table 6.5.
- Patterns within a third of the yearly low tend to act as reversals most often—Table 6.5.
- Candle color confirmation works best in a bull market—Table 6.6.

7

Abandoned Baby, Bearish

Behavior and Rank

Theoretical: Bearish reversal.

Actual bull market: Bearish reversal 69% of the time (ranking 14).

Actual bear market: Bullish continuation 52% of the time (ranking 48).

Frequency: 96th out of 103.

Overall performance over time: 64th out of 103.

Perhaps the saddest thing about the abandoned baby candlestick is that although its name just begs me to crack a joke about it, I can't think of anything; so I'll just have to stick to the facts.

I found only 24 abandoned babies in the first database of over a million candlesticks; adding three additional databases, covering over 4.7 million candle lines in all, the total came to 238. If you looked at one stock quote per day, you would find one abandoned baby every 78 years, on average, assuming you lived that long.

The psychology behind the pattern begins with an upward price trend. The bulls are in control of the market, confirmed by a white candle line as the first in the pattern. The next day price gaps higher but falters and forms a doji. The bulls and bears are struggling for control of the market. The third day tells which side won: the bears. A black candle appears after price gaps lower, signaling the start of a downward price trend.

The rank seems steeped in contradiction. In a bull market, the candlestick acts as a bearish reversal; but in a bear market, it acts as a bullish continuation. The reason for this is most likely the low sample count for bear markets: 27

patterns versus 211 for bull markets. Trust the bull market numbers but beware the bear market results.

The bull market reversal rate is quite high, perhaps because of where price closes in the pattern (near the low). Downward moves take between two and four days to break out. Of course, during that time anything can happen. In a bull market, the pattern ranks 14 out of 103 for performance, where 1 is best.

Identification Guidelines

Figure 7.1 shows what a bearish abandoned baby looks like. The three-candle pattern begins with a white candle, but it need not be a tall one, according to most sources I checked (one disagreed, saying the first day was a tall white candle).

The middle day is a doji whose lower shadow gaps above the adjacent candles' shadows. One reference disagreed, saying that it was sufficient for the doji's lower shadow to be above the first day's close. However, the shadow

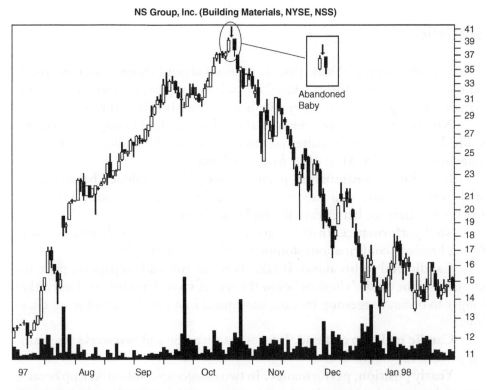

Figure 7.1 An abandoned baby appears after an extended upward price trend and correctly predicts a reversal.

Table 7.1
Identification Guidelines

Characteristic	Discussion
Number of candle lines	Three.
Price trend	Upward leading to the first candle.
First day	A white candle, either short or tall.
Second day	A doji whose lower shadow gaps above the prior and following days' highs (above their upper shadows).
Last day	A black candle, either short or tall, with the upper shadow remaining below the doji's lower shadow.

length (causing overlapping shadows) is what separates this candle pattern from others, such as the evening doji star.

The final day is a black candle whose upper shadow does not overlap the doji. That means price gaps lower and remains below the prior day's low at the close of trading.

I found abandoned baby patterns that obeyed the identification guidelines outlined in Table 7.1.

Statistics

Table 7.2 shows general statistics. Be cautious about forming opinions based on the bear market statistics. Only 27 candlesticks qualified, too few to be of significance, especially since they split between two breakout directions.

Number found. I used additional databases to find enough patterns to study. Even so, this candle pattern is rare. Out of over 4.7 million candlesticks, I uncovered just 238. Most came from a bull market.

Reversal or continuation performance. The abandoned baby candlestick performs quite well except in bull market/down breakouts. The bear market numbers are better than the bull market ones.

S&P performance. In all categories, performance of the abandoned baby (using breakout confirmation) stomped on the S&P 500 index.

Candle end to breakout. It takes between two and six days for price to close above the candle's high or below the candle's low. Upward breakouts take longer to occur, suggesting that the downward move is closer to the candle's low.

Candle end to trend end. It takes between one and two weeks (median) for price to hit the trend end.

Yearly position, performance. In two categories (bull market/up breakouts and bear market/down breakouts), performance is best when the breakout occurs within a third of the yearly low. Those two relate to trading with the

Table 7.2
General Statistics

Description	Bull Market, Up Breakout	Bear Market, Up Breakout*	Bull Market, Down Breakout	Bear Market, Down Breakout*
Number found	65	14	146	13
Reversal (R), continuation (C) performance	7.04% C	9.32% C	−5.59% R	−8.15% R
Standard & Poor's 500 change	1.59%	1.90%	−0.60%	−1.25%
Candle end to breakout (median, days)	6	6	4	2
Candle end to trend end (median, days)	7	10	6	14
Number of breakouts near the 12-month low (L), middle (M), or high (H)	L 7, M 9, H 36	L 4, M 6, H 4	L 19, M 41, H 61	L 10, M 1, H 2
Percentage move for each 12-month period	L 6.35%, M 5.71%, H 6.08%	L 4.21%, M 10.67%, H 8.41%	L −5.37%, M −8.92%, H −4.80%	L −9.21%, M −1.35%, H −7.33%
Candle end + 1 day	1.19%	0.49%	−0.76%	−1.86%
Candle end + 3 days	2.87%	3.31%	−1.72%	−3.12%
Candle end + 5 days	3.99%	4.84%	−1.77%	−0.20%
Candle end + 10 days	4.16%	5.34%	−1.83%	−0.96%
10-day performance rank	29	24	69	96

*Fewer than 30 samples.

market trend. The contratrend guys, bear market/up breakouts and bull market/down breakouts, do better when the breakout is in the middle of the yearly trading range.

Performance over time. This candle performs quite well except for bear market/down breakouts, which falter from three to five days. The ranking reflects that, too, because performance slides to 96 out of 103 where 1 is best.

Table 7.3 shows height statistics.

Candle height. Tall bull market patterns outperform and short bear market patterns do well. To determine whether the candle is short or tall, compute its height from highest high to lowest low price in the candle pattern and divide by the breakout price. If the result is higher than the median, then you have a tall candle; otherwise it's short.

For example, if Snake sees a candle with a high of 63 and a low of 61 in a bull market with a downward breakout, is the candle short or tall? The height is 63 − 61, or 2, so the measure is 2/61, or 3.3%. That represents a short candle.

Table 7.3
Height Statistics

Description	Bull Market, Up Breakout	Bear Market, Up Breakout*	Bull Market, Down Breakout	Bear Market, Down Breakout*
Median candle height as a percentage of breakout price	4.26%	4.27%	4.04%	6.47%
Short candle, performance	5.20%	9.71%	−4.74%	−10.17%
Tall candle, performance	8.66%	8.44%	−6.76%	−6.00%
Percentage meeting price target (measure rule)	54%	57%	53%	46%
Median upper shadow as a percentage of breakout price	0.00%	0.00%	0.00%	0.00%
Short upper shadow, performance	6.92%	6.15%	−5.89%	−4.76%
Tall upper shadow, performance	7.25%*	18.66%	−4.83%	−10.05%
Median lower shadow as a percentage of breakout price	0.00%	0.57%	0.00%	1.12%
Short lower shadow, performance	5.56%	6.92%	−4.83%	−4.43%
Tall lower shadow, performance	7.81%	12.93%	−6.25%	−9.96%

*Fewer than 30 samples.

Measure rule. Use the measure rule to help predict how far price will rise or fall. Compute the height of the candle and multiply it by the appropriate percentage shown in the table; then apply it to the breakout price.

Suppose Snake sees another abandoned baby with a high price of 90 and a low of 85. The height is 5 (90 − 85). For upward breakouts, the price target would be 90 + (5 × 54%), or 92.70. For downward breakouts, the target would be 85 − (5 × 53%), or 82.35.

Shadows. The table's results pertain to the last candle line in the pattern. To determine whether the shadow is short or tall, look at the median in the table for your market condition and breakout direction. If the median is 0.00% (meaning a lot of the patterns showed no upper shadow on the last candle line) and the last candle line has a shadow, then it's a tall candle. Otherwise, compute the height of the shadow and divide by the breakout price. Compare the result to the median in the table. Tall shadows have a percentage higher than the median.

Upper shadow performance. Candles with tall upper shadows work better than short ones except bull market/down breakouts.

Lower shadow performance. Abandoned babies with tall lower shadows outperform across the board.

Table 7.4 shows volume statistics.

Table 7.4
Volume Statistics

Description	Bull Market, Up Breakout	Bear Market, Up Breakout*	Bull Market, Down Breakout	Bear Market, Down Breakout*
Rising candle volume, performance	7.82%	5.84%	−5.97%	−10.26%
Falling candle volume, performance	6.21%*	10.64%	−5.28%	−5.96%
Above-average candle volume, performance	5.26%*	7.45%	−6.27%	−5.59%
Below-average candle volume, performance	7.81%	13.10%	−4.96%	−13.47%
Heavy breakout volume, performance	6.45%	14.74%	−5.33%	−11.08%
Light breakout volume, performance	7.54%	5.71%	−5.78%	−5.62%

*Fewer than 30 samples.

Candle volume trend. A rising volume trend is wonderful for performance in all cases except the low sample count bear market/up breakout category. Those do better if volume is trending down (falling).

Average candle volume. The best performance occurs if the average volume of the three-line candle formation is below the prior one-month average. Only the bull market/down breakout column shows better results with above-average candle volume.

Breakout volume. Breakout-day volume performance tracks the market condition. In a bull market, light breakout volume leads to better performance. In a bear market, the roles reverse, with heavy breakout volume leading to better performance.

Trading Tactics

I split trading tactics into two basic studies, one concerning reversal rates and the other concerning performance. Of the two, reversal rates are more important, because it's better to trade in the direction of the trend and let price run as far as it can.

Table 7.5 gives tips to find the trend direction.

Confirmation reversal rates. If you want to detect a reversal, then wait for price to close lower a day after the abandoned baby completes. That works 91% of the time in a bull market. Of course, a lower close also means you're closer to a breakout (which would confirm the reversal), so this may be a self-fulfilling prophecy. It's like shooting at a target. Whatever you hit, you call the target.

Table 7.5
Reversal Rates

Description	Bull Market	Bear Market*
Closing price confirmation reversal rate	91%	69%
Candle color confirmation reversal rate	90%	67%
Opening gap confirmation reversal rate	88%	59%
Reversal rate: trend up, breakout down	69%	48%
Continuation rate: trend up, breakout up	31%	52%
Percentage of reversals (R)/ continuations (C) for each 12-month low (L), middle (M), or high (H)	L 73% R/27% C, M 82% R/18% C, H 63% R/37% C	L 71% R/29% C, M 14% R/86% C, H 33% R/67% C

*Fewer than 30 samples.

Reversal, continuation rates. This candle sports one of the higher reversal percentages, 69% in a bull market. In a bear market, the numbers are not as impressive: 48% act as reversals.

Yearly range reversals. In a bull market, reversals occur most often in the middle of the yearly price range. In a bear market, those within a third of the yearly low show the most reversals.

Table 7.6 shows performance indicators that can give hints as to how your stock will behave after the breakout from a candle pattern.

Confirmation, performance. Since the price trend is up and we are looking for reversals, only downward breakouts apply.

The best performance comes from using an opening price gap the day after the candle completes as the confirmation method. That method places you into the trade soonest and results in the best performance, by far.

Moving average. Candles with breakouts above the 50-trading-day moving average result in better performance than do those with breakouts below the moving average. The one exception comes from bull market/down breakouts.

Closing position. A close in the lowest third does well for those candles that follow the market trend: bull market/up breakouts and bear market/down breakouts. The contratrend movers do better with the closing price in the middle of the last candle line of the pattern.

Sample Trade

Figure 7.2 shows this chapter's sample trade. It begins on the left with an abandoned baby that resulted in a reversal of just one day. If you shorted the stock at the lower open, it would have been a costly mistake. The only remarkable thing about this baby is the four-price doji. That's a doji in which the open, high, low, and closing prices are the same. It appears as a horizontal

Table 7.6
Performance Indicators

Description	Bull Market, Up Breakout	Bear Market, Up Breakout*	Bull Market, Down Breakout	Bear Market, Down Breakout*
Closing price confirmation, performance	N/A	N/A	−6.03%	−8.45%
Candle color confirmation, performance	N/A	N/A	−6.10%	−8.11%
Opening gap confirmation, performance	N/A	N/A	−7.32%	−11.43%
Breakout above 50-day moving average, performance	7.23%	12.16%	−5.28%	−10.47%
Breakout below 50-day moving average, performance	5.02%*	3.70%	−6.63%	−5.94%
Last candle: close in highest third, performance	7.12%*	1.06%	−3.42%*	0.00%
Last candle: close in middle third, performance	4.76%*	12.07%	−6.43%	−6.42%
Last candle: close in lowest third, performance	7.53%	7.96%	−5.41%	−9.50%

N/A means not applicable.
*Fewer than 30 samples.

line on the chart. The four-price doji is rare except in thinly traded stocks, and it doesn't have much significance: Traders cannot make up their minds which direction they want price to move.

In this example, price resumes the uptrend, leaving Snake, who shorted the abandoned baby, to settle with his broker. A northern doji appears at point A, followed the next day by a bearish belt hold, a tall black candle that serves as confirmation that the doji was a valid reversal signal. Incidentally, the difference between the opening and closing prices in the doji at A (and later at B) is just a penny, despite how thick it appears on the chart. I allow that kind of flexibility in a doji.

Oddly, price moves up in the following two days, ending with another doji (obscured by the circle). The small black candle the next day confirms the doji, but the downtrend lasts only that day. The next day begins the abandoned baby near point B.

Price climbs to a gravestone doji that marks the second highest peak on the chart (B). "Second highest" is key, because the abandoned baby pattern marks a failed attempt at a new high. Some analysts call this a 2B pattern. It occurs when price attempts a new high and fails or rises slightly higher to make a new high before running out of steam and reversing.

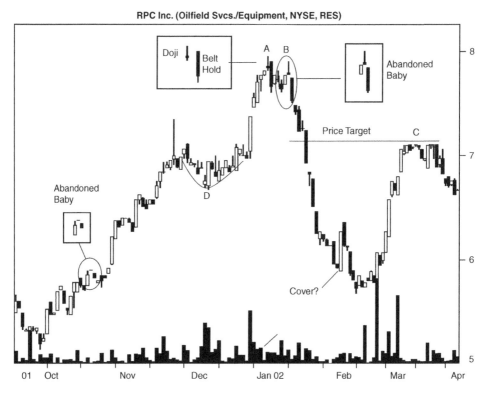

Figure 7.2   An abandoned baby reinforces the belief that the uptrend has ended.

Whatever you want to call it, the abandoned baby and the attempt but failure to set a new high are the nail in the coffin. Price doesn't meander lower; rather, it drops like a drug addict trying to fly off a skyscraper.

Let's crunch some numbers. Is the candle a tall one? The highest high is at 7.91 and the lowest low in the candle is 7.51 for a height of 40 cents. Assuming a downward breakout, the height to breakout value is 0.40/7.51, or 5.33%. Since this candle pattern appears in a bear market (March 2000 to October 2002 was a bear market in the S&P 500), Table 7.3 says that the median is 6.47%. Thus, this candle is short.

The measure rule works only 46% of the time. We know the candle height is 40 cents, so subtract it from the lowest low in the candle to get a target of 7.51 − 0.40, or 7.11. This target coincides with the flat top at point C, shown in the figure. This method uses the full height, in case you failed to notice.

You can multiply the 40-cent height by 46% to get a closer, more reliable target. Subtracting the new height of .18 (46% × 0.40 or 0.18) from the candle low gives a price target of 7.33.

Running through Table 7.4 of volume statistics, we find that a rising volume trend in a bear market from a candle with a downward breakout means a larger decline (but it's based on few samples, so it's unreliable and we are dealing with probabilities, anyway).

Candle volume was light during the three-day candle compared with the prior month's average. Table 7.4 says candles with below-average volume outperform.

Finally, breakout-day volume was light. The breakout occurred the day after the candle ended (a close below the lowest low in the candle) and volume on that day was lighter than average. This suggested weaker performance.

Looking at the figure, I would expect price to stall or even reverse at the congestion zone above point D, about 7. That was also near the target price of 7.11. Thus, I would probably make my target 7.11 because it's an odd number (avoid round numbers like 7, where everyone will place an order). However, price kept tumbling.

With a strong downtrend under way, I would hold until the tall white candle (a bullish engulfing pattern that eats the prior six candle lines), highlighted in Figure 7.2 ("Cover?"), scared me out of the trade.

For Best Performance

The following list offers tips and observations to help choose candles that perform well. Consult the associated table for more information.

- Use the identification guidelines to help select the pattern—Table 7.1.
- Candles within a third of the yearly low perform best when they follow the market trend (bull market/up breakout or bear market/down breakout)—Table 7.2.
- Select tall candles in a bull market—Table 7.3.
- Use the measure rule to predict a price target—Table 7.3.
- Candles with tall lower shadows outperform—Table 7.3.
- Volume gives performance clues—Table 7.4.
- The candle breaks out downward most often in a bull market—Table 7.5.
- Opening gap confirmation works best—Table 7.6.

8

Abandoned Baby, Bullish

Behavior and Rank

Theoretical: Bullish reversal.

Actual bull market: Bullish reversal 70% of the time (ranking 13).

Actual bear market: Bullish reversal 55% of the time (ranking 34).

Frequency: 92nd out of 103.

Overall performance over time: 9th out of 103.

The bullish version of the abandoned baby is a reversal candlestick pattern that is rare but works well. In a historical price series, you see them frequently in thinly traded stocks where gaps occur often.

The psychology behind the candlestick begins with a downtrend where the bears are joyous over the declining price. This party atmosphere translates into a black candle. The next day, price gaps lower and stays lower throughout the day, but closes at or near the opening price, forming a doji. The doji means indecision. Will price move higher or lower the next day? If the answer is higher and the bulls force price to gap upward, then you have a bullish abandoned baby.

Downward breakouts are the star of this baby. They score first and fifth for performance in bear and bull markets, respectively. Of course that means the candle pattern acts not as a reversal but as a continuation of the downward price trend in the bear scenario. That places the overall rank at 9, which I consider excellent (1 is best out of 103 candles).

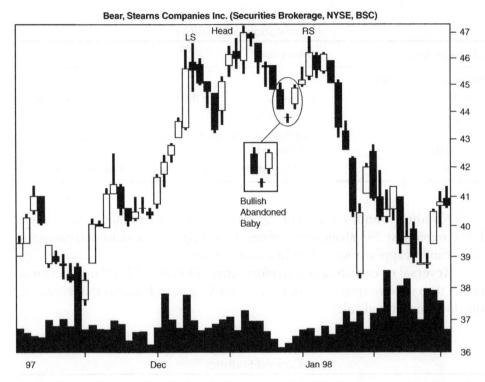

Figure 8.1 A bullish abandoned baby occurs as a short-term reversal pattern in a head-and-shoulders top.

Identification Guidelines

Figure 8.1 shows an example of the bullish abandoned baby. This one appears as the right armpit of a head-and-shoulders top chart pattern. Price enters the candlestick by trending down in a series of black candle lines and then the doji gaps lower, suggesting indecision (or perhaps indigestion for traders trying to make a buck during their lunch hour). The next day, price gaps higher and forms a white candle. Price rises after that in a series of white candles and peaks at the right shoulder (RS).

Table 8.1 lists the identification guidelines. Most of the entries are self-explanatory. The middle candle is a doji whose shadow does not overlap the shadow from the day before or the day after. The third day is a white candle whose lower shadow remains above the prior day's (doji's) shadow. This allows the doji to appear abandoned on the price chart. The length of the doji's shadow (and overlap with surrounding shadows) is what separates the bullish abandoned baby from the morning doji star.

Statistics

Table 8.2 shows general statistics.

Table 8.1
Identification Guidelines

Characteristic	Discussion
Number of candle lines	Three.
Price trend	Downward leading to the start of the candlestick pattern.
First day	Black candle.
Second day	Doji that gaps below the shadows of the candle lines on either side.
Last day	A white candle whose shadow gaps above the doji.

Number found. Using four databases of over 4.7 million candle lines, I discovered just 293 abandoned babies. Prorating the standard database says these candles appear more often in a bear market.

Reversal or continuation performance. Downward breakouts perform better than upward ones. Another way of looking at it: Patterns that continue the downward trend rule!

Table 8.2
General Statistics

Description	Bull Market, Up Breakout	Bear Market, Up Breakout	Bull Market, Down Breakout	Bear Market, Down Breakout
Number found	184	17	78	14
Reversal (R), continuation (C) performance	6.77% R	6.88% R	−8.69% C	−13.62% C
Standard & Poor's 500 change	1.14%	0.79%	−1.89%	−2.10%
Candle end to breakout (median, days)	3	4	7	6
Candle end to trend end (median, days)	7	10	10	10
Number of breakouts near the 12-month low (L), middle (M), or high (H)	L 26, M 42, H 79	L 3, M 9, H 5	L 16, M 24, H 22	L 7, M 2, H 5
Percentage move for each 12-month period	L 11.22%, M 4.09%, H 7.16%	L 11.60%, M 7.75%, H 3.56%	L −6.19%, M −12.87%, H −7.77%	L −17.82%, M −17.70%, H −6.03%
Candle end + 1 day	0.68%	0.90%	−1.08%	−1.11%
Candle end + 3 days	1.89%	1.00%	−3.20%	−4.35%
Candle end + 5 days	2.04%	2.25%	−4.30%	−5.55%
Candle end + 10 days	2.59%	2.44%	−6.04%	−10.31%
10-day performance rank	64	64	5	1

S&P performance. Comparing the performance of the S&P 500 with the breakout confirmation performance, the candle works better in all market conditions and breakout directions.

Candle end to breakout. It takes between three and seven days before price closes above/below the top/bottom of the candle pattern. Downward breakouts take longer, probably because price closes near the high of the pattern.

Candle end to trend end. The median time for price to reach the trend end is about 10 days. Bull market/up breakouts take just a week to finish trending.

Yearly position, performance. The best-performing patterns appear within a third of the yearly low in all cases except for bull market/down breakouts. Those do better if the breakout is in the middle of the yearly trading range.

Performance over time. I call this a robust performer because performance improves in each of the time slots and over the various categories. Look at the size of the performance numbers after 10 days of moving lower. Mouthwatering!

The performance rank confirms the good performance for downward breakouts, in which the candle pattern scores 1 (best) and 5 out of 103 candle types. Tell your friends.

Table 8.3 shows height statistics.

Candle height. Tall candles outperform. To determine whether the candle is short or tall, compute its height from highest high to lowest low price in the candle pattern and divide by the breakout price. If the result is higher than the median, then you have a tall candle; otherwise it's short.

Suppose that Josh sees an abandoned baby with a high of 50 and a low of 47. Is the candle short or tall? The height is $50 - 47$, or 3, so the measure would be 3/50, or 6%. For an upward breakout in a bull market, the candle is tall.

Measure rule. Use the measure rule to help predict how far price will rise or fall. Compute the height of the candle and multiply it by the appropriate percentage shown in the table; then apply it to the breakout price.

If Josh has an abandoned baby with a high of 56 and low of 51, then what are the expected price targets in a bull market? The height is $56 - 51$, or 5. Since price only reaches the target 50% of the time, adjust the height by how often it hits the target: $5 \times 50\%$, or 2.50. For upward breakouts, the target becomes $2.50 + 56$, or 58.50. For downward breakouts, the target is $51 - (5 \times 55\%)$, or 48.25.

Shadows. The results in Table 8.3 pertain to the last candle line in the pattern. To determine whether the shadow is short or tall, compute the height of the shadow and divide by the breakout price. Compare the result to the median in the table. Tall shadows have a percentage higher than the median.

Table 8.3
Height Statistics

Description	Bull Market, Up Breakout	Bear Market, Up Breakout*	Bull Market, Down Breakout	Bear Market, Down Breakout*
Median candle height as a percentage of breakout price	4.23%	6.68%	4.09%	6.06%
Short candle, performance	5.17%	3.93%	−5.70%	−10.36%
Tall candle, performance	9.06%	11.44%	−14.41%	−18.10%
Percentage meeting price target (measure rule)	50%	47%	55%	71%
Median upper shadow as a percentage of breakout price	0.00%	0.31%	0.00%	1.00%
Short upper shadow, performance	6.39%	5.72%	−7.40%	−11.52%
Tall upper shadow, performance	7.08%	7.94%	−9.83%	−15.69%
Median lower shadow as a percentage of breakout price	0.00%	0.05%	0.00%	0.00%
Short lower shadow, performance	5.82%	6.54%	−8.57%	−14.72%
Tall lower shadow, performance	9.84%	7.13%	−9.09%*	−12.71%

*Fewer than 30 samples.

Do not worry about a median of 0.00%. That only means many candle lines had no shadow.

Upper shadow performance. Candles with tall upper shadows work better than do those with short ones in all categories.

Lower shadow performance. Tall lower shadows also suggest better performance except for bear market/down breakouts.

Table 8.4 shows volume statistics.

Candle volume trend. Candles with a rising volume trend perform better than do those with a falling trend except in bull market/up breakouts.

Average candle volume. Heavy candle volume results in the best post-breakout performance after an upward breakout, but worst performance after a downward breakout.

Breakout volume. Candles with heavy breakout-day volume perform better across the board.

Trading Tactics

Figures 8.1 and 8.2 show examples of when the bullish abandoned baby candlestick pattern appears at the end of a short-term downtrend. This is not always the case, of course, but it occurs frequently enough that it caught

Table 8.4
Volume Statistics

Description	Bull Market, Up Breakout	Bear Market, Up Breakout*	Bull Market, Down Breakout	Bear Market, Down Breakout*
Rising candle volume, performance	6.11%	7.95%	−10.03%	−15.43%
Falling candle volume, performance	7.63%	6.21%	−7.33%	−10.17%
Above-average candle volume, performance	8.00%	8.11%	−8.42%*	−12.72%
Below-average candle volume, performance	5.76%	4.46%	−8.79%	−16.29%
Heavy breakout volume, performance	7.81%	9.68%	−10.63%	−17.44%
Light breakout volume, performance	6.14%	5.01%	−7.10%	−10.14%

*Fewer than 30 samples.

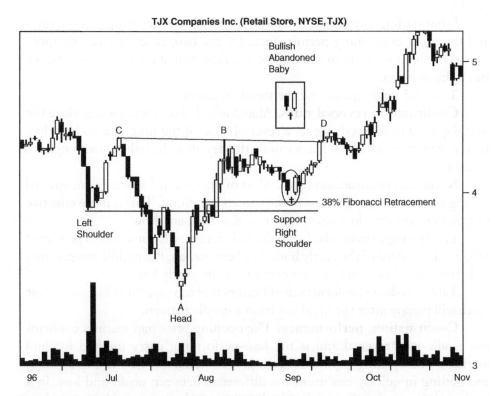

Figure 8.2 Underlying support and a 38% retracement of the uptrend helps this abandoned baby break out upward.

Table 8.5
Reversal Rates

Description	Bull Market	Bear Market*
Closing price confirmation reversal rate	93%	75%
Candle color confirmation reversal rate	89%	80%
Opening gap confirmation reversal rate	81%	50%
Reversal: trend down, breakout up	70%	55%
Continuation: trend down, breakout down	30%	45%
Percentage of reversals (R)/ continuations (C) for each 12-month low (L), middle (M), or high (H)	L 62% R/38% C, M 64% R/36% C, H 78% R/22% C	L 30% R/70% C, M 82% R/18% C, H 50% R/50% C

*Fewer than 30 samples.

my attention. Thus, if price breaks out upward, then buy. Just make sure you look for overhead resistance, because price has a tendency to reverse quickly.

I split trading tactics into two basic studies, one concerning reversal rates and the other concerning performance. Of the two, reversal rates are more important, because it's better to trade in the direction of the trend and let price run as far as it can.

Table 8.5 gives tips to find the trend direction.

Confirmation reversal rates. Abandoned babies with a lower close the next day tend to correctly signal a reversal 93% of the time in a bull market. In a bear market, wait for a black candle the day after the baby ends to signal a reversal.

Reversal, continuation rates. Most of the time, price breaks out upward (acting as a reversal), regardless of the market condition. This is more effective in a bull market than in a bear market, as the numbers show.

Yearly range reversals. In a bull market, reversals come out to play most often within a third of the yearly high. In a bear market, the middle range shows more reversals, but continuations occur near the yearly low.

Table 8.6 shows performance indicators that can give hints as to how your stock will behave after the breakout from a candle pattern.

Confirmation, performance. The opening price gap method confirms the candle as a reversal and is the best-performing entry method for bull markets. The opening gap method works well because it gets you in soonest, and getting in quickly can mean the difference between profit and loss. In a bear market, wait for price to close higher the next day before taking a position. That results in the best performance.

Moving average. Breakouts below the 50-trading-day moving average perform better than do those above the moving average.

Table 8.6
Performance Indicators

Description	Bull Market, Up Breakout	Bear Market, Up Breakout*	Bull Market, Down Breakout	Bear Market, Down Breakout*
Closing price confirmation, performance	7.90%	9.17%	N/A	N/A
Candle color confirmation, performance	7.42%	7.14%	N/A	N/A
Opening gap confirmation, performance	8.52%	8.17%	N/A	N/A
Breakout above 50-day moving average, performance	6.52%	5.80%	−6.94%*	−5.97%
Breakout below 50-day moving average, performance	6.99%	7.95%	−9.82%	−21.99%
Last candle: close in highest third, performance	5.73%	5.90%	−9.12%	−13.57%
Last candle: close in middle third, performance	10.85%	6.94%	−7.98%*	−8.17%
Last candle: close in lowest third, performance	2.96%	15.49%	−4.11%*	−16.96%

N/A means not applicable.
*Fewer than 30 samples.

Closing position. Where price closes in the last candle line shows no consistent trend across the categories.

Sample Trade

Figure 8.2 shows the sample trade that Josh made. When he trades, he tries to guess where price will reverse before taking a position. Many times, a chart pattern helps call the turn. In this example, seeing the left shoulder and head, he guesses where a right shoulder would appear, both in price and time. The symmetry of properly formed head-and-shoulders formations as well as other chart patterns helps take the guesswork out of price prediction. Just imagine where a pattern will complete, based on what you see.

In a well-behaved head-and-shoulders formation, the right shoulder finds support near the price level of the left shoulder and almost the same distance from the head. When the abandoned baby appears, it represents an early buy signal.

Combined with a 38% retracement of the move from A to B (shown as the middle horizontal line in the figure), all Josh has to do is wait for price to close above the highest high in the candle pattern. Two days after the tall white candle of the abandoned baby, price stages a breakout. He has a buy order in place, making entry automatic and at a perfect price.

If he had waited for the traditional buy signal from the head-and-shoulders bottom, a close above the neckline (the line joining peaks C and B, ending at D), he would have bought in during formation of a gravestone doji. That candlestick predicted a weakening of the up move. Coupled with the tall white candle of the prior day, it also hinted that a minor high would form. That's what happened, and price eased lower over the next two weeks before staging a recovery.

For Best Performance

The following list offers tips and observations to help choose candles that perform well. Consult the associated table for more information.

- Use the identification guidelines to help select the pattern—Table 8.1.
- Candles within a third of the yearly low perform best after an upward breakout—Table 8.2.
- Select tall candles—Table 8.3.
- Use the measure rule to predict a price target—Table 8.3.
- Candles with tall upper shadows outperform—Table 8.3.
- Volume gives performance clues—Table 8.4.
- Abandoned babies form at the end of short downtrends—Trading Tactics discussion.
- The candle breaks out upward most often—Table 8.5.
- Patterns within a third of the yearly high tend to act as reversals frequently in a bull market—Table 8.5.
- Opening gap confirmation works best in a bull market—Table 8.6.
- Breakouts below the 50-day moving average lead to the best performance—Table 8.6.

9

Above the Stomach

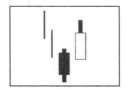

Behavior and Rank

Theoretical: Bullish reversal.

Actual bull market: Bullish reversal 66% of the time (ranking 17).

Actual bear market: Bullish reversal 67% of the time (ranking 18).

Frequency: 32nd out of 103.

Overall performance over time: 31st out of 103.

It is refreshing to find a candle pattern that performs well and yet there are a gazillion of them in my database. The statistics are solid because of the high sample counts.

Above the stomach is a candle pattern that appears in a downtrend and begins with a black candle. The bears are enthusiastic until the next day when the bulls wrest control of the stock. Price opens above the middle of the black candle's body and closes above the middle, too. Not only are the bulls in control but they are not ceding any ground to the bears. Price climbs from there, but often the rise is brief, especially if the primary trend is downward.

As the rankings show, above the stomach is a refreshing change from other candle patterns that I have looked at. It works best as a bullish reversal in either bull or bear markets. For performance, it's in the lower reaches of the atmosphere, with an overall rank of 31 out of 103 where 1 is best. That's quite good.

Identification Guidelines

When researching this candlestick pattern on the Internet, I found a one-sentence description and a thumbnail drawing at www.nisonmarketscan.com,

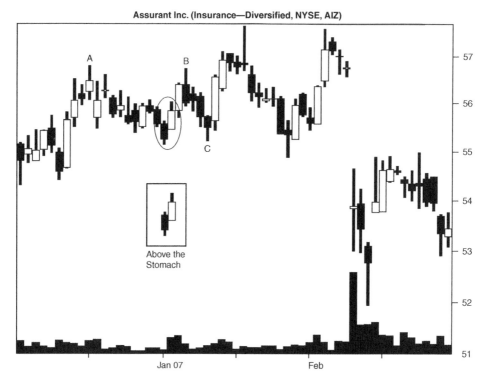

Figure 9.1   Price rises after an above-the-stomach candle pattern, but hits over-head resistance (A) at B and drops to C.

but that was enough. Figure 9.1 shows an example. Price enters the stomach after a downtrend that begins at A, forming a black candle as the first line in the two-bar pattern. A white candle follows with price opening and closing above the middle of the black candle's body. Price breaks out upward in this example and rises to B, where it encounters resistance at the price of A. Selling pressure pushes the stock down to C before bullish buying props it up again.

This rise-retrace pattern seems to be typical for the above the stomach pattern. However, the decline to C is usually not as severe as that shown here (meaning price often retraces only a fraction of the move up to B, not a full retracement as is shown here).

What should you look for when searching for an above-the-stomach? Table 9.1 lists the identification guidelines, all of which need little further explanation except for the last one. After a black candle appears on the first day of the candlestick pattern, a white candle appears. Price in the white candle must open at or above the middle of the black candle's body and close at or above the middle as well.

Statistics

Table 9.2 shows general statistics.

Table 9.1
Identification Guidelines

Characteristic	Discussion
Number of candle lines	Two.
Price trend	Downward.
First day	Black candle.
Second day	White candle opening and closing at or above the midpoint of the prior black candle's body.

Table 9.2
General Statistics

Description	Bull Market, Up Breakout	Bear Market, Up Breakout	Bull Market, Down Breakout	Bear Market, Down Breakout
Number found	9,276	1,969	4,721	963
Reversal (R), continuation (C) performance	6.82% R	10.02% R	−5.17% C	−9.12% C
Standard & Poor's 500 change	1.39%	1.09%	−0.83%	−2.95%
Candle end to breakout (median, days)	3	3	5	5
Candle end to trend end (median, days)	7	8	7	8
Number of breakouts near the 12-month low (L), middle (M), or high (H)	L 2,183, M 2,481, H 3,734	L 734, M 642, H 562	L 1,550, M 1,381, H 1,305	L 473, M 327, H 149
Percentage move for each 12-month period	L 8.13%, M 6.41%, H 6.38%	L 13.90%, M 9.11%, H 7.25%	L −6.05%, M −4.82%, H −4.55%	L −9.67%, M −8.62%, H −8.64%
Candle end + 1 day	0.79%	1.35%	−1.14%	−1.78%
Candle end + 3 days	1.65%	2.78%	−2.36%	−3.91%
Candle end + 5 days	2.18%	3.68%	−2.95%	−4.95%
Candle end + 10 days	2.74%	3.50%	−3.05%	−4.86%
10-day performance rank	59	51	33	33

Number found. I found 16,929 samples, so I did not need to resort to additional databases. That was enough to overload my spreadsheet. Most of the patterns came from a bull market.

Reversal or continuation performance. Since price trends downward into the pattern, an upward breakout is a reversal and a downward breakout is a continuation of the downtrend. The candle pattern performs better in a bear market, and upward breakouts do better than their corresponding downward breakout brothers (meaning that reversals perform better than continuations).

S&P performance. The candle pattern performs much better than the S&P 500 over the same periods.

Candle end to breakout. It takes between three and five days for price to break out, but the time is longer for downward breakouts. This makes sense because the close is usually nearer the candle's top than the bottom.

Candle end to trend end. It takes a median of seven or eight days to reach the trend end. Bear markets take a day longer than bull markets, perhaps because they travel farther and score better performance.

Yearly position, performance. Above-the-stomach candles appear most often near the yearly low, except for bull market/up breakouts, where a slight majority appear within a third of the yearly high. Performance is best when the breakout is near the yearly low in all categories.

Performance over time. Between 5 and 10 days, the performance suffers in a bear market (two columns), so this is not a robust performer. A well-performing candle would show higher performance numbers over time and in all categories.

The performance rank confirms the midlist performance. Downward breakouts show better performance than upward ones when compared to other candle types.

Table 9.3 shows height statistics.

Candle height. Tall candles outperform. To determine whether the candle is short or tall, compute its height from highest high to lowest low price in the candle pattern and divide by the breakout price. If the result is higher than the median then you have a tall candle; otherwise it's short.

If Jake sees an above-the-stomach candle with a high of 18 and a low of 17, is the candle short or tall? The height is $18 - 17$, or 1, so the measure would be 1/18, or 5.6% for an upward breakout. Assuming a bull market, the candle is tall.

Measure rule. Use the measure rule to help predict how far price will rise or fall. Compute the height of the candle and multiply it by the appropriate percentage shown in the table; then apply it to the breakout price.

Jake sees another above the stomach candle with the highest high at 75 and the lowest low at 71. What are the price targets? The height is $75 - 71$, or 4. The upward target would be (for a bull market) $75 + (61\% \times 4)$, or 77.44. The downward target would be $71 - (53\% \times 4)$ or 68.88.

Shadows. The results in Table 9.3 pertain to the last candle line in the pattern. To determine whether the shadow is short or tall, compute the height

Table 9.3
Height Statistics

Description	Bull Market, Up Breakout	Bear Market, Up Breakout	Bull Market, Down Breakout	Bear Market, Down Breakout
Median candle height as a percentage of breakout price	3.82%	6.42%	3.69%	6.24%
Short candle, performance	5.41%	7.32%	−4.11%	−7.85%
Tall candle, performance	8.60%	12.87%	−6.65%	−10.63%
Percentage meeting price target (measure rule)	61%	57%	53%	55%
Median upper shadow as a percentage of breakout price	0.44%	0.90%	0.44%	0.92%
Short upper shadow, performance	6.27%	8.44%	−4.82%	−7.85%
Tall upper shadow, performance	7.26%	11.42%	−5.43%	−10.28%
Median lower shadow as a percentage of breakout price	0.58%	0.81%	0.63%	0.88%
Short lower shadow, performance	5.86%	8.53%	−4.42%	−8.75%
Tall lower shadow, performance	7.92%	11.62%	−6.10%	−9.54%

of the shadow and divide by the breakout price. Compare the result to the median in the table. Tall shadows have a percentage higher than the median.

Candles with tall shadows perform better than those with shorter ones.

Table 9.4 shows volume statistics.

Candle volume trend. Excluding the tie in bear market/down breakouts, rising volume wins in two of three columns. Falling volume works slightly better in bull market/down breakouts.

Average candle volume. Candles with above-average volume perform well in all cases except bull market/down breakouts. Those do better if candle volume is light.

Breakout volume. In all categories heavy breakout-day volume suggests better performance postbreakout.

Trading Tactics

Like most bullish candles, this one does better as part of a downward retracement in an upward price trend. Be cautious about trading this one when the primary trend is downward. Price may make a lasting reversal, but the odds suggest otherwise.

Should price break out downward from this candle when the primary trend is also downward, then consider closing out any long positions and opening a short. Price is likely to continue moving lower.

Table 9.4
Volume Statistics

Description	Bull Market, Up Breakout	Bear Market, Up Breakout	Bull Market, Down Breakout	Bear Market, Down Breakout
Rising candle volume, performance	7.02%	10.22%	−5.13%	−9.13%
Falling candle volume, performance	6.57%	9.82%	−5.19%	−9.13%
Above-average candle volume, performance	6.97%	10.46%	−4.91%	−9.30%
Below-average candle volume, performance	6.65%	9.36%	−5.41%	−8.92%
Heavy breakout volume, performance	7.54%	11.18%	−5.18%	−10.09%
Light breakout volume, performance	6.07%	8.75%	−5.17%	−7.64%

In an upward trend with a downward breakout, trading is a tougher call. *Usually*, and I stress the word, price recovers in a few weeks after having dropped little, but the exception will burn you at the stake.

I split trading tactics into two basic studies, one concerning reversal rates and the other concerning performance. Of the two, reversal rates are more important, because it's better to trade in the direction of the trend and let price run as far as it can.

Table 9.5 gives tips to find the trend direction.

Confirmation reversal rates. If you want to detect a reversal, wait for price to close higher the next day. That works between 87% and 88% of the time.

Reversal, continuation rates. The breakout is upward from the stomach pattern most often.

Table 9.5
Reversal Rates

Description	Bull Market	Bear Market
Closing price confirmation reversal rate	88%	87%
Candle color confirmation reversal rate	85%	87%
Opening gap confirmation reversal rate	75%	74%
Reversal: trend down, breakout up	66%	67%
Continuation: trend down, breakout down	34%	33%
Percentage of reversals (R)/continuations (C) for each 12-month low (L), middle (M), or high (H)	L 58% R/42% C, M 64% R/36% C, H 74% R/26% C	L 61% R/39% C, M 66% R/34% C, H 79% R/21% C

Table 9.6
Performance Indicators

Description	Bull Market, Up Breakout	Bear Market, Up Breakout	Bull Market, Down Breakout	Bear Market, Down Breakout
Closing price confirmation, performance	6.60%	9.63%	N/A	N/A
Candle color confirmation, performance	6.55%	9.41%	N/A	N/A
Opening gap confirmation, performance	7.44%	11.28%	N/A	N/A
Breakout above 50-day moving average, performance	6.34%	8.54%	−4.75%	−7.44%
Breakout below 50-day moving average, performance	7.49%	11.45%	−5.35%	−9.56%
Last candle: close in highest third, performance	6.96%	9.82%	−5.50%	−9.39%
Last candle: close in middle third, performance	6.88%	11.08%	−4.96%	−8.26%
Last candle: close in lowest third, performance	6.25%	8.33%	−4.97%	−10.28%

N/A means not applicable.

Yearly range reversals. Reversals occur frequently within a third of the yearly high.

Table 9.6 shows performance indicators that can give hints as to how your stock will behave after the breakout from a candle pattern.

Confirmation, performance. Among the confirmation types, the opening gap method works best as a signal for reversal patterns. That means buying the stock if price gaps open higher the day after the candle pattern ends.

Moving average. Candles with breakouts below the 50-trading-day moving average do better than do those with breakouts above the average.

Closing position. Price closes all over the place in the last candle, so it's no help in predicting performance.

Sample Trade

Figure 9.2 shows a trade setup that intrigued Jake. Price moved in a straight-line run from B to A. As expected, the stock then retraces a portion of that move. Most retraces reverse between 38% and 62% of the prior up move, and that's what happens here.

Sometimes Jake likes to place a buy order at the 62% retracement mark, and sometimes he'll wait to be sure price rebounds. If price closes below the

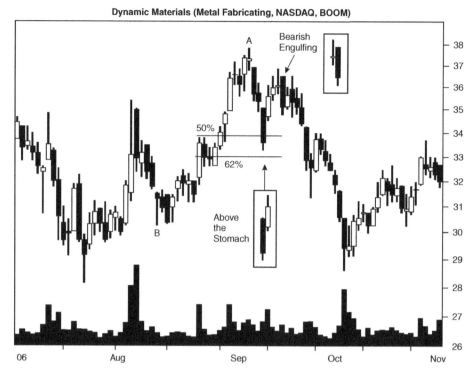

Figure 9.2   Price retraces over 50% of the move from B to A but stays above Jake's buy order.

62% retracement level, then he is confident that price is heading lower. An upward turn doesn't happen all of the time, so it's a risky bet.

In this stock, he places a buy order at the 62% value, but price remains above it, so his buy order doesn't execute. He sees the above-the-stomach candle pattern and toys with trading the reversal.

He decides to evaluate the pattern first. Tall candles outperform, but is this a tall candle? The high is at 36.10 and the low at 33.25 for a height-to-breakout price of 2.85/36.10 or 7.9%. For a bull market with an upward breakout, that represents a tall candle. If price were to climb the average amount, it would move up 6.82% (from Table 9.2) above the candle high of 36.10, to 38.56. That's higher than the peak at A (37.84).

Looking at volume, the trend is rising, so that is good news. Candle volume is above average, so that also suggests good performance. Since the breakout has not occurred yet, Jake can't gauge breakout volume.

The best entry method is an opening gap (Table 9.6), so that's what he decides to use. The next day, price gaps open higher and he receives a fill 2 cents above that, or 35.67. He decides to play it conservatively and looks for a $2 gain per share, to 37.67, slightly below the high at A of 37.84. He places a sell order for that price because he knows trying to time the sale when it approaches an old high is difficult. It's best to have an order to sell already in place.

On the downside, he feels that if price drops below the stomach low, he'll sell. The low was at 33.25 so his stop is at 33.24, a penny below the low. That would represent a potential loss of 2.43 with a possible gain of 2. The win/loss ratio is below 1 when he wanted a minimum of 2 to 1.

He moves his stop closer, to 34.09, a penny below the last candle in the stomach. That means a potential giveback of 1.58 with a $2 gain. That still isn't great, but since he is already in the trade, it will have to do. Putting the stop closer he considers too risky.

The stock moves higher the next day, forming a high wave candle (a potential reversal since it appears at the top of an uptrend) followed by a bearish engulfing pattern. A bearish turn is all he needs to know. He cancels the sell order at 37.67 and sells at the open the next day, receiving a fill at 35.14, for a loss of 53 cents per share, not including commissions.

Looking over the trade, he realizes he made two mistakes. First, he decided to trade the above-the-stomach candle pattern instead of looking elsewhere for a more promising trade based on the 62% Fibonacci retracement (this stock didn't drop to 62%). And second, he evaluated the stop-loss location *after* he placed the trade. The good news is that he was able to exit sooner than he planned when the bearish engulfing candle appeared.

For Best Performance

The following list offers tips and observations to help choose candles that perform well. Consult the associated table for more information.

- Use the identification guidelines to help select the pattern—Table 9.1.
- Candles within a third of the yearly low perform best—Table 9.2.
- Select tall candles—Table 9.3.
- Use the measure rule to predict a price target—Table 9.3.
- Candles with tall upper and lower shadows outperform—Table 9.3.
- Volume gives performance clues—Table 9.4.
- Trade this candle as part of a downward retracement in an uptrend—Trading Tactics discussion.
- The candle breaks out upward most often—Table 9.5.
- Patterns within a third of the yearly high tend to act as reversals most often—Table 9.5.
- Opening gap confirmation works best—Table 9.6.
- Breakouts below the 50-day moving average lead to the best performance—Table 9.6.

10

Advance Block

Behavior and Rank

Theoretical: Bearish reversal.
Actual bull market: Bullish continuation 64% of the time (ranking 15).
Actual bear market: Bullish continuation 61% of the time (ranking 20).
Frequency: 65th out of 103.
Overall performance over time: 54th out of 103.

The advance block is theoretically a bearish candle that is supposed to function as a reversal. However, my tests and results from at least one other researcher show that it acts as a continuation of the prevailing trend most often. When combined with other technical factors like overhead resistance or a downtrending market or industry, then even a dud like this one has value as a reversal.

In the pattern, price forms three consecutive white candles, so the bulls are in control. Bearish selling pressure causes price to gap lower at each open, but then buying demand takes over and price closes higher by day's end.

On the second and third days, the bears kick up a fuss and force price well below the intraday highs, leaving tall upper shadows on the candles. This is a warning that the bears are gaining control. However, the long upper shadows are a bear trap. Price may dip for a time, but most often the bulls enter with stun guns and immobilize the bears. This allows price to rise, eventually closing above the high of the candlestick pattern and staging an upward breakout.

As a bullish continuation pattern it ranks high for behavior, 15 and 20 for bull and bear markets, respectively, where 1 is best out of 103 candle types. Performance, however, is mediocre at best with the overall rank set at 54. The pattern performs better after a downward breakout.

Identification Guidelines

Figure 10.1 shows a weak example of an advance block. I say "weak" because price moves up for only one day into the start of the candlestick pattern and continues higher for three more days, completing the candle. The bodies get shorter even as the upper shadows grow in length, both warning of a slowing uptrend and a possible reversal.

Bullish parties owning the stock will be getting nervous as price peaks at A. The spinning top or high wave candle that appears the next day doesn't help. Both candles are neutral patterns, but the line on the chart has a black body. Price moves lower, bottoming at B, but closing higher with a white candle that day. Is the downtrend over? Only time will tell.

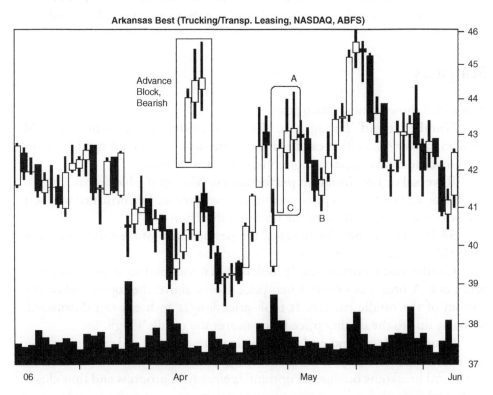

Figure 10.1 Price forms an advance block but fails to close below the pattern's low. The breakout is upward in this example despite a reversal of the brief uptrend.

Table 10.1
Identification Guidelines

Characteristic	Discussion
Number of candle lines	Three.
Price trend	Upward leading to the start of the candlestick pattern.
Candle color	White for all three candles.
Open	Price must open within the previous body.
Body	Tends to get shorter from the first candle to the last candle, but this is an observation, not a requirement.
Shadows	Taller on days 2 and 3.

Waiting for the breakout—when price closes above A in this example—would put you into the stock at the highest candle on the chart, near 46. This is exactly the wrong time to be bullish, because price drops thereafter. Trading is tricky.

Table 10.1 shows identification guidelines for the candle pattern. Most are self-explanatory. Look for three white candles. The middle and last candles must open within the prior candle's body and have shadows at least as long as their own bodies. In other words, look for long shadows on candles 2 and 3.

Statistics

Table 10.2 shows general statistics.

Number found. The advance block is somewhat rare. I uncovered 1,564 of them in over 4.7 million candle lines. Prorating the standard database indicates that the candle appears more often in a bear market.

Reversal or continuation performance. Most of the blocks had upward breakouts, and that means price continued the uptrend. Performance was best in a bear market, regardless of the breakout direction.

S&P performance. In all cases, the performance of the candle beat the S&P 500 over the same periods.

Candle end to breakout. It took between four and six days for price to break out. A breakout occurs when price closes above the top or below the bottom of the candle pattern. It took price longer to break out downward, probably due to the closing price being nearer the candle's high.

Candle end to trend end. The median time to trend end ranges between seven and nine days. Upward breakouts reach the trend end sooner than do downward breakouts because an uptrend is already in progress and thus closer to the end.

Yearly position, performance. The majority of candles appear within a third of the yearly high. However, performance is best when the breakout is

Table 10.2
General Statistics

Description	Bull Market, Up Breakout	Bear Market, Up Breakout	Bull Market, Down Breakout	Bear Market, Down Breakout
Number found	796	210	440	127
Reversal (R), continuation (C) performance	5.82% C	7.01% C	−5.14% R	−9.42% R
Standard & Poor's 500 change	1.30%	0.44%	−0.99%	−3.01%
Candle end to breakout (median, days)	4	4	6	6
Candle end to trend end (median, days)	7	7	9	9
Number of breakouts near the 12-month low (L), middle (M), or high (H)	L 70, M 132, H 468	L 27, M 59, H 114	L 60, M 104, H 208	L 26, M 30, H 71
Percentage move for each 12-month period	L 8.94%, M 6.04%, H 5.38%	L 9.00%, M 9.61%, H 5.36%	L −6.74%, M −5.06%, H −4.83%	L −11.46%, M −6.28%, H −10.19%
Candle end + 1 day	0.74%	1.10%	−0.98%	−1.89%
Candle end + 3 days	1.59%	2.11%	−2.22%	−3.52%
Candle end + 5 days	1.79%	2.86%	−2.57%	−4.93%
Candle end + 10 days	2.59%	3.46%	−3.07%	−4.76%
10-day performance rank	65	52	32	37

near the yearly low. This is true in all categories except for bear market/up breakouts. Those perform better when the breakout is in the middle of the yearly trading range.

Performance over time. Performance stumbled between days 5 and 10 in bear market/down breakouts. A robust candle pattern would show higher numbers in each time period and across each category. That weak performance reflects in the rankings, but even so, the pattern shows the best rank after a downward breakout.

Table 10.3 shows height statistics.

Candle height. Tall candles outperform. To determine whether the candle is short or tall, compute its height from highest high to lowest low price in the candle pattern and divide by the breakout price. If the result is higher than the median, then you have a tall candle; otherwise it's short.

Suppose Jacob sees an advance block with a high of 40 and a low of 38. Is the candle short or tall? The height is 40 − 38, or 2, so the measure would be 2/40, or 5%. In a bull market with an upward breakout, the candle is tall.

Table 10.3
Height Statistics

Description	Bull Market, Up Breakout	Bear Market, Up Breakout	Bull Market, Down Breakout	Bear Market, Down Breakout
Median candle height as a percentage of breakout price	4.13%	5.08%	4.42%	5.38%
Short candle, performance	4.56%	5.78%	−4.90%	−6.27%
Tall candle, performance	7.74%	8.46%	−5.57%	−10.78%
Percentage meeting price target (measure rule)	53%	51%	51%	51%
Median upper shadow as a percentage of breakout price	1.00%	1.15%	1.11%	1.35%
Short upper shadow, performance	4.65%	6.23%	−4.88%	−6.74%
Tall upper shadow, performance	7.49%	7.95%	−5.59%	−12.11%
Median lower shadow as a percentage of breakout price	0.33%	0.60%	0.31%	0.39%
Short lower shadow, performance	4.57%	6.19%	−4.70%	−8.20%
Tall lower shadow, performance	7.12%	7.91%	−5.61%	−10.47%

Measure rule. Use the measure rule to help predict how far price will rise or fall. Compute the height of the candle and multiply it by the appropriate percentage shown in the table; then apply it to the breakout price.

What are the price targets for Jacob's candle? The upward target would be $(2 \times 53\%) + 40$, or 41.06 and the downward target would be $38 - (2 \times 51\%)$, or 36.98.

Shadows. The table's results pertain to the last candle line in the pattern. To determine whether the shadow is short or tall, compute the height of the shadow and divide by the breakout price. Compare the result to the median in the table. Tall shadows have a percentage higher than the median.

Candles with tall shadows perform better than do those with short ones. Table 10.4 shows volume statistics.

Candle volume trend. A falling volume trend suggests better performance postbreakout. That means candles with falling volume perform better than do those with rising volume.

Average candle volume. Heavy candle volume works best in all categories except downward breakouts in a bull market, but even there the numbers are close.

Breakout volume. Heavy breakout volume works best at predicting performance in all breakout directions and market conditions. This is a trend we have seen with other candles. It suggests that breakout-day volume could be

Table 10.4
Volume Statistics

Description	Bull Market, Up Breakout	Bear Market, Up Breakout	Bull Market, Down Breakout	Bear Market, Down Breakout
Rising candle volume, performance	5.79%	6.76%	−4.96%	−9.29%
Falling candle volume, performance	5.83%	7.17%	−5.32%	−9.49%
Above-average candle volume, performance	6.24%	7.33%	−5.13%	−9.47%
Below-average candle volume, performance	5.50%	6.75%	−5.15%	−9.38%
Heavy breakout volume, performance	6.85%	7.48%	−5.71%	−11.56%
Light breakout volume, performance	4.73%	6.38%	−4.72%	−8.72%

an important consideration when trading candlesticks, that is, if you wait for the breakout before trading. However, the delay can be costly.

Trading Tactics

As we saw in Figure 10.1 price may drop for a few days, but 64% of the time price breaks out upward. The 64% number comes from combining the bull and bear market reversal numbers and comparing them to the bull/bear continuation numbers.

Price is especially vulnerable to drop if any of the following occur:

- Price approaches the same level as an old high.
- There is a straight-line price run of several weeks' duration.
- There is a steep price move up, trending above 60 degrees or so.
- The advance block appears as part of an upward retracement in a downward price trend.

The last situation may sound confusing, so I show this scenario in Figure 10.2. The primary trend is downward; then an upward retracement occurs and the advance block appears. The downtrend can be expected to resume.

I split trading tactics into two basic studies, one concerning reversal rates and the other concerning performance. Of the two, reversal rates are more important, because it's better to trade in the direction of the trend and let price run as far as it can.

Figure 10.2 The advance block appears in an upward retracement of a downward price trend.

Table 10.5 gives tips to find the trend direction.

Confirmation reversal rates. To help detect a reversal, look for price to close lower a day after the advance block ends. However, that only works between 56% and 58% of the time. I consider it unreliable because it's too close to random to be meaningful.

Table 10.5
Reversal Rates

Description	Bull Market	Bear Market
Closing price confirmation reversal rate	56%	58%
Candle color confirmation reversal rate	55%	58%
Opening gap confirmation reversal rate	47%	45%
Reversal rate: trend up, breakout down	36%	39%
Continuation rate: trend up, breakout up	64%	61%
Percentage of reversals (R)/ continuations (C) for each 12-month low (L), middle (M), or high (H)	L 46% R/54% C, M 44% R/56% C, H 31% R/69% C	L 49% R/51% C, M 34% R/66% C, H 38% R/62% C

Table 10.6
Performance Indicators

Description	Bull Market, Up Breakout	Bear Market, Up Breakout	Bull Market, Down Breakout	Bear Market, Down Breakout*
Closing price confirmation, performance	N/A	N/A	−7.34%	−10.61%
Candle color confirmation, performance	N/A	N/A	−7.20%	−10.88%
Opening gap confirmation, performance	N/A	N/A	−7.26%	−9.95%
Breakout above 50-day moving average, performance	5.73%	6.55%	−5.00%	−9.42%
Breakout below 50-day moving average, performance	6.80%	12.46%*	−5.50%	−9.44%
Last candle: close in highest third, performance	5.98%	7.23%	−7.01%	−6.15%*
Last candle: close in middle third, performance	6.19%	7.01%	−5.91%	−10.06%
Last candle: close in lowest third, performance	4.17%	6.76%	−4.73%	−19.26%*

N/A means not applicable.
*Fewer than 30 samples.

Reversal, continuation rates. Comparing the price trend immediately before the advance block to the breakout direction, we find that most patterns act as continuations of the price trend. The breakout is often upward.

Yearly range reversals. In a bull market, continuations occur most often when the breakout price is within a third of the yearly high. In a bear market, the middle of the yearly trading range does better.

Table 10.6 shows performance indicators that can give hints as to how your stock will behave after the breakout from a candle pattern.

Confirmation, performance. Since a downward breakout represents a reversal of the uptrend, that is the direction I looked at for candle confirmation. Within their bull or bear market columns, the performance difference between the numbers is slight. In a bull market, closing price confirmation works best. That means waiting for a lower close the next day before taking a position. In a bear market, candle color works slightly better. Trade (sell short or sell a long holding) only if a black candle appears the day after the advance block.

Moving average. Blocks with a close below the 50-trading-day moving average perform better than do those with closes above the moving average.

Closing position. A close in the middle of the candle during bull market/ up breakouts and bear market/down breakouts suggests better postbreakout performance. When the close is near the candle line's high (and we are looking at the last candle line in the advance block here) in bear market/up breakouts and bull market/down breakouts, performance improves.

Sample Trade

Jacob is a novice investor who owned the stock shown in Figure 10.3. As price climbed to the high at A, he called the stock market an easy game. He was rich. He told his friends, bragging that he had the golden touch and couldn't lose. But price bumped against a ceiling of overhead resistance (at A) three times (forming a triple top chart pattern) and then turned down.

He stopped talking to his friends about his investments. He became moody, irritable, and short-tempered. He rode the stock down to 53 in early June and promised that when he recovered his lost paper profit, he would sell.

Price started climbing again. His mood lifted. Then the advance block formed and that was the excuse he was looking for. When the stock opened lower the next day (at B), he dumped his holdings.

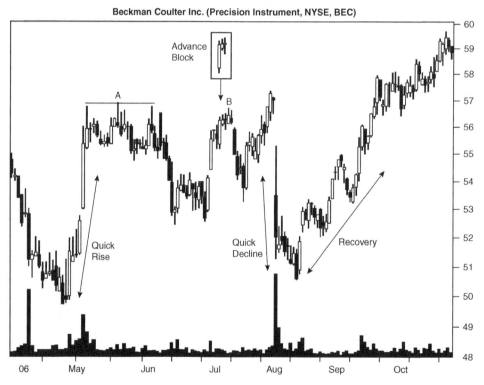

Figure 10.3 A sell signal appears when an advance block approaches overhead resistance.

In the coming days, as price tumbled, he congratulated himself on his perfect timing and wondered how far the stock would plummet. As the chart shows, it recovered to a new high and then gapped lower in a quick decline that mirrored the quick rise during May.

This is a trading setup that he'd seen many times before—a quick decline follows a quick rise. Then a recovery phase takes over that often, but not always, lifts price above the high between the rise/decline phases. So, he bought back in during late August.

He's feeling good about his investments again. He's bragging to his friends about how easy it is to make a killing in the stock market. And that means just one thing: He's going to get slaughtered.

For Best Performance

The following list offers tips and observations to help choose candles that perform well. Consult the associated table for more information.

- Use the identification guidelines to help select the pattern—Table 10.1.
- Candles within a third of the yearly low perform best under most conditions—Table 10.2.
- Select tall candles—Table 10.3.
- Use the measure rule to predict a price target—Table 10.3.
- Candles with tall upper and lower shadows outperform—Table 10.3.
- Volume gives performance clues—Table 10.4.
- For a reversal, look for an upward retracement in a downward price trend—Trading Tactics discussion and Figure 10.2.
- The advance block candle pattern breaks out upward most often—Table 10.5.
- Patterns within a third of the yearly high tend to act as continuations frequently in a bull market—Table 10.5.
- Breakouts below the 50-day moving average lead to the best performance—Table 10.6.

11

Below the Stomach

Behavior and Rank

Theoretical: Bearish reversal.
Actual bull market: Bearish reversal 60% of the time (ranking 27).
Actual bear market: Bearish reversal 65% of the time (ranking 20).
Frequency: 38th out of 103.
Overall performance over time: 59th out of 103.

If there is an above-the-stomach candle pattern, then there should be a below the stomach one also . . . and there is. I found enough of this pattern using two databases that I didn't need to boost the candle search to the full 4.7 million lines.

Below the stomach begins with a tall white candle in an uptrend, and the bulls are excited. Price is moving up! But the next day opens lower and stays below the midpoint of the white candle's body. When the bulls fail to roll price to higher ground and keep it there, it means only one thing: Price is going down. It does, 60% of the time.

The behavioral rank is quite good, scoring 20 (bear market) and 27 (bull market) out of 103, with 1 being best. Performance, however, is helium balloon light, with the overall rank at 59. This candle pattern does best after an upward breakout.

Identification Guidelines

I found this candle pattern on the web site, www.nisonmarketscan.com. Figure 11.1 shows what a below-the-stomach candlestick looks like. Price trends up leading to the pattern and then a tall white candle appears. However, the next day, price opens below the middle of the white candle's body and also closes there. In this case, it is a doji that appears near the middle of the white candle (it opens below it by half a penny and closes slightly below that, too). That sets the stage for a trend change and down price goes, slowly at first as if it's undecided which direction to take. Price forms a series of descending scallop chart patterns on the way down, the bottom of each finding support at rising windows.

The below-the-stomach candle pictured in Figure 11.1 is unusual because of the doji that appears instead of a taller black candle, but it still meets the identification guidelines listed in Table 11.1. Most of the guidelines are self-explanatory. The second candle line in the pattern can be any color just as long as it opens below the middle of the white candle's body and closes at or below the middle.

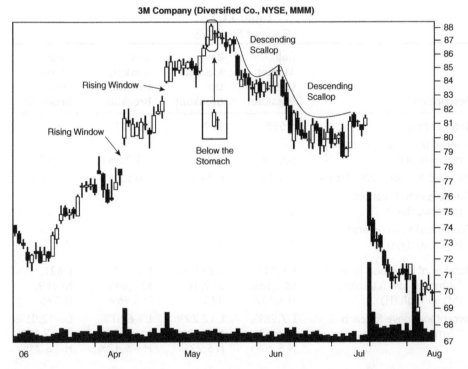

Figure 11.1   A below-the-stomach candle pattern appears at the peak of an up-trend.

Table 11.1
Identification Guidelines

Characteristic	Discussion
Number of candle lines	Two.
Price trend	Upward leading to the start of the candlestick.
First day	A tall white day.
Second day	The candle opens below the middle of the white candle's body and closes at or below the middle, too.

Statistics

Table 11.2 shows general statistics.

Number found. I found 19,500 patterns to give a solid base to the statistics. Prorating them using the standard database indicates that they appear more often in a bear market.

Table 11.2
General Statistics

Description	Bull Market, Up Breakout	Bear Market, Up Breakout	Bull Market, Down Breakout	Bear Market, Down Breakout
Number found	6,598	969	10,094	1,839
Reversal (R), continuation (C) performance	5.02% C	7.27% C	−5.26% R	−9.48% R
Standard & Poor's 500 change	1.34%	0.74%	−0.55%	−2.06%
Candle end to breakout (median, days)	5	5	3	3
Candle end to trend end (median, days)	7	8	6	7
Number of breakouts near the 12-month low (L), middle (M), or high (H)	L 1,043, M 1,588, H 3,137	L 237, M 279, H 443	L 2,344, M 2,643, H 3,969	L 621, M 589, H 596
Percentage move for each 12-month period	L 7.98%, M 5.68%, H 5.26%	L 12.29%, M 7.38%, H 5.72%	L −6.51%, M −5.83%, H −5.42%	L −12.05%, M −8.92%, H −8.24%
Candle end + 1 day	1.04%	1.65%	−0.56%	−1.30%
Candle end + 3 days	2.16%	3.66%	−1.39%	−2.44%
Candle end + 5 days	2.70%	4.25%	−1.57%	−3.07%
Candle end + 10 days	3.33%	4.81%	−1.55%	−3.42%
10-day performance rank	48	32	79	61

Reversal or continuation performance. The best performance comes in a bear market, regardless of the breakout direction. Pound for pound, reversals perform better than continuations.

S&P performance. As is the case with most candlestick patterns, the candle creams the S&P 500's move over the same periods.

Candle end to breakout. It takes between three and five days for price to break out. Downward breakouts take less time to occur, and that's likely due to price closing near the bottom of the pattern.

Candle end to trend end. The median time to trend end ranges between six and eight days. The end comes sooner for below the stomach patterns with downward breakouts. Since the downward trend is already under way, it follows that the downward trend end comes sooner.

Yearly position, performance. The majority of below the stomach patterns occur within a third of the yearly high (except bear market/down breakouts, which are more numerous near the yearly low), but performance is best within a third of the yearly low.

Performance over time. The candle falls short of being robust because of a performance decline from five to 10 days in bull market/down breakouts.

The performance rank shows that upward breakouts perform better than downward breakouts.

Table 11.3 shows height statistics.

Candle height. Tall candles perform better than short ones. To determine whether the candle is short or tall, compute its height from highest high to lowest low price in the candle pattern and divide by the breakout price. If the result is higher than the median, then you have a tall candle; otherwise it's short.

Will sees a stomach with a high price of 53 and a low of 51. Is it tall or short? The height is $53 - 51$, or 2, so the measure would be 2/53, or 3.8% for an upward breakout. In a bull market, the candle is tall. The downward breakout measure would be 2/51, or 3.9%, which is also tall.

Measure rule. Use the measure rule to help predict how far price will rise or fall. Compute the height of the candle and multiply it by the appropriate percentage shown in the table; then apply it to the breakout price.

What are the price targets for Will's candle? The upward target is $(2 \times 60\%) + 53$, or 54.20 and the downward target is $51 - (2 \times 57\%)$, or 49.86.

Shadows. The results in Table 11.3 pertain to the last candle line in the pattern. To determine whether the shadow is short or tall, compute the height of the shadow and divide by the breakout price. Compare the result to the median in the table. Tall shadows have a percentage higher than the median.

Upper shadow performance. Tall upper shadows perform better than short ones in all categories.

Lower shadow performance. Bull market/up breakouts show better performance with a short lower shadow, but the other categories do better with tall shadows.

Table 11.3
Height Statistics

Description	Bull Market, Up Breakout	Bear Market, Up Breakout	Bull Market, Down Breakout	Bear Market, Down Breakout
Median candle height as a percentage of breakout price	3.25%	4.67%	3.65%	5.31%
Short candle, performance	3.94%	6.27%	−4.14%	−7.38%
Tall candle, performance	6.96%	8.56%	−7.15%	−12.14%
Percentage meeting price target (measure rule)	60%	56%	57%	57%
Median upper shadow as a percentage of breakout price	0.57%	0.84%	0.51%	0.85%
Short upper shadow, performance	4.42%	7.03%	−4.66%	−8.53%
Tall upper shadow, performance	5.60%	7.53%	−5.88%	−10.46%
Median lower shadow as a percentage of breakout price	0.13%	0.57%	0.27%	0.58%
Short lower shadow, performance	5.42%	6.69%	−4.46%	−8.40%
Tall lower shadow, performance	4.84%	7.79%	−5.98%	−10.48%

Table 11.4 shows volume statistics.

Candle volume trend. Performance after the breakout is best if volume trended downward leading to the candle pattern. The exception to this is the bear market/down breakout category, which does better with rising volume.

Average candle volume. Candles with above-average volume show better postbreakout performance in all categories except bear market/up breakouts. Those perform better with light candle volume.

Breakout volume. Heavy breakout-day volume works best across the board but is especially potent in a bear market.

Trading Tactics

Figure 11.2 shows an example of a below-the-stomach candle formation appearing in a trading range. Overhead resistance appears at the top of the channel, set up by a down-sloping trendline drawn along the peaks. Below the pattern a support zone exists, creating a floor that will take some digging before price can tunnel through.

Table 11.4
Volume Statistics

Description	Bull Market, Up Breakout	Bear Market, Up Breakout	Bull Market, Down Breakout	Bear Market, Down Breakout
Rising candle volume, performance	5.49%	7.01%	−5.64%	−9.87%
Falling candle volume, performance	6.03%	7.57%	−5.85%	−9.11%
Above-average candle volume, performance	5.64%	6.72%	−5.69%	−9.67%
Below-average candle volume, performance	4.63%	7.72%	−4.94%	−9.25%
Heavy breakout volume, performance	6.59%	8.26%	−5.98%	−10.41%
Light breakout volume, performance	3.72%	6.01%	−4.78%	−8.69%

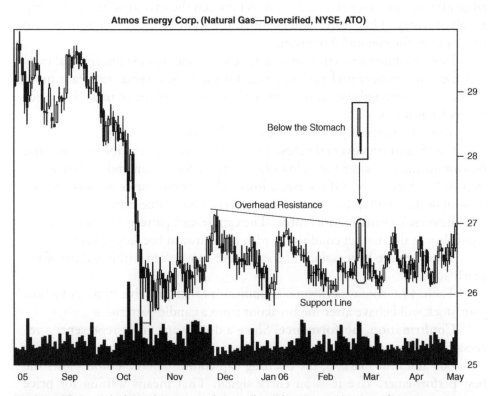

Figure 11.2 A below-the-stomach candlestick appears in a trading range, suggesting price will drop to the bottom of the channel and then rebound.

Table 11.5
Reversal Rates

Description	Bull Market	Bear Market
Closing price confirmation reversal rate	86%	87%
Candle color confirmation reversal rate	80%	84%
Opening gap confirmation reversal rate	72%	71%
Reversal rate: trend up, breakout down	60%	65%
Continuation rate: trend up, breakout up	40%	35%
Percentage of reversals (R)/continuations (C) for each 12-month low (L), middle (M), or high (H)	L 69% R/31% C, M 62% R/38% C, H 56% R/44% C	L 72% R/28% C, M 68% R/32% C, H 57% R/43% C

When the stomach reversal begins at the top of the channel, the price target would be the bottom of the channel. That works well in this situation, but it's not always this easy. When price nears the channel boundary, look for signs of a reversal. If the signs appear, then close out your short position.

The channel can slope in any direction, often at 45 degrees to the horizontal (and sometimes more). Price bounces between the two trendlines, climbing a wall of worry. The steeper the channel, the more likely it is that price will break out of the channel downward.

I split trading tactics into two basic studies, one concerning reversal rates and the other concerning performance. Of the two, reversal rates are more important, because it's better to trade in the direction of the trend and let price run as far as it can.

Table 11.5 gives tips to find the trend direction.

Confirmation reversal rates. To detect a reversal, wait for price to close downward the day after the below-the-stomach formation ends. That works over 86% of the time. Of course, a lower close means price is closer to the bottom of the candle, thereby making a reversal more likely anyway.

Reversal, continuation rates. The candlestick pattern acts as a reversal, regardless of the market conditions, with a downward breakout likely.

Yearly range reversals. Reversals occur most often within a third of the yearly low.

Table 11.6 shows performance indicators that can give hints as to how your stock will behave after the breakout from a candle pattern.

Confirmation, performance. Since a downward move represents a reversal of the uptrend, downward breakouts are the ones I focused on. For both bull and bear markets, the opening gap confirmation method shows the best performance. Use it as an entry signal. That means waiting for price to gap open lower the day after the stomach completes before trading the stock.

Table 11.6
Performance Indicators

Description	Bull Market, Up Breakout	Bear Market, Up Breakout	Bull Market, Down Breakout	Bear Market, Down Breakout
Closing price confirmation, performance	N/A	N/A	−5.50%	−9.66%
Candle color confirmation, performance	N/A	N/A	−5.53%	−9.64%
Opening gap confirmation, performance	N/A	N/A	−6.02%	−10.35%
Breakout above 50-day moving average, performance	5.66%	6.82%	−5.57%	−8.71%
Breakout below 50-day moving average, performance	2.97%	9.98%	−6.04%	−10.62%
Last candle: close in highest third, performance	5.60%	6.12%	−5.29%	−8.77%
Last candle: close in middle third, performance	4.57%	7.80%	−5.45%	−9.40%
Last candle: close in lowest third, performance	5.24%	7.24%	−5.15%	−9.64%

N/A means not applicable.

Moving average. Most often, candles with breakouts below the moving average perform better than do those with breakouts above the average. The exception is bull market/up breakouts.

Closing position. Where price closes in the last line of the candle shows no consistent trend across the categories.

Sample Trade

Figure 11.3 shows a trading setup Will is contemplating. Price has climbed for a few days leading into the stomach pattern and then the candle takes price down to C. C is the bottom of a support zone set up by valleys beginning at A and touching the horizontal line three times before the stomach appears. Having such clearly defined support makes it simpler to judge how far price is likely to fall.

After finding support at C, price bounces up to the middle of the tall black candle. Tall candles show resistance or support along the body 39% of the time, and this is an example.

Will wants to know how far price is likely to fall. Seeing support at line AC and having the bottom of candlestick C stop near there, he understands

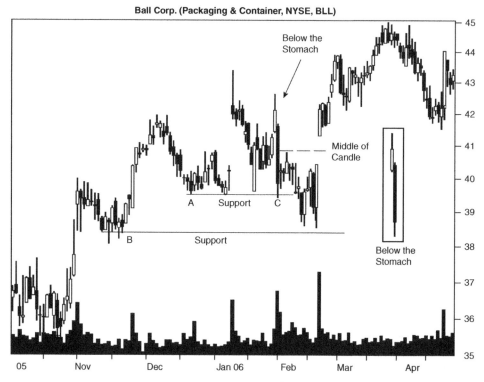

Figure 11.3 A search for underlying support reveals how far price is likely to fall.

price would have to work its way through that support. If that happened, how far would price fall?

A lower support zone appeared at B, created by a congestion of candles in November. Not shown, but the support zone extended backward in time as far as April 2005. Thus, support zone B is a likely turning point (but there's no guarantee, of course).

If Will shorts the stock below support at C and buys it back near the level of B, would that be enough profit? Let's put it this way: I would look elsewhere for a more profitable opportunity.

For Best Performance

The following list offers tips and observations to help choose candles that perform well. Consult the associated table for more information.

- Use the identification guidelines to help select the pattern—Table 11.1.
- Candles within a third of the yearly low perform best—Table 11.2.
- Select tall candles—Table 11.3.
- Use the measure rule to predict a price target—Table 11.3.

- Candles with tall upper shadows outperform—Table 11.3.
- Volume gives performance clues—Table 11.4.
- Channels can help predict turning points—Trading Tactics discussion.
- The below-the-stomach candle breaks out downward most often —Table 11.5.
- Patterns within a third of the yearly low frequently act as reversals— Table 11.5.
- Opening gap confirmation works best—Table 11.6.

12

Belt Hold, Bearish

Behavior and Rank

Theoretical: Bearish reversal.

Actual bull market: Bearish reversal 68% of the time (ranking 16).

Actual bear market: Bearish reversal 69% of the time (ranking 17).

Frequency: 19th out of 103.

Overall performance over time: 63rd out of 103.

The bearish belt hold is a candlestick pattern that surprises me because it works as a bearish reversal over twice as often as it does a continuation, ranking 16 and 17 for bull and bear markets, respectively. However, the length of the price drop after the candle depends on the situation and your skill at eking out a profit. In fact, the best performance over time comes from patterns with upward breakouts. They rank 33 and 39 out of 103 candles in bull and bear markets, respectively. The overall rank is an unexciting 63.

The candle is a study in bullish enthusiasm gone wrong. In my trading, I'll study the charts after the market closes and plan a trade. Overnight, anything can happen, and I know that it's best not to place a trade until an hour after the stock market opens. By then, everything will have settled down and direction is established.

Sometimes, though, the opportunity is so compelling that I just place the market order blindly the night before. If others do the same, price may open at the high for the day. Then the bears take over and push price down. The belt hold candlestick is an example of that behavior. Price opens at the high and closes near the low, leaving a tall black candle to print on the chart.

Identification Guidelines

Figure 12.1 shows an example of a belt hold. This is not a perfect example because some may quibble about the price trend leading to the belt hold. However, the setup is typical for the candlestick and it appears frequently in the charts I looked at. If you erase the black belt hold candle, you'll see that price is indeed trending up, so it qualifies as a belt hold. In any case, the belt hold opens at the high and closes near the low, forming a black opening marubozu candle. The only difference between a black opening marubozu and a bearish belt hold is the requirement of an uptrend for the belt hold. That segues to identification guidelines.

Table 12.1 lists identification guidelines, and they are self-explanatory. One source I checked says that the belt hold should gap well above the prior candle, but other (multiple) sources do not mention the gap requirement. If you want a gap, then look for a gap. The following statistical analysis does *not* depend on a gap. It follows the guidelines listed in Table 12.1.

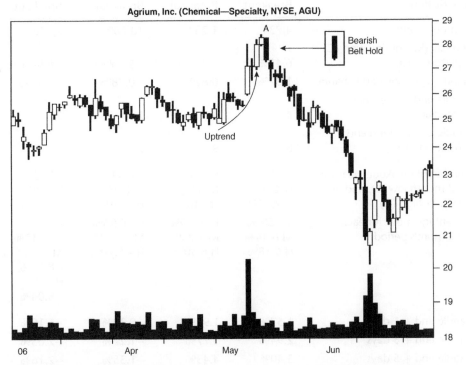

Figure 12.1   A bearish belt hold appears after an uptrend, opening at the high for the day and closing near the low.

Table 12.1
Identification Guidelines

Characteristic	Discussion
Number of candle lines	One.
Price trend	Upward leading to the candle line.
Configuration	Price opens at the high and closes near the low, creating a tall black candle.

Statistics

Table 12.2 shows general statistics.

Number found. As one might expect, the belt hold candle is as plentiful as ants at a picnic. I found 19,198 of them using only one of four databases. Most came from a bull market.

Table 12.2
General Statistics

Description	Bull Market, Up Breakout	Bear Market, Up Breakout	Bull Market, Down Breakout	Bear Market, Down Breakout
Number found	4,734	1,287	10,269	2,908
Reversal (R), continuation (C) performance	6.41% C	7.29% C	−5.90% R	−8.98% R
Standard & Poor's 500 change	1.87%	0.82%	−0.78%	−1.98%
Candle end to breakout (median, days)	4	4	2	2
Candle end to trend end (median, days)	8	9	7	7
Number of breakouts near the 12-month low (L), middle (M), or high (H)	L 524, M 896, H 2,161	L 233, M 398, H 636	L 1,695, M 2,249, H 4,345	L 756, M 940, H 1,166
Percentage move for each 12-month period	L 7.59%, M 6.44%, H 6.18%	L 10.19%, M 7.24%, H 6.50%	L −6.96%, M −6.21%, H −5.70%	L −11.13%, M −8.71%, H −8.04%
Candle end + 1 day	1.57%	1.94%	−0.70%	−1.19%
Candle end + 3 days	2.94%	3.77%	−1.22%	−2.03%
Candle end + 5 days	3.40%	4.43%	−1.35%	−2.16%
Candle end + 10 days	3.92%	4.58%	−1.07%	−2.15%
10-day performance rank	33	39	93	80

Reversal or continuation performance. The best performance comes from the belt hold candle in a bear market. A falling market makes it easier for a stock to tumble. However, you can pull your hair out wondering why performance does so well in a bear market when the breakout is *upward* (price climbs higher than it does in a bull market, when the market trend should be pushing the stock up, too).

S&P performance. Comparing the S&P 500 with the breakout confirmation numbers, the table shows that candle performance beats the S&P 500 by a Grand Canyon (huge) margin.

Candle end to breakout. Downward breakouts take only two days compared to four days for upward breakouts, most likely because the close is near the candle's low.

Candle end to trend end. It takes between seven and nine days for the price trend to end, as measured from the day after the end of the belt hold to the swing low or swing high. Notice that downward breakouts reach the swing low slightly faster than upward breakouts reach the swing high. That could be because downward moves show higher velocity (I proved this using chart patterns).

Yearly position, performance. Candles with breakouts near the yearly high appear more often than do those in the other two ranges. However, performance is best when the breakout is within a third of the yearly low.

Performance over time. The belt hold stumbles twice from 5 to 10 days, both with downward breakouts, so the belt hold is not a robust candle. Robust candles show increasing performance numbers across all time periods and all categories.

The performance rank confirms the finding, with downward breakouts ranking worse than upward ones. The upward breakout performance, when compared to other candles, is unremarkable.

Table 12.3 shows height statistics.

Candle height. Tall candles perform better than short ones across the board. To determine whether the candle is short or tall, compute its height from high to low price in the candle pattern and divide by the breakout price. If the result is higher than the median, then you have a tall candle; otherwise it's short.

If Alice sees a belt hold with a high of 17 and a low of 16, is the candle short or tall in a bull market with a downward breakout? The height is 17 − 16, or 1, so the measure is 1/16, or 6.3%. The candle is tall.

Measure rule. Use the measure rule to help predict how far price will rise or fall. Compute the height of the candle and multiply it by the appropriate percentage shown in the table; then apply it to the breakout price.

What are Alice's price targets? The upward target would be $(1 \times 75\%) +$ 17, or 17.75, and the downward target would be $16 - (1 \times 71\%)$, or 15.29.

Lower shadow performance. To determine whether the shadow is short or tall, compute the height of the shadow and divide by the breakout price.

Table 12.3
Height Statistics

Description	Bull Market, Up Breakout	Bear Market, Up Breakout	Bull Market, Down Breakout	Bear Market, Down Breakout
Median candle height as a percentage of breakout price	2.43%	3.18%	2.67%	3.56%
Short candle, performance	5.16%	6.03%	−4.81%	−7.51%
Tall candle, performance	7.92%	8.69%	−7.32%	−10.65%
Percentage meeting price target (measure rule)	75%	74%	71%	71%
Median lower shadow as a percentage of breakout price	0.25%	0.36%	0.25%	0.36%
Short lower shadow, performance	5.74%	6.60%	−5.43%	−8.34%
Tall lower shadow, performance	7.11%	7.98%	−6.41%	−9.64%

Compare the result to the median in the table. Tall shadows have a percentage higher than the median.

Candles with tall lower shadows perform better than do those with short shadows.

Table 12.4 shows volume statistics.

Candle volume trend. Candles with below-average volume outperform those with heavy volume.

Breakout volume. Heavy breakout-day volume suggests better performance in all categories. We see this in many candlestick patterns: Breakout-day volume is one of the best predictors of performance.

Table 12.4
Volume Statistics

Description	Bull Market, Up Breakout	Bear Market, Up Breakout	Bull Market, Down Breakout	Bear Market, Down Breakout
Above-average candle volume, performance	6.26%	6.85%	−5.85%	−8.95%
Below-average candle volume, performance	6.50%	7.51%	−5.94%	−9.00%
Heavy breakout volume, performance	6.93%	7.80%	−6.31%	−9.89%
Light breakout volume, performance	5.93%	6.81%	−5.64%	−8.30%

Trading Tactics

Congestion has lots to do with sinus trouble, but also everything to do with price breaking out of a support zone. Figure 12.2 shows an example of price trending up and touching the top of the trading range, reversing, and returning to the bottom of the range. Price hitting overhead resistance at C is not my point. What is important is that price drops to A and B, where it finds support before rebounding.

The figure teaches two lessons. First, if price leaves a support zone (and pretend that it *did* escape in the example) and returns, don't expect it to fall far. Second, price has to have something to reverse. If price doesn't climb far, then do not expect it to fall far. This is especially true if the belt hold occurs inside a trading range. Usually, the belt hold will not force price downward out of the trading range.

I split trading tactics into two basic studies, one concerning reversal rates and the other concerning performance. Of the two, reversal rates are more important, because it's better to trade in the direction of the trend and let price run as far as it can.

Table 12.5 gives tips to find the trend direction.

Figure 12.2 Price attempts to leave congestion but reverses at a belt hold candlestick and drops back to the bottom of the support zone.

Table 12.5
Reversal Rates

Description	Bull Market	Bear Market
Closing price confirmation reversal rate	96%	95%
Candle color confirmation reversal rate	90%	91%
Opening gap confirmation reversal rate	79%	79%
Reversal rate: trend up, breakout down	68%	69%
Continuation rate: trend up, breakout up	32%	31%
Percentage of reversals (R)/ continuations (C) for each 12-month low (L), middle (M), or high (H)	L 76% R/24% C, M 72% R/28% C, H 67% R/33% C	L 76% R/24% C, M 70% R/30% C, H 65% R/35% C

Confirmation reversal rates. If you wait for price to close lower the day after a belt hold, the chance is 95% or higher that price will reverse. That really doesn't say much, though, because a lower close will often place the close below the belt hold's low, and that confirms a reversal. So, I wouldn't get too excited.

Reversal, continuation rates. The belt hold candle pattern acts as a reversal more than two out of three times. It performs best as a reversal in a bear market. Expect a downward breakout.

Yearly range reversals. Reversals occur most often within a third of the yearly low.

Table 12.6 shows performance indicators that can give hints as to how your stock will behave after the breakout from a candle pattern.

Confirmation, performance. Since a downward move means a reversal of the uptrend, that is the direction I focused on. For both bull and bear

Table 12.6
Performance Indicators

Description	Bull Market, Up Breakout	Bear Market, Up Breakout	Bull Market, Down Breakout	Bear Market, Down Breakout
Closing price confirmation, performance	N/A	N/A	−5.12%	−8.09%
Candle color confirmation, performance	N/A	N/A	−5.36%	−8.33%
Opening gap confirmation, performance	N/A	N/A	−6.24%	−9.07%
Breakout above 50-day moving average, performance	6.31%	7.01%	−5.70%	−8.07%
Breakout below 50-day moving average, performance	7.29%	8.35%	−6.41%	−10.35%

N/A means not applicable.

markets, opening gap confirmation gives the best performance. That means trading if price gaps open lower following the belt hold.

Moving average. Breakouts below the 50-trading-day moving average result in performance that's better than performance after breakouts above the moving average.

Sample Trade

Alice knows that price typically rises not in a prolonged straight-line run, but in more of a staircase pattern—a rise, a retracement, and another move up. When she sees the stock pictured in Figure 12.3, the technical evidence suggests the decline is over when price begins recovering after B.

The move from D to B retraced between 50% and 62% of the move up from C to D, right where she expected the turn. On this basis, she is all set to buy the stock; but two things stop her. What are they?

First, the belt hold as a tall black candle following a tall white one suggests a bearish shift in sentiment. Second, a trendline drawn downward from the high at D means overhead resistance. If price could push through this ceiling, the rise might have a chance of being a lasting one. To Alice, the evidence suggests that waiting to see what price does next is the prudent course.

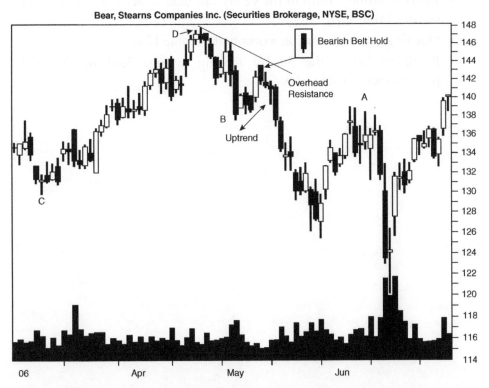

Figure 12.3 Overhead resistance puts an end to this uptrend.

As the chart shows, price turns and heads lower after the belt hold. At A, price bumps up against trendline resistance several times before turning lower. Alice made the right choice to skip the trade.

For Best Performance

The following list offers tips and observations to help choose candles that perform well. Consult the associated table for more information.

- Use the identification guidelines to help select the pattern—Table 12.1.
- Candles within a third of the yearly low perform best—Table 12.2.
- Select tall candles—Table 12.3.
- Use the measure rule to predict a price target—Table 12.3.
- Candles with tall lower shadows outperform—Table 12.3.
- Volume gives performance clues—Table 12.4.
- Look for overhead resistance and underlying support before trading—Trading Tactics discussion.
- The candle breaks out downward most often—Table 12.5.
- Patterns within a third of the yearly low tend to act as reversals most often—Table 12.5.
- Opening gap confirmation works best—Table 12.6.
- Breakouts below the 50-day moving average lead to the best performance—Table 12.6.

13

Belt Hold, Bullish

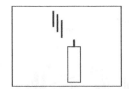

Behavior and Rank

Theoretical: Bullish reversal.

Actual bull market: Bullish reversal 71% of the time (ranking 11).

Actual bear market: Bullish reversal 71% of the time (ranking 14).

Frequency: 22nd out of 103.

Overall performance over time: 62nd out of 103.

I expected more from a bullish belt hold candlestick, but with one of the higher reversal rates (71%), I shouldn't complain. Sometimes called a white opening marubozu (in a downtrend) or white opening shaven bottom, the bullish belt hold is a mediocre performer. Candles with downward breakouts do quite well (ranking 36 and 28 out of 103), but the upward breakout numbers yank the overall performance rank down to 62.

The psychology behind the pattern begins with a falling price trend, so the bears are in control. Then the belt hold appears. Price opens at the low for the day and climbs, forming a tall white candle when price closes near the high. The bears run for cover as if the park ranger were hunting them. When coupled with underlying support, the belt hold marks a reliable turning point in the price trend. However, as we will see, this is not always the case, especially during extensive downtrends. The belt hold seems to work best as part of a retracement in an uptrend. I'll explain that in the Trading Tactics section of this chapter.

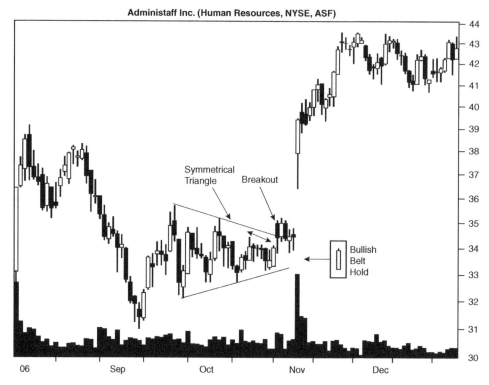

Figure 13.1 A bullish belt hold signals an upward breakout from a symmetrical triangle.

Identification Guidelines

Figure 13.1 shows a bullish belt hold. Looking at the daily highs, the candlestick forms as part of a short-term downtrend near the apex of a symmetrical triangle (illustrated by the diagonal arrow). Price opens at the low and closes near the day's high, leaving a tall white candle on the chart. The next day price continues the uptrend. Price eventually breaks out of the triangle and gaps upward in a powerful rally.

Table 13.1 lists identification guidelines, and most are self-explanatory. Look for a tall white candle that appears in a downtrend. The downtrend is

Table 13.1
Identification Guidelines

Characteristic	Discussion
Number of candle lines	One.
Price trend	Downward leading to the candlestick.
Configuration	A tall white candle with price opening at the low and closing near the high.

what separates the bullish belt hold from a white opening marubozu. In a belt hold, price should open at the low and close near the high. That means it has no lower shadow and a short upper shadow.

Statistics

Table 13.2 shows general statistics.

Number found. In my trading closet, I found 14,542 belt holds, with most appearing in a bull market. I'm thinking of donating them.

Reversal or continuation performance. The best performance from a belt hold is in a bear market, regardless of the breakout direction. You may find that as odd as I do, but it happens frequently in candles.

S&P performance. Postbreakout performance of the belt hold candle draws loops around the S&P 500.

Candle end to breakout. It takes between two and four days for price to close above the top (upward breakouts) or below the bottom (downward

Table 13.2
General Statistics

Description	Bull Market, Up Breakout	Bear Market, Up Breakout	Bull Market, Down Breakout	Bear Market, Down Breakout
Number found	7,836	2,496	3,172	1,038
Reversal (R), continuation (C) performance	6.77% R	8.06% R	−5.86% C	−9.31% C
Standard & Poor's 500 change	1.63%	0.70%	−1.22%	−2.85%
Candle end to breakout (median, days)	2	2	4	4
Candle end to trend end (median, days)	7	7	7	8
Number of breakouts near the 12-month low (L), middle (M), or high (H)	L 1,424, M 1,630, H 2,939	L 671, M 799, H 980	L 806, M 783, H 921	L 334, M 336, H 346
Percentage move for each 12-month period	L 8.40%, M 6.51%, H 6.16%	L 10.06%, M 7.86%, H 7.15%	L −6.84%, M −5.96%, H −5.47%	L −11.21%, M −9.35%, H −7.76%
Candle end + 1 day	0.75%	0.90%	−1.56%	−2.09%
Candle end + 3 days	1.37%	1.59%	−2.78%	−4.16%
Candle end + 5 days	1.70%	2.04%	−3.09%	−4.53%
Candle end + 10 days	2.05%	1.86%	−2.92%	−5.20%
10-day performance rank	85	75	36	28

breakouts) of a belt hold. Since price closes near the top of the candle, it doesn't take long for an upward breakout to occur. Downward breakouts, however, have farther to travel so they take longer.

Candle end to trend end. The median length from the day after the belt hold to the trend end is about a week.

Yearly position, performance. The majority of belt holds appear within a third of the yearly high. However, performance is best when they appear within a third of the yearly low.

Performance over time. The belt hold is not a solid performer. It falters during bear market/up breakouts and bull market/down breakouts between days 5 and 10. By contrast, robust candle patterns show increasing numbers over all time periods and in all categories.

The performance rank shows that downward breakouts have a higher rank than upward breakouts, meaning they perform better when compared to other candles.

Table 13.3 shows height statistics.

Candle height. Tall candles perform better than short ones in all categories. To determine whether the candle is short or tall, compute its height from high to low price in the candle pattern and divide by the breakout price. If the result is higher than the median, then you have a tall candle; otherwise it's short.

Mary has a belt hold left over from a dress with a high price of 78 and a low of 76. Is the candle short or tall? The height is $78 - 76$ or 2, so the measure would be 2/78, or 2.6%. For an upward breakout in a bull market, the candle is short.

Table 13.3
Height Statistics

Description	Bull Market, Up Breakout	Bear Market, Up Breakout	Bull Market, Down Breakout	Bear Market, Down Breakout
Median candle height as a percentage of breakout price	2.78%	3.64%	2.57%	3.47%
Short candle, performance	5.56%	6.63%	−4.88%	−7.56%
Tall candle, performance	8.29%	9.71%	−7.09%	−11.33%
Percentage meeting price target (measure rule)	74%	71%	71%	73%
Median upper shadow as a percentage of breakout price	0.23%	0.37%	0.25%	0.39%
Short upper shadow, performance	6.23%	6.92%	−5.50%	−8.55%
Tall upper shadow, performance	7.33%	9.28%	−6.23%	−10.13%

Table 13.4
Volume Statistics

Description	Bull Market, Up Breakout	Bear Market, Up Breakout	Bull Market, Down Breakout	Bear Market, Down Breakout
Above-average candle volume, performance	6.92%	8.35%	−6.16%	−9.74%
Below-average candle volume, performance	6.65%	7.81%	−5.67%	−8.98%
Heavy breakout volume, performance	7.42%	8.86%	−6.17%	−10.37%
Light breakout volume, performance	6.20%	7.39%	−5.61%	−8.24%

Measure rule. Use the measure rule to help predict how far price will rise or fall. Compute the height of the candle and multiply it by the appropriate percentage shown in the table; then apply it to the breakout price.

What are the price targets for Mary's belt hold? The upward target would be (2 × 74%) + 78, or 79.48, and the downward target would be 76 − (2 × 71%), or 74.58.

Upper shadow performance. To determine whether the shadow is short or tall, compute the height of the shadow and divide by the breakout price. Compare the result to the median in the table. Tall shadows have a percentage higher than the median. Candles with tall upper shadows score better performance than short ones.

Table 13.4 shows volume statistics.

Average candle volume. Heavy candle volume results in good performance in all categories when compared to candles with below-average candle volume.

Breakout volume. Breakout-day volume is my personal pet. Many candlesticks work best if breakout-day volume is heavy, and the belt hold is no exception.

Trading Tactics

After researching how belt holds behave, I found two interesting scenarios. The first is when belt holds appear in downtrends, and Figure 13.2 shows an example. The primary price trend is downward after peaking in October near the belt hold at A. That one, incidentally, occurs as a retracement in an uptrend. Those are low-risk, high-reward setups.

Figure 13.2 The bullish belt hold that appears in late December breaks out downward.

The belt hold that occurs in late December has a downward breakout. Many of the other belt holds pointed to by arrows perform poorly in this downtrend. Thus, do not expect a belt hold to reverse a primary downtrend. By primary, I mean a trend usually several months long. The short-term trend should be downward in the few days before the belt hold. If the trend is ever a question, cover the belt hold and ask if the high price is trending down over the prior few days.

Figure 13.3 shows the last trading tactic. If a belt hold appears as a reversal candle at the bottom of a short-term retracement in a primary uptrend, then buy. That's a mouthful, so I'll dissect it for you.

Look for price to be trending upward over several months. During the uptrend, price often pauses by sliding down before climbing higher. If a belt hold appears during one of those slides, then it represents a buying opportunity. The chart shows this rise, retrace, rise behavior, and the belt hold appears at the bottom of the retracement.

I split trading tactics into two basic studies, one concerning reversal rates and the other concerning performance. Of the two, reversal rates are more important, because it's better to trade in the direction of the trend and let price run as far as it can.

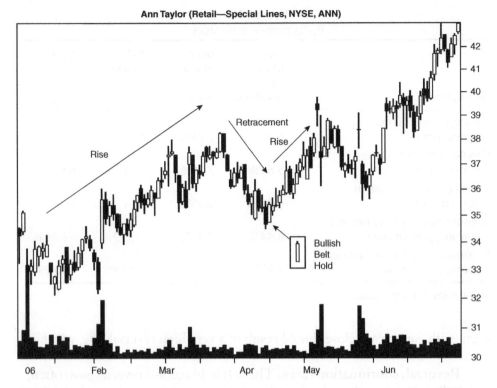

Ann Taylor (Retail—Special Lines, NYSE, ANN)

Figure 13.3 A downward retrace of the primary uptrend represents a delicious trading setup.

Table 13.5 gives tips to find the trend direction.

Confirmation reversal rates. Use a higher closing price the next day to confirm a reversal. That usually means price has closed above the top of the belt hold. If that occurs, then price has broken out upward and reversed the downtrend, by definition. Thus, with the close near the top of the candle to

Table 13.5
Reversal Rates

Description	Bull Market	Bear Market
Closing price confirmation reversal rate	96%	96%
Candle color confirmation reversal rate	93%	91%
Opening gap confirmation reversal rate	80%	80%
Reversal: trend down, breakout up	71%	71%
Continuation: trend down, breakout down	29%	29%
Percentage of reversals (R)/ continuations (C) for each 12-month low (L), middle (M), or high (H)	L 64% R/36% C, M 68% R/32% C, H 76% R/24% C	L 67% R/33% C, M 70% R/30% C, H 74% R/26% C

Table 13.6
Performance Indicators

Description	Bull Market, Up Breakout	Bear Market, Up Breakout	Bull Market, Down Breakout	Bear Market, Down Breakout
Closing price confirmation, performance	5.72%	7.06%	N/A	N/A
Candle color confirmation, performance	5.81%	7.28%	N/A	N/A
Opening gap confirmation, performance	6.82%	8.55%	N/A	N/A
Breakout above 50-day moving average, performance	6.44%	7.41%	−5.39%	−6.89%
Breakout below 50-day moving average, performance	7.21%	8.78%	−6.18%	−10.29%

N/A means not applicable.

begin with, an upward close should result in a very high reversal rate, which it does.

Reversal, continuation rates. The belt hold acts as a reversal most often, with bull and bear markets showing the same rate. Expect an upward breakout.

Yearly range reversals. Reversals occur most often within a third of the yearly high.

Table 13.6 shows performance indicators that can give hints as to how your stock will behave after the breakout from a candle pattern.

Confirmation, performance. What confirmation method works best for the belt hold? Answer: opening gap. Since the price trend leading to the belt hold is downward, buying if price gaps higher gets you into a winning trade sooner than do the other methods.

Moving average. Candles with breakouts below the 50-trading-day moving average result in better performance than do candles with breakouts above the moving average.

Sample Trade

Figure 13.4 shows a sample trade. For months, price bumped against overhead resistance that batted it back down—until December. Then price shoots out of the congestion zone, but Mary isn't about to chase price higher. As an experienced trader, she knows better. She waits.

In about a week, price returns in a move called a throwback (so called because price throws back to the breakout price). Then a bullish belt hold appears and marks the turning point—the end of the throwback. Price gaps

Black Hill Corp. (Electric Utility—West, NYSE, BKH)

Figure 13.4   This belt hold appears at the end of a throwback to a breakout from a resistance zone.

open (opening gap confirmation buy signal), and that represents a low-risk, high-reward opportunity. Mary buys the stock within a minute of the open. Not only does she make money on the stock but on the dividends from the electric utility as well.

For Best Performance

The following list offers tips and observations to help choose candles that perform well. Consult the associated table for more information.

- Use the identification guidelines to help select the pattern—Table 13.1.
- Candles within a third of the yearly low perform best—Table 13.2.
- Select tall candles—Table 13.3.
- Use the measure rule to predict a price target—Table 13.3.
- Candles with tall upper shadows outperform—Table 13.3.
- Volume gives performance clues—Table 13.4.

- Avoid belt holds in a primary downtrend. Look for them as part of a retracement in an uptrend—Trading Tactics discussion.
- The candle breaks out upward most often—Table 13.5.
- Patterns within a third of the yearly high tend to act as reversals most often—Table 13.5.
- Opening gap confirmation works best—Table 13.6.
- Breakouts below the 50-day moving average lead to the best performance—Table 13.6.

14

Breakaway, Bearish

Behavior and Rank

Theoretical: Bearish reversal.

Actual bull market: Bearish reversal 63% of the time (ranking 23).

Actual bear market: Bearish reversal 89% of the time (ranking 2).

Frequency: 98th out of 103.

Overall performance over time: 11th out of 103.

Wow. Talk about a rare pattern. I looked over 4.7 million candle lines and found a massive 36 examples of a bearish breakaway candlestick. The implications of this are twofold. First, it's unlikely you'll ever see one in a stock; and second, even if one does appear you probably won't recognize it. You could cheat and use my free Patternz program that recognizes all of the candles in this book. You can find it at my web site: ThePatternSite.com. This chapter is an abbreviated one because too few samples were found.

According to Gregory Morris in his book, *Candlestick Charting Explained: Timeless Techniques for Trading Stocks and Futures* (McGraw-Hill, 1992, 1995; originally published as *CandlePower*), he found mention only of the bullish variety of the breakaway in Japanese literature, so he created the bearish breakaway.

The psychology behind this pattern is that buying pressure pushes up the stock, creating a tall white candle followed by a gap. From there, the march upward gets dicey. The next three bodies tend to be smaller, but they still have higher closes. The last day in the candlestick pattern slaps the bulls awake. It's a black candle that sacrifices much of the gains in the prior three days when it closes in the gap between the first and second candle lines in the pattern.

Before I forget, the small figure at the top of the first page of this chapter shows a candle line that is half white and half black. That means the candle line can be either color.

Looking at the frequency rank, you can see how rare this pattern is: a ranking of 98 out of 103, where 1 has the highest frequency. I would like to be positive and say that this candle is a winner, but I believe that the performance ranks listed are misleading. There are just too few samples to make the numbers reliable or believable. Nevertheless, the candle shows an overall performance rank of 11.

Identification Guidelines

Figure 14.1 shows an example of a bearish breakaway candlestick pattern. It's a complicated pattern because it's composed of so many lines. This breakaway forms in an uptrend and breaks out downward, just as theory predicts. The pattern starts and ends with a tall candle. The middle three candles are usually smaller, and candle three (the middle one in the five-line pattern) can be either white or black. The other candles are the color as represented in the chart. Table 14.1 has the complete list of identification guidelines.

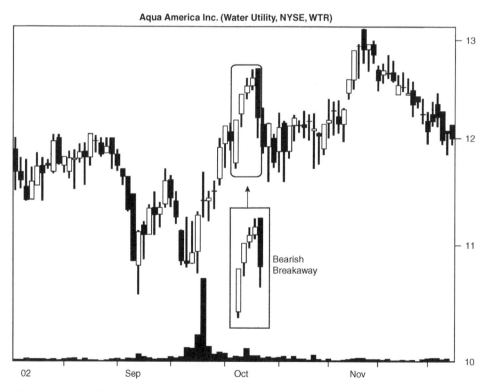

Figure 14.1   This is one of the few examples of a bearish breakaway candlestick pattern.

Table 14.1
Identification Guidelines

Characteristic	Discussion
Number of candle lines	Five.
Price trend	Upward leading to the start of the candle pattern.
First day	A tall white candle.
Second day	A white candle that has a gap between the two candle bodies, but the shadows can overlap.
Third day	A candle with a higher close, but the candle can be any color.
Fourth day	A white candle with a higher close.
Last day	A tall black candle with a close within the gap between the first two candle bodies. Ignore the shadows on the first two candles for citing the gap.

Table 14.1 lists identification guidelines, and most are self-explanatory. Use the figures that accompany the chapter as guidance. The only tricky stuff here is the gap between the first and second candles. It's a gap between the two bodies, so ignore the shadows. The last day must close between the two bodies of the first two candles in the pattern.

Since this candle pattern is so rare, some candle experts allow leeway in interpretation of the identification guidelines. For example, I've seen illustrations that claim to be a breakaway candle with only four lines instead of five. For the record, I used the guidelines set forth by Table 14.1 only. Maybe that's why I found only 36.

Sample Trade

Figure 14.2 shows the sample trade. Price moves up inside an ascending broadening wedge chart pattern. The top trendline is easy enough to draw—just connect the peaks with a line. But the bottom trendline is open to interpretation because the start of it doesn't begin with the lowest low on the chart. If you connect the lowest low in July with the same valley in early September, then the chart pattern would look like a rising wedge.

Regardless, Jeff draws the two trendlines as shown. The bearish breakaway candlestick pattern appears and price touches the top trendline before reversing. The trendline touch and reversal pattern suggests that price will fall to the other side of the wedge. Before shorting the stock, Jeff asks two questions.

First, how far will price drop? The target is below 40 (it changes upward each day with the rising trendline) and an entry price is 42.

Second, how far will price rise if the trade goes bad? Price often rises to make a double top. Thus, Jeff expects price could climb back to the old high at 43.

Figure 14.2 Overhead resistance reverses the uptrend, sending price to the other side of the ascending broadening wedge.

Even if the trade evolved perfectly, he stands to make less than $2 or lose $1. The win-loss ratio is not compelling enough to justify a trade. Jeff knows that selling short in a rising price trend is a crazy thing to do, especially when price is making new highs. It's far easier to make money shorting a stock in a downward price trend when the stock is making new yearly lows. He will look elsewhere for a more promising trade.

15

Breakaway, Bullish

Behavior and Rank

Theoretical: Bullish reversal.

Actual bull market: Bullish reversal 59% of the time (ranking 31).

Actual bear market: Bullish reversal 71% of the time (ranking 12).

Frequency: 97th out of 103.

Overall performance over time: 45th out of 103.

I found a few more samples of the bullish variety of the breakaway candlestick than the bearish variety. Nevertheless, the bullish breakaway is rare, and with so few samples, it's difficult to assess how well it works. As a result, this is an abbreviated chapter.

The bullish breakaway represents a change from a bearish mood to a bullish one. Price forms a tall black candle in a downtrend and then the candle lines continue lower with prices closing down each day until a tall white candle puts an end to any more bearish talk. In one day, price retakes the ground lost during the prior three days. After that, anything can happen, but the breakout is usually upward.

The frequency rank says it all. This pattern is so rare that I found just 41, too few to shoot any statistics. With so few uncovered, it's a wonder how they discovered this pattern to begin with. Perhaps it's more common in other security types such as futures.

Performance over time is so-so except for downward breakouts. Those perform quite well, if you can believe the few samples (and you really can't).

The overall rank is an unexciting 45 out of 103, where 1 is best. If I were a rooster, I wouldn't crow about it.

Identification Guidelines

Figure 15.1 shows an example of a bullish breakaway candlestick pattern. This one appears in a long decline, and that is the first indication that the reversal may not last. An upward breakout from the candlestick formation occurs on a tall white candle, and the next day (point A) price hits overhead resistance set up by the valleys in August. Combined with the existing bearish trend in the stock, the pressure is too much; the rise reverses, eventually reaching a new low in October.

As with most complex candle patterns, the identification guidelines represent a long list, and Table 15.1 shows them. Many are self-explanatory. The only tricky part of this candle pattern is the gap between the first and second days and how the last candle line must close within that gap.

Ignore shadows when forming the gap and placing the closing price of the last day within that gap. Use the charts in this chapter as interpretation

Figure 15.1   A bullish breakaway pattern appears in a downward price trend, leading to a rise that soon falters.

Table 15.1
Identification Guidelines

Characteristic	Discussion
Number of candle lines	Five.
Price trend	Downward leading to the start of the candle pattern.
First day	A tall black candle.
Second day	A black candle that has a gap between the two candle bodies, but the shadows can overlap.
Third day	A candle with a lower close, but the candle can be any color.
Fourth day	A black candle with a lower close.
Last day	A tall white candle with a close within the gap between the first two candles. Ignore the shadows on the first two candles for citing the gap.

guides. You may not need them, though, because this pattern is as rare as a dodo bird. The bird may be extinct, or maybe it's just good at hiding—just like the bullish breakaway candle.

Trading Tactics

Figure 15.1 shows an example of a breakaway candlestick in a long downtrend. Notice how price does not climb far after the breakout before resuming the downtrend.

To increase the chance of a successful trade, look for setups like the one shown in Figure 15.2. Here, the prevailing price trend is upward. The breakaway candle appears when price takes a breather from the up move. Price drops, forms the candlestick pattern, and then resumes trending upward. This technique, when applied to other candlestick types as well, will help fatten your wallet or purse, sometimes with money!

Sample Trade

Figure 15.3 shows the sample trade for this chapter. The bullish breakaway candlestick formation ends at D. If Sandy uses candle color as the confirmation signal, then she would buy the stock at A, a day after a white candle (the candle pattern ends at D, confirms the next day with a white candle, and she buys a day later). But is that the right play?

Knowing that overhead resistance is a ceiling formed by the two peaks at B (and extending backward in time), then Sandy can reasonably assume price

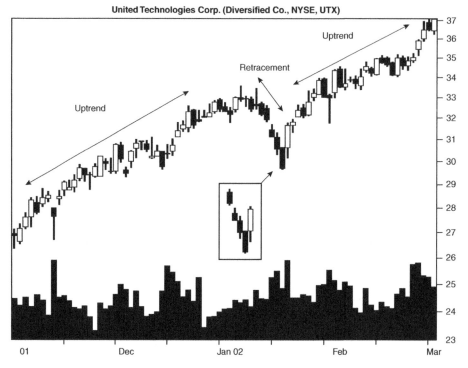

Figure 15.2 A successful breakaway candlestick formation appears as part of a downward retracement in an uptrend.

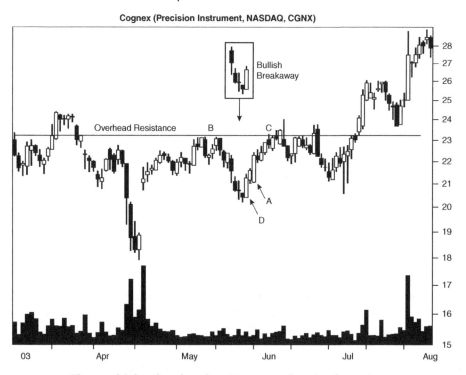

Figure 15.3 Overhead resistance stalls price for a time.

will stall or reverse there. That means price will rise to 23 (the peaks at B are slightly higher, but let's be safe).

If she buys at the open at A, that would put her into the trade at 21.05. If everything were to go perfectly, she would make about $2 a share.

What about risk? How far could price drop before she should exit? Stop placement is a lengthy subject that is beyond the scope of this book. However, she could place a stop below the low the day before D. That would be 20.19 (a penny below the low) and that would mean a potential loss of 86 cents a share. If she believed in the breakaway candlestick, then perhaps a closer stop would be prudent—perhaps the low at D or even the low a day later, when the candle pattern confirmed. That would stop her out at 20.39 or 20.99, respectively. The closer the stop, the higher the risk of being stopped out.

Let's use the middle stop location, a penny below D, or 20.39. With a buy price of 21.05, that means a potential loss of 66 cents and a reward of $2. That's about a 3 to 1 reward-to-risk ratio, which is quite good. The trade might be worth taking.

16

Candle, Black

Behavior and Rank

Theoretical: Reversal or continuation.

Actual bull market: Continuation 52% of the time (ranking 41).

Actual bear market: Continuation 53% of the time (ranking 45).

Frequency: 3rd out of 103.

Overall performance over time: 82nd out of 103.

In the preceding two chapters I complained about candlesticks that had too few samples. This one has too many. I had to split the results from just 500 stocks into two spreadsheets to contain them all, and I had to reboot my machine after waiting 45 minutes to save the spreadsheet that held the results.

You could call this the three bears pattern, because the height of the black candle is not too tall and not too short. In other words, it's normal size with shadows smaller than the body. It appears frequently and works best as a continuation of the short-term trend.

With so many samples, the behavior results are refreshing in that the candle works as a continuation in both bull and bear markets, showing nearly the same rates. This reminds me of out-of-sample testing where you formulate a theory using one set of data and test the theory out on the other set.

The frequency rank is top-notch, scoring 3 out of 103 where 1 is best. That means black candles are as numerous as mosquitoes at a baseball game. However, the overall performance rank is lousy at 82.

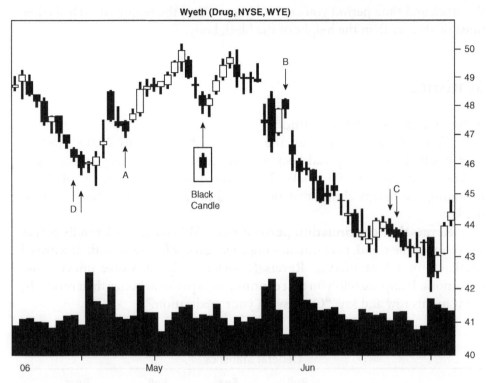

Figure 16.1 A black candle appears near the bottom of a short-term retracement. The arrows point to additional black candles.

Identification Guidelines

Figure 16.1 shows examples of black candles pointed to by arrows. The black candles appear in downtrends, uptrends and, well, wherever they want. Candles A and B act as reversals. Candles C and D act as continuations of the existing trend.

Table 16.1 lists identification guidelines. Look for a black candle of normal size. To explain what *normal* means would take too much room, so just use your common sense. The candle should not appear too short or too tall for

Table 16.1
Identification Guidelines

Characteristic	Discussion
Number of candle lines	One.
Color	Black.
Configuration	A normal-size candle with shadows that do not exceed the body height.

the stock and time period you are looking at. Also, the length of each shadow must be shorter than the height of the black body.

Statistics

Table 16.2 shows general statistics.

Number found. I limited the number of candles to 20,000, just so they would fit in my spreadsheet without crashing it. It may interest you to know that in just 500 stocks, I uncovered more than 67,300 of them. Prorating the results shows that black candles appear more often in a bear market.

Reversal or continuation performance. When the black candle acts as a reversal of the trend, performance improves except for those with downward breakouts in a bear market. Reversals perform slightly worse under those conditions. If anyone tells you that continuations perform better than reversals, point to this row and say, "Go easy on your medication."

Table 16.2
General Statistics

Description	Bull Market, Up Breakout	Bear Market, Up Breakout	Bull Market, Down Breakout	Bear Market, Down Breakout
Number found	4,972	1,639	9,652	3,737
Reversal (R), continuation (C) performance	4.07% C 4.44% R	4.90% C 5.96% R	−6.24% C −6.53% R	−13.46% C −12.17% R
Standard & Poor's 500 change	1.41%	0.81%	−0.94%	−3.00%
Candle end to breakout (median, days)	3	3	2	2
Candle end to trend end (median, days)	7	6	7	8
Number of breakouts near the 12-month low (L), middle (M), or high (H)	L 1,076, M 1,377, H 2,519	L 500, M 500, H 639	L 2,566, M 2,873, H 4,213	L 1,514, M 1,102, H 1,121
Percentage move for each 12-month period	L 5.34%, M 4.25%, H 3.95%	L 7.42%, M 5.39%, H 4.52%	L −6.98%, M −6.47%, H −6.06%	L −15.37%, M −13.25%, H −10.23%
Candle end + 1 day	1.40%	1.90%	−0.91%	−1.73%
Candle end + 3 days	2.04%	2.79%	−1.59%	−3.22%
Candle end + 5 days	1.76%	2.00%	−1.91%	−4.06%
Candle end + 10 days	0.28%	−1.24%	−2.46%	−6.00%
10-day performance rank	100	97	48	19

S&P performance. The black candle performs better than the S&P 500 over the same periods—that is, from the breakout date to the swing high or low date, depending on the breakout direction.

Candle end to breakout. It takes two to three days for price to either close above the top of the black candle or close below the bottom of it. You would expect downward breakouts to take less time because the close is often nearer the bottom of the candle than the top.

Candle end to trend end. I measured the time from the day after the candle ends to the trend high or low. The median time varied from six to eight days.

Yearly position, performance. Most candles appear within a third of the yearly high except for bear market/down breakouts. Those occur most often near the yearly low. Performance is best when the breakout is within a third of the yearly low, in all categories.

Performance over time. Downward breakouts hold up well over time, but upward ones suffer from 3 to 10 days. Thus, the candle is a much better performer after a downward breakout than after an upward one. The performance rank confirms that assessment with a rank for downward breakouts (48) half that of upward breakouts (100).

Table 16.3 shows height statistics.

Candle height. Tall candles outperform. To determine whether the candle is short or tall, compute its height from high to low price in the candle

Table 16.3
Height Statistics

Description	Bull Market, Up Breakout	Bear Market, Up Breakout	Bull Market, Down Breakout	Bear Market, Down Breakout
Median candle height as a percentage of breakout price	2.07%	2.97%	2.22%	3.31%
Short candle, performance	3.35%	4.18%	−4.87%	−9.63%
Tall candle, performance	5.58%	7.18%	−8.46%	−16.84%
Percentage meeting price target (measure rule)	75%	72%	80%	84%
Median upper shadow as a percentage of breakout price	0.42%	0.52%	0.46%	0.66%
Short upper shadow, performance	3.77%	4.73%	−5.53%	−10.89%
Tall upper shadow, performance	4.89%	6.39%	−7.40%	−15.08%
Median lower shadow as a percentage of breakout price	0.46%	0.69%	0.45%	0.66%
Short lower shadow, performance	3.67%	4.79%	−5.45%	−11.21%
Tall lower shadow, performance	5.02%	6.31%	−7.52%	−14.71%

Table 16.4
Volume Statistics

Description	Bull Market, Up Breakout	Bear Market, Up Breakout	Bull Market, Down Breakout	Bear Market, Down Breakout
Above-average candle volume, performance	4.41%	5.77%	−6.26%	−13.22%
Below-average candle volume, performance	4.19%	5.35%	−6.44%	−12.70%
Heavy breakout volume, performance	4.54%	6.02%	−6.74%	−13.78%
Light breakout volume, performance	4.04%	5.14%	−6.11%	−12.11%

pattern and divide by the breakout price. If the result is higher than the median, then you have a tall candle; otherwise it's short.

Justin sees a black candle with a high of 89 and a low of 88. Is the candle short or tall? The height is 89 − 88, or 1, so the measure for an upward breakout would be 1/89, or 1.1%. In a bull market, the candle is short.

Measure rule. Use the measure rule to help predict how far price will rise or fall. Compute the height of the candle and multiply it by the appropriate percentage shown in the table; then apply it to the breakout price.

What are the price targets for Justin's candle? The upward target would be (1 × 75%) + 89, or 89.75, and the downward target would be 88 − (1 × 80%) or 87.20.

Shadows. To determine whether the shadow is short or tall, compute the height of the shadow and divide by the breakout price. Compare the result to the median in the table. Tall shadows have a percentage higher than the median.

Candles with tall shadows perform better than do those with short shadows in all categories.

Table 16.4 shows volume statistics.

Average candle volume. Candles with above-average volume perform better than do those with below-average volume except for bull market/down breakouts.

Breakout volume. Look for heavy breakout-day volume because it suggests better performance when compared to light breakout volume.

Trading Tactics

I split trading tactics into two basic studies, one concerning reversal rates and the other concerning performance. Of the two, reversal rates are more

Table 16.5
Reversal Rates

Description	Bull Market	Bear Market
Reversal rate: trend up, breakout down	65%	70%
Continuation rate: trend up, breakout up	35%	30%
Reversal: trend down, breakout up	33%	31%
Continuation: trend down, breakout down	67%	69%
Percentage of reversals (R)/continuations (C) for each 12-month low (L), middle (M), or high (H)	L 42% R/58% C, M 46% R/54% C, H 52% R/48% C	L 41% R/59% C, M 46% R/54% C, H 55% R/45% C

important, because it's better to trade in the direction of the trend and let price run as far as it can.

Table 16.5 gives tips to find the trend direction.

Reversal, continuation rates. Since the candle is black, you would expect price to break out downward more often than upward, and that's what we see. If you know the trend leading to the candle, then you can use the table to determine the likely outcome. For example, look for a downward breakout 65% of the time if price trends upward to the candle in a bull market.

Yearly range reversals. Reversals occur most often near the yearly high, but the numbers (52% and 55%) are close to random (50%). Continuations appear most often within a third of the yearly low.

Table 16.6 shows performance indicators that can give hints as to how your stock will behave after the breakout from a black candle.

Confirmation, performance. Which confirmation method works best? In all categories, the opening gap confirmation method gets you in soonest and results in the best performance. If price gaps open a day after the black candle, trade in the direction of the gap.

Moving average. Candles with breakouts below the 50-trading-day moving average perform better than do those with breakouts above the moving average.

Closing position. Since we are dealing with a black candle, none closed near the top of the candle. Black candles in a bull market do better when the close is near the candle's middle. In a bear market, a close near the low works best.

Sample Trade

Figure 16.2 shows the sample trade. If Justin were looking to buy this stock and saw the black candle in late December, it would be a clue to a reversal. He would *not* buy the stock just because a black candle appeared. However,

Table 16.6
Performance Indicators

Description	Bull Market, Up Breakout	Bear Market, Up Breakout	Bull Market, Down Breakout	Bear Market, Down Breakout
Closing price confirmation, performance	5.49%	8.97%	−5.53%	−11.32%
Candle color confirmation, performance	5.42%	8.92%	−5.59%	−11.35%
Opening gap confirmation, performance	6.30%	11.43%	−6.33%	−11.68%
Breakout above 50-day moving average, performance	4.18%	4.93%	−6.22%	−10.61%
Breakout below 50-day moving average, performance	4.42%	6.35%	−6.53%	−14.52%
Last candle: close in highest third, performance	0.00%	0.00%	0.00%	0.00%
Last candle: close in middle third, performance	4.31%	4.99%	−6.40%	−12.72%
Last candle: close in lowest third, performance	4.25%	5.70%	−6.37%	−12.92%

Figure 16.2 A black candle at a support zone suggests a reversal of the downtrend.

when coupled with the support zone set up by congestion in September and October, a turn is more likely. Once price rises above the top of the candle shadows (not just the black candle, but the group of five candles surrounding the black one); that is the buy signal.

Does Justin buy this stock? No. He is afraid of a pullback to overhead resistance followed by a resumption of the downtrend. That's what happened in 87% of the 10,878 cases I looked at. In this example, it's best to walk away from the trade, and that's what he does.

For Best Performance

The following list offers tips and observations to help choose candles that perform well. Consult the associated table for more information.

- Use the identification guidelines to help select the pattern—Table 16.1.
- Candles within a third of the yearly low perform best—Table 16.2.
- Select tall candles—Table 16.3.
- Use the measure rule to predict a price target—Table 16.3.
- Candles with tall upper and lower shadows outperform—Table 16.3.
- Volume gives performance clues—Table 16.4.
- The black candle breaks out downward most often—Table 16.5.
- Opening gap confirmation works best—Table 16.6.
- Breakouts below the 50-day moving average lead to the best performance—Table 16.6.

17

Candle,
Short Black

Behavior and Rank

Theoretical: Reversal or continuation (indecision).

Actual bull market: Reversal 52% of the time (ranking 47).

Actual bear market: Continuation 53% of the time (ranking 44).

Frequency: 50th out of 103.

Overall performance over time: 66th out of 103.

The short black candlestick is just as it sounds, short and black. What I find surprising is that it's somewhat rare. I had to use all four databases of over 4.7 million candle lines to unearth enough samples for a reliable analysis.

As one might expect, the short black candle is neither a reversal nor a continuation pattern. Price opens at one level, moves up and down a small amount, and then closes lower. The change from high to low is small and the shadows of the candlestick remain smaller than the height of the body. Those conditions account for the rarity.

Performance from this candle pattern is about what you would expect. Over 10 days, the stock moves little, placing the overall rank at 66 where 1 is best out of 103 candles. Even when you sort the rank into bull and bear markets, and into up and down breakouts, the performance ranges between middle of the road and awful.

Figure 17.1 This short black candle functions as a reversal in a short-term down-trend.

Identification Guidelines

Figure 17.1 shows an example of a short black candle. This one appears at the turning point of a short-term retracement of the uptrend from A to B. Price makes a lower low about a week later, but who's counting?

Table 17.1 lists identification guidelines, and most are self-explanatory. When the main feature of a candle is its height, it's difficult to describe what *short* means without devolving into pattern recognition theory. Let's just say

Table 17.1
Identification Guidelines

Characteristic	Discussion
Number of candle lines	One.
Color	Black.
Configuration	A short candle with upper and lower shadows each shorter than the body.

use your common sense when determining height. Compare the height to other candles in the stock. The body should be short but not doji short. Each shadow should be shorter than the height of the body. If you see a number of them in a stock, remember that this candle is comparatively rare, so wipe those black specks off your eyeglasses.

Statistics

Table 17.2 shows general statistics.

Number found. I found fewer short black candles than I expected, but 5,593 is certainly more than other rare candlesticks. Most appeared in a bull market.

Reversal or continuation performance. Candles with upward breakouts did better as reversals, and those with downward breakouts performed better as continuations.

Table 17.2
General Statistics

Description	Bull Market, Up Breakout	Bear Market, Up Breakout	Bull Market, Down Breakout	Bear Market, Down Breakout
Number found	1,885	486	2,547	675
Reversal (R), continuation (C) performance	6.83% C 7.98% R	8.05% C 11.86% R	−7.11% C −6.92% R	−11.37% C −10.37% R
Standard & Poor's 500 change	1.60%	1.14%	−0.66%	−2.16%
Candle end to breakout (median, days)	2	2	1	1
Candle end to trend end (median, days)	8	8	7	6
Number of breakouts near the 12-month low (L), middle (M), or high (H)	L 387, M 434, H 902	L 158, M 152, H 167	L 648, M 643, H 1,044	L 245, M 188, H 227
Percentage move for each 12-month period	L 9.19%, M 7.00%, H 6.77%	L 12.76%, M 10.89%, H 7.37%	L −8.18%, M −7.21%, H −6.29%	L −10.34%, M −12.36%, H −8.53%
Candle end + 1 day	1.53%	1.97%	−1.21%	−2.20%
Candle end + 3 days	2.43%	3.35%	−1.71%	−2.91%
Candle end + 5 days	2.59%	3.71%	−1.68%	−2.30%
Candle end + 10 days	2.66%	3.61%	−1.25%	−1.86%
10-day performance rank	61	49	86	85

S&P performance. The candle beat the return from the S&P 500 over the same period.

Candle end to breakout. Only one or two days passed before price closed either above the high or below the candlestick's low. Downward breakouts took a day less than upward breakouts, probably because we are dealing with a black candle and not a white one. The closing price is likely closer to the low than the high.

Candle end to trend end. It took a median six to eight days after the candle to find the end of the price trend. Downward breakouts found the end quicker, probably because of the black candle suggesting a downtrend already is progress.

Yearly position, performance. The candle appears most often within a third of the yearly high in all cases except for bear market/down breakouts. Those occur more often near the yearly low. Performance is best within a third of the yearly low except for bear market/down breakouts. Those pesky critters do better when the breakout resides in the middle of the yearly trading range.

Performance over time. I see lots of faults in the performance numbers. The candle pattern shows weakness from 5 to 10 days in bear market/up breakouts and from 3 to 10 days for candles with downward breakouts (two categories).

According to the performance rank, the pattern performs better after upward breakouts than downward ones.

Table 17.3 shows height statistics.

Candle height. This may sound stupid when discussing *short* black candles, but tall ones perform substantially better than short ones. What is meant by short and tall in this respect? Take the height from high to low price and divide by the breakout price. If the result is greater than the median listed in the table, then you have a tall candle.

Suppose Oliver sees a short black candle with a high of 88 and a low of 87.50. Is the candle short or tall? The height is 50 cents, so the measure would be 0.50/88, or 0.6%. The candle is short (assume bull market/up breakout).

Measure rule. Use the measure rule to help predict how far price will rise or fall. Compute the height of the candle and multiply it by the appropriate percentage shown in the table; then apply it to the breakout price. Since the percentages are all above 90%, you can just use the full candle height in the computation, and you should be fine.

Shadows. To determine whether the shadow is short or tall, compute the height of the shadow and divide by the breakout price. Compare the result to the median in the table. Tall shadows have a percentage higher than the median.

Candles with tall shadows perform better than do those with short shadows.

Table 17.4 shows volume statistics.

Table 17.3
Height Statistics

Description	Bull Market, Up Breakout	Bear Market, Up Breakout	Bull Market, Down Breakout	Bear Market, Down Breakout
Median candle height as a percentage of breakout price	1.22%	1.65%	1.30%	1.70%
Short candle, performance	5.65%	7.55%	−5.73%	−8.16%
Tall candle, performance	10.18%	13.36%	−8.94%	−14.48%
Percentage meeting price target (measure rule)	95%	95%	93%	93%
Median upper shadow as a percentage of breakout price	0.32%	0.37%	0.34%	0.41%
Short upper shadow, performance	6.13%	9.00%	−5.93%	−8.56%
Tall upper shadow, performance	9.30%	11.37%	−8.59%	−13.76%
Median lower shadow as a percentage of breakout price	0.34%	0.43%	0.34%	0.43%
Short lower shadow, performance	6.07%	8.09%	−5.89%	−8.67%
Tall lower shadow, performance	9.39%	12.40%	−8.51%	−13.72%

Average candle volume. Light (below-average) candle volume results in the best performance except for downward breakouts in a bear market. There, heavy candle volume performs better post breakout.

Breakout volume. Most candles do best on heavy breakout volume, but not short black candles. Light volume works better in two categories: bear market/up breakouts and bull market/down breakouts.

Table 17.4
Volume Statistics

Description	Bull Market, Up Breakout	Bear Market, Up Breakout	Bull Market, Down Breakout	Bear Market, Down Breakout
Above-average candle volume, performance	6.92%	9.57%	−6.21%	−10.97%
Below-average candle volume, performance	7.65%	10.28%	−7.29%	−10.90%
Heavy breakout volume, performance	8.25%	9.78%	−6.82%	−12.12%
Light breakout volume, performance	6.92%	10.25%	−7.11%	−10.21%

Trading Tactics

I split trading tactics into two basic studies, one concerning reversal rates and the other concerning performance. Of the two, reversal rates are more important, because it's better to trade in the direction of the trend and let price run as far as it can.

Table 17.5 gives tips to find the trend direction.

Reversal, continuation rates. Based on the percentages in the table, I would not try to predict the breakout direction on the price trend leading to the candle. Yes, a downward breakout occurs most often, but the numbers are not much above random.

Yearly range reversals. The numbers hover around 50% (random). If you hold a bazooka to the head of statisticians, they would say that reversals tend to occur most often near the yearly high, based on the data in the table.

Table 17.6 shows performance indicators that can give hints as to how your stock will behave after the breakout from the candle.

Confirmation, performance. The opening gap method works best in all categories. I have found that the opening gap method (where you trade in the direction of the opening day's gap) works best for most candle types.

Moving average. Candles with breakouts below the 50-trading-day moving average perform better than do those with breakouts above the moving average.

Closing position. Since we are dealing with black candles, none had a close in the top third of the candle. When the close is nearer the low price, the candle tends to outperform. This is true in all cases except for bull market/down breakouts, but the numbers are close.

Sample Trade

Figure 17.2 shows a short black candle that appears in a brief downtrend leading to the breakout from a descending triangle chart pattern. This candle rests on

Table 17.5
Reversal Rates

Description	Bull Market	Bear Market
Reversal rate: trend up, breakout down	59%	56%
Continuation rate: trend up, breakout up	41%	44%
Reversal: trend down, breakout up	44%	40%
Continuation: trend down, breakout down	56%	60%
Percentage of reversals (R)/continuations (C) for each 12-month low (L), middle (M), or high (H)	L 46% R/54% C, M 52% R/48% C, H 54% R/46% C	L 42% R/58% C, M 48% R/52% C, H 52% R/48% C

Table 17.6
Performance Indicators

Description	Bull Market, Up Breakout	Bear Market, Up Breakout	Bull Market, Down Breakout	Bear Market, Down Breakout
Closing price confirmation, performance	6.67%	8.73%	−6.19%	−9.97%
Candle color confirmation, performance	6.45%	8.96%	−6.43%	−9.79%
Opening gap confirmation, performance	7.61%	11.29%	−7.13%	−10.78%
Breakout above 50-day moving average, performance	7.42%	8.23%	−6.79%	−8.91%
Breakout below 50-day moving average, performance	7.49%	11.95%	−7.28%	−12.64%
Last candle: close in highest third, performance	0.00%	0.00%	0.00%	0.00%
Last candle: close in middle third, performance	7.39%	9.57%	−7.03%	−9.57%
Last candle: close in lowest third, performance	7.46%	10.33%	−7.01%	−11.38%

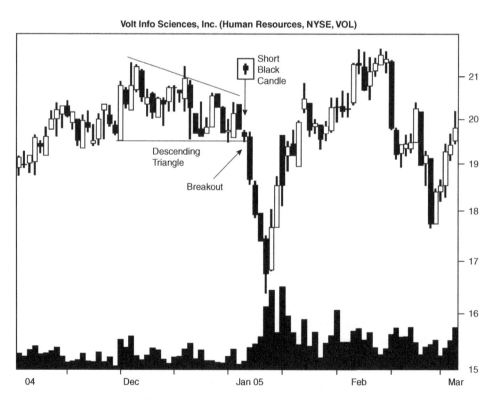

Figure 17.2 A short black candle appears a day before the breakout from a descending triangle chart pattern.

the support line, suggesting indecision about what direction to take. It reminds me of Oliver—a guy reluctant to ask for directions.

The next day the bears make the decision for him and push price down in a tall black candle. Over the next few days, volume trends higher even as price trends lower, more than fulfilling the measure rule for both the short black candlestick and the descending triangle.

This is an example of a short black candle appearing in a downtrend. Table 17.5 indicates that combination tends to break out downward more often than not, and that's what happened in this case.

For Best Performance

The following list offers tips and observations to help choose candles that perform well. Consult the associated table for more information.

- Use the identification guidelines to help select the pattern—Table 17.1.
- Candles within a third of the yearly low perform best, except for bear market/down breakouts—Table 17.2.
- Select tall candles—Table 17.3.
- Use the measure rule to predict a price target—Table 17.3.
- Candles with tall upper or lower shadows outperform—Table 17.3.
- Volume gives performance clues—Table 17.4.
- The candle breaks out downward most often—Table 17.5.
- Opening gap confirmation works best—Table 17.6.
- Breakouts below the 50-day moving average lead to the best performance—Table 17.6.

18

Candle, Short White

Behavior and Rank

Theoretical: Reversal or continuation (indecision).

Actual bull market: Reversal 52% of the time (ranking 45).

Actual bear market: Reversal 51% of the time (ranking 42).

Frequency: 54th out of 103.

Overall performance over time: 85th out of 103.

You're driving down the road, completely lost, and you come to a fork in the road. Which branch do you take? A short white candle is just like that. It cannot make up its mind whether it's a reversal or a continuation pattern. The numbers favor a reversal slightly more often, though, at 51% (bear market) and 52% (bull market).

As you might expect, the overall performance after 10 days ranks the pattern at 85 out of 103 where 1 is best. No breakout direction shows much of an improvement in performance, either.

Identification Guidelines

Figure 18.1 shows an example of a short white candlestick acting as a reversal of the upward price trend. This short white candle appears at the end of a three-candle pattern called a deliberation.

If you miss recognizing the deliberation, how can you guess that the uptrend is pooping out? Since I like mountain climbing, let me put it in those terms. The summit attempt begins when price gaps out of a congestion region

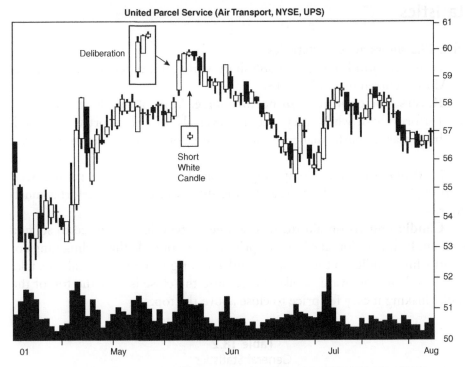

Figure 18.1   A short white candlestick acts as a reversal this time.

and forms the first day of a deliberation candlestick pattern. The next day, price closes higher but the white candle grows shorter. A white candle appears on the last day, and it is, well, short, as if the climbing team is struggling with the high altitude and low oxygen. That's what I notice about the pattern: a series of white candles, each shorter than the previous one, telling me the uptrend is ending.

A storm closes in from the east in the form of a black candle, small at the start but growing fiercer the next day (i.e., a taller black candle). That spells the end of the summit attempt and the start of a downward price trend.

Table 18.1 lists identification guidelines. Look for a short white candle with upper and lower shadows, each shorter than the body. The body should not be a doji; otherwise they'd call it a doji.

Table 18.1
Identification Guidelines

Characteristic	Discussion
Number of candle lines	One.
Color	White.
Configuration	A short candlestick with each shadow shorter than the body height.

Statistics

Table 18.2 shows general statistics.

Number found. I dug up 4,886 short white candlesticks in my prospecting. Most occurred in a bull market.

Reversal or continuation performance. Most of the short white candles perform best when they act as reversals of the short-term trend. The bear market performance numbers are stronger than the bull market ones.

S&P performance. Comparing the candle performance with the S&P 500 over the same periods, we see that the short white candle performs much better.

Candle end to breakout. It took one or two days for price to stage a breakout. It should not take long for price to close outside the trading range of a short white candle, so the results sound about right. Upward breakouts take a day less than downward breakouts, because the close is near the top of the candle, making it easy for price to close above the top.

Table 18.2
General Statistics

Description	Bull Market, Up Breakout	Bear Market, Up Breakout	Bull Market, Down Breakout	Bear Market, Down Breakout
Number found	2,215	614	1,615	442
Reversal (R), continuation (C) performance	6.96% C 7.72% R	8.77% C 10.03% R	−6.79% C −6.93% R	−10.18% C −10.72% R
Standard & Poor's 500 change	1.40%	0.61%	−0.84%	−2.27%
Candle end to breakout (median, days)	1	1	2	2
Candle end to trend end (median, days)	7	8	8	8
Number of breakouts near the 12-month low (L), middle (M), or high (H)	L 427, M 545, H 1,032	L 178, M 194, H 234	L 332, M 414, H 708	L 125, M 147, H 164
Percentage move for each 12-month period	L 9.64%, M 6.98%, H 6.58%	L 12.90%, M 9.18%, H 7.68%	L −7.81%, M −7.24%, H −6.42%	L −9.58%, M −11.76%, H −9.86%
Candle end + 1 day	1.25%	1.64%	−1.26%	−2.01%
Candle end + 3 days	1.96%	2.04%	−2.00%	−2.69%
Candle end + 5 days	1.94%	1.80%	−2.17%	−2.82%
Candle end + 10 days	1.95%	2.21%	−2.05%	−2.62%
10-day performance rank	90	68	61	75

Candle end to trend end. The median time from the day after the white candle to the trend end is about eight days.

Yearly position, performance. The majority of short white candles appear within a third of the yearly high. Performance is best when the candle has a breakout within a third of the yearly low. That's true for all categories except for bear market/down breakouts. Those do better when the breakout is in the middle of the yearly trading range.

Performance over time. Yuck. Every column shows weakness from one period to the next. For example, in bull market/up breakouts, it occurs between days 3 and 5. After 10 days, the price movement over that span is not impressive at all. A good number would be an average of 6% with some posting 10%. I may be a herbivore, but a 10% move in 10 days is the kind of beef I can sink my teeth into!

The performance rank is disappointing but not surprising for a single-line candlestick pattern. The best showing is 61 out of 103 where 1 is best. That occurs in candles with downward breakouts in bull markets.

Table 18.3 shows height statistics.

Candle height. Tall candles performed significantly better than short ones. Even though short white candles are, well, short, the taller of the short ones perform better. To determine whether the candle is short or tall, compute its height from high to low price in the candle and divide by the breakout price.

Table 18.3
Height Statistics

Description	Bull Market, Up Breakout	Bear Market, Up Breakout	Bull Market, Down Breakout	Bear Market, Down Breakout
Median candle height as a percentage of breakout price	1.26%	1.60%	1.24%	1.50%
Short candle, performance	5.49%	7.42%	–5.76%	–8.87%
Tall candle, performance	9.88%	11.58%	–8.49%	–12.42%
Percentage meeting price target (measure rule)	95%	92%	93%	93%
Median upper shadow as a percentage of breakout price	0.34%	0.39%	0.34%	0.41%
Short upper shadow, performance	5.79%	7.61%	–5.95%	–9.10%
Tall upper shadow, performance	9.38%	11.36%	–8.12%	–11.99%
Median lower shadow as a percentage of breakout price	0.33%	0.41%	0.33%	0.36%
Short lower shadow, performance	5.94%	7.73%	–5.93%	–9.38%
Tall lower shadow, performance	9.18%	11.28%	–8.23%	–11.70%

Table 18.4
Volume Statistics

Description	Bull Market, Up Breakout	Bear Market, Up Breakout	Bull Market, Down Breakout	Bear Market, Down Breakout
Above-average candle volume, performance	7.24%	10.15%	–6.62%	–10.75%
Below-average candle volume, performance	7.33%	9.03%	–6.92%	–10.40%
Heavy breakout volume, performance	7.95%	10.25%	–6.61%	–9.66%
Light breakout volume, performance	6.88%	8.81%	–6.94%	–10.93%

If the result is higher than the median, then you have a tall candle; otherwise it's short.

For example, say Guido sees a short white candle with an upward breakout in a bull market with a high price of 10 and a low of 9.75. Is the candle short or tall? The height would be $10 - 9.75$, or 0.25, so the measure would be 0.25/10, or 2.5%. The candle is tall.

Measure rule. Use the measure rule to help predict how far price will rise or fall. Compute the height of the candle and multiply it by the appropriate percentage shown in the table; then apply it to the breakout price. Since the success rates are all above 90%, you don't need to adjust the height by the percentage shown in the table to get a nearer target unless you want to.

What are the price targets for Guido's candle? The upward target would be $0.25 + 10$, or 10.25, and the downward target would be $9.75 - 0.25$, or 9.50.

Shadows. To determine whether the shadow is short or tall, compute the height of the shadow and divide by the breakout price. Compare the result to the median in the table. Tall shadows have a percentage higher than the median.

Candles with tall shadows perform better than do those with short ones. Table 18.4 shows volume statistics.

Average candle volume. Candle volume tracks the market conditions. Candles with above-average volume tend to do well in a bear market; those with light volume do better in a bull market.

Breakout volume. Heavy breakout-day volume propels stocks higher after upward breakouts, but light breakout-day volume does better for downward breakouts.

Trading Tactics

I split trading tactics into two basic studies, one concerning reversal rates and the other concerning performance. Of the two, reversal rates are more

Table 18.5
Reversal Rates

Description	Bull Market	Bear Market
Reversal rate: trend up, breakout down	45%	44%
Continuation rate: trend up, breakout up	55%	56%
Reversal: trend down, breakout up	61%	60%
Continuation: trend down, breakout down	39%	40%
Percentage of reversals (R)/ continuations (C) for each 12-month low (L), middle (M), or high (H)	L 54% R/46% C, M 53% R/47% C, H 50% R/50% C	L 56% R/44% C, M 51% R/49% C, H 47% R/53% C

important, because it's better to trade in the direction of the trend and let price run as far as it can.

Table 18.5 gives tips to find the trend direction.

Reversal, continuation rates. A short white candle acts as a reversal most often when the trend is downward into the candlestick. They break out upward 60% to 61% of the time.

Yearly range reversals. Sorting where the reversal occurs in the yearly price range is unrevealing. Both continuations and reversals hover around the random mark, 50%. Based on the numbers in the table, reversals tend to happen more often within a third of the yearly low.

Table 18.6 shows performance indicators that can give hints as to how your stock will behave after the breakout from a candle pattern.

Confirmation, performance. All categories do better with the opening gap method of confirmation except bear market/down breakouts. Those do better if you wait for the candle color to determine the direction. If price is trending upward, look for a black candle to signal a reversal a day later. If price is trending downward, trade only after a white candle appears the next day.

Moving average. Candles with breakouts below the 50-trading-day moving average perform better than do those with breakouts above the moving average.

Closing position. Short candles with a close in the middle third of the intraday range perform better than those with closes in the other thirds except for bear market/up breakouts. Those do better when the close is near the candle's high, but the numbers are close.

Sample Trade

Figure 18.2 shows a short white candle that appears in an uptrend. In this example, price bumps against overhead resistance set up by twin peaks in October and extending backward in time. The ceiling proves too thick to

Table 18.6
Performance Indicators

Description	Bull Market, Up Breakout	Bear Market, Up Breakout	Bull Market, Down Breakout	Bear Market, Down Breakout
Closing price confirmation, performance	6.20%	7.79%	−6.56%	−9.81%
Candle color confirmation, performance	6.13%	7.78%	−6.62%	−9.98%
Opening gap confirmation, performance	7.19%	10.64%	−7.34%	−9.79%
Breakout above 50-day moving average, performance	6.87%	8.06%	−6.47%	−10.20%
Breakout below 50-day moving average, performance	8.02%	11.27%	−7.41%	−10.83%
Last candle: close in highest third, performance	7.19%	9.35%	−6.75%	−10.44%
Last candle: close in middle third, performance	7.71%	9.33%	−7.15%	−10.61%
Last candle: close in lowest third, performance	0.00%	0.00%	0.00%	0.00%

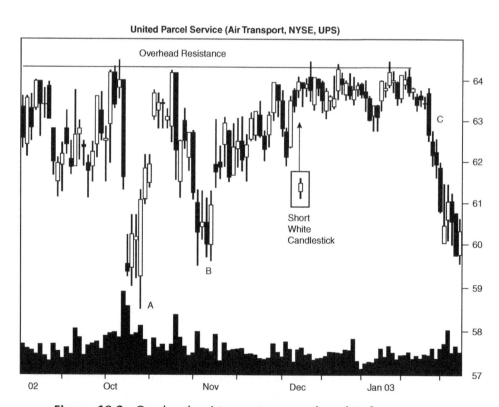

Figure 18.2 Overhead resistance stops any thought of an up move.

pierce, and despite repeated attempts, price can't drill through. About six weeks after the appearance of the short white candle, price begins sliding off a cliff.

If Guido owns this stock, should he sell? That depends on many factors. If price continues down to 0, then selling when it became clear that the stock couldn't pierce overhead resistance would have saved him a bundle.

When trying to make a selling decision, look for underlying support to determine how far price is likely to drop. It may drop even farther, so keep that in mind, but at least you can get an idea of the possible magnitude. Can you tolerate a drop of 5%? How about 15% or 30%?

It usually takes more than one candle pattern for me to exit a position, but that depends on the circumstances. I will combine other technical indicators to determine when to sell. For example, the chart shows an ascending triangle with a downward breakout. I didn't draw the lower trendline of the triangle, but connect bottoms A and B with an up-sloping trendline and extend it upward until price crosses it (near C).

At C, price closes lower in a tall black candle. This candle broke out of a congestion region in January that formed a small peak near 64. With price unable to pierce overhead resistance, coupled with price closing below the up-sloping trendline, I would sell the stock the next day.

For Best Performance

The following list offers tips and observations to help choose candles that perform well. Consult the associated table for more information.

- Use the identification guidelines to help select the pattern—Table 18.1.
- Candles within a third of the yearly low perform best except for bear market/down breakouts—Table 18.2.
- Select tall candles—Table 18.3.
- Use the measure rule to predict a price target—Table 18.3.
- Candles with tall upper and lower shadows outperform—Table 18.3.
- Volume gives performance clues—Table 18.4.
- The candle breaks out upward most often—Table 18.5.
- Opening gap confirmation works best except for bear market/down breakouts—Table 18.6.
- Breakouts below the 50-day moving average lead to the best performance—Table 18.6.

19

Candle, White

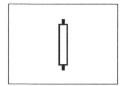

Behavior and Rank

Theoretical: Reversal or continuation (indecision).
Actual bull market: Continuation 51% of the time (ranking 45).
Actual bear market: Continuation 50% of the time (ranking 53).
Frequency: 4th out of 103.
Overall performance over time: 68th out of 103.

A white candlestick is one of those candles you don't pay much attention to, and with good reason. Little happens with this candle line. As the numbers show, the candle acts as a continuation of the existing trend half the time—random, in other words.

Tepid bullish sentiment appears in a white candle, with price opening below where it closes. Long shadows are indicative of fighting among the bulls and bears for control, but the candlestick pattern known as the white candle does not suffer from those skirmishes. Its shadows remain shorter than the body, and the body is of normal length. Thus, the white candle's appearance gives few clues about whether price will reverse. Some type of candle has to be the foot soldier, one that waits in the foxhole for a strong candle pattern to appear and take command. The white candlestick waits for orders with rifle loaded.

The good news is that the white candle is plentiful. It has a frequency rank of 4 out of 103 where 1 is best. The overall performance is midrange, though: 68. Splitting the performance into its components, we find that the candle does best in a bear market after a downward breakout, while upward breakouts perform worst.

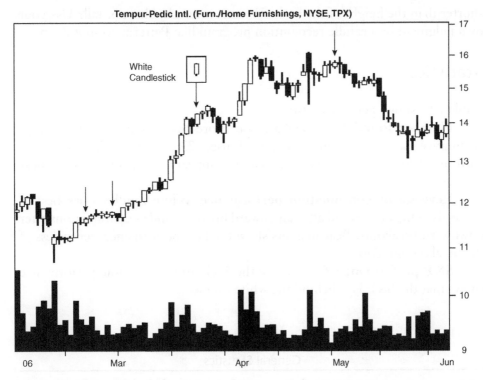

Figure 19.1   A white candlestick appears near the end of the trend. Arrows point to other white candles.

Identification Guidelines

Figure 19.1 shows a number of white candles, pointed to by arrows on the chart. What you may notice is that their height varies. Some look short, whereas the one highlighted in March looks tall or at least taller than the others. The program I used to find white candles measures the average candle height before deciding whether a candle is tall, short, or just right. Thus, what appears to be a short white candle is neither short nor tall, but average height.

Table 19.1 lists identification guidelines. The candle cannot be unduly short or tall, but must be a normal-size white candle with shadows that are

Table 19.1
Identification Guidelines

Characteristic	Discussion
Number of candle lines	One.
Color	White.
Configuration	A candle of normal size, neither short nor tall, with each shadow shorter than the body.

shorter than the height of the body. What is meant by short or tall? Use your own judgment or a candle recognition program like Patternz to spot them.

Statistics

Table 19.2 shows general statistics.

Number found. One database was more than enough to find a representative sample of white candles. I used 23,665. Prorating the standard database indicates that the candle appears most often in a bear market.

Reversal or continuation performance. White candles work best as reversals of the price trend after an upward breakout and as continuations after downward breakouts. Bear markets show the best performance, regardless of the breakout direction.

S&P performance. Comparing the S&P 500 with candle performance shows that the S&P lags behind the white candle.

Table 19.2
General Statistics

Description	Bull Market, Up Breakout	Bear Market, Up Breakout	Bull Market, Down Breakout	Bear Market, Down Breakout
Number found	10,749	4,021	6,365	2,530
Reversal (R), continuation (C) performance	6.34% C 7.19% R	6.96% C 9.19% R	−5.92% C −5.90% R	−11.30% C −10.34% R
Standard & Poor's 500 change	1.49%	0.78%	−1.15%	−3.09%
Candle end to breakout (median, days)	2	2	3	3
Candle end to trend end (median, days)	7	6	7	8
Number of breakouts near the 12-month low (L), middle (M), or high (H)	L 1,706, M 2,562, H 5,513	L 1,080, M 1,212, H 1,660	L 1,236, M 1,686, H 2,971	L 841, M 751, H 905
Percentage move for each 12-month period	L 8.27%, M 6.57%, H 6.36%	L 11.34%, M 8.17%, H 6.12%	L −6.43%, M −6.03%, H −5.75%	L −13.78%, M −10.50%, H −8.99%
Candle end + 1 day	0.88%	1.43%	−1.39%	−2.04%
Candle end + 3 days	1.60%	2.02%	−2.44%	−3.97%
Candle end + 5 days	1.80%	1.84%	−2.57%	−4.43%
Candle end + 10 days	1.96%	1.48%	−2.20%	−4.82%
10-day performance rank	89	85	56	35

Candle end to breakout. It takes two or three days for price to break out—to close either above or below the white candle. Upward breakouts take one less day than downward breakouts because the close is nearer the top of the candle than the bottom.

Candle end to trend end. Upward breakouts reach the trend end sooner than do downward breakouts, but the median says they take about a week.

Yearly position, performance. The majority of white candles appear within a third of the yearly high. However, the best performance comes from candles within a third of the yearly low.

Performance over time. In two out of the four categories shown in the table, performance deteriorates over time. For example, between 3 and 10 days after the candlestick ends in a bear market, leading to an upward breakout, performance suffers.

The performance rank shows that downward breakouts perform better than upward ones. In a bear market with a downward breakout, the rank of 35 out of 103 with 1 being best is almost tasty. Almost.

Table 19.3 shows height statistics.

Candle height. Tall candles perform substantially better than short ones. What is meant by short or tall? Measure the height of the candle from high to low price and divide by the breakout price. If the result is greater than the median listed in the table, then you have a tall candle.

Table 19.3
Height Statistics

Description	Bull Market, Up Breakout	Bear Market, Up Breakout	Bull Market, Down Breakout	Bear Market, Down Breakout
Median candle height as a percentage of breakout price	2.19%	2.97%	2.18%	3.12%
Short candle, performance	4.93%	5.75%	−4.50%	−8.04%
Tall candle, performance	9.04%	10.41%	−7.79%	−13.82%
Percentage meeting price target (measure rule)	81%	78%	78%	81%
Median upper shadow as a percentage of breakout price	0.44%	0.62%	0.48%	0.71%
Short upper shadow, performance	5.57%	6.50%	−5.15%	−8.82%
Tall upper shadow, performance	7.99%	9.45%	−6.81%	−12.79%
Median lower shadow as a percentage of breakout price	0.45%	0.61%	0.42%	0.57%
Short lower shadow, performance	5.54%	6.71%	−5.20%	−9.49%
Tall lower shadow, performance	8.03%	9.23%	−6.75%	−12.11%

Table 19.4
Volume Statistics

Description	Bull Market, Up Breakout	Bear Market, Up Breakout	Bull Market, Down Breakout	Bear Market, Down Breakout
Above-average candle volume, performance	6.82%	8.35%	−5.94%	−11.36%
Below-average candle volume, performance	6.57%	7.64%	−5.88%	−10.35%
Heavy breakout volume, performance	7.38%	8.68%	−6.45%	−11.85%
Light breakout volume, performance	6.09%	7.33%	−5.52%	−9.93%

Suppose Fred is looking at a white candle with a height of 2 and an upward breakout price of 49 in a bull market. The height to breakout measure would be 2/49, or 4.1%. Fred has a tall candle.

Measure rule. Use the measure rule to help predict how far price will rise or fall. Compute the height of the candle and multiply it by the appropriate percentage shown in the table; then apply it to the breakout price.

Say Fred is considering buying a stock showing a white candle in a bull market. What are the price targets if the candle has a high of 49 and a low of 47? The height is 49 − 47, or 2, so the upward target would be (2 × 81%) + 49, or 50.62. The downward target would be 47 − (2 × 78%), or 45.44.

Shadows. To determine whether the shadow is short or tall, compute the height of the shadow and divide by the breakout price. Compare the result to the median in the table. Tall shadows have a percentage higher than the median.

Candles with tall shadows perform better than do those with short shadows.

Table 19.4 shows volume statistics.

Average candle volume. Heavy (above-average) candle volume leads to better postbreakout performance across the board when compared to white candles with below-average volume.

Breakout volume. Similarly, candles with heavy breakout-day volume give better performance than do candles with light breakout volume.

Trading Tactics

I split trading tactics into two basic studies, one concerning reversal rates and the other concerning performance. Of the two, reversal rates are more important, because it's better to trade in the direction of the trend and let price run as far as it can.

Table 19.5
Reversal Rates

Description	Bull Market	Bear Market
Reversal rate: trend up, breakout down	38%	40%
Continuation rate: trend up, breakout up	62%	60%
Reversal: trend down, breakout up	65%	63%
Continuation: trend down, breakout down	35%	37%
Percentage of reversals (R)/continuations (C) for each 12-month low (L), middle (M), or high (H)	L 53% R/47% C, M 50% R/50% C, H 47% R/53% C	L 51% R/49% C, M 50% R/50% C, H 48% R/52% C

Table 19.5 gives tips to find the trend direction.

Reversal, continuation rates. If you know the short-term trend before the candle, you can predict the breakout direction. White candles make it easy. Regardless of the existing trend, expect an upward breakout between 60% (bear market) and 65% (bull market) of the time. That, of course, does not tell how long the trend will last, only that price first closed above the top of the candle most often.

Yearly range reversals. Separating where a reversal occurs in the yearly price range shows results that are essentially random. Reversals occur slightly more often in a bull market when the breakout price is within a third of the yearly low.

Table 19.6 shows performance indicators that can give hints as to how your stock will behave after the breakout from a candle pattern.

Confirmation, performance. The opening gap confirmation method, where the trade depends on the direction price gaps open the next day, works best in all categories except for bear market/down breakouts. In that category, the results are close with candle color coming out on top. That means waiting for a black candle to appear before trading (in the expectation of a reversal of the uptrend).

Moving average. Candles with breakouts below the 50-day moving average perform better than do those with breakouts above the moving average.

Closing position. None of the candles had a close in the lowest third of the candle line. A close in the middle of the candle works best most often. The lone exception is bull market/down breakouts, which do better if the close is near the candle's high.

Sample Trade

Figure 19.2 shows the sample trade. Imagine that Fred wants to buy Teradyne at point 2. Has price changed trend from down to up? The day after point 2, a white candle appears that also completes a two-day above-the-stomach candle

Table 19.6
Performance Indicators

Description	Bull Market, Up Breakout	Bear Market, Up Breakout	Bull Market, Down Breakout	Bear Market, Down Breakout
Closing price confirmation, performance	5.87%	7.16%	−6.61%	−10.39%
Candle color confirmation, performance	5.86%	7.17%	−6.62%	−10.42%
Opening gap confirmation, performance	7.16%	9.56%	−6.82%	−10.32%
Breakout above 50-day moving average, performance	6.46%	6.70%	−5.84%	−9.22%
Breakout below 50-day moving average, performance	7.27%	10.23%	−6.02%	−12.36%
Last candle: close in highest third, performance	6.66%	7.84%	−5.94%	−10.55%
Last candle: close in middle third, performance	6.69%	8.20%	−5.78%	−11.22%
Last candle: close in lowest third, performance	0.00%	0.00%	0.00%	0.00%

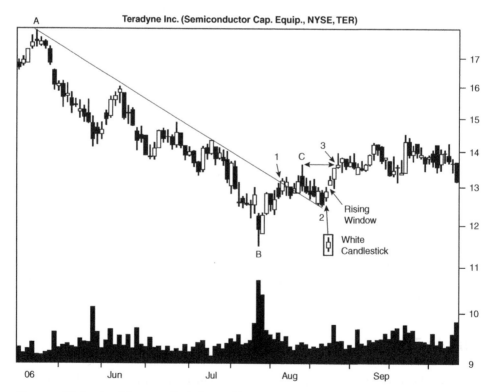

Figure 19.2   A white candle followed by price gapping upward hints at a trend change.

pattern. The combination suggests a short-term change in the downtrend. The next day, price gaps higher at the open, forming a rising window (see the chart). The window is small, but a gap is a gap, regardless of how tall it is, and it represents a weak support zone. As the chart shows, the gap fills the next day when price spikes downward.

Returning to the trend change question, here's a three-step method to help determine if the trend has changed.

Draw a trendline from the highest high on the chart (A) along the subsequent highs toward the lowest low (B, which is always after the highest high) such that price does not intersect the trendline until *after* the lowest low. I show the trendline as A2. Look for price to close above the trendline. That occurs at point 1, and it is the first indication of a trend change.

Price should test the low by attempting to make a new low but failing. It's okay if price moves slightly below the recent low and then rebounds. What's important is that it tries to trend lower and can't hold it. I show the attempt at point 2. Price doesn't come close to the low at B, but it tries to.

Price should recover to close above the high between the lowest low and the test of that low. The lowest low is at B, the test of the low is at 2, the high between those two points is at C, and a close above C occurs at 3. Once price closes higher, it fulfills the three steps of a trend change. At point 3, price has changed trend from down to up.

Tests show that the method works well—not always, but it adds value to a trader's toolbox.

For Best Performance

The following list offers tips and observations to help choose candles that perform well. Consult the associated table for more information.

- Use the identification guidelines to help select the pattern—Table 19.1.
- Candles within a third of the yearly low perform best—Table 19.2.
- Select tall candles—Table 19.3.
- Use the measure rule to predict a price target—Table 19.3.
- Candles with tall upper and lower shadows outperform—Table 19.3.
- Volume gives performance clues—Table 19.4.
- The candle breaks out upward most often—Table 19.5.
- Opening gap confirmation works best except for bear market/downward breakouts—Table 19.6.
- Breakouts below the 50-day moving average lead to the best performance—Table 19.6.

20

Concealing Baby Swallow

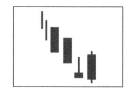

Behavior and Rank

Theoretical: Bullish reversal.
Actual bull market: Bearish continuation 75% of the time (ranking 3).
Actual bear market: None found.
Frequency: 103rd out of 103.
Overall performance over time: 101st out of 103.

Concealing baby swallow is a good name for this candle pattern because you will be hard-pressed to find it in a historical or real-time stock price series. Out of over 4.7 million candle lines, I found only four examples of it, too few to tabulate statistics or formulate trading tactics.

This candlestick pattern is supposed to act as a reversal, but my magnificent four candles say otherwise (75% act as continuations). Even the psychology behind the pattern supports continuation, in my view. Price trends downward leading to the start of the concealing baby swallow and two tall black marubozu candle lines appear. On the third day, price gaps open lower but price recovers sometime during the day, leaving a tall upper shadow behind when the bears force price down again. The final day engulfs the third day completely, including the shadows, but closes below the open (another black candle). The last two days would be bullish if the final candle were white, forming a bullish engulfing pattern. Since both are black candles, I don't view that as particularly bullish.

As the numbers show, the pattern ranks as the worst in terms of frequency (dead last), and overall performance isn't much better—101 out of 103 where 1 is best. This is due, in part, to the lack of bear market samples.

Identification Guidelines

Figure 20.1 shows what a concealing baby swallow looks like. This is an example of the candle pattern acting as a continuation of the downtrend. All four candles are black in the pattern. The first two are tall and without shadows. The third day might be classified as an inverted hammer but I didn't place such a restriction on it. The final day engulfs the entire third day, including the shadows. As the chart shows, I allow ties on the high and low prices of the last two days (in this example, the high price matches).

I follow the identification guidelines listed in Table 20.1. If something is not mentioned there, it's allowed as far as I'm concerned. For example, many ideal drawings of this pattern do not show shadows on the last day, but their actual chart examples do have shadows. I allow shadows, and I also allow the shadow to engulf the prior day's shadow, not just the last day's body engulfing the shadows of the prior day.

Figure 20.2 shows another example of a concealing baby swallow. The candles look short because they depend on the average candle height leading to the candle pattern. You can see where the last day matches the price range of the prior day. I think that's okay. It's like eating a strawberry. If the berry

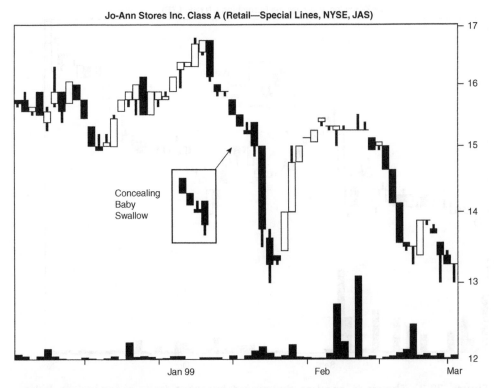

Figure 20.1 A concealing baby swallow appears, but price breaks out downward.

Table 20.1
Identification Guidelines

Characteristic	Discussion
Number of candle lines	Four.
Price trend	Downward leading to the start of the candle pattern.
First and second day	Two long black candles without any shadows (both are black marubozu candles).
Third day	A black day with a tall upper shadow. The candle gaps open downward and yet trades into the body of the prior day.
Last day	Another black day that completely engulfs the prior day, including the shadows.

is much smaller than your mouth, you can fit it in. If the berry equals the size of your mouth, you can still fit it in, but just don't try swallowing it before chewing.

Figure 20.3 shows the final example of a concealing baby swallow. This one is different from the others because the breakout is upward. Thus, it acts as a reversal of the downtrend. The last two days have matching high prices,

Figure 20.2 Shown is another downward breakout from a concealing baby swallow.

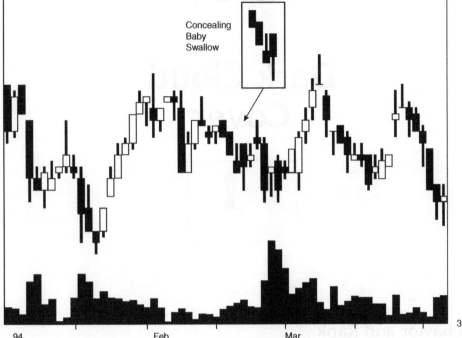

Figure 20.3   A concealing baby swallow acts as a reversal.

but that's just a coincidence, not a requirement. Notice how the lower shadow on the last day helps engulf the third day in this example.

Trading Tactics

I don't have any trading tactics to discuss for two reasons. First, it's unlikely you'll ever see this candle pattern in stocks (but maybe it appears in futures or other markets), and, second, I can't find enough samples to form a trading strategy, anyway. I suggest you look elsewhere for a more exciting candle pattern.

21

Dark Cloud Cover

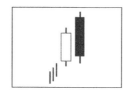

Behavior and Rank

Theoretical: Bearish reversal.

Actual bull market: Bearish reversal 60% of th time (ranking 28).

Actual bear market: Bearish reversal 63% of the time (ranking 24).

Frequency: 46th out of 103.

Overall performance over time: 22nd out of 103.

I like the candle name "dark cloud cover." It reminds me of weekends during college when I used to read a book under cloudy skies in Syracuse, New York, at home, hoping some hot chick would come talk to me. The only things that visited were bugs.

Dark cloud cover begins in an upward price trend with bulls forcing the stock higher. A tall white candle appears, suggesting additional gains, and the next day cooperates when price gaps open higher than the prior day's peak. However, the bears take over and selling pressure pushes price to close near the day's low, completing the candle.

The overall performance rank is 22 out of 103 where 1 is best, which is very good. Upward breakouts are responsible for making the overall performance as delicious as it is. The behavior (reversal) rankings also hold up with numbers in the 20s.

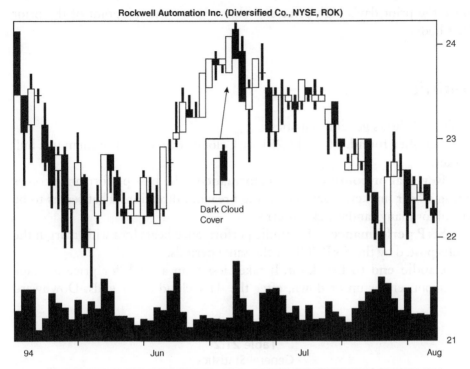

Figure 21.1   This dark cloud cover acts as a reversal of the uptrend.

Identification Guidelines

Figure 21.1 shows what dark cloud cover looks like. Price follows a rising trend moving into the candle pattern. A tall white candle appears followed by a black one. Think of the pattern as a puffy white cloud chasing a black storm cloud. When the two-line pattern completes, price reverses in this example and begins a long journey lower.

Table 21.1 lists identification guidelines, and most are self-explanatory. The tricky part comes with the second candle line. The black candle opens

Table 21.1
Identification Guidelines

Characteristic	Discussion
Number of candle lines	Two.
Price trend	Upward leading to the start of the candle pattern.
First day	A tall white candle.
Second day	A black candle with the open above the prior high and a close below the midpoint of the prior day's body.

above the prior day's high price and closes below the midpoint of the prior day's body.

Statistics

Table 21.2 shows general statistics.

Number found. I found 6,281 dark cloud covers, most of them in a bull market.

Reversal or continuation performance. The best performance comes during a bear market, regardless of the breakout direction. That seems to be typical for many candlestick patterns.

S&P performance. The candle performance beats by a wide margin the results posted by the S&P 500 for the same periods.

Candle end to breakout. It takes less than a week for price to stage a breakout, either up or down, after the dark cloud cover ends. Downward

Table 21.2
General Statistics

Description	Bull Market, Up Breakout	Bear Market, Up Breakout	Bull Market, Down Breakout	Bear Market, Down Breakout
Number found	2,134	340	3,239	568
Reversal (R), continuation (C) performance	6.98% C	8.08% C	−6.46% R	−10.60% R
Standard & Poor's 500 change	1.53%	0.80%	−0.71%	−2.46%
Candle end to breakout (median, days)	5	4	3	3
Candle end to trend end (median, days)	8	8	7	9
Number of breakouts near the 12-month low (L), middle (M), or high (H)	L 284, M 464, H 1,206	L 74, M 101, H 163	L 609, M 809, H 1,514	L 141, M 182, H 239
Percentage move for each 12-month period	L 8.08%, M 6.02%, H 6.94%	L 11.17%, M 7.70%, H 7.28%	L −6.82%, M −6.56%, H −6.40%	L −12.33%, M −10.70%, H −9.93%
Candle end + 1 day	1.36%	2.17%	−0.79%	−1.01%
Candle end + 3 days	2.82%	4.36%	−1.71%	−1.40%
Candle end + 5 days	3.56%	5.10%	−2.20%	−2.45%
Candle end + 10 days	4.59%	5.36%	−2.06%	−4.47%
10-day performance rank	19	23	60	39

breakouts take less time to break out than upward ones, probably because price closes nearer to the candle's low price.

Candle end to trend end. The median time from candle end to trend end varies from seven to nine days.

Yearly position, performance. Most dark cloud cover patterns form within a third of the yearly high. However, the best performance comes from candles within a third of the yearly low.

Performance over time. The percentages that dark cloud cover posts after 10 days are quite good. However, it would be better if price didn't get blown away from 5 to 10 days in bull market/down breakouts.

Downward breakouts are soft according to the 10-day performance rank when compared to other candle types. Upward breakouts are where this puppy excels.

Table 21.3 shows height statistics.

Candle height. Tall candles perform better than short ones. To determine whether the candle is short or tall, compute its height from highest high to lowest low price in the candle pattern and divide by the breakout price. If the result is higher than the median, then you have a tall candle; otherwise it's short.

For example, say Sally sees dark cloud cover with a high at 160 and the low is 157. Is the candle short or tall? The height is 160 – 157, or 3. Assuming

Table 21.3
Height Statistics

Description	Bull Market, Up Breakout	Bear Market, Up Breakout	Bull Market, Down Breakout	Bear Market, Down Breakout
Median candle height as a percentage of breakout price	3.80%	4.93%	3.94%	5.01%
Short candle, performance	5.03%	5.57%	−4.65%	−7.51%
Tall candle, performance	9.75%	10.82%	−9.04%	−13.78%
Percentage meeting price target (measure rule)	59%	58%	56%	62%
Median upper shadow as a percentage of breakout price	0.12%	0.24%	0.13%	0.25%
Short upper shadow, performance	6.17%	7.08%	−5.82%	−7.90%
Tall upper shadow, performance	7.67%	9.09%	−7.03%	−12.95%
Median lower shadow as a percentage of breakout price	0.35%	0.52%	0.35%	0.52%
Short lower shadow, performance	6.10%	8.39%	−5.63%	−10.20%
Tall lower shadow, performance	7.83%	7.80%	−7.31%	−10.97%

a downward breakout in a bull market, the measure is 3/157, or 1.9%, so the candle is short.

Measure rule. Use the measure rule to help predict how far price will rise or fall. Compute the height of the candle and multiply it by the appropriate percentage shown in the table; then apply it to the breakout price.

What are the two price targets for Sally's candle? The upward target would be (3 × 59%) + 160, or 161.77, and the downward target would be 157 − (3 × 56%), or 155.32.

Shadows. The results in the table pertain to the last candle line in the pattern. To determine whether the shadow is short or tall, compute the height of the shadow and divide by the breakout price. Compare the result to the median in the table. Tall shadows have a percentage higher than the median.

Upper shadow performance. Candles with tall upper shadows perform better than do those with short shadows.

Lower shadow performance. Most of the categories show better results with tall lower shadows. The lone exception is bear market/up breakouts, which show better performance if the lower shadow is short.

Table 21.4 shows volume statistics.

Candle volume trend. A falling volume trend suggests good performance across the board except for bull market/down breakouts. Those do better with a rising volume trend within the candle.

Average candle volume. Candles with above-average volume result in better performance when compared to those with below-average volume.

Breakout volume. Heavy breakout-day volume is the gold standard, and the numbers confirm this. Postbreakout performance is best if the breakout-day volume is above the one-month average.

Table 21.4
Volume Statistics

Description	Bull Market, Up Breakout	Bear Market, Up Breakout	Bull Market, Down Breakout	Bear Market, Down Breakout
Rising candle volume, performance	6.59%	7.88%	−6.54%	−9.28%
Falling candle volume, performance	7.31%	8.29%	−6.38%	−11.55%
Above-average candle volume, performance	7.79%	8.90%	−6.90%	−10.61%
Below-average candle volume, performance	6.30%	7.45%	−6.10%	−10.59%
Heavy breakout volume, performance	7.72%	8.82%	−7.13%	−11.10%
Light breakout volume, performance	6.10%	7.12%	−5.97%	−10.23%

Trading Tactics

Figure 21.2 shows an example of a dark cloud cover pattern that occurs as part of an upward retracement of the downward (primary) price trend. Price forms lower peaks and lower valleys, signaling a downward price trend. Dark cloud cover appears at the peak of an upward move, but the primary trend is still down. These situations, where the price trend for a few days leads up to the candlestick pattern but the longer-term price trend is downward, represent a low-risk, high-reward opportunity to profit.

Avoid trading dark cloud cover in an upward price trend of a few months' duration. Price may reverse, but the odds of a sustained decline are against you, especially in a bull market.

I split trading tactics into two basic studies, one concerning reversal rates and the other concerning performance. Of the two, reversal rates are more important, because it's better to trade in the direction of the trend and let price run as far as it can.

Table 21.5 gives tips to find the trend direction.

Confirmation reversal rates. To help detect a reversal, look for price to close lower the day after the candle ends. That works over 80% of the time, but it doesn't say how far price will drop.

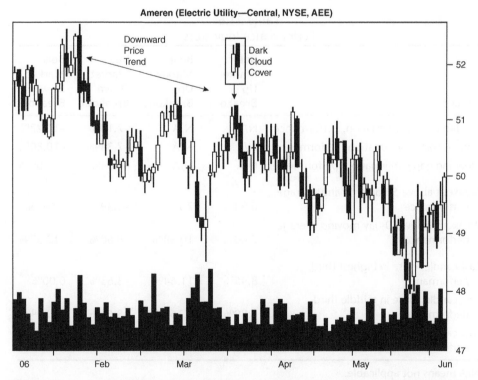

Figure 21.2 Dark cloud cover appears as a reversal in a downward price trend.

Table 21.5
Reversal Rates

Description	Bull Market	Bear Market
Closing price confirmation reversal rate	83%	86%
Candle color confirmation reversal rate	80%	83%
Opening gap confirmation reversal rate	69%	71%
Reversal rate: trend up, breakout down	60%	63%
Continuation rate: trend up, breakout up	40%	37%
Percentage of reversals (R)/continuations (C) for each 12-month low (L), middle (M), or high (H)	L 68% R/32% C, M 64% R/36% C, H 56% R/44% C	L 66% R/34% C, M 64% R/36% C, H 59% R/41% C

Reversal, continuation rates. The pattern acts as a reversal most often with a downward breakout.

Yearly range reversals. Reversals occur frequently within a third of the yearly low.

Table 21.6 shows performance indicators that can give hints as to how your stock will behave after the breakout from a candle pattern.

Confirmation, performance. As we have seen with other candle types, the opening gap confirmation performance results in the best trading signal.

Table 21.6
Performance Indicators

Description	Bull Market, Up Breakout	Bear Market, Up Breakout	Bull Market, Down Breakout	Bear Market, Down Breakout
Closing price confirmation, performance	N/A	N/A	−7.18%	−11.22%
Candle color confirmation, performance	N/A	N/A	−7.34%	−10.80%
Opening gap confirmation, performance	N/A	N/A	−7.64%	−12.00%
Breakout above 50-day moving average, performance	6.94%	7.77%	−6.39%	−9.65%
Breakout below 50-day moving average, performance	7.60%	10.58%	−6.60%	−12.37%
Last candle: close in highest third, performance	8.45%*	11.64%*	−3.63%*	0.00%*
Last candle: close in middle third, performance	5.80%	6.16%	−5.64%	−6.80%
Last candle: close in lowest third, performance	7.16%	8.42%	−6.57%	−11.14%

N/A means not applicable.
*Fewer than 30 samples.

If you suspect a downward breakout, look for price to gap open lower the day after the candle pattern before taking a position.

Moving average. Candles with breakouts below the 50-trading-day moving average result in better performance than those with breakouts above the moving average.

Closing position. Candles with upward breakouts perform better when the close in the last candle line of the pattern is near its high, but that is exceedingly rare. Those with downward breakouts do better if the close is near the candle line's low.

Sample Trade

As mentioned in the Trading Tactics section, an upward retracement in a downward price trend represents a low-risk, high-reward opportunity. Figure 21.3 shows a variation of that setup.

Price peaks at point A, makes a strong move down, and then recovers to B, a lower peak. The same scenario occurs again with price backtracking and then rising to a lower peak at C. A trendline connecting peaks A, B, and C slopes downward. Notice the exhaustion gap that occurs just before a shooting

Figure 21.3 Overhead resistance suggests a major turning point.

star (C). The star and gap accompanied by high volume suggests a bearish turn. That's what happens.

Connecting valleys E and F is another trendline, forming the large symmetrical triangle, ABC-EF. After C, price drops to close the rising window (the exhaustion gap) and then tries again to make a new high at D but fails. That's when dark cloud cover appears.

The dark cloud cover is an early warning that the breakout could be downward from the triangle, but it's not a guarantee. Two days later, price closes below the candle pattern, confirming the downward move. Since the breakout occurred on high volume, the move might be a lasting one. Price eventually breaks out downward from the symmetrical triangle, too, and then continues lower.

For Best Performance

The following list offers tips and observations to help choose candles that perform well. Consult the associated table for more information.

- Use the identification guidelines to help select the pattern—Table 21.1.
- Candles within a third of the yearly low perform best—Table 21.2.
- Select tall candles—Table 21.3.
- Use the measure rule to predict a price target—Table 21.3.
- Candles with tall upper shadows outperform—Table 21.3.
- Volume gives performance clues—Table 21.4.
- Trade dark cloud cover that appears as an upward retracement in a downward price trend—Trading Tactics discussion.
- The candle breaks out downward most often—Table 21.5.
- Patterns within a third of the yearly low frequently act as reversals —Table 21.5.
- Opening gap confirmation works best—Table 21.6.
- Breakouts below the 50-day moving average lead to the best performance—Table 21.6.

22

Deliberation

Behavior and Rank

Theoretical: Bearish reversal.

Actual bull market: Bullish continuation 77% of the time (ranking 2).

Actual bear market: Bullish continuation 75% of the time (ranking 4).

Frequency rank: 48th out of 103.

Overall performance over time: 93rd out of 103.

The first thing I thought was, "Deliberation! What a cool name but lousy performance." For a candle pattern that is supposed to act as a reversal, it doesn't. In fact, over 75% of the time price stages an upward breakout that continues the upward price trend. Upon closer inspection, I figured out why. In some cases, the pattern can be quite tall. To qualify as a reversal, price has to close below the candlestick's low. That can be difficult.

The reverse argument is that the candle is only three days tall and a true price reversal should last longer than that. I agree, and that's why you see this pattern listed as a continuation. A visual check of the results confirms that this candle functions as a continuation pattern.

The deliberation candle pattern begins in an uptrend, so the bulls are in control. Their buying pressure pushes price up for two days, forming long white candles. On the third day, however, the bears counterattack. By day's end, the candle body is small even though it might support tall shadows. The small body emphasizes confusion and indecision over direction, a loss of bullish momentum when compared to the prior two days.

Nevertheless, I consider even a small white body to be bullish (but there is no rule that I could find to prevent the third day in the pattern from being black, which would be bearish, indeed). The day after the pattern ends is key. Since bullish momentum is slowing, judging by the shrinking body size, a black candle or other confirming pattern might put the bears in control to complete a reversal. Otherwise, expect price to continue trending up.

The numbers confirm the poor performance, with an overall rank of 93 out of 103 where 1 is best. Separating the overall rank into its component parts, we find that downward breakouts show very good performance but upward breakouts yank the rank back down. What appears to be happening is that price doesn't reverse immediately after an upward breakout, but sometimes does so within a week. That often means a small rise before price tumbles. As we will see in the statistics section, the performance over one, three, five, and ten days shows meager gains as if the deliberation does not act as a reversal but perhaps warns of one coming.

Identification Guidelines

Figure 22.1 shows two examples of the deliberation candlestick pattern. Look closely at the deliberation in November. The breakout from this candle pattern

Figure 22.1 Two examples of deliberation; the first is a continuation of the up-trend, and the second is a reversal.

Cabot Corp. (Chemical—Diversified, NYSE, CBT)

Figure 22.2   A deliberation that should act as a reversal but doesn't.

is actually upward when price closes above the high in the three-day pattern. It acts as a continuation of the uptrend even though a trend reversal occurs two days later. This is an example of why the performance of the candle is so poor. Price climbs a small amount after the candle ends only to reverse in a few days.

The December deliberation shows price closing below the bottom of the candlestick, so the breakout is downward. Thus, the trend reverses after the candlestick.

Figure 22.2 shows another deliberation at D. If I were trading this candle, I would be concerned about overhead resistance set up by the trendline connecting peaks A, B, and C. With the appearance of the deliberation as price approaches the trendline, my bet would be on price reversing. Instead, price breaks out upward and moves closer to the trendline before reversing, but only for a few days. Price consolidates in a loose pattern and then resumes the uptrend, pushing through trendline resistance with a tall white candle.

Table 22.1 lists identification guidelines. Look for three white candles, each sporting a higher open and higher close. The first two candles should have tall bodies; the third candle line should be small and should open near where the prior candle closed. One source I checked indicated the third candle can be black or white, but other sources disagreed. I allow only white candles. Some sources require a gap above the prior day's close on the last day, but I do not.

Table 22.1
Identification Guidelines

Characteristic	Discussion
Number of candle lines	Three.
Price trend	Upward leading to the start of the candle pattern.
First and second days	Two long-bodied white candles.
Third day	A small body that opens near the second day's close.
Open and close	Each candle opens and closes higher than the previous ones' opens and closes.

Statistics

Table 22.2 shows general statistics.

Number found. I located 7,733 deliberations in the four databases I used. Prorating the standard database suggests deliberations appear most often in a bear market.

Table 22.2
General Statistics

Description	Bull Market, Up Breakout	Bear Market, Up Breakout	Bull Market, Down Breakout	Bear Market, Down Breakout
Number found	4,898	1,049	1,437	349
Reversal (R), continuation (C) performance	5.65% C	5.67% C	−5.16% R	−7.19% R
Standard & Poor's 500 change	1.12%	0.24%	−1.11%	−2.98%
Candle end to breakout (median, days)	4	4	9	8
Candle end to trend end (median, days)	7	7	11	11
Number of breakouts near the 12-month low (L), middle (M), or high (H)	L 402, M 901, H 3,098	L 139, M 348, H 555	L 212, M 322, H 755	L 84, M 105, H 159
Percentage move for each 12-month period	L 7.61%, M 5.58%, H 5.44%	L 8.46%, M 6.05%, H 4.93%	L −4.97%, M −5.24%, H −5.14%	L −6.71%, M −7.82%, H −7.05%
Candle end + 1 day	0.43%	0.23%	−1.43%	−1.69%
Candle end + 3 days	0.82%	0.53%	−3.24%	−4.06%
Candle end + 5 days	1.12%	0.92%	−4.24%	−5.56%
Candle end + 10 days	1.82%	1.29%	−5.24%	−6.72%
10-day performance rank	97	89	6	12

Reversal or continuation performance. Deliberations in a bear market performed better than did those in a bull market.

S&P performance. Candle performance beats the results from the S&P 500 over the same periods.

Candle end to breakout. Downward breakouts took much longer than did upward breakouts. Why? Because a downward breakout required a close below the candle's low price and that can be far from the current price. Upward breakouts need only close above the candle's high.

Candle end to trend end. It takes between 7 and 11 days to reach the trend end, longer for downward breakouts. Upward breakouts are moving in an existing uptrend, but downward breakouts have to start a new trend.

Yearly position, performance. The candle appears most often near the yearly high. Upward breakouts show the best performance within a third of the yearly low. That's typical for most candle types. Downward breakouts show the best performance comes from the middle of the yearly trading range, which is unusual.

Performance over time. The deliberation is a robust candlestick pattern, and by that I mean performance improves over time and in each category. What makes the rank so poor is that the gains over time (upward breakouts) are so meager. If they were 5% or 6%, then this candle would be near the top of the rankings, not the bottom at 93 (1 is best out of 103 candles).

Table 22.3 shows height statistics.

Table 22.3
Height Statistics

Description	Bull Market, Up Breakout	Bear Market, Up Breakout	Bull Market, Down Breakout	Bear Market, Down Breakout
Median candle height as a percentage of breakout price	6.03%	7.49%	6.50%	8.31%
Short candle, performance	4.46%	4.94%	−4.95%	−5.75%
Tall candle, performance	7.26%	6.52%	−5.45%	−9.26%
Percentage meeting price target (measure rule)	36%	29%	31%	32%
Median upper shadow as a percentage of breakout price	0.56%	0.76%	0.78%	0.91%
Short upper shadow, performance	4.80%	5.17%	−4.85%	−6.26%
Tall upper shadow, performance	6.64%	6.21%	−5.52%	−8.18%
Median lower shadow as a percentage of breakout price	0.60%	0.82%	0.55%	0.86%
Short lower shadow, performance	4.78%	5.01%	−4.99%	−6.14%
Tall lower shadow, performance	6.60%	6.30%	−5.33%	−8.56%

Candle height. Tall candles perform better than short ones. To determine whether the candle is short or tall, compute its height from highest high to lowest low price in the candle pattern and divide by the breakout price. If the result is higher than the median, then you have a tall candle; otherwise it's short.

Suppose Jim sees a deliberation with a high of 93 and low of 87. Is the candle short or tall? The height is $93 - 87$, or 6, so the measure would be 6/93, or 6.5%. Assuming a bull market with an upward breakout, the candle is tall.

Measure rule. Use the measure rule to help predict how far price will rise or fall. Compute the height of the candle pattern and multiply it by the appropriate percentage shown in the table; then apply it to the breakout price.

What are Jim's price targets for his candle? The upward target would be $(6 \times 36\%) + 93$, or 95.16, and the downward breakout would be $87 - (6 \times 31\%)$, or 85.14.

Shadows. The table's results pertain to the last candle line in the pattern. To determine whether the shadow is short or tall, compute the height of the shadow and divide by the breakout price. Compare the result to the median in the table. Tall shadows have a percentage higher than the median.

Candles with tall shadows perform better than do those with short ones. Table 22.4 shows volume statistics.

Candle volume trend. The volume trend performance follows the breakout direction. Upward breakouts do better with a rising volume trend, and downward breakouts do better with a falling volume trend.

Average candle volume. Above-average volume works best for upward breakouts and below-average volume excels for downward breakouts.

Breakout volume. Deliberations showing heavy breakout volume perform best across all categories.

Table 22.4
Volume Statistics

Description	Bull Market, Up Breakout	Bear Market, Up Breakout	Bull Market, Down Breakout	Bear Market, Down Breakout
Rising candle volume, performance	5.77%	5.73%	−5.05%	−7.18%
Falling candle volume, performance	5.56%	5.61%	−5.27%	−7.21%
Above-average candle volume, performance	5.70%	5.69%	−4.53%	−6.49%
Below-average candle volume, performance	5.57%	5.64%	−6.13%	−8.27%
Heavy breakout volume, performance	6.09%	5.97%	−5.40%	−8.07%
Light breakout volume, performance	5.11%	5.30%	−4.86%	−6.05%

Trading Tactics

Figure 22.3 shows a deliberation that pulls back into the base of a descending triangle. If you want to trade a deliberation as a reversal, then look for them in a declining price trend. That means the primary trend (at least a month long, usually much longer) should be downward but the shorter trend (days or weeks) is upward leading to the candle pattern.

The chart shows an example. Price trends lower from the October high, breaks out downward from the triangle, and then moves lower. The deliberation appears as part of an upward retracement in a downward price trend.

Avoid trading deliberation candlesticks as reversals when the prevailing (longer-term) price trend is upward. Those tend to break out upward most often.

If a deliberation appears as part of a classic chart pattern, such as the right shoulder of a head-and-shoulders top or the second/third top of a double/triple top, then a reversal is more likely. If you can identify those situations properly, the deliberation works well as a reversal candlestick.

I split trading tactics into two basic studies, one concerning reversal rates and the other concerning performance. Of the two, reversal rates are more

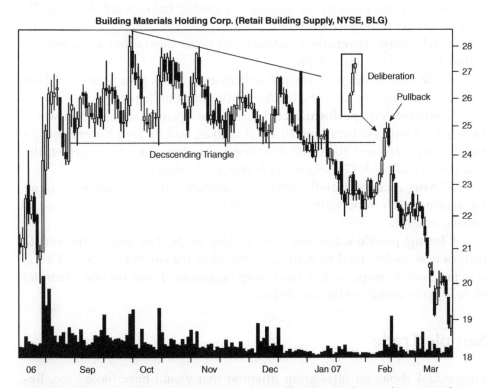

Figure 22.3 A deliberation appears as a pullback to a descending triangle.

Table 22.5
Reversal Rates

Description	Bull Market	Bear Market
Closing price confirmation reversal rate	37%	38%
Candle color confirmation reversal rate	36%	38%
Opening gap confirmation reversal rate	28%	29%
Reversal rate: trend up, breakout down	23%	25%
Continuation rate: trend up, breakout up	77%	75%
Percentage of reversals (R)/continuations (C) for each 12-month low (L), middle (M), or high (H)	L 35% R/65% C, M 26% R/74% C, H 20% R/80% C	L 38% R/62% C, M 23% R/77% C, H 22% R/78% C

important, because it's better to trade in the direction of the trend and let price run as far as it can.

Table 22.5 gives tips to find the trend direction.

Confirmation reversal rates. To help predict a reversal, wait for price to close lower the day after the candle ends. Unfortunately, this works just over a third of the time.

Reversal, continuation rates. Most of the patterns acted as continuations of the uptrend due to the difficulty of closing below a tall three-candle pattern. Expect an upward breakout.

Yearly range reversals. Continuations occur most often when price is within a third of the yearly high.

Table 22.6 shows performance indicators that can give hints as to how your stock will behave after the breakout from this candle pattern.

Confirmation, performance. Usually the opening gap method works best, but not with deliberations. In a bull market, waiting for a lower close the next day to determine the trend direction works best. In a bear market, the next day's candle color (black) works better as a trading signal.

Moving average. Candles with breakouts below the 50-trading-day moving average result in performance better than those with breakouts above the moving average.

Closing position. Candles with a close in the last line of the candle pattern near its low tend to perform better than the other two areas. This is true in all cases except for bull market/up breakouts. Those do best when the close is in the middle of the candle line.

Sample Trade

Figure 22.4 shows an interesting situation that would have fooled me. Before I get to that, though, look at the March deliberation. Price trends up

Table 22.6
Performance Indicators

Description	Bull Market, Up Breakout	Bear Market, Up Breakout	Bull Market, Down Breakout	Bear Market, Down Breakout
Closing price confirmation, performance	N/A	N/A	−7.80%	−9.70%
Candle color confirmation, performance	N/A	N/A	−7.63%	−9.71%
Opening gap confirmation, performance	N/A	N/A	−7.51%	−9.11%
Breakout above 50-day moving average, performance	5.60%	5.51%	−4.73%	−7.18%
Breakout below 50-day moving average, performance	6.87%	7.87%	−6.26%	−7.21%
Last candle: close in highest third, performance	5.52%	5.67%	−4.75%	−6.93%
Last candle: close in middle third, performance	5.98%	5.54%	−5.37%	−7.15%
Last candle: close in lowest third, performance	5.08%	6.06%	−5.47%	−7.71%

N/A means not applicable.

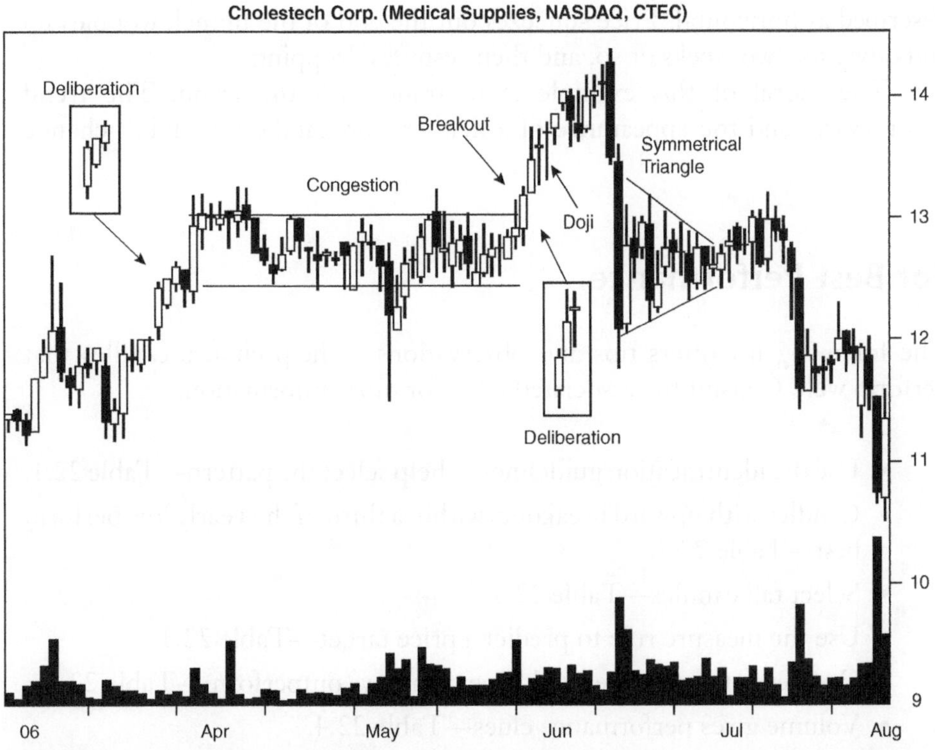

Figure 22.4 A deliberation appears at the breakout from a consolidation region.

into the candle pattern, and at the end a black candle appears with a lower close. However, the next day price breaks out upward, confirming the deliberation as a continuation pattern. Was that a clue to how the May deliberation would work?

Avoid expecting a lasting reversal from a deliberation in a prolonged uptrend. This uptrend began in January 2006, well before the May deliberation appears. Although one could argue that the uptrend is getting tired (price moved horizontally for two months), I consider that a risky bet. The trend is up, so avoid going short.

A long congestion zone of price turnover churns the stock during April and May. Then price closes above the top of the congestion zone, staging an upward breakout. During the breakout process, a deliberation appears. If this were my trade, I would assume that the candle means price will fall back to the top of the congestion zone before continuing higher.

That's not what happens, though. After the deliberation completes, a doji forms, suggesting that the bulls and bears are undecided as to which way price should go. The next day, price closes above the top of the deliberation, confirming the pattern as a continuation. As the chart shows, the stock continues to rise for about two weeks before two huge black candles appear in a show of bearish power. The black candles are the final two lines of a three outside down candlestick pattern.

After that, a small symmetrical triangle takes shape with a breakout best described as horizontal. Price squeezes out the end of the funnel, wobbles up and down for two weeks or so, and then resumes dropping.

The moral of this example is to trade with the trend. The trend was upward, and the appearance of a deliberation candlestick didn't change that.

For Best Performance

The following list offers tips and observations to help choose candles that perform well. Consult the associated table for more information.

- Use the identification guidelines to help select the pattern—Table 22.1.
- Candles with upward breakouts within a third of the yearly low perform best—Table 22.2.
- Select tall candles—Table 22.3.
- Use the measure rule to predict a price target—Table 22.3.
- Candles with tall upper and lower shadows outperform—Table 22.3.
- Volume gives performance clues—Table 22.4.

- Trade deliberations as reversals only as part of an upward retracement in a primary downtrend—Trading Tactics discussion.
- The candle breaks out upward most often—Table 22.5.
- Patterns within a third of the yearly high frequently act as continuations—Table 22.5.
- Breakouts below the 50-day moving average lead to the best performance—Table 22.6.

23

Doji, Dragonfly

Behavior and Rank

Theoretical: Indecision to bullish reversal (during a decline).
Actual bull market: Reversal 50% of the time (ranking 54).
Actual bear market: Continuation 51% of the time (ranking 50).
Frequency: 44th out of 103.
Overall performance over time: 98th out of 103.

I assumed that any doji would be rare and rarer still would be a dragonfly doji. I was wrong. I used two databases to log the candle pattern and found over 30,000, so I chopped it down to a more manageable 20,000.

The dragonfly opens at or near the high for the day and then price dives, forming a long lower shadow. The bears try all day to hold price underwater, but the bulls bounce off the bottom and surface again, ending where they began, at or near the opening price.

Performance for this candle depends on how it's supposed to act. That's unclear. It depends on which source you read. Some say it's a bearish reversal of the uptrend, while others claim it's a bullish reversal of the downtrend. Still others don't mention behavior at all, leaving the reader to guess.

I'll make the call and say that it acts as a reversal. Based on what I actually measured, performance is random, or nearly so, in both bull and bear markets. This random performance places it near the bottom of the overall ranking: 98 out of 103.

Identification Guidelines

Figure 23.1 shows an example of what many dragonfly catchers may recognize as a good trading setup. Price drops leading to the dragonfly, making an extended move down (the more oversold the better, so use indicators to confirm this). The dragonfly doji, with its long lower shadow and high volume, suggests the smart money is accumulating the stock. When everyone else tries to climb aboard, the price should rise.

The next day, a bullish engulfing candle confirms the buying sentiment, and it's off to the stock races. On a larger scale, a measured move down chart pattern helps predict the turn, with the second leg down approximating the drop and duration of the first leg. Price would be expected to climb back into the corrective phase marked AB on the chart. Research shows that price stops within the corrective phase 35% of the time, the highest of the four categories looked at.

How do you correctly identify a dragonfly doji? Table 23.1 lists the guidelines. Look for a long lower shadow topped by opening and closing prices that are at or very near the high for the day. I allow some play between the open, high, and close because a strict reading would eliminate too many doji.

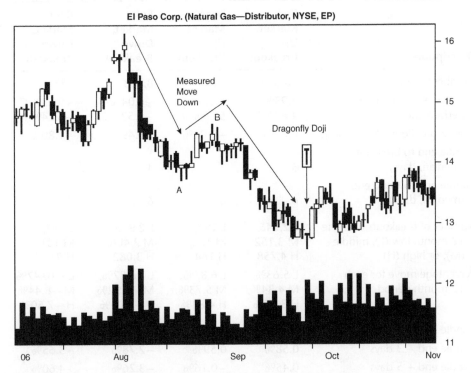

Figure 23.1 A dragonfly doji in a downward price trend acts as a reversal.

Table 23.1
Identification Guidelines

Characteristic	Discussion
Number of candle lines	One.
Configuration	Price opens and closes at or near the high for the day while having a long lower shadow.

Statistics

Table 23.2 shows general statistics.

Number found. I limited the number to 20,000 dragonfly doji so my supercomputer could handle the 74 megabyte spreadsheet. Even so, it choked once and I had to reboot. Prorating the standard database shows that the dragonfly appears more often in a bear market.

Reversal or continuation performance. Upward breakouts show the best performance as reversals of the downtrend, and downward breakouts

Table 23.2
General Statistics

Description	Bull Market, Up Breakout	Bear Market, Up Breakout	Bull Market, Down Breakout	Bear Market, Down Breakout
Number found	10,656	533	8,388	423
Reversal (R), continuation (C) performance	3.93% C 4.60% R	5.27% C 5.88% R	−6.04% C −5.52% R	−9.13% C −8.24% R
Standard & Poor's 500 change	0.81%	−0.02%	−0.49%	−1.80%
Candle end to breakout (median, days)	3	3	4	3
Candle end to trend end (median, days)	6	6	6	7
Number of breakouts near the 12-month low (L), middle (M), or high (H)	L 2,746, M 3,152, H 4,758	L 197, M 172, H 164	L 2,900, M 2,406, H 3,082	L 197, M 131, H 95
Percentage move for each 12-month period	L 5.63%, M 4.34%, H 3.76%	L 6.87%, M 5.73%, H 4.84%	L −6.87%, M −5.92%, H −5.05%	L −10.47%, M −8.44%, H −7.50%
Candle end + 1 day	0.21%	0.40%	−1.63%	−2.05%
Candle end + 3 days	0.58%	0.59%	−2.78%	−3.65%
Candle end + 5 days	0.45%	−0.16%	−3.26%	−4.60%
Candle end + 10 days	−0.46%	−1.74%	−3.89%	−5.02%
10-day performance rank	102	98	17	30

do better as continuations. Bear markets show better performance than bull markets.

S&P performance. Compare the performance of the S&P 500 with that of the dragonfly doji and you'll find that the candlestick performs better—much better, in fact.

Candle end to breakout. It takes about three days for price to either close above the top of the doji or close below the bottom.

Candle end to trend end. Half the candles reach the trend end in a week or less.

Yearly position, performance. Dragonflies in bull markets appear more often near the yearly high, while those in bear markets appear more often within a third of the yearly low. Performance is best when the candle has a breakout within a third of the yearly low.

Performance over time. Performance of dragonfly doji with upward breakouts is terrible. There's no consistent rise in performance over time as you see after downward breakouts. This contributes to the poor performance rank for upward breakouts. The percentage change 10 days after a downward breakout is quite good, and the ranks of 17 and 30 reflect that. A rank of 1 is best out of 103.

Table 23.3 shows height statistics.

Candle height. Tall candles outperform. To use this in your trading, compute the candle height from high to low price and divide by the breakout price (for upward breakouts, use the candle's high; for downward breakouts, use the candle's low). If the result is greater than the percentage listed in the table, then you have a tall candle.

Table 23.3
Height Statistics

Description	Bull Market, Up Breakout	Bear Market, Up Breakout	Bull Market, Down Breakout	Bear Market, Down Breakout
Median candle height as a percentage of breakout price	2.17%	2.86%	2.15%	2.89%
Short candle, performance	3.43%	4.54%	−4.95%	−7.90%
Tall candle, performance	6.01%	7.85%	−7.31%	−10.47%
Percentage meeting price target (measure rule)	78%	77%	77%	80%
Median lower shadow as a percentage of breakout price	1.96%	2.63%	1.94%	2.62%
Short lower shadow, performance	3.45%	4.51%	−4.90%	−7.66%
Tall lower shadow, performance	5.71%	7.70%	−7.19%	−10.56%

Table 23.4
Volume Statistics

Description	Bull Market, Up Breakout	Bear Market, Up Breakout	Bull Market, Down Breakout	Bear Market, Down Breakout
Above-average candle volume, performance	4.46%	5.59%	−5.59%	−8.13%
Below-average candle volume, performance	4.21%	5.56%	−5.88%	−9.02%
Heavy breakout volume, performance	4.89%	5.89%	−6.11%	−10.11%
Light breakout volume, performance	3.87%	5.33%	−5.58%	−7.68%

If Sam catches a dragonfly doji with a high of 50 and a low of 49, is it short or tall? The height is 50 − 49, or 1. For an upward breakout in a bull market, the measure is 1/50, or 2.0%. Sam has a short candle. Trade tall candles for the best results.

Measure rule. Use the measure rule to help predict how far price will rise or fall. Compute the height of the candle and multiply it by the appropriate percentage shown in the table; then apply it to the breakout price.

What are Sam's price targets for his dragonfly? The upward target would be $(1 \times 78\%) + 50$, or 50.78 and the downward target would be $49 − (1 \times 77\%)$, or 48.23.

Lower shadow performance. To determine whether the shadow is short or tall, compute the height of the shadow and divide by the breakout price. Compare the result to the median in the table. Tall shadows have a percentage higher than the median. Tall lower shadows perform better than short ones.

Table 23.4 shows volume statistics.

Average candle volume. Heavy candle volume (above average) suggests better postbreakout performance for doji with upward breakouts. Downward breakouts do better with light (below average) candle volume.

Breakout volume. Heavy breakout-day volume suggests better performance in all categories, a trend we have seen in many other candles. If you wait for the breakout, make sure it occurs on high volume for the best likelihood of better performance.

Trading Tactics

I split trading tactics into two basic studies, one concerning reversal rates and the other concerning performance. Of the two, reversal rates are more

Table 23.5
Reversal Rates

Description	Bull Market	Bear Market
Reversal rate: trend up, breakout down	43%	42%
Continuation rate: trend up, breakout up	57%	58%
Reversal: trend down, breakout up	56%	54%
Continuation: trend down, breakout down	44%	46%
Percentage of reversals (R)/continuations (C) for each 12-month low (L), middle (M), or high (H)	L 50% R/50% C, M 52% R/48% C, H 49% R/51% C	L 53% R/47% C, M 46% R/54% C, H 46% R/54% C
Black body reversal rate	50%	51%
White body reversal rate	51%	43%

important, because it's better to trade in the direction of the trend and let price run as far as it can.

Table 23.5 gives tips to find the trend direction.

Reversal, continuation rates. Use the trend leading to the doji to help determine the likely breakout direction. For example, if price trends upward leading to the doji, expect an upward breakout 57% of the time in a bull market. Price breaks out upward most often. Tell your friends.

Yearly range reversals. The numbers hover near random, so this doesn't mean much.

Body color reversal rate. The body color also doesn't give much of a hint as to the reversal rate. A white body in a bear market acts as a continuation 57% of the time (or a reversal 43% of the time). Performance of the remainder is random. Even though doji are not supposed to have a body color (because the opening and closing prices are the same), I allow a few pennies' difference between the two, and that colors the body.

Table 23.6 shows performance indicators that can give hints as to how your stock will behave after the breakout from a dragonfly candle pattern.

Confirmation, performance. Since a dragonfly doji in a downtrend is supposed to be bullish (act as a reversal), and many candle players place added emphasis on that setup, I only looked for confirmation under upward breakout conditions.

The best performance comes from opening gap confirmation—that is, waiting for price to gap open upward the next day before buying the stock.

Moving average. Candles with breakouts below the moving average work better than do those with breakouts above the moving average.

Body color performance. Candles with white bodies work better after upward breakouts, and black bodies work better after downward breakouts.

Table 23.6
Performance Indicators

Description	Bull Market, Up Breakout	Bear Market, Up Breakout	Bull Market, Down Breakout	Bear Market, Down Breakout
Closing price confirmation, performance	3.00%	4.58%	N/A	N/A
Candle color confirmation, performance	4.03%	5.75%	N/A	N/A
Opening gap confirmation, performance	4.10%	6.28%	N/A	N/A
Breakout above 50-day moving average, performance	4.03%	5.41%	−5.25%	−7.72%
Breakout below 50-day moving average, performance	4.77%	5.87%	−6.29%	−9.78%
Black body, performance	4.26%	5.54%	−5.81%	−9.04%
White body, performance	4.52%	5.69%	−5.66%	−7.91%

N/A means not applicable.

Sample Trade

Figure 23.2 shows an example of how to use a doji in a successful trade. The stock drops from a high level down to a lower one, where it moves horizontally in a rectangle bottom chart pattern (i.e., price bounces between two horizontal trendlines). The top trendline represents overhead resistance and the bottom one is support. Think of those two lines not just as lines but as regions or zones. Price may pierce them briefly before returning for additional sideways work.

A dragonfly doji appears as the right shoulder low of a head-and-shoulders bottom chart pattern, which typically predicts an upward breakout. Since the price trend leading to the doji is downward, what is the probability of an upward breakout? Table 23.5 gives the answer: 56% since 2006 was a bull market. Coupled with underlying support and the head-and-shoulders chart pattern, this setup represents a low-risk trade.

Sam decides to wait for an upward breakout before trading. The breakout occurs at point A when price closes above the top of the doji. He places a buy order to execute at the opening price the next day.

How far is price likely to rise? Based on the top of the rectangle, overhead resistance may kill the uptrend when price rises to the value of B. If everything works as planned, price will reverse at about 40.50. That does not leave much profit. But, if Sam can buy 1,000 shares at less than 39.50 and sell at 40.50, he'll make a grand.

The following day, the market opens at 39.35 and his order fills. Over the coming days, price rises, just as he hoped. Should he place a sell order at 40.50 and capture the profit or leave it alone and hope for a continued rise?

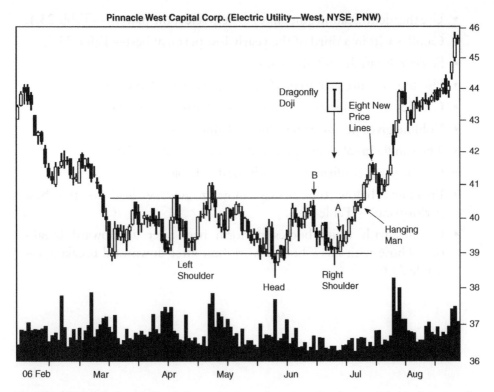

Figure 23.2 A dragonfly doji occurs in a downward price trend that is part of a head-and-shoulders bottom chart pattern.

As price rises so does volume, and that's a good sign. However, the candles are getting shorter and that's a sign of weakening bullish momentum. To add to his worries, a hanging man appears and that's a concern, so he places a stop a penny below the low of the candle line.

The next day, price rises, forming a tall candle on good volume. He breathes a sigh of relief and continues the search for the next possible sell point. It comes in the form of eight new price lines, a candle pattern with eight consecutively higher highs. This one ends with a black candle. So, he places a stop a penny below the black candle, and the next day price hits it and takes him out at 41.29. Thus, he made over $1,900 in about two weeks.

What lessons can Sam learn from this trade? If he was any good, he'd have stayed in and sold near 46. How could he have made that happen? And what about a stop-loss order when he first placed the trade? The answers are, of course, left to Sam to figure out.

For Best Performance

The following list offers tips and observations to help choose candles that perform well. Consult the associated table for more information.

- Use the identification guidelines to help select the pattern—Table 23.1.
- Candles within a third of the yearly low perform best—Table 23.2.
- Select tall candles—Table 23.3.
- Use the measure rule to predict a price target—Table 23.3.
- Candles with tall lower shadows outperform—Table 23.3.
- Volume gives performance clues—Table 23.4.
- The candle breaks out upward most often—Table 23.5.
- Opening gap confirmation works best—Table 23.6.
- Breakouts below the 50-day moving average lead to the best performance—Table 23.6.
- Candles with white bodies perform best after an upward breakout. Those with black bodies work best after downward breakouts—Table 23.6.

24

Doji, Gapping Down

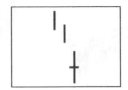

Behavior and Rank

Theoretical: Bearish continuation.

Actual bull market: Bullish reversal 56% of the time (ranking 37).

Actual bear market: Bullish reversal 54% of the time (ranking 36).

Frequency: 57th out of 103.

Overall performance over time: 88th out of 103.

The only thing different between a gapping-down doji and a regular doji is the gap. That is, a price gap appears between the doji and the prior day.

A doji represents a stalemate between bulls and bears. In this case, price trends lower into the candle (for one day at least) and that favors the bears, but the bulls counterattack and fight all day to gain control. At the end of the trading day, price closes at or near where it opened, with neither bulls nor bears in firm control. What happens after that is anyone's guess, but the numbers favor a reversal—the bulls will take over. That goes against the common belief that the gapping-down doji is a bearish continuation pattern.

The rankings support this confusion in behavior. The reversal rates are not outstanding, only 54% to 56%, which is quite close to random (50%). The overall performance ranking is 88 out of 103 where 1 is best. When compared to other candles, performance leaves much to be desired.

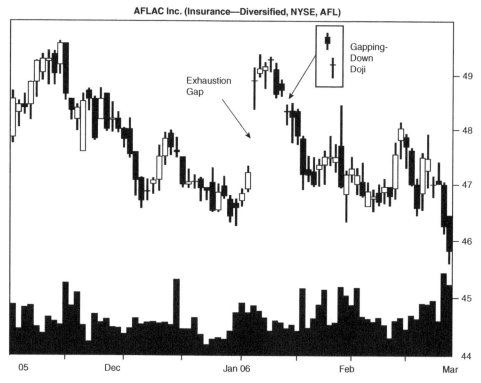

Figure 24.1 A gapping-down doji appears as part of a downward price trend.

Identification Guidelines

Figure 24.1 shows a gapping-down doji that takes shape after prices gapped upward (the exhaustion gap) on news of a broker upgrading the stock. My book, *Encyclopedia of Chart Patterns* (John Wiley & Sons, 2nd ed., 2005) reviews the likely course after a stock upgrade. The typical pattern has price rising for one to three weeks, followed by a decline. That is exactly the pattern we see here. Price gaps upward on the upgrade, coasts higher for three days, and then starts down. In a few weeks, price returns to the launch price, then wobbles up and down for over a month before heading lower.

Table 24.1 lists identification guidelines. Look for price to gap lower, and the gap should include the shadows, meaning that no overlap should occur between today's upper shadow and the prior day's lower shadow. A doji forms, with today's open and close at or near the same price.

Statistics

Table 24.2 shows general statistics.

Table 24.1
Identification Guidelines

Characteristic	Discussion
Number of candle lines	One.
Price trend	Downward (price gaps lower from the prior day).
Configuration	Price opens and closes at or near the same price for the day (a doji) but today's upper shadow remains below the prior day's lower shadow, leaving a price gap on the chart.

Number found. I found 17,603 gapping-down doji using four databases containing over 4.7 million candle lines. Most came from a bull market. Notice how many break out upward versus downward. On that basis alone, the results suggest the doji acts as a reversal of the downward price trend.

Reversal or continuation performance. The best performance comes from a doji in a bear market, regardless of the breakout direction. Reversals perform better than continuations.

Table 24.2
General Statistics

Description	Bull Market, Up Breakout	Bear Market, Up Breakout	Bull Market, Down Breakout	Bear Market, Down Breakout
Number found	8,888	993	6,879	843
Reversal (R), continuation (C) performance	7.54% R	9.90% R	−5.87% C	−8.17% C
Standard & Poor's 500 change	1.20%	0.53%	−0.37%	−1.73%
Candle end to breakout (median, days)	2	1	2	1
Candle end to trend end (median, days)	8	8	5	6
Number of breakouts near the 12-month low (L), middle (M), or high (H)	L 2,743, M 2,873, H 3,272	L 433, M 317, H 243	L 2,253, M 2,192, H 2,434	L 368, M 288, H 187
Percentage move for each 12-month period	L 8.65%, M 7.69%, H 6.84%	L 10.53%, M 7.52%, H 12.24%	L −6.65%, M −5.83%, H −5.41%	L −12.65%, M −6.19%, H −7.21%
Candle end + 1 day	1.25%	1.59%	−1.31%	−1.74%
Candle end + 3 days	1.84%	1.74%	−2.02%	−2.20%
Candle end + 5 days	2.05%	2.01%	−2.10%	−2.33%
Candle end + 10 days	2.52%	2.43%	−1.93%	−1.78%
10-day performance rank	68	65	66	87

S&P performance. The table shows the performance of the S&P 500 from the doji to the trend end. The index underperforms by a large margin.

Candle end to breakout. It takes just a few days for price to close either above or below the candlestick's shadows. Bull markets take a day longer than bear markets to break out, regardless of the breakout direction. While trying to figure out why, I stopped banging my head against the wall because it hurt.

Candle end to trend end. The median time ranges between five and eight days with downward breakouts taking less time to reach the trend end. This makes sense when you factor in the downward trend already under way. Upward breakouts would start a new trend and thus take longer to reach the trend end.

Yearly position, performance. Candles in a bull market appear most often within a third of the yearly high, and candles in a bear market frequently appear closer to the yearly low. The best performance comes from candles within a third of the yearly low except for bear market/up breakouts, which do better when the breakout is near the yearly high.

Performance over time. The gapping down doji stumbles between days 5 and 10 for downward breakouts, meaning performance deteriorates. Performance over time is poor for the four categories, too, so that leads to worse than usual ranking numbers. A rank of 1 is best out of 103 candles.

Table 24.3 shows height statistics.

Table 24.3
Height Statistics

Description	Bull Market, Up Breakout	Bear Market, Up Breakout	Bull Market, Down Breakout	Bear Market, Down Breakout
Median candle height as a percentage of breakout price	0.48%	0.75%	0.61%	0.76%
Short candle, performance	7.35%	9.68%	−5.66%	−7.12%
Tall candle, performance	7.64%	10.10%	−6.01%	−9.39%
Percentage meeting price target (measure rule)	95%	92%	93%	92%
Median upper shadow as a percentage of breakout price	0.00%	0.00%	0.00%	0.00%
Short upper shadow, performance	7.50%	9.16%	−5.84%	−7.22%
Tall upper shadow, performance	7.59%	10.68%	−5.91%	−9.36%
Median lower shadow as a percentage of breakout price	0.00%	0.00%	0.00%	0.00%
Short lower shadow, performance	7.62%	8.48%	−5.84%	−7.36%
Tall lower shadow, performance	7.49%	11.05%	−5.89%	−9.05%

Candle height. Gapping-down doji are short, judging by the medians listed in the table. When the candle is taller than the median, it tends to perform better, but this is not a guarantee.

To determine whether the candle is short or tall, compute its height from high to low price and divide by the breakout price. If the result is higher than the median, then you have a tall candle; otherwise it's short.

Suppose Joan is looking at a doji that has a high price of 51 and a low of 50. Is the doji short or tall? The height is 51 – 50, or 1, and let's suppose the breakout is upward in a bull market. The measure would be 1/51, or 1.96%. Joan has a tall candle.

Measure rule. Use the measure rule to help predict how far price will rise or fall. Compute the height of the candle and multiply it by the appropriate percentage shown in the table; then apply it to the breakout price.

What are the price targets for Joan's doji? The upward target would be $(1 \times 95\%) + 51$, or 51.95, and the downward target would be $50 - (1 \times 93\%)$, or 49.07. Since the success rate of the measure rule is over 90%, you can just use the full height to get a target. The new targets would be 52 and 49.

Shadows. To determine whether the shadow is short or tall, compute the height of the shadow and divide by the breakout price. Compare the result to the median in the table. Tall shadows have a percentage higher than the median.

Do not be alarmed by a median shadow height of zero. That just means there were no upper or lower shadows for at least half of the doji.

Upper shadow performance. Candles with tall upper shadows outperform their short shadow brothers.

Lower shadow performance. Candles with tall lower shadows also perform better than their short counterparts in all cases except bull market/up breakouts.

Table 24.4 shows volume statistics.

Table 24.4
Volume Statistics

Description	Bull Market, Up Breakout	Bear Market, Up Breakout	Bull Market, Down Breakout	Bear Market, Down Breakout
Above-average candle volume, performance	7.63%	7.90%	−5.87%	−8.38%
Below-average candle volume, performance	7.48%	11.61%	−5.87%	−8.03%
Heavy breakout volume, performance	8.00%	10.19%	−6.02%	−8.66%
Light breakout volume, performance	7.23%	9.72%	−5.75%	−7.77%

Average candle volume. Heavy (above-average) candle volume works best in two of four categories, with one tie. The exception is bear market/up breakouts. In that case, light candle volume results in better postbreakout performance—and by a large margin, too.

Breakout volume. As with most other candlestick types, heavy breakout-day volume suggests better postbreakout performance. The gapping-down doji follows the crowd by showing better performance if the candle had heavy breakout volume than light.

Trading Tactics

If you can identify an exhaustion gap, then expect a reversal. An exhaustion gap occurs at the end of a trend, usually on high volume. A continuation gap (a gap that continues the price trend, usually in a straight-line trend and usually on high volume) may precede the exhaustion gap, so look for at least two gaps in the same trend. The exhaustion gap may be unusually wide and is not followed by a series of new highs or lows (i.e., the trend ends). After the gap, price enters a consolidation region and the gap usually closes within a week.

Figure 24.1 shows an exhaustion gap in an upward trend. The gap is unusually wide and price consolidates afterward. The gap that occurs during the gapping-down doji is a breakaway gap because price is breaking away from the congestion zone, does not close quickly, and continues trending downward.

I split trading tactics into two basic studies, one concerning reversal rates and the other concerning performance. Of the two, reversal rates are more important, because it's better to trade in the direction of the trend and let price run as far as it can.

Table 24.5 gives tips to find the trend direction.

Table 24.5
Reversal Rates

Description	Bull Market	Bear Market
Closing price confirmation reversal rate	94%	94%
Candle color confirmation reversal rate	86%	72%
Opening gap confirmation reversal rate	78%	69%
Reversal: trend down, breakout up	56%	54%
Continuation: trend down, breakout down	44%	46%
Percentage of reversals (R)/continuations (C) for each 12-month low (L), middle (M), or high (H)	L 55% R/45% C, M 57% R/43% C, H 57% R/43% C	L 54% R/46% C, M 52% R/48% C, H 57% R/43% C
Black body reversal rate	56%	57%
White body reversal rate	56%	48%

Confirmation reversal rates. To help detect a reversal, wait for price to close higher the day after the doji. That works 94% of the time in signaling a reversal, but it isn't an indication of how far price may trend in the new direction.

Reversal, continuation rates. Based on price closing above the top of the candle (an upward breakout), 56% act as reversals of the downtrend in a bull market and 54% act as reversals in a bear market. These numbers are why I consider the gapping-down doji to be a reversal candle and not a continuation. Expect an upward breakout, but the results are close to random, which is 50%.

Yearly range reversals. Reversals in a bull market are split almost evenly across the yearly price range. The bear market shows reversals occurring most often when the breakout is within a third of the yearly high.

Body color reversal rate. In a bear market, a black-bodied doji (for those doji in which the open and close are a few pennies apart, which I allow) shows a higher tendency to reverse than a white body does.

Table 24.6 shows performance indicators that can give hints as to how your stock will behave after the breakout from this candle pattern.

Confirmation, performance. If we assume that this candle works as a continuation of the bearish price trend, which confirmation method works

Table 24.6
Performance Indicators

Description	Bull Market, Up Breakout	Bear Market, Up Breakout	Bull Market, Down Breakout	Bear Market, Down Breakout
Closing price confirmation, performance	N/A	N/A	−5.46%	−7.27%
Candle color confirmation, performance	N/A	N/A	−5.81%	−9.54%
Opening gap confirmation, performance	N/A	N/A	−6.28%	−10.98%
Breakout above 50-day moving average, performance	7.18%	10.26%	−5.55%	−6.88%
Breakout below 50-day moving average, performance	7.84%	9.62%	−6.07%	−9.01%
Last candle: close in highest third, performance	7.52%	10.12%	−5.73%	−8.42%
Last candle: close in middle third, performance	7.59%	9.84%	−6.07%	−8.04%
Last candle: close in lowest third, performance	7.35%	9.52%	−5.46%	−8.53%
Black body, performance	7.55%	12.44%	−5.95%	−8.85%
White body, performance	7.45%	6.53%	−5.20%	−7.58%

N/A means not applicable.

best? In both bull and bear markets, the opening gap method is the best choice (i.e., short the stock if price gaps open lower).

Moving average. Candles with breakouts below the 50-trading-day moving average perform better than do those candles with breakouts above the moving average in all cases except for bear market/up breakouts.

Closing position. Where price closes in the doji shows no consistent trend through the various categories.

Body color performance. Doji with black bodies show better performance than do those with white bodies, regardless of the market condition or breakout direction.

Sample Trade

Joan has followed the stock of Blyth Inc. for years (see Figure 24.2), and in early May she spots a buying opportunity. A gapping-down doji appears at a support zone and that suggests higher prices. Why?

First, based on the statistics in this chapter, the doji acts as a reversal more often than a continuation. To compute this, she uses the numbers for

Figure 24.2   A gapping-down doji represents a buying opportunity.

the bull market listed in Table 24.2 (8,888 plus 993 for upward breakouts as a percentage of all doji, 17,603), and finds that a reversal occurs 56% of the time.

Second, price reversed direction at 20 twice in the past, at points A and B. Plus, 20 is a round number and that also lends support (the reason being that more people buy or sell at a round number like 20 than at odd numbers such as 19.93 or 20.03).

A stop placed below the low at B would work well, she feels. Since the low is at 19.81, she puts the stop at 19.77, a few pennies below the round 19.80 number.

How much could she make? A trendline drawn along the peaks suggests a descending triangle chart pattern. If price climbs to the line and then reverses, the dashed line would be the sell price. Unfortunately, a down-sloping trendline makes it difficult to pinpoint a target price because the line moves lower each day. Looking elsewhere, she sees several peaks near 22—a round number again. That overhead resistance zone is the target, she decides.

Since a descending triangle breaks out downward 64% of the time (the number is calculated from results in *Encyclopedia of Chart Patterns*), she decides to wait for an upward breakout from the doji before placing the trade.

The day after the doji, price closes higher, staging an upward breakout. The next day, she places a buy order at the open and receives a fill at 20.30. She uses the lower of the peaks at the overhead resistance line near 22 to set a target price of 21.89, a penny below the March peak and an odd number. The stop is set at 19.77. If the trade works, she'll make over $1.50 per share. If it goes badly, she'll lose about 55 cents. That's a yummy reward-to-risk ratio of nearly 3 to 1.

Day by day she watches the stock and almost pulls the trigger when it stumbles about a week after she bought. Fortunately, she hangs on and waits for price to hit her target, selling the stock the day before it starts a large move down in June.

For Best Performance

The following list offers tips and observations to help choose candles that perform well. Consult the associated table for more information.

- Use the identification guidelines to help select the pattern—Table 24.1.
- Candles within a third of the yearly low perform best except in bear market/up breakouts—Table 24.2.
- Select tall candles—Table 24.3.
- Use the measure rule to predict a price target—Table 24.3.
- Candles with tall upper shadows outperform—Table 24.3.

- Volume gives performance clues—Table 24.4.
- Determine the gap type to help gauge breakout direction—Trading Tactics discussion.
- The candle breaks out upward most often—Table 24.5.
- Opening gap confirmation works best—Table 24.6.
- Black candles perform better than white ones—Table 24.6.

25

Doji, Gapping Up

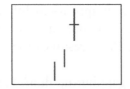

Behavior and Rank

Theoretical: Bullish continuation.

Actual bull market: Bearish reversal 57% of the time (ranking 34).

Actual bear market: Bearish reversal 58% of the time (ranking 32).

Frequency: 49th out of 103.

Overall performance over time: 92nd out of 103.

The gapping-up doji is supposed to act as a bullish continuation pattern, but my tests show otherwise. Price reverses the uptrend 57% of the time. Many of you will start squealing like stuck pigs at that, claiming that the performance is taken out of context. You're right. The numbers in this chapter do not include what nearby candles are saying, how bullish or bearish they may be. But the numbers do give an indication of how this candle behaves if you ignore the surrounding price landscape. That kind of information is invaluable. When trading on this or any other candle pattern, always consider what preceding candles are saying. If many are screaming "Reversal!" then you should listen.

The gapping-up doji is no different from other doji patterns in that it represents a struggle between the bulls and the bears, one that ends in a stalemate. The stock opens and price may rise, tumble, or go nowhere at all, but at market end, the closing price is very near or at the opening price. Little has changed except for the passing of money from trader to trader. The doji represents indecision, a windsock that cannot make up its mind about which way the wind is blowing.

Identification Guidelines

Figure 25.1 shows two examples of gapping-up doji. The one in June appears after breaking out of congestion (circled) when price gaps up at A. The rising window is a breakaway gap because it leaves a congestion area on strong volume. Then rising window B occurs, and it's an exhaustion gap. Following that, the gapping-up doji appears. The doji marks the end of the uptrend, as the chart shows and as the exhaustion gap predicted.

The second gapping-up doji appears in July and it is in the midst of a straight-line move up. Whereas the doji at B acts as a reversal, this one acts as a continuation candlestick. Price resumes the move higher after the doji completes.

How do you recognize a gapping-up doji? Table 25.1 lists identification guidelines. Price gaps upward and forms a doji, which can be any of the doji varieties, such as a gravestone, dragonfly, long-legged, four-price, and so on. In a doji, the opening and closing prices are at or near the same value. The shadows can be tall or short; it doesn't matter. However, in this pattern price must gap above the prior day and that includes the shadows. By that I mean today's lower shadow must be above yesterday's upper shadow, leaving a price gap on the chart.

Figure 25.1   Two gapping-up doji appear. The one in June acts as a reversal, but the one in July acts as a continuation pattern.

Table 25.1
Identification Guidelines

Characteristic	Discussion
Number of candle lines	One.
Price trend	Upward (price gaps up from the prior day).
Configuration	Price opens and closes at or near the same price for the day (a doji), but today's lower shadow remains above the prior day's upper shadow, leaving a price gap on the chart.

Statistics

Table 25.2 shows general statistics.

Number found. Using over 4.7 million candle lines, I excavated 17,176 gapping-up doji. Most appear in a bull market.

Reversal or continuation performance. The strong performance in a bear market may be due to the dearth of candles when compared to the bull

Table 25.2
General Statistics

Description	Bull Market, Up Breakout	Bear Market, Up Breakout	Bull Market, Down Breakout	Bear Market, Down Breakout
Number found	6,553	761	8,831	1,031
Reversal (R), continuation (C) performance	6.19% C	7.08% C	−5.89% R	−8.80% R
Standard & Poor's 500 change	1.09%	0.31%	−0.29%	−1.66%
Candle end to breakout (median, days)	2	2	2	1
Candle end to trend end (median, days)	6	6	7	8
Number of breakouts near the 12-month low (L), middle (M), or high (H)	L 1,090, M 1,497, H 2,661	L 236, M 271, H 240	L 1,664, M 2,070, H 3,347	L 393, M 325, H 291
Percentage move for each 12-month period	L 8.26%, M 6.58%, H 6.32%	L 10.57%, M 6.63%, H 5.68%	L −7.88%, M −6.40%, H −5.72%	L −13.05%, M −7.47%, H −7.54%
Candle end + 1 day	1.36%	2.03%	−1.10%	−1.35%
Candle end + 3 days	2.13%	2.65%	−1.37%	−1.96%
Candle end + 5 days	2.33%	2.61%	−1.33%	−2.15%
Candle end + 10 days	2.35%	2.02%	−1.03%	−2.13%
10-day performance rank	74	72	94	81

market samples. However, I have seen other candle types with the same trends. Candlesticks in a bear market perform better than do those in a bull market.

S&P performance. Comparing the performance of the S&P 500 to that of the gapping-up doji, we see that the candle results in substantially better performance.

Candle end to breakout. It takes a day or two for price to close either above the top of the doji or below the bottom.

Candle end to trend end. The time to the trend end ranges between six and eight days, with downward breakouts taking longer than upward ones. This is caused by price being in an uptrend already (well along on its way to the trend end).

Yearly position, performance. Where the candle appears shows no consistent trend from category to category. However, those with breakouts within a third of the yearly low perform better than do those in the other ranges.

Performance over time. In three of four categories, performance suffers from 5 to 10 days. With weak numbers posted after 10 days, the performance rank suffers, too. Doji with upward breakouts perform better than do those with downward breakouts, according to the rank.

Table 25.3 shows height statistics.

Candle height. For a single candle line, the median height divided by the breakout price is small, as you would expect. However, when you sort the doji candles' performance according to their height/breakout price results, we find

Table 25.3
Height Statistics

Description	Bull Market, Up Breakout	Bear Market, Up Breakout	Bull Market, Down Breakout	Bear Market, Down Breakout
Median candle height as a percentage of breakout price	0.98%	0.99%	0.71%	0.71%
Short candle, performance	4.90%	5.87%	−4.83%	−6.62%
Tall candle, performance	7.39%	8.52%	−6.61%	−10.67%
Percentage meeting price target (measure rule)	92%	91%	93%	93%
Median upper shadow as a percentage of breakout price	0.36%	0.11%	0.00%	0.00%
Short upper shadow, performance	5.05%	5.90%	−5.15%	−7.06%
Tall upper shadow, performance	7.01%	8.13%	−6.29%	−10.05%
Median lower shadow as a percentage of breakout price	0.00%	0.00%	0.00%	0.00%
Short lower shadow, performance	7.36%	5.86%	−5.53%	−7.25%
Tall lower shadow, performance	5.53%	8.24%	−6.30%	−10.26%

that tall candles substantially outperform short ones. This result is consistent with other candle types. In fact, candle height is one of the best predictors of performance.

To determine whether the candle is short or tall, compute its height from high to low price and divide by the breakout price. If the result is higher than the median, then you have a tall candle; otherwise it's short.

Rich sees a gapping-up doji in a stock with a high price of 98 and a low of 95. Is the candle short or tall? The height is 98 − 95, or 3, so the measure is 3/98, or 3.1%, for an upward breakout. The doji is a tall candle.

Measure rule. Use the measure rule to help predict how far price will rise or fall. Compute the height of the candle and multiply it by the appropriate percentage shown in the table; then apply it to the breakout price.

What are the price targets for Rich's candle? The upward target would be 98 + (3 × 92%), or 100.76, and the downward target would be 95 − (3 × 93%), or 92.21.

Since the measure rule works over 90% of the time, you can use the full height to gauge how far price is likely to move instead of multiplying it by the percentage meeting the price target. In that case, the targets would be 101 and 92.

Shadows. To determine whether the shadow is short or tall, compute the height of the shadow and divide by the breakout price. Compare the result to the median in the table. Tall shadows have a percentage higher than the median. Don't worry about a zero median. That simply means I found an abundance of doji with no shadows.

Upper shadow performance. Candles with tall upper shadows outperform those with short ones.

Lower shadow performance. Candles with tall lower shadows outperform in all categories except for bull market/up breakouts.

Table 25.4 shows volume statistics.

Table 25.4
Volume Statistics

Description	Bull Market, Up Breakout	Bear Market, Up Breakout	Bull Market, Down Breakout	Bear Market, Down Breakout
Above-average candle volume, performance	7.02%	7.43%	−6.27%	−8.63%
Below-average candle volume, performance	5.61%	6.79%	−5.64%	−8.93%
Heavy breakout volume, performance	7.64%	7.94%	−6.70%	−8.98%
Light breakout volume, performance	5.07%	6.29%	−5.56%	−8.71%

Average candle volume. Heavy (above-average) candle volume results in the best postbreakout performance in all cases except bear market/down breakout, which does better with light candle volume.

Breakout volume. Heavy breakout-day volume is better for performance than light volume, as the results show.

Trading Tactics

I find it easier to determine what happens with a gapping-up doji when I consider the gap type. Figure 25.1 shows a breakaway gap (at A), so called because price breaks away from the congestion area on higher volume. The stock continues to make new highs and the gap does not close quickly.

An exhaustion gap (at B) appears near the end of the upward price trend, not coming from a congestion zone, but entering one. Price stops making continual highs and moves horizontally or reverses. The gap closes quickly (in a few days), meaning price retraces far enough to cover the gap. Exhaustion gaps can be unusually tall and sometimes follow continuation or breakaway gaps. Continuation gaps occur in the middle of strong price trends.

I split trading tactics into two basic studies, one concerning reversal rates and the other concerning performance. Of the two, reversal rates are more important, because it's better to trade in the direction of the trend and let price run as far as it can.

Table 25.5 gives tips to find the trend direction.

Confirmation reversal rates. To help determine when price might reverse downward, wait for price to close lower the next day. That works to detect a reversal at least 93% of the time.

Table 25.5
Reversal Rates

Description	Bull Market	Bear Market
Closing price confirmation reversal rate	93%	94%
Candle color confirmation reversal rate	85%	82%
Opening gap confirmation reversal rate	78%	69%
Reversal rate: trend up, breakout down	57%	58%
Continuation rate: trend up, breakout up	43%	42%
Percentage of reversals (R)/continuations (C) for each 12-month low (L), middle (M), or high (H)	L 60% R/40% C, M 58% R/42% C, H 56% R/44% C	L 62% R/38% C, M 55% R/45% C, H 55% R/45% C
Black body reversal rate	61%	62%
White body reversal rate	48%	50%

Reversal, continuation rates. The numbers show that more patterns act as reversals of the uptrend. Expect a downward breakout, but that happens just 57% of the time in a bull market.

Yearly range reversals. Reversals occur most often within a third of the yearly low.

Body color reversal rate. Doji with black bodies have higher reversal rates than their white counterparts. Body color is possible because I allow a doji to have a few pennies' difference between the opening and closing prices, coloring its body.

Table 25.6 shows performance indicators that can give hints as to how your stock will behave after the breakout from a candle pattern.

Confirmation, performance. Since price is supposed to break out upward, that is the direction I looked at. The best performance comes from opening gap confirmation, which means buy if price opens higher the day after the doji.

Moving average. Candles with breakouts below the 50-trading-day moving average perform better than do those with breakouts above the moving average.

Closing position. Where price closes shows no consistent trend among the various categories.

Table 25.6
Performance Indicators

Description	Bull Market, Up Breakout	Bear Market, Up Breakout	Bull Market, Down Breakout	Bear Market, Down Breakout
Closing price confirmation, performance	5.44%	6.48%	N/A	N/A
Candle color confirmation, performance	4.95%	6.15%	N/A	N/A
Opening gap confirmation, performance	6.19%	9.51%	N/A	N/A
Breakout above 50-day moving average, performance	6.80%	5.81%	−6.00%	−8.18%
Breakout below 50-day moving average, performance	7.23%	9.64%	−7.34%	−9.92%
Last candle: close in highest third, performance	3.81%	8.59%	−6.24%	−7.61%
Last candle: close in middle third, performance	7.15%	6.38%	−5.65%	−7.87%
Last candle: close in lowest third, performance	6.83%	7.93%	−6.11%	−10.73%
Black body, performance	6.11%	7.86%	−5.79%	−10.28%
White body, performance	6.43%	6.51%	−6.33%	−7.27%

N/A means not applicable.

Body color performance. Candles with white bodies perform better in a bull market, while those with black bodies do better in a bear market.

Sample Trade

Rich is a gap trader. He searches for consolidation areas and price gaps on high volume that push price up. Figure 25.2 shows an example of a trade he is considering. During March, price moves sideways in a consolidation or congestion pattern (circled), churning away on elevated, but not nosebleed high, volume. The small bodies and tall shadows suggest indecision.

When price shoots upward and forms the gapping-up doji, he is ready. In his checklist is a note to look for overhead resistance. In this case, the peak at A represents resistance that might kill the new trend. Since the top of the doji was at 47.25 and the peak at A was at 48.11, that doesn't leave much room for a profit when commissions, slippage, and undershoot (price not making it to the same price as A) are taken into consideration.

Rich shakes his head and says, "Too risky."

He is right, as the chart shows. Price forms a tall white candle followed by a spinning top or high wave candle (after the gapping-up doji). The tall white

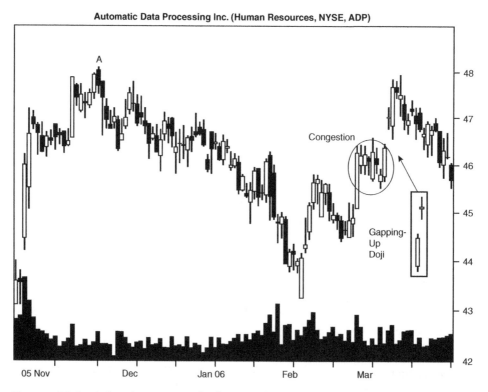

Figure 25.2 A breakaway gap looks promising, but overhead resistance stops the advance.

candle is bullish, except that very tall candles (146% above the average height) often mark a minor high or low within a day (this white candle qualifies as an unusually tall candle). The spinning top suggests indecision, and since it is black, that isn't positive, either.

When Rich looks back at the chart a month later, he smiles because he made the right choice. Sometimes the best trade you can make is none at all.

For Best Performance

The following list offers tips and observations to help choose candles that perform well. Consult the associated table for more information.

- Use the identification guidelines to help select the pattern—Table 25.1.
- Candles within a third of the yearly low perform best—Table 25.2.
- Select tall candles—Table 25.3.
- Use the measure rule to predict a price target—Table 25.3.
- Candles with tall upper shadows outperform—Table 25.3.
- Volume gives performance clues—Table 25.4.
- Determine the gap type (exhaustion or breakaway) before trading—Trading Tactics discussion.
- The candle breaks out downward most often—Table 25.5.
- Patterns within a third of the yearly low tend to act as reversals most often—Table 25.5.
- Opening gap confirmation works best—Table 25.6.
- Breakouts below the 50-day moving average lead to the best performance—Table 25.6.

26

Doji, Gravestone

Behavior and Rank

Theoretical: Indecision to bearish (during an uptrend) reversal.
Actual bull market: Bearish reversal 51% of the time (ranking 52).
Actual bear market: Bearish reversal 51% of the time (ranking 43).
Frequency: 42nd out of 103.
Overall performance over time: 77th out of 103.

The gravestone doji has such an evocative name that it conjures up all sorts of images. It can occur in an uptrend or downtrend, but its forte is to act as a bearish reversal of the uptrend. That's the theory, but there's just one problem: It doesn't work. About half the time price continues the existing trend and half the time it doesn't. Performance is random. Some might complain that the gravestone doji, being a doji, really shows indecision. That's certainly true in this case, because price can't make up its mind which way to go.

The psychology behind the pattern is the same as for other doji candles. Price opens at or very near the low for the day, and bullish buying demand pushes the stock up. Eventually, bearish selling pressure overwhelms buying demand and sends price lower, ending the day at the opening price. The tall upper shadow suggests a lasting bearish turn, but that's a fantasy.

The candle doesn't act as a reversal, and it doesn't act as a continuation. The overall rank of 77 out of 103, where 1 is best, means performance is lacking. Perhaps the only good thing about this candle is its name. We'll take a closer look at the numbers later to see if we can salvage anything from this candle.

Identification Guidelines

Figure 26.1 shows a good example of how a gravestone doji should act as a lasting reversal but doesn't. In this example, a large descending triangle chart pattern forms. Sixty-four percent of the time price breaks out downward from this type of chart pattern. With a gravestone doji appearing at the top trendline, I would expect price to reverse and stage a downward breakout. That doesn't happen. Yes, price does move lower over the next two days, but then it breaks out upward (from the descending triangle) on the second day when price closes above the down-sloping trendline.

My impression of a gravestone doji is just that: death of the uptrend. Perhaps I'm being too hard on the gravestone. It's just a single candle line with random behavior. The statistics will tell us more about the candle, but, first, how do you identify it?

Table 26.1 lists identification guidelines. They are simple enough. Look for a candle with the open, low, and closing price at or near the same value. The upper shadow should be long.

Figure 26.1   A bearish gravestone doji appears at a point where price should turn down, but price breaks out upward instead.

Table 26.1
Identification Guidelines

Characteristic	Discussion
Number of candle lines	One.
Configuration	Price opens and closes at or very near the daily low with a tall upper shadow.

Statistics

Table 26.2 shows general statistics.

Number found. I used only two databases to find well over 30,000 candles. In trying to save the spreadsheet, it locked up my machine. I cut the number of samples nearly in half, but the spreadsheet remained over 100 megabytes. But you didn't want to read about my problems, did you?

Most doji candles appear in a bull market; few show in a bear market.

Table 26.2
General Statistics

Description	Bull Market, Up Breakout	Bear Market, Up Breakout	Bull Market, Down Breakout	Bear Market, Down Breakout
Number found	7,996	431	10,562	616
Reversal (R), continuation (C) performance	5.87% C 6.81% R	7.95% C 9.80% R	−5.97% C −5.69% R	−8.74% C −6.81% R
Standard & Poor's 500 change	1.14%	0.37%	−0.37%	−1.79%
Candle end to breakout (median, days)	4	3	3	2
Candle end to trend end (median, days)	6	7	6	6
Number of breakouts near the 12-month low (L), middle (M), or high (H)	L 2,132, M 2,182, H 3,682	L 165, M 137, H 129	L 3,544, M 3,060, H 3,958	L 227, M 207, H 182
Percentage move for each 12-month period	L 7.91%, M 6.35%, H 5.54%	L 10.86%, M 8.31%, H 7.64%	L −7.06%, M −5.80%, H −5.09%	L −10.82%, M −6.93%, H −6.27%
Candle end + 1 day	1.79%	2.59%	−0.33%	−0.48%
Candle end + 3 days	2.95%	3.74%	−1.01%	−1.04%
Candle end + 5 days	3.43%	4.58%	−1.17%	−1.03%
Candle end + 10 days	3.86%	5.09%	−1.01%	−0.99%
10-day performance rank	37	27	95	95

Reversal or continuation performance. Reversals work better if the breakout is upward. That means the best performance comes when price is trending *down* into the gravestone doji and turns up (reverses) after the candlestick. Downward breakouts from gravestone doji work better as continuations of the price trend (price trends *down* into the candlestick).

S&P performance. Compare the candle's performance with the S&P 500's, and we see that the gravestone doji results in better performance even though both cover the same period.

Candle end to breakout. Most single candle lines take several days to break out, and this doji takes between two and four days. Downward breakouts take less time than upward ones because price is at or near the candle's low.

Candle end to trend end. Measuring from the day after the doji to the trend end, we find that the median is six or seven days.

Yearly position, performance. Candles in a bull market appear more often within a third of the yearly high. Those in a bear market show near the yearly low. The best performance comes from candles with breakouts within a third of the yearly low.

Performance over time. The candle stumbles during 5 to 10 days after a downward breakout. The performance numbers are low enough to push the performance rank into dismal territory. The upward breakout rankings are respectable, though.

Table 26.3 shows height statistics.

Candle height. Tall candles outperform short ones. To determine whether the candle is short or tall, compute its height from high to low price

Table 26.3
Height Statistics

Description	Bull Market, Up Breakout	Bear Market, Up Breakout	Bull Market, Down Breakout	Bear Market, Down Breakout
Median candle height as a percentage of breakout price	2.25%	2.83%	2.39%	2.68%
Short candle, performance	5.27%	7.92%	−4.97%	−5.88%
Tall candle, performance	8.24%	10.07%	−7.44%	−10.51%
Percentage meeting price target (measure rule)	78%	79%	77%	78%
Median upper shadow as a percentage of breakout price	2.05%	2.63%	2.21%	2.56%
Short upper shadow, performance	5.22%	7.90%	−4.87%	−5.90%
Tall upper shadow, performance	8.08%	10.04%	−7.41%	−10.28%

Table 26.4
Volume Statistics

Description	Bull Market, Up Breakout	Bear Market, Up Breakout	Bull Market, Down Breakout	Bear Market, Down Breakout
Above-average candle volume, performance	6.45%	9.01%	−5.69%	−7.28%
Below-average candle volume, performance	6.14%	8.72%	−5.86%	−7.76%
Heavy breakout volume, performance	7.20%	10.27%	−5.95%	−7.27%
Light breakout volume, performance	5.36%	7.69%	−5.71%	−7.80%

in the candle pattern and divide by the breakout price. If the result is higher than the median, then you have a tall candle; otherwise it's short.

For example, if Janet sees a gravestone doji with a high at 113 and a low at 110, is it short or tall? The height is 113 − 110, or 3, so the measure would be 3/113, or 2.7%. In a bull market with an upward breakout, the candle is tall.

Measure rule. Use the measure rule to help predict how far price will rise or fall. Compute the height of the candle and multiply it by the appropriate percentage shown in the table; then apply it to the breakout price.

What are Janet's price targets? The upward target would be (3 × 78%) + 113, or 115.34, and the downward target would be 110 − (3 × 77%), or 107.69.

Shadows. To determine whether the shadow is short or tall, compute the height of the shadow and divide by the breakout price. Compare the result to the median in the table. Tall shadows have a percentage higher than the median. Candles with tall upper shadows suggest better performance than do those with short shadows.

Table 26.4 shows volume statistics.

Average candle volume. Upward breakouts do best when the candle shows above-average volume, and downward breakouts do best with below-average volume.

Breakout volume. Heavy breakout-day volume suggests good performance in all categories except bear market/down breakout. In many candle types, heavy breakout-day volume works better than low breakout volume.

Trading Tactics

If you see a gravestone doji appear as part of a congestion region, usually an area of horizontal price movement, ignore the doji. The chances are that price will continue moving horizontally instead of beginning a new trend. In fact,

Table 26.5
Reversal Rates

Description	Bull Market	Bear Market
Reversal rate: trend up, breakout down	56%	59%
Continuation rate: trend up, breakout up	44%	41%
Reversal: trend down, breakout up	42%	41%
Continuation: trend down, breakout down	58%	59%
Percentage of reversals (R)/continuations (C) for each 12-month low (L), middle (M), or high (H)	L 50% R/50% C, M 51% R/49% C, H 52% R/48% C	L 52% R/48% C, M 49% R/51% C, H 52% R/48% C
Black body reversal rate	51%	49%
White body reversal rate	50%	53%

the best way to interpret a gravestone doji is to believe that price will continue the existing trend (up, down, or sideways) because that's what happens about half the time anyway.

I split trading tactics into two basic studies, one concerning reversal rates and the other concerning performance. Of the two, reversal rates are more important, because it's better to trade in the direction of the trend and let price run as far as it can.

Table 26.5 gives tips to find the trend direction.

Reversal, continuation rates. I looked at the four combinations of trend before and after the doji and measured how often each combination occurred. The two most frequent combinations are a reversal from up to down and a continuation of the downtrend. Thus, if you see a doji in a bear market at the top of an uptrend, there's a 59% chance that price will reverse. Use the table to determine how likely it is that the trend will reverse for your situation.

Yearly range reversals. Reversals seem sprinkled over the yearly price range about evenly, so the numbers don't say much except that the candle's behavior is random.

Body color reversal rate. Candle color comes from allowing the doji to have a body a few pennies high instead of equal opening and closing prices. However, the color does not give much of a hint about the likelihood of a reversal.

Table 26.6 shows performance indicators that can give hints as to how your stock will behave after the breakout from a candle pattern.

Confirmation, performance. I show only reversals of the uptrend to test the various confirmation methods. The best performance comes from opening gap confirmation. That means waiting for price to gap open lower the next day before trading.

Moving average. Breakouts below the 50-trading-day moving average result in better performance than breakouts above the moving average.

Table 26.6
Volume Statistics

Description	Bull Market, Up Breakout	Bear Market, Up Breakout	Bull Market, Down Breakout	Bear Market, Down Breakout
Closing price confirmation, performance	N/A	N/A	−4.83%	−6.67%
Candle color confirmation, performance	N/A	N/A	−5.39%	−7.22%
Opening gap confirmation, performance	N/A	N/A	−5.53%	−8.09%
Breakout above 50-day moving average, performance	5.94%	7.92%	−5.45%	−6.79%
Breakout below 50-day moving average, performance	6.93%	10.23%	−6.19%	−8.30%
Black body, performance	6.35%	8.57%	−5.85%	−7.76%
White body, performance	5.72%	9.22%	−5.44%	−7.21%

N/A means not applicable.

Body color performance. Doji with black bodies (when you allow a few pennies as a doji body size) perform better than white ones. This is true in all cases except for bear market/up breakouts.

Sample Trade

Janet looked at the setup in Figure 26.2 and liked what she saw. Price formed a congestion zone from September to October and then broke out upward, cresting at A. Then the slide began, making another lower high at B. Two lines connecting the peaks and valleys form a channel that confines price as it moves lower.

When the gravestone doji appears at the upper channel line at the end of January, Janet expects a reversal of the small uptrend (of three advancing white candles) with a target decline to the opposite side of the channel. Since price is trending downward toward the congestion zone from September/October (the top of it is highlighted in the chart by the dashed line), she expects price to reverse or stall there (at C).

The day after the doji, she watches price move below the doji's low, and that is the confirmation she is looking for. It isn't breakout confirmation, because that requires a close, but with the channel so narrow, she can't afford to wait. She shorts the stock at 34.89 with a target of 33 (a round number near C).

Figure 26.2 A gravestone doji appears at the top of a down-sloping channel, suggesting a reversal of the uptrend leading to the doji.

As luck would have it, price meets her target the same day. Since the candle line is so tall, she decides to hold on for additional declines. She recognizes that if price were to rebound, it would likely stall somewhere within the tall black body, perhaps around 34, a known resistance zone set up by the two valleys in January (D and E). That would still leave her with a profit.

She extends the lower channel line downward from C and sees that price follows it lower, below the channel line. She hasn't sold yet but will when price closes above that lower channel line, or perhaps sooner.

For Best Performance

The following list offers tips and observations to help choose candles that perform well. Consult the associated table for more information.

- Use the identification guidelines to help select the pattern—Table 26.1.
- Candles within a third of the yearly low perform best—Table 26.2.
- Select tall candles—Table 26.3.

- Use the measure rule to predict a price target—Table 26.3.
- Candles with tall upper shadows outperform—Table 26.3.
- Volume gives performance clues—Table 26.4.
- Ignore doji in congestion areas—Trading Tactics discussion.
- The candle breaks out downward most often—Table 26.5.
- Opening gap confirmation works best—Table 26.6.
- Breakouts below the 50-day moving average lead to the best performance—Table 26.6.

27

Doji,
Long-Legged

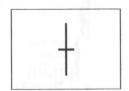

Behavior and Rank

Theoretical: Indecision.
Actual bull market: Bullish continuation 51% of the time (ranking 49).
Actual bear market: Bullish reversal 50% of the time (ranking 47).
Frequency: 41st out of 103.
Overall performance over time: 37th out of 103.

If there is a candle pattern that acts randomly, then the long-legged doji is it. It functions as a continuation pattern 50.5% of the time, reinforced with a review of hundreds of charts. Sometimes a long-legged doji marks the turning point perfectly, but at other times price continues trending without pausing for breath.

As to pattern psychology, the long-legged doji represents the struggle between the bulls and the bears with neither winning. At times during the day, the bulls are euphoric because price is climbing to the sky, and at other times the bears are in full control as they push price down toward the earth's core. By day's end, however, the price ends where it began, leaving behind tall shadows and sweaty brows.

The overall performance rank is quite good at 37 out of 103 with 1 being the best. That's due to the price move after 10 days coupled with robust performance during the prior measurement periods. I discuss statistics later. Let's first concentrate on identifying the candle.

Figure 27.1   A long-legged doji appears as a reversal.

Identification Guidelines

Figure 27.1 shows an example of a long-legged doji. Both the upper and lower shadows of the doji are taller than the average shadow length and the opening and closing prices of the doji are the same. In this example, price breaks out downward from the rectangle bottom chart pattern and trends lower until hitting the doji. Then, the indecision evident in the doji candlestick translates into a reversal when price opens lower the next day but closes up strongly and continues higher.

Table 27.1 lists identification guidelines. The candle line is a doji, meaning the opening and closing prices are either the same or very close to each

Table 27.1
Identification Guidelines

Characteristic	Discussion
Number of candle lines	One.
Configuration	The opening and closing prices should be the same or nearly so, with long upper and lower shadows.

other. The upper and lower shadows should be longer than the average shadow height, but the body need not be in the middle of the candlestick. If it is, then that's a rickshaw man candlestick. The statistics in this chapter include the rickshaw man candles because they are also long-legged doji candles.

Statistics

Table 27.2 shows general statistics.

Number found. I discovered 16,968 long-legged doji, and they are a handsome lot. Prorating the standard database, we find that the pattern occurs most often in a bull market.

Reversal or continuation performance. Performance of long-legged doji with upward breakouts improves when they act as reversals. Downward breakouts do better as continuations. Bear market performance beats the bull market numbers.

Table 27.2
General Statistics

Description	Bull Market, Up Breakout	Bear Market, Up Breakout	Bull Market, Down Breakout	Bear Market, Down Breakout
Number found	8,189	662	7,480	637
Reversal (R), continuation (C) performance	6.28% C 6.88% R	8.98% C 10.30% R	−5.79% C −5.38% R	−11.06% C −9.75% R
Standard & Poor's 500 change	1.27%	0.52%	−0.58%	−2.87%
Candle end to breakout (median, days)	4	3	4	4
Candle end to trend end (median, days)	7	8	7	8
Number of breakouts near the 12-month low (L), middle (M), or high (H)	L 1,763, M 1,895, H 3,140	L 211, M 233, H 207	L 2,250, M 1,808, H 2,133	L 267, M 192, H 168
Percentage move for each 12-month period	L 8.47%, M 6.02%, H 6.01%	L 11.95%, M 9.36%, H 8.34%	L −6.70%, M −5.54%, H −4.81%	L −11.22%, M −11.23%, H −8.89%
Candle end + 1 day	1.15%	1.56%	−1.01%	−1.29%
Candle end + 3 days	2.17%	3.23%	−1.96%	−3.12%
Candle end + 5 days	2.75%	3.82%	−2.36%	−3.65%
Candle end + 10 days	3.56%	4.62%	−2.39%	−4.26%
10-day performance rank	45	38	49	46

S&P performance. By a wide margin, the candle performance beats the the S&P 500 over the same measurement periods.

Candle end to breakout. It takes three or four days for price to break out (close above the top or below the bottom of the doji).

Candle end to trend end. The median time from a day after the candle to the trend end is about a week. Candles in a bear market take a day longer than do those in a bull market.

Yearly position, performance. Performance is best when the breakout is within a third of the yearly low. That's true in all cases except for bear market/down breakouts. Those do better when the breakout is in the middle of the yearly trading range, but the numbers are nearly identical.

Performance over time. The doji is a robust candle. By that I mean performance increases over each time interval and in every category. The performance after 10 days could be higher (6% or more), and that's why each performance rank is middling (1 is best out of 103).

Table 27.3 shows height statistics.

Candle height. If there is one thing a long-legged doji can hang its hat on, it's that tall candles perform better than short ones. That is the case in all categories and the performance difference is substantial. To determine whether a doji is short or tall, measure the height from high to low price and divide by the breakout price; then compare the result with the table. If your result is

Table 27.3
Height Statistics

Description	Bull Market, Up Breakout	Bear Market, Up Breakout	Bull Market, Down Breakout	Bear Market, Down Breakout
Median candle height as a percentage of breakout price	3.37%	4.63%	3.45%	4.66%
Short candle, performance	5.01%	7.43%	−4.70%	−8.52%
Tall candle, performance	9.77%	13.35%	−7.42%	−13.85%
Percentage meeting price target (measure rule)	68%	67%	64%	67%
Median upper shadow as a percentage of breakout price	1.57%	2.13%	1.69%	2.33%
Short upper shadow, performance	5.08%	7.41%	−4.71%	−8.35%
Tall upper shadow, performance	9.30%	12.94%	−7.26%	−13.66%
Median lower shadow as a percentage of breakout price	1.62%	2.15%	1.60%	2.13%
Short lower shadow, performance	5.11%	7.68%	−4.67%	−9.18%
Tall lower shadow, performance	9.42%	12.32%	−7.37%	−12.41%

Table 27.4
Volume Statistics

Description	Bull Market, Up Breakout	Bear Market, Up Breakout	Bull Market, Down Breakout	Bear Market, Down Breakout
Above-average candle volume, performance	6.71%	10.37%	−5.61%	−10.64%
Below-average candle volume, performance	6.44%	8.75%	−5.56%	−10.21%
Heavy breakout volume, performance	7.60%	10.39%	−5.90%	−12.30%
Light breakout volume, performance	5.48%	8.82%	−5.33%	−8.78%

higher than the median height-to-breakout value listed in the table, then you have a tall candle.

For example, say Jim has a long-legged doji with a high of 47 and a low of 46. Is the candle short or tall? The height is 47 − 46, or 1, so the measure would be 1/47, or 2.1%. For a doji with an upward breakout in a bull market, the candle is short.

Measure rule. Use the measure rule to help predict how far price will rise or fall. Compute the height of the candle and multiply it by the appropriate percentage shown in the table; then apply it to the breakout price.

What are the price targets for Jim's candle? The upward target is 47 + (1 × 68%), or 47.68, and the downward target is 46 − (1 × 64%), or 45.36.

Shadows. To determine whether the shadow is short or tall, compute the height of the shadow and divide by the breakout price. Compare the result to the median in the table. Tall shadows have a percentage higher than the median. Candles with tall shadows perform better than short ones.

Table 27.4 shows volume statistics.

Average candle volume. Candles with above-average volume perform better than do those with below-average volume.

Breakout volume. Above-average breakout-day volume is good for performance, as the numbers show. It beats the performance of candles with light breakout volume.

Trading Tactics

I looked at hundreds of long-legged doji and could not find any significant pattern to where they appear or how they behave. In other words, they are just random price bars on the chart, holding little or no significance as far as

Table 27.5
Reversal Rates

Description	Bull Market	Bear Market
Reversal rate: trend up, breakout down	47%	49%
Continuation rate: trend up, breakout up	53%	51%
Reversal: trend down, breakout up	52%	51%
Continuation: trend down, breakout down	48%	49%
Percentage of reversals (R)/continuations (C) for each 12-month low (L), middle (M), or high (H)	L 48% R/52% C, M 50% R/50% C, H 50% R/50% C	L 45% R/55% C, M 55% R/45% C, H 50% R/50% C
Black body reversal rate	50%	50%
White body reversal rate	47%	49%

I can tell. Sometimes they act as trend reversals, but at other times price fails to reverse when it should have. I would not depend on these candles showing you anything but grief if you use them to predict the trend direction.

I split trading tactics into two basic studies, one concerning reversal rates and the other concerning performance. Of the two, reversal rates are more important, because it's better to trade in the direction of the trend and let price run as far as it can.

Table 27.5 gives tips to find the trend direction.

Reversal, continuation rates. The numbers are quite close to 50%, especially in a bear market. You can use the trend direction leading to the doji to help predict the breakout direction, but with the numbers so close to each other, it might be a useless exercise. However, price breaks out upward more often than downward.

Yearly range reversals. The numbers are close enough to 50% that they offer no tips on how to select a reversal based on where it appears in the yearly trading range.

Body color reversal rate. The white-bodied doji shows a slight tendency to act as a continuation pattern. I allow a few pennies' difference between the open and close in the doji, so that's why some have a body color.

Table 27.6 shows performance indicators that can give hints as to how your stock will behave after the breakout from a candle pattern.

Confirmation, performance. Across the board the opening gap confirmation method results in the best performance with one exception: bear market/down breakouts. Those do slightly better with candle color confirmation. If price forms a black candle after the doji, then consider shorting the stock. For opening gap confirmation, wait for price to gap open to determine the trend direction before making a trade.

Moving average. Candles with breakouts below the 50-trading-day moving average result in better performance than do those above the average.

Table 27.6
Performance Indicators

Description	Bull Market, Up Breakout	Bear Market, Up Breakout	Bull Market, Down Breakout	Bear Market, Down Breakout
Closing price confirmation, performance	6.51%	10.68%	−6.40%	−11.04%
Candle color confirmation, performance	6.48%	10.50%	−6.43%	−11.19%
Opening gap confirmation, performance	7.14%	12.31%	−6.93%	−11.15%
Breakout above 50-day moving average, performance	6.26%	8.50%	−5.16%	−8.77%
Breakout below 50-day moving average, performance	7.18%	11.85%	−5.92%	−11.71%
Last candle: close in highest third, performance	6.14%	10.04%	−4.73%	−7.04%
Last candle: close in middle third, performance	6.65%	9.35%	−5.63%	−10.24%
Last candle: close in lowest third, performance	6.03%	11.46%	−5.49%	−14.78%
Black body, performance	6.60%	10.20%	−5.68%	−9.97%
White body, performance	6.45%	7.70%	−4.99%	−11.44%

Closing position. Candles in a bull market perform better when the close is in the middle third of the candle. In a bear market, candles with closes in the lowest third of the candle work best.

Body color performance. Performance of a black candle is best except for bear market/down breakouts. Those do better if the doji has a white body. This assumes that you allow a few pennies' difference between the opening and closing prices, as I do.

Sample Trade

Figure 27.2 shows a trade Jim is considering. Price moved horizontally during November and then shot up, reaching A and then backtracking to D before resuming the uptrend. When price rounds down at B, he draws a trendline connecting the points A and B and extends it into the future. At D, he draws a line parallel to AB beginning at D (the dashed line). The assumption is that price will rise to touch the top trendline and fall to touch the bottom one before rebounding. He knows that this method is just a guess, but it's better than nothing.

When he sees the long-legged doji at C, he considers shorting the stock if it closes below the doji's low. He doesn't do so, though. Why?

Figure 27.2 Jim decides not to trade the long-legged doji at C.

After price touched point E, he erased the dashed trendline and replaced it with line DE, forming the bottom of an up-sloping channel. This channel is the key to answering the question. Each day that price takes to cross the channel, the bottom trendline will climb, leaving less profit. Since he can't predict how long price will take to cross the channel, he decides not to trade it. "Diminishing returns," he says. "You don't short up-sloping channels, only down-sloping ones."

When price nears the trendline at G, he considers buying the stock but decides against doing that, too. Price has advanced too far back across the channel to be worth the risk of a trade (i.e., the closing price is too high).

At H, he decides to buy the stock and does so after the long-legged doji. He's still in the trade as I write this. I should also tell you that this is a fictitious trade, so it will be a buy-and-hold forever for Jim.

For Best Performance

The following list offers tips and observations to help choose candles that perform well. Consult the associated table for more information.

- Use the identification guidelines to help select the pattern—Table 27.1.
- Candles within a third of the yearly low perform best—Table 27.2.
- Select tall candles—Table 27.3.
- Use the measure rule to predict a price target—Table 27.3.
- Candles with tall upper or lower shadows outperform—Table 27.3.
- Volume gives performance clues—Table 27.4.
- The candle breaks out upward most often—Table 27.5.
- Opening gap confirmation works best except for bear market/down breakouts—Table 27.6.
- Breakouts below the 50-day moving average lead to the best performance—Table 27.6.

28

Doji, Northern

Behavior and Rank

Theoretical: Bearish reversal.
Actual bull market: Bullish continuation 51% of the time (ranking 48).
Actual bear market: Bullish continuation 52% of the time (ranking 49).
Frequency: 6th out of 103.
Overall performance over time: 83rd out of 103.

Having worked through just over half of the doji patterns now, I am struck with one thought: They don't work well. I was hoping that they would show a reversal of major significance, but they don't. They work as one knowledgeable about candles might expect: Indecision in the minds of traders means price can go anywhere after the doji.

The candles act randomly, so why dignify them with a name in the first place? That's a good question, and one I don't have an answer for. But I will tell you this: A lot of people see these candles and put too much faith in them acting as reversals. As their behavior statistics show, the northern doji acts as a continuation slightly more often than as a reversal. Together, they are just a percentage point or two above random behavior, which would be 50%. Overall performance ranks them at 83 out of 103. That's well away from the number one position, where performance is best.

Nothing is magical about the northern doji. It's just a garden-variety doji that appears in an uptrend. Price in the doji opens and moves up or down or not at all and closes where it opened. If the trend leading to the doji is up, then it's a northern doji and perhaps another type of doji as well (like gravestone, dragonfly, long-legged, and so on). From there, anything goes. Traders may push price upward (which statistics say is the more likely direction) or downward. The direction may lie with the general market or industry trends, currents that push price along.

Identification Guidelines

Figure 28.1 shows two examples of northern doji, chosen because of their reversal capability. They are showing off, and I wanted to give them some airtime. This is how a northern doji is supposed to behave.

The first doji in June bumps up against overhead resistance. The upward retracement stops at 63% of the down move from A to B, right where you would expect it to. Price cooperates by reversing and heading back down.

The second doji, the one on June 30, 2006, also stops at overhead resistance but this zone is off the chart to the left. The picture looks like a complex head-and-shoulders top—that is, a head-and-shoulders pattern inside another set of shoulders. The late June doji appears as the second set of shoulders to the right of the head. For reference, A is the head and the two doji candles form the two right shoulders.

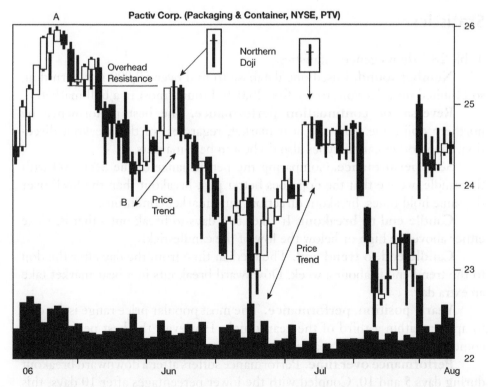

Figure 28.1 Two northern doji appear after an upward price trend.

Table 28.1
Identification Guidelines

Characteristic	Discussion
Number of candle lines	One.
Price trend	Upward leading to the doji.
Configuration	A doji. Price opens and closes at or near the same price.

This highlights one of the things that I find valuable in trading stocks using candles and chart patterns. Sometimes you can guess how price will behave by imagining a chart pattern like a head-and-shoulders completing. Seeing a right shoulder form where you expected the shoulder to appear allows you to make better and more timely trading decisions.

Table 28.1 lists identification guidelines. Look for a doji in an upward price trend. A doji is a single candle line in which the opening and closing prices are the same or nearly so. Beyond that, anything goes—like shadow length, for example (none at all or very long shadows—it doesn't matter). The next section describes how they behave, modeled like clay only using numbers.

Statistics

Table 28.2 shows general statistics.

Number found. I used one database to find over 50,000 northern doji, so I limited my selections to the first 20,000. I found most in a bull market.

Reversal or continuation performance. The best performance by northern doji came from the bear market, regardless of the breakout direction. Many other candle types also do best in bear markets.

S&P performance. Comparing the performance of the S&P 500 with the candle, we see that the doji does better post breakout than the S&P over the same hold times, breakout directions, and market conditions.

Candle end to breakout. It takes two days to break out—that is, close either above the high or below the low of the candlestick.

Candle end to trend end. The median time from the day after the doji to the trend end is about a week. Downward breakouts in a bear market take an extra day.

Yearly position, performance. The most popular price range is for doji to appear within a third of the yearly high. However, the best performance comes from doji near the yearly low.

Performance over time. Performance suffers after a downward breakout during days 5 and 10. Coupled with the lower percentages after 10 days, this results in the lousy performance rankings. Good percentage changes after 10

Table 28.2
General Statistics

Description	Bull Market, Up Breakout	Bear Market, Up Breakout	Bull Market, Down Breakout	Bear Market, Down Breakout
Number found	8,126	2,088	7,844	1,942
Reversal (R), continuation (C) performance	7.97% C	8.15% C	−6.25% R	−8.09% R
Standard & Poor's 500 change	1.45%	0.35%	−0.92%	−2.63%
Candle end to breakout (median, days)	2	2	2	2
Candle end to trend end (median, days)	7	7	7	8
Number of breakouts near the 12-month low (L), middle (M), or high (H)	L 1,366, M 1,996, H 4,764	L 367, M 541, H 1,180	L 1,584, M 2,140, H 4,120	L 383, M 541, H 1,018
Percentage move for each 12-month period	L 10.15%, M 7.93%, H 7.60%	L 12.18%, M 8.87%, H 7.12%	L −7.04%, M −6.36%, H −6.02%	L −10.56%, M −8.20%, H −7.49%
Candle end + 1 day	1.30%	1.44%	−1.13%	−1.28%
Candle end + 3 days	2.30%	2.49%	−1.71%	−2.20%
Candle end + 5 days	2.65%	2.77%	−1.74%	−2.26%
Candle end + 10 days	3.17%	3.16%	−1.20%	−1.90%
10-day performance rank	53	54	88	84

days would be in the 5% to 6% range. A rank of 1 is best out of 103 candles, so the northern doji ranks well down the list.

Table 28.3 shows height statistics.

Candle height. Tall candles perform better than short ones. Candle height is one of the best predictors of performance, and it works for all breakout directions and market conditions. Measure the height of the doji from high to low price and divide by the breakout price. If the result is greater than the median listed in the table, then you have a tall candle.

Phil wants to know if his northern doji is short or tall. It has a high of 133 and a low of 130, so the height is 133 − 130, or 3. For an upward breakout in a bull market, the measure would be 3/133, or 2.3%, which is tall.

Measure rule. Use the measure rule to help predict how far price will rise or fall. Compute the height of the candle and multiply it by the appropriate percentage shown in the table; then apply it to the breakout price.

What are the price targets for Phil's doji? The upward target would be 133 + (3 × 88%), or 135.64. The downward target would be 130 − (3 × 85%), or 127.45.

Table 28.3
Height Statistics

Description	Bull Market, Up Breakout	Bear Market, Up Breakout	Bull Market, Down Breakout	Bear Market, Down Breakout
Median candle height as a percentage of breakout price	1.79%	2.15%	1.85%	2.21%
Short candle, performance	6.36%	7.13%	−5.33%	−7.07%
Tall candle, performance	10.15%	9.42%	−7.54%	−9.42%
Percentage meeting price target (measure rule)	88%	85%	85%	86%
Median upper shadow as a percentage of breakout price	0.72%	0.85%	0.91%	1.07%
Short upper shadow, performance	6.89%	7.33%	−5.64%	−7.12%
Tall upper shadow, performance	9.19%	9.09%	−6.98%	−9.23%
Median lower shadow as a percentage of breakout price	0.79%	0.97%	0.66%	0.83%
Short lower shadow, performance	6.89%	7.76%	−5.60%	−7.38%
Tall lower shadow, performance	9.24%	8.60%	−7.02%	−8.90%

Shadows. To determine whether the shadow is short or tall, compute the height of the shadow and divide by the breakout price. Compare the result to the median in the table. Tall shadows have a percentage higher than the median. Candles with tall shadows perform better than do those with short shadows.

Table 28.4 shows volume statistics.

Table 28.4
Volume Statistics

Description	Bull Market, Up Breakout	Bear Market, Up Breakout	Bull Market, Down Breakout	Bear Market, Down Breakout
Above-average candle volume, performance	7.92%	8.24%	−6.44%	−8.23%
Below-average candle volume, performance	7.99%	8.11%	−6.17%	−8.02%
Heavy breakout volume, performance	8.66%	9.01%	−6.63%	−8.05%
Light breakout volume, performance	7.36%	7.37%	−6.05%	−8.11%

Average candle volume. Candles with above-average volume work better most often than do those with below-average volume. The exception occurs in bull market/up breakouts.

Breakout volume. Heavy breakout-day volume suggests better performance in all cases except for bear market/down breakouts.

Trading Tactics

I split trading tactics into two basic studies, one concerning reversal rates and the other concerning performance. Of the two, reversal rates are more important, because it's better to trade in the direction of the trend and let price run as far as it can.

Table 28.5 gives tips to find the trend direction.

Confirmation reversal rates. To help detect a reversal of the uptrend, wait for price to close lower the next day. That works between 79% (bear markets) and 82% (bull markets) of the time.

Reversal, continuation rates. The numbers confirm that the northern doji is more comfortable as a continuation pattern. Price breaks out upward more often but only by a paper-thin margin.

Yearly range reversals. Sorting where the reversals occur in the yearly price range shows no outstanding numbers. Reversals occur most often within a third of the yearly low in a bull market. Continuations occur most frequently within a third of the yearly high.

Body color reversal rate. Since I allow a few pennies between the opening and closing prices, the doji can have a body color. The numbers in the table show how often price reverses according to candle color. In short, you can't tell if a doji will reverse based on candle color.

Table 28.5
Reversal Rates

Description	Bull Market	Bear Market
Closing price confirmation reversal rate	82%	79%
Candle color confirmation reversal rate	77%	77%
Opening gap confirmation reversal rate	60%	58%
Reversal rate: trend up, breakout down	49%	48%
Continuation rate: trend up, breakout up	51%	52%
Percentage of reversals (R)/continuations (C) for each 12-month low (L), middle (M), or high (H)	L 54% R/46% C, M 52% R/48% C, H 46% R/54% C	L 51% R/49% C, M 50% R/50% C, H 46% R/54% C
Black body reversal rate	50%	48%
White body reversal rate	47%	49%

Table 28.6
Performance Indicators

Description	Bull Market, Up Breakout	Bear Market, Up Breakout	Bull Market, Down Breakout	Bear Market, Down Breakout
Closing price confirmation, performance	N/A	N/A	−6.34%	−7.78%
Candle color confirmation, performance	N/A	N/A	−6.46%	−7.83%
Opening gap confirmation, performance	N/A	N/A	−7.37%	−8.73%
Breakout above 50-day moving average, performance	7.84%	7.73%	−6.09%	−7.60%
Breakout below 50-day moving average, performance	8.74%	10.43%	−6.76%	−9.65%
Last candle: close in highest third, performance	7.49%	7.71%	−6.40%	−8.04%
Last candle: close in middle third, performance	8.32%	8.11%	−6.28%	−8.02%
Last candle: close in lowest third, performance	7.95%	8.86%	−6.15%	−8.21%
Black body, performance	8.27%	8.24%	−6.31%	−7.97%
White body, performance	7.50%	8.00%	−6.14%	−8.28%

N/A means not applicable.

Table 28.6 shows performance indicators that can give hints as to how your stock will behave after the breakout from a candle pattern.

Confirmation, performance. Only downward breakouts appear in the table, because those represent a reversal of the uptrend. The opening gap confirmation method works best. That means trading only if price gaps open lower the day after the doji.

Moving average. Candles with breakouts below the 50-trading-day moving average show better performance than do those with breakouts above the moving average.

Closing position. Where price closes in the doji shows no consistent trend between the four columns.

Body color performance. Black candles perform better than white ones in all cases except for bear market/down breakouts.

Sample Trade

Phil looks for profit opportunities wherever the market allows him to part someone from a few bucks. Figure 28.2 shows an example. Price peaks three

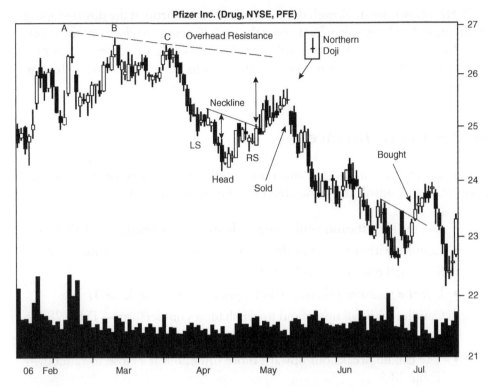

Figure 28.2 A northern doji appears after a head-and-shoulders bottom.

times at A, B, and C, forming a triple top, three falling peaks, or if you connect the two major valleys, a symmetrical triangle chart pattern.

After C, price drops and forms a head-and-shoulders bottom reversal pattern. The height of this chart pattern from the head to the neckline directly above projected upward from the breakout price (where the stock pierces the neckline) results in the measure rule target (shown by the vertical arrows). Price makes it about halfway to the target before a northern doji appears.

Normally, Phil would ignore the doji because their performance is dismal, but his wife wants a new Mercedes and he is short on bucks. Overhead resistance set up by the ABC line (and the price of the apex of the symmetrical triangle) would provide a ceiling and that would also come close to the head-and-shoulders price target. That would be the preferred entry point for a short sale. However, price does not cooperate—it gaps lower the next day. Since price confirms the bearish northern doji as a reversal, Phil shorts the stock midway up the black candle.

He expects the stock to drop down to the head level, and if it closes below that it would qualify as a busted head-and-shoulders bottom. Those chart patterns he has traded before with much success. A powerful decline often follows a busted pattern, so going short doesn't bother him in this trading setup.

He follows the stock each day until price breaks through the down-sloping trendline in late June, when he decides the time has come to close out the short.

Coupled with profits from other trades, he is able to purchase that new Mercedes for his wife. Upon receiving it, she rolls her eyes and says, "It's the wrong color."

For Best Performance

The following list offers tips and observations to help choose candles that perform well. Consult the associated table for more information.

- Use the identification guidelines to help select the pattern—Table 28.1.
- Candles within a third of the yearly low perform best—Table 28.2.
- Select tall candles—Table 28.3.
- Use the measure rule to predict a price target—Table 28.3.
- Candles with tall upper and lower shadows outperform—Table 28.3.
- Volume gives performance clues—Table 28.4.
- The candle breaks out upward more often, but it's close to random—Table 28.5.
- Opening gap confirmation works best—Table 28.6.
- Breakouts below the 50-day moving average lead to the best performance—Table 28.6.

29

Doji, Southern

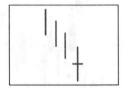

Behavior and Rank

Theoretical: Bullish reversal.
Actual bull market: Bullish reversal 52% of the time (ranking 48).
Actual bear market: Bullish reversal 51% of the time (ranking 40).
Frequency: 8th out of 103.
Overall performance over time: 78th out of 103.

A southern doji is an unremarkable candlestick except that it acts as a reversal *slightly* more often than as a continuation. I emphasize the word *slightly* because the numbers (51% and 52% reversal rates) are close enough to 50% that I consider the behavior random. Nevertheless, the candle tells a tale if you listen.

The candle represents the struggle of bulls and bears in a downward price trend. The bears are trying to force price lower and the bulls want to prop it up. Who wins? Neither one until the next day or perhaps later. Only then can we know which side has taken control. Thus, do not depend on this candle being a reversal until the next day confirms it. And even then the new direction might be fake.

Identification Guidelines

Figure 29.1 shows two southern doji candles. Let's discuss the one at A first. Price trends downward into the candle line and exits downward, too. That

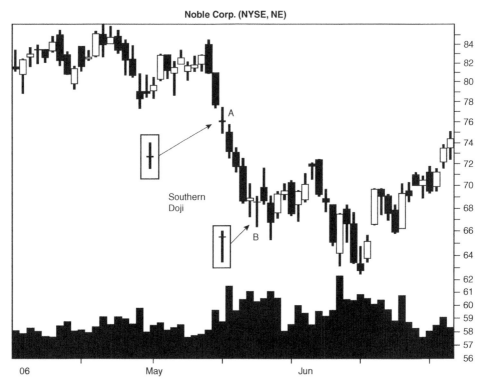

Figure 29.1 Two southern doji candles appear in a declining price trend. Doji A acts as a continuation pattern and B as a reversal.

means it acts as a continuation of the downtrend. Within the candle line, the opening and closing prices are near each other, leaving a cross to print on the chart.

The southern doji at B is different, isn't it? Price trends downward into the candle line, but this time price exits upward out of the pattern. In fact, price closes above the top of the candle, too, at the first white candle that comes along. Candle B acts as a reversal of the downtrend. It also has the opening and closing prices at or near each other, forming a cross.

How do you identify a southern doji? Table 29.1 lists identification guidelines. A doji is a candlestick with the opening and closing prices at or

Table 29.1
Identification Guidelines

Characteristic	Discussion
Number of candle lines	One.
Price trend	Downward leading to the doji.
Configuration	A doji. The open and close are near in price to each other.

very near each other. I allow a few pennies between the opening and closing prices so as not to exclude too many patterns, especially when a doji is involved in a multiline candle. Shadow length doesn't matter. In a southern doji, price trends downward into the candlestick. That's all it takes to identify a southern doji.

Statistics

Table 29.2 shows general statistics.

Number found. I limited the number of southern doji to 20,000 to keep the spreadsheet manageable. Most of them appeared in a bull market.

Reversal or continuation performance. The best-performing doji come from a bear market, regardless of the breakout direction. That behavior agrees with many other candle types, but I cannot explain why.

S&P performance. Performance of the candle beats the S&P 500 over the same time periods.

Table 29.2
General Statistics

Description	Bull Market, Up Breakout	Bear Market, Up Breakout	Bull Market, Down Breakout	Bear Market, Down Breakout
Number found	8,185	2,127	7,679	2,009
Reversal (R), continuation (C) performance	8.22% R	9.33% R	−6.24% C	−8.34% C
Standard & Poor's 500 change	1.72%	0.78%	−0.92%	−2.41%
Candle end to breakout (median, days)	2	2	2	2
Candle end to trend end (median, days)	8	9	6	6
Number of breakouts near the 12-month low (L), middle (M), or high (H)	L 2,480, M 2,505, H 3,200	L 657, M 667, H 803	L 2,817, M 2,444, H 2,418	L 769, M 656, H 584
Percentage move for each 12-month period	L 9.71%, M 7.79%, H 7.76%	L 12.43%, M 9.48%, H 7.70%	L −6.67%, M −6.40%, H −5.75%	L −10.92%, M −7.98%, H −6.71%
Candle end + 1 day	1.28%	1.56%	−1.18%	−1.49%
Candle end + 3 days	2.33%	2.52%	−1.80%	−2.37%
Candle end + 5 days	2.73%	2.92%	−1.78%	−2.58%
Candle end + 10 days	3.15%	3.51%	−1.37%	−1.76%
10-day performance rank	54	50	83	88

Candle end to breakout. It takes price two days to either close above the high or close below the low of the candlestick.

Candle end to trend end. The median ranges from six to nine days. Downward breakouts take less time to reach the trend end than do upward breakouts, because the downward trend is already in progress.

Yearly position, performance. Upward breakouts form most often near the yearly high, and downward breakouts are more numerous near the yearly low. Performance is best when the breakout is within a third of the yearly low.

Performance over time. Performance over time falters from 3 to 10 days in bull market/down breakouts and from 5 to 10 days in bear market/down breakouts. That's why the performance rank (83, 88, respectively) is so poor (1 is best out of 103).

Table 29.3 shows height statistics.

Candle height. Tall candles work better than short ones. To use this finding, subtract the low from the high price in the doji and divide by the breakout price (either the high for upward breakouts or the low for downward ones). If the result is greater than the median shown in the table, then you have a tall doji.

Sharon has her eye on a stock when it forms a southern doji that has a low of 25 and a high of 26. Is the candle short or tall (assume a bull market with an

Table 29.3
Height Statistics

Description	Bull Market, Up Breakout	Bear Market, Up Breakout	Bull Market, Down Breakout	Bear Market, Down Breakout
Median candle height as a percentage of breakout price	1.89%	2.34%	1.89%	2.42%
Short candle, performance	6.73%	7.73%	−5.37%	−7.16%
Tall candle, performance	10.28%	11.44%	−7.47%	−9.91%
Percentage meeting price target (measure rule)	90%	87%	84%	84%
Median upper shadow as a percentage of breakout price	0.71%	0.87%	0.85%	1.10%
Short upper shadow, performance	7.46%	8.28%	−5.65%	−7.45%
Tall upper shadow, performance	9.11%	10.59%	−6.93%	−9.41%
Median lower shadow as a percentage of breakout price	0.88%	1.17%	0.72%	0.99%
Short lower shadow, performance	7.06%	8.06%	−5.60%	−7.54%
Tall lower shadow, performance	9.59%	10.77%	−6.99%	−9.32%

Table 29.4
Volume Statistics

Description	Bull Market, Up Breakout	Bear Market, Up Breakout	Bull Market, Down Breakout	Bear Market, Down Breakout
Above-average candle volume, performance	8.35%	9.98%	−5.95%	−8.94%
Below-average candle volume, performance	8.17%	9.01%	−6.36%	−8.04%
Heavy breakout volume, performance	8.88%	10.05%	−6.69%	−9.40%
Light breakout volume, performance	7.74%	8.80%	−5.94%	−7.50%

upward breakout)? The height is $26 - 25$, or 1, so the measure would be 1/26, or 3.8%; the candle is tall.

Measure rule. Use the measure rule to help predict how far price will rise or fall. Compute the height of the candle and multiply it by the appropriate percentage shown in the table; then apply it to the breakout price.

What are the two price targets for Sharon's candle according to the measure rule? The upward target is $26 + (1 \times 90\%)$, or 26.90, and the downward target is $25 - (1 \times 84\%)$, or 24.16.

Shadows. To determine whether the shadow is short or tall, compute the height of the shadow and divide by the breakout price. Compare the result to the median in the table. Tall shadows have a percentage higher than the median. Candles with tall shadows perform better than do candles with short shadows.

Table 29.4 shows volume statistics.

Average candle volume. Candles with above-average volume perform better than do those with below-average volume in all categories except bull market/down breakouts.

Breakout volume. Heavy breakout volume also works best for the various market conditions and breakout directions.

Trading Tactics

Since the breakout from a southern doji is upward when it works as a reversal, avoid trading (buying) them when the primary trend is downward. They perform best as reversals in a short-term downward retracement of an upward price trend.

I split trading tactics into two basic studies, one concerning reversal rates and the other concerning performance. Of the two, reversal rates are more

Table 29.5
Reversal Rates

Description	Bull Market	Bear Market
Closing price confirmation reversal rate	83%	83%
Candle color confirmation reversal rate	81%	80%
Opening gap confirmation reversal rate	61%	61%
Reversal: trend down, breakout up	52%	51%
Continuation: trend down, breakout down	48%	49%
Percentage of reversals (R)/continuations (C) for each 12-month low (L), middle (M), or high (H)	L 47% R/53% C, M 51% R/49% C, H 57% R/43% C	L 46% R/54% C, M 50% R/50% C, H 58% R/42% C
Black body reversal rate	50%	51%
White body reversal rate	54%	53%

important, because it's better to trade in the direction of the trend and let price run as far as it can.

Table 29.5 gives tips to find the trend direction.

Confirmation reversal rates. To detect a reversal of the downtrend, wait for price to close higher the day after a southern doji. That works 83% of the time.

Reversal, continuation rates. The table shows how often the doji acts as a reversal of the downtrend. It's nearly random regardless of the bull/bear market condition.

Yearly range reversals. Sorting reversals and continuations into the yearly price range, we find that reversals occur most often within a third of the yearly high.

Body color reversal rate. Since I allow a few pennies between the opening and closing prices, the body can have a color—but it doesn't do much to improve the detection of a reversal, as the results show. They all hover around random (50%).

Table 29.6 shows performance indicators that can give hints as to how your stock will behave after the breakout from a candle pattern.

Confirmation, performance. I used the confirmation methods on reversals only. The best-performing method is opening gap confirmation. That means waiting for price to gap open higher after the doji before trading.

Moving average. Candles with breakouts below the 50-trading-day moving average result in performance better than those with breakouts above the moving average.

Closing position. Southern doji with closing prices within the top third of the candle result in better performance than the other ranges except in bear market/down breakouts. Those do best when the close is in the middle of the candle.

Table 29.6
Performance Indicators

Description	Bull Market, Up Breakout	Bear Market, Up Breakout	Bull Market, Down Breakout	Bear Market, Down Breakout
Closing price confirmation, performance	7.27%	8.68%	N/A	N/A
Candle color confirmation, performance	7.24%	8.51%	N/A	N/A
Opening gap confirmation, performance	8.03%	9.86%	N/A	N/A
Breakout above 50-day moving average, performance	7.95%	8.40%	−5.84%	−6.56%
Breakout below 50-day moving average, performance	8.48%	10.28%	−6.43%	−9.11%
Last candle: close in highest third, performance	8.50%	9.52%	−6.33%	−8.11%
Last candle: close in middle third, performance	8.25%	9.18%	−6.23%	−8.69%
Last candle: close in lowest third, performance	7.75%	9.27%	−6.18%	−8.05%
Black body, performance	8.20%	9.58%	−6.36%	−8.20%
White body, performance	8.27%	8.86%	−5.97%	−8.62%

N/A means not applicable.

Body color performance. White candles do best when the breakout is in line with the market trend—bull market/up breakouts and bear market/down breakouts. Black candles work best for the other two categories—bear market/up breakouts and bull market/down breakouts.

Sample Trade

Figure 29.2 shows a southern doji in a stock that interests Sharon. She saw the tall white candle in November and thought it was a data error, but two independent sources showed the same thing. When a southern doji appears in December, she believes that an Adam and Eve double bottom has formed.

When price gaps above the doji the next day (point A), she pounces and buys the stock. At the end of the day, price remains well above the top of the doji, so she places a stop-loss order at a penny below the bottom of the doji.

The next day, at point B, she is stopped out of the trade. What did she do wrong? Her instincts were correct in that price did make a double bottom. Unfortunately, her desire to keep losses small meant she placed the stop too close.

Figure 29.2   Sharon bets that the southern doji will result in a profitable trade.

Here's a tip on how to place a stop. Use a volatility stop. For the prior 22 trading days (about one month), measure the difference between the high and low price each day and average them. Multiply the average by 2, and then subtract the result from the current low price. Place a stop no closer than the resulting value.

For example, at the southern doji, the high-low volatility was 55 cents for the prior month. Two times that is 1.10. The current low of the doji is 27.16, so subtracting 1.10 from the low gives a stop of 26.06, or 5% below the current low. Place a stop no closer than 26.06; otherwise you risk being stopped out by normal price movement.

For Best Performance

The following list offers tips and observations to help choose candles that perform well. Consult the associated table for more information.

- Use the identification guidelines to help select the pattern—Table 29.1.
- Candles within a third of the yearly low perform best—Table 29.2.

- Select tall candles—Table 29.3.
- Use the measure rule to predict a price target—Table 29.3.
- Candles with tall upper and lower shadows outperform—Table 29.3.
- Volume gives performance clues—Table 29.4.
- Select southern doji as reversals in a short-term downward retracement of the upward price trend—Trading Tactics discussion.
- The candle breaks out upward most often—Table 29.5.
- Patterns within a third of the yearly high tend to act as reversals most often—Table 29.5.
- Opening gap confirmation works best—Table 29.6.
- Breakouts below the 50-day moving average lead to the best performance—Table 29.6.

30

Doji Star, Bearish

Behavior and Rank

Theoretical: Bearish reversal.

Actual bull market: Bullish continuation 69% of the time (ranking 8).

Actual bear market: Bullish continuation 67% of the time (ranking 11).

Frequency: 43rd out of 103.

Overall performance over time: 51st out of 103.

The bearish doji star reminds me of powering a bicycle uphill. My speed is higher at the bottom than when I crest the hill. With this candlestick pattern, price narrows from the first day to the second, showing a loss of momentum. This narrowing is a warning of a coming reversal—in theory.

In technical terms, the market trends upward, leading to a bullish white candle—a candle that closes well above the open, making it a tall, robust one. The next day, price gaps higher in a continuation of the bullish trend, but soon runs into selling pressure. Price trades in a narrow range all day as bulls and bears fight it out. When the battle is over, a doji prints on the chart.

Unfortunately, it rarely works that way. Most often, price just continues upward, closing above the candle high in a few days, never having reversed at all.

The 69% (bull market) and 67% (bear market) rates confirm the behavior not as a bearish reversal but as a bullish continuation pattern. Overall performance ranks 51 out of 103 with 1 being best, so this one is way down the list.

Identification Guidelines

Figure 30.1 shows a good example of a doji star pattern and how it is supposed to work. After an uptrend, a doji follows a long white candle and then price drops. This doji star forms the head of a head-and-shoulders top. When price pierces the support line (neckline), price tumbles for several days before pulling back to the base of the head-and-shoulders formation and then resumes the slide.

Table 30.1 shows the identification guidelines for the doji star pattern. The characteristics are self-explanatory except for the following: The doji's body should remain above the close posted by the prior day. This forms a price gap between the bodies, even though the shadows may overlap. I do not allow ties between the price of the doji's body and that of the prior day's body.

In my tests, I began with a doji shadow height less than the average shadow height for each stock, but dismal were the number of doji star patterns qualifying (375). So I changed the algorithm to compare the total shadow height (sum of both upper and lower shadows) with the prior day's body height. If the combined shadow height was taller than the prior day's body, I excluded

Figure 30.1 This doji star forms the head of a head-and-shoulders top chart pattern.

Table 30.1
Identification Guidelines

Characteristic	Discussion
Number of candle lines	Two.
Price trend	Upward leading to the pattern.
First day	A long white candle.
Body gap	Price gaps higher, forming a body that is above the first day's body.
Second day	A doji. The open and close are at or near the same price.
Doji shadows	Avoid excessively long shadows on the doji. The sum of the doji shadows is less than the body height of the prior day.

the candle. Simply put, when searching for a doji star, make sure the shadows on the doji look reasonable in length—not too long, whatever that may mean to you.

Statistics

Table 30.2 shows general statistics.

Number found. I found 11,810 doji stars on a cloudless night, separated into bull and bear markets, up and down breakouts. Most came from a bull market.

Reversal or continuation performance. Sorting performance by reversals and continuations, we see that the best performance comes from patterns in a bear market, regardless of the breakout direction (i.e., regardless of whether the doji acted as a reversal or continuation).

S&P performance. The doji candle performed better than the S&P 500 over the same period.

Candle end to breakout. Downward breakouts took two to three days longer to occur than upward breakouts. That is because price is closer to the top of the pattern than the bottom.

Candle end to trend end. The median time from candle end to trend end is 6 to 10 days. Downward breakouts take longer because price has to start a new trend whereas upward breakouts are closer to the end of an existing trend.

Yearly position, performance. The majority of bearish doji stars appeared within a third of the yearly high. However, the best performance came from those near the yearly low.

Performance over time. The bearish doji star is a robust pattern, meaning that performance improves over time and in each category. Unfortunately, the upward breakout percentage changes are too low to help the performance rank. Downward breakouts rank quite well.

Table 30.2
General Statistics

Description	Bull Market, Up Breakout	Bear Market, Up Breakout	Bull Market, Down Breakout	Bear Market, Down Breakout
Number found	7,410	737	3,305	358
Reversal (R), continuation (C) performance	6.01% C	7.17% C	−5.59% R	−9.02% R
Standard & Poor's 500 change	1.05%	0.04%	−0.91%	−2.95%
Candle end to breakout (median, days)	3	3	6	5
Candle end to trend end (median, days)	6	7	10	10
Number of breakouts near the 12-month low (L), middle (M), or high (H)	L 888, M 1,499, H 4,106	L 145, M 213, H 373	L 607, M 759, H 1,543	L 97, M 111, H 145
Percentage move for each 12-month period	L 7.51%, M 5.68%, H 5.83%	L 10.46%, M 6.56%, H 6.05%	L −6.81%, M −5.29%, H −5.23%	L −11.01%, M −9.10%, H −8.32%
Candle end + 1 day	0.54%	0.69%	−1.35%	−1.95%
Candle end + 3 days	1.28%	1.52%	−2.86%	−3.99%
Candle end + 5 days	1.62%	1.94%	−3.65%	−4.92%
Candle end + 10 days	2.09%	2.50%	−4.09%	−5.77%
10-day performance rank	80	63	14	24

Table 30.3 shows height statistics.

Candle height. Candles taller than the median outperform in all situations. To determine whether the candle is short or tall, compute its height from highest high to lowest low price in the candle pattern and divide by the breakout price. If the result is higher than the median, then you have a tall candle; otherwise it's short.

Doug has a bearish doji star with a high at 87 and a low at 85. Is the candle short or tall? The height is 87 − 85, or 2, so the measure is 2/87, or 2.3%. In a bull market with an upward breakout the candle is short.

Measure rule. Use the measure rule to help predict how far price will rise or fall. Compute the height of the candle pattern and multiply it by the appropriate percentage shown in the table; then apply it to the breakout price.

What price targets does Doug's candle predict? The upward target is 87 + (2 × 53%), or 88.06, and the downward target is 85 − (2 × 49%), or 84.02.

Table 30.3
Height Statistics

Description	Bull Market, Up Breakout	Bear Market, Up Breakout	Bull Market, Down Breakout	Bear Market, Down Breakout
Median candle height as a percentage of breakout price	4.21%	4.97%	4.42%	5.62%
Short candle, performance	4.82%	5.87%	−4.66%	−8.13%
Tall candle, performance	8.03%	9.05%	−7.08%	−10.33%
Percentage meeting price target (measure rule)	53%	55%	49%	54%
Median upper shadow as a percentage of breakout price	0.52%	0.61%	0.62%	0.81%
Short upper shadow, performance	5.21%	6.33%	−4.97%	−7.95%
Tall upper shadow, performance	6.89%	7.97%	−6.28%	−10.05%
Median lower shadow as a percentage of breakout price	0.64%	0.88%	0.65%	0.97%
Short lower shadow, performance	5.15%	6.46%	−4.91%	−7.62%
Tall lower shadow, performance	6.92%	7.99%	−6.27%	−10.67%

Shadows. The table's results pertain to the last candle line in the pattern (the doji). To determine whether the shadow is short or tall, compute the height of the shadow and divide by the breakout price. Compare the result to the median in the table. Tall shadows have a percentage higher than the median.

Shadow performance. Candles with tall upper or lower shadows perform better than do those with short ones.

Table 30.4 shows volume statistics.

Candle volume trend. Candles with a falling volume trend perform better than do those with a rising trend in all categories.

Average candle volume. I compared the average candle volume for the two-day pattern with the one-month average and separated the performance results into above-average and below-average volume rows, which the table shows. Candles with below-average volume show better performance, with the exception of those in a bull market with an upward breakout. Those perform better if the candle pattern shows heavy volume.

Breakout volume. Candles with heavy breakout volume result in the best performance across the board.

Table 30.4
Volume Statistics

Description	Bull Market, Up Breakout	Bear Market, Up Breakout	Bull Market, Down Breakout	Bear Market, Down Breakout
Rising candle volume, performance	5.76%	6.39%	−5.38%	−7.70%
Falling candle volume, performance	6.14%	7.69%	−5.71%	−9.82%
Above-average candle volume, performance	6.45%	6.89%	−5.54%	−8.60%
Below-average candle volume, performance	5.54%	7.49%	−5.65%	−9.57%
Heavy breakout volume, performance	6.78%	7.54%	−6.23%	−10.17%
Light breakout volume, performance	5.20%	6.78%	−5.07%	−7.77%

Trading Tactics

Figure 30.2 shows a reliable trading setup. In a downtrend that is usually at least a month long, a doji star sometimes appears just below a trendline like the one shown. Price bumps against overhead resistance, and usually within a week or so the decline resumes. The breakout may be upward, but it doesn't last long and the primary downtrend continues.

In cases where price pushes above the down-sloping trendline—that is, the upward breakout is a lasting one—it signals an extended advance, one worth hopping aboard.

I split trading tactics into two basic studies, one concerning reversal rates and the other concerning performance. Of the two, reversal rates are more important, because it's better to trade in the direction of the trend and let price run as far as it can.

Table 30.5 gives tips to find the trend direction.

Confirmation reversal rates. To help detect a reversal of the uptrend, wait for price to close lower after the bearish doji star. Unfortunately, that method works only randomly—50% in a bull market and 53% in a bear market.

Reversal, continuation rates. Over two-thirds of the time the bearish doji star acts as a continuation pattern, not a reversal. Expect an upward breakout.

Yearly range reversals. Continuation patterns populate the highest third of the yearly price range. Do not expect a reversal to occur.

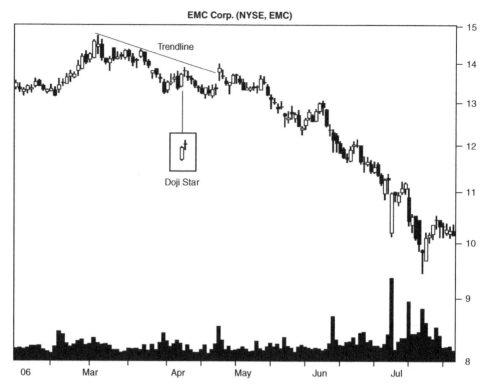

EMC Corp. (NYSE, EMC)

Figure 30.2 Resistance above this doji star, coupled with a downward breakout, suggests a resumption of the decline.

Table 30.6 shows performance indicators that can give hints as to how your stock will behave after the breakout from this candle pattern.

Confirmation, performance. Since we are looking for reversals, only the downward breakout direction applies to all confirmation methods. If you wait for price to gap open lower the day after the doji star, the average decline

Table 30.5
Reversal Rates

Description	Bull Market	Bear Market
Closing price confirmation reversal rate	50%	53%
Candle color confirmation reversal rate	49%	50%
Opening gap confirmation reversal rate	39%	38%
Reversal rate: trend up, breakout down	31%	33%
Continuation rate: trend up, breakout up	69%	67%
Percentage of reversals (R)/ continuations (C) for each 12-month low (L), middle (M), or high (H)	L 41% R/59% C, M 34% R/66% C, H 27% R/73% C	L 40% R/60% C, M 34% R/66% C, H 28% R/72% C

Table 30.6
Performance Indicators

Description	Bull Market, Up Breakout	Bear Market, Up Breakout	Bull Market, Down Breakout	Bear Market, Down Breakout
Closing price confirmation, performance	N/A	N/A	−7.45%	−9.77%
Candle color confirmation, performance	N/A	N/A	−7.57%	−9.85%
Opening gap confirmation, performance	N/A	N/A	−7.46%	−10.73%
Breakout above 50-day moving average, performance	5.97%	6.85%	−5.19%	−8.29%
Breakout below 50-day moving average, performance	6.76%	9.67%	−6.42%	−10.58%
Last candle: close in highest third, performance	5.87%	7.56%	−5.69%	−8.15%
Last candle: close in middle third, performance	6.03%	6.56%	−5.56%	−10.15%
Last candle: close in lowest third, performance	6.21%	7.60%	−5.52%	−8.09%

N/A means not applicable.

to the trend low is 10.73%, the best of the bunch for a bear market. In a bull market, candle color works best as the confirmation method. That means trading only if a black candle appears the day after the doji star ends. Also notice that the numbers are close to each other, so it probably doesn't matter which method you use.

Moving average. Breakouts from bearish doji stars below the 50-day moving average lead to the best performance.

Closing position. Where price closes in the doji candle line (the last line in the candle) matters little for performance.

Sample Trade

Doug likes to search for support and resistance zones and then trade off those areas. For example, Figure 30.3 shows a trading setup that he finds appealing. A bearish doji star appears after a month's worth of price steadily climbing. (The move up the price mountain began in early May at a leisurely pace but quickened as June approached. Then the doji star appeared.)

The three peaks labeled A, B, and C are at nearly the same level, posing a barrier to any upward move—a ceiling, if you will, which Doug loves. He

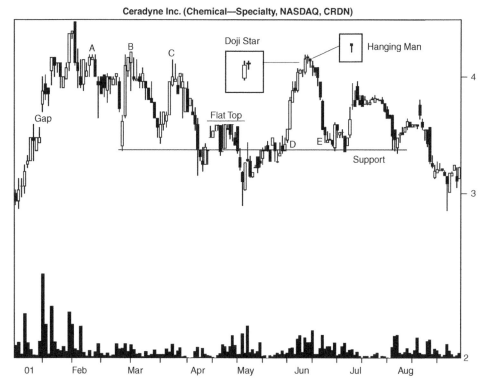

Figure 30.3   This doji star correctly predicts a reversal.

shorts the stock using the opening gap method on the day a hanging man appears.

How far will price fall? Use the measure rule for the doji star to get an idea. Subtract the candle low (the lower of the two price bars, 4.02) from the high (the higher of the two price bars, 4.22) for a height of 20 cents, and then subtract the height from the candle low. That gives a target of 3.82 (about 9% below the current close).

The measure rule works only 54% of the time (bear market/down breakout), so for a more likely target multiply the candle height by 54% and project the new height downward. That would give a closer target of 3.91.

Measure rules are fine, but I prefer to look for support zones. The flat top in April looks like a tasty landing zone. The flat top has a price of about 3.55, or 15% below the current close.

So what happens? As the chart shows, price can't pierce overhead resistance (peaks A, B, C), so it tumbles. Then price digs through the flat top as if it isn't there, finding support at a lower level. The decline mirrors the rise, making the path look like a bell-shaped curve (D to E). Such price mirrors happen from time to time and are worth factoring into your trading. Doug closes out his trade on the first tall white candle a few days after point E.

For Best Performance

The following list offers tips and observations to help choose candles that perform well. Consult the associated table for more information.

- Use the identification guidelines to help select the pattern—Table 30.1.
- Candles within a third of the yearly low perform best—Table 30.2.
- Select tall candles—Table 30.3.
- Use the measure rule to predict a price target—Table 30.3.
- Candles with tall upper or lower shadows outperform—Table 30.3.
- Volume gives performance clues—Table 30.4.
- Look for a bearish doji star to appear as an upward retracement in a downward price trend—Trading Tactics discussion.
- The candle breaks out upward most often—Table 30.5.
- Patterns within a third of the yearly high tend to act as continuations most often—Table 30.5.
- Breakouts below the 50-day moving average lead to the best performance—Table 30.6.

31

Doji Star, Bullish

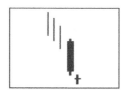

Behavior and Rank

Theoretical: Bullish reversal.
Actual bull market: Bearish continuation 64% of the time (ranking 16).
Actual bear market: Bearish continuation 71% of the time (ranking 8).
Frequency: 53rd out of 103.
Overall performance over time: 49th out of 103.

The bullish doji star is a two-candle line pattern that occurs after a downtrend. The first line is a tall black candle, suggesting a strong downward thrust. The bears are confident that the stock is going down...until the next line appears. It's a doji, and it signals indecision. The bulls and bears struggle for direction all day, but at the close, price is little changed from the open. This causes concern for the bears. They assumed the strong price downdraft would continue, but the appearance of the doji changed that. If price reverses the downtrend, as the doji star predicts, then the bulls will win out and the shorts will run for cover, helping push price upward.

That's the theory, but as its actual behavior shows, the bullish doji star isn't bullish after all. Price continues down 64% of the time in a bull market and even more in a bear market: 71%. The overall rank comes in at 49, so this pattern is a midlist performer when compared to other candle types.

Identification Guidelines

Figure 31.1 shows what a bullish doji star looks like on the daily price chart. In this example, price tumbles about four points from the June peak and forms a doji star upon meeting underlying support at B, midway along the tall white candle, and at C, from the cluster of price tops earlier in the year. The twin support zones were strong enough to reverse prices and end the swift decline. From there, price made a V-shaped recovery and attempted to make a new yearly high in October, but failed.

Notice at A how price reverses (at the black candle pointed to in the chart) when it finds support midway down the tall white candle. The reversal doesn't last long, but tall candles, either black or white, sometimes act as weak support or resistance areas.

Table 31.1 shows identification guidelines for this pattern. Most are self-explanatory. Shadows on the doji should not be excessively long. What does that mean? I added the height of the upper and lower shadows on the doji and discarded any doji star if its height exceeded the length of the black body the day before the doji. This method allowed locating many doji stars while still maintaining the spirit of the "no long shadows" guideline. Cool, huh?

Figure 31.1   Price reverses at the bullish doji star after hitting underlying support.

Table 31.1
Identification Guidelines

Characteristic	Discussion
Number of candle lines	Two.
Price trend	Downward leading to the candle.
First day	A tall black candle.
Body gap	The closing price of the first day is above the body of the doji.
Second day	A doji. The opening and closing prices of the doji remain below the prior day's close, even though the shadows may overlap.
Doji shadows	Discard patterns with unusually long doji shadows.

Statistics

Table 31.2 shows general statistics.

Table 31.2
General Statistics

Description	Bull Market, Up Breakout	Bear Market, Up Breakout	Bull Market, Down Breakout	Bear Market, Down Breakout
Number found	3,034	302	5,341	717
Reversal (R), continuation (C) performance	6.76% R	8.61% R	−5.57% C	−9.20% C
Standard & Poor's 500 change	1.91%	1.37%	−0.46%	−2.05%
Candle end to breakout (median, days)	6	5	3	3
Candle end to trend end (median, days)	10	11	6	6
Number of breakouts near the 12-month low (L), middle (M), or high (H)	L 687, M 779, H 1,141	L 98, M 100, H 99	L 1,814, M 1,553, H 1,253	L 363, M 204, H 140
Percentage move for each 12-month period	L 7.74%, M 6.35%, H 6.58%	L 13.37%, M 7.24%, H 6.44%	L −5.95%, M −5.36%, H −5.08%	L −10.75%, M −9.08%, H −6.63%
Candle end + 1 day	1.41%	2.21%	−0.58%	−0.94%
Candle end + 3 days	3.03%	3.98%	−1.26%	−1.90%
Candle end + 5 days	3.93%	4.91%	−1.39%	−2.40%
Candle end + 10 days	5.10%	5.46%	−1.31%	−1.68%
10-day performance rank	9	22	85	89

Number found. Most bullish doji stars occur in a bull market and have a downward breakout, handily beating the other categories. Together, I found 9,394 of them.

Reversal or continuation performance. The best performance comes from candles in a bear market, regardless of the breakout direction.

S&P performance. The table shows the average rise or decline as measured in the S&P 500 index from the date of the candle breakout to the trend high or low, depending on the breakout direction. The candle performance handily beats the results of the S&P in all categories.

Candle end to breakout. It takes price between three and six days to stage a breakout—a close either above the higher of the two price bars in the candle or below the lower of the two lines. Downward moves take less time to break out because price is nearer the candle's low.

Candle end to trend end. From the candle end to the trend end, it takes price a median of six to 11 days to make the journey. The time is shorter for downward breakouts because the downtrend is already well along.

Yearly position, performance. Candles within a third of the yearly low perform best.

Performance over time. Downward breakouts suffer performance degradation from 5 to 10 days after the candle ends. This decline and the anemic numbers posted after 10 days is why the rankings are so poor. Upward breakouts do quite well in the ranking, but it's not enough to improve the overall rank from 49 (1 is best out of 103).

Table 31.3 shows height statistics.

Candle height. In all four categories, tall candles outperform short ones. Trade only tall candles. To determine whether the candle is short or tall, compute its height from highest high to lowest low price in the candle pattern and divide by the breakout price. If the result is higher than the median, then you have a tall candle; otherwise it's short.

Stinky Pete is considering trading a bullish doji star with a high of 110 and a low of 105. Is the candle short or tall? The height is 110 – 105, or 5, so the measure would be 5/110, or 4.5%. In a bull market with an upward breakout the candle is tall.

Measure rule. Use the measure rule to help predict how far price will rise or fall. Compute the height of the candle pattern and multiply it by the appropriate percentage shown in the table; then apply it to the breakout price.

What are Stinky Pete's price targets? The upward target would be 110 + (5 × 59%), or 112.95, and the downward target would be 105 – (5 × 51%), or 102.45.

Shadows. The table's results pertain to the last candle line in the pattern. To determine whether the shadow is short or tall, compute the height of the shadow and divide by the breakout price. Compare the result to the median in the table. Tall shadows have a percentage higher than the median.

Table 31.3
Height Statistics

Description	Bull Market, Up Breakout	Bear Market, Up Breakout	Bull Market, Down Breakout	Bear Market, Down Breakout
Median candle height as a percentage of breakout price	4.17%	5.71%	4.27%	6.19%
Short candle, performance	5.60%	7.49%	−4.74%	−7.35%
Tall candle, performance	8.69%	10.33%	−6.86%	−12.07%
Percentage meeting price target (measure rule)	59%	55%	51%	56%
Median upper shadow as a percentage of breakout price	0.59%	0.88%	0.64%	1.05%
Short upper shadow, performance	6.04%	7.27%	−5.05%	−7.89%
Tall upper shadow, performance	7.42%	10.19%	−6.06%	−10.85%
Median lower shadow as a percentage of breakout price	0.61%	0.96%	0.52%	0.81%
Short lower shadow, performance	6.08%	7.29%	−5.06%	−7.70%
Tall lower shadow, performance	7.47%	9.84%	−6.07%	−10.91%

Shadow performance. Candles with tall upper or lower shadows perform better than their short counterparts.

Table 31.4 shows volume statistics.

Candle volume trend. A rising volume trend works better than a falling trend in bull market/up breakouts and bear market/down breakouts. A falling

Table 31.4
Volume Statistics

Description	Bull Market, Up Breakout	Bear Market, Up Breakout	Bull Market, Down Breakout	Bear Market, Down Breakout
Rising candle volume, performance	7.05%	8.04%	−5.49%	−9.54%
Falling candle volume, performance	6.53%	9.13%	−5.61%	−8.96%
Above-average candle volume, performance	6.78%	8.95%	−5.26%	−9.70%
Below-average candle volume, performance	6.74%	8.26%	−5.82%	−8.78%
Heavy breakout volume, performance	7.34%	9.30%	−5.67%	−10.23%
Light breakout volume, performance	6.13%	8.13%	−5.47%	−8.22%

volume trend works in the other two categories: bear market/up breakouts and bull market/down breakouts.

Average candle volume. Candles with above-average volume perform better than do those with light volume in all cases except for bull market/down breakouts.

Breakout volume. Breakout-day volume heavier than normal leads to better performance in all categories.

Trading Tactics

I looked at doji star patterns that acted as reversals of the downward price trend. Nearly all of them reversed when approaching or hitting major underlying support set up by minor highs, lows, or trendlines. Figure 31.2 shows an example for a short-term decline.

The congestion regions A and B support price as the doji forms as part of the doji star pattern. After finding support, price reverses the downtrend and heads higher, but not for long. Within a week price is easing lower again, eventually bottoming at 58.

I split trading tactics into two basic studies, one concerning reversal rates and the other concerning performance. Of the two, reversal rates are more

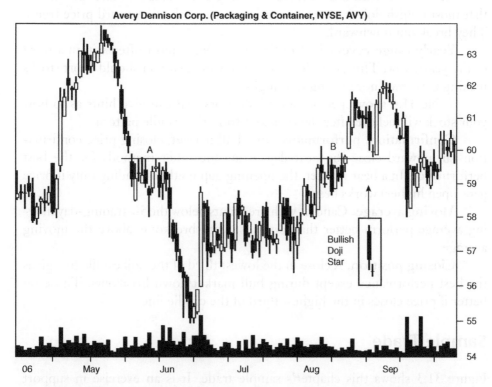

Figure 31.2   A bullish doji star appears, and price reverses direction.

Table 31.5
Reversal Rates

Description	Bull Market	Bear Market
Closing price confirmation reversal rate	57%	50%
Candle color confirmation reversal rate	57%	47%
Opening gap confirmation reversal rate	43%	36%
Reversal: trend down, breakout up	36%	30%
Continuation: trend down, breakout down	64%	70%
Percentage of reversals (R)/ continuations (C) for each 12-month low (L), middle (M), or high (H)	L 27% R/73% C, M 33% R/67% C, H 48% R/52% C	L 21% R/79% C, M 33% R/67% C, H 41% R/59% C

important, because it's better to trade in the direction of the trend and let price run as far as it can.

Table 31.5 gives tips to find the trend direction.

Confirmation reversal rates. If you wait for price to close higher the day after the doji star ends, you have a 57% chance of seeing a reversal occur in a bull market. In a bear market, the chance is 50%, which is random. I don't think this presents any earth-shaking trading tip.

Reversal, continuation rates. Looking at the breakout direction shows that most bullish doji stars act as continuations of the downward price trend. They break out downward.

Yearly range reversals. Continuations occur most often within a third of the yearly low. This goes along with the view that you should short stocks making new lows, not making new highs.

Table 31.6 shows performance indicators that can give hints as to how your stock will behave after the breakout from this candle pattern.

Confirmation, performance. In a bull market, closing price confirmation (an upward close the next day) beats the other methods for the best performance. In a bear market, the opening gap method (trading only if price gaps open higher) works best.

Moving average. Candles with breakouts below the 50-trading-day moving average perform better than do those with breakouts above the moving average.

Closing position. A close in the lowest third of the doji candle line gives the best performance except during bull market/down breakouts. Those do better if price closes in the highest third of the candle line.

Sample Trade

Figure 31.3 shows this chapter's sample trade. It is an exercise in support zones. After price changes trend at point A, it makes two peaks at B and C.

Table 31.6
Performance Indicators

Description	Bull Market, Up Breakout	Bear Market, Up Breakout	Bull Market, Down Breakout	Bear Market, Down Breakout
Closing price confirmation, performance	7.88%	12.25%	N/A	N/A
Candle color confirmation, performance	7.69%	11.47%	N/A	N/A
Opening gap confirmation, performance	7.79%	12.54%	N/A	N/A
Breakout above 50-day moving average, performance	6.70%	7.05%	−4.64%	−7.62%
Breakout below 50-day moving average, performance	6.88%	10.35%	−5.75%	−9.64%
Last candle: close in highest third, performance	6.87%	8.70%	−5.71%	−8.51%
Last candle: close in middle third, performance	6.46%	7.86%	−5.43%	−9.28%
Last candle: close in lowest third, performance	7.08%	9.62%	−5.61%	−9.71%

N/A means not applicable.

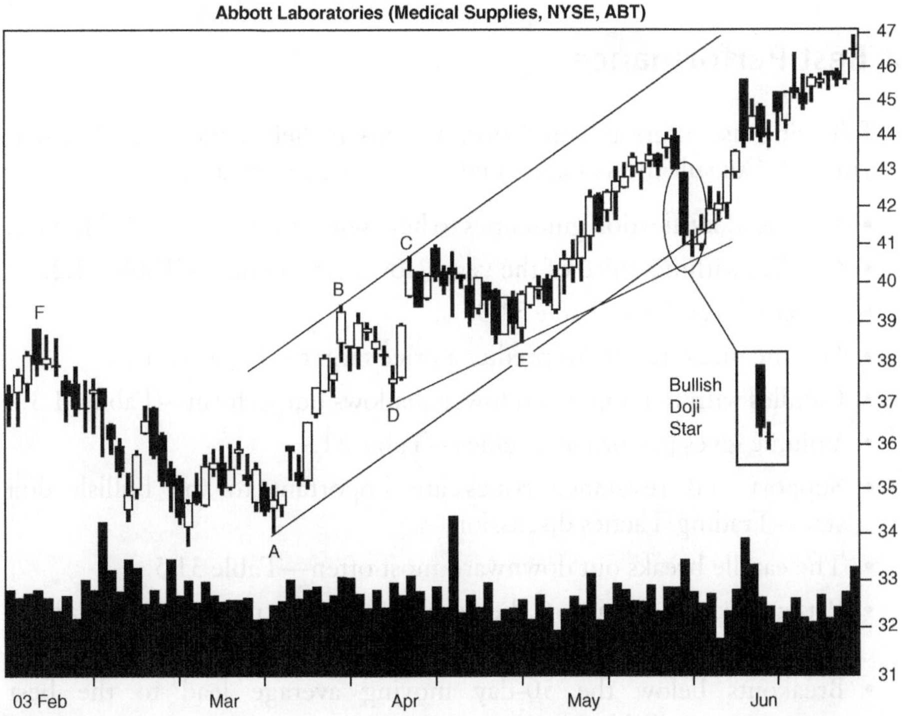

Figure 31.3 After reaching underlying support, the bullish doji star suggests that the downtrend will reverse.

This outlines the top of the price channel and A marks the lower boundary. Drawing a trendline connecting B and C would show the top of the channel and a line parallel to it starting from A would mark the bottom of the channel.

Notice how the bullish doji star appears near the bottom of this channel. Another trendline connecting the lows at D and E and projected into the future nearly intersects the bottom of the doji star pattern. The high just after peak C (near 41) also gives support to the doji star candle.

The confluence of the trendlines, support at C, and the doji star all suggest the price trend will reverse, maybe not immediately, but soon. Since the trend over the prior few months has been up, as illustrated by the rising price channel, and since price is now at the bottom of that channel, trading the doji star is a low-risk setup.

What if Stinky Pete buys the stock and price drops? How far will price tumble? The congestion at E, combined with the prior peak at F, suggests that 39 would be a likely stopping place. That would be the downside or risk to the trade. Upside or reward would be the top of the channel, about 47. The doji closed at 41. Thus, the risk is 2 points (41 − 39) and the potential reward is 6 (47 − 41), so the reward-to-risk ratio is 3 to 1.

If Stinky Pete could look into the future, he would see that price will peak at 46.94, just pennies from the 47 target. After the peak, price will drop in a near straight-line run to a low of 37.65 (about level with D), slightly below the 39 target.

For Best Performance

The following list offers tips and observations to help choose candles that perform well. Consult the associated table for more information.

- Use the identification guidelines to help select the pattern—Table 31.1.
- Candles within a third of the yearly low perform best—Table 31.2.
- Select tall candles—Table 31.3.
- Use the measure rule to predict a price target—Table 31.3.
- Candles with tall upper and lower shadows outperform—Table 31.3.
- Volume gives performance clues—Table 31.4.
- Support and resistance zones are important to the bullish doji star—Trading Tactics discussion.
- The candle breaks out downward most often—Table 31.5.
- Patterns within a third of the yearly low tend to act as continuations most often—Table 31.5.
- Breakouts below the 50-day moving average lead to the best performance—Table 31.6.

32

Doji Star, Collapsing

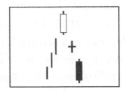

Behavior and Rank

Theoretical: Bearish reversal.

Actual bull market: Bearish reversal 63% of the time (ranking 24).

Actual bear market: None found.

Frequency: 101st out of 103.

Overall performance over time: 97th out of 103.

If you watched your trading screen set to the one-minute scale, you would see a collapsing doji star every 3.3 years, on average. That's how rare this candle pattern is. In over 4.7 million candle lines I found 16, with none coming from a bear market. That's too few to run a statistical analysis or even to present trading tactics.

A collapsing doji star acts as a reversal 63% of the time—that's what my 16 candles tell me. The bulls drive price upward, peaking with a white candle. Then price gaps lower and forms a doji. This is a bearish move because of the falling window (the gap), but the doji suggests indecision among traders. Which way will price go? The next day answers the question with another falling window. A black candle appears.

With three days in the candle pattern trending lower, starting from a white candle and ending with a black one, the bears control the stock. That's the psychology behind the pattern.

The overall performance rank is a dismal 97 out of 103, where 1 is best, and that's because of the two zeros I put in for the bear market results. In a bull market, the performance rank is 24 for a reversal (bull market/down breakouts) and 80 for continuations (bull market/up breakouts).

What should you look for as you sit for years in front of a computer monitor waiting for one to appear?

Identification Guidelines

Figure 32.1 shows a collapsing doji star. This one appears as part of an upward retracement in a downward trend. That means the primary trend is downward but price bumps up periodically, just to keep traders on their toes.

Table 32.1 lists the identification guidelines. This candlestick pattern is a three-candle-line formation that illustrates the change from bullish to bearish sentiment. The first candle is white and it appears in an uptrend. Following that, a doji gaps below the white candle's lower shadow, and it represents neutrality between the bulls and the bears. A doji has the opening and closing prices at or near the same value.

On the final day of the candle, price gaps lower and a black candle line prints on the chart. Again, there should be a gap between the shadows of the candle lines.

Figure 32.1 A collapsing doji star appears after an upward retracement during a downtrend.

Table 32.1
Identification Guidelines

Characteristic	Discussion
Number of candle lines	Three.
Price trend	Upward leading to the start of the candle pattern.
First day	A white candle.
Second day	A doji that gaps below yesterday's candle, including the shadows.
Last day	A black day that gaps below the doji, including the shadows.

Figure 32.2 shows another example of a collapsing doji star. Many of the candles in this stock do not have shadows, which I find odd. It may be due to the low price and the separation between the bid and asked prices. This stock showed three collapsing doji stars, so my guess is the lack of shadows allowed the stars to shine.

Price moves up at a steady pace and then tops out at the start of the collapsing doji star with a white candle. Price gaps lower and forms the doji,

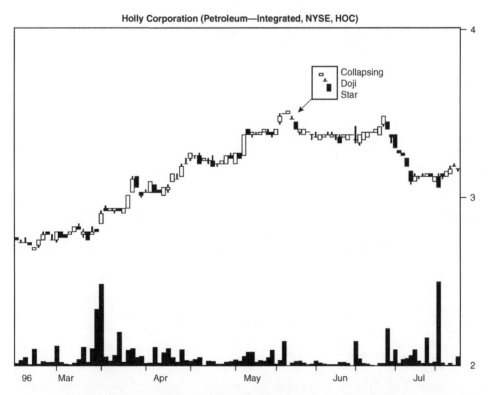

Holly Corporation (Petroleum—Integrated, NYSE, HOC)

Collapsing
Doji
Star

Figure 32.2   A collapsing doji star marks the end of an uptrend.

followed by another gap, and ends with the black candle. From there, price moves down some, then horizontally, but eventually trends lower.

If you allowed the shadows to overlap, you would find many more patterns. My interpretation of the rare literature on the candlestick pattern suggests that's not allowed, but I could be wrong. In any case, don't expect to see a collapsing doji star anytime soon. Speaking of collapsing stars, did you know that black holes are out of sight?

33

Downside Gap
Three Methods

Behavior and Rank

Theoretical: Bearish continuation.

Actual bull market: Bullish reversal 62% of the time (ranking 25).

Actual bear market: Bullish reversal 59% of the time (ranking 30).

Frequency: 84th out of 103.

Overall performance over time: 26th out of 103.

The downside gap three methods candlestick pattern is rare despite a search of over 4.7 million candles. This candlestick is supposed to act as a continuation pattern but doesn't. Nearly two-thirds of the time in a bull market price reverses the downtrend, and that's a big surprise. The overall performance rank is 26, which is very good (1 is best out of 103 candles).

If you know what an area or common gap is, this candlestick pattern surrounds it. Price trends downward with the bears in full control. Two black candles print on the chart sharing a gap between them, emphasizing the bearish momentum. Then the bulls stage a palace coup and force price up, wresting control from the bears.

The theory for this pattern suggests the uptick is only short covering, and once that's done, price will resume the downtrend. I'm sure that's true in some cases, but based on the numbers, that's not the way to bet.

Identification Guidelines

Figure 33.1 shows an example of a downside gap three methods candle pattern that forms in a strong downtrend. After the candle pattern completes, a shooting star prints but price does not close above the top of the three methods formation (A). Price eases lower, eventually closing below the bottom of the three methods candle (B) and staging a downward breakout. With price entering the pattern headed down and exiting down, this three methods candle acts as a continuation of the downtrend.

Table 33.1 lists identification guidelines. Not much has been written about this candle pattern, probably because it's so rare. The first two days are tall black-bodied candles with a gap between them that includes the shadows (meaning no overlapping shadows). If you count the gap as between the bodies and allow overlapping shadows, you will find more patterns. The last day is a white candle that opens in the body of the second black candle and closes within the body of the first black candle.

The statistics in this chapter obey the identification guidelines listed in Table 33.1, including no overlapping shadows and a white candle that begins and ends within the prior candles' bodies. Sounds gory, doesn't it, like something from an *Alien* movie?

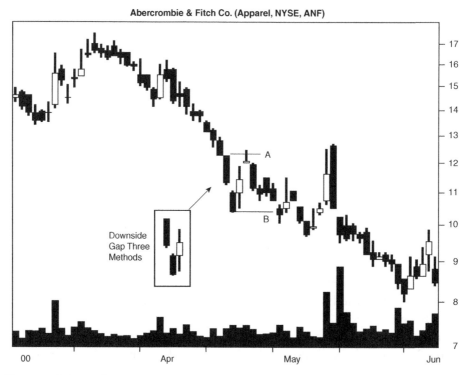

Figure 33.1   A downside gap three methods candlestick pattern in which price breaks out downward, continuing the trend.

Table 33.1
Identification Guidelines

Characteristic	Discussion
Number of candle lines	Three.
Price trend	Downward leading to the candle pattern.
First day	A long black-bodied candle.
Second day	Another long black-bodied candle with a gap between today and yesterday, including the shadows (meaning no overlapping shadows).
Third day	Price forms a white candle. The candle opens within the body of the second day and closes within the body of the first candle, thus closing the gap between the two black candles.

Statistics

Table 33.2 shows general statistics.

Number found. The stringent guidelines calling for the last (white) candle to open and close within the bodies of the black candles limited the number found to 464. Prorating the results from the standard database shows that this candlestick appears more often in a bear market.

Reversal or continuation performance. The best performance occurred in a bear market, regardless of the breakout direction. You might guess that this is due to few samples, but other candle types also show the same result.

S&P performance. The candlestick pattern beats the performance of the S&P 500 over the same periods. That should not be a surprise, because it's like comparing the time of a world-class sprinter to my time in the 100-meter dash. He's going to beat me every time unless I epoxy his track shoes to the starting block.

Candle end to breakout. It takes between 4 and 10 days for price to reach the breakout. Upward breakouts take substantially less time than downward ones, perhaps because price is closer to the top of the candle pattern than the bottom.

Candle end to trend end. Downward breakouts take slightly longer to reach the end of the trend than do upward breakouts.

Yearly position, performance. In three out of four categories, the best performance comes when the breakout is within a third of the yearly low. However, the sample counts are few for the other ranges, so temper your enthusiasm. In a bull market, 74% act as reversals when they are within a third of the yearly low.

Performance over time. Performance is quite good in all columns except for bear market/up breakouts. Performance suffers from 3 to 10 days and that drops the rank down, too.

Table 33.2
General Statistics

Description	Bull Market, Up Breakout	Bear Market, Up Breakout	Bull Market, Down Breakout	Bear Market, Down Breakout
Number found	240	46	146	32
Reversal (R), continuation (C) performance	6.48% R	7.65% R	−5.17% C	−8.96% C
Standard & Poor's 500 change	1.67%	0.94%	−0.76%	−3.53%
Candle end to breakout (median, days)	4	4	10	7
Candle end to trend end (median, days)	9	9	11	10
Number of breakouts near the 12-month low (L), middle (M), or high (H)	L 46, M 62, H 94	L 10, M 19, H 16	L 46, M 49, H 27	L 16, M 11, H 5
Percentage move for each 12-month period	L 7.24%, M 8.43%, H 5.05%	L 9.22%, M 8.17%, H 6.19%	L −6.20%, M −4.97%, H −3.56%	L −10.89%, M −6.21%, H −8.47%
Candle end + 1 day	0.64%	1.29%	−1.38%	−2.07%
Candle end + 3 days	1.52%	2.50%	−2.47%	−4.15%
Candle end + 5 days	2.43%	2.13%	−3.36%	−4.89%
Candle end + 10 days	3.08%	1.98%	−4.97%	−5.02%
10-day performance rank	55	73	8	29

Downward breakouts are the star of this candle. The performance rank is quite high, peaking at 8 out of 103 candles where 1 is best.

Table 33.3 shows height statistics.

Candle height. Tall candles perform better than short ones except for bear market/down breakouts, which have short candles outperforming. To determine whether the candle is short or tall, compute its height from highest high to lowest low price in the candle pattern and divide by the breakout price. If the result is higher than the median, then you have a tall candle; otherwise it's short.

Cheryl sees a downside gap three methods candle that interests her because it appears at a support zone. The top of the tallest candle is at 55 and the bottom of the lowest one is at 50. Is the candle short or tall? The height is 55 − 50, or 5, so the measure would be 5/55, or 9.1%. In a bull market with an upward breakout, the candle is tall.

Measure rule. Use the measure rule to help predict how far price will rise or fall. Compute the height of the candle and multiply it by the appropriate percentage shown in the table; then apply it to the breakout price.

Table 33.3
Height Statistics

Description	Bull Market, Up Breakout	Bear Market, Up Breakout*	Bull Market, Down Breakout	Bear Market, Down Breakout*
Median candle height as a percentage of breakout price	5.61%	10.40%	6.72%	8.78%
Short candle, performance	4.30%	6.60%	−4.63%	−9.32%
Tall candle, performance	9.14%	9.18%	−6.03%	−8.43%
Percentage meeting price target (measure rule)	50%	24%	26%	56%
Median upper shadow as a percentage of breakout price	0.20%	0.52%	0.21%	0.58%
Short upper shadow, performance	7.12%	6.47%	−4.62%	−8.56%
Tall upper shadow, performance	5.96%	9.15%	−5.59%	−9.55%
Median lower shadow as a percentage of breakout price	0.00%	0.20%	0.14%	0.40%
Short lower shadow, performance	7.59%	6.91%	−4.88%	−9.87%
Tall lower shadow, performance	5.32%	8.62%	−5.43%	−7.74%

*Fewer than 30 samples.

What are the price targets for Cheryl's candle? The upward target would be 55 + (5 × 50%), or 57.50, and the downward target would be 50 − (5 × 26%), or 48.70.

Shadows. The following results pertain to the last candle line in the pattern. To determine whether the shadow is short or tall, compute the height of the shadow and divide by the breakout price. Compare the result to the median in the table. Tall shadows have a percentage higher than the median.

Upper shadow performance. Candles with tall upper shadows usually perform better than short ones, and that's true in all cases except for bull market/up breakouts.

Lower shadow performance. Do not be alarmed about a 0.00% median. That only means a large number of candles had no lower shadow.

Candles with tall lower shadows perform better than short ones in bear market/up breakouts and bull market/down breakouts. Short shadows work better in bull market/up breakouts and bear market/down breakouts.

Table 33.4 shows volume statistics.

Table 33.4
Volume Statistics

Description	Bull Market, Up Breakout	Bear Market, Up Breakout*	Bull Market, Down Breakout	Bear Market, Down Breakout*
Rising candle volume, performance	6.65%	7.78%	−4.01%	−8.69%
Falling candle volume, performance	6.18%	7.15%	−7.35%	−10.36%
Above-average candle volume, performance	6.76%	8.60%	−3.99%	−9.17%
Below-average candle volume, performance	6.09%	6.35%	−7.56%	−8.54%
Heavy breakout volume, performance	7.69%	9.45%	−4.55%	−10.75%
Light breakout volume, performance	5.28%	5.90%	−6.21%	−6.29%

*Fewer than 30 samples.

Candle volume trend. Upward breakouts perform best post breakout if volume trends upward within the candle. Downward breakouts do better after falling volume.

Average candle volume. Volume that is higher than the one-month average results in the best performance in all categories except bull market/down breakout. That category does better if the candle shows lighter than average volume.

Breakout volume. Heavy breakout-day volume suggests better performance across the board except for bull market/down breakouts. Those do better after light volume.

Trading Tactics

Figure 33.2 shows an example of the setup I see many times when I look for the downside gap three methods pattern. The three methods form at or near the end of an inverted and ascending scallop. Sometimes the three methods are a few weeks early; other times they are dead on as in this case. They represent a low-risk trading opportunity when price rises after the candle breaks out upward.

I split trading tactics into two basic studies, one concerning reversal rates and the other concerning performance. Of the two, reversal rates are more important, because it's better to trade in the direction of the trend and let price run as far as it can.

Figure 33.2 A downside gap three methods candlestick formation appears at the end of an inverted and ascending scallop.

Table 33.5 gives tips to find the trend direction.

Confirmation reversal rates. Since the price trend is downward, wait for price to close upward to confirm a reversal. That works between 78% (bear markets) and 84% (bull markets) of the time.

Table 33.5
Reversal Rates

Description	Bull Market	Bear Market*
Closing price confirmation reversal rate	84%	78%
Candle color confirmation reversal rate	81%	78%
Opening gap confirmation reversal rate	77%	56%
Reversal: trend down, breakout up	62%	59%
Continuation: trend down, breakout down	38%	41%
Percentage of reversals (R)/ continuations (C) for each 12-month low (L), middle (M), or high (H)	L 50% R/50% C, M 56% R/44% C, H 78% R/22% C	L 38% R/62% C, M 63% R/37% C, H 76% R/24% C

*Fewer than 30 samples.

Table 33.6
Performance Indicators

Description	Bull Market, Up Breakout	Bear Market, Up Breakout*	Bull Market, Down Breakout	Bear Market, Down Breakout*
Closing price confirmation, performance	N/A	N/A	−8.02%	−12.22%
Candle color confirmation, performance	N/A	N/A	−8.32%	−12.11%
Opening gap confirmation, performance	N/A	N/A	−7.61%	−13.31%
Breakout above 50-day moving average, performance	4.71%	6.29%	−3.98%*	−3.80%
Breakout below 50-day moving average, performance	8.23%	9.31%	−5.24%	−9.24%
Last candle: close in highest third, performance	6.64%	7.04%	−4.44%	−8.96%
Last candle: close in middle third, performance	4.19%*	12.19%	−11.37%	−8.96%
Last candle: close in lowest third, performance	0.00%	0.00%	0.00%	0.00%

N/A means not applicable.
*Fewer than 30 samples.

Reversal, continuation rates. The vast majority of the time, price breaks out upward, regardless of the market direction. Upward breakouts occur more often in a bull market than in a bear one.

Yearly range reversals. Price is more likely to reverse the downtrend if the breakout appears within a third of the yearly high.

Table 33.6 shows performance indicators that can give hints as to how your stock will behave after the breakout from a candle pattern.

Confirmation, performance. The opening gap method works well in a bear market. You'd short only if price gaps downward at the open the next day.

In a bull market, candle color confirmation works best. That means if a black candle appears the day after the downside gap three methods, then consider selling short.

Moving average. Candles with breakouts below the 50-trading-day moving average do better than those with breakouts above the moving average.

Closing position. None of the candles had a close in the lowest third (probably because the candle is a white one). When price closes in the middle of the candle line, it tends to either tie or outperform a close near the candle's high. However, the high price works best in bull market/up breakouts.

Sample Trade

Cheryl spotted the chart pattern in Figure 33.3 just before she turned off her computer for the day. A downside gap three methods appeared in mid-August. When she looks at it the next day, she sees the candlestick and trendline resistance. A trendline connecting peaks A, B, and C shows what concerns her. She reasons that price will have a difficult time piercing the line. "But you never know," she says. If the breakout is upward, she'll go long. What about the downside?

Support has appeared in the form of prior minor lows. A horizontal trendline connecting them means the downside gap three methods is caught in a dual trendline vice squeezing price. The breaking of this tightening congestion zone will probably represent a forceful move, regardless of the direction. "But that is just a guess," Cheryl admits.

The next day, when price closes lower in a tall black candle, it breaks through the support line and that tells her price is going down. She shorts the stock and receives a fill at 79.25.

Price drops for about two weeks and then pulls back to the bottom of the support area (D), now overhead resistance; but this doesn't worry her. "I

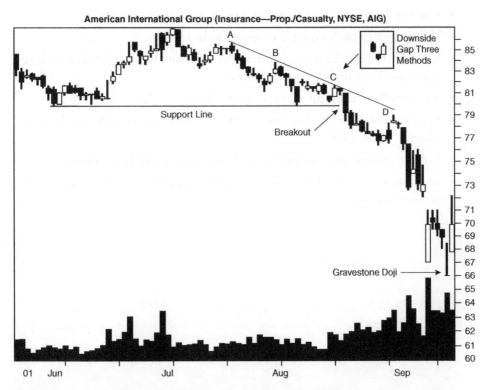

Figure 33.3 A downside gap three methods pattern hits overhead resistance. A trade is signaled when price closes below the support line.

know price will continue down," she says. How does she know? "Overhead resistance. Besides, that's how pullbacks work."

I see this often in chart patterns. Price breaks out downward from a chart pattern and then pulls back to the breakout price. The stock continues lower 87% of the time.

That's what happens to Cheryl's stock. Price peaks at D during the pullback and then resumes the downtrend.

When price makes a gravestone doji and then opens higher, she figures the decline is dead and closes out her position at 67.80, for a 14% gain.

For Best Performance

The following list offers tips and observations to help choose candles that perform well. Consult the associated table for more information.

- Use the identification guidelines to help select the pattern—Table 33.1.
- Candles within a third of the yearly low perform best except for bull market/up breakouts—Table 33.2.
- Select tall candles except for bear market/down breakouts—Table 33.3.
- Use the measure rule to predict a price target—Table 33.3.
- Volume gives performance clues—Table 33.4.
- Look for the candle to appear near the end of an inverted and ascending scallop—Trading Tactics discussion.
- The candle breaks out upward most often—Table 33.5.
- Patterns within a third of the yearly high tend to act as reversals most often—Table 33.5.
- Candle color confirmation works best in a bull market—Table 33.6.
- Breakouts below the 50-day moving average lead to the best performance—Table 33.6.

34

Downside Tasuki Gap

Behavior and Rank

Theoretical: Bearish continuation.
Actual bull market: Bullish reversal 54% of the time (ranking 42).
Actual bear market: Bearish continuation 51% of the time (ranking 52).
Frequency: 68th out of 103.
Overall performance over time: 23rd out of 103.

The downside Tasuki gap is a close relative of the downside gap three methods candlestick. The differences are subtle but important. In a bull market, three methods acts as a reversal 62% of the time, and the Tasuki gap also acts as a reversal but just 54% of the time. The downside Tasuki gap is supposed to be a continuation pattern, but the percentages are close enough to random (50%) that it could be a continuation if more samples were found. Overall performance is very good, placing the rank at 23 out of 103 candle patterns where 1 is best.

The downside Tasuki gap occurs in a downtrend with price forming two black candles. Price gaps between them, and, to my mind, it's an exhaustion gap. Exhaustion gaps close within a week 64% of the time in a bull market, and that may happen in this case, but the Tasuki gap formation does not close it the next day. Price forms a white candle as the bulls struggle to retake control. Price moves into the gap but does not cover it completely. After that, anything can happen. The theory says that the bulls give up and the bears push price lower. My testing says that not only do the bulls retain control, but they push price above the top of the first candle, closing higher more than half the time.

Identification Guidelines

Figure 34.1 shows a downside Tasuki gap that occurs one day after price forms a minor peak, so it's a weak example (the downtrend should be longer). This candle pattern resumes the downward price trend that began at the high in early April, but one that forms a straight-line plunge into the ground, mirroring the takeoff that occurred in March.

In the Tasuki gap, price forms two black candles with a gap between them. The candles always appear tall in the pictures I've seen of this candlestick, but the identification guidelines accompanying those sources do not specify tall candles. Thus, I allow short or tall candles in this pattern, although a check of my results shows that most are, in fact, tall candles and not short ones.

Table 34.1 lists identification guidelines. The gap that appears between the two black candles should include the shadows, meaning that they do not overlap. The last day is a white day that opens within the body of the second day and closes somewhere between the gap of the first two candles but does not close the gap. In other words, the closing price of the third day must remain below the close of the first day and above the open of the second day. The upper shadow of the third day can be as tall as weeds at an abandoned house.

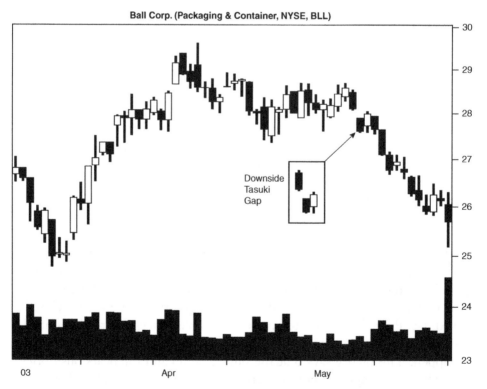

Figure 34.1 A downside Tasuki gap begins a downward price trend.

Table 34.1
Identification Guidelines

Characteristic	Discussion
Number of candle lines	Three.
Price trend	Downward leading to the start of the candlestick pattern.
First day	A black candle.
Second day	Price forms another black candle with a down gap between the first and second days. There should be no overlapping shadows.
Last day	Price forms a white candle that opens within the body of the second candle and closes within the gap set by the first and second day, but does not completely close the gap. Ignore the shadows.

Statistics

Table 34.2 shows general statistics.

Number found. I located 1,164 Tasuki gaps, which makes this pattern somewhat rare. Prorating the standard database shows that these candles occur more often in a bear market.

Reversal or continuation performance. The best performance comes from a bear market, regardless of the breakout direction.

S&P performance. Performance of the candle beats the performance of the S&P 500 over the same period, in all categories.

Candle end to breakout. It takes six days for price to either close above the top or close below the bottom of this candle pattern, thus staging a breakout.

Candle end to trend end. The median time to reach the end of the trend ranges between 8 and 11 days. Downward breakouts take less time to reach the trend end than do upward breakouts, probably because the prevailing trend is downward, so the trend is well along.

Yearly position, performance. Candles within a third of the yearly low perform better than the other ranges in all categories except for bull market/down breakouts, but even there the numbers are close.

Performance over time. This candle pattern stumbles from three to five days in bear market/down breakouts. That might be responsible for the high rank number, 86, which is well below the other categories. A rank of 1 is best out of 103 candles.

Table 34.3 shows height statistics.

Candle height. Tall candle patterns outperform in all categories, so look for tall ones. To determine whether the candle is short or tall, compute its height from highest high to lowest low price in the candle pattern and divide by the breakout price. If the result is higher than the median, then you have a tall candle; otherwise it's short.

Table 34.2
General Statistics

Description	Bull Market, Up Breakout	Bear Market, Up Breakout	Bull Market, Down Breakout	Bear Market, Down Breakout
Number found	488	125	423	128
Reversal (R), continuation (C) performance	5.43% R	7.38% R	−5.66% C	−9.94% C
Standard & Poor's 500 change	2.00%	1.52%	−0.87%	−3.75%
Candle end to breakout (median, days)	6	6	6	6
Candle end to trend end (median, days)	11	10	9	8
Number of breakouts near the 12-month low (L), middle (M), or high (H)	L 93, M 125, H 220	L 34, M 48, H 41	L 145, M 137, H 86	L 60, M 50, H 17
Percentage move for each 12-month period	L 6.98%, M 5.92%, H 4.51%	L 11.44%, M 7.33%, H 5.09%	L −5.56%, M −5.64%, H −5.49%	L −11.28%, M −9.92%, H −6.68%
Candle end + 1 day	1.04%	1.98%	−0.68%	−1.80%
Candle end + 3 days	2.30%	3.42%	−1.84%	−3.34%
Candle end + 5 days	3.05%	4.64%	−2.28%	−2.74%
Candle end + 10 days	4.16%	4.69%	−2.93%	−4.34%
10-day performance rank	30	35	34	86

Scott has a downside Tasuki gap with a high of 97 and a low of 94. Is his candle short or tall? The height is 97 − 94, or 3, so the measure would be 3/97, or 3.1%, and that represents a short candle (assume bull market/up breakout).

Measure rule. Use the measure rule to help predict how far price will rise or fall. Compute the height of the candle pattern and multiply it by the appropriate percentage shown in the table; then apply it to the breakout price.

What are Scott's price targets? The upward target would be (3 × 36%) + 97, or 98.08 and the downward target would be 94 − (3 × 32%), or 93.04.

Shadows. The table's results pertain to the last candle line in the pattern. To determine whether the shadow is short or tall, compute the height of the shadow and divide by the breakout price. Compare the result to the median in the table. Tall shadows have a percentage higher than the median.

Both upper and lower shadows, when tall, perform better than their short brothers and sisters. The one exception occurs in a bear market after a downward breakout of the upper shadow. A short shadow in that situation suggests better performance.

Table 34.4 shows volume statistics.

Table 34.3
Height Statistics

Description	Bull Market, Up Breakout	Bear Market, Up Breakout	Bull Market, Down Breakout	Bear Market, Down Breakout
Median candle height as a percentage of breakout price	6.06%	8.24%	6.59%	10.47%
Short candle, performance	4.92%	5.64%	−4.67%	−7.74%
Tall candle, performance	6.09%	9.08%	−7.15%	−12.26%
Percentage meeting price target (measure rule)	36%	34%	32%	44%
Median upper shadow as a percentage of breakout price	0.48%	0.78%	0.53%	0.98%
Short upper shadow, performance	4.86%	5.50%	−4.73%	−10.10%
Tall upper shadow, performance	6.03%	9.04%	−6.63%	−9.77%
Median lower shadow as a percentage of breakout price	0.31%	0.46%	0.34%	0.36%
Short lower shadow, performance	4.84%	5.99%	−5.21%	−8.33%
Tall lower shadow, performance	5.97%	8.74%	−6.14%	−11.56%

Candle volume trend. Rising candle volume within the Tasuki pattern leads to the best performance in all categories.

Average candle volume. Volume less than the average results in better postbreakout performance except from patterns with upward breakouts in a bear market.

Table 34.4
Volume Statistics

Description	Bull Market, Up Breakout	Bear Market, Up Breakout	Bull Market, Down Breakout	Bear Market, Down Breakout
Rising candle volume, performance	5.46%	7.83%	−5.67%	−10.21%
Falling candle volume, performance	5.39%	6.56%	−5.66%	−9.37%
Above-average candle volume, performance	5.37%	7.81%	−5.54%	−9.37%
Below-average candle volume, performance	5.52%	6.66%	−5.87%	−11.00%
Heavy breakout volume, performance	5.49%	7.87%	−6.13%	−10.86%
Light breakout volume, performance	5.37%	6.72%	−5.04%	−7.76%

Breakout volume. Heavy candle volume on the breakout day suggests better performance across the board. By that I mean candles with heavy breakout volume outperform those with light volume.

Trading Tactics

Figure 33.2 in the preceding chapter shows an example of an inverted and ascending scallop with a downside gap three methods candle ending the pattern. The downside Tasuki gap also appears in place of the three methods pattern in some inverted and ascending scallop chart patterns. Both act the same, meaning that price resumes the uptrend most often.

In another trading setup, if price races from the top of the chart to the bottom and then forms a downside Tasuki gap, the chances improve that the candle pattern will act as a reversal. I see this often in the charts. The time is usually quick, four to six weeks to make the plunge (but be flexible). After the candle pattern completes, price recovers.

I split trading tactics into two basic studies, one concerning reversal rates and the other concerning performance. Of the two, reversal rates are more important, because it's better to trade in the direction of the trend and let price run as far as it can.

Table 34.5 gives tips to find the trend direction.

Confirmation reversal rates. To help confirm a reversal, wait for price to close higher the day after the Tasuki candle ends.

Reversal, continuation rates. More patterns act as reversals in a bull market. Continuations hold a slight lead in a bear market, but the numbers are about random.

Yearly range reversals. Reversals occur most often when the breakout is within a third of the yearly high.

Table 34.6 shows performance indicators that can give hints as to how your stock will behave after the breakout from a candle pattern.

Table 34.5
Reversal Rates

Description	Bull Market	Bear Market
Closing price confirmation reversal rate	70%	79%
Candle color confirmation reversal rate	69%	73%
Opening gap confirmation reversal rate	63%	63%
Reversal: trend down, breakout up	54%	49%
Continuation: trend down, breakout down	46%	51%
Percentage of reversals (R)/ continuations (C) for each 12-month low (L), middle (M), or high (H)	L 39% R/61% C, M 48% R/52% C, H 72% R/28% C	L 36% R/64% C, M 49% R/51% C, H 71% R/29%* C

*Fewer than 30 samples.

Table 34.6
Performance Indicators

Description	Bull Market, Up Breakout	Bear Market, Up Breakout	Bull Market, Down Breakout	Bear Market, Down Breakout
Closing price confirmation, performance	N/A	N/A	−8.15%	−13.65%
Candle color confirmation, performance	N/A	N/A	−8.55%	−12.30%
Opening gap confirmation, performance	N/A	N/A	−8.49%	−13.79%
Breakout above 50-day moving average, performance	5.60%	5.83%	−4.08%	−7.43%*
Breakout below 50-day moving average, performance	5.29%	8.94%	−5.92%	−10.12%
Last candle: close in highest third, performance	5.28%	6.85%	−5.54%	−10.20%
Last candle: close in middle third, performance	5.69%	8.98%	−5.25%	−9.43%
Last candle: close in lowest third, performance	6.57%*	3.61%*	−10.36%*	−11.93%*

N/A means not applicable.
*Fewer than 30 samples.

Confirmation, performance. I searched for the best method to confirm price continuing lower after a downside Tasuki gap. The best results came from opening gap confirmation in a bear market, where you short the stock after a lower gap open the day after the Tasuki pattern completes. In a bull market, candle color works slightly better. That means waiting for a black candle to appear the day after the Tasuki ends before trading.

Moving average. Candles with breakouts below the 50-trading-day moving average result in better performance than do those with breakouts above the moving average. This is true in all categories except for bull market/up breakouts.

Closing position. A close in the lowest third of the last candle line in the pattern often results in better performance; but since the samples are few, don't trust those results. The middle third works best for bear market/up breakouts.

Sample Trade

Scott has followed the stock shown in Figure 34.2 for several months, waiting for a buying opportunity. It comes when price touches the support line for the third time and then forms a downside Tasuki gap. Price closes the gap a day later, suggesting the gap was an exhaustion gap that appears at the end of trends. That suggests price is going to rise.

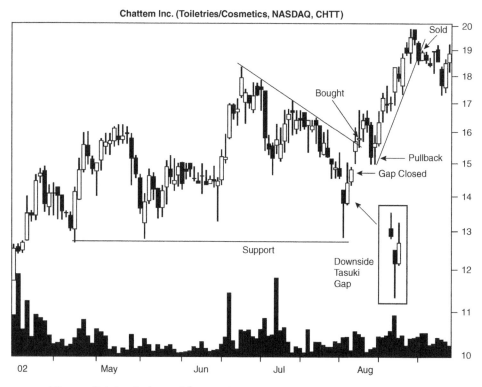

Chattem Inc. (Toiletries/Cosmetics, NASDAQ, CHTT)

Figure 34.2   A downside Tasuki gap marks the end of the decline.

Since Scott believes that price is moving up, why not buy the stock immediately? "Overhead resistance," he says. The figure shows this as a downsloping trendline. He waits for price to close above the line before taking a position in the stock. Price cooperates the next day by creating a tall white candle that closes just above the trendline. He buys at the market open a day later.

Each day, he follows the stock, watching it move higher. Over time, price moves up in a channel, bounded on the top and bottom by parallel trendlines (only the bottom one appears in the figure). When price closes below the bottom trendline, that is his sell signal. He sells his position and makes about 20% on the trade.

For Best Performance

The following list offers tips and observations to help choose candles that perform well. Consult the associated table for more information.

- Use the identification guidelines to help select the pattern—Table 34.1.
- Candles within a third of the yearly low perform best most often—Table 34.2.
- Select tall candles—Table 34.3.

- Use the measure rule to predict a price target—Table 34.3.
- Candles with tall upper or lower shadows outperform—Table 34.3.
- Volume gives performance clues—Table 34.4.
- Inverted and ascending scallops sometimes spawn Tasuki gaps—Trading Tactics discussion.
- A large downward move in about four to six weeks that forms a downside Tasuki gap is likely to rebound—Trading Tactics discussion.
- Patterns within a third of the yearly high tend to act as reversals most often—Table 34.5.
- Breakouts below the 50-day moving average lead to the best performance except for bull market/up breakouts—Table 34.6.

35

Engulfing, Bearish

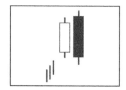

Behavior and Rank

Theoretical: Bearish reversal.
Actual bull market: Bearish reversal 79% of the time (ranking 5).
Actual bear market: Bearish reversal 82% of the time (ranking 5).
Frequency: 11th out of 103.
Overall performance over time: 91st out of 103.

Bearish engulfing candlesticks are about as numerous as bees in a hive. I logged over 30,000 (candlesticks, not bees) in one database before I quit looking. What's more exciting, though, is that they work quite well as reversals, but that tells only part of the story. The rank of 5 as bearish reversals is very close to the best (1) out of 103 candlestick patterns. Unfortunately, although price may reverse it doesn't go far. Check out the overall performance ranking of 91. Ouch! Again, 1 is best out of 103. This candle pattern is like the time the fuel pump on my Chevette broke. As soon as I started an uphill climb, the car died. Don't depend on price after a reversal from this candle going anywhere, either.

Price trends upward leading to the first white candle in this pattern. With the bulls in control, a tall black candle appears that opens higher than the body of the first candle, indicating that the bulls still think they are masters of the domain. Then the bears come in and knock price down, with it closing below the body of the first day in a strong push of selling pressure. Price continues lower the vast majority of the time.

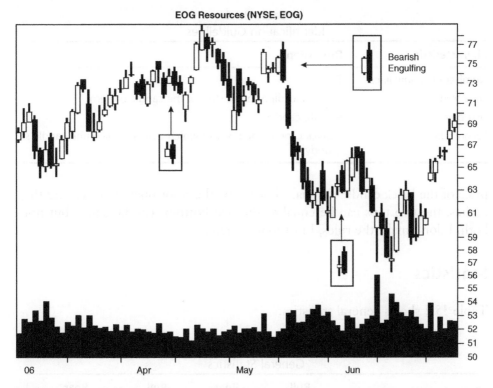

Figure 35.1 Three bearish engulfing patterns, with two showing reversals and one not.

Identification Guidelines

Figure 35.1 shows three examples of a bearish engulfing pattern. The first one in April appears after price trends up one day. This is a weak uptrend—more of a consolidation, really—so there's not much to reverse. Price breaks out downward nevertheless.

The middle bearish engulfing pattern is more successful. Price gaps lower and continues down for almost two weeks before finding solid ground upon which to stand.

The last engulfing pattern occurs near June. Price trends up leading to the candle pattern and continues moving up after the end, too. The shadows of the first candle are not engulfed and that's okay. It's an engulfed body that's important with this candle pattern.

Table 35.1 lists identification guidelines. This two-candle pattern begins with a white candle, followed by a black one. The black candle has a body that's taller than the white candle's body and it overlaps. That means the opening price of the black candle is equal to or above the prior close and the closing

Table 35.1
Identification Guidelines

Characteristic	Discussion
Number of candle lines	Two.
Price trend	Upward leading to the start of the candle pattern.
First day	A white candle.
Second day	A black candle, the body of which overlaps the white candle's body.

price of the black candle is equal to or below the prior open. Concerning the bodies, the two tops can be equal *or* the two bottoms can be equal, but not both. I don't make the rules; I just follow them.

Statistics

Table 35.2 shows general statistics.

Table 35.2
General Statistics

Description	Bull Market, Up Breakout	Bear Market, Up Breakout	Bull Market, Down Breakout	Bear Market, Down Breakout
Number found	3,059	933	11,745	4,263
Reversal (R), continuation (C) performance	2.79% C	3.67% C	−6.80% R	−11.26% R
Standard & Poor's 500 change	1.11%	0.38%	−1.06%	−2.69%
Candle end to breakout (median, days)	4	4	2	2
Candle end to trend end (median, days)	5	5	8	9
Number of breakouts near the 12-month low (L), middle (M), or high (H)	L 402, M 727, H 1,930	L 172, M 260, H 501	L 2,155, M 3,163, H 6,427	L 1,131, M 1,255, H 1,877
Percentage move for each 12-month period	L 3.73%, M 2.86%, H 2.63%	L 4.96%, M 3.44%, H 3.43%	L −7.39%, M −6.77%, H −6.68%	L −14.48%, M −10.70%, H −10.23%
Candle end + 1 day	1.27%	1.77%	−0.79%	−1.24%
Candle end + 3 days	2.01%	2.95%	−1.69%	−2.73%
Candle end + 5 days	1.36%	2.29%	−2.39%	−3.85%
Candle end + 10 days	−1.56%	−2.11%	−3.56%	−5.92%
10-day performance rank	103	100	25	21

Number found. I limited the number of candle patterns under study to 20,000 to keep things manageable. Most engulfing patterns came from a bull market.

Reversal or continuation performance. Candles with downward breakouts show the best performance. Those are also reversals.

S&P performance. Comparing the candle performance with the S&P 500, we see that the candle wallops the S&P's performance over the same period.

Candle end to breakout. It takes between two and four days for price to break out. Downward breakouts take about half the time to break out compared to upward ones. That's because price closes nearer the low than the high.

Candle end to trend end. It takes between five and nine days for price to reach the trend end. Upward breakouts take less time to reach the trend end because the uptrend is already well along.

Yearly position, performance. Most of the bearish engulfing candles break out within a third of the yearly high. However, performance is best when the breakout is near the yearly low.

Performance over time. If you will recall, the reversal rate listed at the opening of this chapter was near the top of the list (5, where 1 is best). Looking at performance over time from the table tells you why the candle pattern ranks 91 out of 103. Performance does not climb over time and even goes negative when it should not. Downward breakouts do well but upward ones are pathetic. In fact, the bull market/up breakout rank is the worst of any candle pattern.

Table 35.3 shows height statistics.

Candle height. Tall candles perform substantially better than short ones. To determine whether the candle is short or tall, compute its height from highest high to lowest low price in the candle pattern and divide by the breakout price. If the result is higher than the median, then you have a tall candle; otherwise it's short.

Rusty is considering shorting a stock that shows a bearish engulfing candle pattern with a high price of 37 and a low of 36. Is his candle tall? The height is $37 - 36$, or 1, and the measure is 1/37, or 2.7%. That is above the median listed for bull market/upward breakouts, so the candle is tall.

Measure rule. Use the measure rule to help predict how far price will rise or fall. Compute the height of the candle and multiply it by the appropriate percentage shown in the table; then apply it to the breakout price.

What are Rusty's price targets for his candle? The upward target becomes $(1 \times 45\%) + 37$, or 37.45, and the downward target would be $36 - (1 \times 74\%)$, or 35.26.

Shadows. The following results pertain to the last candle line in the pattern. To determine whether the shadow is short or tall, compute the height of the shadow and divide by the breakout price. Compare the result to the median in the table. Tall shadows have a percentage higher than the median.

Table 35.3
Height Statistics

Description	Bull Market, Up Breakout	Bear Market, Up Breakout	Bull Market, Down Breakout	Bear Market, Down Breakout
Median candle height as a percentage of breakout price	2.62%	3.49%	3.07%	4.17%
Short candle, performance	2.19%	2.90%	−5.36%	−8.94%
Tall candle, performance	3.59%	4.55%	−8.73%	−13.95%
Percentage meeting price target (measure rule)	45%	41%	74%	76%
Median upper shadow as a percentage of breakout price	0.23%	0.27%	0.21%	0.30%
Short upper shadow, performance	2.57%	3.33%	−6.43%	−9.96%
Tall upper shadow, performance	3.02%	3.98%	−7.19%	−12.57%
Median lower shadow as a percentage of breakout price	0.45%	0.62%	0.37%	0.56%
Short lower shadow, performance	2.50%	3.22%	−6.21%	−10.72%
Tall lower shadow, performance	3.11%	4.13%	−7.47%	−11.84%

Candles with tall upper or lower shadows perform better than do those with short shadows.

Table 35.4 shows volume statistics.

Candle volume trend. A rising volume trend works better in all categories but one. Bull market/down breakouts work better with falling volume.

Table 35.4
Volume Statistics

Description	Bull Market, Up Breakout	Bear Market, Up Breakout	Bull Market, Down Breakout	Bear Market, Down Breakout
Rising candle volume, performance	2.80%	3.86%	−6.75%	−11.75%
Falling candle volume, performance	2.78%	3.51%	−6.86%	−10.80%
Above-average candle volume, performance	2.56%	3.61%	−6.81%	−11.24%
Below-average candle volume, performance	2.89%	3.69%	−6.80%	−11.28%
Heavy breakout volume, performance	3.06%	4.22%	−7.12%	−11.82%
Light breakout volume, performance	2.57%	3.24%	−6.55%	−10.83%

Average candle volume. Candles with below-average volume perform better than do those with above-average volume in all cases except bull market/down breakouts.

Breakout volume. Candles with heavy breakout volume perform best across the board.

Trading Tactics

Figure 35.2 shows upward retracements in a downward price trend. Price peaks in May and then heads down in a stair-step decline. Along the way, three bearish engulfing patterns occur at the top of the upward retracements. They provide good trading signals to short the stock. Since the primary trend is downward, look for the brief upward retracements and take a position once price begins trending lower.

I split trading tactics into two basic studies, one concerning reversal rates and the other concerning performance. Of the two, reversal rates are more important, because it's better to trade in the direction of the trend and let price run as far as it can.

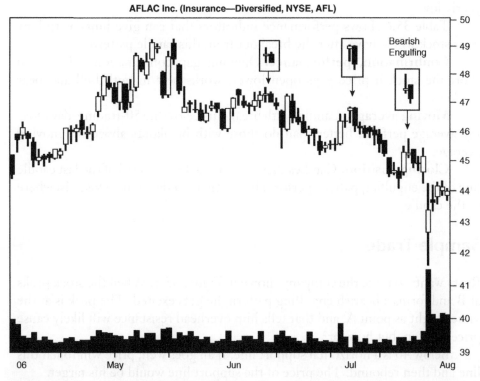

Figure 35.2 Bearish engulfing patterns in a downtrend present good trading opportunities.

Table 35.5
Reversal Rates

Description	Bull Market	Bear Market
Closing price confirmation reversal rate	95%	95%
Candle color confirmation reversal rate	92%	94%
Opening gap confirmation reversal rate	86%	87%
Reversal rate: trend up, breakout down	79%	82%
Continuation rate: trend up, breakout up	21%	18%
Percentage of reversals (R)/ continuations (C) for each 12-month low (L), middle (M), or high (H)	L 84% R/16% C, M 81% R/19% C, H 77% R/23% C	L 87% R/13% C, M 83% R/17% C, H 79% R/21% C

Table 35.5 gives tips to find the trend direction.

Confirmation reversal rates. To confirm that a reversal will occur, wait for price to close lower the day after the engulfing pattern ends. That method works 95% of the time.

Reversal, continuation rates. Looking at the breakout direction, the candle acts as a reversal more often. Expect a downward breakout.

Yearly range reversals. Most reversals occur within a third of the yearly low.

Table 35.6 shows performance indicators that can give hints as to how your stock will behave after the breakout from this candle pattern.

Confirmation, performance. Opening gap confirmation, where you short the stock if price gaps open lower, works best in both bull and bear markets.

Moving average. Candles with breakouts below the 50-trading-day moving average perform better than do those with breakouts above the moving average.

Closing position. Candles that close in the lowest third of the last candle line of the engulfing pattern perform better than do those that close elsewhere in the candle.

Sample Trade

Rusty wants to trade the company shown in Figure 35.3. When the stock peaks at B and forms a bearish engulfing pattern, he gets excited. The peak is at the same height as point A, and that tells him overhead resistance will likely cause price to drop, but how far?

Below 40 is a horizontal support line. If all goes well, price will touch this line and then rebound. The price of the support line would be his target.

The next day, price gaps lower at the open and he sells short the stock (using opening gap confirmation). On that day, a white candle forms and it

Table 35.6
Performance Indicators

Description	Bull Market, Up Breakout	Bear Market, Up Breakout	Bull Market, Down Breakout	Bear Market, Down Breakout
Closing price confirmation, performance	N/A	N/A	−6.09%	−10.29%
Candle color confirmation, performance	N/A	N/A	−6.06%	−10.59%
Opening gap confirmation, performance	N/A	N/A	−6.71%	−10.75%
Breakout above 50-day moving average, performance	2.69%	3.59%	−6.61%	−10.08%
Breakout below 50-day moving average, performance	3.36%	4.09%	−7.19%	−13.11%
Last candle: close in highest third, performance	2.50%	2.97%*	−6.08%	−10.24%
Last candle: close in middle third, performance	2.75%	3.64%	−6.45%	−9.41%
Last candle: close in lowest third, performance	2.81%	3.71%	−6.87%	−11.68%

N/A means not applicable.
*Fewer than 30 samples.

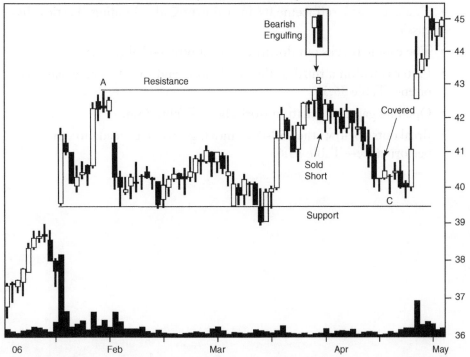

Figure 35.3   Price hits overhead resistance and forms a bearish engulfing candle.

concerns him because the bulls are regaining control. Coupled with a long lower shadow, it confirms this bullish belief. Nevertheless, he decides to wait out the stock. For safety, he places a stop a penny above the high at B.

Price eases lower over time. When a gravestone doji appears at C, near underlying support, he believes the risk of a rise is much greater than the potential reward of an additional decline. The next day he closes out his short position for a near $2 profit per share.

"On a million shares, that's a nice chunk of change," he says. That's true, but it's too bad he didn't short a million shares.

For Best Performance

The following list offers tips and observations to help choose candles that perform well. Consult the associated table for more information.

- Use the identification guidelines to help select the pattern—Table 35.1.
- Candles within a third of the yearly low perform best—Table 35.2.
- Select tall candles—Table 35.3.
- Use the measure rule to predict a price target—Table 35.3.
- Candles with tall upper or lower shadows outperform—Table 35.3.
- Volume gives performance clues—Table 35.4.
- Trade upward retracements in a downtrend—Trading Tactics discussion.
- The candle breaks out downward most often—Table 35.5.
- Patterns within a third of the yearly low tend to act as reversals most often—Table 35.5.
- Opening gap confirmation works best—Table 35.6.
- Breakouts below the 50-day moving average lead to the best performance—Table 35.6.

36

Engulfing, Bullish

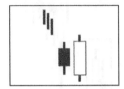

Behavior and Rank

Theoretical: Bullish reversal.

Actual bull market: Bullish reversal 63% of the time (ranking 22).

Actual bear market: Bullish reversal 62% of the time (ranking 25).

Frequency: 12th out of 103.

Overall performance over time: 84th out of 103.

The bullish engulfing pattern acts as a reversal almost two-thirds of the time (62% to 63%), but its performance suffers. It ranks 84 out of 103 where 1 is best. Downward breakouts show respectable performance, but upward breakouts yank the rank back like a bungee cord on the rebound. The candlestick appears most often at minor lows but less often at major turning points.

The psychology behind the pattern begins with a downward price trend leading to the engulfing pattern. The bears have control of the bank. A black candle prints on the chart as the opening move by the bears, but after price opens lower, the bulls storm the bank, taking over. Their buying demand pushes price up above the prior black body. At the close, the bulls still control the bank and price remains above the prior black body, completing the bullish engulfing candlestick.

Identification Guidelines

Figure 36.1 shows an example of where you will often see an engulfing pattern. Price moves up in a stair-step rise. At the bottom of the step, a bullish engulfing

317

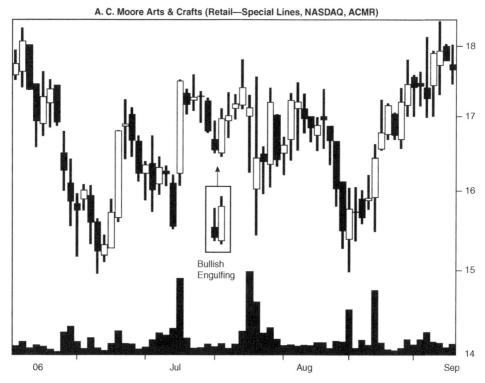

A. C. Moore Arts & Crafts (Retail—Special Lines, NASDAQ, ACMR)

Figure 36.1   A bullish engulfing pattern occurs in a downward retracement of the upward trend.

pattern sometimes appears. It's a signal for price to climb to the next step and that's what happens. Price moves higher, eventually closing above the top of the two-day candle pattern and staging an upward breakout. Table 36.1 lists what to look for when searching for bullish engulfing patterns.

The candle pattern consists of two candle lines. The first line is black and the second white. The white candle engulfs or overlaps the black candle's body. That means the white candle opens at or below the black body and closes at or

Table 36.1
Identification Guidelines

Characteristic	Discussion
Number of candle lines	Two.
Price trend	Downward leading to the start of the candlestick pattern.
First day	A black candle.
Second day	A white candle opens below the prior body and closes above that body, too. Price need not engulf the shadows.

above the black body. The tops of the bodies or the bottoms of the bodies can share the same price, but not both. Ignore the shadows in this candle pattern.

Statistics

Table 36.2 shows general statistics.

Number found. I cut the sample size from a gazillion candle patterns to 20,000. Prorating the standard database reveals that the bullish engulfing pattern occurs more often in a bear market.

Reversal or continuation performance. The best-performing engulfing candles appear in a bear market. This isn't a fluke, because it occurs with many other candle types as well.

S&P performance. Comparing the candle breakout to the trend high or low with the performance of the S&P 500 over the same periods, we see that the engulfing candle does substantially better in all cases.

Table 36.2
General Statistics

Description	Bull Market, Up Breakout	Bear Market, Up Breakout	Bull Market, Down Breakout	Bear Market, Down Breakout
Number found	8,923	3,617	5,225	2,235
Reversal (R), continuation (C) performance	4.60% R	5.75% R	−5.91% C	−9.68% C
Standard & Poor's 500 change	1.32%	0.59%	−1.31%	−3.28%
Candle end to breakout (median, days)	2	2	4	4
Candle end to trend end (median, days)	6	6	8	8
Number of breakouts near the 12-month low (L), middle (M), or high (H)	L 2,130, M 2,589, H 4,204	L 1,083, M 1,161, H 1,373	L 1,696, M 1,680, H 1,849	L 896, M 718, H 621
Percentage move for each 12-month period	L 5.50%, M 4.63%, H 4.25%	L 7.56%, M 5.56%, H 4.84%	L −6.89%, M −5.84%, H −5.32%	L −12.12%, M −8.56%, H −8.31%
Candle end + 1 day	0.62%	0.95%	−1.34%	−1.88%
Candle end + 3 days	0.89%	1.22%	−2.69%	−4.11%
Candle end + 5 days	0.80%	0.92%	−3.32%	−5.02%
Candle end + 10 days	−0.05%	−1.18%	−3.77%	−6.31%
10-day performance rank	101	96	20	14

Candle end to breakout. It takes two to four days for price to break out. Upward breakouts take less time than downward ones because the close is nearer to the top of the candle.

Candle end to trend end. Upward breakouts take two days less time to reach the trend end than downward breakouts. Since the prevailing trend is downward, I find the result unusual. However, with price closing near the top of the second candle, a new uptrend would already be underway, so maybe that explains the shorter time.

Yearly position, performance. Most bullish engulfing candles appear within a third of the yearly high except for bear market/down breakouts. Those show more often near the yearly low. Candles within a third of the yearly low perform best.

Performance over time. First the good news. Performance after a downward breakout is exemplary. Performance increases over each measurement period, resulting in excellent performance rankings. The bad news is the bull market performance is dreadful. Price actually drops from days 5 to 10, so the performance rank suffers, too.

Table 36.3 shows height statistics.

Candle height. Tall patterns perform better than short ones. To determine whether the candle is short or tall, compute its height from highest high to lowest low price in the candle pattern and divide by the breakout price. If

Table 36.3
Height Statistics

Description	Bull Market, Up Breakout	Bear Market, Up Breakout	Bull Market, Down Breakout	Bear Market, Down Breakout
Median candle height as a percentage of breakout price	3.17%	4.42%	3.06%	4.36%
Short candle, performance	3.83%	4.62%	−4.82%	−8.07%
Tall candle, performance	5.64%	7.08%	−7.35%	−11.71%
Percentage meeting price target (measure rule)	60%	54%	63%	67%
Median upper shadow as a percentage of breakout price	0.37%	0.49%	0.48%	0.67%
Short upper shadow, performance	4.32%	5.26%	−5.52%	−9.34%
Tall upper shadow, performance	4.92%	6.28%	−6.34%	−10.05%
Median lower shadow as a percentage of breakout price	0.24%	0.34%	0.24%	0.35%
Short lower shadow, performance	4.28%	5.23%	−5.51%	−9.23%
Tall lower shadow, performance	4.94%	6.28%	−6.33%	−10.16%

the result is higher than the median, then you have a tall candle; otherwise it's short.

John sees a bullish engulfing candle with a high of 77 and a low of 73. Is the candle short or tall? The height is 77 − 73, or 4, so the measure would be (assuming bull market/upward breakout) 4/77, or 5.2%. That is well above the median listed, so the candle is tall.

Measure rule. Use the measure rule to help predict how far price will rise or fall. Compute the height of the candle pattern and multiply it by the appropriate percentage shown in the table; then apply it to the breakout price.

What price targets can John expect? The upward target would be (4 × 60%) + 77, or 79.40, and the downward target would be 73 − (4 × 63%), or 70.48.

Shadows. The table's results pertain to the last candle line in the pattern. To determine whether the shadow is short or tall, compute the height of the shadow and divide by the breakout price. Compare the result to the median in the table. Tall shadows have a percentage higher than the median. Candles with tall upper or lower shadows perform better than do those with short shadows.

Table 36.4 shows volume statistics.

Candle volume trend. A rising volume trend within the candle leads to better performance in all categories except bear market/down breakout. Those show better postbreakout performance if volume trends lower within the candle pattern.

Average candle volume. Heavy (above-average) candle volume results in better postbreakout performance across the board. In many cases, however, the performances with above-average and below-average volume are close, so the results are not as startling as they may seem.

Table 36.4
Volume Statistics

Description	Bull Market, Up Breakout	Bear Market, Up Breakout	Bull Market, Down Breakout	Bear Market, Down Breakout
Rising candle volume, performance	4.61%	5.83%	−6.02%	−9.61%
Falling candle volume, performance	4.59%	5.64%	−5.78%	−9.76%
Above-average candle volume, performance	4.69%	6.07%	−5.95%	−10.06%
Below-average candle volume, performance	4.54%	5.53%	−5.89%	−9.43%
Heavy breakout volume, performance	4.90%	6.47%	−6.30%	−10.82%
Light breakout volume, performance	4.34%	5.20%	−5.53%	−8.45%

Breakout volume. Candles with heavy breakout volume perform better than do those with light volume.

Trading Tactics

Figure 36.2 shows a bullish engulfing candlestick that appears when price is trending downward. By this I mean the primary, longer-term trend, not the minor ripples that appear within the tide. It's rare that the engulfing pattern will act as a major turning point, so don't depend on it doing so.

In this example, price moves higher, staging an upward breakout, but price resumes the downward trend soon after. Anyone taking a long position in this stock would lose money if they didn't sell quickly. Avoid going long when the primary price trend is downward.

I split trading tactics into two basic studies, one concerning reversal rates and the other concerning performance. Of the two, reversal rates are more important, because it's better to trade in the direction of the trend and let price run as far as it can.

Table 36.5 gives tips to find the trend direction.

Confirmation reversal rates. To help detect a reversal of the downward price trend, wait for price to close higher the day after the engulfing candle

Figure 36.2   Avoid trading a bullish engulfing candle when the primary trend is down.

Table 36.5
Reversal Rates

Description	Bull Market	Bear Market
Closing price confirmation reversal rate	89%	90%
Candle color confirmation reversal rate	86%	86%
Opening gap confirmation reversal rate	71%	70%
Reversal: trend down, breakout up	63%	62%
Continuation: trend down, breakout down	37%	38%
Percentage of reversals (R)/ continuations (C) for each 12-month low (L), middle (M), or high (H)	L 56% R/44% C, M 61% R/39% C, H 69% R/31% C	L 55% R/45% C, M 62% R/38% C, H 69% R/31% C

ends. That is a reliable method, but it does not tell how long the new trend will last.

Reversal, continuation rates. Look for an upward breakout most often.

Yearly range reversals. Candles within a third of the yearly high tend to reverse more often than do those in the other ranges.

Table 36.6 shows performance indicators that can give hints as to how your stock will behave after the breakout from a candle pattern.

Table 36.6
Performance Indicators

Description	Bull Market, Up Breakout	Bear Market, Up Breakout	Bull Market, Down Breakout	Bear Market, Down Breakout
Closing price confirmation, performance	4.33%	5.52%	N/A	N/A
Candle color confirmation, performance	4.43%	5.63%	N/A	N/A
Opening gap confirmation, performance	5.67%	8.15%	N/A	N/A
Breakout above 50-day moving average, performance	4.35%	5.24%	−5.35%	−7.46%
Breakout below 50-day moving average, performance	4.91%	6.41%	−6.15%	−10.54%
Last candle: close in highest third, performance	4.67%	5.76%	−5.99%	−9.82%
Last candle: close in middle third, performance	4.30%	5.64%	−5.66%	−9.24%
Last candle: close in lowest third, performance	3.95%	6.44%	−5.58%	−9.20%

N/A means not applicable.

Confirmation, performance. Opening gap confirmation works better than the other methods. That means trading the day after the engulfing candle ends only if price gaps open higher.

Moving average. Candles with breakouts below the 50-trading-day moving average do better than do those with breakouts above the moving average.

Closing position. A close in the highest third of the last candle line in the pattern suggests better performance than a close elsewhere in the line except for bear market/up breakouts. Performance from those candles does best if the close is near the candle line's low.

Sample Trade

Figure 36.3 shows a trade that John made. Price trends downward into A and then bounces up and returns to B. That's when a bullish engulfing candlestick appears. When price moves above the top of the engulfing pattern, John buys the stock, receiving a fill at 71.30.

It's rare for price to trend upward in a straight-line run, so a return to a trendline connecting the lows of A and B is expected. That's what happens.

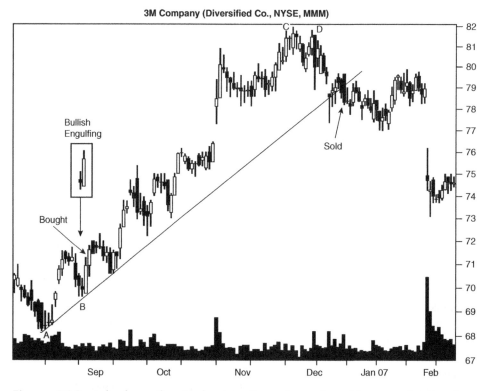

Figure 36.3 John buys the stock when the primary trend is up and sells when price closes below the trendline.

John decides that if price closes below the trendline, he will get out. The sale will likely not be at the high, but at least he can keep most of his profit intact.

In subsequent months price moves up, loosely following the trendline upward. In mid-October price gaps higher, and John considers redrawing the trendline but decides against it. (That turns out to be a mistake, because a steeper trendline would have taken him out at a higher price.)

Price peaks to the right of C and then forms a lower high at D. A lower peak is a clue that the trend has changed from up to down. Why? "Because price attempted to make a new high and failed. The weakness suggests the bulls are tired," John says.

Price gaps downward in December but closes above the trendline. Four days later, price finally closes below the line. He sells the next day at the open and receives a fill of 78.31, making almost 10% on the trade.

For Best Performance

The following list offers tips and observations to help choose candles that perform well. Consult the associated table for more information.

- Use the identification guidelines to help select the pattern—Table 36.1.
- Candles within a third of the yearly low perform best—Table 36.2.
- Select tall candles—Table 36.3.
- Use the measure rule to predict a price target—Table 36.3.
- Candles with tall upper or lower shadows outperform—Table 36.3.
- Volume gives performance clues—Table 36.4.
- Avoid engulfing candles that appear in a downward primary trend—Trading Tactics discussion.
- The candle breaks out upward most often—Table 36.5.
- Patterns within a third of the yearly high tend to act as reversals most often—Table 36.5.
- Opening gap confirmation works best—Table 36.6.
- Breakouts below the 50-day moving average lead to the best performance—Table 36.6.

37

Evening Doji Star

Behavior and Rank

Theoretical: Bearish reversal.

Actual bull market: Bearish reversal 71% of the time (ranking 12).

Actual bear market: Bearish reversal 71% of the time (ranking 15).

Frequency: 81st out of 103.

Overall performance over time: 30th out of 103.

The evening doji star, sometimes called a southern cross, is a rare candlestick pattern, but its performance is decent. Nearly three-quarters of the candles show downward breakouts after an uptrend; that is, they act as reversals.

The candle pattern shows the change from bullish to bearish sentiment in three candle lines. The first candle, a tall white one, appears after bulls push price upward. Then buying demand for more stock causes price to gap upward but the bears come out of hibernation and fight back. Price stalls and forms a doji, a pattern that says the bulls and bears are stalemated. The next day, the bears receive reinforcements and price gaps lower, forming a black candle that closes well into the white candle. After that, price continues lower, completing the reversal.

Identification Guidelines

Figure 37.1 shows an example of an evening doji star candlestick. This one forms as the last peak in a broadening top chart pattern. Price crosses the chart pattern from side to side and trends up to the evening doji star in September.

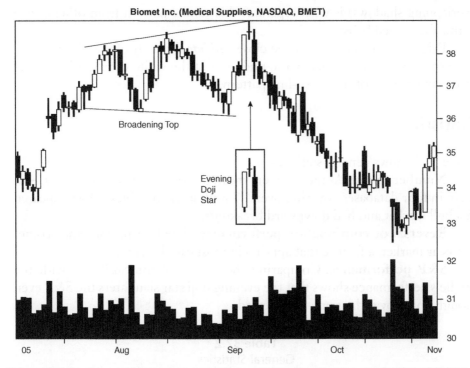

Figure 37.1   An evening doji star reaches overhead resistance, and price reverses.

There, a rainbow transition from bull to bear market occurs and price tumbles down a steep slope of falling black candles.

How do you identify the evening doji star? Table 37.1 lists the guidelines. The first candle is a tall white one. Following that, a doji appears whose body is above the white candle's body, leaving a gap between the bodies but not necessarily the shadows. A doji is a candle in which the opening and closing prices are the same or nearly so.

A day later, another gap sends price lower into a black candle. Again, the bodies cannot overlap but the shadows can. The shadow length (causing

Table 37.1
Identification Guidelines

Characteristic	Discussion
Number of candle lines	Three.
Price trend	Upward leading to the start of the candle pattern.
First day	A tall white day.
Second day	A doji that gaps above the bodies of the two adjacent candle lines. The shadows are not important; only the doji body need remain above the surrounding candles.
Last day	A tall black candle that closes at or below the midpoint (well into the body) of the white candle.

overlapping shadows) is what separates this candle pattern from others, such as the abandoned baby.

Price in the black candle must close *well into* the body of the white candle. I interpret that to mean below the midpoint of the white candle. Figure 37.1 shows an example of the three-line pattern.

Statistics

Table 37.2 shows general statistics.

Number found. As the numbers show, this pattern is rare. I found 774 of them in four databases covering over 4.7 million candle lines. Most appeared in a bull market and had downward breakouts.

Reversal or continuation performance. The best performance comes in a bear market, a feature that appears in most candle types.

S&P performance. Comparing the results of the S&P 500 with the candle's performance shows that the evening doji star slaughters the S&P even though both cover the same time period.

Table 37.2
General Statistics

Description	Bull Market, Up Breakout	Bear Market, Up Breakout	Bull Market, Down Breakout	Bear Market, Down Breakout
Number found	199	28	480	67
Reversal (R), continuation (C) performance	6.03% C	6.63% C	−6.08% R	−11.02% R
Standard & Poor's 500 change	1.62%	1.75%	−64%	−2.07%
Candle end to breakout (median, days)	6	7	3	3
Candle end to trend end (median, days)	8	12	7	9
Number of breakouts near the 12-month low (L), middle (M), or high (H)	L 22, M 44, H 106	L 6, M 10, H 12	L 85, M 102, H 242	L 23, M 19, H 25
Percentage move for each 12-month period	L 4.71%, M 5.00%, H 6.17%	L 8.06%, M 9.35%, H 5.04%	L −7.42%, M −6.27%, H −5.58%	L −8.46%, M −14.75%, H −9.54%
Candle end + 1 day	1.90%	1.52%	−0.72%	−0.16%
Candle end + 3 days	3.54%	4.93%	−1.43%	−0.88%
Candle end + 5 days	4.17%	4.95%	−1.68%	−1.58%
Candle end + 10 days	4.79%	6.20%	−1.70%	−3.66%
10-day performance rank	15	19	73	57

Candle end to breakout. It takes between three and seven days for price to close either above the highest price in the candle pattern (including the shadows) or below the lowest price. Downward breakouts take less time to break out because price is nearer the bottom of the candle than the top.

Candle end to trend end. The median time to reach the trend end ranges between 7 and 12 days. Downward breakouts take less time, probably because price has already made the turn lower, so the trend is already well along.

Yearly position, performance. The table shows that most of the evening doji stars appear within a third of the yearly high. The performance over the yearly trading range shows no consistent trend, and that's unusual for a candle pattern. Often, the yearly low has the best performance, but not with this candle. The odd results are likely due to the dearth of samples.

Performance over time. The evening doji star is a robust candle, meaning that performance improves over time and in each category. Upward breakouts display outstanding percentage changes, and they show in the performance ranks of 15 and 19, where 1 is best out of 103 candles. Downward breakouts have much less inspiring numbers, and their ranks reflect that.

Table 37.3 shows height statistics.

Candle height. Tall candles show the best performance. To determine whether the candle is short or tall, compute its height from highest high to

Table 37.3
Height Statistics

Description	Bull Market, Up Breakout	Bear Market, Up Breakout*	Bull Market, Down Breakout	Bear Market, Down Breakout
Median candle height as a percentage of breakout price	4.25%	5.26%	4.71%	5.88%
Short candle, performance	4.99%	6.61%	−5.13%	−8.56%
Tall candle, performance	7.62%	6.64%	−7.25%	−13.63%
Percentage meeting price target (measure rule)	52%	57%	48%	48%
Median upper shadow as a percentage of breakout price	0.10%	0.40%	0.16%	0.28%
Short upper shadow, performance	6.73%	10.77%	−6.03%	−11.70%
Tall upper shadow, performance	5.50%	3.96%	−6.12%	−10.40%
Median lower shadow as a percentage of breakout price	0.20%	0.34%	0.22%	0.24%
Short lower shadow, performance	5.32%	5.13%	−5.31%	−9.04%
Tall lower shadow, performance	6.56%	7.73%	−6.72%	−13.45%

*Fewer than 30 samples.

lowest low price in the candle pattern and divide by the breakout price. If the result is higher than the median, then you have a tall candle; otherwise it's short.

Gabe finds an evening doji star candlestick formation with the highest high at 37 and the lowest low at 34. Is his candle short or tall? The height is 37 − 34, or 3, so the measure is 3/37, or 8.1%. In a bull market with an upward breakout it's a tall candle.

Measure rule. Use the measure rule to help predict how far price will rise or fall. Compute the height of the candle pattern and multiply it by the appropriate percentage shown in the table; then apply it to the breakout price.

What are the price targets for Gabe's candle? The upward target would be (3 × 52%) + 37, or 38.56, and the downward target would be 34 − (3 × 48%), or 32.56.

Shadows. The table's results pertain to the last candle line in the pattern. To determine whether the shadow is short or tall, compute the height of the shadow and divide by the breakout price. Compare the result to the median in the table. Tall shadows have a percentage higher than the median.

Upper shadow performance. Candles with short upper shadows result in better performance except for bull market/down breakouts. The results are unusual because most candle types perform better with tall shadows.

Lower shadow performance. Candles with tall lower shadows perform better than do those with short shadows.

Table 37.4 shows volume statistics.

Candle volume trend. A falling volume trend within the candle pattern suggests good postbreakout performance. However, there is one

Table 37.4
Volume Statistics

Description	Bull Market, Up Breakout	Bear Market, Up Breakout*	Bull Market, Down Breakout	Bear Market, Down Breakout
Rising candle volume, performance	5.72%	4.64%	−6.77%	−10.45%
Falling candle volume, performance	6.27%	8.18%	−5.39%	−11.56%
Above-average candle volume, performance	6.05%	5.70%	−6.31%	−11.67%
Below-average candle volume, performance	6.02%	8.12%	−5.84%	−9.94%
Heavy breakout volume, performance	7.05%	6.17%	−6.24%	−12.12%
Light breakout volume, performance	4.74%	6.83%	−5.94%	−9.77%

*Fewer than 30 samples.

exception to this: bull market/down breakouts. They do better after a rising volume trend.

Average candle volume. Candles with above-average candle volume work better than do those with below-average volume except for upward breakouts in a bear market.

Breakout volume. Heavy breakout-day volume scores best almost across the board. The lone exception is (drumroll, please) bear market/up breakouts. Those perform better after light breakout volume.

Trading Tactics

Figure 37.2 shows an example of a setup I see often. Price begins to swing up at A, crests at B and forms the evening doji star, and then retraces to C. The average B to C retracement of the move up from A to B is 50%. That's an average, so each pattern will vary. What's clear from the chart is that once price breaks out, there isn't much downside remaining.

I split trading tactics into two basic studies, one concerning reversal rates and the other concerning performance. Of the two, reversal rates are more important, because it's better to trade in the direction of the trend and let price run as far as it can.

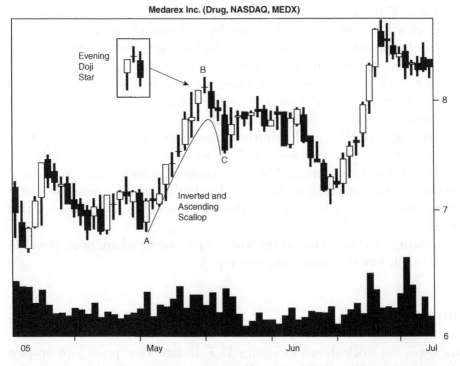

Figure 37.2 An evening doji star appears at the top of an inverted and ascending scallop chart pattern.

Table 37.5
Reversal Rates

Description	Bull Market	Bear Market*
Closing price confirmation reversal rate	92%	91%
Candle color confirmation reversal rate	90%	85%
Opening gap confirmation reversal rate	81%	81%
Reversal rate: trend up, breakout down	71%	71%
Continuation rate: trend up, breakout up	29%	29%
Percentage of reversals (R)/ continuations (C) for each 12-month low (L), middle (M), or high (H)	L* 79% R/21% C, M 70% R/30% C, H 70% R/30% C	L 79% R/21% C, M 66% R/34% C, H 68% R/32% C

*Fewer than 30 samples.

Table 37.5 gives tips to find the trend direction.

Confirmation reversal rates. To help detect a reversal of the uptrend, wait for price to close lower the day after the candle ends. That works over 90% of the time.

Reversal, continuation rates. Price breaks out downward most often.

Yearly range reversals. If you can believe the low sample count, breakouts within a third of the yearly low show the highest reversal rates.

Table 37.6 shows performance indicators that can give hints as to how your stock will behave after the breakout from this candle pattern.

Confirmation, performance. In a bull market, the best performance comes by using the opening gap confirmation method. That's when you short the stock if the candle gaps open lower. In a bear market, waiting for a black candle to appear after the end of the evening doji star—candle color confirmation—results in the best performance.

Moving average. Candles with breakouts below the 50-trading-day moving average result in performance that's better than those candles with breakouts above the moving average. The one exception comes from the low sample count bull market/up breakout category. Most other candle types show better performance when the breakout is below the moving average, so keep that in mind.

Closing position. Due to the low sample count, where price closes in the last candle line shows no consistent trend.

Sample Trade

Gabe owns the stock shown in Figure 37.3. In late May, price gaps upward and he is excited. "Finally!" he says. Price forms a series of tall white candles, hesitating only briefly along the way before marching upward again.

Table 37.6
Performance Indicators

Description	Bull Market, Up Breakout	Bear Market, Up Breakout*	Bull Market, Down Breakout	Bear Market, Down Breakout
Closing price confirmation, performance	N/A	N/A	−5.99%	−8.37%
Candle color confirmation, performance	N/A	N/A	−6.13%	−11.93%
Opening gap confirmation, performance	N/A	N/A	−7.38%	−10.04%
Breakout above 50-day moving average, performance	6.18%	6.05%	−5.63%	−10.48%
Breakout below 50-day moving average, performance	4.60%*	10.53%	−6.92%	−11.79%
Last candle: close in highest third, performance	3.94%*	−7.44%	0.00%	0.00%
Last candle: close in middle third, performance	6.07%*	6.92%	−7.48%	−7.88%*
Last candle: close in lowest third, performance	6.09%	6.68%	−5.96%	−11.43%

N/A means not applicable.
*Fewer than 30 samples.

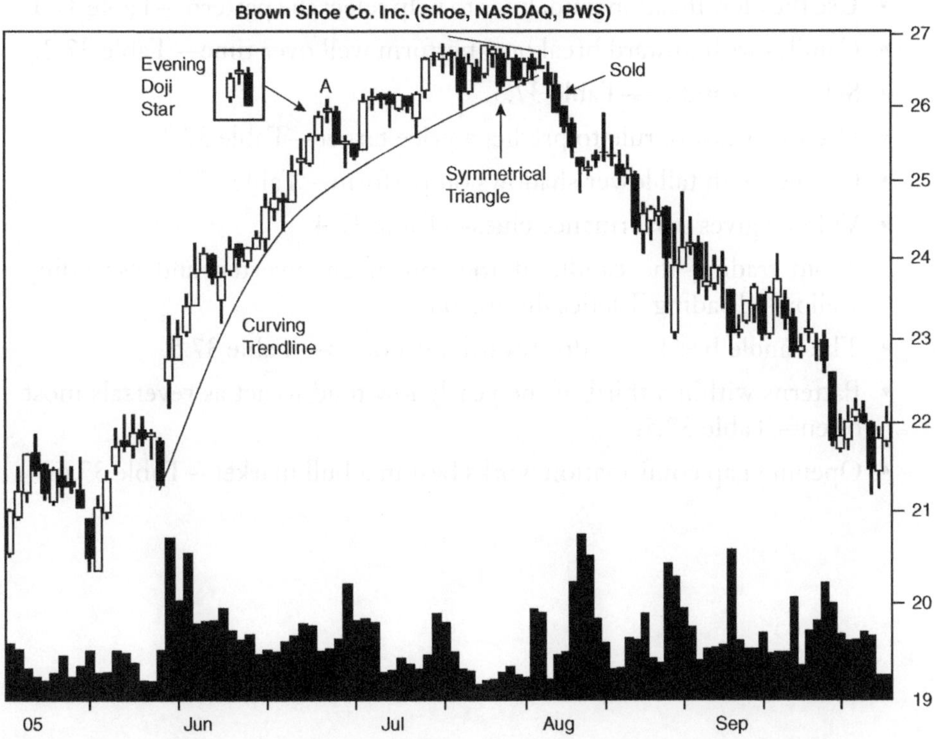

Figure 37.3 Price follows a curving trendline of support.

When he sees the evening doji star form at A, he becomes concerned. How far will price drop? "If it closes below the trendline, then that will be the sell signal," he says. "I'm not married to the stock, so I'm not afraid to sell it." That's good advice. Marriage should be between people, not between you and your stock portfolio.

Price breaks out downward from the evening doji star but the next day forms a tall white candle with price advancing again. Gabe smiles because he guessed properly.

As the lazy summer days ease by, he watches the stock. In late July, he sees the candles becoming shorter, narrowing to a point in a classic symmetrical triangle chart pattern. If the breakout from this pattern is upward, he can relax. A downward breakout, though, means a sale.

Price drops out of the triangle, closing below the curving trendline. That is the sell signal and one Gabe isn't going to miss. He sells the stock and saves himself the pain of watching his profits drop along with the stock.

For Best Performance

The following list offers tips and observations to help choose candles that perform well. Consult the associated table for more information.

- Use the identification guidelines to help select the pattern—Table 37.1.
- Candles with upward breakouts perform well over time—Table 37.2.
- Select tall candles—Table 37.3.
- Use the measure rule to predict a price target—Table 37.3.
- Candles with tall lower shadows outperform—Table 37.3.
- Volume gives performance clues—Table 37.4.
- Avoid trading the candle at the top of an inverted and ascending scallop—Trading Tactics discussion.
- The candle breaks out downward most often—Table 37.5.
- Patterns within a third of the yearly low tend to act as reversals most often—Table 37.5.
- Opening gap confirmation works best in a bull market—Table 37.6.

38

Evening Star

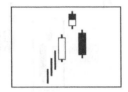

Behavior and Rank

Theoretical: Bearish reversal.
Actual bull market: Bearish reversal 72% of the time (ranking 10).
Actual bear market: Bearish reversal 72% of the time (ranking 11).
Frequency: 71st out of 103.
Overall performance over time: 4th out of 103.

I compared the performance of reversals for the evening star with the evening doji star. My guess was that the evening doji star would perform better. That's not the case. The evening star ranks 10 and 11 for reversals whereas the evening doji star ranks 12 and 15. The overall performance for the evening star is an amazing 4 where 1 is best and 103 is worst.

The evening star candlestick appears with the bulls in control. Their buying demand pushes price upward, forming a tall white candle. The next day, price gaps higher, illustrating the enthusiasm the bulls have for the stock. The hype is short-lived, though, because the candle body remains small—a result of an argument with the bears. The next day price gaps lower and forms a black candle. This confirms that the bears have taken control.

Identification Guidelines

What does an evening star look like? Figure 38.1 shows the answer. This example caps an uptrend and illustrates the change in outlook from bullish to bearish. In the evening star pattern, a white candle suggests a solid move up

Airgas, Inc. (Chemical—Specialty, NYSE, ARG)

Evening
Star

06   Apr   May   Jun

Figure 38.1 An evening star appears at the top of an upward trend and acts as a reversal.

when coupled with the existing upward price trend. The small candle of the second day means indecision as if the bulls are not quite sure what will come next. The final candle seals the fate when price gaps lower and forms a black candle, handing control to the bears.

Table 38.1 lists identification guidelines. Look for a three-candle pattern with the middle candle gapping above the bodies of the adjacent ones. If the middle candle is a doji, then refer to the evening doji star instead of the evening star candlestick. The final day should close well into the body of the

Table 38.1
Identification Guidelines

Characteristic	Discussion
Number of candle lines	Three.
Price trend	Upward leading to the start of the candle pattern.
First day	A tall white candle.
Second day	A small-bodied candle that gaps above the bodies of the adjacent candles. It can be either black or white.
Last day	A tall black candle that gaps below the prior candle and closes at least halfway down the body of the white candle.

white candle (i.e., the first day of the evening star). By that I mean it has to close at or below the middle of the white body. I do not require price to close in the body of the first day, but it has to close at least halfway down the white candlestick's body.

Statistics

Table 38.2 shows general statistics.

Number found. I expected to find more than 903 candle patterns out of the 4.7 million lines that I searched. Prorating the standard database revealed that the candle occurs more often in a bear market.

Reversal or continuation performance. Like many other candle types, the evening star does best in a bear market, regardless of the breakout direction.

S&P performance. The performance of the evening star is much better than the move of the S&P 500 over the same periods.

Candle end to breakout. Downward breakouts take less time to break out because the closing price is nearer to the bottom of the candle than the top.

Table 38.2
General Statistics

Description	Bull Market, Up Breakout	Bear Market, Up Breakout	Bull Market, Down Breakout	Bear Market, Down Breakout
Number found	188	63	491	161
Reversal (R), continuation (C) performance	6.18% C	9.92% C	−6.22% R	−11.63% R
Standard & Poor's 500 change	1.53%	2.05%	−0.54%	−2.44%
Candle end to breakout (median, days)	6	7	3	2
Candle end to trend end (median, days)	10	8	7	6
Number of breakouts near the 12-month low (L), middle (M), or high (H)	L 27, M 31, H 118	L 18, M 19, H 26	L 76, M 121, H 261	L 47, M 60, H 53
Percentage move for each 12-month period	L 8.43%, M 5.44%, H 5.88%	L 13.08%, M 8.77%, H 8.94%	L −5.22%, M −7.69%, H −5.88%	L −11.59%, M −12.97%, H −10.18%
Candle end + 1 day	1.80%	2.99%	−0.57%	−1.80%
Candle end + 3 days	3.38%	5.06%	−1.48%	−3.02%
Candle end + 5 days	4.36%	6.59%	−1.83%	−2.92%
Candle end + 10 days	5.37%	8.77%	−1.57%	−4.34%
10-day performance rank	7	4	78	44

Candle end to trend end. After the candle ends, it takes between 6 and 10 days to reach the trend end. Upward breakouts take longer than downward ones. The reason downward breakouts take less time is that the downtrend is already under way, so price is closer to the trend end.

Yearly position, performance. Most breakouts occur near the yearly high, with the exception being bear market/down breakouts. Those break out most often in the middle of the yearly price range. Upward breakouts show the best performance when they occur within a third of the yearly low. Downward breakouts do best when the breakout is in the middle of the yearly range. Most other candle types show the best performance when the breakout is near the yearly low.

Performance over time. For a candle with such good overall performance the results are not that impressive. Sure, the monster numbers posted in an upward breakout are wonderful, but there's weakness after downward breakouts during days 5 to 10 (bull market) and 3 to 5 (bear market). The 10-day performance is downright terrible for bull market/down breakouts. That's why the category ranks a distant 78 when compared to the other 102 candles (a rank of 1 is best).

Table 38.3 shows height statistics.

Table 38.3
Height Statistics

Description	Bull Market, Up Breakout	Bear Market, Up Breakout	Bull Market, Down Breakout	Bear Market, Down Breakout
Median candle height as a percentage of breakout price	4.81%	6.95%	5.27%	7.54%
Short candle, performance	5.31%	6.93%	−5.51%	−8.20%
Tall candle, performance	7.42%	13.35%	−7.22%	−16.26%
Percentage meeting price target (measure rule)	50%	43%	44%	46%
Median upper shadow as a percentage of breakout price	0.23%	0.37%	0.25%	0.32%
Short upper shadow, performance	6.26%	7.98%	−5.86%	−9.06%
Tall upper shadow, performance	6.09%	12.07%	−6.63%	−14.65%
Median lower shadow as a percentage of breakout price	0.36%	0.77%	0.34%	0.49%
Short lower shadow, performance	4.99%	7.59%	−6.30%	−9.92%
Tall lower shadow, performance	7.54%	12.12%	−6.13%	−13.39%

Candle height. Tall candles perform better than short ones. To determine whether the candle is short or tall, compute its height from highest high to lowest low price in the candle pattern and divide by the breakout price. If the result is higher than the median, then you have a tall candle; otherwise it's short.

Mark is looking at an evening star with a high price of 27 and a low of 25. Is the candle short or tall? The height is $27 - 25$, or 2, so the measure is $2/27$, or 7.4%. After an upward breakout in a bull market, the candle is tall.

Measure rule. Use the measure rule to help predict how far price will rise or fall. Compute the height of the candle pattern and multiply it by the appropriate percentage shown in the table; then apply it to the breakout price.

What are the price targets for Mark's candle? The upward target would be $(2 \times 50\%) + 27$, or 28, and the downward target would be $25 - (2 \times 44\%)$, or 24.12.

Shadows. The table's results pertain to the last candle line in the pattern. To determine whether the shadow is short or tall, compute the height of the shadow and divide by the breakout price. Compare the result to the median in the table. Tall shadows have a percentage higher than the median.

Upper shadow performance. Tall upper shadows work better than short ones in all cases except for bull market/up breakouts.

Lower shadow performance. Tall lower shadows also work well except for bull market/down breakouts.

Table 38.4 shows volume statistics.

Table 38.4
Volume Statistics

Description	Bull Market, Up Breakout	Bear Market, Up Breakout	Bull Market, Down Breakout	Bear Market, Down Breakout
Rising candle volume, performance	6.64%	10.50%*	−6.59%	−13.93%
Falling candle volume, performance	5.90%	9.56%	−5.86%	−9.99%
Above-average candle volume, performance	6.08%	11.43%	−6.65%	−13.54%
Below-average candle volume, performance	6.30%	7.31%*	−5.75%	−9.67%
Heavy breakout volume, performance	6.64%	9.95%	−6.54%	−12.09%
Light breakout volume, performance	5.53%	9.86%*	−5.92%	−11.05%

*Fewer than 30 samples.

    Candle volume trend. Candles with a rising volume trend perform better than do candles with a falling volume trend.

    Average candle volume. Heavy (above-average) candle volume suggests good postbreakout performance in all cases except bull market/up breakout. Those perform better after below-average candle volume.

    Breakout volume. Candles with heavy breakout volume perform better than do those with light volume.

Trading Tactics

Figure 38.2 shows price trending down from the October high. The swift decline planes out in early November and shows a slight upward tilt. Then an evening star appears. The breakout from this pattern is downward, suggesting a resumption of the downward primary trend.

    Consider looking for this type of setup, where an evening star appears in a predominantly downward price trend. Remember, the few days leading to the evening star should trend upward, not downward. Wait for confirmation before taking a position and do other research before shorting a stock.

Figure 38.2 An upward retracement in a downward price trend can lead to a profitable trading opportunity.

Table 38.5
Reversal Rates

Description	Bull Market	Bear Market
Closing price confirmation reversal rate	92%	90%
Candle color confirmation reversal rate	89%	92%
Opening gap confirmation reversal rate	77%	78%
Reversal rate: trend up, breakout down	72%	72%
Continuation rate: trend up, breakout up	28%	28%
Percentage of reversals (R)/ continuations (C) for each 12-month low (L), middle (M), or high (H)	L* 74% R/26% C, M 80% R/20% C, H 69% R/31% C	L* 72% R/28% C, M* 76% R/24% C, H* 67% R/33% C

*Fewer than 30 samples.

I split trading tactics into two basic studies, one concerning reversal rates and the other concerning performance. Of the two, reversal rates are more important, because it's better to trade in the direction of the trend and let price run as far as it can.

Table 38.5 gives tips to find the trend direction.

Confirmation reversal rates. To help confirm a reversal, wait for price to close lower the day after the evening star in bull markets. For bear markets, candle color works best. Trade if a black candle appears the day after the evening star completes.

Reversal, continuation rates. The breakout is downward 72% of the time.

Yearly range reversals. Sorting where reversals and continuations appear, we find that most reversals occur in the middle third of the yearly trading range. Compared to other candle types, that is an unusual result (typically, anywhere but the middle third does well), probably due to the low sample counts.

Table 38.6 shows performance indicators that can give hints as to how your stock will behave after the breakout from a candle pattern.

Confirmation, performance. The opening gap method works best. That's when you short the stock based on price gapping lower at the open.

Moving average. Candles with breakouts above the 50-day moving average work better for bull market/up breakouts and bear market/down breakouts. Candles in the other two categories—bear market/up breakout and bull market/down breakout—do better if the breakout is below the moving average.

Closing position. A close in the middle third of the last candle line in the evening star means better performance if the breakout is upward. Candles with downward breakouts do better if the close is in the lowest third of the candle line.

Table 38.6
Performance Indicators

Description	Bull Market, Up Breakout	Bear Market, Up Breakout	Bull Market, Down Breakout	Bear Market, Down Breakout
Closing price confirmation, performance	N/A	N/A	−6.28%	−12.20%
Candle color confirmation, performance	N/A	N/A	−6.13%	−12.64%
Opening gap confirmation, performance	N/A	N/A	−7.30%	−12.68%
Breakout above 50-day moving average, performance	6.17%	9.83%	−6.08%	−12.08%
Breakout below 50-day moving average, performance	5.33%*	10.27%*	−6.50%	−10.98%
Last candle: close in highest third, performance	0.00%*	0.00%*	−1.41%*	0.00%*
Last candle: close in middle third, performance	8.14%*	14.75%*	−4.35%	−9.74%*
Last candle: close in lowest third, performance	5.92%	8.25%	−6.43%	−11.78%

N/A means not applicable.
*Fewer than 30 samples.

Sample Trade

Mark decides in June to short the stock shown in Figure 38.3. Why? Price made a new high in late April, but the stock had been easing upward slightly for about six weeks, almost becoming a flat base. The breakout from this consolidation region was a sharp move downward that ended in a very tall black candle (AB). The candle pierced a region of support that formed in February. The support zone, once pierced, became overhead resistance, and I show that as a horizontal line.

Since the AB candle is tall, Mark expects price to climb but reverse somewhere up the candle's body. That happens at the peak between the lows at B and C. When price climbs again after C and forms an evening star right at overhead resistance, he believes that price will drop from there.

He draws a trendline connecting the valleys at B and C and extends the down-sloping trendline into the future. If price drops to the trendline, it should stop near 24 at the time, or even lower as time passes. He decides to short the stock if price closes below the bottom of the evening star. Two days after the candle is completed, price hits his order and fills.

As price drops, he follows the stock closely day after day, and is pleased to see that it sinks through his 24 target price without flinching. When a series of small candles appears in June, he figures that a move up is more likely than a continued decline, so he closes out his position.

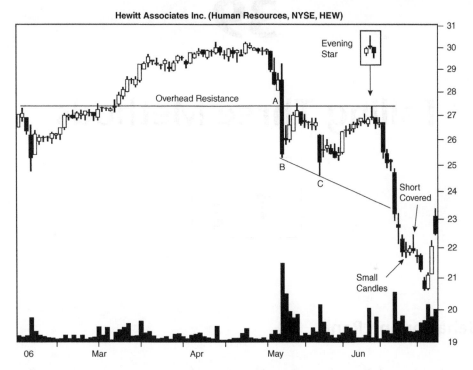

Figure 38.3 Overhead resistance stops the short-term move up, and an evening star announces a resumption of the downtrend.

For Best Performance

The following list offers tips and observations to help choose candles that perform well. Consult the associated table for more information.

- Use the identification guidelines to help select the pattern—Table 38.1.
- Candles within a third of the yearly low perform best in a bull market—Table 38.2.
- Select tall candles—Table 38.3.
- Use the measure rule to predict a price target—Table 38.3.
- Volume gives performance clues—Table 38.4.
- Search for an upward retracement in a primary downtrend—Trading Tactics discussion.
- The candle breaks out downward most often—Table 38.5.
- Patterns within the middle third of the yearly price range tend to act as reversals most often—Table 38.5.
- Opening gap confirmation works best—Table 38.6.

39

Falling Three Methods

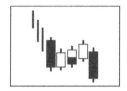

Behavior and Rank

Theoretical: Bearish continuation.

Actual bull market: Bearish continuation 71% of the time (ranking 7).

Actual bear market: Bearish continuation 67% of the time (ranking 15).

Frequency: 91st out of 103.

Overall performance over time: 89th out of 103.

The falling three methods is a complicated and rare pattern. Because of its scarcity, some take liberties with the number of candle lines composing the pattern. I do not. In researching this candle pattern, I discovered that it represents a support or resistance zone that can project days or weeks into the future. On the slim chance that you may find this pattern in one of your stocks, it predicts a continuation of the downtrend and also sets up overhead resistance. Since this pattern is so rare (I found just 64 examples), I exclude the Statistics section.

The psychology behind this pattern begins with a downward price trend leading to the candle. The bears have control of the ball and push price toward the goal with a tall black candle printing on the chart. Then the bulls fight back in a series of three small candles, the middle of which can be either black or white, and the three trend upward—not far, but price does ease somewhat higher. As bear reinforcements join the fray from the sidelines, another tall black candle completes the pattern and down price goes.

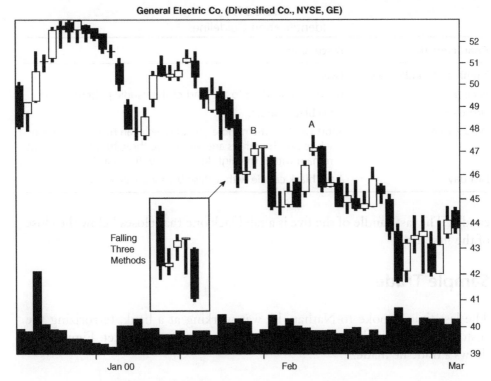

General Electric Co. (Diversified Co., NYSE, GE)

Figure 39.1 A falling three methods candle formation appears in a downtrend, with point A finding overhead resistance set up by the candle pattern at B.

Identification Guidelines

Figure 39.1 shows a falling three methods candle pattern. Price trends downward into the candlestick and then hesitates by forming three small candles that trend upward against the prevailing downtrend. It reminds me of salmon swimming upstream at spawning time. The last candle in the series of five resumes the downtrend.

A larger version of the falling three methods is a chart pattern called a measured move down. The three small candles represent the corrective phase. A downtrending price often turns up to the corrective phase and then turns lower. It's gratifying that the performance of the larger chart pattern translates so well onto the smaller scale. Here, too, price retraces (A) to the site of the corrective phase, B, and then reverses.

The falling three methods is a complicated candle pattern, and Table 39.1 lists the identification guidelines. The candle appears in a downward price trend and the first line is a tall black candle. Following that, three smaller candles appear, the middle of which can be any color but the others are white. All three trend upward but remain within the trading (high-low) range of the first

Table 39.1
Identification Guidelines

Characteristic	Discussion
Number of candle lines	Five.
Price trend	Downward leading to the start of the candle pattern.
First day	A tall black candle.
Days 2 to 4	Short candles, the middle one of which can be either black or white but the others are white. The three trend upward but remain within the high-low range of the first day.
Last day	A tall black candle with a close below the first day's close.

candle. The last candle of the five is a tall black one that closes below the close of the first day.

Sample Trade

The last time I spoke to Nathan, he was working at a bank, terrorizing the customers. Now, he has turned his attention to the stock market. Figure 39.2 shows a trade he made.

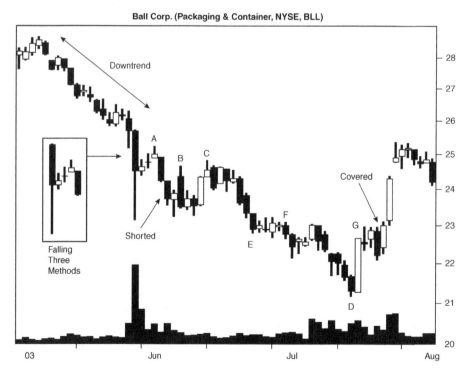

Figure 39.2   Price finds overhead resistance at B and C set up by the falling three methods candle pattern.

Price trended lower in May and formed a long black candle that became the first line in a falling three methods pattern. The next three small days remained within the body of the first candle, and the final candle in the pattern posted a close below the first day's close. The candlestick was an example of a continuation pattern, or so Nathan hoped.

The day after the falling three methods completed, price trended lower so he shorted the stock. When price returned (B) to the price level of the small three candles within the falling three methods (A), he wasn't worried. It happened again at C before price finally turned lower and started trending.

He followed the stock closely and recognized a measured move down chart pattern (CD) with a mild corrective phase (EF). In that chart pattern, price often returns to the corrective phase before moving lower.

When the tall candle appeared at G, he regretted not taking profits but was not convinced the downtrend was over. However, when price moved above the three-day flat top to the right of G, he closed out his short position. He made about a dollar a share.

40

Hammer

Behavior and Rank

Theoretical: Bullish reversal.

Actual bull market: Bullish reversal 60% of the time (ranking 26).

Actual bear market: Bullish reversal 59% of the time (ranking 29).

Frequency: 36th out of 103.

Overall performance over time: 65th out of 103.

The hammer is a popular candlestick if only for its name. The single candle line appears in a downtrend with a small body and long lower shadow. During the trading day, the bears force price much lower, but by day's end, the bulls have managed a recovery by pushing price back up.

Since the hammer acts as a reversal of the downtrend, you would expect a white hammer to be more bullish and result in better performance than a black one. It does, as we will see. Speaking of performance, a ranking of 26 (bull market) as a bullish reversal is very good. The pattern is plentiful, but the overall performance rank is 65. That is disappointing since 1 is best out of 103 candles. It means the pattern is on the far side of "good" when compared to other candles for performance over 10 days.

Identification Guidelines

Figure 40.1 shows a black hammer that appears after a swift downtrend. A white candle precedes this hammer and that's the first indication that the bears are growing tired. The long lower shadow on the hammer means the bulls have

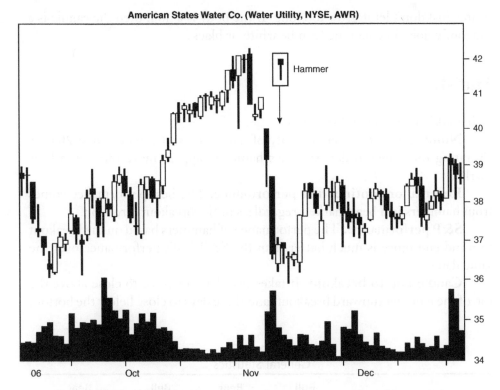

Figure 40.1 A hammer acts as a reversal after a severe downtrend.

pushed back another down day to close near the day's high, but price still closes lower than on the prior day. The next two days extend the confusion as small bodies and long lower shadows suggest a base upon which to launch a new attempt higher. That happens on the third day after the hammer when a tall white candle pushes price upward. That begins the new trend from downward to sideways with a slight upward bias.

The hammer shown in Figure 40.1 conforms to the identification guidelines listed in Table 40.1. A hammer has a lower shadow that is between two and three times the body height, but no longer. A small nubbin of upper shadow

Table 40.1
Identification Guidelines

Characteristic	Discussion
Number of candle lines	One.
Price trend	Downward leading to the candle pattern.
Configuration	Has a lower shadow between two and three times the height of a small body and little or no upper shadow. Body color is unimportant.

is fine; just don't let it grow too long. If the body is a doji, then the candle is a dragonfly doji. The hammer can be white or black.

Statistics

Table 40.2 shows general statistics.

Number found. I found plenty of hammers, so I used the first 20,000. Prorating the standard database says hammers appear more often in a bear market.

Reversal or continuation performance. The best performance comes from hammers in a bear market, regardless of the breakout direction.

S&P performance. The performance of hammers based on the breakout to trend end move is much better than the S&P 500's performance over the same dates.

Candle end to breakout. It takes two days for price to close above the top of the hammer (upward breakout) and three days to close below the bottom

Table 40.2
General Statistics

Description	Bull Market, Up Breakout	Bear Market, Up Breakout	Bull Market, Down Breakout	Bear Market, Down Breakout
Number found	10,115	1,936	6,606	1,343
Reversal (R), continuation (C) performance	7.51% R	9.44% R	−6.10% C	−9.69% C
Standard & Poor's 500 change	1.53%	0.75%	−0.83%	−2.41%
Candle end to breakout (median, days)	2	2	3	3
Candle end to trend end (median, days)	8	8	6	7
Number of breakouts near the 12-month low (L), middle (M), or high (H)	L 2,500, M 2,882, H 3,854	L 649, M 655, H 619	L 2,020, M 1,941, H 2,064	L 583, M 450, H 305
Percentage move for each 12-month period	L 8.89%, M 7.14%, H 6.96%	L 12.12%, M 9.04%, H 7.91%	L −6.81%, M −6.07%, H −5.46%	L −11.34%, M −9.42%, H −7.76%
Candle end + 1 day	0.97%	1.32%	−1.50%	−2.38%
Candle end + 3 days	1.83%	2.15%	−2.45%	−3.67%
Candle end + 5 days	2.11%	2.22%	−2.57%	−3.92%
Candle end + 10 days	2.29%	2.12%	−2.25%	−4.12%
10-day performance rank	76	70	53	48

(downward breakout). Downward breakouts take a day longer because price has to move nearly the height of the candle to break out.

Candle end to trend end. The candle end to the trend end takes between six and eight days. Downward breakouts take less time to reach the trend end probably because the downward trend is already well underway.

Yearly position, performance. Hammers within a third of the yearly low perform better than hammers in the other ranges.

Performance over time. In half of the categories, performance suffers from day 5 to 10. The performance after 10 days is not impressive, either, resulting in poor performance rankings. Good performance would show a percentage change of 6% or more after 10 days.

Table 40.3 shows height statistics.

Candle height. Tall candles outperform short ones. To determine whether the candle is short or tall, compute its height from high to low price in the candle and divide by the breakout price. If the result is higher than the median, then you have a tall candle; otherwise it's short.

Phillip likes hammers—wooden, steel, and candle types. Is his candle short or tall if the hammer has a high at 39 and a low at 38? The height is 39 − 38, or 1, so the measure is 1/39, or 2.6%. That represents a tall candle (assume bull market/up breakout).

Measure rule. Use the measure rule to help predict how far price will rise or fall. Compute the height of the candle and multiply it by the appropriate percentage shown in the table; then apply it to the breakout price.

What are the price targets for Phillip's candle? The upward target would be 39 + (1 × 88%), or 39.88, and the downward target would be 38 − (1 × 82%), or 37.18.

Table 40.3
Height Statistics

Description	Bull Market, Up Breakout	Bear Market, Up Breakout	Bull Market, Down Breakout	Bear Market, Down Breakout
Median candle height as a percentage of breakout price	1.99%	2.81%	1.96%	2.84%
Short candle, performance	5.84%	7.52%	−5.09%	−8.01%
Tall candle, performance	9.94%	11.92%	−7.60%	−12.00%
Percentage meeting price target (measure rule)	88%	85%	82%	84%
Median lower shadow as a percentage of breakout price	1.38%	1.93%	1.35%	1.97%
Short lower shadow, performance	5.88%	7.51%	−5.09%	−8.03%
Tall lower shadow, performance	9.88%	11.97%	−7.62%	−11.93%

Table 40.4
Volume Statistics

Description	Bull Market, Up Breakout	Bear Market, Up Breakout	Bull Market, Down Breakout	Bear Market, Down Breakout
Above-average candle volume, performance	7.83%	9.77%	−6.02%	−9.94%
Below-average candle volume, performance	7.33%	9.24%	−6.14%	−9.54%
Heavy breakout volume, performance	8.18%	10.01%	−6.44%	−10.94%
Light breakout volume, performance	7.02%	9.05%	−5.86%	−8.62%

Shadows. To determine whether the shadow is short or tall, compute the height of the shadow and divide by the breakout price. Compare the result to the median in the table. Tall shadows have a percentage higher than the median. Candles with tall lower shadows perform better than do those with short shadows.

Table 40.4 shows volume statistics.

Average candle volume. Heavy (above-average) candle volume suggests better postbreakout performance in all categories except bull market/down breakouts. Those do better after light candle volume.

Breakout volume. Heavy breakout volume means better performance across the board.

Trading Tactics

The best-performing hammers are those that occur during a downward retracement of the primary (longer-term) upward trend. Those that occur in a primary downtrend tend to have price rise for a few days but that's it—price tumbles thereafter.

I split trading tactics into two basic studies, one concerning reversal rates and the other concerning performance. Of the two, reversal rates are more important, because it's better to trade in the direction of the trend and let price run as far as it can.

Table 40.5 gives tips to find the trend direction.

Confirmation reversal rates. To help detect a reversal, wait for price to close higher the day after the hammer. That means a reversal will occur over 90% of the time. That may be misleading because a reversal occurs when price closes above the top of the pattern. Waiting for a higher close just might guarantee that, but it says nothing about how long the reversal will last.

Table 40.5
Reversal Rates

Description	Bull Market	Bear Market
Closing price confirmation reversal rate	93%	92%
Candle color confirmation reversal rate	88%	88%
Opening gap confirmation reversal rate	73%	70%
Reversal: trend down, breakout up	60%	59%
Continuation: trend down, breakout down	40%	41%
Percentage of reversals (R)/ continuations (C) for each 12-month low (L), middle (M), or high (H)	L 55% R/45% C, M 60% R/40% C, H 65% R/35% C	L 53% R/47% C, M 59% R/41% C, H 67% R/33% C
Black body reversal rate	57%	56%
White body reversal rate	67%	64%

Reversal, continuation rates. Hammers break out upward more often, but the numbers seem too close to random (50%).

Yearly range reversals. Hammers within a third of the yearly high reverse most often.

Body color reversal rate. White-bodied hammers act as reversals more often than black ones.

Table 40.6 shows performance indicators that can give hints as to how your stock will behave after the breakout from a candle pattern.

Confirmation, performance. Opening gap confirmation results in the best performance. Trade only if price gaps open higher the day after the hammer.

Moving average. Candles with breakouts below the 50-trading-day moving average result in better performance than do those with breakouts above it.

Closing position. Candles with price closing in the middle of the hammer result in the best performance.

Body color performance. White candles perform better than black ones in all cases except for bear market/up breakouts.

Sample Trade

Phillip likes the company whose stock appears in Figure 40.2. The stock has been following a trendline connecting the lows at A and B. When he sees the black hammer the day before C, he takes a keen interest. Why?

Price is nearing the trendline extended upward from B to C. Even though the top of the candle has a small upper shadow and one could argue that the downtrend leading to it wasn't robust, he feels it still qualifies as a hammer.

Table 40.6
Performance Indicators

Description	Bull Market, Up Breakout	Bear Market, Up Breakout	Bull Market, Down Breakout	Bear Market, Down Breakout
Closing price confirmation, performance	6.25%	7.93%	N/A	N/A
Candle color confirmation, performance	6.34%	8.29%	N/A	N/A
Opening gap confirmation, performance	7.24%	9.55%	N/A	N/A
Breakout above 50-day moving average, performance	7.13%	8.09%	−5.49%	−7.77%
Breakout below 50-day moving average, performance	7.84%	10.46%	−6.39%	−10.49%
Last candle: close in highest third, performance	7.50%	9.41%	−6.07%	−9.41%
Last candle: close in middle third, performance	7.54%	9.55%	−6.21%	−10.74%
Last candle: close in lowest third, performance	0.00%	0.00%	0.00%	0.00%
Black body, performance	7.41%	9.66%	−6.06%	−9.61%
White body, performance	7.65%	9.06%	−6.20%	−9.87%

N/A means not applicable.

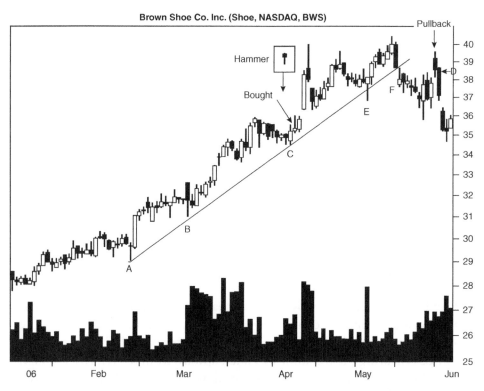

Figure 40.2 Phillip buys the stock after it bounces off support.

After the hammer, he waits for the next close to determine the breakout direction. A white candle closes above the top of the hammer at C, indicating that price is staging an upward breakout. He buys the stock at the open the next day, receiving a fill at 35.22.

Phillip watches the stock gap upward two days later, retrace to the bottom of the tall white candle, and then continue moving up. At E, price forms a bullish engulfing pattern with a lower shadow that pierces the trendline. But since it doesn't close below the line, he isn't worried.

At F, price *does* close below the trendline, but Phillip is paralyzed and takes no action. Day by day price moves lower until a turn comes. Price attempts to pull back to the trendline and almost makes it. The next day, D, he decides to sell and receives a fill at the opening price of 38.65. He has made almost 10% on the trade.

For Best Performance

The following list offers tips and observations to help choose candles that perform well. Consult the associated table for more information.

- Use the identification guidelines to help select the pattern—Table 40.1.
- Candles within a third of the yearly low perform best—Table 40.2.
- Select tall candles—Table 40.3.
- Use the measure rule to predict a price target—Table 40.3.
- Candles with tall lower shadows outperform—Table 40.3.
- Volume gives performance clues—Table 40.4.
- Trade hammers only as part of a downward retracement of the primary uptrend—Trading Tactics discussion.
- The candle breaks out upward most often—Table 40.5.
- Patterns within a third of the yearly high tend to act as reversals most often—Table 40.5.
- Trade white hammers—Table 40.5.
- Opening gap confirmation works best—Table 40.6.
- Breakouts below the 50-day moving average lead to the best performance—Table 40.6.

41

Hammer, Inverted

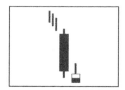

Behavior and Rank

Theoretical: Bullish reversal.

Actual bull market: Bearish continuation 65% of the time (ranking 13).

Actual bear market: Bearish continuation 67% of the time (ranking 13).

Frequency: 61st out of 103.

Overall performance over time: 6th out of 103.

The first surprise with the inverted hammer is that it acts as a continuation more often than a reversal, despite convention saying otherwise. The second surprise is that sources I checked on this pattern cannot decide what the configuration is. One source says, "The upper shadow should be at least two times the length of the body," while another says, "Upper shadow [is] usually no more than twice as long as the real body." Of the six independent sources I checked, three said the shadow should be shorter than twice the body and three said it should be longer. No wonder candlesticks are subject to interpretation; few can agree on what they should look like.

When I thought of an inverted hammer, I guessed that it was a single candle line, a hammer candle flipped upside down. It's not, according to numerous sources I checked, but some suggest it's a single candle line. I tested the two-line variety. The candle pattern begins in a downtrend. The bears form a tall black candle followed by a small body with a long upper shadow. It appears near the low of the black candle. The small body suggests indecision, but the tall upper shadow means a bearish downward thrust. With price continuing lower two-thirds of the time, the markets seem to agree with my assessment.

The overall performance rank of the candle pattern is 6 out of 103 candles where 1 is best. Thus, this is one of the best-performing candles. Even such strong performance has its peculiarities, though. The inverted hammer performs better after an upward breakout, not a downward one.

Identification Guidelines

Figure 41.1 shows an inverted hammer, but one that appears at the end of a congestion area, so it's not a classic example. The candle pattern occurs in early December as a two-line pattern when price tries to pull out of a sharp dive. Price does for a few days but the downtrend resumes.

After over a decade of analyzing and searching for chart patterns, my eyes are pulled to the diamond bottom that precedes the inverted hammer. It's a small one and thus not powerful. Price eases downward out of the pattern, suggesting the downtrend will continue. That's what happens and the inverted hammer confirms it, too.

What are the identification guidelines for this pattern? Table 41.1 lists them. The candlestick is a two-line candle with the first being a tall black

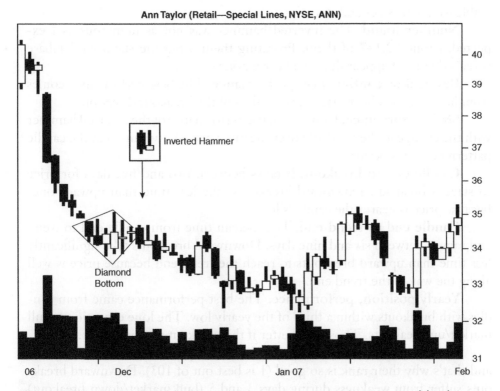

Figure 41.1 An inverted hammer appears in a congestion area and leads to a continuation of the downtrend.

Table 41.1
Identification Guidelines

Characteristic	Discussion
Number of candle lines	Two.
Price trend	Downward leading to the candle pattern.
First day	A tall black candle with a close near the low of the day.
Second day	A small-bodied candle with a tall upper shadow and little or no lower shadow. Body cannot be a doji (otherwise it's a gravestone doji). The open must be below the prior day's close. Candle color is unimportant.

candle that closes near its low. The second day is a small-bodied candle that opens below the prior close and has a tall upper shadow. I did not place any limit on shadow length. If it has a lower shadow, it's small in comparison to the entire candle length.

Statistics

Table 41.2 shows general statistics.

Number found. The inverted hammer was not as numerous as I expected. I found 2,147 of them. Prorating them using the standard database reveals that most appear during a bear market.

Reversal or continuation performance. The best performance comes from hammers in a bear market, regardless of the breakout direction.

S&P performance. Comparing the performance of the inverted hammer with the change in the S&P 500 over the same periods, we find that the candle pattern performs better.

Candle end to breakout. It takes between two and five days for price to stage a breakout. Downward breakouts take less time than upward ones because price is nearer the candle's low.

Candle end to trend end. The median time from candle end to trend end ranges between six and nine days. Downward breakouts take significantly less time than upward breakouts to reach the trend end because price is well along the way to the trend end.

Yearly position, performance. The best performance came from candles with breakouts within a third of the yearly low. The lone exception is bull market/up breakouts. Those did better if the breakout was midrange.

Performance over time. Upward breakouts post monster rises over time and that's why their rank is so good (1 is best out of 103). Downward breakouts suffer from weakness during days 3 and 5 (bull market/down breakout) and their percentage changes over time are weak. Their rankings suffer as a result.

Table 41.2
General Statistics

Description	Bull Market, Up Breakout	Bear Market, Up Breakout	Bull Market, Down Breakout	Bear Market, Down Breakout
Number found	587	152	1,097	311
Reversal (R), continuation (C) performance	6.77% R	10.12% R	−5.91% C	−11.51% C
Standard & Poor's 500 change	2.18%	2.32%	−0.53%	−1.98%
Candle end to breakout (median, days)	5	4	3	2
Candle end to trend end (median, days)	9	8	6	6
Number of breakouts near the 12-month low (L), middle (M), or high (H)	L 127, M 188, H 230	L 59, M 49, H 39	L 350, M 372, H 290	L 155, M 107, H 45
Percentage move for each 12-month period	L 8.45%, M 8.59%, H 5.85%	L 12.25%, M 9.79%, H 7.86%	L −7.47%, M −5.87%, H −4.76%	L −13.62%, M −8.65%, H −3.04%
Candle end + 1 day	1.73%	3.87%	−0.50%	−1.17%
Candle end + 3 days	3.37%	5.60%	−1.01%	−1.93%
Candle end + 5 days	4.31%	7.60%	−0.81%	−2.66%
Candle end + 10 days	5.03%	7.74%	−1.00%	−3.40%
10-day performance rank	10	9	96	63

Table 41.3 shows height statistics.

Candle height. Tall inverted hammers pound the dickens out of the short ones in terms of performance. To determine whether the candle is short or tall, compute its height from highest high to lowest low price in the candle pattern and divide by the breakout price. If the result is higher than the median, then you have a tall candle; otherwise it's short.

Stone saw an inverted hammer with a high of 69 and a low of 67. Is his candle short or tall? The height is 69 − 67, or 2, so the measure is 2/69, or 2.9%. In a bull market with an upward breakout, the candle is short.

Measure rule. Use the measure rule to help predict how far price will rise or fall. Compute the height of the candle pattern and multiply it by the appropriate percentage shown in the table; then apply it to the breakout price.

What are the price targets for Stone's candle? The upward target is 69 + (2 × 68%), or 70.36, and the downward target is 67 − (2 × 57%), or 65.86.

Upper shadow performance. To determine whether the shadow is short or tall, compute the height of the shadow and divide by the breakout price.

Table 41.3
Height Statistics

Description	Bull Market, Up Breakout	Bear Market, Up Breakout	Bull Market, Down Breakout	Bear Market, Down Breakout
Median candle height as a percentage of breakout price	3.52%	5.37%	3.76%	5.72%
Short candle, performance	5.38%	8.64%	−4.42%	−8.39%
Tall candle, performance	8.82%	11.40%	−8.20%	−15.30%
Percentage meeting price target (measure rule)	68%	65%	57%	61%
Median upper shadow as a percentage of breakout price	1.40%	2.28%	1.45%	2.32%
Short upper shadow, performance	5.51%	10.13%	−4.82%	−8.47%
Tall upper shadow, performance	8.48%	10.11%	−7.37%	−15.00%

Compare the result to the median in the table. Tall shadows have a percentage higher than the median.

Candles with tall upper shadows perform better than do those with short ones in all cases except for bear market/up breakouts, but even there the numbers are close.

Table 41.4 shows volume statistics.

Candle volume trend. Candles with rising volume work better than do those with falling volume.

Table 41.4
Volume Statistics

Description	Bull Market, Up Breakout	Bear Market, Up Breakout	Bull Market, Down Breakout	Bear Market, Down Breakout
Rising candle volume, performance	6.85%	11.32%	−6.14%	−11.76%
Falling candle volume, performance	6.70%	9.12%	−5.72%	−11.26%
Above-average candle volume, performance	6.80%	10.66%	−5.30%	−11.26%
Below-average candle volume, performance	6.76%	9.46%	−6.41%	−11.79%
Heavy breakout volume, performance	7.45%	11.67%	−6.20%	−11.46%
Light breakout volume, performance	6.12%	8.43%	−5.64%	−11.59%

Average candle volume. Candles with upward breakouts and above-average candle volume perform better than do those with below-average volume. Downward breakouts show the reverse, with below-average volume performing better.

Breakout volume. Heavy breakout volume works best in all cases except for bear market/down breakouts.

Trading Tactics

For the best performance from this candle, trade it only in a downward retracement of the primary uptrend. Price breaks out upward from the candle pattern, and the existing current pulls price along to higher ground. You want to avoid depending on this candle acting as a reversal of the primary downtrend, because there the chances are that price will move up but not for long.

I split trading tactics into two basic studies, one concerning reversal rates and the other concerning performance. Of the two, reversal rates are more important, because it's better to trade in the direction of the trend and let price run as far as it can.

Table 41.5 gives tips to find the trend direction.

Confirmation reversal rates. Waiting for price to close higher after the candle ends confirms a reversal just 57% of the time in a bull market. That's fairly close to random (50%).

Reversal, continuation rates. Based on the breakout direction, where price closes above the top of the candle pattern or below the bottom, we see that the pattern acts as a continuation about two-thirds of the time. The numbers tell you how often you'll be stopped out if you place a stop at either end of the candle pattern. The candle breaks out downward more often.

Yearly range reversals. Continuations occur frequently when the breakout price is within a third of the yearly low.

Table 41.5
Reversal Rates

Description	Bull Market	Bear Market
Closing price confirmation reversal rate	57%	55%
Candle color confirmation reversal rate	56%	54%
Opening gap confirmation reversal rate	42%	43%
Reversal: trend down, breakout up	35%	33%
Continuation: trend down, breakout down	65%	67%
Percentage of reversals (R)/ continuations (C) for each 12-month low (L), middle (M), or high (H)	L 27% R/73% C, M 34% R/66% C, H 44% R/56% C	L 28% R/72% C, M 31% R/69% C, H 46% R/54% C

Table 41.6
Performance Indicators

Description	Bull Market, Up Breakout	Bear Market, Up Breakout	Bull Market, Down Breakout	Bear Market, Down Breakout
Closing price confirmation, performance	7.22%	12.55%	N/A	N/A
Candle color confirmation, performance	7.36%	11.80%	N/A	N/A
Opening gap confirmation, performance	7.38%	13.02%	N/A	N/A
Breakout above 50-day moving average, performance	6.10%	10.14%	−5.49%	−9.13%
Breakout below 50-day moving average, performance	7.39%	9.99%	−6.06%	−12.00%
Last candle: close in highest third, performance	0.00%	0.00%	0.00%	0.00%
Last candle: close in middle third, performance	7.41%	11.83%	−6.95%	−10.56%
Last candle: close in lowest third, performance	6.59%	9.54%	−5.67%	−11.71%

N/A means not applicable.

Table 41.6 shows performance indicators that can give hints as to how your stock will behave after the breakout from a candle pattern.

Confirmation, performance. The opening gap confirmation method works best in both markets. That's where you buy the stock if price gaps open higher the day after the candle ends.

Moving average. Candles with breakouts below the 50-trading-day moving average perform better than do those above the moving average. This applies to all categories except for bear market/up breakouts.

Closing position. Use the close in the last candle line of the inverted hammer. Candles with price closing in the middle of the candle outperform those closing in the other two ranges except for bear market/down breakouts. Those do better when the candle closes near its low. None showed closes near the high.

Sample Trade

Stone recognizes the inverted hammer shown in Figure 41.2. Since price is likely to continue moving down according to the statistics, he searches for underlying support. A solid horizontal line beneath some of the bottoms suggests that the area might be a good buying opportunity. If price reverses, he would be buying near the turning point with the target a few dollars higher (about 23, near the peaks).

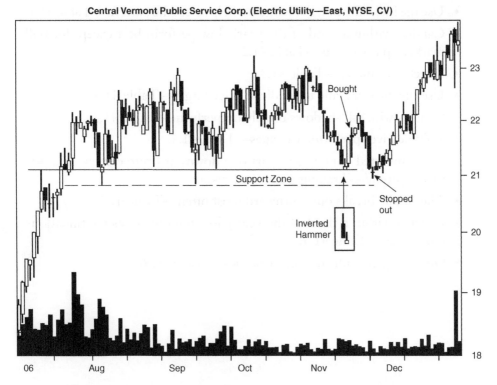

Figure 41.2 An inverted hammer appears at a support zone.

With this in mind, he waits for the closing price to determine the trade direction. The next day, price makes a tall white candle that closes above the top of the hammer, staging an upward breakout. That means go long. At the open the next day, Stone buys the stock and receives a fill at 21.73.

For safety, he places a stop a penny below the inverted hammer's low, at 21.09. "The solid horizontal trendline represents a support zone, so if price drops below that, then the chances increase that price is going down," he says.

In this case, however, price curled around and dropped through his stop price, taking him out of the trade. Then the stock reversed and made a straight-line run upward after that.

"In retrospect, I should have used the dashed line as a support area and placed a stop below that," Stone says. In that scenario, he might have waited to place the trade and perhaps bought in at the bullish doji star instead of being stopped out there.

For Best Performance

The following list offers tips and observations to help choose candles that perform well. Consult the associated table for more information.

- Use the identification guidelines to help select the pattern—Table 41.1.
- Candles within a third of the yearly low perform best except for bull market/up breakouts—Table 41.2.
- Select tall candles—Table 41.3.
- Use the measure rule to predict a price target—Table 41.3.
- Candles with tall shadows usually outperform—Table 41.3.
- Volume gives performance clues—Table 41.4.
- Select inverted hammers as part of a downward retracement in a primary uptrend—Trading Tactics discussion.
- The candle breaks out downward most often—Table 41.5.
- Patterns within a third of the yearly low tend to act as continuations most often—Table 41.5.
- Opening gap confirmation works best—Table 41.6.

42

Hanging Man

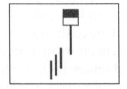

Behavior and Rank

Theoretical: Bearish reversal.

Actual bull market: Bullish continuation 59% of the time (ranking 23).

Actual bear market: Bullish continuation 59% of the time (ranking 23).

Frequency: 16th out of 103.

Overall performance over time: 87th out of 103.

The hanging man is a widely known candlestick that is supposed to act as a reversal of the uptrend, but guess what? It doesn't 59% of the time. Of course, that's not far above random (50%) behavior. The overall performance is a lousy 87 out of 103 candles where 1 is best, so this one is well down the list. Downward breakouts (reversals) show a better performance rank than upward breakouts, as we will see in the Statistics section. The performance-over-time numbers are lackluster, so regardless of what direction price breaks out, it tends not to move far before reaching the trend end (the first minor high or low that comes along).

As to the psychology behind the candle, the bulls have control during the push up to the hanging man. Price opens at or near the day's high, but during the trading session, selling pressure forces price lower. At day's end, though, the bulls have managed to recover their losses and price is again close to the high, forming a small-bodied candle with a long lower shadow.

To my way of thinking, a long lower shadow means the bulls have burned off the selling pressure and price is likely to rise. That's not the conventional wisdom, though, which says that traders have many long positions and are dying to take profits, and any selling the next day will begin a downward slide. If traders are dying to take profits, maybe that's why they call it a hanging man (that's a pun, of course).

Identification Guidelines

Figure 42.1 shows an example of a hanging man. Price trends upward in a straight-line run from the December low, and along the way price gaps higher. Then the hanging man appears. One could argue that the gap upward is the last attempt at the summit, and inclement weather in the form of selling pressure the next day would push the climbers back down to base camp. Of course, that doesn't happen. Price gaps open lower, confirming the hanging man as a reversal, and price trends well below the close but ends near where it began, creating what looks to be a doji but is really a high wave candle. In the next few days, price moves *up* instead of down. In this example, the hanging man acts as a continuation and not a reversal, despite the lower open the next day. Have we identified the candle properly?

Table 42.1 lists identification guidelines. This is a simple candle. Look

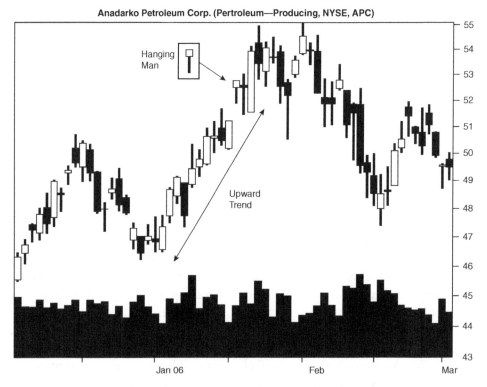

Figure 42.1 A hanging man in an uptrend fails to reverse.

Table 42.1
Identification Guidelines

Characteristic	Discussion
Number of candle lines	One.
Price trend	Upward leading to the start of the hanging man.
First day	Price opens at or near the high, forms a long lower shadow, and closes near, but not at, the high. A small body remains, either white or black, near the top of the trading range with a long lower shadow.

for a small body at or near the high with a long lower shadow. The candle can be any color, and if it has an upper shadow, it should be small relative to the height of the candle line.

Statistics

Table 42.2 shows general statistics.

Table 42.2
General Statistics

Description	Bull Market, Up Breakout	Bear Market, Up Breakout	Bull Market, Down Breakout	Bear Market, Down Breakout
Number found	8,367	3,440	5,805	2,388
Reversal (R), continuation (C) performance	6.31% C	6.92% C	−6.10% R	−8.68% R
Standard & Poor's 500 change	1.25%	0.53%	−1.19%	−2.49%
Candle end to breakout (median, days)	2	2	2	2
Candle end to trend end (median, days)	7	6	8	8
Number of breakouts near the 12-month low (L), middle (M), or high (H)	L 1,036, M 1,940, H 5,391	L 623, M 1,103, H 1,714	L 860, M 1,438, H 3,507	L 566, M 703, H 1,119
Percentage move for each 12-month period	L 7.67%, M 6.16%, H 6.16%	L 9.44%, M 7.15%, H 6.07%	L −6.97%, M −5.95%, H −6.00%	L −10.85%, M −8.02%, H −8.22%
Candle end + 1 day	0.84%	1.01%	−1.48%	−2.02%
Candle end + 3 days	1.36%	1.58%	−2.32%	−3.20%
Candle end + 5 days	1.51%	1.55%	−2.34%	−3.46%
Candle end + 10 days	1.64%	1.50%	−2.04%	−3.60%
10-day performance rank	93	83	62	59

Number found. I limited selection to 20,000 candles, meaning a hanging man appears on nearly every street corner. If you prorate the standard database, you will find that the hanging man appears more often in a bear market.

Reversal or continuation performance. The best performance comes from a hanging man in a bear market, regardless of the breakout direction.

S&P performance. Comparing candle performance with the S&P 500 over the same periods, the hanging man outperforms the index.

Candle end to breakout. It takes two days for price to close either above the top or below the bottom of the hanging man.

Candle end to trend end. Measured from a day after the hanging man to the trend end, it takes about a week to reach the trend end. Upward breakouts take less time to top out because the uptrend is already well along.

Yearly position, performance. Most hanging man candles appear within a third of the yearly high, but the best performance comes from those near the yearly low.

Performance over time. In two out of four categories performance deteriorates over time. After 10 days, the move is substantially less than what one would hope (like a 6% or higher move). The results are why the performance ranks are lousy. If there is a silver lining to the hanging man, it's that downward breakouts perform marginally better than upward ones.

Table 42.3 shows height statistics.

Candle height. Tall hanging man candles perform better than short ones across the board. To determine whether the candle is short or tall, compute its height from high to low price in the candle and divide by the breakout price. If the result is higher than the median, then you have a tall candle; otherwise it's short.

Table 42.3
Height Statistics

Description	Bull Market, Up Breakout	Bear Market, Up Breakout	Bull Market, Down Breakout	Bear Market, Down Breakout
Median candle height as a percentage of breakout price	1.71%	2.24%	1.74%	2.30%
Short candle, performance	4.75%	5.64%	−4.81%	−7.31%
Tall candle, performance	8.28%	8.38%	−7.77%	−10.29%
Percentage meeting price target (measure rule)	85%	82%	85%	86%
Median lower shadow as a percentage of breakout price	1.17%	1.55%	1.17%	1.56%
Short lower shadow, performance	4.83%	5.78%	−4.89%	−7.39%
Tall lower shadow, performance	8.10%	8.20%	−7.63%	−10.17%

Table 42.4
Volume Statistics

Description	Bull Market, Up Breakout	Bear Market, Up Breakout	Bull Market, Down Breakout	Bear Market, Down Breakout
Above-average candle volume, performance	6.03%	6.96%	−6.19%	−8.36%
Below-average candle volume, performance	6.43%	6.90%	−6.07%	−8.80%
Heavy breakout volume, performance	6.89%	7.83%	−6.61%	−9.27%
Light breakout volume, performance	5.89%	6.35%	−5.81%	−8.34%

Brittany is considering trading a hanging man that has a high of 87 and a low of 86. Is her candle short or tall? The height is 87 − 86, or 1, so the measure would be 1/87, or 1.1%. In a bull market with an upward breakout, her candle is short.

Measure rule. Use the measure rule to help predict how far price will rise or fall. Compute the height of the candle and multiply it by the appropriate percentage shown in the table; then apply it to the breakout price.

What are Brittany's price targets? The upward target would be 87 + (1 × 85%), or 87.85, and the downward target would be 86 − (1 × 85%), or 85.15.

Lower shadow performance. To determine whether the shadow is short or tall, compute the height of the shadow and divide by the breakout price. Compare the result to the median in the table. Tall shadows have a percentage higher than the median. Candles with tall shadows perform better than do those with short ones.

Table 42.4 shows volume statistics.

Average candle volume. Candles that follow the market trend (bull market/up breakouts and bear market/down breakouts) do better if volume is below average. The other columns (bear market/up breakouts and bull market/down breakouts) do better if the candle has above-average volume.

Breakout volume. Heavy breakout volume means better postbreakout performance across the board. Candles with heavy breakout volume perform better than do those with light breakout volume.

Trading Tactics

Avoid the hanging man as a bearish reversal when the primary trend is upward. Any downward breakout is apt to be short-lived. Continuations of the uptrend, however, work well. Price breaks out upward and keeps going up.

Table 42.5
Reversal Rates

Description	Bull Market	Bear Market
Closing price confirmation reversal rate	70%	70%
Candle color confirmation reversal rate	68%	69%
Opening gap confirmation reversal rate	50%	50%
Reversal rate: trend up, breakout down	41%	41%
Continuation rate: trend up, breakout up	59%	59%
Percentage of reversals (R)/ continuations (C) for each 12-month low (L), middle (M), or high (H)	L 45% R/55% C, M 43% R/57% C, H 39% R/61% C	L 48% R/52% C, M 39% R/61% C, H 39% R/61% C
Black body reversal rate	45%	44%
White body reversal rate	35%	36%

For reversals, the hanging man candle does best as part of an upward retracement when the primary price trend is downward.

I split trading tactics into two basic studies, one concerning reversal rates and the other concerning performance. Of the two, reversal rates are more important, because it's better to trade in the direction of the trend and let price run as far as it can.

Table 42.5 gives tips to find the trend direction.

Confirmation reversal rates. To help detect a reversal, wait for price to close lower the day after the hanging man. That method works 70% of the time.

Reversal, continuation rates. Based on the breakout direction, most hanging man candles act as continuations. In other words, price closes above the candlestick high most often, resuming the uptrend already in progress. Thus, expect an upward breakout.

Yearly range reversals. Continuations occur most often when the breakout price is within a third of the yearly high.

Body color reversal rate. A hanging man with a black body tends to reverse more often than do those with a white body. Notice that all of the numbers are below 50%, meaning that continuations are more prevalent. Hanging man candles with white bodies tend to act as continuation patterns 65% of the time in a bull market.

Table 42.6 shows performance indicators that can give hints as to how your stock will behave after the breakout from a candle pattern.

Confirmation, performance. The best performance for reversals comes from the opening gap method of confirmation. That's when you wait for price to gap open lower before taking a position.

Moving average. Candles with breakouts below the 50-trading-day moving average perform better than do those with breakouts above the moving average.

Table 42.6
Performance Indicators

Description	Bull Market, Up Breakout	Bear Market, Up Breakout	Bull Market, Down Breakout	Bear Market, Down Breakout
Closing price confirmation, performance	N/A	N/A	−6.38%	−8.35%
Candle color confirmation, performance	N/A	N/A	−6.49%	−8.23%
Opening gap confirmation, performance	N/A	N/A	−6.67%	−8.76%
Breakout above 50-day moving average, performance	6.25%	6.48%	−5.93%	−8.45%
Breakout below 50-day moving average, performance	6.63%	8.74%	−6.62%	−9.23%
Last candle: close in highest third, performance	6.23%	6.84%	−6.12%	−8.63%
Last candle: close in middle third, performance	6.59%	7.18%	−6.05%	−8.79%
Last candle: close in lowest third, performance	0.00%	0.00%	0.00%	0.00%
Black body, performance	6.41%	7.11%	−5.94%	−8.73%
White body, performance	6.20%	6.67%	−6.37%	−8.59%

N/A means not applicable.

Closing position. A close in the middle of the candle results in the best performance in all cases except bull market/down breakouts. Those do better when the close is near the hanging man's high price. None of the candles closed in the lowest third.

Body color performance. Black candles perform better than white ones in all categories except for bull market/down breakouts. White candles perform better in that situation.

Sample Trade

Brittany owns the stock shown in Figure 42.2. Price over time shows a horizontal base and a down-sloping top, forming a descending triangle chart pattern. When the hanging man appears at the top of the triangle, she thinks that price will reverse, but it is too soon to sell.

Price often bounces off the bottom trendline before staging an upward breakout (as opposed to curling down from the top trendline and then shooting upward). If an upward breakout happens, selling at the hanging man signal would be a mistake.

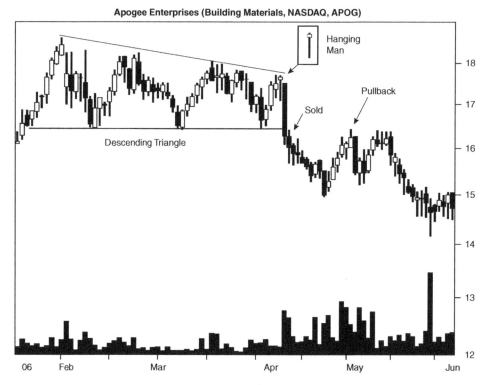

Figure 42.2 A hanging man at the top of a descending triangle suggests price weakness.

The candle high is at 17.58 and the low is at 17.08, for a height-to-breakout value of 2.9%. Thus, the candle is tall, and that means price is more likely to move farther after the breakout (but no guarantee and no hint of the direction).

The day after the hanging man, a tall black candle prints on the chart and price closes below the triangle. That confirms the hanging man sell signal. When price opens the next day, Brittany sells the stock because the odds suggest a downward move of sizable proportions.

About two weeks later, the stock pulls back to the breakout price (as it does 54% of the time). Price then resumes dropping until slipping below 13 and rebounding (not shown).

In case you don't like the upper shadow on the hanging man, I don't, either, but the difference between the high and the close is just four cents. That's close enough for government work, as they say, and it's a valid hanging man candle.

For Best Performance

The following list offers tips and observations to help choose candles that perform well. Consult the associated table for more information.

- Use the identification guidelines to help select the pattern—Table 42.1.
- Candles within a third of the yearly low perform best—Table 42.2.
- Select tall candles—Table 42.3.
- Use the measure rule to predict a price target—Table 42.3.
- Candles with tall lower shadows outperform—Table 42.3.
- Volume gives performance clues—Table 42.4.
- As a bearish reversal, avoid trading the hanging man in a primary uptrend—Trading Tactics discussion.
- The candle breaks out upward most often—Table 42.5.
- Patterns within a third of the yearly high tend to act as continuations most often—Table 42.5.
- Opening gap confirmation works best—Table 42.6.
- Breakouts below the 50-day moving average lead to the best performance—Table 42.6.

43

Harami, Bearish

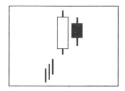

Behavior and Rank

Theoretical: Bearish reversal.

Actual bull market: Bullish continuation 53% of the time (ranking 36).

Actual bear market: Bearish reversal 50% of the time (ranking 46).

Frequency: 26th out of 103.

Overall performance over time: 72nd out of 103.

I had high hopes for the bearish harami, but with a reversal rate of just 47% (bull market), that's too close to random to be useful. The overall performance rank of 72 out of 103, where 1 is best, is not inspiring, either.

The experts are undecided on what is a bearish harami. Some claim that the body color is not important, but their pictures do not show a gray body (standard usage when either a black or white candle will do). One said the first candle should be a white and another source seems undecided. At first I ignored the different-colored bodies, but then I changed my mind. I'll discuss identification guidelines later.

Pattern psychology begins with the bulls pushing price upward, eventually forming a tall white candle. The next day's small body falls within the range of the prior body, with the bears forcing price lower at the open and closing lower still—a black candle. The belief is that price will move lower, but as I mentioned, that happens almost randomly or with a slight tendency to continue the uptrend.

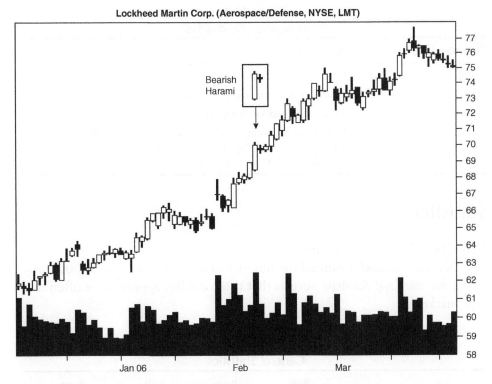

Lockheed Martin Corp. (Aerospace/Defense, NYSE, LMT)

Bearish
Harami

Figure 43.1   A bearish harami appears in an uptrend and price fails to reverse.

Identification Guidelines

Figure 43.1 shows an example of a bearish harami. The second day is not a doji (the difference between the open and close is eight cents) but it looks like one on this scale. The first day is a tall white candle, which is followed by a small black one. The black candle's body resides within the body of the white candle.

I chose the figure to illustrate the typical behavior of a bearish harami. Price continues higher slightly more often than it reverses. Although my statistics use only the white/black combination shown, an earlier test that allowed a black first candle was actually closer to random performance than the way I define the harami now.

Table 43.1 lists identification guidelines. The small black candle on the second day must have a body that fits inside the body of the white candle. The tops of the bodies can be the same, or the bottoms of the bodies can share the same price, but not both. Ignore the shadows, and the second day cannot be a doji (if it is, then the pattern is a bearish harami cross).

Table 43.1
Identification Guidelines

Characteristic	Discussion
Number of candle lines	Two.
Price trend	Upward leading to the candle pattern.
First day	A tall white candle. Some ignore the candle color, but I don't.
Second day	A small black candle. The open and close must be within the body of the first day, but ignore the shadows. Either the tops or the bottoms of the bodies can be equal but not both.

Statistics

Table 43.2 shows general statistics.

Number found. I limited the number of patterns found to 20,000. Prorating the standard database reveals that these candles appear more often in a bear market.

Table 43.2
General Statistics

Description	Bull Market, Up Breakout	Bear Market, Up Breakout	Bull Market, Down Breakout	Bear Market, Down Breakout
Number found	8,122	2,342	7,189	2,347
Reversal (R), continuation (C) performance	6.03% C	6.83% C	−5.97% R	−9.32% R
Standard & Poor's 500 change	1.41%	0.70%	−0.98%	−2.68%
Candle end to breakout (median, days)	4	4	4	4
Candle end to trend end (median, days)	7	7	8	9
Number of breakouts near the 12-month low (L), middle (M), or high (H)	L 865, M 1,783, H 4,776	L 440, M 707, H 1,177	L 1,001, M 1,823, H 3,778	L 560, M 767, H 995
Percentage move for each 12-month period	L 7.47%, M 5.98%, H 5.69%	L 11.09%, M 7.00%, H 5.58%	L −6.20%, M −6.50%, H −5.69%	L −10.14%, M −9.20%, H −8.98%
Candle end + 1 day	0.93%	1.00%	−1.01%	−1.58%
Candle end + 3 days	1.89%	2.38%	−2.03%	−2.87%
Candle end + 5 days	2.30%	2.50%	−2.42%	−3.62%
Candle end + 10 days	2.73%	2.61%	−2.31%	−4.01%
10-day performance rank	60	61	51	50

Reversal or continuation performance. A bearish harami in a bear market gives the best performance.

S&P performance. Comparing the performance of the S&P 500 versus the candle, we see that the harami beats the S&P in all categories.

Candle end to breakout. It takes four days for price to close either above the top of the harami or below the bottom.

Candle end to trend end. From candle end to trend end takes a median of seven to nine days. Downward breakouts take a day or two longer than upward ones because of the upward trend already in progress.

Yearly position, performance. Most of the bearish harami formations appear within a third of the yearly high, a situation I have found with many candle types. The best performance comes from those near the yearly low except for bull market/down breakouts. Those do best when the breakout is in the middle third of the yearly trading range.

Performance over time. Only one category stumbles, and that's between days 5 and 10 of bull market/down breakouts. The poor rank numbers are the result of low-percentage moves over time. If the stocks moved, say, 6% or so during the 10 trading days, then their rank would show dramatic improvement.

Table 43.3 shows height statistics.

Candle height. Tall candles perform substantially better than short ones, so trade only tall ones. To determine whether the candle is short or tall,

Table 43.3
Height Statistics

Description	Bull Market, Up Breakout	Bear Market, Up Breakout	Bull Market, Down Breakout	Bear Market, Down Breakout
Median candle height as a percentage of breakout price	3.08%	4.26%	3.03%	4.37%
Short candle, performance	4.73%	5.35%	−4.80%	−7.98%
Tall candle, performance	7.73%	8.42%	−7.52%	−10.88%
Percentage meeting price target (measure rule)	63%	58%	64%	64%
Median upper shadow as a percentage of breakout price	0.45%	0.65%	0.49%	0.76%
Short upper shadow, performance	5.36%	6.00%	−5.36%	−8.30%
Tall upper shadow, performance	6.73%	7.64%	−6.61%	−10.38%
Median lower shadow as a percentage of breakout price	0.63%	0.92%	0.62%	0.91%
Short lower shadow, performance	5.24%	6.12%	−5.43%	−8.12%
Tall lower shadow, performance	6.91%	7.56%	−6.56%	−10.62%

compute its height from highest high to lowest low price in the candle pattern and divide by the breakout price. If the result is higher than the median, then you have a tall candle; otherwise it's short.

Schmidt is considering trading a bearish harami candle with a high of 63 and a low of 61. Is the candle short or tall? The height is 63 − 61, or 2, so the measure would be 2/63, or 3.2%. For a bull market with an upward breakout, it's a tall candle.

Measure rule. Use the measure rule to help predict how far price will rise or fall. Compute the height of the candle pattern and multiply it by the appropriate percentage shown in the table; then apply it to the breakout price.

What are Schmidt's price targets for his candle? The upward target would be 63 + (2 × 63%), or 64.26, and the downward breakout target would be 61 − (2 × 64%), or 59.72.

Shadows. The table's results pertain to the last candle line in the pattern. To determine whether the shadow is short or tall, compute the height of the shadow and divide by the breakout price. Compare the result to the median in the table. Tall shadows have a percentage higher than the median.

Candles with tall upper or lower shadows perform better than do those with short shadows.

Table 43.4 shows volume statistics.

Candle volume trend. Candles in bull markets show the best performance if volume falls during the candle. Candles in bear markets do best after rising candle volume.

Average candle volume. Candles with above-average volume lead to the best postbreakout performance in all cases except bear market/up breakouts. Those do better after light (below-average) candle volume.

Table 43.4
Volume Statistics

Description	Bull Market, Up Breakout	Bear Market, Up Breakout	Bull Market, Down Breakout	Bear Market, Down Breakout
Rising candle volume, performance	5.94%	6.91%	−5.94%	−9.51%
Falling candle volume, performance	6.07%	6.79%	−5.99%	−9.23%
Above-average candle volume, performance	6.26%	6.78%	−6.06%	−9.68%
Below-average candle volume, performance	5.85%	6.87%	−5.91%	−9.05%
Heavy breakout volume, performance	6.61%	7.72%	−6.32%	−10.41%
Light breakout volume, performance	5.29%	5.95%	−5.74%	−8.54%

Breakout volume. Heavy breakout volume suggests better performance across the board. By that I mean candles with heavy breakout volume perform better than do those with light breakout volume.

Trading Tactics

A down-sloping channel or even a trendline drawn along the peaks sets up this trading tactic. If price appears at the top of the channel where a bearish harami resides, then price is more likely to break out downward. This also works for up-sloping channels, but the decline may not be enough to cause a downward breakout.

I split trading tactics into two basic studies, one concerning reversal rates and the other concerning performance. Of the two, reversal rates are more important, because it's better to trade in the direction of the trend and let price run as far as it can.

Table 43.5 gives tips to find the trend direction.

Confirmation reversal rates. To help determine a reversal of the up-trend, wait for price to close lower the next day. That method works 72% of the time, but it doesn't say how far price will move.

Reversal, continuation rates. In a bull market, the pattern acts as a continuation more often than a reversal. Expect an upward breakout. In a bear market, the behavior is random.

Yearly range reversals. Sorting the reversals into where they occur in the yearly price range shows no significant trend. The results are too close to random.

Table 43.6 shows performance indicators that can give hints as to how your stock will behave after the breakout from a candle pattern.

Confirmation, performance. Use opening gap confirmation as a trading signal because it works best. That means waiting for price to gap open lower the day after the harami before trading.

Table 43.5
Reversal Rates

Description	Bull Market	Bear Market
Closing price confirmation reversal rate	72%	72%
Candle color confirmation reversal rate	69%	71%
Opening gap confirmation reversal rate	56%	58%
Reversal rate: trend up, breakout down	47%	50%
Continuation rate: trend up, breakout up	53%	50%
Percentage of reversals (R)/ continuations (C) for each 12-month low (L), middle (M), or high (H)	L 54% R/46% C, M 51% R/49% C, H 44% R/56% C	L 56% R/44% C, M 52% R/48% C, H 46% R/54% C

Table 43.6
Performance Indicators

Description	Bull Market, Up Breakout	Bear Market, Up Breakout	Bull Market, Down Breakout	Bear Market, Down Breakout
Closing price confirmation, performance	N/A	N/A	−6.89%	−10.07%
Candle color confirmation, performance	N/A	N/A	−6.92%	−10.01%
Opening gap confirmation, performance	N/A	N/A	−7.50%	−10.38%
Breakout above 50-day moving average, performance	5.94%	6.31%	−5.90%	−8.72%
Breakout below 50-day moving average, performance	6.31%	9.85%	−6.19%	−10.65%
Last candle: close in highest third, performance	5.98%	6.38%	−5.77%	−9.31%
Last candle: close in middle third, performance	5.85%	6.74%	−5.80%	−9.17%
Last candle: close in lowest third, performance	6.26%	7.16%	−6.22%	−9.49%

N/A means not applicable.

Moving average. Breakouts below the 50-trading-day moving average mean performance that is better than from candles with breakouts above the moving average.

Closing position. Using the last candle line as the reference, a close in the lowest third of the line suggests performance that is better than a close elsewhere in the candle.

Sample Trade

Schmidt owns stock in the company pictured in Figure 43.2. Price started trending in February, bouncing like a ball off a trendline drawn along the lows. Price peaked at A and then retraced to B before making another attempt at the summit.

Price *does* make a higher high at the black candle of the bearish harami but fails to continue moving up. Overhead resistance blocks price from rising much and the harami correctly signals a reversal.

What does Schmidt do? He waits. He knows that price is likely to bounce off the trendline, and if it doesn't, then he will evaluate it again at that time.

As bad luck would have it, a tall black candle punches through trendline support at C. That is the sell signal. He sells the stock at the open the next day.

Figure 43.2 A bearish harami appears as price attempts to trend higher but fails.

Notice that a bullish (not bearish) harami with the last day being a Takuri line appears on the day he sells. Both suggest a bullish turn, and that's what happens. Price pulls back to D, and then resumes the downtrend.

For Best Performance

The following list offers tips and observations to help choose candles that perform well. Consult the associated table for more information.

- Use the identification guidelines to help select the pattern—Table 43.1.
- Candles within a third of the yearly low perform best except for bull market/down breakouts—Table 43.2.
- Select tall candles—Table 43.3.
- Use the measure rule to predict a price target—Table 43.3.
- Candles with tall upper or lower shadows outperform—Table 43.3.
- Volume gives performance clues—Table 43.4.

- If the harami appears at the top of a trend channel, then expect a downward breakout—Trading Tactics discussion.
- The candle breaks out upward most often—Table 43.5.
- Opening gap confirmation works best—Table 43.6.
- Breakouts below the 50-day moving average lead to the best performance—Table 43.6.

44

Harami, Bullish

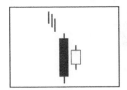

Behavior and Rank

Theoretical: Bullish reversal.
Actual bull market: Bullish reversal 53% of the time (ranking 43).
Actual bear market: Bullish reversal 51% of the time (ranking 41).
Frequency: 25th out of 103.
Overall performance over time: 38th out of 103.

The bullish harami acts as a reversal just three percentage points above random. That's not encouraging. In actual trading, you won't be able to tell the difference. Sometimes price will move up and sometimes not. Do not depend on this candlestick pointing the way. Performance over time is respectable, with an overall rank of 38 out of 103 where 1 is best.

The psychology behind the bullish harami begins with a downward price trend. Selling pressure appears as a tall black candle. The bears are excited, but the next day price trends in a narrow range, forming a small white candle that is within the body of the prior day's black candle. Since the candle is white, perhaps the situation isn't as dire as the bears would have everyone believe. In coming days, the shorts start covering and price rises . . . in theory.

Identification Guidelines

Figure 44.1 shows an example of a bullish harami. Price trended upward until peaking at A and then retraced the move, bottoming at the bullish harami.

383

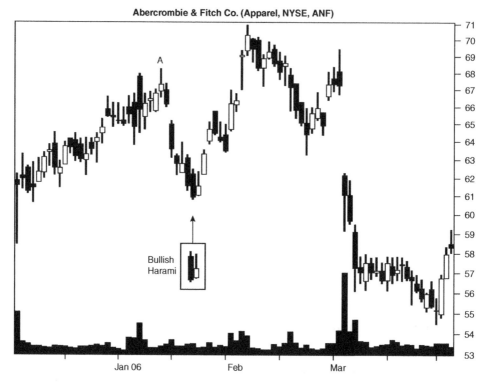

Figure 44.1   A bullish harami acts as a reversal of the downtrend.

Price found support and moved higher, confirming this harami as a bullish reversal pattern.

Table 44.1 lists identification guidelines. I allow only the black-white color combination in my tests of the bullish harami even though others allow different body color. Thus, there is some confusion about identification with this candle. The white candle body resides within the body of the black candle. If the tops of the bodies share the same price then the body bottoms cannot, and vice versa.

Table 44.1
Identification Guidelines

Characteristic	Discussion
Number of candle lines	Two.
Price trend	Downward leading to the candle pattern.
First day	A tall black candle.
Second day	A small-bodied white candle. The body must be within the prior candle's body. The tops or bottoms of the two bodies can be the same price but not both.

Statistics

Table 44.2 shows general statistics.

Number found. I limited my surveillance to 20,000 patterns. Prorating the standard database reveals that the pattern appears most often in a bear market.

Reversal or continuation performance. The best performance comes from harami formations in a bear market, regardless of the breakout direction.

S&P performance. The performance of the bullish harami beats results from the S&P 500 over the same period.

Candle end to breakout. It takes three or four days for price to close above the top or below the bottom of the harami.

Candle end to trend end. From candle end to trend end, the median ranges between six and nine days. Downward breakouts have a shorter period to the trend end and that's because the downtrend is already well along.

Yearly position, performance. Candles with breakouts within a third of the yearly low perform better than candles in the other ranges.

Table 44.2
General Statistics

Description	Bull Market, Up Breakout	Bear Market, Up Breakout	Bull Market, Down Breakout	Bear Market, Down Breakout
Number found	8,163	2,315	7,318	2,204
Reversal (R), continuation (C) performance	7.11% R	9.71% R	−5.72% C	−10.40% C
Standard & Poor's 500 change	1.84%	1.51%	−0.93%	−2.64%
Candle end to breakout (median, days)	3	3	4	3
Candle end to trend end (median, days)	9	9	6	7
Number of breakouts near the 12-month low (L), middle (M), or high (H)	L 1,816, M 2,280, H 3,439	L 825, M 734, H 729	L 2,322, M 2,349, H 2,160	L 1,012, M 750, H 420
Percentage move for each 12-month period	L 8.36%, M 6.88%, H 6.69%	L 12.74%, M 9.66%, H 7.24%	L −6.15%, M −6.00%, H −5.15%	L −12.03%, M −9.69%, H −8.65%
Candle end + 1 day	1.23%	2.06%	−0.94%	−1.52%
Candle end + 3 days	2.38%	3.76%	−1.92%	−2.87%
Candle end + 5 days	2.95%	4.22%	−2.06%	−3.62%
Candle end + 10 days	3.29%	4.05%	−1.99%	−4.00%
10-day performance rank	50	45	65	51

Table 44.3
Height Statistics

Description	Bull Market, Up Breakout	Bear Market, Up Breakout	Bull Market, Down Breakout	Bear Market, Down Breakout
Median candle height as a percentage of breakout price	3.25%	5.04%	3.45%	5.13%
Short candle, performance	5.54%	7.32%	−4.70%	−8.21%
Tall candle, performance	9.16%	12.28%	−7.06%	−12.99%
Percentage meeting price target (measure rule)	69%	66%	59%	61%
Median upper shadow as a percentage of breakout price	0.68%	1.12%	0.74%	1.14%
Short upper shadow, performance	6.16%	8.05%	−5.10%	−8.79%
Tall upper shadow, performance	8.11%	11.39%	−6.39%	−12.04%
Median lower shadow as a percentage of breakout price	0.58%	0.89%	0.54%	0.87%
Short lower shadow, performance	6.17%	8.79%	−5.19%	−9.05%
Tall lower shadow, performance	8.11%	10.65%	−6.30%	−11.85%

Performance over time. Performance stumbles in the inner two columns during days 5 to 10. Coupled with tepid performance after 10 days (good performance would be a move of over 6%), that accounts for the weak performance ranks.

Table 44.3 shows height statistics.

Candle height. Tall harami candles perform better than short ones across the board. To determine whether the candle is short or tall, compute its height from highest high to lowest low price in the candle pattern and then divide by the breakout price. If the result is higher than the median, then you have a tall candle; otherwise it's short.

Instead of working, Clint flipped to his favorite stock chart and spotted a bullish harami. Is his candle tall if it has a high of 39 and a low of 37? The height is 39 − 37, or 2, so the measure is 2/39, or 5.1%. In a bull market with an upward breakout the candle is tall.

Measure rule. Use the measure rule to help predict how far price will rise or fall. Compute the height of the candle pattern and multiply it by the appropriate percentage shown in the table; then apply it to the breakout price.

What are the price targets for Clint's candle? The upward target would be 39 + (2 × 69%), or 40.38, and the downward target would be 37 − (2 × 61%), or 35.78.

Table 44.4
Volume Statistics

Description	Bull Market, Up Breakout	Bear Market, Up Breakout	Bull Market, Down Breakout	Bear Market, Down Breakout
Rising candle volume, performance	7.22%	9.44%	−5.80%	−10.11%
Falling candle volume, performance	7.04%	9.89%	−5.67%	−10.57%
Above-average candle volume, performance	6.99%	9.90%	−5.67%	−10.36%
Below-average candle volume, performance	7.22%	9.52%	−5.76%	−10.43%
Heavy breakout volume, performance	7.79%	10.80%	−5.87%	−10.80%
Light breakout volume, performance	6.48%	8.81%	−5.57%	−9.92%

Shadows. The table's results pertain to the last candle line in the pattern. To determine whether the shadow is short or tall, compute the height of the shadow and divide by the breakout price. Compare the result to the median in the table. Tall shadows have a percentage higher than the median.

Candles with tall upper or lower shadows perform better than those with short shadows.

Table 44.4 shows volume statistics.

Candle volume trend. Candle volume splits along breakout directions. In other words, a rising volume trend works better in a bull market. Falling volume leads to better performance in a bear market.

Average candle volume. Light (below-average) candle volume leads to the best postbreakout performance in all categories except bear market/up breakout. That category does better if the candle shows above-average volume.

Breakout volume. Heavy breakout volume leads to good performance across the board.

Trading Tactics

The bullish harami works best as a reversal of the downward retracement in a primary uptrend. While harami candles sometimes reverse the primary downtrend, more often price climbs little before sinking. It's best to avoid trading this one in a primary downtrend or confirm the reversal with other indicators and techniques. In all situations, if price breaks out downward from the harami, expect the downtrend to continue.

I split trading tactics into two basic studies, one concerning reversal rates and the other concerning performance. Of the two, reversal rates are more

Table 44.5
Reversal Rates

Description	Bull Market	Bear Market
Closing price confirmation reversal rate	76%	75%
Candle color confirmation reversal rate	75%	74%
Opening gap confirmation reversal rate	61%	59%
Reversal: trend down, breakout up	53%	51%
Continuation: trend down, breakout down	47%	49%
Percentage of reversals (R)/ continuations (C) for each 12-month low (L), middle (M), or high (H)	L 44% R/56% C, M 49% R/51% C, H 61% R/39% C	L 45% R/55% C, M 49% R/51% C, H 63% R/37% C

important, because it's better to trade in the direction of the trend and let price run as far as it can.

Table 44.5 gives tips to find the trend direction.

Confirmation reversal rates. To help confirm a reversal of the downtrend, wait for price to close higher the day after the harami ends. That works about 75% of the time.

Reversal, continuation rates. Based on a downward price trend leading to the candle along with the breakout direction, the bullish harami acts as a reversal most often, but the numbers are close to random. Expect an upward breakout, but be prepared if it doesn't happen.

Yearly range reversals. Separating the reversal/continuation behavior into the yearly price range, we see that the pattern behaves as a reversal the higher up the price range the breakout resides. For example, those harami candles with breakouts within a third of the yearly high act as reversals 61% of the time in a bull market and 63% of the time in a bear market.

Table 44.6 shows performance indicators that can give hints as to how your stock will behave after the breakout from this candle pattern.

Confirmation, performance. Opening gap confirmation gives the best performance yet again. In that method, wait for price to gap open higher the day after the harami ends before buying the stock.

Moving average. Candles with breakouts below the 50-trading-day moving average perform better than do those with breakouts above the moving average.

Closing position. For fun, I looked at performance related to where price closed in the last day of the harami. Most often (three out of four categories), when the white candle closes within the highest third of its intraday trading range, postbreakout performance improves. When the close is in the middle third, harami formations in the bear market/up breakout combination do better. That's a useful performance tip.

Table 44.6
Performance Indicators

Description	Bull Market, Up Breakout	Bear Market, Up Breakout	Bull Market, Down Breakout	Bear Market, Down Breakout
Closing price confirmation, performance	7.48%	10.76%	N/A	N/A
Candle color confirmation, performance	7.27%	10.61%	N/A	N/A
Opening gap confirmation, performance	7.98%	12.32%	N/A	N/A
Breakout above 50-day moving average, performance	6.99%	8.07%	−5.16%	−8.40%
Breakout below 50-day moving average, performance	7.22%	10.90%	−5.89%	−10.93%
Last candle: close in highest third, performance	7.29%	9.47%	−5.81%	−10.66%
Last candle: close in middle third, performance	7.15%	10.03%	−5.79%	−10.41%
Last candle: close in lowest third, performance	6.47%	9.43%	−5.32%	−9.87%

N/A means not applicable.

Sample Trade

Figure 44.2 shows a trade Clint made while on the job. Price began its uphill run at A and peaked at B before retracing a portion of the climb and ending in a bullish harami.

Clint is a sophisticated investor who yearns to be a full-time trader. He looks at the extent of the rise from A to B and then calculates where a 38% Fibonacci retracement would be (shown). The harami bottoms at that retracement level. If the bullish harami acts as a reversal, the resulting pattern on the chart will be an inverted and ascending scallop, a pattern he has traded before.

Next, he calculates where his stop should be. He bases the stop location (shown) on price volatility, taking twice the average difference between each day's high and low price over the prior 22 trading days and subtracting that number from the current low. Place a stop closer and you risk being stopped out on normal price volatility.

How high will price rise? Like the candlestick measure rule, he takes the difference between the high at B and the low at A and multiplies it by 61% (because that's how often the full measure works for scallops) to get a target of 13.13.

The height of the harami divided by the breakout price is 3.1%, making it a short candle (bad for performance). The upper shadow is 0.52% high, so

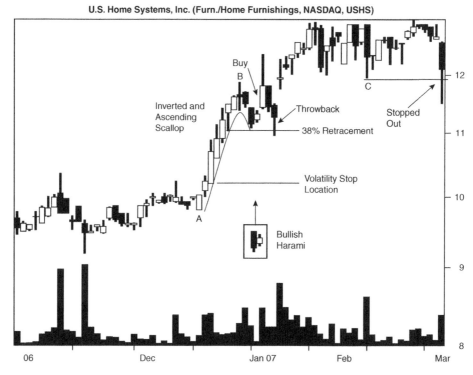

Figure 44.2 A bullish harami marks the end of an inverted and ascending scallop.

it's short (bad for performance). The lower shadow height/breakout price is
0.35%, so it's also short (bad). The harami is within a third of the yearly high,
suggesting it has a better chance of acting as a reversal (good), but performance
would be better if it was near the yearly low. The harami is above the 50-day
moving average (bad). Candle volume is trending downward (bad) and looks
to be below average, too (good). Breakout volume is heavy (good). Based on
the statistics, the results are three good and five or six bad, depending on how
you count.

When price gaps open upward the next day, he buys despite the statistical
analysis. "A buy signal is a buy signal," he says. Price throws back to the right lip
of the scallop, behavior that happens 61% of the time, before gapping higher
and recovering.

The series of long shadows on the bottom of the candles during late
January and into February with small shadows on top he interprets as bullish.
"The long black candles and smaller white ones are troublesome, though,"
he admits.

When tall candle C forms and price climbs away from it, he places a stop
a penny below C. He draws a trendline (not shown) upward along the lows
starting at C, and thinks that if price closes below the line, that would also be
a sell signal. It turns out that price stops him out and also pierces the trendline
the same day.

Price eventually reaches a high of 13.16, three cents above his price target. If he had placed a sell stop there, he would have made substantially more money.

For Best Performance

The following list offers tips and observations to help choose candles that perform well. Consult the associated table for more information.

- Use the identification guidelines to help select the pattern—Table 44.1.
- Candles within a third of the yearly low perform best—Table 44.2.
- Select tall candles—Table 44.3.
- Use the measure rule to predict a price target—Table 44.3.
- Candles with tall upper or lower shadows outperform—Table 44.3.
- Volume gives performance clues—Table 44.4.
- Trade harami as reversals of the downward retracement in a primary uptrend—Trading Tactics discussion.
- The candle breaks out upward most often—Table 44.5.
- Patterns within a third of the yearly high tend to act as reversals most often—Table 44.5.
- Opening gap confirmation works best—Table 44.6.
- Breakouts below the 50-day moving average lead to the best performance—Table 44.6.

45

Harami Cross, Bearish

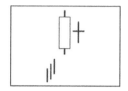

Behavior and Rank

Theoretical: Bearish reversal.
Actual bull market: Bullish continuation 57% of the time (ranking 25).
Actual bear market: Bullish continuation 56% of the time (ranking 33).
Frequency: 45th out of 103.
Overall performance over time: 80th out of 103.

My numbers show that the bearish harami cross acts as a continuation pattern most often, despite claims that it's a reversal, but I will concede that performance is close to random (50%). The overall performance is 80, too, which puts it near the end of the list of 103, where 1 is best.

The psychology behind the pattern starts with an uptrend leading to a tall white candle. The bulls have control of the ball, but the next day a doji appears. The trading range of that day may be wide (but still less than the range of the prior day) as the bulls and bears try to move the ball toward the end zone. At day's end, price is where it started, with the teams hitting the showers and nothing to show for a day's work but a tie. To my way of thinking, anything can happen a day later, but it favors a resumption of the uptrend and that's what happens most often.

Identification Guidelines

Figure 45.1 shows a bearish harami cross. Price forms a rectangle bottom with prices sandwiched between two horizontal trendlines. On exit from this chart

El Paso Corp. (Natural Gas—Distributor, NYSE, EP)

Bearish
Harami
Cross

Rectangle Bottom

Figure 45.1 A bearish harami cross appears during the breakout from a rectangle bottom.

pattern, the bearish harami cross appears after a strong uptrend that moves price from the bottom of the rectangle to the top. This bearish harami cross is not bearish at all. Rather, price leaves a congestion area and zips up, surfing a rising volume trend.

Table 45.1 lists identification guidelines. A bearish harami cross is a two-candle pattern, the first being a tall white candle line and the second being a doji. The high and low of the doji must be within the high-low range of the prior white candle. Put the combination in an uptrend and you have a bearish harami cross.

Table 45.1
Identification Guidelines

Characteristic	Discussion
Number of candle lines	Two.
Price trend	Upward leading to the start of the candle pattern.
First day	A tall white candle.
Second day	A doji (open and close are equal or nearly so) with a trading range inside the price range of the prior day.

Statistics

Table 45.2 shows general statistics.

Number found. I stopped counting at 20,000 harami patterns. Most come from a bull market.

Reversal or continuation performance. The best performance comes from bearish harami cross formations in a bear market—behavior we have seen from many other candlestick types as well.

S&P performance. The harami cross gives substantially better results than the change in the S&P 500 over the same periods.

Candle end to breakout. It takes three or four days for price to close either above the highest high or below the lowest low in the candle pattern.

Candle end to trend end. The median time to the trend end is about a week.

Yearly position, performance. Candles with breakouts within a third of the yearly low show the best performance of the three ranges.

Table 45.2
General Statistics

Description	Bull Market, Up Breakout	Bear Market, Up Breakout	Bull Market, Down Breakout	Bear Market, Down Breakout
Number found	10,693	756	7,945	606
Reversal (R), continuation (C) performance	5.73% C	8.82% C	−5.52% R	−7.32% R
Standard & Poor's 500 change	1.01%	0.15%	−0.47%	−1.79%
Candle end to breakout (median, days)	4	3	4	4
Candle end to trend end (median, days)	6	7	7	8
Number of breakouts near the 12-month low (L), middle (M), or high (H)	L 1,845, M 2,725, H 5,906	L 193, M 228, H 335	L 1,981, M 2,220, H 3,596	L 201, M 208, H 197
Percentage move for each 12-month period	L 7.25%, M 5.74%, H 5.37%	L 12.31%, M 7.47%, H 8.48%	L −6.09%, M −6.03%, H −5.06%	L −9.36%, M −7.38%, H −6.29%
Candle end + 1 day	0.71%	0.95%	−1.03%	−1.61%
Candle end + 3 days	1.54%	2.03%	−2.08%	−2.61%
Candle end + 5 days	1.93%	2.37%	−2.51%	−2.80%
Candle end + 10 days	2.43%	2.91%	−2.60%	−3.13%
10-day performance rank	73	56	41	70

Table 45.3
Height Statistics

Description	Bull Market, Up Breakout	Bear Market, Up Breakout	Bull Market, Down Breakout	Bear Market, Down Breakout
Median candle height as a percentage of breakout price	2.75%	3.92%	2.78%	3.84%
Short candle, performance	4.76%	8.77%	−4.77%	−6.78%
Tall candle, performance	7.18%	8.89%	−6.63%	−7.99%
Percentage meeting price target (measure rule)	69%	67%	68%	66%
Median upper shadow as a percentage of breakout price	0.00%	0.29%	0.00%	0.27%
Short upper shadow, performance	5.93%	10.42%	−5.36%	−7.11%
Tall upper shadow, performance	5.59%	7.67%	−5.62%	−7.42%
Median lower shadow as a percentage of breakout price	0.58%	0.82%	0.52%	0.52%
Short lower shadow, performance	5.01%	9.66%	−5.12%	−6.97%
Tall lower shadow, performance	6.41%	8.10%	−5.87%	−7.49%

Performance over time. The candle is a robust performer, meaning that the numbers increase over time and in each category. Unfortunately, after 10 days, the percentage change is not high enough to push the performance rank to better levels.

Table 45.3 shows height statistics.

Candle height. Tall candles work best across the board. To determine whether the candle is short or tall, compute its height from highest high to lowest low price in the candle pattern and divide by the breakout price. If the result is higher than the median, then you have a tall candle; otherwise it's short.

Morgan sees a bearish harami cross with a high price of 83 and a low of 80. Is it short or tall? The height is 83 − 80, or 3, so the measure would be 3/83, or 3.6%. In a bull market with an upward breakout, she has a tall candle.

Measure rule. Use the measure rule to help predict how far price will rise or fall. Compute the height of the candle pattern and multiply it by the appropriate percentage shown in the table; then apply it to the breakout price.

Morgan wants to know what the price targets are for her candle. The upward target would be 83 + (3 × 69%), or 85.07, and the downward target would be 80 − (3 × 68%), or 77.96.

Shadows. The table's results pertain to the last candle line in the pattern. To determine whether the shadow is short or tall, compute the height of the shadow and divide by the breakout price. Compare the result to the median

Table 45.4
Volume Statistics

Description	Bull Market, Up Breakout	Bear Market, Up Breakout	Bull Market, Down Breakout	Bear Market, Down Breakout
Rising candle volume, performance	5.45%	6.92%	−5.30%	−7.17%
Falling candle volume, performance	5.83%	9.36%	−5.61%	−7.37%
Above-average candle volume, performance	5.89%	7.04%	−5.49%	−7.52%
Below-average candle volume, performance	5.61%	10.05%	−5.55%	−7.20%
Heavy breakout volume, performance	6.49%	8.03%	−5.87%	−7.62%
Light breakout volume, performance	4.95%	9.53%	−5.30%	−7.14%

in the table. Tall shadows have a percentage higher than the median. Do not be alarmed about a 0.00% median. That just means a number of candles had no shadow.

Upper shadow performance. Candles with upward breakouts and short upper shadows perform better than do those with tall shadows. Downward breakouts show the reverse behavior, with tall shadows outperforming those candles with short shadows.

Lower shadow performance. Candles with tall lower shadows perform better than do those with short shadows except for bear market/up breakouts.

Table 45.4 shows volume statistics.

Candle volume trend. Candles with falling volume worked better than did those with rising volume in all categories.

Average candle volume. When volume is compared to the 30-day average, we find that above-average volume worked better for candles in bull market/up breakouts and bear market/down breakouts. Bear market/up breakouts and bull market/down breakouts did better when the candles showed below-average volume.

Breakout volume. Heavy breakout volume meant better performance post breakout across the board except for one category: bear market/up breakouts.

Trading Tactics

For the best reversal performance, trade the bearish harami cross only in an upward retracement of a primary downtrend. A downward breakout joins with

Table 45.5
Reversal Rates

Description	Bull Market	Bear Market
Closing price confirmation reversal rate	66%	69%
Candle color confirmation reversal rate	65%	66%
Opening gap confirmation reversal rate	54%	53%
Reversal rate: trend up, breakout down	43%	44%
Continuation rate: trend up, breakout up	57%	56%
Percentage of reversals (R)/ continuations (C) for each 12-month low (L), middle (M), or high (H)	L 52% R/48% C, M 45% R/55% C, H 38% R/62% C	L 51% R/49% C, M 48% R/52% C, H 37% R/63% C

the primary trend, and down price goes. In an upward price trend, the breakout may still be downward, but price will drop for only a week or so before the current pulls it back up.

I split trading tactics into two basic studies, one concerning reversal rates and the other concerning performance. Of the two, reversal rates are more important, because it's better to trade in the direction of the trend and let price run as far as it can.

Table 45.5 gives tips to find the trend direction.

Confirmation reversal rates. To help determine a reversal, wait for price to close lower after the harami cross ends. That works about two out of three times.

Reversal, continuation rates. I counted the number of patterns with upward and downward breakouts. Most acted as continuations of the uptrend that existed before the start of the harami. Expect an upward breakout.

Yearly range reversals. Sorting the harami within the yearly trading range, we find that continuations occurred most often within a third of the yearly high.

Table 45.6 shows performance indicators that can give hints as to how your stock will behave after the breakout from a candle pattern.

Confirmation, performance. Candles with opening gap confirmation perform better than the other varieties in a bull market. Opening gap means trading only when price gaps lower the next day.

Candles in a bear market do better with closing price confirmation. Wait for price to close lower the day after the harami cross before trading.

Moving average. Candles with breakouts below the 50-trading-day moving average perform better than do those with breakouts above the moving average.

Closing position. Where price closes in the last line of the candlestick formation shows no consistent trend.

Table 45.6
Performance Indicators

Description	Bull Market, Up Breakout	Bear Market, Up Breakout	Bull Market, Down Breakout	Bear Market, Down Breakout
Closing price confirmation, performance	N/A	N/A	−6.33%	−9.27%
Candle color confirmation, performance	N/A	N/A	−6.35%	−9.09%
Opening gap confirmation, performance	N/A	N/A	−6.72%	−9.08%
Breakout above 50-day moving average, performance	5.64%	8.52%	−5.23%	−6.86%
Breakout below 50-day moving average, performance	6.27%	10.77%	−6.13%	−8.43%
Last candle: close in highest third, performance	5.81%	7.50%	−5.34%	−7.58%
Last candle: close in middle third, performance	5.64%	10.03%	−5.44%	−6.98%
Last candle: close in lowest third, performance	5.73%	9.32%	−6.02%	−7.68%

N/A means not applicable.

Sample Trade

Figure 45.2 shows a congestion area (circled) that forms near the price of the August peak. At first Morgan sees the small candles as having no real direction. Then the harami cross appears. The harami mirrors the tall black candle three days earlier, but since it is within a congestion area she doesn't give it much thought. However, when price climbs above the harami and above the congestion area, she buys just before the close that day.

Price moves upward following a trendline that Morgan has drawn connecting the lows. When price moves horizontally in late December accompanied by small trendless candles, she grows concerned. A spinning top closes below the trendline, and that is her sell signal. She sells the next day because she believes a downtrend is beginning. She is a few days early, but her instincts are correct. Price drops well below her purchase price.

For Best Performance

The following list offers tips and observations to help choose candles that perform well. Consult the associated table for more information.

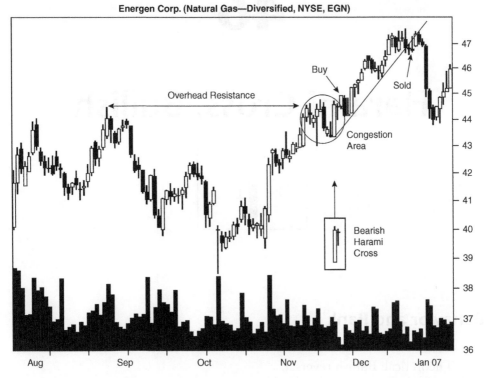

Figure 45.2 A bearish harami cross appears at the end of a congestion area.

- Use the identification guidelines to help select the pattern—Table 45.1.
- Candles within a third of the yearly low perform best—Table 45.2.
- Select tall candles—Table 45.3.
- Use the measure rule to predict a price target—Table 45.3.
- Volume gives performance clues—Table 45.4.
- Trade reversals only in an upward retracement of a primary downtrend—Trading Tactics discussion.
- The candle breaks out upward most often—Table 45.5.
- Patterns within a third of the yearly high tend to act as continuations most often—Table 45.5.
- Opening gap confirmation works best in a bull market—Table 45.6.

46

Harami Cross, Bullish

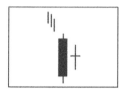

Behavior and Rank

Theoretical: Bullish reversal.

Actual bull market: Bearish continuation 55% of the time (ranking 32).

Actual bear market: Bearish continuation 56% of the time (ranking 32).

Frequency: 47th out of 103.

Overall performance over time: 50th out of 103.

The bullish harami cross is a slimmed-down version of a bullish harami pattern. Instead of a white candle, the second day of the harami cross is a doji. The harami cross is supposed to act as a bullish reversal, but my testing finds that it acts as a bearish continuation pattern. This candle pattern performs less well (overall rank of 50) than the regular bullish harami (overall rank of 38).

The psychology behind the cross pattern is the same as for a bullish harami. The bears are in control of the stock, forcing price lower. Then a tall black candle prints on the chart, suggesting more downside ahead. A doji appears. The trading range of the doji is shorter than that exhibited by the black candle, and the bears are worried. When price ends the day where it started, both the bulls and the bears are confused. This indecision isn't settled until the next day or the next when price finally decides on a direction. Only then will we know if the harami cross is bullish or bearish, whether it acts as a reversal or continuation.

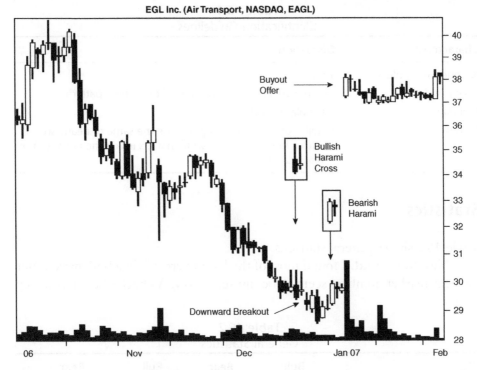

EGL Inc. (Air Transport, NASDAQ, EAGL)

Buyout
Offer →

Bullish
Harami
Cross

Bearish
Harami

Downward Breakout →

06   Nov   Dec   Jan 07   Feb

Figure 46.1 A typical bullish harami cross acting as a continuation candle pattern.

Identification Guidelines

Figure 46.1 shows a good example of the bullish harami cross acting as a continuation pattern. This one appears in an extended downtrend. After such a long decline, many might expect a reversal to occur; but that's not what happens. Price breaks out lower and the downtrend resumes. Price bottoms three days later and then bounces. Price seems to pause at 30, at round number resistance, and then word comes down the blower that the company has received a buyout offer. The bears scatter. Price jumps up to 37 plus and then hangs around for about a month before the buyout falls through (not shown). This sends price right back down to near 30, delighting the bears.

Notice the bearish harami that appears two days before the announcement. It isn't bearish after all.

Table 46.1 lists identification guidelines. Look for two candle lines, the first one a tall black candle and the second a doji with a price range that squeezes inside the range of the prior day (inside the black candle's price range). Marry the combination with a downward price trend and you have a bullish harami cross.

Table 46.1
Identification Guidelines

Characteristic	Discussion
Number of candle lines	Two.
Price trend	Downward leading to the start of the candle pattern.
First day	A tall black candle.
Second day	A doji (open and closing prices are the same or nearly so) with a high-low price range that fits inside the range of the black candle.

Statistics

Table 46.2 shows general statistics.

Number found. I found most of the harami crosses in a bull market, but the bear market numbers seem to be unusually low. A check of the frequency

Table 46.2
General Statistics

Description	Bull Market, Up Breakout	Bear Market, Up Breakout	Bull Market, Down Breakout	Bear Market, Down Breakout
Number found	8,381	623	10,212	784
Reversal (R), continuation (C) performance	7.01% R	9.70% R	−5.99% C	−9.45% C
Standard & Poor's 500 change	1.48%	0.46%	−0.43%	−1.48%
Candle end to breakout (median, days)	4	4	4	3
Candle end to trend end (median, days)	8	8	6	6
Number of breakouts near the 12-month low (L), middle (M), or high (H)	L 2,362, M 2,134, H 2,565	L 279, M 185, H 151	L 3,619, M 2,646, H 2,330	L 434, M 215, H 118
Percentage move for each 12-month period	L 8.52%, M 6.60%, H 6.29%	L 12.54%, M 9.03%, H 7.52%	L −6.86%, M −5.83%, H −5.15%	L −11.02%, M −10.40%, H −5.64%
Candle end + 1 day	1.18%	1.82%	−0.83%	−1.07%
Candle end + 3 days	2.44%	3.75%	−1.71%	−2.50%
Candle end + 5 days	3.10%	4.59%	−1.96%	−3.06%
Candle end + 10 days	3.89%	4.52%	−1.84%	−3.16%
10-day performance rank	36	40	68	68

indicates that the harami cross is indeed rare in a bear market. I limited the number of harami crosses to 20,000.

Reversal or continuation performance. The best performance comes from candles in a bear market, regardless of the breakout direction. We've seen this behavior in many other candle types.

S&P performance. The candle pattern performs better than the S&P 500 over the same periods.

Candle end to breakout. It takes about four days for price to close either above the top of the candle or below the bottom of it.

Candle end to trend end. The table shows that the median time to trend end is six to eight days. Downward breakouts take less time for price to reach the trend end because the downtrend is already well along.

Yearly position, performance. Harami crosses appear within a third of the yearly low (except for bull market/up breakouts) and that's where they perform best most often.

Performance over time. Performance stumbles in the two middle columns during days 5 to 10. Upward breakouts show a good performance rank, but downward breakouts are weak (meaning the percentage changes are low, leading to a poor rank).

Table 46.3 shows height statistics.

Table 46.3
Height Statistics

Description	Bull Market, Up Breakout	Bear Market, Up Breakout	Bull Market, Down Breakout	Bear Market, Down Breakout
Median candle height as a percentage of breakout price	2.82%	4.28%	2.91%	4.33%
Short candle, performance	5.69%	8.00%	−5.04%	−7.95%
Tall candle, performance	8.84%	12.19%	−7.28%	−11.41%
Percentage meeting price target (measure rule)	74%	73%	68%	70%
Median upper shadow as a percentage of breakout price	0.55%	0.62%	0.63%	0.75%
Short upper shadow, performance	6.37%	8.20%	−5.30%	−8.16%
Tall upper shadow, performance	7.58%	10.58%	−6.67%	−10.25%
Median lower shadow as a percentage of breakout price	0.17%	0.35%	0.00%	0.28%
Short lower shadow, performance	6.56%	7.62%	−6.40%	−8.98%
Tall lower shadow, performance	7.26%	10.96%	−5.74%	−9.68%

Candle height. Tall candles outperform, so select them when trading this pattern. To determine whether the candle is short or tall, compute its height from highest high to lowest low price in the candle pattern and divide by the breakout price. If the result is higher than the median, then you have a tall candle; otherwise it's short.

Randy sees a bullish harami cross with a high of 13 and a low of 12. Is the candle short or tall? The height is $13 - 12$, or 1, so the measure is 1/13, or 7.7%. In a bull market with an upward breakout the candle is tall.

Measure rule. Use the measure rule to help predict how far price will rise or fall. Compute the height of the candle pattern and multiply it by the appropriate percentage shown in the table; then apply it to the breakout price.

What are the two targets for Randy's candle? The upward target would be $(1 \times 74\%) + 13$, or 13.74, and the downward target would be $12 - (1 \times 68\%)$, or 11.32.

Shadows. The table's results pertain to the last candle line in the pattern. To determine whether the shadow is short or tall, compute the height of the shadow and divide by the breakout price. Compare the result to the median in the table. Tall shadows have a percentage higher than the median.

Upper shadow performance. Candles with tall upper shadows perform better than do those with short shadows in all categories.

Lower shadow performance. Candles with tall lower shadows also show improved performance except for bull market/down breakouts. Those do better with short shadows. Most candle types perform better with tall lower shadows.

Table 46.4 shows volume statistics.

Table 46.4
Volume Statistics

Description	Bull Market, Up Breakout	Bear Market, Up Breakout	Bull Market, Down Breakout	Bear Market, Down Breakout
Rising candle volume, performance	7.39%	9.51%	−6.11%	−10.07%
Falling candle volume, performance	6.82%	9.78%	−5.94%	−9.23%
Above-average candle volume, performance	6.99%	11.09%	−5.82%	−9.53%
Below-average candle volume, performance	7.02%	8.62%	−6.09%	−9.39%
Heavy breakout volume, performance	7.63%	10.84%	−6.23%	−9.70%
Light breakout volume, performance	6.44%	8.41%	−5.81%	−9.23%

Candle volume trend. The harami cross with a rising volume pattern between the two candles suggests better performance after the breakout except in the bear market/up breakout category. That column does better with a falling trend.

Average candle volume. Above-average candle volume means better performance in bull markets, and below-average volume works better for candles with downward breakouts.

Breakout volume. Heavy breakout-day volume suggests better performance across the board.

Trading Tactics

Avoid expecting a lasting reversal when the primary trend is downward. That happens, but it's more likely that price will move up for a few days to a week before resuming the downward move. If you want to trade the bullish harami cross as a reversal, then find them in a downward retracement of the upward move. The upward breakout joins with the primary uptrend and both move with the market current higher.

I split trading tactics into two basic studies, one concerning reversal rates and the other concerning performance. Of the two, reversal rates are more important, because it's better to trade in the direction of the trend and let price run as far as it can.

Table 46.5 gives tips to find the trend direction.

Confirmation reversal rates. To help confirm a reversal, wait for price to close higher the day after the cross ends. That boosts the reversal rate to 71% in a bull market. That may sound like reasonable advice, but what it's doing is pushing price above the top of the pattern. If it closes there, then a reversal has occurred, by definition. So, waiting a day for confirmation may be a self-fulfilling prophecy.

Table 46.5
Reversal Rates

Description	Bull Market	Bear Market
Closing price confirmation reversal rate	71%	69%
Candle color confirmation reversal rate	70%	66%
Opening gap confirmation reversal rate	57%	53%
Reversal: trend down, breakout up	45%	44%
Continuation: trend down, breakout down	55%	56%
Percentage of reversals (R)/ continuations (C) for each 12-month low (L), middle (M), or high (H)	L 39% R/61% C, M 45% R/55% C, H 52% R/48% C	L 39% R/61% C, M 46% R/54% C, H 56% R/44% C

Table 46.6
Performance Indicators

Description	Bull Market, Up Breakout	Bear Market, Up Breakout	Bull Market, Down Breakout	Bear Market, Down Breakout
Closing price confirmation, performance	7.16%	9.72%	N/A	N/A
Candle color confirmation, performance	7.12%	9.72%	N/A	N/A
Opening gap confirmation, performance	7.59%	11.53%	N/A	N/A
Breakout above 50-day moving average, performance	6.54%	8.70%	−5.27%	−6.73%
Breakout below 50-day moving average, performance	7.35%	10.68%	−6.22%	−10.20%
Last candle: close in highest third, performance	7.45%	9.59%	−5.89%	−8.41%
Last candle: close in middle third, performance	7.16%	9.97%	−5.79%	−9.21%
Last candle: close in lowest third, performance	6.53%	9.43%	−6.25%	−10.17%

N/A means not applicable.

Reversal, continuation rates. Looking at the breakout direction, we see that the pattern acts as a continuation most often, regardless of the bull or bear market. Expect a downward breakout slightly more often than an upward one.

Yearly range reversals. Sorting the reversals and continuations into where they occur in the yearly price range, we find that continuations appear within a third of the yearly low 61% of the time.

Table 46.6 shows performance indicators that can give hints as to how your stock will behave after the breakout from this candle pattern.

Confirmation, performance. Opening gap confirmation, where you buy the stock if price gaps open higher after the doji (expecting an upward breakout), results in the best trading signal.

Moving average. When the candle's breakout is below the 50-trading-day moving average, the candle tends to perform better after the breakout in all cases.

Closing position. Where price closes in the last line of the candle gives no consistent performance hints.

Sample Trade

Randy watched the rounding turn develop as Ann dropped from her perch at 45; a portion of it appears in Figure 46.2. He thinks of buying the stock

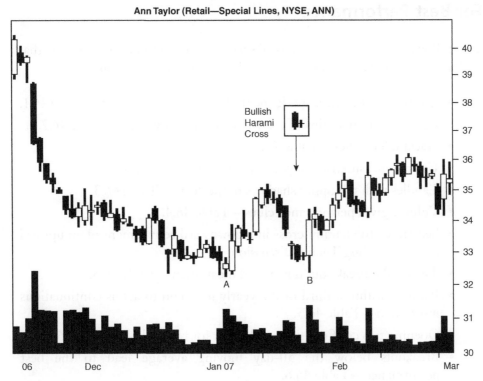

Ann Taylor (Retail—Special Lines, NYSE, ANN)

Figure 46.2 A bearish harami cross appears as part of a double bottom chart pattern.

sometime after point A but realizes that a sharp updraft often leads to a retracement that carries price almost back to the low.

He waits.

Sure enough, price rolls over and heads down in mid-January. Then a bearish harami cross appears after price gaps down. Is this a sign of more bearish enthusiasm, indicating a resumption of the downtrend? Only time will tell. The answer comes the next day in the form of a tall white candle (B)—bullish.

Since price touched the low at B and rebounded (farther down than Randy expected but still following his rounding bottom pattern), he buys the stock. The stock cooperates by confirming the double bottom when price closes above the peak between valleys A and B and then continuing higher like a helium balloon untethered (well, maybe with the child still hanging on).

During February, the stock runs into some trouble but recovers. About a month later (not shown in the figure), Randy sells the stock when it looks as if price is rounding over after reaching the 39 price target he set, picked because of a congestion zone formed at that price in November 2006 (a portion of that appears on the far left).

For Best Performance

The following list offers tips and observations to help choose candles that perform well. Consult the associated table for more information.

- Use the identification guidelines to help select the pattern—Table 46.1.
- Candles within a third of the yearly low perform best—Table 46.2.
- Select tall candles—Table 46.3.
- Use the measure rule to predict a price target—Table 46.3.
- Candles with tall upper shadows outperform—Table 46.3.
- Volume gives performance clues—Table 46.4.
- Search for the harami cross in a downward retracement of an upward move—Trading Tactics discussion.
- The candle breaks out downward most often—Table 46.5.
- Patterns within a third of the yearly low tend to act as continuations most often—Table 46.5.
- Opening gap confirmation works best for reversals—Table 46.6.
- Breakouts below the 50-day moving average lead to the best performance—Table 46.6.

47

High Wave

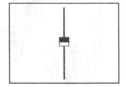

Behavior and Rank

Theoretical: Indecision.
Actual bull market: Reversal 51% of the time (ranking 51).
Actual bear market: Reversal 52% of the time (ranking 39).
Frequency: 17th out of 103.
Overall performance over time: 67th out of 103.

The high wave candle is another random pattern pretending to have significance to traders. To be exact, it functions as a reversal 51.1% of the time and that means it breaks out in any direction it feels like. Overall performance ranks 67, so that's well down the list from 1 (best) to 103 (worst) candles.

The psychology behind the pattern represents a futile struggle between the bulls and the bears to win control of the stock. Price drops during the day well below the open and also climbs well above it, too, but the end result is a small body sandwiched between two long shadows.

I read somewhere that a tall white candle trending up to a high wave means a reversal. I tested this and found that they were right! But the reversal rate was 50.4%. Yawn. That's worse than not depending on a tall white candle to lead the way.

Identification Guidelines

Figure 47.1 shows two examples of high wave candles. The first one appears after a tall white candle and it acts as a reversal of the uptrend. The high

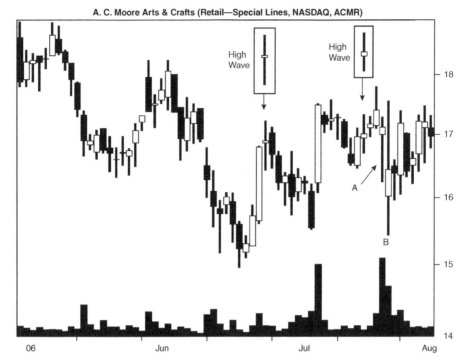

Figure 47.1   Two high wave candles appear; the first one signals the end of an uptrend and the second lies buried within the trend.

wave is a warning that the bulls have run out of energy to push price higher. Two tall black candles lead the way downward starting the next day, forming a three outside down bearish candle pattern. That's a bearish engulfing pattern followed by a lower close, confirming the downtrend.

The second high wave candle is just another drop in a pond. It appears after the start of an uptrend. It's also a warning that the bulls are enervated, but they still push price higher the next day and a day later, too. Notice the two white candles that appear next (marked A and B). Price drops and yet the candles are white. This is as it should be, but I wonder how much better candles would be if the color were tied to whether price closed higher or lower than the previous day.

Table 47.1 lists identification guidelines. This is a simple candle to recognize. Look for tall shadows and a small body. That's it. The candle appears

Table 47.1
Identification Guidelines

Characteristic	Discussion
Number of candle lines	One.
Configuration	Tall upper and lower shadows with a small body. Body can be either black or white.

regardless of the price trend leading to it, and body color is unimportant. The difference between a high wave candle and a spinning top is the shadow length. Spinning tops have shorter shadows. High wave candles have unusually long shadows.

Statistics

Table 47.2 shows general statistics.

Number found. I cut off my search at 20,000 candles. Prorating the standard database, I found that more high wave candles appear in a bear market than in a bull market.

Reversal or continuation performance. The best performance comes from patterns in a bear market, and reversals give the best results most often.

S&P performance. If you wait for the breakout from a high wave candle before taking a position and then ride price until the trend ends, you will have better performance than investing in the S&P 500 over the same periods.

Table 47.2
General Statistics

Description	Bull Market, Up Breakout	Bear Market, Up Breakout	Bull Market, Down Breakout	Bear Market, Down Breakout
Number found	7,100	3,137	6,445	3,318
Reversal (R), continuation (C) performance	6.38% C 7.04% R	6.90% C 8.73% R	−5.80% C −5.95% R	−10.11% C −9.50% R
Standard & Poor's 500 change	1.65%	1.19%	−1.07%	−2.92%
Candle end to breakout (median, days)	3	2	3	3
Candle end to trend end (median, days)	8	7	7	7
Number of breakouts near the 12-month low (L), middle (M), or high (H)	L 1,293, M 1,877, H 3,930	L 875, M 1,042, H 1,220	L 1,491, M 1,948, H 3,006	L 1,116, M 1,081, H 1,121
Percentage move for each 12-month period	L 8.36%, M 6.33%, H 6.45%	L 11.19%, M 7.25%, H 6.56%	L −6.63%, M −6.03%, H −5.52%	L −10.95%, M −10.08%, H −8.70%
Candle end + 1 day	1.29%	1.79%	−1.13%	−1.61%
Candle end + 3 days	2.24%	2.90%	−1.99%	−2.91%
Candle end + 5 days	2.48%	2.89%	−2.07%	−3.24%
Candle end + 10 days	2.64%	2.61%	−1.72%	−3.38%
10-day performance rank	62	60	71	64

Candle end to breakout. It takes about three days for price to close either above the high or below the candlestick's low.

Candle end to trend end. It takes about a week for price to reach the trend end.

Yearly position, performance. This candlestick appears most often within a third of the yearly high. However, performance is best when it appears near the yearly low.

Performance over time. The two inner columns show weakness from days 3 to 10 (bear market/up breakouts) and days 5 to 10 (bull market/down breakouts). The percentage change after 10 days is unremarkable, resulting in mediocre rankings of between 60 and 71 (1 is best out of 103).

Table 47.3 shows height statistics.

Candle height. Tall candles outperform short ones. To determine whether the candle is short or tall, compute its height from high to low price and divide by the breakout price. If the result is higher than the median, then you have a tall candle; otherwise it's short.

George spots a high wave candle with a high of 87 and a low of 86. The height is 87 − 86, or 1, so the measure would be 1/87, or 1.1%. In a bull market with an upward breakout, the candle is short.

Measure rule. Use the measure rule to help predict how far price will rise or fall. Compute the height of the candle and multiply it by the appropriate percentage shown in the table; then apply it to the breakout price.

Table 47.3
Height Statistics

Description	Bull Market, Up Breakout	Bear Market, Up Breakout	Bull Market, Down Breakout	Bear Market, Down Breakout
Median candle height as a percentage of breakout price	2.46%	3.56%	2.48%	3.55%
Short candle, performance	5.03%	6.02%	−4.74%	−8.39%
Tall candle, performance	8.97%	10.09%	−7.45%	−11.54%
Percentage meeting price target (measure rule)	77%	73%	73%	75%
Median upper shadow as a percentage of breakout price	1.12%	1.51%	1.16%	1.63%
Short upper shadow, performance	5.20%	6.28%	−4.96%	−8.40%
Tall upper shadow, performance	8.60%	9.67%	−7.07%	−11.42%
Median lower shadow as a percentage of breakout price	1.08%	1.60%	1.06%	1.54%
Short lower shadow, performance	5.10%	6.30%	−4.79%	−8.64%
Tall lower shadow, performance	8.82%	9.68%	−7.35%	−11.19%

Table 47.4
Volume Statistics

Description	Bull Market, Up Breakout	Bear Market, Up Breakout	Bull Market, Down Breakout	Bear Market, Down Breakout
Above-average candle volume, performance	6.83%	8.19%	−5.84%	−9.74%
Below-average candle volume, performance	6.60%	7.56%	−5.91%	−9.81%
Heavy breakout volume, performance	7.34%	8.68%	−6.12%	−10.48%
Light breakout volume, performance	6.15%	7.12%	−5.67%	−9.18%

What are the price targets for George's candle? The upward target would be (1 × 77%) + 87, or 87.77, and the downward target would be 86 − (1 × 73%), or 85.27.

Shadows. To determine whether the shadow is short or tall, compute the height of the shadow and divide by the breakout price. Compare the result to the median in the table. Tall shadows have a percentage higher than the median.

Candles with tall upper or lower shadows perform better than do those with short shadows.

Table 47.4 shows volume statistics.

Average candle volume. Candles with above-average volume and upward breakouts perform better than do those with below-average volume. Downward breakouts show the reverse: Candles with below-average volume perform better.

Breakout volume. Heavy breakout volume suggests good performance after the breakout, across the board.

Trading Tactics

I split trading tactics into two basic studies, one concerning reversal rates and the other concerning performance. Of the two, reversal rates are more important, because it's better to trade in the direction of the trend and let price run as far as it can.

Table 47.5 gives tips to find the trend direction.

Reversal, continuation rates. This category shows how often price reverses or continues the trend. In a bull market, a high wave candle acts as a reversal of the downtrend most often. In a bear market, the high wave candle also acts as a reversal but this time the trend is up to down. In either case, the reversal rate is close to random (50%).

Table 47.5
Reversal Rates

Description	Bull Market	Bear Market
Reversal rate: trend up, breakout down	49%	53%
Continuation rate: trend up, breakout up	51%	47%
Reversal: trend down, breakout up	54%	50%
Continuation: trend down, breakout down	46%	50%
Percentage of reversals (R)/ continuations (C) for each 12-month low (L), middle (M), or high (H)	L 50% R/50% C, M 51% R/49% C, H 52% R/48% C	L 49% R/51% C, M 52% R/48% C, H 53% R/47% C
Black body reversal rate	51%	51%
White body reversal rate	51%	52%

Yearly range reversals. The reversal and continuation rates are close to random, so the results are no help.

Body color reversal rate. The reversal rate does not change much when sorted by body color.

Table 47.6 shows performance indicators that can give hints as to how your stock will behave after the breakout from this candle pattern.

Confirmation, performance. The opening gap method to enter a trade results in the best performance across the board. That means you trade in the direction of the opening gap the next day, assuming it has a gap.

Moving average. As we have seen in many candle patterns, taking a position in a candle below the 50-trading-day moving average results in the best postbreakout performance across the board.

Closing position. A close in the highest third of the candle scores best for postbreakout performance in bull markets. Candles in bear markets do better when the close is near the candle's low.

Body color performance. A white high wave candle performs best most often. The exception occurs in a bull market with an upward breakout. There, a black candle works slightly better.

Sample Trade

Figure 47.2 shows a trade I made. Everyone who trades the markets frequently enough makes mistakes, and this is one of mine. I trade chart patterns with candles helping me enter or exit a position.

On the weekly scale (not shown), a double bottom with a tall left side appeared. My thinking was that the stock would become a Big W chart pattern—the right side would mirror the height of the left. So, I bought the stock.

Table 47.6
Performance Indicators

Description	Bull Market, Up Breakout	Bear Market, Up Breakout	Bull Market, Down Breakout	Bear Market, Down Breakout
Closing price confirmation, performance	6.43%	8.46%	−6.29%	−9.53%
Candle color confirmation, performance	6.38%	8.22%	−6.36%	−9.71%
Opening gap confirmation, performance	7.30%	9.33%	−6.99%	−10.13%
Breakout above 50-day moving average, performance	6.42%	6.77%	−5.66%	−8.75%
Breakout below 50-day moving average, performance	7.28%	9.47%	−6.11%	−10.71%
Last candle: close in highest third, performance	7.38%	7.59%	−6.40%	−9.14%
Last candle: close in middle third, performance	6.66%	7.80%	−5.90%	−9.78%
Last candle: close in lowest third, performance	6.32%	8.32%	−5.51%	−10.21%
Black body, performance	6.79%	7.79%	−5.76%	−9.72%
White body, performance	6.62%	7.86%	−6.01%	−9.85%

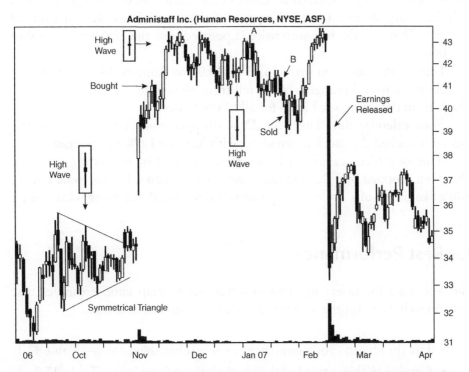

Figure 47.2 A symmetrical triangle leads to a strong up move that peaks with a high wave candle.

When I bought, the candles were not particularly telling. The large gap up (a rising window in candlespeak) would lend support if price dropped that far (it didn't in this case). Tall white candles on the climb were a good sign but, based on the symmetrical triangle breakout, I was late getting in. That's on the daily scale, which Figure 47.2 shows. On the weekly scale, I bought after price confirmed a double bottom chart pattern—a good entry.

I placed a stop at 36.33 or about 10% below the buy price. A stop based on volatility would be farther (12.6%) below, and if you based it on the minor low it would be 16% below. The upside target would be a rise to 53, the middle of a tall black candle back in May 2006 (not shown). Tall candles are often resistance zones.

Price retraced a bit in the few days after I bought, and then it moved up again with more tall white candles that led to the high wave. After that, many small bodies appeared, reminding me of fire ants after I kick their nest. They run around trying to bite anything they can, showing no consistent direction.

Price moved horizontally, bouncing between 41 and 43 for almost two months. I waited patiently. Another high wave candle appeared in the middle of the congestion area and the candle became just another ripple on the pond.

The day before the peak at A, I placed a buy order to expand my position. Why? If price did break out of this congestion region, I felt it would likely rise and hit my target price (that didn't occur, either, as the meager climb in early February shows). I wanted a piece of that move but only if it climbed to 43.55. That was the buy stop price, a penny above the high on November 22, 2006.

I raised the first stop from 36.33 to 40.03 on January 18 (B) because "I thought price would plunge when it fell through support, so I put in a stop." That's from the notebook I keep for all of my trades.

Four calendar days later, the Dow dropped over 100 points and the undertow sucked this stock down along with it. I lost 1.6% on the trade.

The long black candle in February was caused by an earnings release. The stock dropped over 22% in one session on the news. I guess some traders didn't like the results. At least they missed taking me down along with them.

For Best Performance

The following list offers tips and observations to help choose candles that perform well. Consult the associated table for more information.

- Use the identification guidelines to help select the pattern—Table 47.1.
- Candles within a third of the yearly low perform best—Table 47.2.
- Select tall candles—Table 47.3.

- Use the measure rule to predict a price target—Table 47.3.
- Candles with tall upper or lower shadows outperform—Table 47.3.
- Volume gives performance clues—Table 47.4.
- In a bull market, the candle breaks out upward most often—Table 47.5.
- Opening gap confirmation works best—Table 47.6.
- Breakouts below the 50-day moving average lead to the best performance—Table 47.6.

48

Homing Pigeon

Behavior and Rank

Theoretical: Bullish reversal.

Actual bull market: Bearish continuation 56% of the time (ranking 31).

Actual bear market: Bearish continuation 57% of the time (ranking 26).

Frequency: 34th out of 103.

Overall performance over time: 21st out of 103.

A bullish harami is a close cousin to the homing pigeon. The only difference is the second candle in a homing pigeon is black instead of white. That simple color change makes all the difference. The bullish harami is a reversal that works 53% of the time. A homing pigeon works 56% of the time but as a continuation pattern, not a reversal. Both are close to random, so you probably won't be able to tell the difference anyway.

Overall performance is quite good, ranking 21 out of 103, where 1 is best. The frequency rank is also good, so you can find plenty of them in the price landscape.

A homing pigeon occurs in a downtrend when the bears control the board. A tall black candle appears followed by a smaller black candle. The body of the second candle is engulfed by the first candle's body. All of the sources I checked say this combination represents a bullish reversal of the downtrend, but I don't see how. Two black candles in a downtrend tell me price will continue lower. The real surprise is that price drops only 56% of the time.

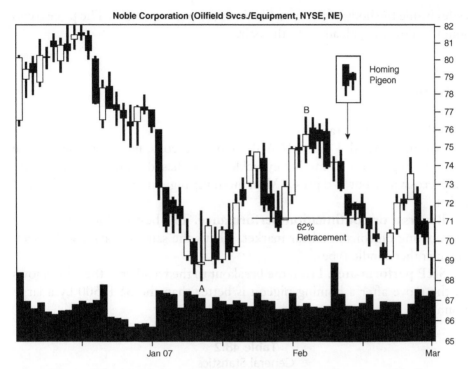

Figure 48.1 A homing pigeon appears in a downtrend and hits a 62% Fibonacci retracement line, where price should reverse but doesn't.

Identification Guidelines

Figure 48.1 shows an example of the typical behavior of a homing pigeon. Price climbs from A to B and then reverses. In many uptrends, price will hit a 62% retracement of the AB move and then rebound. That's what the homing pigeon is supposed to signal: a reversal of the downtrend. However, in this example, price continues lower, lengthening a string of black candles until price nears the previous low at A. Only then do you see a rebound.

Table 48.1 lists identification guidelines. Look for a pair of black candles; the first is a tall one and the second is shorter such that the body of the second

Table 48.1
Identification Guidelines

Characteristic	Discussion
Number of candle lines	Two.
Price trend	Downward leading to the start of the candle pattern.
First day	A tall black body.
Second day	A short black body that is inside the body of the first day.

nestles inside the body of the first. Shadows are not important. The price trend should be downward leading to the pair.

Statistics

Table 48.2 shows general statistics.

Number found. I found 16,670 homing pigeons, not including the one that's building a nest in my honeysuckle. Ants chased away another nesting in my crossvine, but I digress. Most homing pigeons come from the bull market.

Reversal or continuation performance. The best performance comes from homing pigeons in a bear market. That's the same behavior we've seen in many other candle types.

S&P performance. From the breakout to the trend end, the table shows that the move after a homing pigeon is better than the S&P 500 by a large amount.

Table 48.2
General Statistics

Description	Bull Market, Up Breakout	Bear Market, Up Breakout	Bull Market, Down Breakout	Bear Market, Down Breakout
Number found	6,033	1,319	7,556	1,762
Reversal (R), continuation (C) performance	6.84% R	9.81% R	−5.86% C	−10.63% C
Standard & Poor's 500 change	1.87%	1.49%	−0.71%	−2.14%
Candle end to breakout (median, days)	4	4	3	3
Candle end to trend end (median, days)	9	9	6	6
Number of breakouts near the 12-month low (L), middle (M), or high (H)	L 1,554, M 1,720, H 2,438	L 502, M 461, H 332	L 2,557, M 2,409, H 2,168	L 856, M 577, H 295
Percentage move for each 12-month period	L 8.55%, M 6.90%, H 6.54%	L 13.05%, M 9.50%, H 7.05%	L −6.42%, M −6.12%, H −5.12%	L −12.02%, M −10.16%, H −8.18%
Candle end + 1 day	1.36%	2.18%	−0.82%	−1.43%
Candle end + 3 days	2.64%	4.47%	−1.57%	−3.02%
Candle end + 5 days	3.40%	5.05%	−1.81%	−3.52%
Candle end + 10 days	3.79%	4.76%	−1.71%	−3.89%
10-day performance rank	39	33	72	54

Candle end to breakout. It takes three or four days for price to break out. Upward breakouts take a day longer than downward ones because price closes nearer the candle's low.

Candle end to trend end. Downward breakouts take six days and upward breakouts take nine to reach the trend end. The difference is that a downtrend is under way, making a downward move closer to the trend end.

Yearly position, performance. Candles with breakouts within a third of the yearly low show the best performance. That's also where many of them reside.

Performance over time. The 72 performance rank highlights the one category that has a performance problem. It occurs from day 5 to 10 where performance drops. All of the percentages over 10 days could use a bit of a lift, though. Good performance is 6% or more over that time.

Table 48.3 shows height statistics.

Candle height. Tall candles perform better than short ones. To determine whether the candle is short or tall, compute its height from highest high to lowest low price in the candle pattern and divide by the breakout price. If the result is higher than the median, then you have a tall candle; otherwise it's short.

Colombo spots a homing pigeon and discovers that it has a high price of 37 and a low of 35. Is it short or tall? In a bull market with an upward breakout,

Table 48.3
Height Statistics

Description	Bull Market, Up Breakout	Bear Market, Up Breakout	Bull Market, Down Breakout	Bear Market, Down Breakout
Median candle height as a percentage of breakout price	3.56%	5.45%	3.70%	5.82%
Short candle, performance	5.32%	7.40%	−4.48%	−8.02%
Tall candle, performance	9.34%	12.63%	−7.90%	−13.88%
Percentage meeting price target (measure rule)	68%	65%	57%	59%
Median upper shadow as a percentage of breakout price	0.63%	1.09%	0.65%	1.07%
Short upper shadow, performance	5.89%	8.15%	−5.19%	−9.19%
Tall upper shadow, performance	7.94%	11.40%	−6.52%	−12.11%
Median lower shadow as a percentage of breakout price	0.73%	1.15%	0.66%	1.10%
Short lower shadow, performance	5.70%	8.60%	−4.96%	−9.11%
Tall lower shadow, performance	8.38%	11.26%	−6.96%	−12.31%

Table 48.4
Volume Statistics

Description	Bull Market, Up Breakout	Bear Market, Up Breakout	Bull Market, Down Breakout	Bear Market, Down Breakout
Rising candle volume, performance	7.38%	10.22%	−5.85%	−10.47%
Falling candle volume, performance	6.96%	9.59%	−5.87%	−10.71%
Above-average candle volume, performance	7.00%	10.78%	−5.80%	−10.99%
Below-average candle volume, performance	6.72%	8.94%	−5.91%	−10.28%
Heavy breakout volume, performance	7.79%	10.58%	−6.08%	−11.51%
Light breakout volume, performance	5.96%	9.12%	−5.66%	−9.56%

the height would be 37 − 35, or 2, and the measure would be 2/37, or 5.4%. The candle is tall.

Measure rule. Use the measure rule to help predict how far price will rise or fall. Compute the height of the candle pattern and multiply it by the appropriate percentage shown in the table; then apply it to the breakout price.

What are Colombo's price targets? The upward target would be $(2 \times 68\%) + 37$, or 38.36, and the downward target would be $35 − (2 \times 57\%)$, or 33.86.

Shadows. The table's results pertain to the last candle line in the pattern. To determine whether the shadow is short or tall, compute the height of the shadow and divide by the breakout price. Compare the result to the median in the table. Tall shadows have a percentage higher than the median. Homing pigeons with tall upper or lower shadows perform better than do those with short shadows.

Table 48.4 shows volume statistics.

Candle volume trend. Upward breakouts do best if the homing pigeon shows a rising volume trend. Downward breakouts do better after a falling volume trend.

Average candle volume. Candles with above-average volume work better in all cases except for bull market/down breakouts.

Breakout volume. Candles with heavy breakout volume do better than those with light volume.

Trading Tactics

If you know what an inverted and ascending scallop looks like (picture the letter J flipped upside down and backward), then a homing pigeon on the

Table 48.5
Reversal Rates

Description	Bull Market	Bear Market
Closing price confirmation reversal rate	67%	68%
Candle color confirmation reversal rate	67%	67%
Opening gap confirmation reversal rate	52%	51%
Reversal: trend down, breakout up	44%	43%
Continuation: trend down, breakout down	56%	57%
Percentage of reversals (R)/ continuations (C) for each 12-month low (L), middle (M), or high (H)	L 38% R/62% C, M 42% R/58% C, H 53% R/47% C	L 37% R/63% C, M 44% R/56% C, H 53% R/47% C

right bottom edge often leads to a reversal. The scallop should appear in an established uptrend of several months' duration. In technical terms, the homing pigeon appears as a downward retracement in an uptrend. If the retracement is about 38% of the prior uptrend when the homing pigeon appears, there is a better chance that price will reverse.

If a homing pigeon appears in an established downtrend several months long, then expect the downtrend to continue. Any up move is likely to be short-lived. That's not always the case, of course, but it's rare that a homing pigeon acts as a reversal of the primary downtrend.

I split trading tactics into two basic studies, one concerning reversal rates and the other concerning performance. Of the two, reversal rates are more important, because it's better to trade in the direction of the trend and let price run as far as it can.

Table 48.5 gives tips to find the trend direction.

Confirmation reversal rates. To help detect a reversal of the downtrend in a bull market, wait for either a higher close the day after the homing pigeon or a white candle.

Reversal, continuation rates. Expect the breakout to be downward, but it's not much better than random (50%).

Yearly range reversals. If a homing pigeon has a breakout within a third of the yearly low, it's nearly twice as likely to be a continuation pattern as a reversal.

Table 48.6 shows performance indicators that can give hints as to how your stock will behave after the breakout from a candle pattern.

Confirmation, performance. Performance improves if you wait for price to gap open higher after the homing pigeon rather than using the other confirmation methods.

Moving average. A homing pigeon with a breakout below the 50-trading-day moving average results in the best performance. This is the same result that we've seen from many other candle types.

Table 48.6
Performance Indicators

Description	Bull Market, Up Breakout	Bear Market, Up Breakout	Bull Market, Down Breakout	Bear Market, Down Breakout
Closing price confirmation, performance	7.39%	12.20%	N/A	N/A
Candle color confirmation, performance	7.52%	11.73%	N/A	N/A
Opening gap confirmation, performance	7.95%	12.78%	N/A	N/A
Breakout above 50-day moving average, performance	6.84%	8.10%	−4.94%	−8.49%
Breakout below 50-day moving average, performance	6.84%	11.02%	−6.17%	−11.12%
Last candle: close in highest third, performance	6.95%	10.35%	−6.25%	−10.75%
Last candle: close in middle third, performance	6.76%	9.84%	−5.79%	−10.29%
Last candle: close in lowest third, performance	6.91%	9.56%	−5.82%	−10.93%

N/A means not applicable.

Closing position. If the closing price in the last candle is within a third of the candle's high price, then postbreakout performance improves in all categories except for bear market/down breakouts. Those do better if the close is within a third of the candle's low.

Sample Trade

At the start of 2007, I was getting nervous about my utility holdings. They had been trending upward since April 2006. With signs in the utility average that it was about to change trend and with many utility stocks showing weakness, I sold all of my utility holdings. Figure 48.2 shows one of them.

Notice the tall black candle at B. The long upper shadow meant the bulls tried to keep price up but failed. A group of small candles that followed suggested indecision from traders, but the closing price eased lower over time. The tall shadows on those candles I interpreted as bearish. Those signs (and others) were enough to kick me out of the stock at A.

I did ponder how far price might fall and realized that it might drop to the support zone (shown) before rebounding. However, I thought that unlikely since the average was also struggling, as were the other utility stocks. I felt that price would eventually make its way lower. I didn't want to give back too much of my gains in case I was right. You never go broke taking a profit.

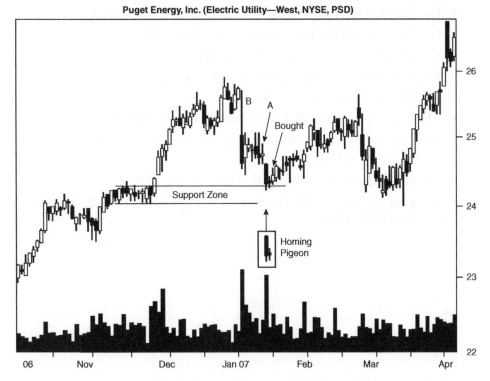

Puget Energy, Inc. (Electric Utility—West, NYSE, PSD)

Figure 48.2 A homing pigeon appears at a support zone offering a low-risk trade.

Colombo looked at things differently. He saw a homing pigeon form at the support zone. That meant a low-risk opportunity with a large reward. When price gapped open higher the day after the homing pigeon ended, he bought.

Price moved up in a chain of small candles with long lower shadows, an underlying bullish force pushing price higher. Price tumbled back to the support zone in March when the general market stumbled, but Colombo wasn't worried. He felt that the tight knot of support from the November zone would be enough to hold price. He was right.

For Best Performance

The following list offers tips and observations to help choose candles that perform well. Consult the associated table for more information.

- Use the identification guidelines to help select the pattern—Table 48.1.
- Candles within a third of the yearly low perform best—Table 48.2.
- Select tall candles—Table 48.3.

- Use the measure rule to predict a price target—Table 48.3.
- Candles with tall shadows outperform—Table 48.3.
- Volume gives performance clues—Table 48.4.
- Reversals from homing pigeons occur on the right of an inverted and ascending scallop—Trading Tactics discussion.
- The candle breaks out downward most often—Table 48.5.
- Patterns within a third of the yearly low tend to act as continuations frequently—Table 48.5.
- Opening gap confirmation works best—Table 48.6.
- Breakouts below the 50-day moving average lead to the best performance—Table 48.6.

49

Identical Three Crows

Behavior and Rank

Theoretical: Bearish reversal.
Actual bull market: Bearish reversal 79% of the time (ranking 4).
Actual bear market: Bearish reversal 72% of the time (ranking 10).
Frequency: 83rd out of 103.
Overall performance over time: 24th out of 103.

The identical three crows have an outstanding reversal record: Almost 80% of the time price reverses the uptrend in a bull market. Why is that? Because the pattern is so tall that you often get a close under the low of the pattern (a downward breakout) before you get a close above the highest high in the pattern (an upward breakout).

The overall performance is a very good 24 out of 103, where 1 is best. Separating the performance by categories, we find that the rise after an upward breakout is top-notch. The performance after a downward breakout is startlingly bad—price goes almost nowhere.

The psychology behind the identical three crows pattern begins with an uptrend leading to the pattern. The bulls have control and are pushing price higher. Then a tall black candle appears, then another and yet another, each opening where the other closed and all pointing lower. Downward momentum grows as the bears take over from bulls scurrying for cover.

After the pattern ends anything can happen, but price often makes a lower low for a few days and then bounces up (retracing a good portion of the three crows pattern), rounds over, and heads down again. Whether it clears the low it made after the three crows depends on the general market, industry, and company conditions. Usually price *will* post a new low but one that doesn't drop much farther. If it did, the measure rule hit rate would be much higher, like 70% or 80% and not 30%.

Identification Guidelines

Figure 49.1 shows price forming a straight-line run out of a congestion region in early August (B) leading to the highest peak on the chart. Following that, an identical three crows pattern appears and leads price lower.

If I were trading this pattern, I would expect the stock to return to the launch price of about 28 and stop there, perhaps making a complex head-and-shoulders top. It does stop at 28 for a few days, forming a homing pigeon (two candle lines) and a ladder bottom that encompasses five candle lines ending with the white one highlighted in the figure. Both candle patterns are bullish if you believe the theory, and if price moves up a significant amount, then I would agree. But in this case a bearish engulfing candle at A ends with a tall black candle, and price punches through support.

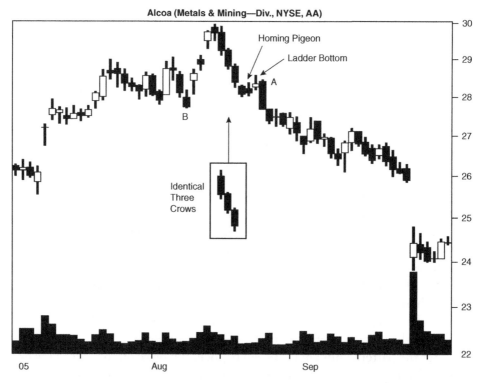

Figure 49.1   Identical three crows pattern leads price lower.

Table 49.1
Identification Guidelines

Characteristic	Discussion
Number of candle lines	Three.
Price trend	Upward leading to the start of the pattern.
Configuration	Look for three tall black candles, the last two each opening at or near the prior close.

Notice how price retraces a portion of the downward move after the crows end. This is typical, but the extent of the rise varies widely from pattern to pattern.

Table 49.1 lists identification guidelines, and they are a bit confusing if you examine enough sources. I look for three tall candles with the last two each opening near where the prior candle closed. The pattern looks like a straight-line run headed lower. The variations from other sources say that the candles should be similar in size and that they should close near their lows. I did not place those restrictions on the pattern. This one is rare enough without them.

Statistics

Table 49.2 shows general statistics.

Number found. I found 921 patterns, making this a rare candle despite the search of over 4.7 million candle lines. Most appear in a bull market and have a downward breakout, as the table shows.

Reversal or continuation performance. The bear market shows the best performance of the three crows.

S&P performance. The performance of the three crows beats the S&P 500 over the same period.

Candle end to breakout. Downward breakouts take less time to reach the breakout price than do upward breakouts. This makes sense since price is at the bottom of the candle and has to close above the top of the pattern for an upward breakout.

Candle end to trend end. It takes between 5 and 15 days to reach the trend end, with downward breakouts taking less time than upward breakouts. Downward breakouts reach the trend end sooner because the downtrend is well along. The percentage drop over time (the last several lines in the table) also confirms this theory by posting meager or no declines.

Yearly position, performance. Candles with the best performance come from the middle of the yearly price range except for bull market/up breakouts. Most other candle types show better performance when the breakout is within a third of the yearly low.

Table 49.2
General Statistics

Description	Bull Market, Up Breakout	Bear Market, Up Breakout	Bull Market, Down Breakout	Bear Market, Down Breakout
Number found	178	16	686	41
Reversal (R), continuation (C) performance	4.83% C	8.15% C	−5.45% R	−7.74% R
Standard & Poor's 500 change	1.92%	0.75%	−0.47%	−2.09%
Candle end to breakout (median, days)	13	9	3	2
Candle end to trend end (median, days)	11	15	5	5
Number of breakouts near the 12-month low (L), middle (M), or high (H)	L 29, M 25, H 90	L 2, M 7, H 6	L 154, M 204, H 195	L 22, M 5, H 14
Percentage move for each 12-month period	L 5.65%, M 2.70%, H 4.93%	L 7.50%, M 10.98%, H 5.86%	L −5.69%, M −5.78%, H −4.86%	L −6.96%, M −10.22%, H −7.90%
Candle end + 1 day	1.66%	2.53%	−0.38%	−0.58%
Candle end + 3 days	3.31%	6.08%	−0.78%	0.50%
Candle end + 5 days	4.62%	8.45%	−1.12%	0.77%
Candle end + 10 days	5.67%	10.03%	−0.88%	−0.41%
10-day performance rank	6	3	99	97

Performance over time. The performance for upward breakouts is very good, especially the 10% move in a bear market. However, downward breakouts post some of the worst results I've seen. Price actually rises in two cases. The performance rank suffers as a result.

Table 49.3 shows height statistics.

Candle height. Tall candles outperform short ones in all cases. To determine whether the candle is short or tall, compute its height from highest high to lowest low price in the candle pattern and divide by the breakout price. If the result is higher than the median, then you have a tall candle; otherwise it's short.

Moe sees identical three crows with a high price of 40 and a low of 35. Is the candle tall or short? The height is 40 − 35, or 5, so the measure would be 5/40, or 13%. In a bull market with an upward breakout the candle is tall.

Measure rule. Use the measure rule to help predict how far price will rise or fall. Compute the height of the candle pattern and multiply it by the appropriate percentage shown in the table; then apply it to the breakout price.

Table 49.3
Height Statistics

Description	Bull Market, Up Breakout	Bear Market, Up Breakout*	Bull Market, Down Breakout	Bear Market, Down Breakout*
Median candle height as a percentage of breakout price	6.82%	9.67%	7.11%	11.64%
Short candle, performance	4.76%	8.09%	−4.69%	−7.61%
Tall candle, performance	4.94%	8.24%	−6.57%	−7.94%
Percentage meeting price target (measure rule)	31%	63%	28%	29%
Median upper shadow as a percentage of breakout price	0.28%	0.05%	0.05%	0.00%
Short upper shadow, performance	4.13%	8.34%	−5.58%	−7.16%
Tall upper shadow, performance	5.36%	8.01%	−5.33%	−8.53%
Median lower shadow as a percentage of breakout price	0.07%	0.00%	0.00%	0.23%
Short lower shadow, performance	4.05%	9.61%	−5.82%	−7.19%
Tall lower shadow, performance	5.30%	6.55%	−5.20%	−8.42%

*Fewer than 30 samples.

What are Moe's price targets? The upward target would be (5 × 31%) + 40, or 41.55, and the downward target would be 35 − (5 × 28%), or 33.60.

Shadows. The table's results pertain to the last candle line in the pattern. To determine whether the shadow is short or tall, compute the height of the shadow and divide by the breakout price. Compare the result to the median in the table. Tall shadows have a percentage higher than the median. Do not let a 0% median alarm you. That just means many candles do not have a shadow.

Candles with tall shadows perform better in bull market/up breakouts and bear market/down breakouts. Candles with short shadows do better in bear market/up breakouts and bull market/down breakouts.

Table 49.4 shows volume statistics.

Candle volume trend. Candles with falling volume perform better than do those with rising volume in all categories except for bear market/up breakouts.

Average candle volume. Candles with above-average volume do better than do those with below-average volume except for bear market/down breakouts.

Breakout volume. Heavy breakout-day volume results in the best performance in all categories.

Table 49.4
Volume Statistics

Description	Bull Market, Up Breakout	Bear Market, Up Breakout*	Bull Market, Down Breakout	Bear Market, Down Breakout*
Rising candle volume, performance	4.38%	9.17%	−5.19%	−7.15%
Falling candle volume, performance	5.49%	3.74%	−5.90%	−9.29%
Above-average candle volume, performance	5.48%	10.80%	−5.70%	−7.71%
Below-average candle volume, performance	4.41%	5.82%	−5.23%	−7.77%
Heavy breakout volume, performance	4.93%	8.54%	−5.63%	−9.66%
Light breakout volume, performance	4.71%	6.28%	−5.15%	−4.92%

*Fewer than 30 samples.

Trading Tactics

If you see an identical three crows pattern in a stock you own form in a primary uptrend, do not be alarmed and panic sell. The chances are that price will break out downward but reverse in just a few days. If you want to sell, you can do so generally at a higher price within a week.

I split trading tactics into two basic studies, one concerning reversal rates and the other concerning performance. Of the two, reversal rates are more important, because it's better to trade in the direction of the trend and let price run as far as it can.

Table 49.5 gives tips to find the trend direction.

Table 49.5
Reversal Rates

Description	Bull Market	Bear Market*
Closing price confirmation reversal rate	97%	100%
Candle color confirmation reversal rate	94%	94%
Opening gap confirmation reversal rate	88%	85%
Reversal rate: trend up, breakout down	79%	72%
Continuation rate: trend up, breakout up	21%	28%
Percentage of reversals (R)/ continuations (C) for each 12-month low (L), middle (M), or high (H)	L* 84% R/16% C, M* 89% R/11% C, H 68% R/32% C	L 92% R/8% C, M 42% R/58% C, H 70% R/30% C

*Fewer than 30 samples.

Confirmation reversal rates. To help confirm an upward reversal, wait for price to close higher the day after the crows formation ends. Although the 100% success rate in a bear market is outstanding, it just means I didn't find any that failed. I'm sure failures are out there somewhere.

Reversal, continuation rates. Based on the price trend leading to the candle pattern and the breakout direction, expect a downward breakout. That occurs when price closes below the bottom of the candle pattern.

Yearly range reversals. The results say that the candle works as a reversal most often in the middle of the price range for bull markets, but the sample size is small. Downward breakouts show a high reversal rate when the breakout is within a third of the yearly low.

Table 49.6 shows performance indicators that can give hints as to how your stock will behave after the breakout from this candle pattern.

Confirmation, performance. The opening gap method (trade only if price gaps open lower the day after the candle pattern ends) works well in both bull and bear markets.

Moving average. The best performance comes when the three crows have a breakout below the 50-trading-day moving average. This is true in all cases except for bull market/up breakouts.

Closing position. Price closes in the lowest third of the black candle in all cases.

Table 49.6
Performance Indicators

Description	Bull Market, Up Breakout	Bear Market, Up Breakout*	Bull Market, Down Breakout	Bear Market, Down Breakout*
Closing price confirmation, performance	N/A	N/A	−4.60%	−6.75%
Candle color confirmation, performance	N/A	N/A	−5.09%	−6.88%
Opening gap confirmation, performance	N/A	N/A	−5.67%	−7.45%
Breakout above 50-day moving average, performance	5.26%	7.60%	−5.19%	−5.52%
Breakout below 50-day moving average, performance	2.57%*	11.11%	−5.54%	−8.56%
Last candle: close in highest third, performance	0.00%	0.00%	0.00%	0.00%
Last candle: close in middle third, performance	0.00%	0.00%	0.00%	0.00%
Last candle: close in lowest third, performance	4.83%	8.15%	−5.45%	−7.74%

N/A means not applicable.
*Fewer than 30 samples.

Sample Trade

Triple tops are easy to spot. You just look for three peaks near the same price, so Moe has no trouble finding the one pictured in Figure 49.2. There's just one problem: It's not a triple top.

Before it can be called a triple top chart pattern, price has to close below the lowest low between the three tops. That doesn't happen, so the chart shows just three peaks near the same price.

Moe watches the stock form the first two peaks and then the third. When the identical three crows fly in, he looks at how far price might decline. The cluster of peaks in February and March forming a support line near 40, a round number, would likely stop the decline, he thinks. Instead of shorting the stock on the basis of the three crows, he decides to wait and see what happens.

Price gaps below a neckline (the dashed line in the chart) drawn connecting the valleys between the three peaks. If Moe were interested in shorting the stock, this would be an early entry signal for an unconfirmed triple top.

Price crosses the confirmation line of the three peaks but doesn't close below it. As price climbs in the coming days, Moe draws a dashed line downward from peaks 2 and 3. When price closes above the line, he buys the stock.

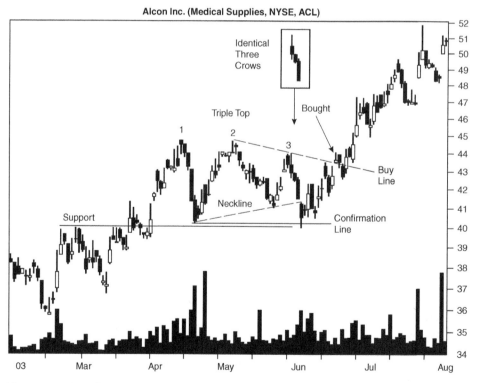

Figure 49.2 Identical three crows appear at the third peak of an unconfirmed triple top.

This chart represents a good example of the identical three crows behavior. Price broke out downward from the candle pattern (by closing lower) but then recovered and flew to a new high.

For Best Performance

The following list offers tips and observations to help choose candles that perform well. Consult the associated table for more information.

- Use the identification guidelines to help select the pattern—Table 49.1.
- Candles in the middle third of the yearly price range perform best except for bull market/up breakouts—Table 49.2.
- Select tall candles—Table 49.3.
- Use the measure rule to predict a price target—Table 49.3.
- Volume gives performance clues—Table 49.4.
- In a primary uptrend, anticipate a downward breakout but expect price to recover quickly—Trading Tactics discussion.
- The candle breaks out downward most often—Table 49.5.
- Opening gap confirmation works best—Table 49.6.
- Breakouts below the 50-day moving average lead to the best performance except for bull market/up breakouts—Table 49.6.

50

In Neck

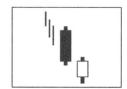

Behavior and Rank

Theoretical: Bearish continuation.
Actual bull market: Bearish continuation 53% of the time (ranking 39).
Actual bear market: Bearish continuation 65% of the time (ranking 17).
Frequency: 62nd out of 103.
Overall performance over time: 17th out of 103.

An in neck is supposed to work as a continuation pattern, and it does but just barely—53% of the time in a bull market. In a bear market is where the pattern shines: 65% of the time price continues lower. The overall performance is very good at 17 out of 103 candles, with 1 being best.

The psychology behind the pattern begins with a downward price trend. The bears push price lower and a tall black candle appears followed by a white candle. Price in the white candle opens lower but closes near the black candle's close. The inability of price to make a strong recovery dismays the bulls who bought in the morning. If they begin to sell the next day, joining the bears already dumping the stock, price will tumble.

Identification Guidelines

Figure 50.1 shows a good example of an in neck pattern. This one appears as part of a straight-line run downward. Just where you would expect price to reverse—at the price of the January low a month earlier (A)—the in neck

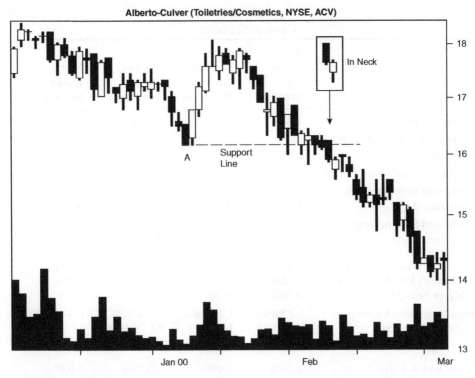

Figure 50.1 An in neck pattern appears in a downward price trend.

presents itself. Price drills through the support, but it takes about a week of loose price action to do so.

How do you recognize an in neck pattern? Table 50.1 lists the identification guidelines. Look for a black and white candle combination in a downtrend. The white candle should open lower than the low of the first candle but close within the black body, near its close.

Statistics

Table 50.2 shows general statistics.

Table 50.1
Identification Guidelines

Characteristic	Discussion
Number of candle lines	Two.
Price trend	Downward leading to the start of the candle pattern.
First day	A long black candle.
Second day	A white candle with an open below the low of the first day and a close that is into the body of the first day but not by much.

Table 50.2
General Statistics

Description	Bull Market, Up Breakout	Bear Market, Up Breakout	Bull Market, Down Breakout	Bear Market, Down Breakout
Number found	1,349	151	1,505	282
Reversal (R), continuation (C) performance	6.88% R	9.34% R	−5.53% C	−11.76% C
Standard & Poor's 500 change	1.92%	1.57%	−0.53%	−2.69%
Candle end to breakout (median, days)	5	4	4	4
Candle end to trend end (median, days)	9	10	6	7
Number of breakouts near the 12-month low (L), middle (M), or high (H)	L 333, M 376, H 500	L 57, M 41, H 48	L 489, M 455, H 373	L 146, M 99, H 35
Percentage move for each 12-month period	L 7.88%, M 7.02%, H 5.99%	L 11.24%, M 8.52%, H 8.15%	L −6.57%, M −5.00%, H −5.07%	L −13.73%, M −10.09%, H −9.37%
Candle end + 1 day	1.06%	1.99%	−0.76%	−0.60%
Candle end + 3 days	2.48%	3.73%	−1.68%	−2.55%
Candle end + 5 days	3.50%	4.82%	−1.94%	−3.98%
Candle end + 10 days	4.45%	6.34%	−2.08%	−5.86%
10-day performance rank	23	16	59	22

Number found. The in neck pattern is somewhat rare. Out of over 4.7 million candle lines, I found only 3,287 of them. Prorating the standard database means that more appear in a bear market.

Reversal or continuation performance. The best performance comes from patterns in a bear market.

S&P performance. The performance of the in neck beats the S&P 500 over the same periods by a wide margin.

Candle end to breakout. It takes four or five days for price to break out. That means a close above the top of the pattern or a close below the pattern's low.

Candle end to trend end. The median time to reach the trend end varies between 6 and 10 days, with downward breakouts taking a few days less time. This makes sense because price completes the pattern near its low, in a downtrend.

Yearly position, performance. Most of the in neck patterns have breakouts that occur within a third of the yearly low. The lone exception, bull

Table 50.3
Height Statistics

Description	Bull Market, Up Breakout	Bear Market, Up Breakout	Bull Market, Down Breakout	Bear Market, Down Breakout
Median candle height as a percentage of breakout price	4.03%	6.68%	4.06%	6.84%
Short candle, performance	5.72%	8.00%	−4.72%	−7.76%
Tall candle, performance	8.43%	11.21%	−6.71%	−16.62%
Percentage meeting price target (measure rule)	61%	54%	53%	59%
Median upper shadow as a percentage of breakout price	0.46%	1.03%	0.50%	1.00%
Short upper shadow, performance	6.09%	8.48%	−5.40%	−9.82%
Tall upper shadow, performance	7.62%	10.55%	−5.65%	−13.56%
Median lower shadow as a percentage of breakout price	0.38%	0.72%	0.21%	0.68%
Short lower shadow, performance	5.97%	8.71%	−5.43%	−8.80%
Tall lower shadow, performance	7.65%	9.98%	−5.61%	−14.68%

market/up breakouts, has them near the yearly high. Candles with breakouts within a third of the yearly low perform best.

Performance over time. This is a robust candle showing increasing performance over time and in all categories, without exception. Its reward is very good performance ranks.

Table 50.3 shows height statistics.

Candle height. Tall candles work better than short ones. To determine whether the candle is short or tall, compute its height from highest high to lowest low price in the candle pattern and divide by the breakout price. If the result is higher than the median, then you have a tall candle; otherwise it's short.

Joe sees an in neck with a high of 87 and a low of 84. Is the candle short or tall? The height is 87 − 84, or 3, so the measure is 3/87, or 3.4%. Assuming an upward breakout in a bull market, Joe's candle is short because it's less than the median.

Measure rule. Use the measure rule to help predict how far price will rise or fall. Compute the height of the candle pattern and multiply it by the appropriate percentage shown in the table; then apply it to the breakout price.

What are the price targets for Joe's candle? The upward target would be (3 × 61%) + 87, or 88.83, and the downward target would be 84 − (3 × 53%), or 82.41.

Table 50.4
Volume Statistics

Description	Bull Market, Up Breakout	Bear Market, Up Breakout	Bull Market, Down Breakout	Bear Market, Down Breakout
Rising candle volume, performance	6.71%	9.68%	−5.63%	−12.24%
Falling candle volume, performance	7.11%	8.76%	−5.42%	−11.16%
Above-average candle volume, performance	6.99%	9.08%	−5.11%	−12.65%
Below-average candle volume, performance	6.78%	9.63%	−5.80%	−10.99%
Heavy breakout volume, performance	7.54%	9.58%	−5.92%	−12.78%
Light breakout volume, performance	6.19%	8.99%	−5.19%	−10.75%

Shadows. The table's results pertain to the last candle line in the pattern. To determine whether the shadow is short or tall, compute the height of the shadow and divide by the breakout price. Compare the result to the median in the table. Tall shadows have a percentage higher than the median.

In neck patterns with tall shadows perform better than do those with short shadows.

Table 50.4 shows volume statistics.

Candle volume trend. A rising volume trend within the candle results in the best performance except for the bull market/up breakout condition. There a falling volume trend works better.

Average candle volume. Candles with above-average volume in bull market/up breakouts and bear market/down breakouts perform better than do those with below-average volume. Bear market/up breakouts and bull market/down breakouts perform better if volume is below average.

Breakout volume. Heavy breakout volume leads to better performance across the board.

Trading Tactics

If you want to trade this candle pattern as a continuation, then look for it when price has been trending downward (the primary trend). Avoid trading it when the primary trend is upward such that the in neck appears as part of a downward retracement in an upward price trend. The downward move from those tends to be short.

I split trading tactics into two basic studies, one concerning reversal rates and the other concerning performance. Of the two, reversal rates are more

Table 50.5
Reversal Rates

Description	Bull Market	Bear Market
Reversal: trend down, breakout up	47%	35%
Continuation: trend down, breakout down	53%	65%
Percentage of reversals (R)/ continuations (C) for each 12-month low (L), middle (M), or high (H)	L 41% R/59% C, M 45% R/55% C, H 57% R/43% C	L 28% R/72% C, M 29% R/71% C, H 58% R/ 42% C

important, because it's better to trade in the direction of the trend and let price run as far as it can.

Table 50.5 gives tips to find the trend direction.

Reversal, continuation rates. Based on the breakout price, the bull market reversal rate is about random. In a bear market, we find more continuations than reversals. Expect a downward breakout.

Yearly range reversals. Separating the yearly price range into thirds, we find that candles with breakouts in the lowest third of the range result in continuation patterns most often.

Table 50.6 shows performance indicators that can give hints as to how your stock will behave after the breakout from a candle pattern.

Table 50.6
Performance Indicators

Description	Bull Market, Up Breakout	Bear Market, Up Breakout	Bull Market, Down Breakout	Bear Market, Down Breakout
Closing price confirmation, performance	N/A	N/A	−6.72%	−12.37%
Candle color confirmation, performance	N/A	N/A	−6.79%	−13.48%
Opening gap confirmation, performance	N/A	N/A	−7.43%	−12.34%
Breakout above 50-day moving average, performance	6.40%	8.33%	−4.68%	−11.69%
Breakout below 50-day moving average, performance	7.14%	9.78%	−5.77%	−11.55%
Last candle: close in highest third, performance	6.77%	9.14%	−5.51%	−11.01%
Last candle: close in middle third, performance	7.01%	9.34%	−5.64%	−11.11%
Last candle: close in lowest third, performance	7.13%	10.64%*	−5.18%	−17.15%*

N/A means not applicable.
*Fewer than 30 samples.

Confirmation, performance. The opening gap method (trade only if price gaps open lower) works best in a bull market. In a bear market, candle color (trade if the next day's candle is black) gives the best trading signal.

Moving average. Breakouts below the 50-trading-day moving average result in the best performance across the board except for bear market/down breakouts.

Closing position. A close within the lowest third of the white candle results in the best postbreakout performance except for bull markets/down breakouts. Those do better if price closes in the middle third of the day's trading range.

Sample Trade

Figure 50.2 shows price changing trend from downward leading to A to horizontal or upward to B. Price climbs after that, peaking in late June and again in July. But price cannot sustain the higher high and it tumbles, gapping lower on its way to C.

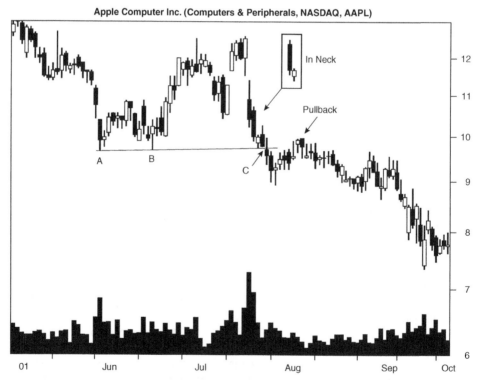

Figure 50.2 When price breaks through a support layer after an in neck pattern, Joe decides to sell.

When Joe looks at his portfolio that evening, he sees the in neck pattern and becomes worried. Will price continue lower? The AB support zone might support price, but if it doesn't then it's time to sell.

Price tries to recover the day after the in neck but forms a black candle. The following day, Joe receives a call from his broker saying he has been stopped out of the stock.

Having a stop in place turns out to be a good move, because Joe has gotten out before the decline really takes hold. A series of small candles occurs during and after the pullback when price returns to the breakout price. The small candles speak of a stock trying to find a trend but easing lower over time. When the smart money returns from summer vacation in mid-August, the tall candles also return and volume climbs even as price drops.

For Best Performance

The following list offers tips and observations to help choose candles that perform well. Consult the associated table for more information.

- Use the identification guidelines to help select the pattern—Table 50.1.
- Candles within a third of the yearly low perform best—Table 50.2.
- Select tall candles—Table 50.3.
- Use the measure rule to predict a price target—Table 50.3.
- Candles with tall upper or lower shadows outperform—Table 50.3.
- Volume gives performance clues—Table 50.4.
- As a continuation pattern, trade this candle when the primary trend is down—Trading Tactics discussion.
- The candle breaks out downward most often—Table 50.5.
- Patterns within a third of the yearly low tend to act as continuations most often—Table 50.5.
- Opening gap confirmation works best in a bull market—Table 50.6.

51

Kicking,
Bearish

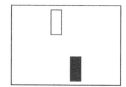

Behavior and Rank

Theoretical: Bearish reversal.

Actual bull market: Bearish reversal 54% of the time (ranking 41).

Actual bear market: Bearish continuation 80% of the time (ranking 1).

Frequency: 102nd out of 103.

Overall performance over time: 102nd out of 103.

I feel like I'm wasting my time looking at a candle that's very rare and if you do find it, it acts little better than random in a bull market. That's an accurate description of the bearish kicking pattern. Out of over 4.7 million candle lines, I found just 116, and only 5 of those came from a bear market. You won't find bear market statistics in this chapter because there's no story to tell.

The overall performance rank is crippled by the dearth of bear market statistics, 102 out of 103, where 1 is best. If you can't find a pattern, it doesn't matter how good the rank is—or the performance.

The psychology behind the pattern begins with a white candle. The bulls are buoyant and push price up, but the next day the bears line up like bullies playing dodgeball. Price gaps lower and forms a black candle.

The kicking pattern is supposed to be a reversal, and if you consider just the two candle lines in the pattern then that is right: Price reverses from being bullish (white candle) to being bearish (black candle). Beyond that, though, performance is almost random in a bull market, but that's based on a tiny sample size. Additional samples might give the kicking candle some, well, kick.

Identification Guidelines

Figure 51.1 shows a bearish kicking candle pattern. Price trends downward starting from the peak in late January at a price of 32.88 (not shown). The trend is a near straight-line run down, and you would expect candle patterns to appear that would foretell of a reversal. However, small candles of indecision form like mushrooms after a drenching rain, but price continues lower anyway.

Then the tall lines of the kicking pattern appear. Does price reverse after the candle? You decide. Price changes from cascading downward to easing lower (or even going horizontal for a time) but then makes another lower low with a tall black candle. That tall candle finally signals an end to the downtrend, at least for a while.

Table 51.1 lists identification guidelines. Look for two marubozu (tall shadowless) candles, the first white and the second black. Price should gap between the candles, meaning the high of the second day is below the low of the first day.

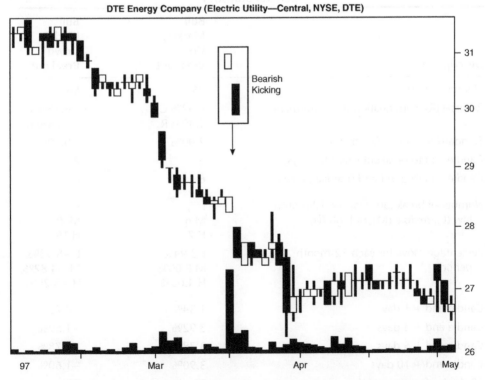

Figure 51.1 A bearish kicking pattern fails to reverse the downtrend.

Table 51.1
Identification Guidelines

Characteristic	Discussion
Number of candle lines	Two.
First day	A white marubozu candle, meaning a tall white candle with no shadows.
Second day	A black marubozu candle, meaning a tall black candle with no shadows. Price should gap below the white candle's low.

Statistics

In this section, I show only bull market statistics because I found just five bear market examples. That's too few to waste precious ink filling in a bunch of zeros in the table. Upward breakouts had only 25 samples, so those results are soft, too.

Table 51.2 shows general statistics.

Table 51.2
General Statistics

Description	Bull Market, Up Breakout	Bull Market, Down Breakout
Number found	25	86
Reversal (R), continuation (C) performance	6.62% C 3.49% R	−6.36% C −5.28% R
Standard & Poor's 500 change	2.00%	−0.10%
Candle end to breakout (median, days)	6	2
Candle end to trend end (median, days)	6	6
Number of breakouts near the 12-month low (L), middle (M), or high (H)	L 7, M 6, H 7	L 24, M 26, H 19
Percentage move for each 12-month period	L 3.94%, M 8.00%, H 4.05%	L −8.93%, M −4.82%, H −3.29%
Candle end + 1 day	1.34%	−0.73%
Candle end + 3 days	3.92%	−1.59%
Candle end + 5 days	3.78%	−1.78%
Candle end + 10 days	3.90%	−1.60%
10-day performance rank	35	77

Number found. I kicked tires and turned over stones but found just 116 kicking patterns, all but 5 from a bull market, despite a search of over 4.7 million candle lines

Reversal or continuation performance. The pattern performs best as a continuation of the existing price trend.

S&P performance. Comparing the performance of the kicking candle with the S&P 500, we see that kicking kicks S&P's butt.

Candle end to breakout. It takes from two to six days for price to break out. The difference between the two is that upward breakouts have to climb up the kicking pattern and close above it, so it takes longer than just a close below the nearby low.

Candle end to trend end. It takes six days to reach the trend end.

Yearly position, performance. The kicking pattern appears frequently in the middle range (downward breakouts) or split between the yearly low and high for upward breakouts. Upward breakouts show the best performance if the breakout is in the middle of the yearly price range; downward breakouts do best near the yearly low. Most candle types show the best performance within a third of the yearly low, and that's also where you find them most often.

Performance over time. Both columns suffer performance issues at various times, so the performance rank suffers, too.

Table 51.3 shows height statistics.

Candle height. Tall candles perform better than short ones. To determine whether the candle is short or tall, compute its height from highest high to lowest low price in the candle pattern and divide by the breakout price. If the result is higher than the median, then you have a tall candle; otherwise it's short.

Chad has a bearish kicking candle with a high of 39 and a low of 37. Is his candle short or tall? The height is $39 - 37$, or 2, so the measure would be 2/39, or 5.1%. In a bull market with an upward breakout, it's a tall candle because it's taller than the median.

Table 51.3
Height Statistics

Description	Bull Market, Up Breakout*	Bull Market, Down Breakout
Median candle height as a percentage of breakout price	3.75%	3.49%
Short candle, performance	3.53%	−4.96%
Tall candle, performance	8.48%	−7.15%
Percentage meeting price target (measure rule)	44%	51%

*Fewer than 30 samples.

Table 51.4
Volume Statistics

Description	Bull Market, Up Breakout*	Bull Market, Down Breakout
Rising candle volume, performance	6.55%	−7.04%
Falling candle volume, performance	3.65%	−4.20%
Above-average candle volume, performance	2.50%	−4.44%
Below-average candle volume, performance	5.85%	−7.07%
Heavy breakout volume, performance	5.28%	−5.35%
Light breakout volume, performance	4.81%	−6.02%

*Fewer than 30 samples.

Measure rule. Use the measure rule to help predict how far price will rise or fall. Compute the height of the candle pattern and multiply it by the appropriate percentage shown in the table; then apply it to the breakout price.

What are the measure rule price targets for Chad's candle? The upward target would be 39 + (2 × 44%), or 39.88, and the downward breakout target would be 37 − (2 × 51%), or 35.98.

No shadow statistics appear because, well, the kicking pattern has no shadows. They were kicked out, you might say.

Table 51.4 shows volume statistics.

Candle volume trend. Candles with a rising volume trend within them do better than do those with a falling trend.

Average candle volume. Candles with below-average volume work better than do those with above-average volume.

Breakout volume. Heavy breakout volume is usually good for performance, but that happens only with upward breakouts. Downward breakouts perform better with light breakout volume.

Trading Tactics

I split trading tactics into two basic studies, one concerning reversal rates and the other concerning performance. Of the two, reversal rates are more important, because it's better to trade in the direction of the trend and let price run as far as it can.

Table 51.5 gives tips to find the trend direction.

Confirmation reversal rates. If you want to detect a reversal, wait for price to close the next day and trade in the direction of the close. For example, if price trends down before the kicking candle and then closes higher after it, buy the stock.

Table 51.5
Reversal Rates

Description	Bull Market*
Closing price confirmation reversal rate	79%
Candle color confirmation reversal rate	62%
Opening gap confirmation reversal rate	66%
Reversal rate: trend up, breakout down	76%
Continuation rate: trend up, breakout up	24%
Reversal rate: trend down, breakout up	20%
Continuation rate: trend down, breakout down	80%
Percentage of reversals (R)/continuations (C) for each 12-month low (L), middle (M), or high (H)	L 52% R/48% C, M 63% R/37% C, H 42% R/58% C

*Fewer than 30 samples.

Reversal, continuation rates. Based on the trend leading to the start of the pattern and the breakout direction, you can see that a downward price trend continues lower 80% of the time. If price trends up, expect a downward breakout.

Yearly range reversals. Splitting the yearly price range into thirds and looking at continuations and reversals, we find that the results are not exceptional. The widest performance difference comes from those in the middle third of the yearly range. Kicking candles act as reversals 63% of the time.

Table 51.6 shows performance indicators that can give hints as to how your stock will behave after the breakout from a candle pattern.

Confirmation, performance. Trading based on candle color results in the best postbreakout performance. That's somewhat unusual for candle

Table 51.6
Performance Indicators

Description	Bull Market, Up Breakout*	Bull Market, Down Breakout
Closing price confirmation, performance	N/A	−5.44%
Candle color confirmation, performance	N/A	−5.86%
Opening gap confirmation, performance	N/A	−4.33%
Breakout above 50-day moving average, performance	4.65%	−4.44%*
Breakout below 50-day moving average, performance	6.08%	−5.60%

N/A means not applicable.
*Fewer than 30 samples.

patterns. Often the opening gap method works best for other candle types. Let the candle color dictate the trade direction (white to go long, for example).

Moving average. When the breakout price from a kicking pattern is below the 50-trading-day moving average, price tends to perform better after the breakout.

Sample Trade

Chad owned stock in the company shown in Figure 51.2. He loved collecting the dividends, especially at the lower tax rate afforded to dividends. What he didn't want to do was sell the stock.

He drew an upward trendline along the valleys as price climbed. A close below the trendline would signal a possible trend change. That's not an automatic sell signal, but it's a good hint of rough weather ahead.

A series of small white candles, many higher than the previous ones, populated the latter half of the trendline. Then the bearish kicking candle appeared. The black candle was especially tall, and that told him that the decline was serious. Referring to Table 51.5, price was trending up before the pattern started, suggesting a downward breakout would occur 76% of the time (which it did).

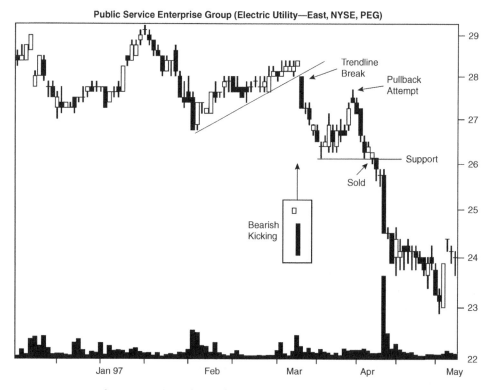

Figure 51.2 A bearish kicking candle signals a sell.

Did Chad sell? No. Why not? When I asked him, he just shrugged. Price pulled back a few weeks later and that was another opportunity to sell. Again, he missed exiting at a good price because he loved his dividends. (Fall in love with your mate, not a stock.)

As price fell again he placed a stop below the March valley, near 26 (shown as the line labeled "Support"), and when price hit his stop, it took him out.

The key to this trade is recognizing the pullback. Those occur often and many novice investors believe they signal a breakout, that price will resume the uptrend. In 87% of the 10,878 pullbacks I looked at, price continued lower.

For Best Performance

The following list offers tips and observations to help choose candles that perform well. Consult the associated table for more information.

- Use the identification guidelines to help select the pattern—Table 51.1.
- Candles within a third of the yearly low after a downward breakout in a bull market perform best—Table 51.2.
- Select tall candles—Table 51.3.
- Use the measure rule to predict a price target—Table 51.3.
- Volume gives performance clues—Table 51.4.
- The candle breaks out downward most often—Table 51.5.
- Candle color confirmation works best—Table 51.6.
- Breakouts below the 50-day moving average lead to the best performance—Table 51.6.

52

Kicking, Bullish

Behavior and Rank

Theoretical: Bullish reversal.
Actual bull market: Bullish reversal 53% of the time (ranking 44).
Actual bear market: Bullish reversal 50% of the time (ranking 48).
Frequency: 100th out of 103.
Overall performance over time: 96th out of 103.

Overall performance from the bullish kicking pattern is better than its bearish sibling. Nevertheless, the bullish kicking is a rare pattern that appears most often in thinly traded stocks. Kicking is supposed to be a reversal, and in my tests that's how it performs. I found just eight bear market patterns, too few to even report on, so I swept them off the statistics tables.

Overall performance is dreadful at 96 out of 103 where 1 is best. Frequency is also almost dead last—100 out of 103. You may cherish this pattern, but you won't find it often.

The psychology behind the pattern begins with the tall black candle. Price opens high and closes low, and that means the bears are in control. The next day, however, price gaps higher and opens at the low and closes at the high, the exact opposite of the prior day. The bulls take over from the bears, but how long the uptrend will continue is anyone's guess.

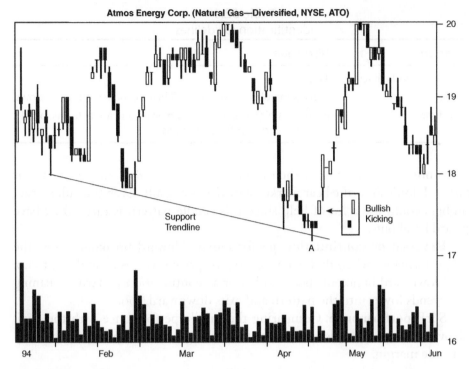

Figure 52.1   A bullish kicking pattern appears after price reaches a support zone, followed by a rebound.

Identification Guidelines

Figure 52.1 shows a good example of a bullish kicking pattern involved in turning a bearish downtrend into a bullish uptrend. What appears to be a hammer at A actually isn't because the body is too tall. However, it still works as an indicator of a possible trend change. Coupled with trendline support drawn beneath the lows, an upturn seems more likely.

The bullish kicking pattern appears and price completes the reversal of the downtrend followed by a series of tall white candles. Volume climbs, molding an irregular landscape of skyscrapers over time that helps price soar. Price continues moving up until reaching the old high and round number resistance at 20 and then dropping back to 18.

Table 52.1 lists identification guidelines. Look for two tall candles, the first black and the second white. Both are missing shadows and a price gap appears between them.

Statistics

Table 52.2 shows general statistics.

Table 52.1
Identification Guidelines

Characteristic	Discussion
Number of candle lines	Two.
First day	A black marubozu candle: a tall black candle with no shadows.
Second day	Price gaps higher and a white marubozu candle forms: a tall white candle with no shadows.

Number found. I unearthed 139 kicking candles, 8 of them from a bear market. I don't show the bear market statistics as a result. Even the bull market numbers could use a lot of help since this candle pattern is rare. Most have upward breakouts.

Reversal or continuation performance. Upward breakouts show the best performance when they act as reversals—price reverses from down to up.

Downward breakouts perform better as continuation patterns, meaning price trends lower into the pattern and exits downward, too.

S&P performance. Comparing the candle performance with the S&P 500 over the same periods, we see that the kicking candle outperforms the S&P by a wide margin.

Table 52.2
General Statistics

Description	Bull Market, Up Breakout	Bull Market, Down Breakout
Number found	100	31
Reversal (R), continuation (C) performance	4.44% C 7.76% R	−2.69% C −2.40% R
Standard & Poor's 500 change	0.94%	0.24%
Candle end to breakout (median, days)	2	6
Candle end to trend end (median, days)	4	6
Number of breakouts near the 12-month low (L), middle (M), or high (H)	L 21, M 21, H 42	L 8, M 7, H 10
Percentage move for each 12-month period	L 8.24%, M 3.90%, H 5.94%	L −1.73%, M −5.16%, H −2.71%
Candle end + 1 day	1.13%	−0.98%
Candle end + 3 days	1.79%	−1.89%
Candle end + 5 days	2.23%	−2.90%
Candle end + 10 days	2.78%	−2.22%
10-day performance rank	57	55

Table 52.3
Height Statistics

Description	Bull Market, Up Breakout	Bull Market, Down Breakout*
Median candle height as a percentage of breakout price	3.58%	3.62%
Short candle, performance	5.37%	−2.67%
Tall candle, performance	8.28%	−4.22%
Percentage meeting price target (measure rule)	52%	42%

*Fewer than 30 samples.

Candle end to breakout. It takes between two and six days for price to close either above the top or below the bottom of the candle. This makes sense because price is at the top of the second candle so an upward breakout should happen quickly.

Candle end to trend end. It takes a median of four to six days for price to reach the trend end. Upward breakouts reach the trend end sooner because the uptrend is already under way.

Yearly position, performance. Most kicking patterns appear within a third of the yearly high. The lowest third of the yearly price range is where you get the best performance for upward breakouts. The middle range works better for downward breakouts.

Performance over time. Downward breakouts falter from 5 to 10 days, hurting the performance rank. The percentage change over 10 days is less than one half of what it should be (6% would be excellent).

Table 52.3 shows height statistics.

Candle height. Tall candles perform better than short ones. To determine whether the candle is short or tall, compute its height from highest high to lowest low price in the candle pattern and divide by the breakout price. If the result is higher than the median, then you have a tall candle; otherwise it's short.

Jack owns a kicking candle with a high of 99 and a low of 97. Is the candle short or tall? The height is 99 − 97, or 2. For an upward breakout, the result would be 2/99, or 2.0%, so it is a short candle.

Measure rule. Use the measure rule to help predict how far price will rise or fall. Compute the height of the candle pattern and multiply it by the appropriate percentage shown in the table; then apply it to the breakout price.

What are the price targets for Jack's candle? The upward target would be 99 + (2 × 52%), or 100.04 and the downward target would be 97 − (2 × 42%), or 96.16.

Table 52.4 shows volume statistics.

Candle volume trend. A falling trend during the kicking pattern suggests better postbreakout performance than does a rising volume trend.

Table 52.4
Volume Statistics

Description	Bull Market, Up Breakout	Bull Market, Down Breakout*
Rising candle volume, performance	6.48%	−4.17%
Falling candle volume, performance	7.04%	−4.96%
Above-average candle volume, performance	9.34%	−4.44%
Below-average candle volume, performance	4.89%	−2.68%
Heavy breakout volume, performance	9.49%	−3.35%
Light breakout volume, performance	5.04%	−2.67%

*Fewer than 30 samples.

Average candle volume. Candles with above-average volume perform better than did those with below-average volume.

Breakout volume. Above-average breakout volume suggests good performance.

Trading Tactics

I split trading tactics into two basic studies, one concerning reversal rates and the other concerning performance. Of the two, reversal rates are more important, because it's better to trade in the direction of the trend and let price run as far as it can.

Table 52.5 gives tips to find the trend direction.

Table 52.5
Reversal Rates

Description	Bull Market
Closing price confirmation reversal rate	83%
Candle color confirmation reversal rate	74%
Opening gap confirmation reversal rate	68%*
Reversal rate: trend up, breakout down	21%*
Continuation rate: trend up, breakout up	79%
Reversal: trend down, breakout up	74%
Continuation: trend down, breakout down	26%*
Percentage of reversals (R)/ continuations (C) for each 12-month low (L), middle (M), or high (H)	L* 59% R/41% C, M* 39% R/61% C, H* 56% R/44% C

*Fewer than 30 samples.

Table 52.6
Performance Indicators

Description	Bull Market, Up Breakout	Bull Market, Down Breakout*
Closing price confirmation, performance	4.82%	N/A
Candle color confirmation, performance	5.15%	N/A
Opening gap confirmation, performance	5.87%	N/A
Breakout above 50-day moving average, performance	6.14%	−3.80%
Breakout below 50-day moving average, performance	7.26%	−4.35%

N/A means not applicable.
*Fewer than 30 samples.

Confirmation reversal rates. Use the closing price of the candle the day after the kicking candle to help determine the reversal direction. For example, if price closes higher, consider buying the stock.

Reversal, continuation rates. Upward breakouts happen most often.

Yearly range reversals. The numbers show the behavior of the kicking candle when the breakout price is sorted into the yearly price ranges. Those within a third of the yearly low act as reversals most often.

Table 52.6 shows performance indicators that can give hints as to how your stock will behave after the breakout from a candle pattern.

Confirmation, performance. The opening gap method results in the best postbreakout performance. That means buy if price gaps open higher after the kicking candle ends.

Moving average. Kicking patterns with breakouts below the 50-trading-day moving average tend to perform better.

Sample Trade

Jack saw price make a new high at D then stumble to A before recovering to E, as shown in Figure 52.2. Overhead resistance pushed price back down to make a higher low at B. A trendline drawn connecting A and B and extended to C touches a bullish kicking pattern.

He considers buying the stock at C when price bounces off the trendline after the black marubozu, but one thing stops him: overhead resistance. He believes that price will rise to the level of E and then curl down again. Depending on when he buys in and assuming he sells at the old high, that would not be enough profit to make the trade work. So, he waits.

Price does climb to the level of E and stalls there for about a week. Then a tall white candle pierces overhead resistance in an upward thrust accompanied by good volume. This is the breakout he has been looking for, so he buys the stock at the open the next day.

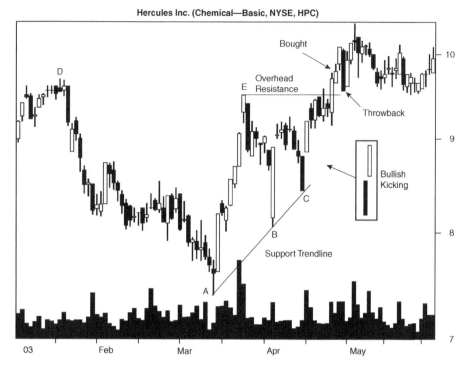

Hercules Inc. (Chemical—Basic, NYSE, HPC)

Figure 52.2   A bullish kicking pattern leads the way higher.

Two days later, price throws back to the breakout price and then has trouble climbing much higher. However (not shown in the figure), eventually the stock moves up to 12 before encountering severe turbulence.

For Best Performance

The following list offers tips and observations to help choose candles that perform well. Consult the associated table for more information.

- Use the identification guidelines to help select the pattern—Table 52.1.
- Candles within a third of the yearly low perform best for upward breakouts—Table 52.2.
- Select tall candles—Table 52.3.
- Use the measure rule to predict a price target—Table 52.3.
- Volume gives performance clues—Table 52.4.
- The candle breaks out upward most often—Table 52.5.
- Opening gap confirmation works best—Table 52.6.
- Breakouts below the 50-day moving average lead to the best performance—Table 52.6.

53

Ladder Bottom

Behavior and Rank

Theoretical: Bullish reversal.

Actual bull market: Bullish reversal 56% of the time (ranking 39).

Actual bear market: Bearish continuation 51% of the time (ranking 51).

Frequency: 80th out of 103.

Overall performance over time: 41st out of 103.

The more rules a candle pattern has for identification, the rarer it becomes. I can't say for sure that performance suffers, but if the reversal rate of 56% in a bull market is any clue, the pattern performs almost randomly. A confirmation technique discussed in the Trading Tactics section boosts the reversal rate to 71%.

The overall performance rank is 41 out of 103, with 1 being best. This is a midlist pattern, and even if it were closer to the best, it appears so infrequently that you might not be able to trade it, anyway.

In this pattern, the bears push price lower in a downward trend leading to the start of the ladder bottom. A series of three tall black candles occurs, followed by another black candle. Then a bullish retracement of the downtrend happens in the form of a white candle that gaps higher. According to the sources I checked, the white candle line need not be a tall one, so I don't put much faith in one candle creating a reversal of a strong downdraft. A check of the charts shows that in a primary downtrend this pattern fails to reverse more often than it succeeds. Price keeps tumbling.

Identification Guidelines

Figure 53.1 shows an example of a ladder bottom. Depending on the sources you check, there are variations in how the pattern appears. None of the written descriptions fully match their drawings, so the contradictions leave a lot to be desired.

In the chart, a downward price trend exists when the ladder bottom begins to take shape. The first three candles are tall black ones, but height is a function of the relative height of prior candles. You can have a short candle appear tall if it's in the midst of doji candles or spinning tops. Each tall black candle should open and close lower than the previous one did.

After three long black candles, a fourth black one appears. The only qualifier on this candle is that it must have an upper shadow. It does not have to post a lower open or close, nor does its body have to be tall. The upper shadow can be any length, too, just as long as it has one.

The final day is a white candle whose price gaps higher—an open above the body of the prior day. The white candle does not have to be tall—but that depends on which source you check. One source says the white candle has to close above the trading range of the prior three days. That requirement would make the pattern almost impossible to find. The other sources have no such stipulation.

Figure 53.1 Price finds traction in a ladder bottom and reverses.

Table 53.1
Identification Guidelines

Characteristic	Discussion
Number of candle lines	Five.
Price trend	Downward leading to the start of the candle pattern.
Days 1 to 3	Tall black candles, each with a lower open and lower close.
Fourth day	A black candle with an upper shadow.
Last day	A white candle that gaps above the body of the prior day.

All of the sources I checked have pictures showing three tall black candles and then a short black candle with a tall upper shadow. A white day appears that also has a tall body and a price gap above the prior body (the open is above the prior open). Programming this picture into my candle recognition software would remove some of the ladder bottoms I found. There might not be enough left for a good statistical analysis. Even the 451 I found are not enough. However, I'm happy with the guidelines I chose to implement. They appear in Table 53.1.

Statistics

Table 53.2 shows general statistics.

Number found. Prorating using the standard database, the candle pattern appears most often in a bull market. I found 451 ladder bottoms using three additional databases for over 4.7 million candle lines in all.

Reversal or continuation performance. Candle performance often varies depending on whether the candle acts as a continuation of the prevailing price trend or a reversal.

The best performance comes from ladders in a bear market. Even though samples are few, I don't expect the ranking to change, because it agrees with so many other candle types.

S&P performance. Using the dates of the candle end to the trend end, I measured the performance of the S&P 500 and found that the performance of the ladder bottom beats the S&P over the same periods.

Candle end to breakout. This describes the median time it takes price to close above or close below the candle pattern. It takes price just over a week to make the breakout journey. That's because this pattern can be tall. Price may complete the candlestick well up the pattern. Thus, whether price continues up or down, it takes time before it breaks out.

Candle end to trend end. How long can you expect price to trend? It varies according to breakout direction and market condition but ranges between 8 and 11 days.

Table 53.2
General Statistics

Description	Bull Market, Up Breakout	Bear Market, Up Breakout	Bull Market, Down Breakout	Bear Market, Down Breakout
Number found	200	45	159	47
Reversal (R), continuation (C) performance	5.13% R	6.28% R	−4.36% C	−9.43% C
Standard & Poor's 500 change	2.24%	3.17%	−0.62%	−2.62%
Candle end to breakout (median, days)	8	7	9	9
Candle end to trend end (median, days)	11	8	9	9
Number of breakouts near the 12-month low (L), middle (M), or high (H)	L 46, M 64, H 66	L 23, M 13, H 9	L 63, M 57, H 30	L 31, M 12, H 2
Percentage move for each 12-month period	L 5.02%, M 5.62%, H 4.24%	L 9.08%, M 5.11%, H 4.02%	L −5.11%, M −4.69%, H −2.87%	L −9.25%, M −11.34%, H −1.46%
Candle end + 1 day	0.85%	0.80%	−0.56%	−1.39%
Candle end + 3 days	1.95%	2.26%	−1.35%	−2.08%
Candle end + 5 days	2.41%	4.28%	−2.06%	−1.89%
Candle end + 10 days	3.92%	6.76%	−2.93%	−7.07%
10-day performance rank	34	14	35	8

Yearly position, performance. Splitting the patterns into where the breakout occurs in the yearly price range shows that most ladders occur within a third of the yearly low (bull market/up breakouts appear more often near the yearly high). Performance is best in the middle range for bull market/up breakouts and bear market/down breakouts. The lowest range does best for the other two categories: bear market/up breakouts and bull market/down breakouts.

Performance over time. The numbers show the price performance over time. The results confirm that the best performance comes from patterns in a bear market. Making 7% (bear market/down breakouts) in 10 days means an annual return of 255%. Impossible, sure, but it's fun to dream. A performance rank of 8 (out of 103, where 1 is best) supports the notion that it's a monster return.

Table 53.3 shows height statistics.

Candle height. To determine whether the candle is short or tall, compute its height from highest high to lowest low price in the candle pattern and divide by the breakout price. If the result is higher than the median, then you have a tall candle; otherwise it's short.

Table 53.3
Height Statistics

Description	Bull Market, Up Breakout	Bear Market, Up Breakout	Bull Market, Down Breakout	Bear Market, Down Breakout
Median candle height as a percentage of breakout price	8.90%	14.23%	8.92%	22.17%
Short candle, performance	4.62%	6.48%*	−3.44%	−8.33%*
Tall candle, performance	5.90%	6.00%*	−5.63%	−11.16%*
Percentage meeting price target (measure rule)	27%	20%	16%	15%
Median upper shadow as a percentage of breakout price	0.74%	1.01%	0.72%	1.64%
Short upper shadow, performance	4.78%	6.27%*	−4.08%	−10.78%*
Tall upper shadow, performance	5.48%	6.28%*	−4.64%	−8.31%*
Median lower shadow as a percentage of breakout price	0.38%	0.65%	0.50%	1.12%
Short lower shadow, performance	5.31%	4.55%*	−4.21%	−9.31%*
Tall lower shadow, performance	4.91%	8.30%*	−4.55%	−9.60%*

*Fewer than 30 samples.

Rusty sees a ladder bottom with a high price of 69 and a low of 63, for a height of 69 − 63, or 6. Is his candle short or tall? For the upward breakout/bull market example, the result would be 6/69, or 8.7%. That's below the 8.9% median, so Rusty's candle is short.

Tall candles perform better than short ones in all cases except bear market/up breakout. That one category uses 44 candles, split between short and tall, so the results are likely to change. Most other candle types do best with tall candles.

Measure rule. Use the measure rule to help predict how far price will rise or fall. Compute the height of the candle pattern and multiply it by the appropriate percentage shown in the table; then apply it to the breakout price.

Based on the measure rule, what are the price targets for Rusty's candle in a bull market? The upward breakout target would be $(6 \times 27\%) + 69$, or 70.62, and the downward breakout target would be $63 − (6 \times 16\%)$, or 62.04.

Shadows. The results pertain to the last candle line in the pattern. To determine whether the shadow is short or tall, compute the height of the shadow and divide by the breakout price. Compare the result to the median in the table. Tall shadows have a percentage higher than the median.

Upper shadow performance. Candles with tall upper shadows show the best postbreakout performance in all categories except for bear market/down breakout. Those few samples do better with a short upper wick.

Table 53.4
Volume Statistics

Description	Bull Market, Up Breakout	Bear Market, Up Breakout	Bull Market, Down Breakout	Bear Market, Down Breakout
Rising candle volume, performance	5.69%	4.89%	−4.13%	−9.32%
Falling candle volume, performance	4.31%	9.96%*	−4.58%	−9.69%*
Above-average candle volume, performance	5.16%	5.93%	−4.57%	−8.16%
Below-average candle volume, performance	5.06%	7.12%*	−3.94%	−12.33%*
Heavy breakout volume, performance	5.67%	6.96%*	−5.08%	−9.37%
Light breakout volume, performance	4.41%	5.33%*	−3.38%	−9.52%*

*Fewer than 30 samples.

Lower shadow performance. Candles with tall lower shadows outperform except in the bull market/up breakout column. Those do better with short shadows.

Table 53.4 shows volume statistics.

Candle volume trend. I used linear regression on volume from the start of the candle pattern to its end to determine whether volume was rising or falling. Often you can tell by looking.

Falling candle volume works best in all cases except for bull market/up breakouts. Those perform better after the breakout if volume trends upward throughout the candle.

Average candle volume. I compared the average volume in the candle to the average of the prior month. Bull markets do better if accompanied by heavy candle volume, and bear markets perform best post breakout if light volume accompanies the candle pattern.

Breakout volume. This is a comparison of the breakout day's volume with the prior one-month average. Heavy breakout volume suggests good postbreakout performance in all categories except bear market/down breakouts. Those do better after light breakout volume (but the sample size is small).

Trading Tactics

Before I discuss the tactics tables, Figure 53.2 shows a ladder bottom that appears as a reversal pattern in an uptrend. Price has risen from the low in November to a peak in January. Then it retraces a portion of that rise, ending at the ladder bottom. Price reverses and the rise resumes.

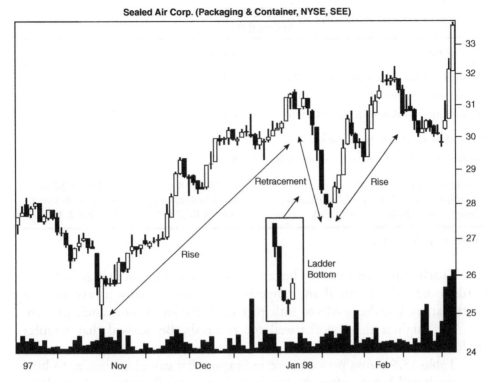

Sealed Air Corp. (Packaging & Container, NYSE, SEE)

Figure 53.2 A ladder bottom appears as part of a retracement in an uptrend.

The situation shown is one of the more reliable ways to trade this pattern—a ladder bottom that appears in a primary uptrend. Avoid depending on price reversing if the primary trend is downward. Those tend to fail about as often as they work.

I split trading tactics into two basic studies, one concerning reversal rates and the other concerning performance. Of the two, reversal rates are more important, because it's better to trade in the direction of the trend and let price run as far as it can.

Table 53.5 gives tips to find the new trend direction.

Confirmation reversal rates. In a bull market, trading on a higher closing the day after the ladder completes results in a reversal rate of 71%. That means price breaks out upward 71% of the time. In a bear market, a white candle a day after the ladder bottom ends results in the best reversal rate.

Reversal, continuation rates. Since you know the price trend leading to the start of a candle pattern, you can use the information in the table to help predict the breakout direction. The higher the percentage above random (50%), the better.

The ladder bottom pattern acts as a reversal in a bull market most often, but the bear market is about random.

Table 53.5
Reversal Rates

Description	Bull Market	Bear Market
Closing price confirmation reversal rate	71%	63%*
Candle color confirmation reversal rate	70%	73%*
Opening gap confirmation reversal rate	60%	52%*
Reversal: trend down, breakout up	56%	49%
Continuation: trend down, breakout down	44%	51%
Percentage of reversals (R)/ continuations (C) for each 12-month low (L), middle (M), or high (H)	L 42% R/58% C, M 53% R/47% C, H 69% R/31% C	L* 43% R/57% C, M* 52% R/48% C, H* 82% R/18% C

*Fewer than 30 samples.

Yearly range reversals. The table shows the yearly price range split into thirds to help determine if any range is more likely to show a reversal or a continuation. Use the results to anticipate the behavior of your candle pattern.

The highest third works well for reversals. Be advised that samples are few.

Table 53.6 shows performance indicators that can give hints as to how your stock will behave after the breakout from a candle pattern. A breakout

Table 53.6
Performance Indicators

Description	Bull Market, Up Breakout	Bear Market, Up Breakout	Bull Market, Down Breakout	Bear Market, Down Breakout
Closing price confirmation, performance	8.02%	14.32%	N/A	N/A
Candle color confirmation, performance	8.48%	12.98%	N/A	N/A
Opening gap confirmation, performance	8.26%	13.80%	N/A	N/A
Breakout above 50-day moving average, performance	5.03%	5.30%*	−2.68%	−7.94%*
Breakout below 50-day moving average, performance	5.09%	6.85%	−4.53%	−9.54%
Last candle: close in highest third, performance	5.18%	7.96%*	−4.22%	−13.22%*
Last candle: close in middle third, performance	4.37%	4.46%*	−4.79%	−6.02%*
Last candle: close in lowest third, performance	7.87%	0.14%*	−2.60%	−8.22%*

N/A means not applicable.
*Fewer than 30 samples.

occurs when price closes either above the top (highest high) or below the bottom (lowest low) of the candlestick.

Confirmation, performance. The numbers show the move from a confirmed candle pattern to the trend end and describe which type of confirmation works best, on average.

Candle color performs best as an entry signal in a bull market (buy after a white candle appears the day after a ladder bottom ends). Closing price confirmation works best in a bear market. That's when you buy if price closes higher the day after the ladder ends.

Moving average. This shows whether it's best to trade a candle pattern with a breakout above or below the 50-trading-day moving average (i.e., a moving average based on price performance over about two and a half calendar months).

If the ladder bottom breakout is below the 50-day moving average, then it signals better postbreakout performance in all categories.

Closing position. The position of the closing price on the last day of the candle formation shows no consistent trend across the various categories.

Sample Trade

Rusty is intrigued with the situation shown in Figure 53.3. Price peaked at A and B, forming a double top and a support zone bounded on the bottom by valley E. (Often support is not a distinct price but a range or zone of prices.) Extending the top support line through the congestion zone at C, he thinks it likely that price might stall at D on the way back down from the high at G. His guess is a good one, but it is off, as the chart shows.

On the decline from peak G, price consolidates at J by forming a series of spinning tops before the downtrend resumes and forms a ladder bottom. Price drops to H, nestled between the two support lines at a 50% retracement of the F to G move.

When the ladder bottom is finished, Rusty believes that price will rise at least to the previous consolidation level at J and, he hopes, to the old high at G. The downside would be a drop to the lower edge of the support zone shown by the horizontal line beginning at E.

A day after the ladder bottom's white candle, he buys. Price climbs in a series of white candles until it hits the congestion level at J. There price forms a tweezers top in the form of a bearish harami at K. Rusty misses the reversal signal, though. He is still hoping price will climb to the old high at G.

Day by day, Rusty watches black candle after black candle appear. He finally jumps off the ladder and sells his position when price drops below the lower support line, booking a small loss.

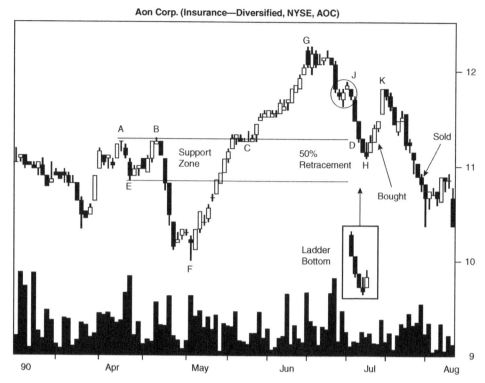

Figure 53.3   A ladder bottom after an upward move leads to a losing trade.

To improve this trade, he could have sold half or all of his position when the bearish harami appeared and confirmed with a black candle the next day.

For Best Performance

The following list offers tips and observations to help choose candles that perform well. Consult the associated table for more information.

- Use the identification guidelines to help select the pattern—Table 53.1.
- The best-performing candles in a bull market with upward breakouts occur in the middle of the yearly price range. Downward breakouts do best within a third of the yearly low—Table 53.2.
- Tall candles work best most often—Table 53.3.
- Use the measure rule to predict a price target—Table 53.3.
- Volume gives performance clues—Table 53.4.
- In a bull market, a higher close the next day often confirms a reversal—Table 53.5.

- Use the price trend leading to the start of the candle to help predict the likely breakout direction. Ladders tend to act as reversals in a bull market—Table 53.5.
- Use candle color as the entry signal in a bull market—Table 53.6.
- Breakouts below the 50-day moving average lead to the best performance—Table 53.6.

54

Last Engulfing Bottom

Behavior and Rank

Theoretical: Bullish reversal.

Actual bull market: Bearish continuation 65% of the time (ranking 14).

Actual bear market: Bearish continuation 67% of the time (ranking 12).

Frequency: 13th out of 103.

Overall performance over time: 48th out of 103.

The last engulfing bottom is yet another example of a dismal failure of a candle to act as a reversal. That's how it's supposed to behave, but my tests show that it acts as a continuation pattern 65% of the time (bull market) and 67% of the time (bear market). That's about two out of three. If you wait for an upward close the next day then you can reverse that. In that situation, price breaks out upward 61% of the time. As a continuation pattern, performance is middling, ranking 48 out of 103 candles where 1 is best.

This candle pattern, which has a white candle followed by a black one, almost screams "bear!" The tall black candle engulfs the white one and somehow it's supposed to be bullish. Anytime I see a tall black candle it sends bearish shivers down my spine, like seeing a black funnel cloud heading for my house. That can't be good news, not for your house and not for the stock. Maybe this acts differently in securities other than stocks. We examine the behavior more closely in the Statistics section.

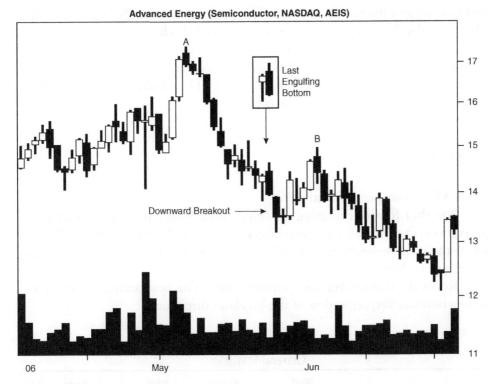

Figure 54.1 A last engulfing pattern acts as a continuation pattern when price breaks out downward.

Identification Guidelines

Figure 54.1 shows a good example of a last engulfing bottom that's not a bottom. Price breaks out downward and then retraces a portion of the move from A before continuing lower. The retracement to B is typical for long downward moves, so don't think it's a delayed reaction to the engulfing pattern.

What do you look for when hunting last engulfing bottoms? Table 54.1 lists identification guidelines. The candle pattern uses two candle lines, the

Table 54.1
Identification Guidelines

Characteristic	Discussion
Number of candle lines	Two.
Price trend	Downward leading to the start of the candle pattern.
First day	A white candle.
Second day	A black candle opens above the prior body and closes below the prior body. Price need not engulf the shadows.

first is white and the second is black. The black candle engulfs the body of the white candle. That means the top of the black body is equal to or above the top of the white body and the black body bottom is equal to or below the bottom of the white body. Between the two candles, both the body tops and bottoms cannot be equal at the same time. The candle pair is similar to a bullish engulfing pattern except for color.

Statistics

Table 54.2 shows general statistics.

Number found. Prorating the standard database, the candle pattern appears most often in a bear market. However, I limited the selection to 20,000, which the table shows. Since the bull market was longer than the bear market, more appear there.

Reversal or continuation performance. The best performance comes from a bear market, regardless of the breakout direction.

Table 54.2
General Statistics

Description	Bull Market, Up Breakout	Bear Market, Up Breakout	Bull Market, Down Breakout	Bear Market, Down Breakout
Number found	5,183	1,723	9,559	3,535
Reversal (R), continuation (C) performance	6.63% R	8.12% R	−5.44% C	−10.20% C
Standard & Poor's 500 change	2.11%	1.09%	−0.82%	−2.53%
Candle end to breakout (median, days)	4	4	2	2
Candle end to trend end (median, days)	9	8	6	6
Number of breakouts near the 12-month low (L), middle (M), or high (H)	L 1,088, M 1,334, H 2,141	L 540, M 558, H 607	L 2,822, M 2,944, H 2,900	L 1,478, M 1,168, H 846
Percentage move for each 12-month period	L 7.68%, M 6.19%, H 6.34%	L 10.50%, M 7.83%, H 6.82%	L −6.00%, M −5.39%, H −5.12%	L −12.31%, M −9.24%, H −8.71%
Candle end + 1 day	1.46%	2.18%	−0.77%	−1.40%
Candle end + 3 days	2.96%	4.43%	−1.16%	−2.35%
Candle end + 5 days	3.58%	5.09%	−1.10%	−2.67%
Candle end + 10 days	3.99%	4.85%	−0.91%	−2.73%
10-day performance rank	31	31	98	74

S&P performance. Using the dates of the candle end to the trend end, I measured the performance of the S&P 500 and found that the candle beats the index by a wide margin.

Candle end to breakout. This describes the median time it takes price to close above or close below the candle pattern. Downward breakouts take half the time of upward ones because the close is near the pattern's low.

Candle end to trend end. How long can you expect price to trend? Again, downward breakouts take less time than do upward breakouts. The reason for this is probably because the downtrend is already underway, placing it closer to the trend end.

Yearly position, performance. Where a candle appears in the yearly price range sometimes affects performance. Upward breakouts appear within a third of the yearly high most often, but it's the yearly low where you'll find the best performance. In fact, the yearly low provides the best performance across the board.

Performance over time. Based on the performance rank, upward breakouts are where the money is to be made. The strength of this pattern softens between five and 10 days in the bear market/up breakout category and sooner (after three days) in the bull market/down breakout column. That weakness suggests this pattern is not a robust performer (or else it would be strong across all time periods and market conditions).

Table 54.3 shows height statistics.

Candle height. To determine whether the candle is short or tall, compute its height from highest high to lowest low price in the candle pattern and divide by the breakout price. If the result is higher than the median, then you have a tall candle; otherwise it's short.

For example, Aniston sees a last engulfing candle on her chart with a high price of 40 and a low of 39. Is the candle pattern short or tall? The height is 40 − 39, or 1, so the computation is 1/40, or 2.5%. Let's assume an upward breakout in a bull market, so the candle is short because the value is less than the median 2.93%.

Why is this important? Because candle height is one of the best predictors of postbreakout performance. Look at the performance results in the table and you'll see that tall candles beat the short in all columns.

Measure rule. Use the measure rule to help predict how far price will rise or fall. Compute the height of the candle pattern and multiply it by the appropriate percentage shown in the table; then apply it to the breakout price.

What are Aniston's price targets for her engulfing pattern, assuming a bull market? The height is 1, so the upward breakout target would be (1 × 70%) + 40, or 40.70 and the downward breakout target would be 39 − (1 × 61%), or 38.39.

Shadows. The shadows pertain to the last candle line in the pattern. To determine whether the shadow is short or tall, compute the height of the shadow and divide by the breakout price. Compare the result to the median in

Table 54.3
Height Statistics

Description	Bull Market, Up Breakout	Bear Market, Up Breakout	Bull Market, Down Breakout	Bear Market, Down Breakout
Median candle height as a percentage of breakout price	2.93%	4.25%	3.13%	4.53%
Short candle, performance	5.23%	6.16%	−4.47%	−8.23%
Tall candle, performance	8.44%	10.29%	−6.71%	−12.57%
Percentage meeting price target (measure rule)	70%	66%	61%	68%
Median upper shadow as a percentage of breakout price	0.26%	0.35%	0.24%	0.36%
Short upper shadow, performance	6.30%	7.67%	−5.22%	−9.29%
Tall upper shadow, performance	6.98%	8.58%	−5.67%	−11.10%
Median lower shadow as a percentage of breakout price	0.40%	0.62%	0.35%	0.52%
Short lower shadow, performance	5.89%	7.31%	−4.92%	−10.05%
Tall lower shadow, performance	7.48%	8.98%	−6.02%	−10.37%

the table. Tall shadows have a percentage higher than the median. Tall upper and lower shadows perform better than their short counterparts.

Table 54.4 shows volume statistics.

Candle volume trend. A falling volume trend works best in all categories except for bear market/down breakouts. Those do better with a rising volume trend in the candle.

Table 54.4
Volume Statistics

Description	Bull Market, Up Breakout	Bear Market, Up Breakout	Bull Market, Down Breakout	Bear Market, Down Breakout
Rising candle volume, performance	6.57%	7.67%	−5.41%	−10.28%
Falling candle volume, performance	6.70%	8.57%	−5.47%	−10.13%
Above-average candle volume, performance	6.67%	8.51%	−5.50%	−10.21%
Below-average candle volume, performance	6.62%	7.87%	−5.40%	−10.20%
Heavy breakout volume, performance	7.29%	8.68%	−5.76%	−11.22%
Light breakout volume, performance	6.01%	7.56%	−5.10%	−8.91%

Average candle volume. Candles with above-average candle volume perform better after the breakout than do those with below-average volume.

Breakout volume. Heavy breakout volume suggests better performance across the board.

Trading Tactics

Trade a last engulfing bottom reversal only when the primary trend is upward. The short downward retracement in the uptrend provides a buying opportunity when price merges with the upward current already underway. Upward breakouts in a primary downtrend tend to be short-lived, so avoid that trading setup.

I split trading tactics into two basic studies, one concerning reversal rates and the other concerning performance. Of the two, reversal rates are more important, because it's better to trade in the direction of the trend and let price run as far as it can.

Table 54.5 gives tips to find the trend direction.

Confirmation reversal rates. If you wait for an upward close the day after the candle pattern ends, price tends to continue moving higher 61% of the time in a bull market and 59% of the time in a bear market. That's the best of the bunch.

Reversal, continuation rates. Since the price trend is down, expect a downward breakout about 65% to 67% of the time.

Yearly range reversals. Patterns with breakouts in the two lowest thirds of the yearly price range act as continuations between 68% and 73% of the time. The highest third also favors continuation of the price trend, but the difference is not as startling.

Table 54.6 shows performance indicators that can give hints as to how your stock will behave after the breakout from a candle pattern.

Confirmation, performance. Candle theory says that when price closes higher after the black candle, it confirms the pattern as a reversal. That turns

Table 54.5
Reversal Rates

Description	Bull Market	Bear Market
Closing price confirmation reversal rate	61%	59%
Candle color confirmation reversal rate	59%	57%
Opening gap confirmation reversal rate	44%	42%
Reversal: trend down, breakout up	35%	33%
Continuation: trend down, breakout down	65%	67%
Percentage of reversals (R)/ continuations (C) for each 12-month low (L), middle (M), or high (H)	L 28% R/72% C, M 31% R/69% C, H 42% R/58% C	L 27% R/73% C, M 32% R/68% C, H 42% R/58% C

Table 54.6
Performance Indicators

Description	Bull Market, Up Breakout	Bear Market, Up Breakout	Bull Market, Down Breakout	Bear Market, Down Breakout
Closing price confirmation, performance	7.15%	10.62%	N/A	N/A
Candle color confirmation, performance	6.98%	10.31%	N/A	N/A
Opening gap confirmation, performance	7.16%	11.56%	N/A	N/A
Breakout above 50-day moving average, performance	6.41%	7.03%	−5.19%	−8.47%
Breakout below 50-day moving average, performance	6.79%	9.26%	−5.54%	−10.65%
Last candle: close in highest third, performance	6.38%	9.64%	−5.75%	−12.97%
Last candle: close in middle third, performance	6.67%	8.29%	−5.60%	−9.02%
Last candle: close in lowest third, performance	6.63%	8.03%	−5.41%	−10.37%

N/A means not applicable.

out to be true. If price closes higher the day after the candle ends, it breaks out upward 61% of the time. In other words, it acts as a reversal 61% of the time. That's quite a turnaround from being a continuation pattern 65% of the time when you don't wait for a higher close.

However, a higher closing price does not lead to the best performance. The opening gap method, where you wait for price to gap open higher, works better, especially in a bear market, as the numbers show.

Moving average. If the breakout price is below the 50-day moving average, postbreakout performance improves over those with breakouts above the moving average.

Closing position. A close within the highest third of the black candle suggests better performance in all categories except bull market/up breakouts. Those do better if price is in the middle third of the candle.

You may wonder how price can close in the top third of a black candle. The answer is the candle must have a long lower shadow. Few patterns qualify, so be skeptical and don't depend on this being accurate.

Sample Trade

Figure 54.2 shows a trade Aniston made in the stock. Price trended lower during March, as the chart shows, and then found support. Price bobbled

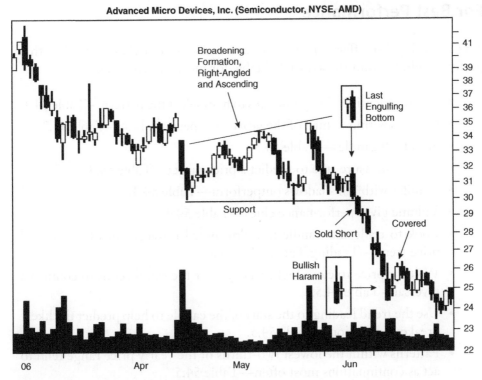

Figure 54.2 A broadening chart pattern appears with a last engulfing bottom pattern pointing the way downward.

up and down, bottoming near the support line but forming higher peaks. Eventually, the pattern became a right-angled and ascending broadening chart pattern.

She followed price as it touched the support line and then formed a last engulfing bottom pattern. The breakout was in the middle third of the yearly price range, suggesting that the breakout would be downward (the last engulfing bottom would act as a continuation of the price trend). The candle was tall, as were both shadows, suggesting good postbreakout performance. The candle was comfortably below the 50-trading-day moving average, which was also good. Volume was rising in the candle (bad), but it was above average and breakout volume was also heavy (both suggest better performance). All of this pointed to, but did not guarantee, a profitable short trade.

She depended on opening gap confirmation the next day as the entry signal. When price gapped lower, she sold the stock short. Each day she got a quote and updated her charts. A spinning top and a series of black candles were all she saw until the bullish harami appeared—her signal to run for cover. When price gapped higher the next day, she covered her short and walked away with a profit in her purse and a smile on her face.

For Best Performance

The following list offers tips and observations to help choose candles that perform well. Consult the associated table for more information.

- Use the identification guidelines to help select the pattern—Table 54.1.
- Candles within a third of the yearly low perform best—Table 54.2.
- Select tall candles—Table 54.3.
- Use the measure rule to predict a price target—Table 54.3.
- Candles with tall shadows outperform—Table 54.3.
- Volume gives performance clues—Table 54.4.
- Look to trade this candle in a downward retracement of an upward price trend—Trading Tactics discussion.
- Wait for price to close higher a day after the candle ends to confirm a reversal—Table 54.5.
- Use the trend leading to the start of the candle to help predict the likely breakout direction—Table 54.5.
- Patterns within the lowest two-thirds of the yearly price range tend to act as continuations most often—Table 54.5.
- Opening gap confirmation works best—Table 54.6.
- Breakouts below the 50-day moving average lead to the best performance—Table 54.6.

55

Last Engulfing Top

Behavior and Rank

Theoretical: Bearish reversal.

Actual bull market: Bullish continuation 68% of the time (ranking 9).

Actual bear market: Bullish continuation 67% of the time (ranking 14).

Frequency: 14th out of 103.

Overall performance over time: 79th out of 103.

The last engulfing top is supposed to act as a reversal candlestick, but my testing shows it acts as a continuation over two-thirds of the time. Even if you wait for a lower close, the reversal rate climbs to just 55%, which is a nickel above random. Do yourself a favor and trade this as a continuation pattern unless technical evidence says otherwise.

The last engulfing top is a continuation pattern that occurs frequently (rank of 14 out of 103 candles where 1 is best) but performance suffers. It ranks 79. Based on the rank, you'll find the best performance after a downward breakout.

The psychology behind this pattern begins with a trend in which the bulls have pushed price upward. A black candle appears as a wake-up call to bulls who have grown fat and lazy from all of the money they've been gorging on. The next day sports a candle that wraps around the black body, engulfing it. It's a white candle and it says the bulls have gotten the message and are ready to tangle with the bears again. If price closes lower the next day, then the chances improve that price will reverse, but that's hardly a guarantee.

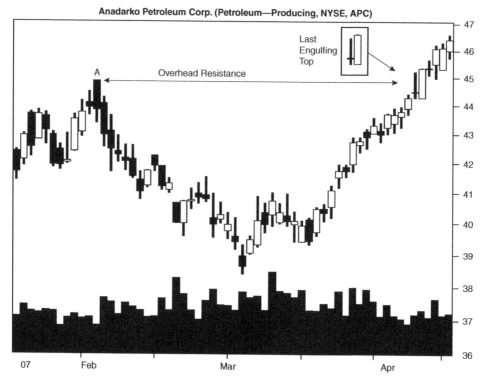

Figure 55.1   A last engulfing top suggests a continuation of the uptrend.

Identification Guidelines

Figure 55.1 shows a last engulfing top that swallows the body of a doji. Many would expect price to reverse because of overhead resistance set up by the peak at A, but that's not what happens. Price continues rising, breaking out upward and tracking what is happening at the gas pump.

Table 55.1 lists identification guidelines. These are the same guidelines as those of a bearish engulfing pattern except for candle color. Look for a white candle to engulf the body of the prior black candle. That means the white body's

Table 55.1
Identification Guidelines

Characteristic	Discussion
Number of candle lines	Two.
Price trend	Upward leading to the start of the candle pattern.
First day	A black candle.
Second day	A white candle, the body of which overlaps the prior black candle's body.

top is at or above the black body's top and the white body's bottom is at or below the prior black body's bottom. Either the body tops or the body bottoms can be equal, but not both. Shadows are not important for candle recognition.

Statistics

Table 55.2 shows general statistics.

Number found. I prorated the results from my standard database (slightly different from the one used here) and found that the last engulfing top appears more often in a bear market. I limited the number of candles to 20,000 so my spreadsheet wouldn't cough up fur balls.

Reversal or continuation performance. The best performance comes from patterns in a bear market, regardless of the breakout direction.

S&P performance. Using the dates of the candle end to the trend end, I measured the performance of the S&P 500 and found that the candle outperforms the index.

Table 55.2
General Statistics

Description	Bull Market, Up Breakout	Bear Market, Up Breakout	Bull Market, Down Breakout	Bear Market, Down Breakout
Number found	10,074	3,475	4,746	1,705
Reversal (R), continuation (C) performance	5.99% C	6.74% C	−5.45% R	−8.22% R
Standard & Poor's 500 change	1.37%	0.49%	−1.31%	−2.73%
Candle end to breakout (median, days)	2	3	4	4
Candle end to trend end (median, days)	7	6	8	9
Number of breakouts near the 12-month low (L), middle (M), or high (H)	L 1,113, M 2,018, H 5,250	L 668, M 1,015, H 1,737	L 687, M 1,104, H 2,319	L 377, M 553, H 740
Percentage move for each 12-month period	L 7.90%, M 5.85%, H 5.62%	L 10.03%, M 6.72%, H 5.82%	L −6.56%, M −5.68%, H −5.23%	L −10.42%, M −7.94%, H −7.53%
Candle end + 1 day	0.67%	0.96%	−1.28%	−1.71%
Candle end + 3 days	1.34%	1.41%	−2.52%	−3.47%
Candle end + 5 days	1.56%	1.58%	−2.92%	−4.08%
Candle end + 10 days	1.90%	1.45%	−2.79%	−4.42%
10-day performance rank	91	86	38	41

Candle end to breakout. It takes between a median of two and four days for price to break out. Since a white candle is the last line in the pattern, an upward breakout has less distance to travel so it takes less time than a downward breakout.

Candle end to trend end. Price trends for about a week before the trend stops. Downward breakouts take longer to reach the trend end than upward breakouts do.

Yearly position, performance. Most last engulfing tops appear within a third of the yearly high, but the best performers hide in the shallow end—within a third of the yearly low.

Performance over time. Compared to other candle results, these numbers are lousy. They also show that the candle pattern is a weak performer. For example, the middle two columns show weakness from 5 to 10 days. If this were a robust performer, the numbers would increase over time under all market conditions and breakout directions. The performance rank confirms that the pattern does better after a downward breakout.

Table 55.3 shows height statistics.

Candle height. Look for tall candles because they outperform. To determine whether the candle is short or tall, compute its height from highest high to lowest low price in the candle pattern and divide by the breakout price. If the result is higher than the median, then you have a tall candle; otherwise it's short.

Table 55.3
Height Statistics

Description	Bull Market, Up Breakout	Bear Market, Up Breakout	Bull Market, Down Breakout	Bear Market, Down Breakout
Median candle height as a percentage of breakout price	2.92%	3.92%	2.80%	3.90%
Short candle, performance	4.69%	5.49%	−4.42%	−7.31%
Tall candle, performance	7.66%	8.12%	−6.79%	−9.23%
Percentage meeting price target (measure rule)	67%	62%	65%	65%
Median upper shadow as a percentage of breakout price	0.32%	0.44%	0.40%	0.62%
Short upper shadow, performance	5.52%	5.95%	−5.13%	−7.74%
Tall upper shadow, performance	6.49%	7.59%	−5.79%	−8.72%
Median lower shadow as a percentage of breakout price	0.24%	0.32%	0.24%	0.34%
Short lower shadow, performance	5.55%	6.26%	−5.26%	−7.64%
Tall lower shadow, performance	6.44%	7.21%	−5.64%	−8.79%

Auntie Em sees a last engulfing top with a high price of 37 and a low of 36. Is the candle short or tall? The height is 37 − 36, or 1, so the result is 1/37, or 2.70%. In a bull market with an upward breakout, the candle is short.

Measure rule. Use the measure rule to help predict how far price will rise or fall. Compute the height of the candle pattern and multiply it by the appropriate percentage shown in the table; then apply it to the breakout price.

Using Auntie Em's example, in a bull market the upward breakout target would be (1 × 67%) + 37, or 37.67, and the downward breakout target would be 36 − (1 × 65%), or 35.35.

Shadows. The results pertain to the last candle line in the pattern. To determine whether the shadow is short or tall, compute the height of the shadow and divide by the breakout price. Compare the result to the median in the table. Tall shadows have a percentage higher than the median. Candles with tall upper and lower shadows perform better than do their short counterparts.

Table 55.4 shows volume statistics.

Candle volume trend. A rising volume trend throughout the candle suggests better postbreakout performance in all cases except bull market/up breakouts. Those do better after falling volume.

Average candle volume. Heavy candle volume is better for performance except in a bull market with a downward breakout. That category does better with below-average volume.

Breakout volume. Heavy breakout volume suggests better performance across all categories.

Table 55.4
Volume Statistics

Description	Bull Market, Up Breakout	Bear Market, Up Breakout	Bull Market, Down Breakout	Bear Market, Down Breakout
Rising candle volume, performance	5.96%	6.85%	−5.53%	−8.41%
Falling candle volume, performance	6.03%	6.60%	−5.35%	−7.98%
Above-average candle volume, performance	6.12%	6.78%	−5.38%	−8.45%
Below-average candle volume, performance	5.92%	6.72%	−5.48%	−8.12%
Heavy breakout volume, performance	6.68%	7.60%	−5.77%	−8.88%
Light breakout volume, performance	5.33%	6.00%	−5.20%	−7.75%

Trading Tactics

If you see this candle form during a primary uptrend, it *may* signal a lasting reversal. However, more likely any turn down will be short-lived and the upward trend will resume. For a safer trade, look for an upward retracement in a downward price trend. When the candle breaks out downward it joins with the existing current and both sail off downstream.

I split trading tactics into two basic studies, one concerning reversal rates and the other concerning performance. Of the two, reversal rates are more important, because it's better to trade in the direction of the trend and let price run as far as it can.

Table 55.5 gives tips to find the trend direction.

Confirmation reversal rates. The last engulfing top acts as a continuation pattern 67.7% of the time. However, if you wait for a lower close the next day, price breaks out downward 55% to 56% of the time. The other confirmation methods give less successful results.

Reversal, continuation rates. Since the price trend is up, expect an upward breakout between 67% and 68% of the time.

Yearly range reversals. Splitting the reversals and continuations into where they occur in the yearly price range, we find that they all behave similarly. Continuations rule regardless of where the candle appears. However, a continuation is most likely to occur within a third of the yearly high.

Table 55.6 shows performance indicators that can give hints as to how your stock will behave after the breakout from a candle pattern.

Confirmation, performance. In a bull market, the opening gap confirmation method leads to the best postbreakout performance. That's when you take a position if price gaps open lower the next day.

In a bear market, wait for a lower close the next day before shorting the stock.

Table 55.5
Reversal Rates

Description	Bull Market	Bear Market
Closing price confirmation reversal rate	55%	56%
Candle color confirmation reversal rate	52%	54%
Opening gap confirmation reversal rate	40%	41%
Reversal rate: trend up, breakout down	32%	33%
Continuation rate: trend up, breakout up	68%	67%
Percentage of reversals (R)/ continuations (C) for each 12-month low (L), middle (M), or high (H)	L 38% R/62% C, M 35% R/65% C, H 31% R/69% C	L 36% R/64% C, M 35% R/65% C, H 30% R/70% C

Table 55.6
Performance Indicators

Description	Bull Market, Up Breakout	Bear Market, Up Breakout	Bull Market, Down Breakout	Bear Market, Down Breakout
Closing price confirmation, performance	N/A	N/A	−6.73%	−9.11%
Candle color confirmation, performance	N/A	N/A	−6.66%	−8.93%
Opening gap confirmation, performance	N/A	N/A	−6.85%	−8.94%
Breakout above 50-day moving average, performance	5.85%	6.35%	−5.36%	−7.66%
Breakout below 50-day moving average, performance	6.95%	9.22%	−5.76%	−9.47%
Last candle: close in highest third, performance	6.01%	6.74%	−5.52%	−8.09%
Last candle: close in middle third, performance	5.93%	6.49%	−5.29%	−8.67%
Last candle: close in lowest third, performance	5.35%	9.04%	−4.40%	−7.30%

N/A means not applicable.

Moving average. Last engulfing tops perform best if the breakout is below the 50-trading-day moving average.

Closing position. A close in the highest third of the last candle line of the engulfing top works best in all markets, regardless of the breakout direction except for bear market/up breakouts Those do better when price closes near the low.

Sample Trade

Auntie Em is shopping for stocks and sees a promising setup pictured in Figure 55.2. Price trends downward from the high at D to the low at A, bounces once like a stone skipping across water, and then bottoms at C. Price rises and forms another valley at B. The ABC formation is an ugly head-and-shoulders bottom chart pattern. By *ugly* I mean the two shoulders do not bottom near the same price.

A neckline drawn connecting the armpits of the pattern provides the traditional buy signal when price closes above it. That happens when price forms a last engulfing top. To Auntie Em, it's another signal that price will continue higher, so she buys the stock the next day.

Price rises in a series of white candles, and she believes it will reach the old high and stall. So she places a sell stop at the price of D, where the tallest

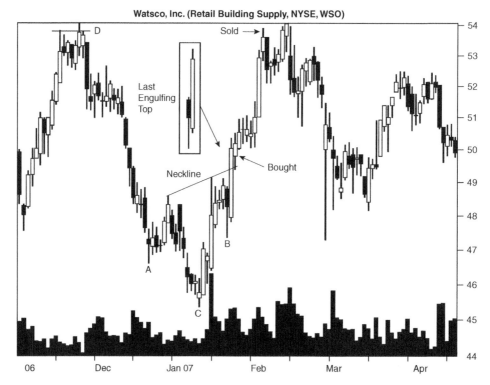

Figure 55.2 A last engulfing top combined with a head-and-shoulders bottom suggests a continued rise.

body ends. In a few days, price reaches her stop and the stock sells for a tidy profit. She plans to use the money for Toto's vet bills.

For Best Performance

The following list offers tips and observations to help choose candles that perform well. Consult the associated table for more information.

- Use the identification guidelines to help select the pattern—Table 55.1.
- Candles within a third of the yearly low perform best—Table 55.2.
- Select tall candles—Table 55.3.
- Use the measure rule to predict a price target—Table 55.3.
- Candles with tall shadows outperform—Table 55.3.
- Volume gives performance clues—Table 55.4.
- Look for the candle in an upward retracement of a downward price trend—Trading Tactics discussion.

- Improve the reversal rate by waiting for a downward close a day after the candle formation ends—Table 55.5.
- The last engulfing top breaks out upward most often—Table 55.5.
- Opening gap confirmation works best in a bull market—Table 55.6.
- Breakouts below the 50-day moving average lead to the best performance—Table 55.6.

56

Long Black Day

Behavior and Rank

Theoretical: Continuation.
Actual bull market: Continuation 53% of the time (ranking 38).
Actual bear market: Continuation 56% of the time (ranking 31).
Frequency: 9th out of 103.
Overall performance over time: 19th out of 103.

Long black days are like clouds. Sometimes they are important but most times you can just ignore them. Every candle tells a story, and a long black day candle's story begins with its tall body. Only the body height matters, not the shadow length, and the body must be taller than the average of the prior week or two. Thus, attach more significance to a few tall black candles as opposed to a chart full of tall candles.

The psychology behind the candle represents a battle between the bulls and bears in which the bears come out on top. Price opens high and closes much lower, creating a black candle and a depressing day for owners of the stock.

I found that the candle acts as a continuation most often and the rank shows it works well (38 in a bull market). It occurs frequently (9th) and the overall performance rank is superb at 19th out of 103 where 1 is best.

Identification Guidelines

Figure 56.1 highlights the only three long black day candles on the chart. That may seem odd, but other black candles are not exceptionally tall when

Figure 56.1   Three long black day candles mark minor highs or lows within a day of their appearance.

compared to prior price action or they have shadows longer than their bodies. Table 56.1 shows the identification guidelines I used.

I look for a black body whose height is at least three times that of the average body during the preceding week or two. That eliminates many candles. Moreover, I don't want to see long shadows. I found a source that said, "The shadow lines are much shorter than the real body." Therefore, I look for shadows shorter than the body height. Since the body height can be huge, so can the shadow height—just make sure it's shorter than the body.

The guidelines I chose helped select the best of the best in hopes of finding a candle with special properties and behavior.

Table 56.1
Identification Guidelines

Characteristic	Discussion
Number of candle lines	One.
Configuration	The candle is black and the body height is at least three times the average body height of recent candles, with shadows shorter than the body.

These guidelines apply only to long black day candles, not the generic long candles used in multiline candle patterns. Those have a different definition. I treat a long black day as a special candle, not as part of other candles.

Statistics

Table 56.2 shows general statistics.

Number found. Using a more complete database to prorate this candle, I found that it appears most often in a bull market. Since this candle is plentiful, I limited selection to 20,000 candle lines.

Reversal or continuation performance. Reversals perform better after upward breakouts and continuations work better after downward breakouts. Patterns in bear markets do better than do those in bull markets.

S&P performance. Using the dates of the candle end to the trend end, I measured the performance of the S&P 500 index and found that the candle beats the S&P, often by a wide margin.

Table 56.2
General Statistics

Description	Bull Market, Up Breakout	Bear Market, Up Breakout	Bull Market, Down Breakout	Bear Market, Down Breakout
Number found	4,567	1,435	10,527	3,471
Reversal (R), continuation (C) performance	6.26% C 6.58% R	7.53% C 8.01% R	−5.48% C −5.38% R	−10.13% C −9.35% R
Standard & Poor's 500 change	2.31%	1.72%	−0.74%	−2.29%
Candle end to breakout (median, days)	5	5	2	2
Candle end to trend end (median, days)	11	11	6	6
Number of breakouts near the 12-month low (L), middle (M), or high (H)	L 775, M 1,086, H 2,076	L 395, M 461, H 562	L 2,536, M 2,980, H 3,924	L 1,302, M 1,116, H 1,009
Percentage move for each 12-month period	L 7.78%, M 6.29%, H 6.07%	L 9.95%, M 7.94%, H 6.45%	L −6.19%, M −5.41%, H −5.16%	L −11.41%, M −9.46%, H −8.75%
Candle end + 1 day	1.76%	2.65%	−0.74%	−1.22%
Candle end + 3 days	3.38%	4.66%	−1.09%	−1.97%
Candle end + 5 days	4.32%	5.83%	−1.25%	−2.26%
Candle end + 10 days	5.11%	6.31%	−0.94%	−2.46%
10-day performance rank	8	17	97	78

Candle end to breakout. Since price closes near the candle's low, it takes less time for price to break out downward than upward.

Candle end to trend end. I checked to be sure the computations for the breakout and trend end numbers were correct. Having four pairs of numbers the same is a bit unusual.

It takes less time to reach the trend end for downward breakouts because the closing price is near the candle's low. An upward breakout would start a new trend, likely taking longer to reach the trend end than a downtrend already in progress.

Yearly position, performance. Most long black day candles appear within a third of the yearly high except for bear market/down breakouts, where a third from the yearly low is popular. Those near the yearly low perform best.

Performance over time. Patterns in a bear market outperform their bull market counterparts. Upward breakouts from this candle pattern are the star performers, and the rank confirms this. The percentages are robust results across all market conditions and breakout directions with one exception: the bull market/down breakout category between 5 and 10 days. The performance numbers show weakness under those conditions.

Table 56.3 shows height statistics.

Candle height. Tall candles outperform across the board, so search for tall candles.

Table 56.3
Height Statistics

Description	Bull Market, Up Breakout	Bear Market, Up Breakout	Bull Market, Down Breakout	Bear Market, Down Breakout
Median candle height as a percentage of breakout price	3.66%	5.44%	3.73%	5.58%
Short candle, performance	5.12%	6.29%	−4.32%	−8.28%
Tall candle, performance	8.17%	9.62%	−6.92%	−11.74%
Percentage meeting price target (measure rule)	62%	55%	54%	58%
Median upper shadow as a percentage of breakout price	0.13%	0.16%	0.13%	0.17%
Short upper shadow, performance	6.35%	7.51%	−5.32%	−9.04%
Tall upper shadow, performance	6.54%	8.16%	−5.54%	−10.64%
Median lower shadow as a percentage of breakout price	0.37%	0.63%	0.31%	0.49%
Short lower shadow, performance	5.90%	7.36%	−4.94%	−9.76%
Tall lower shadow, performance	7.06%	8.34%	−6.01%	−9.93%

Table 56.4
Volume Statistics

Description	Bull Market, Up Breakout	Bear Market, Up Breakout	Bull Market, Down Breakout	Bear Market, Down Breakout
Above-average candle volume, performance	6.31%	8.01%	−5.49%	−10.02%
Below-average candle volume, performance	6.64%	7.52%	−5.34%	−9.54%
Heavy breakout volume, performance	7.01%	8.35%	−5.80%	−10.56%
Light breakout volume, performance	5.71%	7.21%	−4.90%	−8.48%

To determine whether the candle is short or tall, compute its height from high to low price and divide by the breakout price. If the result is above the median, then you have a tall candle; otherwise it's short.

For example, Clyde sees a long black candle with a high of 90 and a low of 89. Is the candle short or tall? The height is 90 – 89, or 1, and for an upward breakout in a bull market the result would be 1/90, or 1.11%. Since that is below the median, the candle is short.

Measure rule. Use the measure rule to help predict how far price will rise or fall. Compute the height of the candle and multiply it by the appropriate percentage shown in the table; then apply it to the breakout price.

What are the price targets for Clyde's candle? Plugging numbers into the formula we get $(1 \times 62\%) + 90$, or 90.62, for the upward breakout direction and $89 – (1 \times 54\%)$, or 88.46, for a downward breakout, both taken in a bull market.

Shadows. To determine whether the shadow is short or tall, compute the height of the shadow and divide by the breakout price. Compare the result to the median in the table. Tall shadows have a percentage higher than the median. Candles with upper and lower shadows taller than the median outperform those candles with shorter shadows.

Table 56.4 shows volume statistics.

Average candle volume. Long black days with above-average volume tend to perform better post breakout except in the bull market/up breakout category.

Breakout volume. Heavy breakout volume results in the best performance across the board.

Trading Tactics

Before I get to trading tactics, let me mention what I found when researching tall candles. I looked at candles taller than 146% of the median height (the

Table 56.5
Reversal Rates

Description	Bull Market	Bear Market
Reversal rate: trend up, breakout down	71%	71%
Continuation rate: trend up, breakout up	29%	29%
Reversal: trend down, breakout up	31%	29%
Continuation: trend down, breakout down	69%	71%
Percentage of reversals (R)/continuations (C) for each 12-month low (L), middle (M), or high (H)	L 39% R/61% C, M 44% R/56% C, H 53% R/47% C	L 38% R/62% C, M 43% R/57% C, H 52% R/48% C

height includes the shadows) over the previous 22 days and found that price peaks within a day of the tall candle 67% of the time and a valley appears within a day of the tall candle 72% of the time. Figures 56.1 and 56.2 both show price forming a peak or valley within a day of the tall black candle (i.e., before or after it).

I split trading tactics into two basic studies, one concerning reversal rates and the other concerning performance. Of the two, reversal rates are more important, because it's better to trade in the direction of the trend and let price run as far as it can.

Table 56.5 gives tips to find the trend direction.

Reversal, continuation rates. This examines the trend leading to the long black day and the resulting breakout direction. The breakout is downward most often, probably because the closing price is near the candle's low.

Yearly range reversals. Most candles acting as continuation patterns occur within a third of the yearly low.

Table 56.6 shows performance indicators that can give hints as to how your stock will behave after the breakout from this candle pattern.

Confirmation, performance. Opening gap confirmation works best. That means trading only if price gaps lower the day after the tall black candle.

Moving average. Long black days with breakouts below the 50-trading-day moving average result in the best performance after the breakout.

Closing position. Since we are dealing with tall black candles, the close is not near the candle's high. Candles with the close near the low tend to perform better after the breakout.

Sample Trade

A successful trade is often the result of a combination of factors, and the one Clyde makes is no exception. Figure 56.2 shows the setup. Price trends down from the high at C to the first cluster of prices at A. It bounces to E and then drops back to B, where it finds support at the A low.

Table 56.6
Performance Indicators

Description	Bull Market, Up Breakout	Bear Market, Up Breakout	Bull Market, Down Breakout	Bear Market, Down Breakout
Closing price confirmation, performance	N/A	N/A	−4.77%	−8.67%
Candle color confirmation, performance	N/A	N/A	−5.17%	−8.91%
Opening gap confirmation, performance	N/A	N/A	−6.26%	−10.70%
Breakout above 50-day moving average, performance	6.23%	7.16%	−5.05%	−8.66%
Breakout below 50-day moving average, performance	6.92%	8.63%	−5.68%	−10.35%
Last candle: close in highest third, performance	0.00%	0.00%	0.00%	0.00%
Last candle: close in middle third, performance	6.27%	7.12%	−4.76%	−8.60%
Last candle: close in lowest third, performance	6.46%	7.90%	−5.46%	−9.89%

N/A means not applicable.

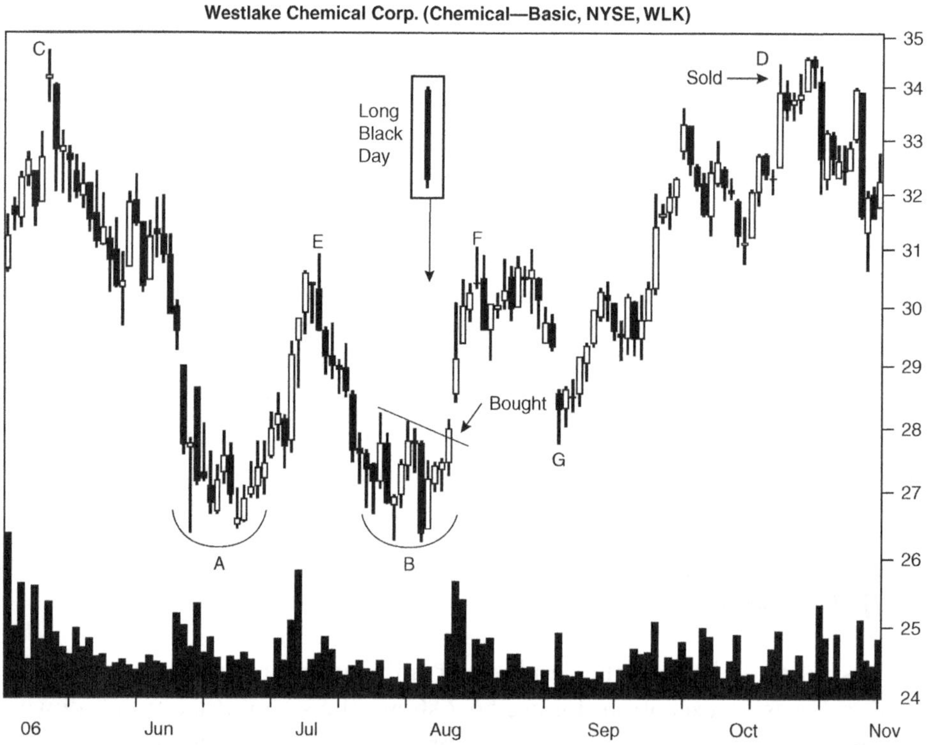

Figure 56.2 A double bottom chart pattern presents a buying opportunity.

A white candle and a higher close follows the long black day at B, suggesting price will recover. Clyde draws a trendline down across the tops and places a buy order for where he expects price to cross the trendline. When it does, he buys the stock.

How far will price rise? Certainly the high at E is possible. A close above that would confirm the double bottom as a valid chart pattern with a rise expected to match the high at C (the site of overhead resistance).

Within days, price climbs to F but then throws back to G. Throwbacks happen 55% of the time in Eve & Eve double bottoms (which is the type shown), so Clyde isn't worried. However, he wisely places a stop below the low at B to protect his position in case things go bad.

When price starts moving up from G, he places a stop slightly below the high price of C and the stock is sold at D.

Clyde is lucky with this trade in two ways. First, when price makes a twin bottom, there is only a 36% chance of it rising to close above the high at E. Second, assuming price will reach the old high at C is often wishful thinking. It pays off in this case, but price will often fall short, sometimes dramatically so.

For Best Performance

The following list offers tips and observations to help choose candles that perform well. Consult the associated table for more information.

- Use the identification guidelines to help select the pattern—Table 56.1.
- Upward breakouts that reverse the downtrend outperform—Table 56.2.
- Candles within a third of the yearly low do best—Table 56.2.
- Select tall candles—Table 56.3.
- Use the measure rule to predict a price target—Table 56.3.
- Candles with tall shadows outperform—Table 56.3.
- Volume gives performance clues—Table 56.4.
- Patterns within a third of the yearly low tend to act as continuations—Table 56.5.
- Opening gap confirmation works best in a bull market—Table 56.6.
- Breakouts below the 50-day moving average lead to the best performance—Table 56.6.

57

Long White Day

Behavior and Rank

Theoretical: Continuation.
Actual bull market: Continuation 58% of the time (ranking 24).
Actual bear market: Continuation 55% of the time (ranking 35).
Frequency: 10th out of 103.
Overall performance over time: 53rd out of 103.

A long *black* day has a continuation rate of 53% and a long *white* day continues the price trend 58% of the time in a bull market. Therefore, a white candle performs a smidgen better than the black one. Both are what I call near random, meaning in actual trading you won't be able to tell if it will be a reversal or continuation until it's too late. Of course, that's true of any candle pattern. The overall performance rank is 53 out of 103 candles, where 1 is best.

A long white day is a study in bullish excitement. Price opens near the low and then climbs, closing near the high for the day. Regardless of the price trend leading to the candle, there's a 74% to 75% chance that the break-out will be upward. Keep that in mind when considering a long white day for a trade.

Identification Guidelines

Figure 57.1 highlights two long white days, the only two on the chart. I define a long white day as one with a body three times the average height of preceding

UIL Holdings Corp. (Electric Utility—East, NYSE, UIL)

Long
White
Day

Figure 57.1 Two long white days appear in an uptrend.

candles over the prior week or two and with shadows shorter than the body.
The two candles on the chart are the only ones that qualify.

These two appear in an upward trend, and since they represent continuation patterns, there's a good chance that they will break out upward, too.
That's what happens here when price (eventually) closes above the top of each
candle, confirming an upward breakout.

Table 57.1 lists identification guidelines. I chose them to help identify
unique candles that might have more significance to traders. Look for an unusually tall white candle with comparatively short shadows. Consider limiting
your selections to a few per chart. If you find too many, then either they won't
have bodies tall enough or your eyes need to be checked.

Table 57.1
Identification Guidelines

Characteristic	Discussion
Number of candle lines	One.
Configuration	A tall white candle with a body three times the average of the prior week or two and with shadows shorter than the body.

Table 57.2
General Statistics

Description	Bull Market, Up Breakout	Bear Market, Up Breakout	Bull Market, Down Breakout	Bear Market, Down Breakout
Number found	11,342	3,479	3,869	1,310
Reversal (R), continuation (C) performance	6.19% C 6.50% R	6.63% C 7.89% R	−5.71% C −6.02% R	−9.58% C −8.70% R
Standard & Poor's 500 change	1.25%	0.46%	−1.35%	−3.22%
Candle end to breakout (median, days)	2	3	6	5
Candle end to trend end (median, days)	6	6	10	11
Number of breakouts near the 12-month low (L), middle (M), or high (H)	L 1,481, M 2,186, H 5,579	L 764, M 1,080, H 1,596	L 733, M 949, H 1,591	L 384, M 367, H 536
Percentage move for each 12-month period	L 7.82%, M 6.23%, H 5.74%	L 10.38%, M 6.66%, H 6.12%	L −6.63%, M −6.24%, H −5.76%	L −11.30%, M −8.32%, H −7.74%
Candle end + 1 day	0.66%	0.71%	−1.58%	−2.08%
Candle end + 3 days	1.26%	1.26%	−3.02%	−4.15%
Candle end + 5 days	1.62%	1.69%	−3.69%	−5.12%
Candle end + 10 days	2.02%	1.49%	−3.91%	−6.21%
10-day performance rank	87	84	16	16

Statistics

Table 57.2 shows general statistics.

Number found. I limited my selection to 20,000 candles. After prorating the numbers using the standard database, I found that most appear in a bull market.

Reversal or continuation performance. Most long white days perform best as reversals. That's true for all categories except bear market/down breakout. Continuations do better under those conditions.

S&P performance. Using the dates of the candle end to the trend end, I measured the performance of the S&P 500 index and found that the candle performs better than the S&P in all cases.

Candle end to breakout. Since price closes near the top of the candle, an upward breakout takes less time than a downward one.

Candle end to trend end. It takes longer to reach the trend end if the breakout is downward. This may be due to the white candle representing an existing upward trend, so some of the upward move has already completed, leaving less time to go compared to a downtrend.

Yearly position, performance. Most long white days appear within a third of the yearly high, but the best performance comes from those with breakouts near the yearly low.

Performance over time. If you think a long white day is a bullish candle, then check again. The table shows that downward breakouts perform substantially better than do their upward breakout counterparts. The performance rank agrees with that assessment. In addition, weakness from 5 to 10 days in the bear market/up breakout column suggests this pattern is not a robust performer.

Table 57.3 shows height statistics.

Candle height. Tall candles perform best, so those are the ones to hunt for. To determine whether the candle is short or tall, compute its height from highest high to lowest low price and divide by the breakout price. If the result is higher than the median, then you have a tall candle; otherwise it's short.

Mike sees a tall white candle with a high at 79 and a low at 77. Is the candle tall or short? Let's assume an upward breakout in a bull market. The height is 79 − 77, or 2, so the measure is 2/79, or 2.53%. The candle is short because it's less than the median.

Table 57.3
Height Statistics

Description	Bull Market, Up Breakout	Bear Market, Up Breakout	Bull Market, Down Breakout	Bear Market, Down Breakout
Median candle height as a percentage of breakout price	3.93%	5.05%	3.86%	4.94%
Short candle, performance	4.86%	5.36%	−4.87%	−7.51%
Tall candle, performance	8.12%	9.14%	−7.33%	−10.71%
Percentage meeting price target (measure rule)	57%	55%	55%	60%
Median upper shadow as a percentage of breakout price	0.32%	0.43%	0.39%	0.54%
Short upper shadow, performance	5.75%	6.29%	−5.36%	−8.39%
Tall upper shadow, performance	6.85%	7.94%	−6.51%	−9.60%
Median lower shadow as a percentage of breakout price	0.16%	0.20%	0.15%	0.18%
Short lower shadow, performance	5.96%	6.84%	−5.57%	−8.39%
Tall lower shadow, performance	6.63%	7.36%	−6.30%	−9.62%

Table 57.4
Volume Statistics

Description	Bull Market, Up Breakout	Bear Market, Up Breakout	Bull Market, Down Breakout	Bear Market, Down Breakout
Above-average candle volume, performance	6.46%	7.31%	−6.19%	−8.94%
Below-average candle volume, performance	5.91%	6.68%	−5.45%	−9.09%
Heavy breakout volume, performance	6.83%	7.68%	−6.36%	−9.59%
Light breakout volume, performance	5.49%	6.27%	−5.47%	−8.33%

Measure rule. Use the measure rule to help predict how far price will rise or fall. Compute the height of the candle and multiply it by the appropriate percentage shown in the table; then apply it to the breakout price.

For Mike's candle, what are the price targets? For upward breakouts in a bull market, the target would be (2 × 57%) + 79, or 80.14. The downward target would be 77 − (2 × 55%), or 75.90.

Shadows. To determine whether the shadow is short or tall, compute the height of the shadow and divide by the breakout price. Compare the result to the median in the table. Tall shadows have a percentage higher than the median. Candles with tall upper and lower shadows perform better than do those with short shadows.

Table 57.4 shows volume statistics.

Average candle volume. Above-average volume leads to better post-breakout performance in all cases except for bear market/down breakouts. Those do better with below-average volume.

Breakout volume. Heavy breakout volume suggests better performance in all categories.

Trading Tactics

I looked at candles taller than 146% of the median height (the height includes the shadows) over the previous 22 days and found that price peaks within a day of (before or after) a tall candle 67% of the time and a valley appears within a day of a tall candle 72% of the time. Thus, if you see a tall white candle in an uptrend, price might drop for a few days—but not break out downward, mind you—before continuing higher.

I split trading tactics into two basic studies, one concerning reversal rates and the other concerning performance. Of the two, reversal rates are more

Table 57.5
Reversal Rates

Description	Bull Market	Bear Market
Reversal rate: trend up, breakout down	26%	28%
Continuation rate: trend up, breakout up	74%	72%
Reversal: trend down, breakout up	75%	75%
Continuation: trend down, breakout down	25%	25%
Percentage of reversals (R)/continuations (C) for each 12-month low (L), middle (M), or high (H)	L 47% R/53% C, M 46% R/54% C, H 40% R/60% C	L 53% R/47% C, M 46% R/54% C, H 41% R/59% C

important, because it's better to trade in the direction of the trend and let price run as far as it can.

Table 57.5 gives tips to find the trend direction.

Reversal, continuation rates. Most times, expect an upward breakout. This is because the price is likely near the top of the candle, making a close above the candle's top easier to obtain. Reversals occur between 25% and 28% of the time.

Yearly range reversals. Continuations occur most often within a third of the yearly high.

Table 57.6 shows performance indicators that can give hints as to how your stock will behave after the breakout from this candle pattern.

Confirmation, performance. Opening gap confirmation results in the best performance. That means you buy the stock if price gaps open higher the day after a tall white candle.

Moving average. Breakouts below the 50-trading-day moving average result in the best performance in all cases.

Closing position. Since price closes near the high, the lowest third shows 0.00%. The results track the market direction. Tall white days in bull markets do better when they close near the candle's high. Bear market candles do better when they close in the middle of the day's trading range.

Sample Trade

Figure 57.2 shows a trade that Mike makes. From the January high, price drops and bottoms at LS, the left shoulder of what will become a head-and-shoulders bottom chart pattern. Price makes a lower valley at the head before climbing to the right shoulder low (RS).

Mike watches the chart pattern develop, and when a long white day breaches the neckline, that is the buy signal. He buys the stock the next day.

His price target is based on the height of the head-and-shoulders chart pattern from the head low to the price of the neckline directly above applied

Table 57.6
Performance Indicators

Description	Bull Market, Up Breakout	Bear Market, Up Breakout	Bull Market, Down Breakout	Bear Market, Down Breakout
Closing price confirmation, performance	5.56%	6.45%	N/A	N/A
Candle color confirmation, performance	5.66%	6.53%	N/A	N/A
Opening gap confirmation, performance	6.82%	8.30%	N/A	N/A
Breakout above 50-day moving average, performance	6.13%	6.49%	−5.77%	−8.16%
Breakout below 50-day moving average, performance	6.83%	9.45%	−6.19%	−10.35%
Last candle: close in highest third, performance	6.31%	7.09%	−6.02%	−8.96%
Last candle: close in middle third, performance	5.99%	7.19%	−5.06%	−9.23%
Last candle: close in lowest third, performance	0.00%	0.00%	0.00%	0.00%

N/A means not applicable.

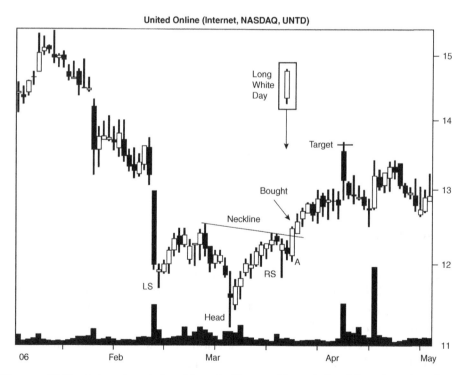

Figure 57.2 A head-and-shoulders bottom with a tall white day signals an upward breakout.

to the breakout price. The breakout price is the value of the stock when price pierces the neckline, moving up.

Mike is lucky and smart to place a limit order at his target price. About two weeks after he bought, price hits his limit and takes him out.

For Best Performance

The following list offers tips and observations to help choose candles that perform well. Consult the associated table for more information.

- Use the identification guidelines to help select the pattern—Table 57.1.
- Candles within a third of the yearly low perform best—Table 57.2.
- Select tall candles—Table 57.3.
- Use the measure rule to predict a price target—Table 57.3.
- Candles with tall shadows outperform—Table 57.3.
- Volume gives performance clues—Table 57.4.
- Patterns within a third of the yearly high tend to act as continuations 59% to 60% of the time—Table 57.5.
- Opening gap confirmation works best—Table 57.6.
- Breakouts below the 50-day moving average lead to the best performance—Table 57.6.

58

Marubozu, Black

Behavior and Rank

Theoretical: Continuation.
Actual bull market: Continuation 53% of the time (ranking 35).
Actual bear market: Continuation 54% of the time (ranking 39).
Frequency: 30th out of 103.
Overall performance over time: 57th out of 103.

The black marubozu appears as often as clouds in Syracuse (meaning a lot), but many will argue that the marubozu is a weak candle pattern. Being a black candle, it shows that the bears have the edge. They push price well below the open, and it closes at the low for the day.

What's unusual about this candle is the lack of shadows at either end. Perhaps they'll turn up when the sun appears.

Performance as a continuation pattern is quite good, ranking 35 in a bull market. The overall performance is just 57th out of 103 candles, where 1 is best. That's midlist and nothing to get excited about.

Identification Guidelines

Figure 58.1 shows what black marubozu candles look like. The marubozu is a tall black candle without any shadows. Body size is a function of the average body size preceding the candle, so even though the first candle is much shorter

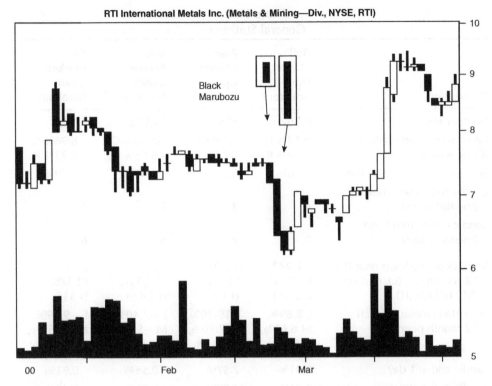

Figure 58.1 Two black marubozu candles act as continuations of the downtrend.

than the second in the figure, it still qualifies as a marubozu. Table 58.1 lists the identification guidelines in case you blinked. They are self-explanatory.

Statistics

Table 58.2 shows general statistics.

Number found. I limited selection to 19,993 candles, seven short of a full load (the seven had incomplete data). What I find unusual about this candle is the scarcity of them in a bear market. You would think that in a bear market, a black marubozu candle would appear as often as hair on a gorilla, but that's not what happens.

Table 58.1
Identification Guidelines

Characteristic	Discussion
Number of candle lines	One.
Configuration	A tall black body with no shadows.

Table 58.2
General Statistics

Description	Bull Market, Up Breakout	Bear Market, Up Breakout	Bull Market, Down Breakout	Bear Market, Down Breakout
Number found	6,362	516	11,943	1,172
Reversal (R), continuation (C) performance	6.12% C 7.28% R	7.12% C 8.42% R	−6.00% C −5.95% R	−8.96% C −8.22% R
Standard & Poor's 500 change	1.76%	0.72%	−0.47%	−1.79%
Candle end to breakout (median, days)	4	3	2	1
Candle end to trend end (median, days)	8	9	5	6
Number of breakouts near the 12-month low (L), middle (M), or high (H)	L 1,242, M 1,451, H 2,155	L 170, M 182, H 161	L 2,939, M 2,937, H 3,474	L 441, M 378, H 335
Percentage move for each 12-month period	L 8.69%, M 6.69%, H 6.15%	L 10.30%, M 7.70%, H 6.42%	L −7.40%, M −5.92%, H −5.57%	L −9.69%, M −8.57%, H −7.84%
Candle end + 1 day	1.91%	2.57%	−0.58%	−0.91%
Candle end + 3 days	3.26%	4.08%	−1.03%	−1.48%
Candle end + 5 days	3.86%	4.96%	−1.06%	−1.43%
Candle end + 10 days	4.39%	5.33%	−0.88%	−1.35%
10-day performance rank	24	25	100	93

Reversal or continuation performance. Upward breakouts from marubozu candles do better as reversals of the downtrend, and downward breakouts do better as continuations of the downtrend.

S&P performance. Using the dates of the candle end to the trend end, I measured the performance of the S&P 500 index and found that the marubozu beats the performance of the S&P.

Candle end to breakout. A black marubozu candle has its close at the bottom of the candle, so a downward breakout (a close below the candle's low) often takes less time. Since a marubozu has no lower shadow, the breakout occurs within a day or two. Upward breakouts take longer because price has to climb up the tall marubozu candle and close above the high.

Candle end to trend end. My guess as to why downward breakouts reach the end of the trend quicker than upward ones is because a downtrend is already in place, so the end is closer than it is for an upward trend that begins after the marubozu ends.

Yearly position, performance. Bull markets tend to have black marubozu candles appear within a third of the yearly high most often. The

Table 58.3
Height Statistics

Description	Bull Market, Up Breakout	Bear Market, Up Breakout	Bull Market, Down Breakout	Bear Market, Down Breakout
Median candle height as a percentage of breakout price	2.26%	3.12%	2.42%	3.29%
Short candle, performance	5.56%	6.63%	−4.94%	−7.19%
Tall candle, performance	8.41%	9.38%	−7.32%	−10.51%
Percentage meeting price target (measure rule)	78%	77%	76%	78%

bear market shows a mixed location. Performance is best for those candles with breakouts within a third of the yearly low.

Performance over time. This is one of the few candles that perform better after an upward breakout than a downward one. The low ranking numbers (1 is best out of 103) are quite good and confirm the performance assessment. However, the weakness shown after downward breakouts in 5 to 10 days (bull market/down breakout) and 3 to 10 days (bear market/down breakout) suggest this candle is not a robust performer. If it were, performance would increase in all market conditions and breakout directions.

Table 58.3 shows height statistics. Since the marubozu lost its shadows, there are no shadow statistics to report.

Candle height. Tall candles perform better than short ones. To determine whether the candle is short or tall, compute its height from high to low price and divide by the breakout price. If the result is higher than the median, then you have a tall candle; otherwise it's short.

For example, Lorenzo finds a black marubozu with a high at 53 and a low at 51. Is the candle short or tall? The height is 53 − 51, or 2, so the result would be 2/53, or 3.77%, for an upward breakout. In a bull market, that represents a tall candle.

Measure rule. Use the measure rule to help predict how far price will rise or fall. Compute the height of the candle and multiply it by the appropriate percentage shown in the table; then apply it to the breakout price.

In Lorenzo's case, the upward breakout target would be (2 × 78%) + 53, or 54.56, and the downward breakout target would be 51 − (2 × 76%), or 49.48.

Table 58.4 shows volume statistics.

Average candle volume. Light candle volume works best for downward breakouts, but upward breakouts do better if candle volume is above average.

Breakout volume. Heavy breakout volume leads to better performance in all categories.

Table 58.4
Volume Statistics

Description	Bull Market, Up Breakout	Bear Market, Up Breakout	Bull Market, Down Breakout	Bear Market, Down Breakout
Above-average candle volume, performance	7.02%	8.27%	−5.73%	−8.56%
Below-average candle volume, performance	6.69%	7.68%	−6.11%	−8.71%
Heavy breakout volume, performance	7.52%	9.09%	−6.12%	−8.93%
Light breakout volume, performance	6.12%	6.89%	−5.87%	−8.37%

Trading Tactics

I split trading tactics into two basic studies, one concerning reversal rates and the other concerning performance. Of the two, reversal rates are more important, because it's better to trade in the direction of the trend and let price run as far as it can.

Table 58.5 gives tips to find the trend direction.

Reversal, continuation rates. Since you know the price trend leading to the black marubozu, the table shows the likely outcome. For example, if Lorenzo sees price trending up to the marubozu, there's a 65% chance that price will reverse and break out downward after the marubozu in a bull market.

Yearly range reversals. The widest performance difference comes in a bear market when the pattern is within a third of the yearly low. Black marubozu patterns tend to act as continuations under those circumstances. That result is also true in a bull market, but the range is narrower.

Table 58.5
Reversal Rates

Description	Bull Market	Bear Market
Reversal rate: trend up, breakout down	65%	69%
Continuation rate: trend up, breakout up	35%	31%
Reversal: trend down, breakout up	34%	30%
Continuation: trend down, breakout down	66%	70%
Percentage of reversals (R)/continuations (C) for each 12-month low (L), middle (M), or high (H)	L 43% R/57% C, M 46% R/54% C, H 50% R/50% C	L 40% R/60% C, M 48% R/52% C, H 54% R/46% C

Table 58.6
Performance Indicators

Description	Bull Market, Up Breakout	Bear Market, Up Breakout	Bull Market, Down Breakout	Bear Market, Down Breakout
Closing price confirmation, performance	6.99%	9.11%	−4.69%	−6.97%
Candle color confirmation, performance	6.78%	8.64%	−5.19%	−7.59%
Opening gap confirmation, performance	7.20%	9.79%	−5.77%	−7.91%
Breakout above 50-day moving average, performance	6.31%	6.85%	−5.51%	−7.66%
Breakout below 50-day moving average, performance	7.67%	9.15%	−6.42%	−9.34%

Table 58.6 shows performance indicators that can give hints as to how your stock will behave after the breakout from this candle pattern.

Confirmation, performance. Opening gap confirmation leads to the best performance after the breakout. That means waiting for price to gap open the next day before taking a position. Trade in the direction of the gap. For example, if price gaps higher at the open, then buy the stock. If it gaps lower, then short.

Moving average. Candles with breakouts below the 50-trading-day moving average result in the best performance.

Sample Trade

Figure 58.2 shows a part of a trade Lorenzo made based on a black marubozu. Price declined into the valley at A and then bounced. The stock eased lower to B, bottoming with a black marubozu after finding support at the price of A.

Lorenzo saw the identical three crows candle pattern for what it was, a double bottom (AB) reversal. He became excited.

He drew a down-sloping trendline along the peaks and reasoned that if price rose above the line, it would likely continue higher. So, he placed a buy stop just above the trendline and bought the stock four days after the black marubozu.

Price climbed in a straight-line run up to C, forming a deliberation candle pattern. He knew price was running out of steam because the last day had a small body and tall upper shadow. He thought about cashing out but decided against it. He didn't need the money, and with the strength shown in the stock (during the deliberation), he thought the inevitable retracement would be shallow.

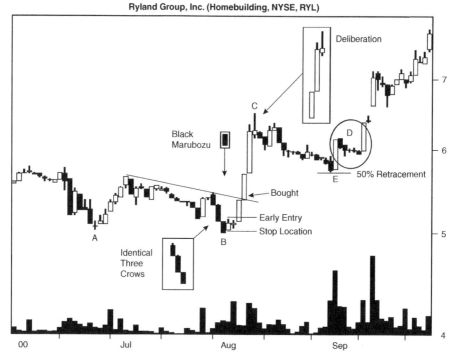

Figure 58.2 A black marubozu forms as the second bottom of a double bottom chart pattern.

Price eased lower, eventually hitting the 50% retracement level of the B to C move. A bullish engulfing pattern followed with its tall white candle (E). Then price backtracked and formed a pseudo rising three methods but with five days between the two tall white candles (circled at D) instead of three. Price continued higher and the next retracement (not shown), also bottomed at 50% of the up move starting at E.

He kept following the stock upward and when it reached wave 5 of an Elliott wave pattern and price started an ABC correction, he sold for a huge gain, doubling his money.

Here's a trading setup that occurs when you see the identical three crows pattern leading to B (three or more black candles with little body overlap and small shadows). The next candle is a white candle and it indicates a potential reversal. Price confirms the reversal (and issues a buy signal) when price closes above the top of the white candle. That occurs in this example two days later (at Early Entry). A stop placed below the white candle (Stop Location) after B often works well.

For Best Performance

The following list offers tips and observations to help choose candles that perform well. Consult the associated table for more information.

- Use the identification guidelines to help select the pattern—Table 58.1.
- Candles within a third of the yearly low perform best—Table 58.2.
- Select tall candles—Table 58.3.
- Use the measure rule to predict a price target—Table 58.3.
- Volume gives performance clues—Table 58.4.
- Use the trend leading to the start of the candle to help predict the likely breakout direction—Table 58.5.
- Opening gap confirmation works best—Table 58.6.
- Breakouts below the 50-day moving average lead to the best performance—Table 58.6.
- The identical three crows pattern is a worthwhile trading setup—Sample Trade.

59

Marubozu, Closing Black

Behavior and Rank

Theoretical: Continuation.

Actual bull market: Continuation 52% of the time (ranking 43).

Actual bear market: Continuation 54% of the time (ranking 37).

Frequency: 18th out of 103.

Overall performance over time: 43rd out of 103.

When I read that a closing black marubozu was a weak candle line, the source wasn't kidding. The candle pattern functions as a continuation just 52% of the time. That's a toothpick's width away from random (50%). The ranking places it 43 in a bull market, both as a continuation pattern and as the overall performance rank. One is best out of 103 candles, so this is well down the list.

The psychology behind the pattern begins with the bulls pushing the stock above the opening price sometime during the day. However, the bears counterattack and down price goes, closing the day at the very low. This turn of events is bearish, because a long black candle prints on the chart, with the bears firmly in control. Whether they can maintain the upper hand in following days remains to be seen. If volume is high enough during the marubozu candle, volume voyeurs claim it's bullish because everyone who wanted to sell has sold, leaving buyers to push the stock up the next day and thereafter.

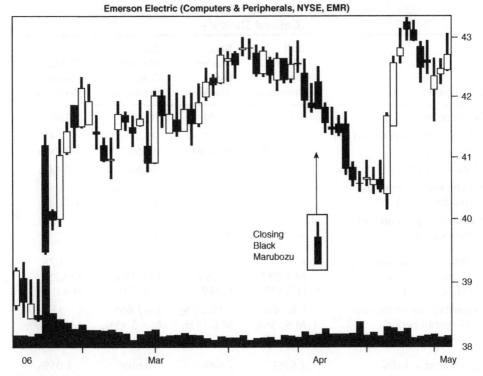

Emerson Electric (Computers & Peripherals, NYSE, EMR)

Closing
Black
Marubozu

Figure 59.1 A closing black marubozu candle suggests the downtrend will continue.

Identification Guidelines

Figure 59.1 shows an example of a closing black marubozu. Price trends downward into this candle pattern but it need not. I checked this and found that price trends downward into the marubozu just 58% of the time. Therefore, you'll find this candle in a rising price trend, too.

Identification is simple and Table 59.1 lists the guidelines. Look for a tall black body with an upper shadow but no lower one. That's all there is to it.

Statistics

Table 59.2 shows general statistics.

Table 59.1
Identification Guidelines

Characteristic	Discussion
Number of candle lines	One.
Configuration	A tall black candle with an upper shadow but no lower shadow.

Table 59.2
General Statistics

Description	Bull Market, Up Breakout	Bear Market, Up Breakout	Bull Market, Down Breakout	Bear Market, Down Breakout
Number found	5,256	1,184	10,776	2,784
Reversal (R), continuation (C) performance	6.10% C 6.93% R	6.96% C 9.57% R	−5.51% C −5.55% R	−9.84% C −9.61% R
Standard & Poor's 500 change	2.33%	1.23%	−0.65%	−2.47%
Candle end to breakout (median, days)	3	4	1	1
Candle end to trend end (median, days)	9	9	5	6
Number of breakouts near the 12-month low (L), middle (M), or high (H)	L 855, M 1,082, H 2,135	L 371, M 380, H 419	L 2,417, M 2,594, H 3,720	L 1,078, M 825, H 831
Percentage move for each 12-month period	L 8.18%, M 6.29%, H 6.11%	L 11.35%, M 8.13%, H 6.84%	L −7.05%, M −5.45%, H −5.16%	L −11.46%, M −8.88%, H −8.92%
Candle end + 1 day	1.97%	2.84%	−0.60%	−1.05%
Candle end + 3 days	3.46%	4.78%	−0.80%	−1.86%
Candle end + 5 days	4.03%	5.60%	−0.74%	−1.73%
Candle end + 10 days	4.52%	5.82%	−0.46%	−1.98%
10-day performance rank	21	20	103	82

Number found. I used 20,000 candles to generate my statistics, and most came from a bull market as the table shows. Even after prorating the numbers using the standard database, the closing black marubozu appears most often in a bull market.

Reversal or continuation performance. Reversals perform better than continuation patterns in all cases except bear market/down breakouts. Continuations under those conditions perform slightly better. The biggest performance difference appears in a bear market after an upward breakout when the marubozu acts as a reversal of the downtrend. Reversals perform 38% better than continuations (that's 9.57% versus 6.96%).

The closing black marubozu performs best in a bear market, regardless of the breakout direction.

S&P performance. Using the dates of the candle end to the trend end, I measured the performance of the S&P 500 index and found that the candle performs better than the index in all cases.

Candle end to breakout. Downward breakouts take a day to occur since price is at the candle's low. Upward breakouts take longer since price has to close above the top of the candle.

Candle end to trend end. Downward breakouts reach the trend end sooner than upward breakouts. This may be due to a black candle appearing partway into a downward trend. Thus, the trend end comes sooner than if the marubozu appears at the start of an uptrend.

Yearly position, performance. Most marubozu candles appear within a third of the yearly high except for bear market/down breakouts. Candles in that category show most often near the yearly low. The best performance occurs when the candles are within a third of the yearly low, too.

Performance over time. Performance after upward breakouts exceeds the returns from downward breakouts. That's somewhat unusual, but the performance rank confirms it. However, the weakness for days 3 to 10 and 3 to 5 in bull market/down breakout and bear market/down breakout numbers suggests this candle is not a robust performer. If it were, then all of the numbers would increase over time. Stick to the long side (upward breakouts) with this candle.

Table 59.3 shows height statistics.

Candle height. Tall patterns perform better than short ones, so be sure to check the height. How do you do this? Compute the candle's height from high to low price and divide by the breakout price. If the result is higher than the median, then you have a tall candle; otherwise it's short.

For example, Leo has a closing black marubozu with a high of 198 and a low of 196. The height is 198 – 196, or 2, and the results would be 2/198 (upward breakouts), or 1%. That's a short candle regardless of the market conditions.

Measure rule. Use the measure rule to help predict how far price will rise or fall. Compute the height of the candle and multiply it by the appropriate percentage shown in the table; then apply it to the breakout price.

Table 59.3
Height Statistics

Description	Bull Market, Up Breakout	Bear Market, Up Breakout	Bull Market, Down Breakout	Bear Market, Down Breakout
Median candle height as a percentage of breakout price	2.49%	3.52%	2.62%	3.65%
Short candle, performance	5.17%	6.42%	−4.49%	−8.33%
Tall candle, performance	8.39%	10.94%	−6.93%	−11.49%
Percentage meeting price target (measure rule)	76%	75%	69%	73%
Median upper shadow as a percentage of breakout price	0.47%	0.58%	0.48%	0.59%
Short upper shadow, performance	5.95%	7.62%	−4.98%	−8.57%
Tall upper shadow, performance	7.32%	9.52%	−6.22%	−11.05%

Table 59.4
Volume Statistics

Description	Bull Market, Up Breakout	Bear Market, Up Breakout	Bull Market, Down Breakout	Bear Market, Down Breakout
Above-average candle volume, performance	6.51%	8.13%	−5.40%	−10.14%
Below-average candle volume, performance	6.59%	8.76%	−5.61%	−9.47%
Heavy breakout volume, performance	7.41%	9.17%	−5.81%	−10.76%
Light breakout volume, performance	5.74%	7.82%	−5.27%	−8.63%

In Leo's example, the upward breakout target would be $(2 \times 76\%) + 198$, or 199.52 (bull market), and the downward breakout target would be $196 - (2 \times 69\%)$, or 194.62.

Upper shadow performance. To determine whether the shadow is short or tall, compute the height of the shadow and divide by the breakout price. Compare the result to the median in the table. Tall shadows have a percentage higher than the median.

Tall upper shadows mean better performance in all categories.

Table 59.4 shows volume statistics.

Average candle volume. Below-average candle volume suggests better postbreakout performance in all cases except bear market/down breakout. That category does better with above-average volume.

Breakout volume. Heavy breakout volume works best across the board.

Trading Tactics

I split trading tactics into two basic studies, one concerning reversal rates and the other concerning performance. Of the two, reversal rates are more important, because it's better to trade in the direction of the trend and let price run as far as it can.

Table 59.5 gives tips to find the trend direction.

Reversal, continuation rates. If you know the trend leading to the candle, the table helps predict the breakout direction. For example, if the trend is up, the chances are 68% that the breakout will be down in a bull market. That's not saying much, since price only needs to close lower the next day (recall that price in the closing black marubozu is at the low).

Yearly range reversals. Separating the behavior across the yearly price range, we see no outstanding trends emerge. The best performance comes

Table 59.5
Reversal Rates

Description	Bull Market	Bear Market
Reversal rate: trend up, breakout down	68%	69%
Continuation rate: trend up, breakout up	32%	31%
Reversal: trend down, breakout up	33%	29%
Continuation: trend down, breakout down	67%	71%
Percentage of reversals (R)/continuations (C) for each 12-month low (L), middle (M), or high (H)	L 41% R/59% C, M 46% R/54% C, H 52% R/48% C	L 39% R/61% C, M 45% R/55% C, H 54% R/46% C

from continuations near the yearly low. That results in the best postbreakout performance in both bull and bear markets.

Table 59.6 shows performance indicators that can give hints as to how your stock will behave after the breakout from this candle pattern.

Confirmation, performance. The opening gap method results in the best performance in all columns. If price gaps higher or lower at the open the day after the marubozu, trade in the direction of the gap.

Moving average. Candles below the 50-trading-day moving average result in the best postbreakout performance.

Sample Trade

Leo owns stock in the utility pictured in Figure 59.2. What should he do with the holding? Let's tear apart the picture starting at point 1. Price peaks here in a bearish tweezers top and price tumbles to the low at C. C will become an important turning point later as price develops.

Table 59.6
Performance Indicators

Description	Bull Market, Up Breakout	Bear Market, Up Breakout	Bull Market, Down Breakout	Bear Market, Down Breakout
Closing price confirmation, performance	6.83%	9.98%	−4.34%	−8.01%
Candle color confirmation, performance	6.65%	9.71%	−4.80%	−8.44%
Opening gap confirmation, performance	6.93%	10.65%	−5.79%	−9.52%
Breakout above 50-day moving average, performance	6.39%	7.16%	−5.20%	−8.65%
Breakout below 50-day moving average, performance	6.95%	10.50%	−5.85%	−10.44%

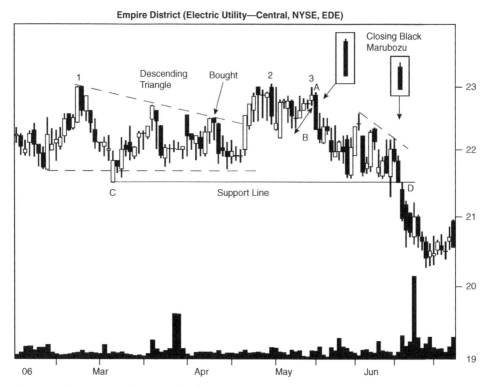

Figure 59.2 Two closing black marubozu candles appear at decisive turning points.

Price moves horizontally for over a month, generally showing lower tops and flat to higher bottoms. If you are familiar with chart patterns, you might recognize this as a symmetrical triangle or even a descending triangle with an outlier at C. I show the descending triangle with dashed lines. A descending triangle is generally a bearish pattern. This one breaks out upward with a tall white candle, eventually forming the three white soldiers candle pattern.

However, a hanging man suggests an end to the uphill run three days before point 2. Price moves horizontally to 2 and that candle engulfs the white hanging man of the prior day. Price plunges the next day, forming a bearish three outside down pattern, meaning it confirms the bearish engulfing pattern. But guess what? Price rises the next day and holds its ground, eventually trending higher at B, with a series of small candles to point 3.

Points 1, 2, and 3 are a triple top chart pattern. If price closes below the low between these three peaks (C), it confirms the triple top as a bearish pattern. Everything hinges on price staying above or dropping below the confirmation (support) line.

Point A is a closing black marubozu, a tall candle that sends price lower and seems to shout, "Sell now!"

Price does drop but not far. For several weeks leading to D, price moves horizontally with a flat bottom and a down-sloping top (dashed line). It's a smaller version of the earlier descending triangle. Price forms another closing black marubozu a day before the breakout at D. At D, price closes below the triple top, confirming the pattern, and also closes below the June descending triangle. Both patterns say to sell.

Should Leo sell the stock? Maybe. Other factors can come into play. If the stock is paying a hefty dividend, he might want to hold. If price drops but not far, it would be a mistake to sell (which turns out to be the case because after the June low, price rises to over 26).

An estimate of the size of the decline based on the height of the triple top projected downward as a maximum decline and the June triangle height projected downward as a minimum would serve as a good target area. That narrow band surrounds the June low. He might decide that if price were to reverse there, it would not be a large enough decline to justify a sale. Of course, if price were to continue down, then holding would be a mistake. In trading stocks, the proper course is not always easy to deduce.

I actually owned this stock. I bought it on April 6 (which turned into a hanging man, shown) and sold it January 16 (not shown). At that time, I thought the world of utilities was ending because everything was headed lower or showing signs of beginning a downward plunge. I was right for about two weeks and then price bumped up to 26 then down to 23 and back to 26 as I write this in April. In short, I cashed out of my utility stocks too soon.

For Best Performance

The following list offers tips and observations to help choose candles that perform well. Consult the associated table for more information.

- Use the identification guidelines to help select the pattern—Table 59.1.
- Candles within a third of the yearly low perform best—Table 59.2.
- Select tall candles—Table 59.3.
- Use the measure rule to predict a price target—Table 59.3.
- Candles with tall upper shadows outperform—Table 59.3.
- Volume gives performance clues—Table 59.4.
- Patterns within a third of the yearly low tend to act as continuations most often—Table 59.5.
- Opening gap confirmation works best—Table 59.6.
- Breakouts below the 50-day moving average lead to the best performance—Table 59.6.

60

Marubozu, Closing White

Behavior and Rank

Theoretical: Continuation.
Actual bull market: Continuation 55% of the time (ranking 33).
Actual bear market: Continuation 55% of the time (ranking 36).
Frequency: 15th out of 103.
Overall performance over time: 70th out of 103.

The closing white marubozu is the polar opposite of the closing black marubozu. Of the two, the white candle is the stronger one, sporting a continuation rate of 55% versus 52% for the black candle (bull market). The overall performance rank is a distant and poor 70 out of 103 candles, where 1 is best.

The psychology behind the closing white marubozu pattern begins with the bulls holding the ball. During the day, the bears steal the ball and price drops below the open, forming a lower shadow. By day's end, however, the bulls have chalked up more points on the scoreboard and price closes at the high for the day. Price can go either up or down the next day, but with such bullish enthusiasm shown in the tall white candle, the tendency is for price to continue moving higher, staging an upward breakout.

Identification Guidelines

Figure 60.1 shows three closing white marubozu candlesticks. The first one occurs in late October and punches out of a minor congestion region formed during the prior week. The comparatively long tail suggests a bullish move,

520

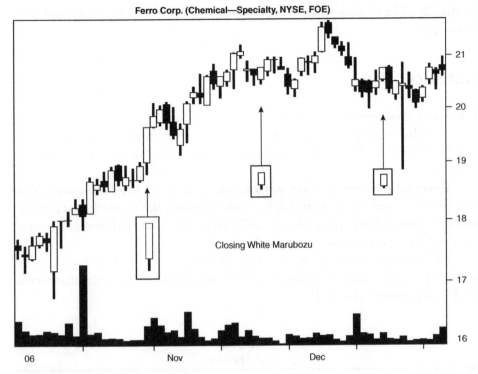

Ferro Corp. (Chemical—Specialty, NYSE, FOE)

Closing White Marubozu

Figure 60.1 Three closing white marubozu candles in various stages of trend development.

because those selling to force price down have done so and exited their positions, leaving buying demand to push price upward.

The middle marubozu appears after a short swing downward. It's part of the recovery team sent in to restore the uptrend. Price moves up for two more days and then eases lower.

The final marubozu (far right) appears a day before things turn ugly. A tall black candle engulfs (bearish engulfing pattern) the closing white marubozu and price heads lower. A few days later, an exceptionally long high wave candle is either a mistake in the data or one frighteningly long candle. The long tail marks the end of the downtrend, though, and price trends higher for the next two months (not shown).

Table 60.1 lists identification guidelines. Look for a tall white body that has a lower shadow but no upper one. That means price closes at the high

Table 60.1
Identification Guidelines

Characteristic	Discussion
Number of candle lines	One.
Configuration	A tall white body with a close at the high and a lower shadow.

for the day. The closing white marubozu can appear in either an uptrend or a downtrend.

Statistics

Table 60.2 shows general statistics.

Number found. This pattern is plentiful so I limited selection to the first 20,000 candle lines. Most appear in a bull market and have an upward breakout.

Reversal or continuation performance. Upward breakouts work best after price reverses the downtrend, but downward breakouts work best if price continues down. Like many other candle types, the best performance comes from marubozu candles in a bear market.

S&P performance. Using the dates of the candle end to the trend end, I measured the performance of the S&P 500 index and found that the marubozu candle outperforms the S&P.

Table 60.2
General Statistics

Description	Bull Market, Up Breakout	Bear Market, Up Breakout	Bull Market, Down Breakout	Bear Market, Down Breakout
Number found	11,726	2,789	4,383	1,102
Reversal (R), continuation (C) performance	5.96% C 6.77% R	6.53% C 7.74% R	−5.83% C −5.76% R	−10.25% C −8.27% R
Standard & Poor's 500 change	1.44%	0.59%	−1.32%	−3.07%
Candle end to breakout (median, days)	2	2	4	4
Candle end to trend end (median, days)	6	6	8	9
Number of breakouts near the 12-month low (L), middle (M), or high (H)	L 1,500, M 2,198, H 5,039	L 622, M 870, H 1,243	L 747, M 952, H 1,755	L 312, M 362, H 413
Percentage move for each 12-month period	L 8.46%, M 6.44%, H 5.66%	L 9.65%, M 6.72%, H 6.02%	L −7.17%, M −6.37%, H −5.51%	L −10.76%, M −9.01%, H −7.97%
Candle end + 1 day	0.53%	0.65%	−1.78%	−2.38%
Candle end + 3 days	1.01%	1.10%	−2.98%	−4.19%
Candle end + 5 days	1.28%	1.13%	−3.39%	−4.79%
Candle end + 10 days	1.53%	1.20%	−3.23%	−5.36%
10-day performance rank	94	90	31	27

Candle end to breakout. Since price closes at the top of the candle, an upward breakout takes just two days. Downward breakouts have to close below the candle's low, so they take twice as long to make the journey.

Candle end to trend end. Upward breakouts take less time to reach the trend end than downward ones, suggesting that the closing white marubozu is in an uptrend most often. With the uptrend long in the tooth, price reaches the end sooner than those just starting a downward trend. (I don't know if that's right, but it sounds good.)

Yearly position, performance. The pattern appears most often within a third of the yearly high. However, the best performance comes from marubozu candles near the yearly low.

Performance over time. This candle performs best after a downward breakout, according to the results, confirmed by the low performance rank (1 is best out of 103 candles). The only chink in the armor comes during a bull market/down breakout from 5 to 10 days when performance softens. The performance is not as robust as it could be.

Table 60.3 shows height statistics.

Candle height. Tall candles outperform short ones, so if you decide to trade a closing white marubozu, stick with a tall one.

To determine whether the candle is short or tall, compute its height from highest high to lowest low price and divide by the breakout price. If the result is higher than the median, then you have a tall candle; otherwise it's short.

For example, Dustin sees a marubozu with a high of 87 and a low of 85 in a bull market with an upward breakout. Is the candle short or tall? The height is 87 − 85, or 2, so the measure is 2/87, or 2.30%. The candle is short, because the result is less than the median.

Table 60.3
Height Statistics

Description	Bull Market, Up Breakout	Bear Market, Up Breakout	Bull Market, Down Breakout	Bear Market, Down Breakout
Median candle height as a percentage of breakout price	2.59%	3.34%	2.52%	3.48%
Short candle, performance	4.92%	5.74%	−4.69%	−7.79%
Tall candle, performance	7.98%	8.53%	−7.18%	−10.44%
Percentage meeting price target (measure rule)	72%	69%	71%	73%
Median lower shadow as a percentage of breakout price	0.45%	0.54%	0.45%	0.57%
Short lower shadow, performance	5.48%	6.42%	−5.15%	−8.13%
Tall lower shadow, performance	7.21%	7.60%	−6.58%	−9.91%

Table 60.4
Volume Statistics

Description	Bull Market, Up Breakout	Bear Market, Up Breakout	Bull Market, Down Breakout	Bear Market, Down Breakout
Above-average candle volume, performance	6.47%	6.99%	−5.91%	−8.73%
Below-average candle volume, performance	6.07%	6.99%	−5.70%	−9.12%
Heavy breakout volume, performance	6.92%	7.50%	−6.34%	−10.29%
Light breakout volume, performance	5.64%	6.48%	−5.34%	−7.79%

Measure rule. Use the measure rule to help predict how far price will rise or fall. Compute the height of the candle and multiply it by the appropriate percentage shown in the table; then apply it to the breakout price.

In Dustin's candle, what are the price targets? For upward breakouts in a bull market the target would be $(2 \times 72\%) + 87$, or 88.44. The downward breakout target would be $85 - (2 \times 71\%)$, or 83.58.

Lower shadow performance. To determine whether the shadow is short or tall, compute the height of the shadow and divide by the breakout price. Compare the result to the median in the table. Tall shadows have a percentage higher than the median. Marubozu candles with tall lower shadows result in better performance after the breakout.

Table 60.4 shows volume statistics.

Average candle volume. Above-average candle volume works best in most cases except for bear market/down breakouts. That case works better if the candle shows below-average volume.

Breakout volume. High breakout volume suggests better postbreakout performance in all cases.

Trading Tactics

I split trading tactics into two basic studies, one concerning reversal rates and the other concerning performance. Of the two, reversal rates are more important, because it's better to trade in the direction of the trend and let price run as far as it can.

Table 60.5 gives tips to find the trend direction.

Reversal, continuation rates. This is a meaningless result because of where price is positioned in the candle. With the close at the candle's high, you would expect an upward price trend leading to the marubozu to result

Table 60.5
Reversal Rates

Description	Bull Market	Bear Market
Reversal rate: trend up, breakout down	28%	29%
Continuation rate: trend up, breakout up	72%	71%
Reversal: trend down, breakout up	73%	73%
Continuation: trend down, breakout down	27%	27%
Percentage of reversals (R)/ continuations (C) for each 12-month low (L), middle (M), or high (H)	L 50% R/50% C, M 48% R/52% C, H 43% R/57% C	L 51% R/49% C, M 46% R/54% C, H 42% R/58% C

in an upward breakout. What's surprising is that upward breakouts occur just 71% to 73% of the time and not more often.

Yearly range reversals. The widest performance gap comes from marubozu candles within a third of the yearly high. They act as continuation patterns most often, regardless of the market conditions (bull or bear).

Table 60.6 shows performance indicators that can give hints as to how your stock will behave after the breakout from this candle pattern.

Confirmation, performance. Opening gap confirmation works best in all cases except for bear market/down breakouts. Those show slightly better performance if the closing price is used as confirmation or a trading signal.

Moving average. Closing white marubozu candles below the 50-trading-day moving average result in the best postbreakout performance across the board.

Table 60.6
Performance Indicators

Description	Bull Market, Up Breakout	Bear Market, Up Breakout	Bull Market, Down Breakout	Bear Market, Down Breakout
Closing price confirmation, performance	4.91%	5.09%	−6.79%	−9.23%
Candle color confirmation, performance	5.14%	5.83%	−6.67%	−8.91%
Opening gap confirmation, performance	6.08%	6.49%	−6.85%	−9.15%
Breakout above 50-day moving average, performance	5.99%	6.48%	−5.55%	−8.04%
Breakout below 50-day moving average, performance	7.18%	8.30%	−6.27%	−10.09%

Sample Trade

Dustin is a swinger, buying near the swing low and selling near the swing high. When he spots the setup pictured in Figure 60.2 he goes to work. He draws a bottom trendline from D to A, slicing through B. That doesn't matter because he'll use the lower trendline only as a gauge to determine when to buy.

Along the top, he connects peaks E and F and sees the two trendlines narrowing, forming a rising wedge chart pattern. The vertical distance between the two lines will be his profit target. The potential loss would be if price drops below A. Therefore, he decides to place his stop there, a few pennies below A, after he buys the stock.

Price makes a Takuri line (at A), with a long lower shadow and a bullish outlook. Since price touched the trendline, Dustin believes price will zip to the other side of the rising wedge chart pattern. So, the next day he buys at the open. That day price forms a closing white marubozu, suggesting a continuation of the uptrend.

As price climbs, he extends the EF line and places a limit order to sell his position at 26. When price touches the order at C, his position is sold for a tidy profit.

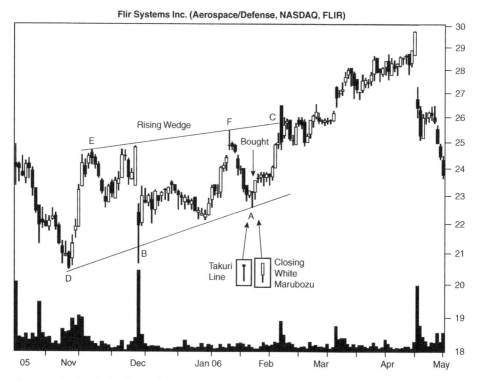

Figure 60.2   A closing white marubozu appears after price touches a trendline.

Is he bothered by the profits he left on the table as price approached 30? "I didn't own the stock anymore, so I didn't care what happened. I was too busy fishing for another trading setup."

For Best Performance

The following list offers tips and observations to help choose candles that perform well. Consult the associated table for more information.

- Use the identification guidelines to help select the pattern—Table 60.1.
- Candles within a third of the yearly low perform best—Table 60.2.
- Select tall candles—Table 60.3.
- Use the measure rule to predict a price target—Table 60.3.
- Candles with tall shadows outperform—Table 60.3.
- Volume gives performance clues—Table 60.4.
- Expect an upward breakout—Table 60.5.
- Patterns within a third of the yearly high tend to act as continuations most often—Table 60.5.
- Opening gap confirmation works best (except for bear market/down breakouts)—Table 60.6.
- Breakouts below the 50-day moving average lead to the best performance—Table 60.6.

61

Marubozu, Opening Black

Behavior and Rank

Theoretical: Continuation.
Actual bull market: Continuation 52% of the time (ranking 42).
Actual bear market: Continuation 53% of the time (ranking 43).
Frequency: 5th out of 103.
Overall performance over time: 58th out of 103.

The opening black marubozu is an inverted version of the closing black marubozu. Price opens at the high for the day and then plummets, recovering like a patient finding strength before death and leaving a lower shadow behind.

The psychology behind the pattern tells little since we are dealing with a single candle line, but the bears rule the day. Price begins heading down after the open, forming a tall black candle. Sometime during the day, the bulls make an appearance and force price up from the day's low, keeping the bears on their toes until the close. A slight majority of the time the trend will continue lower in succeeding days, but with a continuation rate of just 52%, expect a random direction outcome.

The frequency rank is 5 out of 103 candles where 1 is best. That means you'll see a gazillion of them. However, the overall performance rank is 58, so this candle is nothing to get excited about.

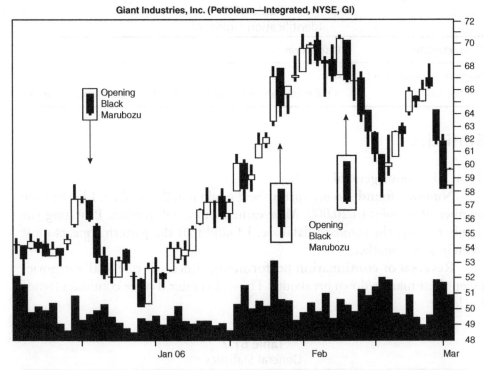

Figure 61.1 Three opening black marubozu candles appear in various stages of trend development.

Identification Guidelines

Figure 61.1 shows several examples of the opening black marubozu candle pattern. The left one in December occurs just after price peaks. Being a black candle, it is most comfortable in a falling price trend, but this need not be the case.

An example of that comes from the middle marubozu candle. Price is trending upward when the opening black marubozu appears. A long white candle forms that suggests a strong upward thrust, but the opening black marubozu the next day seems to say, "Not so fast!" It tries to push price down. The stock stalls for another day while the bulls and bears duke it out, but the uptrend soon resumes.

The last opening black marubozu is similar to the first one. The candle appears near the start of a downtrend, initiating a train of black candles that ends after retracing a good portion of the prior move up from the late December low.

Table 61.1 lists identification guidelines, and they are simplicity itself. Look for a tall black candle, one that has a lower shadow but no upper one.

Table 61.1
Identification Guidelines

Characteristic	Discussion
Number of candle lines	One.
Configuration	A tall black candle with a lower shadow but no upper shadow.

Statistics

Table 61.2 shows general statistics.

Number found. So my spreadsheet could handle the data, I limited the number of samples to 20,000. Most came from a bull market. Prorating the numbers using the standard database, I found that the pattern appears most often in a bear market.

Reversal or continuation performance. Reversals rule in all categories except bear market/down breakouts. Those do better if price continues trending lower.

Table 61.2
General Statistics

Description	Bull Market, Up Breakout	Bear Market, Up Breakout	Bull Market, Down Breakout	Bear Market, Down Breakout
Number found	4,983	2,076	9,299	3,642
Reversal (R), continuation (C) performance	6.15% C 7.12% R	7.38% C 8.33% R	−5.76% C −5.86% R	−9.14% C −8.73% R
Standard & Poor's 500 change	2.03%	1.13%	−0.93%	−2.04%
Candle end to breakout (median, days)	4	4	2	2
Candle end to trend end (median, days)	10	10	6	6
Number of breakouts near the 12-month low (L), middle (M), or high (H)	L 1,022, M 1,406, H 2,555	L 539, M 670, H 867	L 2,518, M 2,890, H 3,891	L 1,264, M 1,253, H 1,125
Percentage move for each 12-month period	L 8.63%, M 6.61%, H 6.24%	L 10.18%, M 7.39%, H 7.33%	L −6.65%, M −5.98%, H −5.31%	L −11.09%, M −8.50%, H −7.64%
Candle end + 1 day	1.46%	1.91%	−0.83%	−1.27%
Candle end + 3 days	2.87%	3.76%	−1.39%	−2.08%
Candle end + 5 days	3.35%	4.28%	−1.48%	−2.38%
Candle end + 10 days	3.78%	4.63%	−1.20%	−2.26%
10-day performance rank	40	37	89	79

S&P performance. Using the dates of the candle end to the trend end, I measured the performance of the S&P 500 and found that the marubozu beats the index by a wide margin.

Candle end to breakout. Since the close is near the candle's low, you would expect to see downward breakouts taking less time, and that's what happens.

Candle end to trend end. The search for the trend end occurs sooner after a downward breakout. The reason for this, I think, is that a downtrend is likely in progress, so instead of measuring the distance from trend start to end, we are measuring the middle to end. Upward breakouts probably start closer to the trend beginning than downward breakouts.

Yearly position, performance. The most popular birthplace is within a third of the yearly high except for bear market/down breakouts, where the lowest third takes a slight lead. The best performance comes from those within a third of the yearly low.

Performance over time. Upward breakouts post respectable numbers, but downward breakouts show a fault from 5 to 10 days. That's when the numbers show weakness, and that means the candle pattern is not as robust as some other candles. A strong showing would mean the numbers increase under all market conditions and breakout directions.

The rankings confirm this assessment. Upward breakouts rank better than downward ones, where 1 is best out of 103 candles.

Table 61.3 shows height statistics.

Table 61.3
Height Statistics

Description	Bull Market, Up Breakout	Bear Market, Up Breakout	Bull Market, Down Breakout	Bear Market, Down Breakout
Median candle height as a percentage of breakout price	2.74%	3.57%	2.85%	3.79%
Short candle, performance	5.39%	6.28%	−4.66%	−7.56%
Tall candle, performance	8.43%	9.87%	−7.33%	−10.64%
Percentage meeting price target (measure rule)	75%	73%	68%	70%
Median lower shadow as a percentage of breakout price	0.57%	0.77%	0.49%	0.66%
Short lower shadow, performance	5.99%	6.65%	−5.17%	−8.54%
Tall lower shadow, performance	7.59%	9.37%	−6.58%	−9.45%

Candle height. Tall candles outperform. To determine whether the candle is short or tall, compute its height from high to low price and divide by the breakout price. If the result is higher than the median, then you have a tall candle; otherwise it's short.

Flintstone sees an opening black marubozu with a high of 47 and a low of 45. Is the candle short or tall? The height is 47 − 45, or 2, so the computation is 2/47, or 4.3%. That means it's a tall candle regardless of the breakout direction or market condition.

Measure rule. Use the measure rule to help predict how far price will rise or fall. Compute the height of the candle and multiply it by the appropriate percentage shown in the table; then apply it to the breakout price.

In Flintstone's case, the upward breakout target in the bull market would be (2 × 75%) + 47, or 48.50 and the downward breakout target would be 45 − (2 × 68%), or 43.64.

Lower shadow performance. To determine whether the shadow is short or tall, compute the height of the shadow and divide by the breakout price. Compare the result to the median in the table. Tall shadows have a percentage higher than the median.

Candles with tall shadows perform better than do those with short shadows.

Table 61.4 shows volume statistics.

Average candle volume. High candle volume is best for performance in all cases except for bull market/down breakouts. The numbers are close, but those (bull market/down breakouts) perform slightly better with below-average volume.

Breakout volume. Heavy breakout volume leads to the best postbreakout performance in all categories.

Table 61.4
Volume Statistics

Description	Bull Market, Up Breakout	Bear Market, Up Breakout	Bull Market, Down Breakout	Bear Market, Down Breakout
Above-average candle volume, performance	6.80%	8.09%	−5.79%	−9.29%
Below-average candle volume, performance	6.66%	7.85%	−5.82%	−8.67%
Heavy breakout volume, performance	7.32%	8.56%	−6.13%	−10.11%
Light breakout volume, performance	6.10%	7.45%	−5.50%	−7.69%

Table 61.5
Reversal Rates

Description	Bull Market	Bear Market
Reversal rate: trend up, breakout down	66%	64%
Continuation rate: trend up, breakout up	34%	36%
Reversal: trend down, breakout up	36%	36%
Continuation: trend down, breakout down	64%	64%
Percentage of reversals (R)/continuations (C) for each 12-month low (L), middle (M), or high (H)	L 42% R/58% C, M 46% R/54% C, H 53% R/47% C	L 41% R/59% C, M 47% R/53% C, H 52% R/48% C

Trading Tactics

I split trading tactics into two basic studies, one concerning reversal rates and the other concerning performance. Of the two, reversal rates are more important, because it's better to trade in the direction of the trend and let price run as far as it can.

Table 61.5 gives tips to find the trend direction.

Reversal, continuation rates. Since the close is near the candle's low, expect a downward breakout most often, which the table shows.

Yearly range reversals. Splitting the behavior into the yearly price range, the widest performance variation occurs when the breakout is within a third of the yearly low. Those act as continuations most often.

Table 61.6 shows performance indicators that can give hints as to how your stock will behave after the breakout from this candle pattern.

Table 61.6
Performance Indicators

Description	Bull Market, Up Breakout	Bear Market, Up Breakout	Bull Market, Down Breakout	Bear Market, Down Breakout
Closing price confirmation, performance	7.15%	9.31%	−5.50%	−8.27%
Candle color confirmation, performance	7.04%	9.00%	−5.71%	−8.58%
Opening gap confirmation, performance	7.32%	10.11%	−6.69%	−9.57%
Breakout above 50-day moving average, performance	6.39%	7.48%	−5.53%	−8.00%
Breakout below 50-day moving average, performance	7.30%	8.71%	−6.02%	−9.59%

Confirmation, performance. The opening gap method of confirmation works best as a buy signal in all cases. Trade in the direction of the gap: Go long if price gaps open higher or short if price gaps lower.

Moving average. A breakout from an opening black marubozu candle results in the best performance when the breakout is below the 50-day moving average.

Sample Trade

Figure 61.2 shows a trade that Flintstone made. He constructed the trend channel by drawing a trendline connecting bottoms A and B and extending the line to C. Along the top, he connected peaks D and E and extended the line into the future. The top trendline would serve as a target. The bottom one would act as support.

Two days after E, an opening black marubozu appeared midtrend, suggesting price had further to tumble. Price continued lower and formed another opening black marubozu the day before touching C.

How did Flintstone know that price would stop at C? He didn't. But even though the tall black candle suggested the downtrend would continue,

Figure 61.2 An opening black marubozu appears near the bottom of a trend channel.

the trendline would act as support and likely (he hoped) reverse the trend. Flintstone bought on the day price touched the trendline at C and showed signs of moving up.

As price climbed, Flintstone extended the top trendline farther along, and after the tall white candle, he place a limit order to sell at the top trendline. Why? Because a minor high appears within a day of an unusually tall candle 67% of the time. Coupled with overhead resistance set up by the trendline, it was a good target.

For Best Performance

The following list offers tips and observations to help choose candles that perform well. Consult the associated table for more information.

- Use the identification guidelines to help select the pattern—Table 61.1.
- Candles within a third of the yearly low perform best—Table 61.2.
- Select tall candles—Table 61.3.
- Use the measure rule to predict a price target—Table 61.3.
- Candles with tall shadows outperform—Table 61.3.
- Volume gives performance clues—Table 61.4.
- Patterns within a third of the yearly low act as continuations most often—Table 61.5.
- Opening gap confirmation works best—Table 61.6.
- Breakouts below the 50-day moving average lead to the best performance—Table 61.6.

62

Marubozu, Opening White

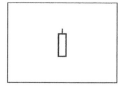

Behavior and Rank

Theoretical: Continuation.

Actual bull market: Continuation 54% of the time (ranking 34).

Actual bear market: Continuation 54% of the time (ranking 38).

Frequency: 7th out of 103.

Overall performance over time: 75th out of 103.

Comparing the opening white marubozu with the opening black marubozu, the white candle is more powerful than the black one. I base this on the continuation rate of 54% for the white candle versus 52% for the black candle (bull market). However, the opening white marubozu is more closely related to a *closing* white marubozu flipped upside down. The colors are the same and so is the shape.

The performance rank is a dismal 75, where 1 is best out of 103 candles. The frequency rank is 7, so these candles are as plentiful as stars on a clear night in the country.

The psychology behind this pattern begins with the bulls driving price higher right from the open. Their buying pressure sends price shooting upward before the bears know what has happened. When the bears awake from hibernation, they force price back down, so what remains is a tall white candle with an upper shadow but no lower one.

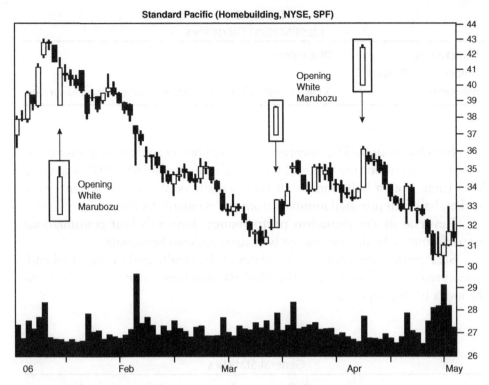

Figure 62.1   Three opening white marubozu candles appear in various stages of trend development.

Identification Guidelines

Figure 62.1 shows three examples of the opening white marubozu candle. The first one in January occurs as part of a downward price trend. That may sound odd for a tall white candle but since it occurs, it must be possible. In fact, I've seen several white candles appear in a declining price trend. That's one reason I'm not so keen on candle color. I'd rather see color based on whether price closed higher or lower from the previous day, not the current day.

The middle marubozu appears in the center of a rising price trend, and the final opening marubozu tops off a short uptrend.

Table 62.1 lists identification guidelines. Look for a tall white body with an upper shadow but no lower shadow. That means price opens at the low for the day and closes much higher, but not at the high.

Statistics

Table 62.2 shows general statistics.

Table 62.1
Identification Guidelines

Characteristic	Discussion
Number of candle lines	One.
Configuration	A tall white candle with an upper shadow but no lower one.

Number found. The opening white marubozu candle is as numerous as geese flying south for the winter. I limited selection to the first 20,000 candles. Most came from a bull market but they actually occur more often in a bear market, based on prorated numbers from the standard database.

Reversal or continuation performance. Reversals beat continuations for performance in all cases except bear market/down breakouts.

S&P performance. Using the dates of the candle end to the trend end, I measured the performance of the S&P 500 and found that the candle beats the index in all categories.

Table 62.2
General Statistics

Description	Bull Market, Up Breakout	Bear Market, Up Breakout	Bull Market, Down Breakout	Bear Market, Down Breakout
Number found	9,146	3,965	4,823	2,066
Reversal (R), continuation (C) performance	5.85% C 6.41% R	6.56% C 8.10% R	−5.90% C −6.08% R	−9.04% C −8.07% R
Standard & Poor's 500 change	1.37%	0.46%	−1.23%	−2.69%
Candle end to breakout (median, days)	2	2	4	4
Candle end to trend end (median, days)	7	7	8	9
Number of breakouts near the 12-month low (L), middle (M), or high (H)	L 1,528, M 2,316, H 5,302	L 888, M 1,254, H 1,823	L 1,108, M 1,375, H 2,340	L 556, M 678, H 823
Percentage move for each 12-month period	L 8.01%, M 6.26%, H 5.56%	L 9.38%, M 6.88%, H 6.43%	L −6.87%, M −6.07%, H −5.69%	L −9.78%, M −8.26%, H −7.86%
Candle end + 1 day	0.85%	1.06%	−1.29%	−1.66%
Candle end + 3 days	1.54%	1.71%	−2.53%	−3.32%
Candle end + 5 days	1.76%	1.85%	−2.91%	−3.82%
Candle end + 10 days	2.06%	1.81%	−2.84%	−4.37%
10-day performance rank	83	76	37	43

Candle end to breakout. Since price closes near the candle's high, it takes less time to break out upward than downward.

Candle end to trend end. Upward breakouts also take slightly less time to reach the trend end than downward breakouts. The reason for this is probably that the white candle is in the middle of an uptrend when it appears, so it's closer to the end. For downward breakouts, price is closer to the start of a trend so it takes longer. I don't know if that's right, but it's the only logical explanation I can think of. How about we blame it on global warming?

Yearly position, performance. Most of the opening white marubozu candles occur within a third of the yearly high, but performance is best if the candle is near the yearly low.

Performance over time. Downward breakouts show better results than upward breakouts, suggesting this candle works better in that direction. The performance ranks (37 and 43) confirm it, too, with 1 being best out of 103 candles.

Between 5 and 10 days, bear market/up breakouts and bull market/down breakouts show weakness. This suggests the candle pattern is not as robust as other candles, because it does not show better results over time in all market conditions and breakout directions.

Table 62.3 shows height statistics.

Candle height. Tall candles outperform. To determine whether the candle is short or tall, compute its height from high to low price in the candle pattern and divide by the breakout price. If the result is higher than the median, then you have a tall candle; otherwise it's short.

Table 62.3
Height Statistics

Description	Bull Market, Up Breakout	Bear Market, Up Breakout	Bull Market, Down Breakout	Bear Market, Down Breakout
Median candle height as a percentage of breakout price	2.87%	3.65%	2.73%	3.70%
Short candle, performance	5.03%	5.92%	−4.94%	−7.43%
Tall candle, performance	7.36%	8.55%	−7.40%	−9.59%
Percentage meeting price target (measure rule)	70%	68%	70%	71%
Median upper shadow as a percentage of breakout price	0.51%	0.64%	0.60%	0.79%
Short upper shadow, performance	5.51%	6.49%	−5.47%	−7.65%
Tall upper shadow, performance	6.65%	7.82%	−6.64%	−9.27%

Table 62.4
Volume Statistics

Description	Bull Market, Up Breakout	Bear Market, Up Breakout	Bull Market, Down Breakout	Bear Market, Down Breakout
Above-average candle volume, performance	6.07%	7.36%	−6.22%	−8.52%
Below-average candle volume, performance	6.02%	6.90%	−5.82%	−8.30%
Heavy breakout volume, performance	6.54%	7.76%	−6.33%	−9.24%
Light breakout volume, performance	5.52%	6.43%	−5.75%	−7.70%

For example, Wilma sees a marubozu with a high price of 69 and a low of 66. Is the candle short or tall? The height is 69 − 66, or 3. In a bull market with an upward breakout, the measure would be 3/69, or 4.3%. That makes the candle a tall one.

Measure rule. Use the measure rule to help predict how far price will rise or fall. Compute the height of the candle and multiply it by the appropriate percentage shown in the table; then apply it to the breakout price.

For Wilma's candle, the upward breakout target would be (3 × 70%) + 69, or 71.10, and the downward breakout target would be 66 − (3 × 70%), or 63.90.

Upper shadow performance. To determine whether the shadow is short or tall, compute the height of the shadow and divide by the breakout price. Compare the result to the median in the table. Tall shadows have a percentage higher than the median. Candles with tall shadows perform better than do those with short shadows.

Table 62.4 shows volume statistics.

Average candle volume. Above-average volume suggests good performance after the breakout in all categories.

Breakout volume. Similarly, heavy breakout volume is good for post-breakout performance.

Trading Tactics

I split trading tactics into two basic studies, one concerning reversal rates and the other concerning performance. Of the two, reversal rates are more important, because it's better to trade in the direction of the trend and let price run as far as it can.

Table 62.5 gives tips to find the trend direction.

Table 62.5
Reversal Rates

Description	Bull Market	Bear Market
Reversal rate: trend up, breakout down	35%	35%
Continuation rate: trend up, breakout up	65%	65%
Reversal: trend down, breakout up	65%	66%
Continuation: trend down, breakout down	35%	34%
Percentage of reversals (R)/continuations (C) for each 12-month low (L), middle (M), or high (H)	L 50% R/50% C, M 48% R/52% C, H 43% R/57% C	L 50% R/50% C, M 48% R/52% C, H 43% R/57% C

Reversal, continuation rates. Price breaks out upward most often, probably because it's closer to the top of the candle than the bottom.

Yearly range reversals. Since both columns show the same results, I rechecked my work. The widest performance difference comes from marubozu patterns within a third of the yearly high. Most often, they act as continuations of the price trend.

Table 62.6 shows performance indicators that can give hints as to how your stock will behave after the breakout from this candle pattern.

Confirmation, performance. The opening gap method of confirmation works best as a trading signal. That means you trade in the direction of the opening price gap the day after the marubozu candle.

Moving average. Candles with breakouts below the moving average result in the best performance, regardless of the breakout direction or market condition.

Table 62.6
Performance Indicators

Description	Bull Market, Up Breakout	Bear Market, Up Breakout	Bull Market, Down Breakout	Bear Market, Down Breakout
Closing price confirmation, performance	5.52%	6.61%	−6.88%	−9.04%
Candle color confirmation, performance	5.59%	6.63%	−6.77%	−9.01%
Opening gap confirmation, performance	6.60%	8.02%	−7.12%	−9.24%
Breakout above 50-day moving average, performance	5.79%	6.63%	−5.91%	−7.38%
Breakout below 50-day moving average, performance	6.91%	8.50%	−6.16%	−9.81%

Sample Trade

Figure 62.2 shows a trade Wilma made. At A, price reached a new low, ending with a southern doji. That's just a doji candle after a downward price trend. In this case, the opening white marubozu candle confirmed a trend reversal. How was Wilma to know that this reversal was a lasting one? If you can answer that correctly 100% of the time or even 75% of the time, then all the money the stock market has to offer is yours for the taking.

Here's what she did. Price climbed to C. A retracement of the downtrend was expected, so this was nothing new. However, when price bottomed at B, it was a higher low. For price to change trend, it has to make a higher low sometime.

In the chart pattern world, I call the AB pattern an ugly double bottom. A traditional double bottom has two valleys at (or near) the same price, but this one shows a higher second bottom. (See my web site, ThePatternSite.com, for specific identification details.) So it's an ugly version of a traditional double bottom.

When price closed above C, that was the buy signal. She bought the stock a day later at the open, then suffered through a few weeks of turbulence before

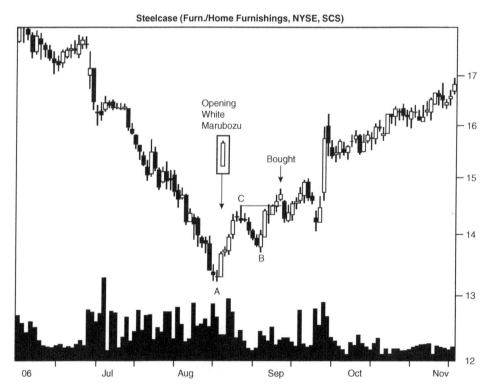

Figure 62.2 An opening white marubozu candle appears the day after price reaches a low.

price started behaving itself. In October, price moved up and up and—well, you get the picture.

For Best Performance

The following list offers tips and observations to help choose candles that perform well. Consult the associated table for more information.

- Use the identification guidelines to help select the pattern—Table 62.1.
- Candles within a third of the yearly low perform best—Table 62.2.
- Select tall candles—Table 62.3.
- Use the measure rule to predict a price target—Table 62.3.
- Candles with tall shadows outperform—Table 62.3.
- Volume gives performance clues—Table 62.4.
- Patterns within a third of the yearly high tend to act as continuations most often—Table 62.5.
- Opening gap confirmation works best—Table 62.6.
- Breakouts below the 50-day moving average lead to the best performance—Table 62.6.

63

Marubozu, White

Behavior and Rank

Theoretical: Continuation.
Actual bull market: Continuation 56% of the time (ranking 30).
Actual bear market: Continuation 56% of the time (ranking 29).
Frequency: 27th out of 103.
Overall performance over time: 71st out of 103.

The white marubozu is a strange candle. It reminds me of a person with no arms for some reason. This candle pattern has no shadows, just a tall white body. As one might expect, white marubozu candles can appear anywhere in a trend, and they signal a continuation of the trend 56% of the time. In a bull market, that places their rank at 30 out of 103 candles, where 1 is best. The overall performance, however, is well back in the pack, at 71. Perhaps they make it up on volume, because this ranks 27 for frequency.

The psychology behind the pattern is a bullish party. Price opens and moves upward as the bullish buying demand sends the stock higher. By day's end, price is locked at the day's high, never having ventured below the opening price and never giving the bears a chance to cause trouble. But the fun might end there, because anything can happen the next day.

Identification Guidelines

Figure 63.1 shows two white marubozu candles grazing in their native habitat. The first one occurs midway through a small uptrend. With such a tall candle,

Figure 63.1 Two white marubozu candles appear in an uptrend.

I would expect price to continue higher, but it doesn't. Price *does* coast higher for two more days but the gain is almost negligible.

Another white marubozu joins the herd near the start of an uptrend, breaking out of September's consolidation area. This time, price continues higher at a steep incline but then levels out.

Table 63.1 lists identification guidelines. Look for a white candle with a body taller than average and no shadows.

Statistics

Table 63.2 shows general statistics.

Table 63.1
Identification Guidelines

Characteristic	Discussion
Number of candle lines	One.
Configuration	A tall white candle without shadows.

Table 63.2
General Statistics

Description	Bull Market, Up Breakout	Bear Market, Up Breakout	Bull Market, Down Breakout	Bear Market, Down Breakout
Number found	12,341	1,418	5,670	571
Reversal (R), continuation (C) performance	5.96% C 6.83% R	7.44% C 8.10% R	−6.04% C −5.77% R	−9.04% C −8.48% R
Standard & Poor's 500 change	1.11%	0.21%	−0.75%	−2.25%
Candle end to breakout (median, days)	2	2	4	4
Candle end to trend end (median, days)	6	7	7	9
Number of breakouts near the 12-month low (L), middle (M), or high (H)	L 2,400, M 3,436, H 6,505	L 305, M 429, H 684	L 1,505, M 1,718, H 2,447	L 169, M 185, H 217
Percentage move for each 12-month period	L 7.72%, M 6.44%, H 5.84%	L 9.34%, M 8.35%, H 6.82%	L −6.56%, M −6.11%, H −5.48%	L −10.62%, M −8.94%, H −7.51%
Candle end + 1 day	0.57%	0.62%	−1.71%	−2.20%
Candle end + 3 days	1.09%	1.19%	−2.81%	−3.95%
Candle end + 5 days	1.29%	1.54%	−3.33%	−4.53%
Candle end + 10 days	1.52%	1.68%	−3.55%	−4.79%
10-day performance rank	95	79	26	36

Number found. The white marubozu is as plentiful as mosquitoes on a camping trip. I limited the number of bites to 20,000. Most appear in a bull market and comparatively few show in a bear market.

Reversal or continuation performance. Reversals perform best after an upward breakout, and continuations do better after a downward breakout.

S&P performance. The white marubozu candle performed better than the S&P 500 index over the same measurement period.

Candle end to breakout. Since price is at the candle's high, it takes just two days to break out upward. Downward breakouts have to travel the height of the candle before closing below it. That takes twice as long as upward breakouts.

Candle end to trend end. The time to reach the trend end varies from six to nine days. Downward breakouts take longer to reach the trend end than upward breakouts. The explanation is probably because most white candles are already in an uptrend, so they are close to the end. Downward breakouts after a white candle would be closer to the start of the trend and thus take longer to reach the end.

Table 63.3
Height Statistics

Description	Bull Market, Up Breakout	Bear Market, Up Breakout	Bull Market, Down Breakout	Bear Market, Down Breakout
Median candle height as a percentage of breakout price	2.42%	3.21%	2.37%	3.17%
Short candle, performance	5.13%	6.56%	−4.77%	−7.58%
Tall candle, performance	7.70%	9.05%	−7.36%	−10.09%
Percentage meeting price target (measure rule)	75%	74%	73%	79%

Yearly position, performance. Most white marubozu candles appear within a third of the yearly high, but the best performance comes from candles near the yearly low.

Performance over time. The white marubozu is a robust performer. In all market conditions and breakout directions, the candle shows stronger performance over time.

When I read that the white marubozu was an "extremely strong candle line," I thought the sources were kidding. They weren't, at least for downward breakouts. Downward breakouts perform more than twice as well as upward ones. The performance ranks agree.

Table 63.3 shows height statistics.

Candle height. Tall candles perform substantially better than short ones regardless of market condition and breakout direction. To determine whether the candle is short or tall, compute its height from high to low price in the candle pattern and divide by the breakout price. If the result is higher than the median, then you have a tall candle; otherwise it's short.

For example, Jacob has a white marubozu with a high price of 30 and a low of 29. Is it short or tall? The height is $30 - 29$, or 1, so the measure would be 1/30, or 3.3%, for an upward breakout. In a bull market, the candle would be tall. In fact, it would be tall in any market.

Measure rule. Use the measure rule to help predict how far price will rise or fall. Compute the height of the candle and multiply it by the appropriate percentage shown in the table; then apply it to the breakout price.

For Jacob's candle, the upward breakout target would be $(1 \times 75\%) + 30$, or 30.75. The downward breakout target would be $29 - (1 \times 73\%)$, or 28.27.

Table 63.4 shows volume statistics.

Average candle volume. High candle volume results in the best post-breakout performance in all cases except for bear market/up breakout. That category does better after below-average candle volume.

Table 63.4
Volume Statistics

Description	Bull Market, Up Breakout	Bear Market, Up Breakout	Bull Market, Down Breakout	Bear Market, Down Breakout
Above-average candle volume, performance	6.49%	7.10%	−6.19%	−8.88%
Below-average candle volume, performance	6.09%	8.19%	−5.67%	−8.53%
Heavy breakout volume, performance	7.08%	8.25%	−6.05%	−9.05%
Light breakout volume, performance	5.48%	7.08%	−5.74%	−8.38%

Breakout volume. Across the board, heavy breakout volume works better than light volume.

Trading Tactics

I split trading tactics into two basic studies, one concerning reversal rates and the other concerning performance. Of the two, reversal rates are more important, because it's better to trade in the direction of the trend and let price run as far as it can.

Table 63.5 gives tips to find the trend direction.

Reversal, continuation rates. Since the candle has a close at the high for the day, an upward breakout is almost a given. Almost. What's surprising is that an upward breakout occurs only between 68% and 72% of the time. That's surprisingly low. Thus, check the price trend leading to the candle

Table 63.5
Reversal Rates

Description	Bull Market	Bear Market
Reversal rate: trend up, breakout down	31%	28%
Continuation rate: trend up, breakout up	69%	72%
Reversal: trend down, breakout up	68%	70%
Continuation: trend down, breakout down	32%	30%
Percentage of reversals (R)/ continuations (C) for each 12-month low (L), middle (M), or high (H)	L 50% R/50% C, M 47% R/53% C, H 41% R/59% C	L 49% R/51% C, M 47% R/53% C, H 39% R/61% C

Table 63.6
Performance Indicators

Description	Bull Market, Up Breakout	Bear Market, Up Breakout	Bull Market, Down Breakout	Bear Market, Down Breakout
Closing price confirmation, performance	4.77%	6.10%	−6.75%	−9.09%
Candle color confirmation, performance	5.10%	6.40%	−6.65%	−9.22%
Opening gap confirmation, performance	5.86%	8.15%	−6.85%	−8.80%
Breakout above 50-day moving average, performance	6.07%	7.41%	−5.53%	−7.35%
Breakout below 50-day moving average, performance	6.87%	8.57%	−6.32%	−10.46%

to help determine the breakout direction. Look for overhead resistance or underlying support that might also help with locating a reversal situation.

Yearly range reversals. The widest difference between reversals and continuations occurs when the breakout price is within a third of the yearly high. The white marubozu acts as a continuation between 59% and 61% of the time. That's the best of the bunch, but it's also not much above random (50%).

Table 63.6 shows performance indicators that can give hints as to how your stock will behave after the breakout from this candle pattern.

Confirmation, performance. Opening gap confirmation works best in all cases except for bear market/down breakouts. Candle color confirmation works better under those conditions.

Moving average. Breakouts below the 50-day moving average result in the best postbreakout performance regardless of breakout direction and market condition.

Sample Trade

Figure 63.2 shows a trading setup that many of us face. Here's how Jacob handled it. He had bought the stock well before the period covered by the chart. At peak B, he thought he had a golden touch. Everything he bought was turning to gold, including this stock. Then price dropped and within two weeks, he had given back over 20%.

Like many novice investors, he swore that when he recovered his "loss" (it really wasn't a loss but a profit giveback, since he had bought much lower) he would sell.

Figure 63.2 A white marubozu appears at overhead resistance. Will price continue higher?

Price moved horizontally from the end of December until late January, when it took off. Then it formed a white marubozu. Was this a reversal signal?

Drawing a trendline from peaks A to B and extending it onward to C, Jacob saw that the trendline matched the top of the marubozu exactly. This suggested that the uptrend was over. Instead of selling, though, he gripped tightly to hope and held on like a mountaineer hanging on to the face of a sheer rock cliff.

Over the next three days, price made higher lows and lower highs—a squeezing movement. However, the last day was a hanging man candle. To Jacob, this meant his investment world was ending. So, he sold the next day at the open. His timing was excellent, because price dropped after he sold.

For Best Performance

The following list offers tips and observations to help choose candles that perform well. Consult the associated table for more information.

- Use the identification guidelines to help select the pattern—Table 63.1.
- Candles within a third of the yearly low perform best—Table 63.2.
- Downward breakouts perform more than twice as well as upward ones—Table 63.2.
- Select tall candles—Table 63.3.
- Use the measure rule to predict a price target—Table 63.3.
- Volume gives performance clues—Table 63.4.
- Patterns within a third of the yearly high tend to act as continuations most often—Table 63.5.
- Opening gap confirmation works best except for the bear market/down breakout category—Table 63.6.
- Breakouts below the 50-day moving average lead to the best performance—Table 63.6.

64

Mat Hold

Behavior and Rank

Theoretical: Bullish continuation.

Actual bull market: Bullish continuation 78% of the time (ranking 1).

Actual bear market: Bullish continuation 67% of the time (ranking 16).

Frequency: 93rd out of 103.

Overall performance over time: 86th out of 103.

The mat hold pattern is one of the more complicated patterns and that's why it's so rare. Its configuration has a lot in common with the rising three methods candle pattern. The difference lies with the second candle, which gaps open higher and remains above the close of the first candle in the mat hold.

The mat hold acts as a continuation pattern 78% of the time (bull market), and since it appears in an upward price trend, expect price to continue moving higher after the breakout—just not for long: 45% appear near the end of the trend.

The continuation rank in a bull market is 1, the best out of 103 candles. Performance, however, is almost last: 86. No doubt with more samples the rankings would change, perhaps dramatically.

The psychology behind the pattern begins with an upward trend leading to the start of the candle formation. Bulls lining up on the runway are ready for takeoff. They push price upward, forming a tall white candle as the first line in the pattern.

Price gaps higher the next day, but bears counterattack and a dogfight ensues. The bears succeed in pushing price lower over the next three days, but not by much. Price remains above the bottom of the first candle.

On the final day of the pattern, the bulls have won the air war and they force price higher in another white candle.

Identification Guidelines

Figure 64.1 shows what a mat hold looks like. The five-candle pattern is a complicated one, but it's easy to find despite being very rare. This one appears near the end of an upward price move. After the candle pattern completes, price breaks out upward and then almost immediately trends horizontally. On a miniature scale, the candle pattern mimics the rise-retrace pattern seen on the larger scale. Price rises, backtracks a portion of the rise, and then resumes moving up.

Table 64.1 lists identification guidelines. Details about identification vary from source to source. I've even seen one author identify as a mat hold a

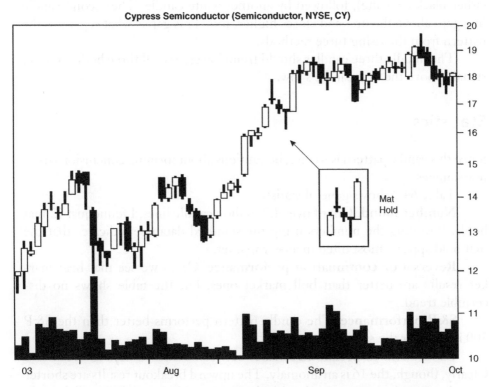

Figure 64.1 Price eases upward after the mat hold completes.

Table 64.1
Identification Guidelines

Characteristic	Discussion
Number of candle lines	Five.
Price trend	Upward leading to the start of the candle pattern.
First day	A long white body.
Second day	Price gaps open upward but closes lower (meaning a small black candle) and yet remains above the prior close. Ignore the shadows.
Days 3 and 4	Day 3 can be any color, but day 4 is black. Both candles have small bodies with the closing price easing lower, but the bodies remain above the low of the first day.
Last day	A white candle with a close above the highs of the prior four candles.

formation that was seven candle lines wide. I did not allow such variations, and that's another reason why I found so few.

Look for five candle lines; the first one is a tall white candle, which is followed by three small bodies, usually all black (but the middle one can be either black or white), followed by another white candle. The second candle line gaps above the first and closes higher, too. This gap is what separates the pattern from the rising three methods.

The middle three candles should trend lower, and all three bodies should remain above the first candle's low.

Statistics

Since this candle pattern is so rare, be cautious about forming conclusions from few samples.

Table 64.2 shows general statistics.

Number found. Out of over 4.7 million candle lines, I found just 52 mat holds. Prorating the numbers using the standard database indicates that the mat hold appears most often in a bear market.

Reversal or continuation performance. Often we see that bear market results are better than bull market ones, but the table shows no discernible trend.

S&P performance. The candle pattern performs better than the S&P 500 index over the same time periods.

Candle end to breakout. It takes between 2 and 16 days to break out. Clearly, though, the 16 is an anomaly. The upward breakout results are shorter times because the patterns ends with the closing price near the candle's high. Thus, an upward breakout is easier to achieve.

Table 64.2
General Statistics

Description	Bull Market, Up Breakout	Bear Market, Up Breakout	Bull Market, Down Breakout	Bear Market, Down Breakout
Number found	31	8	9	4
Reversal (R), continuation (C) performance	5.00% C	5.79% C	−8.47% R	−3.95% R
Standard & Poor's 500 change	0.72%	0.56%	−2.38%	0.27%
Candle end to breakout (median, days)	2	2	7	16
Candle end to trend end (median, days)	4	5	14	12
Number of breakouts near the 12-month low (L), middle (M), or high (H)	L 6, M 11, H 14	L 1, M 2, H 5	L 2, M 0, H 5	L 1, M 2, H 1
Percentage move for each 12-month period	L 6.93%, M 5.39%, H 4.15%	L 5.56%, M 2.89%, H 7.03%	L −7.10%, M 0.00%, H −8.19%	L −0.28%, M −5.39%, H −6.95%
Candle end + 1 day	0.65%	2.14%	−0.41%	−1.18%
Candle end + 3 days	0.79%	−0.39%	−2.60%	−3.43%
Candle end + 5 days	0.47%	−1.42%	−5.75%	−5.66%
Candle end + 10 days	0.72%	−3.71%	−7.21%	−6.89%
10-day performance rank	98	103	2	10

Candle end to trend end. With price moving up into the candle pattern, the trend end comes sooner than if price breaks out downward and has to form a new trend.

Yearly position, performance. Most mat holds appear within a third of the yearly high. That's also where you'll find the best performance. That is counter to the results we've seen for other candle types, which often do best within a third of the yearly low. Blame low sample counts, and I would expect the results to change with additional samples. Mat hold patterns in bull market/up breakouts do better when the breakout is near the yearly low. They also have the most samples of the group (31).

Performance over time. In three of the four columns (the exception being bull market/up breakouts), the results trend downward over time. Even in a bull market after an upward breakout, price shows weakness after three days. Thus, I would be leery about depending on the uptrend continuing for long. The uphill run may flame out as quickly as the one shown in Figure 64.1.

Table 64.3
Height Statistics*

Description	Bull Market, Up Breakout	Bear Market, Up Breakout	Bull Market, Down Breakout	Bear Market, Down Breakout
Median candle height as a percentage of breakout price	5.96%	8.66%	5.50%	8.26%
Short candle, performance	4.00%	4.25%	−8.96%	−0.36%
Tall candle, performance	6.56%	6.56%	−7.52%	−9.24%
Percentage meeting price target (measure rule)	42%	25%	67%	0%
Median upper shadow as a percentage of breakout price	0.51%	0.36%	0.35%	1.12%
Short upper shadow, performance	4.84%	6.20%	−9.92%	−2.63%
Tall upper shadow, performance	5.14%	4.88%	−6.90%	−5.39%
Median lower shadow as a percentage of breakout price	0.23%	0.36%	0.28%	0.15%
Short lower shadow, performance	3.62%	3.94%	−7.92%	−0.36%
Tall lower shadow, performance	6.55%	7.77%	−9.08%	−9.24%

*Fewer than 30 samples.

The performance rank is some of the best (2) and worst (103). Clearly, this pattern does well after a downward breakout if you can believe the low sample count numbers.

Table 64.3 shows height statistics.

Candle height. Tall candles perform better than short ones in all cases except for bull market/down breakouts. Those do better with short candles, but the low sample count is likely to blame for that result.

To determine whether the candle is short or tall, compute its height from highest high to lowest low price in the candle pattern and divide by the breakout price. If the result is higher than the median, then you have a tall candle; otherwise it's short.

Wayne has a mat hold with a high price of 60 and a low of 55. Is the candle short or tall? The height is $60 - 55$, or 5, so the measure for an upward breakout would be 5/60, or 8.3%. In a bull market, it's a tall candle.

Measure rule. Use the measure rule to help predict how far price will rise or fall. Compute the height of the candle pattern and multiply it by the appropriate percentage shown in the table; then apply it to the breakout price.

What are Wayne's target prices? The upward breakout target would be (5 × 42%) + 60, or 62.10, and the downward breakout target would be 55 − (5 × 67%), or 51.65. For the bear market/down breakout category, just use 67% of the height since none of the patterns met their target.

Shadows. The table's results pertain to the last candle line in the pattern. To determine whether the shadow is short or tall, compute the height of the shadow and divide by the breakout price. Compare the result to the median in the table. Tall shadows have a percentage higher than the median.

Upper shadow performance. Tall shadows results in better postbreakout performance in bull market/up breakout and bear market/down breakout categories. The other two categories (bear market/up breakout and bull market/down breakout) work better if the upper shadow is short. Most candle patterns work better with long shadows, so be skeptical of the short shadow performance.

Lower shadow performance. A tall lower shadow leads to better performance across the board.

Table 64.4 shows volume statistics.

Candle volume trend. Falling candle volume results in the best postbreakout performance except for bear market/down breakouts. That category did not have any candles with falling volume.

Average candle volume. Above-average candle volume works best in the bull market/up breakout and bear market/down breakout categories.

Table 64.4
Volume Statistics*

Description	Bull Market, Up Breakout	Bear Market, Up Breakout	Bull Market, Down Breakout	Bear Market, Down Breakout
Rising candle volume, performance	4.87%	4.90%	−8.01%	−3.95%
Falling candle volume, performance	5.19%	6.39%	−9.26%	0.00%
Above-average candle volume, performance	6.83%	5.66%	−4.95%	−9.24%
Below-average candle volume, performance	3.93%	6.67%	−11.27%	−0.36%
Heavy breakout volume, performance	6.75%	6.30%	−8.52%	−9.24%
Light breakout volume, performance	3.04%	5.04%	−8.43%	−0.36%

*Fewer than 30 samples.

Below-average volume results in the best postbreakout performance for bear market/up breakout and bull market/down breakout categories.

Breakout volume. Heavy breakout volume suggests good postbreakout performance across the board.

Trading Tactics

Given that samples are few, Table 64.2 shows that the performance over time is weak. Price may break out upward but the trend end may arrive quickly. A review of the patterns with upward breakouts showed that 45% broke out within days of reaching an important high, 32% were in the middle of an uptrend, and 23% were closer to the start of an uptrend. Keep those numbers in mind when you next spot a mat hold.

I split trading tactics into two basic studies, one concerning reversal rates and the other concerning performance. Of the two, reversal rates are more important, because it's better to trade in the direction of the trend and let price run as far as it can.

Table 64.5 gives tips to find the trend direction.

Reversal, continuation rates. Since the price trend is known to be up leading to the candle pattern, price breaks out upward most often.

Yearly range reversals. Separating reversals/continuations into where they occur in the yearly price range, most continuations occur within a third of the yearly high. Buy high and sell higher.

Table 64.6 shows performance indicators that can give hints as to how your stock will behave after the breakout from this candle pattern.

Confirmation, performance. This shows how well the confirmation methods work. The best trading signal is to use opening gap confirmation; that is, buy the stock if price gaps open higher the next day.

Moving average. The results are mixed, but most other candle types do best if the breakout price is below the 50-day moving average. The bull market numbers agree with that assessment but not the bear market ones.

Table 64.5
Reversal Rates*

Description	Bull Market	Bear Market
Reversal rate: trend up, breakout down	23%	33%
Continuation rate: trend up, breakout up	77%	67%
Percentage of reversals (R)/continuations (C) for each 12-month low (L), middle (M), or high (H)	L 25% R/75% C, M 0% R/100% C, H 26% R/74% C	L 50% R/50% C, M 50% R/50% C, H 17% R/83% C

*Fewer than 30 samples.

Table 64.6
Performance Indicators*

Description	Bull Market, Up Breakout	Bear Market, Up Breakout	Bull Market, Down Breakout	Bear Market, Down Breakout
Closing price confirmation, performance	5.05%	2.76%	N/A	N/A
Candle color confirmation, performance	4.94%	2.28%	N/A	N/A
Opening gap confirmation, performance	6.29%	4.69%	N/A	N/A
Breakout above 50-day moving average, performance	4.65%	5.79%	−6.15%	−11.13%
Breakout below 50-day moving average, performance	15.33%	0.00%	−11.37%	−1.91%

N/A means not applicable.
*Fewer than 30 samples.

Sample Trade

Figure 64.2 shows the setup that concerned Wayne. As price trended up in late April, it approached the level of A, where it had often stalled or even reversed in the past. Should he hold on to his stock or sell it? That's usually a difficult question, but for Wayne it was made easier with the mat hold.

Figure 64.2 A mat hold appears just below overhead resistance.

However, Wayne didn't know that the mat hold pattern often occurs near a trend end. Even so, 55% of the time it occurs in the middle or start of a trend. When price hit B and completed the mat hold, he assumed price would continue rising as the mat hold theoretically predicted. However, nothing is guaranteed in trading, so he raised his stop just in case.

The next day, C, price made a huge upper shadow. The candle is a shooting star. The tall upper shadow meant that the bulls had been taken to the cleaners during the day. They would be gun-shy about buying the stock after being wounded taking a position near the high at C.

A day later, price opened much higher, so Wayne decided to hold on to the stock. Long lower shadows that appeared that day and over the next few days suggested bulls gathering, waiting to make a try for a new high. He didn't see anything that would warn him of a trend change.

A doji formed at D and again a day later, speaking of indecision. At E a bearish last engulfing top appeared, followed by a bearish harami at F. Trendlines drawn along the tops and bottoms showed a small symmetrical triangle. It wasn't a pennant, because those have flagpoles upon which to rest.

Despite the bearish candle signals, including another bearish last engulfing top at G, price broke out upward from the triangle, signaling a resumption of the uptrend. A throwback at H was expected, so Wayne held on to the stock.

For Best Performance

The following list offers tips and observations to help choose candles that perform well. Consult the associated table for more information.

- Use the identification guidelines to help select the pattern—Table 64.1.
- Expect price to reverse soon after the mat hold ends—Table 64.2 and Trading Tactics discussion.
- Select tall candles—Table 64.3.
- Use the measure rule to predict a price target—Table 64.3.
- Candles with tall lower shadows outperform—Table 64.3.
- Volume gives performance clues—Table 64.4.
- Expect an upward breakout—Table 64.5.
- Patterns within a third of the yearly high tend to act as continuations most often—Table 64.5.
- Opening gap confirmation works best—Table 64.6.

65

Matching Low

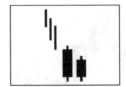

Behavior and Rank

Theoretical: Bullish reversal.

Actual bull market: Bearish continuation 61% of the time (ranking 19).

Actual bear market: Bearish continuation 61% of the time (ranking 21).

Frequency: 58th out of 103.

Overall performance over time: 8th out of 103.

The matching low candle reminds me of when I started studying chart patterns for performance. I found simple techniques to boost reliability. If you want to find matching low candles that act as reversals, then wait for confirmation. That means if price closes higher the day after the matching low, then the chances improve from 39% to 62% that price will break out upward.

The performance over time ranks 8 out of 103 candles where 1 is best. I consider that excellent, but the candle performs better in some markets and breakout directions than others.

The matching low pattern is a small study in finding support areas. The bears have control and price is trending lower. A tall black candle appears, signaling more losses ahead. But the next day, price makes no headway, meaning it closes at the same price as the day before. The bears have slammed into a support zone, an imaginary line drawn on the charts that the bulls say, "You will not cross." If the bulls can hold this line by price either closing higher the next day or showing a white candle, there's a good chance that price will reverse the downtrend.

Figure 65.1 A matching low acted as a continuation of the downward price trend.

Identification Guidelines

Figure 65.1 shows a matching low pattern that occurs as price tumbles. These two black candles in the pattern have long lower shadows (as does the following day) but that bullish feature did not stop price from continuing lower over the coming days.

What I find amusing about the matching low candlestick is that the low price of the day is not what's matching. It is the closing price of the two candles that is the same. The emphasis must be on the bodies of the two candles, because in the candlestick world, the body is more important than the shadows.

Table 65.1 lists identification guidelines. Look for two black candles; the first one has a tall body but the second one can be any size. The key factor is that the closing prices of the two candles must match. Shadows can be any length.

Ideal depictions of the matching low candle pattern from several sources often show two black closing marubozu candles. Those are ones with no lower shadows. In actual figures, shadows sometimes appear. Thus, I allow lower shadows for this candle pattern.

Table 65.1
Identification Guidelines

Characteristic	Discussion
Number of candle lines	Two.
Price trend	Downward leading to the start of the candle pattern.
First day	A tall-bodied black candle.
Second day	A black body with a close that matches the prior close.

Statistics

Table 65.2 shows general statistics.

Number found. The matching low candle is not as prevalent as I expected among the 4.7 million lines examined. I found only 10,283 but expected more. Few appear in a bear market. Even after prorating the numbers using the standard database, the matching low candle appears more often in a bull market.

Table 65.2
General Statistics

Description	Bull Market, Up Breakout	Bear Market, Up Breakout	Bull Market, Down Breakout	Bear Market, Down Breakout
Number found	3,755	288	5,792	448
Reversal (R), continuation (C) performance	7.18% R	11.15% R	−6.09% C	−9.97% C
Standard & Poor's 500 change	1.53%	0.85%	−0.46%	−1.33%
Candle end to breakout (median, days)	5	5	3	3
Candle end to trend end (median, days)	8	9	6	6
Number of breakouts near the 12-month low (L), middle (M), or high (H)	L 1,200, M 1,005, H 1,160	L 137, M 92, H 50	L 2,332, M 1,576, H 1,250	L 276, M 113, H 54
Percentage move for each 12-month period	L 8.39%, M 6.35%, H 6.77%	L 12.92%, M 10.41%, H 9.72%	L −6.62%, M −6.03%, H −5.39%	L −11.42%, M −8.79%, H −8.26%
Candle end + 1 day	1.37%	2.47%	−0.72%	−1.27%
Candle end + 3 days	2.97%	4.89%	−1.44%	−2.76%
Candle end + 5 days	3.86%	5.58%	−1.72%	−3.70%
Candle end + 10 days	4.67%	7.15%	−1.68%	−3.75%
10-day performance rank	17	13	75	55

I expected a downward price trend so prevalent in a bear market to spawn these patterns like salmon reaching their birthplace.

Reversal or continuation performance. Reversals perform better than continuations, and upward breakouts seem to beat their downward breakout counterparts. That is somewhat unusual for candle patterns (the bear market usually posts the best numbers)

S&P performance. The S&P 500 can't hold a candle to the matching low pattern. In other words, the pattern beats the index in all cases.

Candle end to breakout. Downward breakouts take less time to occur because price is closer to the low than the high.

Candle end to trend end. Since price is trending down into the start of the matching low, it's often closer to the end of the trend. That's why downward breakouts post smaller numbers than upward ones.

Yearly position, performance. Most matching low candles appear within a third of the yearly low, and that's also where you'll find the best performance.

Performance over time. The candle pattern shows *almost* robust performance. The one area that could stand improvement is days 5 to 10 of bull market/down breakouts. There the performance numbers drop slightly over those two periods.

The high numbers in the bear market/up breakout are worrisome. They might be correct, but the comparatively low sample counts suggest additional samples might throttle back the results. The candle shines after an upward breakout, posting exceptional rank numbers (17 and 13; 1 is best out of 103 candles). Downward breakouts suffer.

Table 65.3 shows height statistics.

Candle height. Tall candles outperform the short ones in all cases, and the monster numbers they put on the scoreboard are a remarkable sight.

To determine whether the candle is short or tall, compute its height from highest high to lowest low price in the candle pattern and divide by the breakout price. If the result is higher than the median, then you have a tall candle; otherwise it's short.

For example, if Tom has a matching low candlestick with a high price of 70 and a low of 68, is the candle short or tall? The height is 70 − 68, or 2, so the measure is 2/70, or 2.9%. For an upward breakout in a bull market, the candle is short.

Measure rule. Use the measure rule to help predict how far price will rise or fall. Compute the height of the candle pattern and multiply it by the appropriate percentage shown in the table; then apply it to the breakout price.

In Tom's example, what are the price targets? The upward breakout target (bull market) would be (2 × 69%) + 70, or 71.38, and the downward breakout target would be 68 − (2 × 63%), or 66.74.

Shadows. The table's results pertain to the last candle line in the pattern. To determine whether the shadow is short or tall, compute the height of the

Table 65.3
Height Statistics

Description	Bull Market, Up Breakout	Bear Market, Up Breakout	Bull Market, Down Breakout	Bear Market, Down Breakout
Median candle height as a percentage of breakout price	3.44%	5.32%	3.51%	5.70%
Short candle, performance	5.82%	8.93%	−5.01%	−8.64%
Tall candle, performance	9.21%	13.83%	−7.83%	−12.34%
Percentage meeting price target (measure rule)	69%	69%	63%	60%
Median upper shadow as a percentage of breakout price	0.00%	0.77%	0.00%	0.75%
Short upper shadow, performance	7.17%	8.71%	−6.02%	−9.14%
Tall upper shadow, performance	7.19%	13.69%	−6.15%	−10.70%
Median lower shadow as a percentage of breakout price	0.38%	0.80%	0.32%	0.86%
Short lower shadow, performance	6.52%	10.56%	−5.59%	−8.15%
Tall lower shadow, performance	7.74%	11.70%	−6.51%	−11.98%

shadow and divide by the breakout price. Compare the result to the median in the table. Tall shadows have a percentage higher than the median.

I felt as if I was having a heart attack the first time I saw a 0.00% median. That simply means that the candles have an inordinate number of lines with no shadows. Candles with tall shadows perform better than short ones in all categories, and this applies to both upper and lower shadows.

Table 65.4 shows volume statistics.

Candle volume trend. Falling candle volume suggests better postbreakout performance across the board.

Average candle volume. Above-average candle volume means good performance after an upward breakout. Downward breakouts do better following below-average volume.

Breakout volume. Heavy breakout volume leads to good performance in all categories. In fact, breakout volume is often a good predictor of performance in nearly all candle types.

Trading Tactics

For the best performance, look for matching low candles as part of a downward retracement in an uptrend. An upward breakout joins with the primary trend

Table 65.4
Volume Statistics

Description	Bull Market, Up Breakout	Bear Market, Up Breakout	Bull Market, Down Breakout	Bear Market, Down Breakout
Rising candle volume, performance	7.11%	10.87%	−6.04%	−8.82%
Falling candle volume, performance	7.25%	11.32%	−6.13%	−10.88%
Above-average candle volume, performance	7.21%	11.67%	−6.09%	−9.19%
Below-average candle volume, performance	7.16%	10.66%	−6.09%	−10.69%
Heavy breakout volume, performance	8.12%	11.87%	−6.43%	−10.17%
Light breakout volume, performance	6.27%	10.38%	−5.83%	−9.75%

and price climbs like a helium balloon. Maybe not that fast, but you understand the meaning. Avoid relying on a reversal in a primary downtrend. The upward breakout is apt to be short-lived.

I split trading tactics into two basic studies, one concerning reversal rates and the other concerning performance. Of the two, reversal rates are more important, because it's better to trade in the direction of the trend and let price run as far as it can.

Table 65.5 gives tips to find the trend direction.

Confirmation reversal rates. Waiting for a white candle or a higher close the day after a matching low leads to the pattern breaking out upward

Table 65.5
Reversal Rates

Description	Bull Market	Bear Market
Closing price confirmation reversal rate	62%	65%
Candle color confirmation reversal rate	62%	63%
Opening gap confirmation reversal rate	47%	46%
Reversal: trend down, breakout up	39%	39%
Continuation: trend down, breakout down	61%	61%
Percentage of reversals (R)/continuations (C) for each 12-month low (L), middle (M), or high (H)	L 34% R/66% C, M 39% R/61% C, H 48% R/52% C	L 33% R/67% C, M 45% R/55% C, H 48% R/52% C

Table 65.6
Performance Indicators

Description	Bull Market, Up Breakout	Bear Market, Up Breakout	Bull Market, Down Breakout	Bear Market, Down Breakout
Closing price confirmation, performance	7.71%	12.18%	N/A	N/A
Candle color confirmation, performance	7.49%	12.04%	N/A	N/A
Opening gap confirmation, performance	8.27%	12.58%	N/A	N/A
Breakout above 50-day moving average, performance	6.77%	11.55%	−5.36%	−8.04%
Breakout below 50-day moving average, performance	7.53%	10.88%	−6.32%	−10.37%
Last candle: close in highest third, performance	6.77%	12.45%	−6.78%	−10.18%
Last candle: close in middle third, performance	7.27%	8.91%	−6.05%	−10.72%
Last candle: close in lowest third, performance	7.20%	12.22%	−6.04%	−9.31%

N/A means not applicable.

between 62% and 65% of the time (depending on market conditions). Thus, if you are looking for a reversal, then wait a day before taking a position.

Reversal, continuation rates. A downward breakout will occur nearly two out of three times.

Yearly range reversals. Splitting the reversals into where they occur in the yearly price range, we find that the widest difference comes from patterns within a third of the yearly low. They act as continuations 66% or 67% of the time. Thus, if you see a matching low candlestick near the yearly low, then expect a downward breakout.

Table 65.6 shows performance indicators that can give hints as to how your stock will behave after the breakout from this candle pattern.

Confirmation, performance. For the best performance, use the opening gap method. That means buy if price gaps open higher a day after the matching low. That will get you in soonest, and the analysis says it works best.

Moving average. Matching low candles below the 50-day moving average lead to the best postbreakout performance in all cases except for bear market/up breakouts. That category does better if the candle's breakout is above the moving average.

Closing position. Looking at the closing price of the last candle in the pattern, we find that when price closes in the middle third of the candle line, performance improves during bull market/up breakouts and bear market/down breakouts. A closing price near the candle's low works best in the other two categories: bear market/up breakout and bull market/down breakout.

Sample Trade

Figure 65.2 shows a trade that Tom made. Price moved horizontally since early March, but only a portion of it appears on the chart. The flat bottom of the support zone, once pierced, would bring a tasty decline, Tom thought.

Based on the statistics showing that the matching low candle pattern acts as a bearish continuation more often than a reversal, he started looking to enter the trade going short.

At point A, price gapped open lower by a penny and that was his entry signal. He shorted the stock at 15.76.

Three days after opening the trade, the stock pulled back to the base of support, but this did not bother Tom. Pullbacks are just a cost of doing

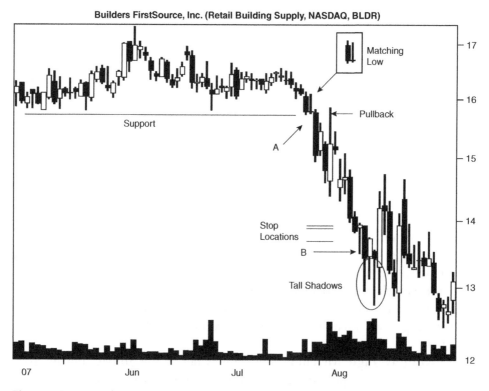

Figure 65.2 A shorting opportunity occurred when price pierced the bottom of a support zone after a matching low candle pattern.

business, and the probability says that the decline will resume. However, there are no guarantees in trading, so he kept a watchful eye on the stock.

Price resumed the downtrend by forming long candles. When it began trending with each high price below the previous, he used the high price as a stop loss location (plus a penny, just to be safe). The cluster of horizontal lines shown on the chart were the stop locations he used. The last one, B, appears just above the top of a Takuri line candle. That candle is the black one in the circled region with the longest lower shadow, and the candle acts as a bullish reversal 66% of the time. When price climbed above the top of this candle, he was stopped out at 13.57. He made about $2 a share.

For Best Performance

The following list offers tips and observations to help choose candles that perform well. Consult the associated table for more information.

- Use the identification guidelines to help select the pattern—Table 65.1.
- Candles within a third of the yearly low perform best—Table 65.2.
- Select tall candles—Table 65.3.
- Use the measure rule to predict a price target—Table 65.3.
- Candles with tall shadows outperform—Table 65.3.
- Volume gives performance clues—Table 65.4.
- Look for matching low candles as part of a downward retracement in an uptrend—Trading Tactics discussion.
- Wait for a higher close or a white candle to confirm the matching low—Table 65.5.
- The candle breaks out downward 61% of the time—Table 65.5.
- Patterns within a third of the yearly low tend to act as continuations most often—Table 65.5.
- Opening gap confirmation works best—Table 65.6.
- Breakouts below the 50-day moving average lead to the best performance most often—Table 65.6.

66

Meeting Lines, Bearish

Behavior and Rank

Theoretical: Bearish reversal.

Actual bull market: Bullish continuation 51% of the time (ranking 44).

Actual bear market: Bullish continuation 53% of the time (ranking 46).

Frequency: 63rd out of 103.

Overall performance over time: 16th out of 103.

According to the sources I checked, meeting lines (sometimes called counterattack lines) are reversal patterns—but you can't tell that from my statistics. I show they act as continuations 51% of the time in a bull market. That's a dollop above random (50%). However, if you wait for price to close lower the next day, then you can boost the chance of a reversal to as high as 70%.

The frequency rank is middle of the road, at 63 out of 103 candles where 1 is best. The overall performance rank at 16 is simply marvelous.

Pattern psychology: Bulls push price higher in an upward trend leading to the start of the meeting lines pattern. Then a tall white candle appears and the bulls are excited. Another promising day of profits! The next day price gaps higher but the bears stage a surprising attack and push price lower, closing near where it closed the day before. This turn has the bulls taking cover. Expecting that a reversal has begun, they are likely right if price makes a lower close the next day or even if another bearish black candle joins the opposition. Otherwise, price goes wherever it pleases, depending on the strength of the warring parties.

Identification Guidelines

Figure 66.1 shows an example of a bearish meeting lines candle pattern in an uptrend that acts not as a reversal but as a continuation pattern. The candle at A closes lower and it's a black candle. Both of those features suggest that a reversal is about to unfold. In fact, the two black candles form a bearish two crows pattern.

Price moves up the next day and forms a shooting star. This is somewhat confusing because price closes higher but the shooting star is a bearish candle. Since the one-day uptrend was not a strong trend leading to the shooting star, there is not much to reverse, and price continues rising, not knowing that it's supposed to turn lower. Sometimes that's the way candles burn, or should I say that's the way candles burn traders.

Table 66.1 lists identification guidelines. The bearish meeting lines candlestick is a two-candle pattern with the first candle being white and the next one black. Both are tall candles, and both close at or near the same price. To adhere to an exact penny-for-penny matching close I believe is too strict, so I allow some leeway, usually no more than two cents. This does not violate the intent of the candle, and if you view the screen from a few miles away, you won't be able to see the difference anyway.

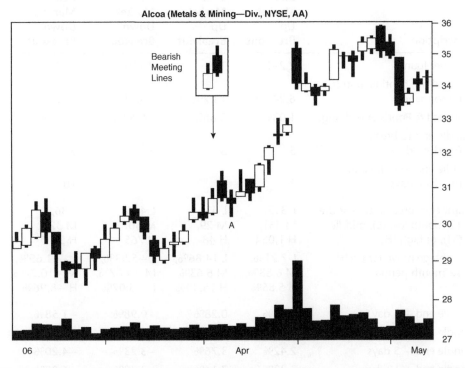

Figure 66.1 Price after a bearish meeting lines pattern continues higher despite reversal confirmation at A.

Table 66.1
Identification Guidelines

Characteristic	Discussion
Number of candle lines	Two.
Price trend	Upward leading to the start of the candle pattern.
First day	A tall white candle.
Second day	A tall black candle that closes at or near the prior day's close.

Statistics

Table 66.2 shows general statistics.

Number found. I found 4,677 bearish meeting lines candle patterns out of over 4.7 million, making the meeting lines a rare pattern. Most appear in a bull market; they are even rarer in a bear market.

Reversal or continuation performance. The best performance comes from patterns in a bear market, but this may be due to the low sample count.

Table 66.2
General Statistics

Description	Bull Market, Up Breakout	Bear Market, Up Breakout	Bull Market, Down Breakout	Bear Market, Down Breakout
Number found	2,291	119	2,160	107
Reversal (R), continuation (C) performance	6.24% C	13.29% C	−6.01% R	−10.24% R
Standard & Poor's 500 change	1.03%	0.68%	−0.53%	−2.50%
Candle end to breakout (median, days)	5	5	5	5
Candle end to trend end (median, days)	7	6	7	10
Number of breakouts near the 12-month low (L), middle (M), or high (H)	L 317, M 461, H 1,054	L 41, M 29, H 48	L 446, M 507, H 765	L 36, M 32, H 38
Percentage move for each 12-month period	L 7.21%, M 6.88%, H 5.85%	L 14.86%, M 6.63%, H 15.40%	L −5.93%, M −4.87%, H −5.07%	L −11.69%, M −10.72%, H −8.96%
Candle end + 1 day	0.74%	0.28%	−0.98%	−1.58%
Candle end + 3 days	2.07%	2.64%	−2.32%	−3.47%
Candle end + 5 days	2.42%	3.76%	−3.23%	−4.20%
Candle end + 10 days	3.33%	7.16%	−3.89%	−6.00%
10-day performance rank	49	12	18	18

However, other candle types also show better performance in a bear market and they have significantly higher sample counts.

S&P performance. The bearish meeting lines pattern outperforms the S&P 500 index over the same measurement periods.

Candle end to breakout. It takes price a median of five days to reach the breakout. Notice that the values are the same across the board. This makes sense because both candles in the meeting lines are tall ones and price closes near the middle of the pattern, so no breakout direction is favored.

Candle end to trend end. Since price is trending up leading to the start of this pattern, it makes sense that we are closer to the end of an uptrend than the beginning, so the uptrend ends sooner than a downward trend (which would begin a new downtrend and take correspondingly longer to reach the trend end). Clear as mud, right?

Yearly position, performance. Most candles appear within a third of the yearly high, but performance is best near the yearly low in most cases, the exception being a bear market/up breakout. That category does better if price is near the yearly high.

Performance over time. The bearish meeting lines candle is a strong, robust performer. Price moves in the trend direction over each time period without a pause. That means the numbers increase over time, suggesting a lasting trend. Notice that the bear market numbers are higher than are their bull market counterparts. The performance ranks agree with that assessment. You might consider avoiding this candle in bull market/up breakouts because of the middling performance.

Table 66.3 shows height statistics.

Candle height. Tall candles perform better than short ones in all cases except for bear market/up breakouts. Short candles perform better under those conditions.

To determine whether the candle is short or tall, compute its height from highest high to lowest low price in the candle pattern and divide by the breakout price. If the result is higher than the median, then you have a tall candle; otherwise it's short.

For example, Wanda sees a meeting lines candle with a high at 39 and a low at 37. Is the candle short or tall? The height is 39 − 37, or 2, so the measure for an upward breakout in a bull market would be 2/39, or 5.1%, making this a tall candle.

Measure rule. Use the measure rule to help predict how far price will rise or fall. Compute the height of the candle pattern and multiply it by the appropriate percentage shown in the table; then apply it to the breakout price.

For Wanda's candle the upward breakout target would be $(2 \times 60\%) + 39$, or 40.20, and the downward breakout target would be $37 − (2 \times 58\%)$, or 35.84.

Shadows. The table's results pertain to the last candle line in the pattern. To determine whether the shadow is short or tall, compute the height of the

Table 66.3
Height Statistics

Description	Bull Market, Up Breakout	Bear Market, Up Breakout	Bull Market, Down Breakout	Bear Market, Down Breakout
Median candle height as a percentage of breakout price	4.04%	6.37%	4.17%	6.65%
Short candle, performance	4.52%	14.35%	−4.23%	−7.47%
Tall candle, performance	8.58%	11.86%	−8.22%	−13.56%
Percentage meeting price target (measure rule)	60%	48%	58%	50%
Median upper shadow as a percentage of breakout price	0.00%	0.13%	0.00%	0.31%
Short upper shadow, performance	5.87%	15.33%	−4.95%	−10.48%
Tall upper shadow, performance	6.57%	11.02%	−6.83%	−10.09%
Median lower shadow as a percentage of breakout price	0.09%	0.54%	0.00%	0.68%
Short lower shadow, performance	6.03%	17.91%	−5.29%	−11.10%
Tall lower shadow, performance	6.35%	7.99%	−6.27%	−9.37%

shadow and divide by the breakout price. Compare the result to the median in the table. Tall shadows have a percentage higher than the median.

Upper shadow performance. A zero median means the candle pattern had many examples with no upper shadow. Usually tall upper shadows suggest better postbreakout performance, but with meeting lines the results are mixed. Bull market numbers are better with tall shadows and the bear market shows improved results after short shadows. This may change with additional samples.

Lower shadow performance. The lower shadows show the same behavior as upper shadows: Bull markets post the best numbers after meeting lines with tall shadows, and results in bear markets show better performance from candles with short shadows.

Table 66.4 shows volume statistics.

Candle volume trend. A falling volume trend results in the best postbreakout performance in all cases except for bull market/down breakouts. Those do better with a rising volume trend.

Average candle volume. Above-average candle volume works best in all categories except bull market/down breakout. That column shows better performance after below-average candle volume.

Breakout volume. Heavy breakout volume results in the best postbreakout performance across the board.

Table 66.4
Volume Statistics

Description	Bull Market, Up Breakout	Bear Market, Up Breakout	Bull Market, Down Breakout	Bear Market, Down Breakout
Rising candle volume, performance	6.22%	9.44%	−6.55%	−8.06%
Falling candle volume, performance	6.27%	14.94%	−5.62%	−11.61%
Above-average candle volume, performance	6.78%	15.20%	−5.59%	−11.04%
Below-average candle volume, performance	5.51%	10.06%	−6.55%	−8.77%
Heavy breakout volume, performance	7.48%	16.24%	−6.16%	−11.39%
Light breakout volume, performance	4.73%	8.59%	−5.89%	−9.19%

Trading Tactics

The best way to trade this pattern is to trade in the direction of the breakout. If the breakout is upward, then consider going long. A downward breakout would suggest either going short or selling an existing holding.

I split trading tactics into two basic studies, one concerning reversal rates and the other concerning performance. Of the two, reversal rates are more important, because it's better to trade in the direction of the trend and let price run as far as it can.

Table 66.5 gives tips to find the trend direction.

Confirmation reversal rates. If you wait for price to close lower the day after a bearish meeting lines pattern, the chances improve to 70% (bull market) and 67% (bear market) that price will continue moving downward. Table 66.5 shows the results for the other two confirmation methods.

If you choose to use confirmation to detect a reversal, then close out your trade if price later moves in an adverse direction. Think of this as a double reversal.

For example, if price closes lower the day after a bearish meeting lines pattern, suggesting a reversal, but then price closes above the top of the meeting lines (over the next several days, not immediately—although that can happen), then cover your short. Price is likely to continue moving higher over the following days.

The same is true of upward breakouts. If price closes higher, suggesting a continuation of the uptrend, but then closes below the meeting

Table 66.5
Reversal Rates

Description	Bull Market	Bear Market
Closing price confirmation reversal rate	70%	67%
Candle color confirmation reversal rate	68%	58%
Opening gap confirmation reversal rate	59%	54%
Reversal rate: trend up, breakout down	49%	47%
Continuation rate: trend up, breakout up	51%	53%
Percentage of reversals (R)/continuations (C) for each 12-month low (L), middle (M), or high (H)	L 58% R/42% C, M 52% R/48% C, H 42% R/58% C	L 47% R/53% C, M 52% R/48%* C, H 44% R/56% C

*Fewer than 30 samples.

lines' low, consider selling a long holding. Price is likely to continue moving lower.

Reversal, continuation rates. The breakout direction is essentially random in both markets, so if you don't wait for confirmation, there's no telling what direction price is likely to break out.

Yearly range reversals. In a bull market, reversals tend to occur most often within a third of the yearly low. In a bear market, continuations occur most often within a third of the yearly high.

Table 66.6 shows performance indicators that can give hints as to how your stock will behave after the breakout from this candle pattern.

Confirmation, performance. Bear market results significantly exceed those of the bull market, but this may be due to the scarcity of samples. In a bull market, the opening gap method results in the best performance. That means waiting for price to gap open lower the next day before taking a position.

For bear markets, candle color works best as confirmation of a trading signal. Take a position in the stock if a black candle appears the next day.

Moving average. Meeting lines with breakouts below the moving average tend to outperform after the breakout in all cases except for bear market/up breakouts. Those do better if the breakout is above the moving average (but samples are few).

Closing position. Checking the closing price in the last candle of the meeting lines, performance is best when price closes within a third of the intraday low in bear markets. The other ranges show no consistent trend, and the bear market results may be due to the low sample counts.

Sample Trade

Wanda sees the trading setup shown in Figure 66.2. Along peaks A and B she draws a trendline and extends it down to the bearish meeting lines candlestick

Table 66.6
Performance Indicators

Description	Bull Market, Up Breakout	Bear Market, Up Breakout	Bull Market, Down Breakout	Bear Market, Down Breakout
Closing price confirmation, performance	N/A	N/A	−7.79%	−13.97%
Candle color confirmation, performance	N/A	N/A	−8.01%	−16.83%
Opening gap confirmation, performance	N/A	N/A	−8.30%	−14.05%
Breakout above 50-day moving average, performance	6.16%	13.76%	−5.14%	−9.69%
Breakout below 50-day moving average, performance	7.45%	9.54%*	−6.03%	−11.02%
Last candle: close in highest third, performance	6.74%	4.74%*	−4.57%	−4.27%*
Last candle: close in middle third, performance	6.35%	8.85%	−7.69%	−7.49%*
Last candle: close in lowest third, performance	6.20%	14.96%	−5.41%	−11.57%

N/A means not applicable.
*Fewer than 30 samples.

pattern. That suggests overhead resistance will prevent price from climbing much higher. Thus, a long position is out of the question unless it becomes apparent that price is staging an upward breakout (i.e., closing above the trendline in a signal of continued price gains).

Along the bottoms, she draws another trendline, this time sloping up and connecting valleys D and E. She extends it forward in time just to anticipate where price might stop if it drops (which happens at G).

The day after the meeting lines complete (F), price closes lower, forming a doji. This suggests indecision on the part of traders, but the lower close says price is more likely to continue downward. How much lower? If price touches the bottom trendline, Wanda can make $1.76 per share if traded perfectly. That's at most 3.7%, and that's without commissions and fees deducted.

She decides to look elsewhere for a more profitable setup. Sometimes the best trade you can make is none at all.

For Best Performance

The following list offers tips and observations to help choose candles that perform well. Consult the associated table for more information.

Figure 66.2 A bearish meeting lines acts as a reversal of the uptrend.

- Use the identification guidelines to help select the pattern—Table 66.1.
- Most candles within a third of the yearly low perform best—Table 66.2.
- Select tall candles except in bear markets with upward breakouts—Table 66.3.
- Use the measure rule to predict a price target—Table 66.3.
- Bull market candles with tall shadows outperform—Table 66.3.
- Volume gives performance clues—Table 66.4.
- Close out a trade if price reverses and then reverses again—Table 66.5.
- A lower close suggests a downward reversal 67% to 70% of the time—Table 66.5.
- Patterns within a third of the yearly low tend to act as reversals most often in a bull market, whereas continuations appear most often within a third of the yearly high in a bear market—Table 66.5.
- Opening gap confirmation works best in a bull market, while candle color confirmation is the better choice in a bear market—Table 66.6.
- Breakouts below the 50-day moving average lead to the best performance most often (except for bear market/up breakouts)—Table 66.6.

67

Meeting Lines, Bullish

Behavior and Rank

Theoretical: Bullish reversal.

Actual bull market: Bullish reversal 56% of the time (ranking 38).

Actual bear market: Bearish continuation 52% of the time (ranking 47).

Frequency: 72nd out of 103.

Overall performance over time: 18th out of 103.

You might think that the bullish meeting lines candle pattern is the opposite of the bearish version, and I'm here to tell you that's the case. The trend leading to the candle pattern is opposite, as are the candle colors. Performance is also opposite. The bullish meeting lines act as reversals 56% of the time, but the bearish varieties are continuations 51% of the time (bull market).

One warning I see with this analysis is that the out-of-sample tests come to different conclusions. In other words, in a bull market the pattern acts as a reversal but in a bear market it's a continuation. The bear market results I believe are flawed because of the low sample counts. Keep that in mind.

Performance rank is very good at 18 out of 103 candles with 1 being best. However, the frequency rank at 72 is a bit soft. You will be able to find these patterns, but it may take a bit of digging, perhaps with a backhoe.

Psychology is opposite, too. With the bullish meeting lines, the bulls are running for cover, being chased by angry bears. Price trends lower and forms a tall black candle. The next day price gaps even lower, signaling another bearish rout, but then the bulls stage an ambush and force price up to close at the same price as the prior day. After that, anything can happen and often does, but price is supposed to continue higher. If you wait for confirmation, then 80% of the time the breakout is upward. That's a startling recovery in a downtrend.

Identification Guidelines

Figure 67.1 shows an example of the bullish meeting lines pattern. It's not a perfect example, because I allow a few cents' overlap between closing prices to keep the sample count above zero. In a perfect world, the closing prices would be equal, but with global peace still a distant dream, this world is far from perfect.

Price trends downward leading to the candle pattern, showing a few doji before the meeting lines. Then price forms a tall black candle followed by a tall white one, sharing the closing price between them like two lovers splitting a wishbone. After that, price closes higher and that signals a reversal of the downtrend. In this example, closing price confirmation works wonderfully, and we'll discuss that again later in this chapter.

Table 67.1 lists identification guidelines. With a good pair of binoculars, this is an easy pattern to spot, but it's a rare bird. Look for two tall-bodied

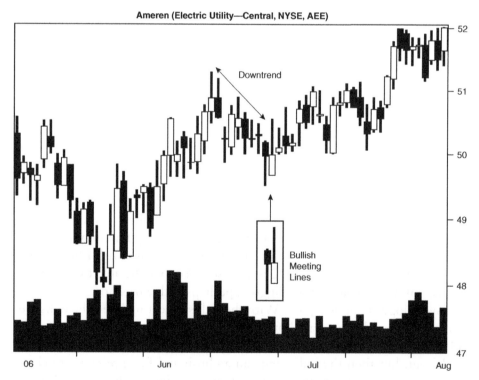

Figure 67.1   A meeting lines candle pattern accurately predicts a trend reversal.

Table 67.1
Identification Guidelines

Characteristic	Discussion
Number of candle lines	Two.
Price trend	Downward leading to the start of the candle pattern.
First day	A tall black candle.
Second day	A tall white candle with a closing price at or near the prior day's close.

candles of opposite color that close at or near the same price. I allow two cents' variation between the closes, and that seems to work well. Excluding that variation would limit the number of samples.

Statistics

Table 67.2 shows general statistics.

Table 67.2
General Statistics

Description	Bull Market, Up Breakout	Bear Market, Up Breakout	Bull Market, Down Breakout	Bear Market, Down Breakout
Number found	2,120	116	1,660	125
Reversal (R), continuation (C) performance	6.99% R	7.92% R	−5.57% C	−10.30% C
Standard & Poor's 500 change	1.48%	1.29%	−0.48%	−3.23%
Candle end to breakout (median, days)	5	5	5	4
Candle end to trend end (median, days)	8	10	6	7
Number of breakouts near the 12-month low (L), middle (M), or high (H)	L 510, M 502, H 650	L 50, M 40, H 23	L 548, M 406, H 338	L 67, M 36, H 20
Percentage move for each 12-month period	L 8.03%, M 6.66%, H 6.40%	L 10.06%, M 8.59%, H 5.04%	L −7.08%, M −4.13%, H −4.82%	L −12.34%, M −8.93%, H −6.08%
Candle end + 1 day	0.94%	2.13%	−0.93%	−1.87%
Candle end + 3 days	2.23%	3.11%	−1.98%	−3.88%
Candle end + 5 days	3.23%	4.23%	−2.26%	−5.11%
Candle end + 10 days	4.29%	5.08%	−2.39%	−3.69%
10-day performance rank	27	28	50	56

Number found. I trapped 4,021 of these candle patterns, but I assure you that none were harmed in the process. I use dolphin-friendly nets, too.

In my standard database, this pattern occurs more often in a bear market. I found that hard to believe based on the few bear market samples shown in the table, so I rechecked the numbers and found that it's correct.

Reversal or continuation performance. The best performance occurs in a bear market, regardless of the breakout direction.

S&P performance. The candle pattern's performance beats the S&P 500 index in all market conditions and breakout directions.

Candle end to breakout. It takes between four and five days for price to break out. A breakout occurs when price closes either above the highest high or below the lowest low in the candle pattern.

Candle end to trend end. Downward breakouts take less time than upward ones to reach the trend end. This makes sense when you consider the existing downward trend. Price is already well down the road to the trend end when the meeting lines pattern appears. For upward breakouts, meeting lines act as reversals and that starts the uptrend, meaning price has longer to go to reach the trend end.

Yearly position, performance. Most meeting lines appear within a third of the yearly low, the one exception being bull market/up breakouts. Those occur frequently near the yearly high. Performance is best when the candles show breakouts within a third of the yearly low.

Performance over time. The meeting lines pattern shows good staying power except in the bear market/down breakout category during days 5 to 10. The numbers suggest that once a trend is under way, price continues to trend.

The performance rank emphasizes that this candle pattern does better after an upward breakout than a downward one. In all cases, 1 is best out of 103 candles.

Table 67.3 shows height statistics.

Candle height. Tall candles perform better than short ones across the board. To determine whether the candle is short or tall, compute its height from highest high to lowest low price in the candle pattern and divide by the breakout price. If the result is higher than the median, then you have a tall candle; otherwise it's short.

For example, Peter sees a meeting lines candle with a high of 83 and a low of 81. Is the candle short or tall? The height is $83 - 81$, or 2; the measure for upward breakouts in a bull market would be 2/83, or 2.4%, so the candle is short.

Measure rule. Use the measure rule to help predict how far price will rise or fall. Compute the height of the candle pattern and multiply it by the appropriate percentage shown in the table; then apply it to the breakout price.

In Peter's case, what are the target prices? For upward breakouts, the target would be $(2 \times 66\%) + 83$, or 84.32. The downward breakout target would be $81 - (2 \times 57\%)$, or 79.86.

Table 67.3
Height Statistics

Description	Bull Market, Up Breakout	Bear Market, Up Breakout	Bull Market, Down Breakout	Bear Market, Down Breakout
Median candle height as a percentage of breakout price	3.90%	7.02%	4.00%	6.80%
Short candle, performance	5.75%	6.91%	−4.94%	−6.91%
Tall candle, performance	8.44%	9.09%	−6.42%	−14.99%
Percentage meeting price target (measure rule)	66%	51%	57%	53%
Median upper shadow as a percentage of breakout price	0.00%	0.88%	0.00%	0.72%
Short upper shadow, performance	6.68%	7.91%	−5.71%	−8.26%
Tall upper shadow, performance	7.25%	7.93%	−5.47%	−12.17%
Median lower shadow as a percentage of breakout price	0.00%	0.36%	0.00%	0.24%
Short lower shadow, performance	6.96%	7.74%	−5.72%	−10.16%
Tall lower shadow, performance	7.03%	8.07%	−5.38%	−10.39%

Shadows. The table's results pertain to the last candle line in the pattern. To determine whether the shadow is short or tall, compute the height of the shadow and divide by the breakout price. Compare the result to the median in the table. Tall shadows have a percentage higher than the median.

A zero median means this candle pattern has an inordinate number of candles with no upper shadows. Candles with tall upper or lower shadows perform better than short ones in all cases except bull market/down breakouts.

Table 67.4 shows volume statistics.

Candle volume trend. A falling volume trend leads to good postbreakout performance in all cases except bear market/up breakouts. Those do better with rising candle volume.

Average candle volume. Average volume follows the same trend as candle volume, with below-average candle volume suggesting better postbreakout performance except for patterns with upward breakouts in a bear market.

Breakout volume. Heavy breakout volume is good for performance under all breakout directions and market conditions.

Trading Tactics

Trade in the direction of the breakout. By that I mean going long when the breakout is upward and shorting or selling a long holding when the breakout

Table 67.4
Volume Statistics

Description	Bull Market, Up Breakout	Bear Market, Up Breakout	Bull Market, Down Breakout	Bear Market, Down Breakout
Rising candle volume, performance	6.73%	8.45%	−5.27%	−8.77%
Falling candle volume, performance	7.29%	7.23%	−5.78%	−12.49%
Above-average candle volume, performance	6.75%	8.16%	−5.33%	−9.68%
Below-average candle volume, performance	7.20%	7.45%	−5.74%	−10.84%
Heavy breakout volume, performance	7.78%	9.41%	−5.92%	−12.00%
Light breakout volume, performance	6.22%	5.27%	−5.30%	−7.51%

is downward. Keep an eye on the primary trend, and if the breakout is in the direction of that trend, then it's more likely to be a lasting one.

I split trading tactics into two basic studies, one concerning reversal rates and the other concerning performance. Of the two, reversal rates are more important, because it's better to trade in the direction of the trend and let price run as far as it can.

Table 67.5 gives tips to find the trend direction.

Confirmation reversal rates. If you wait for price to close higher a day after the bullish meeting lines pattern ends, then the chances improve to 80% that price will break out upward. That's quite an improvement over the current 56% rate when you blindly buy into a bullish meeting lines candle.

Table 67.5
Reversal Rates

Description	Bull Market	Bear Market
Closing price confirmation reversal rate	80%	69%
Candle color confirmation reversal rate	75%	64%
Opening gap confirmation reversal rate	64%	65%
Reversal: trend down, breakout up	56%	48%
Continuation: trend down, breakout down	44%	52%
Percentage of reversals (R)/continuations (C) for each 12-month low (L), middle (M), or high (H)	L 48% R/52% C, M 55% R/45% C, H 66% R/34% C	L 43% R/57% C, M 53% R/47% C, H 53% R/47% C

Table 67.6
Performance Indicators

Description	Bull Market, Up Breakout	Bear Market, Up Breakout	Bull Market, Down Breakout	Bear Market, Down Breakout
Closing price confirmation, performance	7.35%	11.02%	N/A	N/A
Candle color confirmation, performance	7.61%	10.69%	N/A	N/A
Opening gap confirmation, performance	7.93%	11.63%	N/A	N/A
Breakout above 50-day moving average, performance	6.78%	7.28%	−4.77%	−4.66%
Breakout below 50-day moving average, performance	7.23%	8.30%	−5.75%	−10.88%
Last candle: close in highest third, performance	6.83%	7.22%	−5.48%	−11.16%
Last candle: close in middle third, performance	7.58%	9.12%	−5.90%	−8.73%
Last candle: close in lowest third, performance	5.64%	12.23%	−4.46%*	−6.84%*

N/A means not applicable.
*Fewer than 30 samples.

Reversal, continuation rates. The trend leading to the meeting lines candle does little to help predict the breakout direction. In a bull market, expect a reversal. In a bear market, look for a continuation, but don't be surprised in either market if the breakout direction appears random.

Yearly range reversals. In a bull market, reversals occur most often within a third of the yearly high. In a bear market, continuations rule the lower third of the yearly price range but by only a slight advantage.

Table 67.6 shows performance indicators that can give hints as to how your stock will behave after the breakout from this candle pattern.

Confirmation, performance. The opening gap confirmation method leads to the best performance. That means you buy the stock if price gaps open upward a day after the bullish meeting lines candle ends.

Moving average. Postbreakout performance is highest when the breakout is below the 50-day moving average.

Closing position. When price closes in the middle of the last candle line in the pattern, performance improves in a bull market, regardless of the breakout direction. The bear market shows inconsistent results.

Figure 67.2 After a bullish meeting lines pattern, price forms a tall white candle to punch through overhead resistance.

Sample Trade

Figure 67.2 shows the trading setup Peter faced. He saw the bullish meeting lines candle pattern form the day before point A, and then he went to work. He drew an up-sloping trendline along the bottom at E and F, then saw the flat top. Along this top, he drew line D, a long trendline that cut through price. Together, they formed an ascending triangle that suggested an upward breakout. Unfortunately, that chart pattern is not the most reliable—price often climbs 10% or so and then tumbles. With the meeting lines suggesting a reversal, the combination might do the trick for a lasting and profitable trade.

He looked back at June and saw the same pattern, an ascending triangle formed by line BC on the bottom and D on the top. This is an example of the triangle accurately forecasting an upward breakout but then price failing to follow through. Admittedly, a 50-cent move in a $4 stock is nothing to sneeze at, but Peter wanted more.

Nevertheless, past performance is a good clue to future trends. When price formed a tall white candle the day after the meeting lines, he bought the stock at the open the following day. You can see what price did after that. Peter needed a forklift to carry his profits to the bank.

For Best Performance

The following list offers tips and observations to help choose candles that perform well. Consult the associated table for more information.

- Use the identification guidelines to help select the pattern—Table 67.1.
- Candles within a third of the yearly low perform best—Table 67.2.
- Select tall candles—Table 67.3.
- Use the measure rule to predict a price target—Table 67.3.
- Candles with tall shadows usually perform well—Table 67.3.
- Volume gives performance clues—Table 67.4.
- Trade in the direction of the breakout, especially if it agrees with the primary trend direction—Trading Tactics discussion.
- A higher close the day after the meeting lines suggests a reversal 80% of the time in a bull market—Table 67.5.
- Patterns within a third of the yearly high in a bull market tend to act as reversals most often—Table 67.5.
- Opening gap confirmation works best—Table 67.6.
- Breakouts below the 50-day moving average lead to the best performance—Table 67.6.

68

Morning Doji Star

Behavior and Rank

Theoretical: Bullish reversal.

Actual bull market: Bullish reversal 76% of the time (ranking 8).

Actual bear market: Bullish reversal 71% of the time (ranking 13).

Frequency: 78th out of 103.

Overall performance over time: 25th out of 103.

When I saw the 76% reversal rate, I said, "Finally! A candle pattern that works!" However, you have to be careful to trade it under favorable circumstances because the gains over time may not be as impressive as you hope.

The frequency rank is 78th out of 103 candles, where 1 is best, so this one is difficult to find. It's not needle-in-the-haystack difficult, but more like finding a mouse hiding in the garage. You just remove everything that doesn't look like a mouse.

Overall performance is quite good (25) but it varies with the breakout direction. Downward breakouts, for example, perform better than do upward ones.

The psychology behind the pattern is a rainbow transition from bear to bull. Price trends downward leading to the candle, and the bears think they died and went to heaven.

A tall black candle prints on the chart, but change is in the wind. The next day the bears try to force price lower, but at day's end it closes where it began, forming a doji.

The bulls rub their hooves together with glee, knowing that their time has come. The next day, they run out charging at the bears and frighten them off. A tall white candle completes the transition from bearish downtrend to bullish uptrend. Those traders who wait another day for a confirming close will see a reversal 93% of the time in a bull market.

Identification Guidelines

Figure 68.1 shows a good example of a morning doji star candle pattern. Price moves horizontally to A before resuming the downtrend that began in October 2001 at a price of nearly 42 (not shown). Price drops to the doji at B, one that sports a long lower shadow, suggesting the worst is behind it. That's the case when price rebounds the next day and completes the three-day morning doji star with a tall white candle. A higher open, white candle, and higher close all confirm the reversal a day later. Price climbs after that.

Table 68.1 lists identification guidelines. There is some confusion about the configuration of the morning doji star. None of the sources I checked require tall bodies in their recognition rules, but the figures that accompany

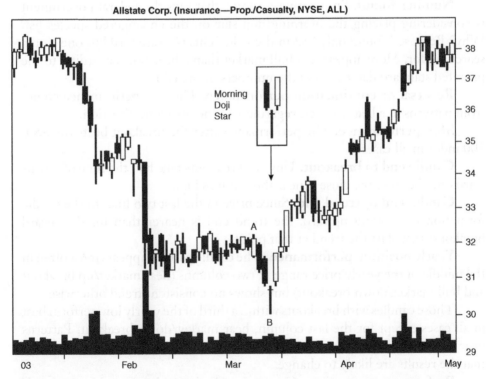

Figure 68.1 The morning doji star acts as a reversal most often, as in this example.

Table 68.1
Identification Guidelines

Characteristic	Discussion
Number of candle lines	Three.
Price trend	Downward leading to the start of the candle pattern.
First day	A tall black candle.
Second day	A doji whose body gaps below the prior body.
Third day	A tall white candle whose body remains above the doji's body.

their descriptions all show tall candles. I allow any doji as the middle candle, whether it has shadows that stretch to Pluto or not. The doji shadow length is what separates this candle from others, such as an abandoned baby (which has no overlapping shadows). The pattern performs quite well as I have defined it.

Statistics

Table 68.2 shows general statistics.

Number found. I'm starting a rumor that says the federal government is considering placing the morning doji star on the endangered species list. Why? Because I found only 932 in the wild. This is a rare bird but one worth searching for. More appear in a bull market than a bear one, according to the prorated standard database and the numbers in the table.

Reversal or continuation performance. The best performance comes from patterns in a bear market, regardless of the breakout direction.

S&P performance. The performance after the breakout beats the S&P 500 index in all cases.

Candle end to breakout. Upward breakouts take half the time of downward ones because the close is near the candle's high.

Candle end to trend end. Since price in the last two lines of the candle formation is trending upward, the trend end is nearer than for downward breakouts that start the trend at that point.

Yearly position, performance. The candle pattern appears most often in the middle of the yearly price range in two columns (bear market/up breakout and bull market/down breakout) but shows no consistent trend otherwise.

Those candles with breakouts within a third of the yearly low perform best in all cases except for the last column, bear market/down breakout. Patterns near the yearly high do best in that situation, but samples are few, meaning that the results are likely to change.

Performance over time. Comparing the large rise posted for reversal/continuation performance (the second row in the table) with the performance after 10 days suggests that the road is a risky one. In a bull market with an

Table 68.2
General Statistics

Description	Bull Market, Up Breakout	Bear Market, Up Breakout	Bull Market, Down Breakout	Bear Market, Down Breakout
Number found	619	82	198	33
Reversal (R), continuation (C) performance	6.32% R	8.69% R	−4.46% C	−10.08% C
Standard & Poor's 500 change	1.24%	0.91%	−0.76%	−4.85%
Candle end to breakout (median, days)	3	3	7	6
Candle end to trend end (median, days)	6	7	9	8
Number of breakouts near the 12-month low (L), middle (M), or high (H)	L 142, M 163, H 245	L 23, M 35, H 24	L 54, M 62, H 50	L 15, M 12, H 6
Percentage move for each 12-month period	L 6.55%, M 5.84%, H 6.45%	L 14.89%, M 5.84%, H 9.20%	L −5.31%, M −3.61%, H −5.15%	L −9.93%, M −7.17%, H −13.11%
Candle end + 1 day	0.77%	0.82%	−1.18%	−1.58%
Candle end + 3 days	1.57%	2.20%	−2.86%	−5.11%
Candle end + 5 days	1.87%	2.37%	−3.27%	−5.74%
Candle end + 10 days	2.10%	2.97%	−3.49%	−6.25%
10-day performance rank	79	55	27	15

upward breakout, the *average* (not the median) time to the trend end is nine days and the average rise over that span is 6.32%. That's if every trader exits at the trend high and buys in at the breakout price (the highest high in the pattern)—a perfect trade. The snapshot of price after 10 days, an average, shows less substantial results, 2.10%. Think of the results as the difference between a perfect swing trader and one who buys and holds for 10 days every time.

The good news is that price increases in every holding period, from 1 to 10 days. The bad news is that the results could be much better, especially for upward breakouts. The performance ranks of 79 and 55 confirm this. The ranks are much better for downward breakouts (27 and 15, where 1 is best out of 103 candles).

Table 68.3 shows height statistics.

Candle height. Tall patterns outperform short ones except for the low-sample-count bear market/down breakout category. To determine whether the candle is short or tall, compute its height from highest high to lowest low price in the candle pattern and divide by the breakout price. If the result is higher than the median, then you have a tall candle; otherwise it's short.

Table 68.3
Height Statistics

Description	Bull Market, Up Breakout	Bear Market, Up Breakout	Bull Market, Down Breakout	Bear Market, Down Breakout
Median candle height as a percentage of breakout price	4.78%	6.55%	5.07%	8.30%
Short candle, performance	5.10%	8.80%	−4.05%	−10.36%*
Tall candle, performance	8.18%	8.49%	−5.16%	−9.69%*
Percentage meeting price target (measure rule)	49%	44%	41%	42%
Median upper shadow as a percentage of breakout price	0.20%	0.26%	0.16%	1.12%
Short upper shadow, performance	6.59%	8.49%	−5.30%	−7.25%*
Tall upper shadow, performance	6.09%	8.84%	−3.74%	−12.96%*
Median lower shadow as a percentage of breakout price	0.17%	0.23%	0.16%	0.25%
Short lower shadow, performance	6.23%	9.13%	−4.45%	−7.64%*
Tall lower shadow, performance	6.41%	8.22%	−4.47%	−13.04%*

*Fewer than 30 samples.

For example, if Johnson has a morning doji star with a high of 37 and a low of 35, is the candle short or tall? The height is 37 − 35, or 2, so the measure would be (assume an upward breakout in a bull market) 2/37, or 5.4%; the candle is tall.

Measure rule. Use the measure rule to help predict how far price will rise or fall. Compute the height of the candle pattern and multiply it by the appropriate percentage shown in the table; then apply it to the breakout price.

For Johnson's candle, what are the target prices? The upward breakout target would be (2 × 49%) + 37, or 37.98, and the downward breakout target would be 35 − (2 × 41%), or 34.18.

Notice how low the hit rates are. This suggests the performance of the morning doji star is, shall we say, lousy. Trade only tall candles to boost your chances of a profitable pattern.

Shadows. The table's results pertain to the last candle line in the pattern. To determine whether the shadow is short or tall, compute the height of the shadow and divide by the breakout price. Compare the result to the median in the table. Tall shadows have a percentage higher than the median.

Upper shadow performance. Upper shadow performance tracks market conditions. By that I mean price in bull markets does best with candles showing short upper shadows, and price in bear markets does better with candles showing tall upper shadows.

Table 68.4
Volume Statistics

Description	Bull Market, Up Breakout	Bear Market, Up Breakout	Bull Market, Down Breakout	Bear Market, Down Breakout*
Rising candle volume, performance	6.16%	8.22%	−5.03%	−9.41%
Falling candle volume, performance	6.57%	9.33%	−3.93%	−10.98%
Above-average candle volume, performance	6.31%	11.10%	−3.73%	−8.25%
Below-average candle volume, performance	6.34%	7.29%	−5.16%	−12.01%
Heavy breakout volume, performance	7.30%	9.30%	−5.61%	−9.93%
Light breakout volume, performance	5.38%	8.14%	−3.39%	−10.28%

*Fewer than 30 samples.

Lower shadow performance. Tall lower shadows lead to the best post-breakout performance in all cases except bear market/up breakouts, which do better with short lower shadows.

Table 68.4 shows volume statistics.

Candle volume trend. A falling volume trend works best for this candle pattern most often. The exception is bull market/down breakouts, which do better after rising volume.

Average candle volume. Below-average candle volume results in the best postbreakout performance in all cases except bear market/up breakouts, which do better if volume is above average.

Breakout volume. Heavy breakout volume leads to the best performance in all cases except for the low sample count column, bear market/down breakout.

Trading Tactics

I examined this pattern closely to uncover how well it worked. Figure 68.2 shows a scenario I find compelling. Price rises, retraces, forms the morning doji star, and then rises again. This rise-retrace setup often leads to profitable moves.

The figure shows the primary trend is up. What you want to avoid is a morning doji star appearing when the primary price trend is down. Those candle patterns tend to either break out downward or break out upward and then reverse soon after.

The rise-retrace pattern shown in Figure 68.2 doesn't always work, either. When trading the morning doji star pattern, look for underlying support that

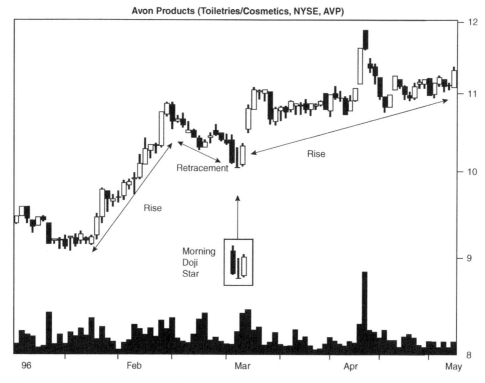

Avon Products (Toiletries/Cosmetics, NYSE, AVP)

Figure 68.2 The morning doji star works best when the primary trend is rising.

might cause price to reverse. Sometimes this comes in the form of a Fibonacci retracement of the uptrend where price stops at 38%, 50%, or 62% of the prior up move. When that occurs, the setup offers a good location to enter a trade. At other times, horizontal price movement beneath the morning doji star helps support price, as do prior peaks and valleys topping out or bottoming near the doji's price.

If no nearby support exists, then it may be best to wait for confirmation. You'll be giving up profit by doing so, but this increases your chances of finding a reversal that works.

I split trading tactics into two basic studies, one concerning reversal rates and the other concerning performance. Of the two, reversal rates are more important, because it's better to trade in the direction of the trend and let price run as far as it can.

Table 68.5 gives tips to find the trend direction.

Confirmation reversal rates. If you wait for price to close higher the day after a morning doji star, you can boost the reversal rate to over 90%. That's not saying much, though, because price is near the pattern's high when the candle formation ends, and a higher close might just seal the deal. If price closes above the high, then the candle pattern is a reversal. Waiting a day for confirmation means less profit.

Reversal, continuation rates. Most patterns break out upward.

Table 68.5
Reversal Rates

Description	Bull Market	Bear Market
Closing price confirmation reversal rate	93%	91%
Candle color confirmation reversal rate	89%	85%
Opening gap confirmation reversal rate	84%	71%
Reversal: trend down, breakout up	76%	71%
Continuation: trend down, breakout down	24%	29%
Percentage of reversals (R)/continuations (C) for each 12-month low (L), middle (M), or high (H)	L 72% R/28% C, M 72% R/28% C, H 83% R/17% C	L* 61% R/39% C, M* 74% R/26% C, H* 80% R/20% C

*Fewer than 30 samples.

Yearly range reversals. A morning doji star within a third of the yearly high works as a reversal at least 80% of the time. These probably fall into the rise-retrace pattern I described at the start of the Trading Tactics section.

Table 68.6 shows performance indicators that can give hints as to how your stock will behave after the breakout from this candle pattern.

Table 68.6
Performance Indicators

Description	Bull Market, Up Breakout	Bear Market, Up Breakout	Bull Market, Down Breakout	Bear Market, Down Breakout
Closing price confirmation, performance	5.70%	9.09%	N/A	N/A
Candle color confirmation, performance	5.59%	9.34%	N/A	N/A
Opening gap confirmation, performance	6.74%	11.56%	N/A	N/A
Breakout above 50-day moving average, performance	6.54%	8.44%	−4.38%	−8.41%*
Breakout below 50-day moving average, performance	5.95%	9.19%	−4.44%	−10.24%
Last candle: close in highest third, performance	6.35%	7.59%	−4.73%	−9.11%*
Last candle: close in middle third, performance	6.07%	13.48%*	−2.91%*	−11.70%*
Last candle: close in lowest third, performance	0.00%*	27.98%*	−3.64%*	0.00%*

N/A means not applicable.
*Fewer than 30 samples.

Confirmation, performance. Opening gap confirmation is the best trading signal. That's when you trade only if price gaps open higher the day after the morning doji star ends.

Moving average. Postbreakout performance is best when the breakout is below the 50-day moving average. The exception to this is in a bull market/up breakout condition, where price above the moving average leads to better performance.

Closing position. I only show these results for completeness. The samples are too few to provide meaningful information.

Sample Trade

Figure 68.3 shows the trading setup that confronted Johnson. Price trended downward to A and bounced to C, then fell back to B. The doji at B marked a pivot point that allowed price to change directions. Support at A, forming an unconfirmed double bottom, added to the likelihood of a price reversal.

A day later, the white candle completed the morning doji star and Johnson bought the stock at the open the next day. With support at A and a morning doji star pattern, Johnson thought that the risk of a loss was much less than the chance of a winning trade.

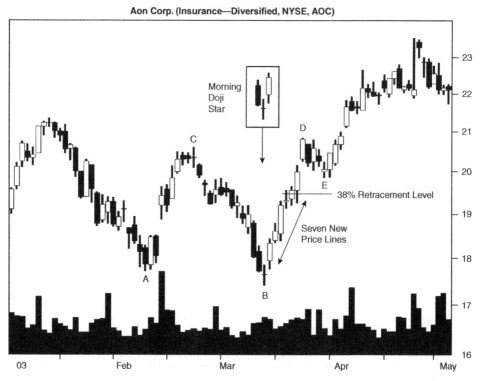

Figure 68.3   A morning doji star finds support and leads to a strong up move.

Price climbed, forming seven consecutively higher highs, one short of an eight new price lines candle pattern, but a strong up move nevertheless. Price topped out at D, close to the price of peak C and near the January peak. Johnson expected overhead resistance set up by these two peaks to stall price, and that's what happened. He was gratified that the retracement from D to E of the move up from B to D fell short of the 38% retracement level. That should mean an especially powerful upturn, so he decided to hold the stock and ride price higher.

For Best Performance

The following list offers tips and observations to help choose candles that perform well. Consult the associated table for more information.

- Use the identification guidelines to help select the pattern—Table 68.1.
- The pattern is a reliable performer over time, but you have to pick your setups—Table 68.2 and Trading Tactics discussion.
- Tall candles work best in most markets—Table 68.3.
- Use the measure rule to predict a price target—Table 68.3.
- Volume gives performance clues—Table 68.4.
- Waiting for price to close higher a day after the candle pattern ends boosts the reversal rate but likely hurts performance—Table 68.5.
- Patterns within a third of the yearly high tend to act as reversals most often—Table 68.5.
- Opening gap confirmation works best—Table 68.6.

69

Morning Star

Behavior and Rank

Theoretical: Bullish reversal.

Actual bull market: Bullish reversal 78% of the time (ranking 6).

Actual bear market: Bullish reversal 65% of the time (ranking 19).

Frequency: 66th out of 103.

Overall performance over time: 12th out of 103.

Even without waiting for confirmation the next day, the morning star is one of the better performers, showing a reversal rate of 78% of the time in a bull market. That's just a whisker better than the 76% reversal rate of the morning doji star.

The overall performance rank is excellent, too, at 12th out of 103 candles where 1 is best. However, much of this success comes from good numbers after a downward breakout.

The morning star is a visual representation of the change from bearish to bullish trend. Price moves lower leading to the start of the candle pattern, forced lower by bearish selling. A tall black candle prints on the chart and the bears know that more downside is in store. The next day, however, a small candle appears (called the star). It can be either black or white, and it's a clue to the trend change. Bears are scratching their heads trying to understand what happened, and bulls are licking their chops. The next day the bulls charge and scare away the bears, leaving a tall white candle to print on the chart.

A. C. Moore Arts & Crafts (Retail—Special Lines, NASDAQ, ACMR)

Figure 69.1   A morning star acts as a reversal pattern most often.

Identification Guidelines

Figure 69.1 shows a morning star candlestick pattern. This one appears after an extended retracement of an upward price trend. Two black candles show, followed by a tall white one. The middle candle, the star of the pattern, sports a tall lower shadow, signaling that the bullish buying demand successfully fought off bearish selling pressure.

Table 69.1 lists identification guidelines. The morning star is a tricky candlestick. The first day is a long black candle followed by a small candle of any color whose body remains below the two candles that surround it. Ignore the shadows in this candlestick pattern. The last day has a body that gaps higher, and I require that price must close at least midway into the black body of the first day, but price can open and close much higher. In other words, the two bodies need not overlap, provided that the white body closes above the middle of the first day.

Statistics

Table 69.2 shows general statistics.

Table 69.1
Identification Guidelines

Characteristic	Discussion
Number of candle lines	Three.
Price trend	Downward leading to the start of the candle pattern.
First day	A tall black candle.
Second day	A small-bodied candle that gaps lower from the prior body. The color can be either black or white.
Third day	A tall white candle that gaps above the body of the second day and closes at least midway into the black body of the first day.

Number found. I found 1,192 morning star patterns. Prorating the standard database shows that this pattern appears more often in a bear market.

Reversal or continuation performance. Morning star patterns perform best in a bear market.

S&P performance. The S&P 500 index does exceedingly well in a bear market, but it still isn't good enough to beat the morning star.

Table 69.2
General Statistics

Description	Bull Market, Up Breakout	Bear Market, Up Breakout	Bull Market, Down Breakout	Bear Market, Down Breakout
Number found	686	209	189	108
Reversal (R), continuation (C) performance	7.08% R	9.46% R	−5.90% C	−11.83% C
Standard & Poor's 500 change	1.62%	1.35%	−1.30%	−5.46%
Candle end to breakout (median, days)	3	2	7	7
Candle end to trend end (median, days)	7	7	9	11
Number of breakouts near the 12-month low (L), middle (M), or high (H)	L 130, M 174, H 322	L 66, M 76, H 63	L 55, M 73, H 57	L 52, M 38, H 15
Percentage move for each 12-month period	L 8.71%, M 7.07%, H 6.59%	L 15.44%, M 8.42%, H 6.85%	L −6.54%, M −6.25%, H −5.20%	L −13.96%, M −11.02%, H −7.99%
Candle end + 1 day	0.56%	1.31%	−1.78%	−2.66%
Candle end + 3 days	1.31%	1.55%	−3.11%	−5.56%
Candle end + 5 days	1.57%	2.02%	−3.98%	−6.86%
Candle end + 10 days	2.33%	1.69%	−4.23%	−8.53%
10-day performance rank	75	77	12	3

Candle end to breakout. Upward breakouts take substantially less time to break out than do downward ones. This is because price closes near the high of the candle.

Candle end to trend end. Upward breakouts also take less time to reach the trend end. This is because price reverses at the star, giving price a head start to the trend end. Downward breakouts would have to work through the tall pattern to reach the trend end. That takes longer.

Yearly position, performance. Since samples are few in this candle pattern, no consistent trend appears as to where the candle shows within the yearly price range. However, performance is best if the morning star has a breakout within a third of the yearly low.

Performance over time. The candle is a reliable performer over time except for weakness shown during days 5 to 10 in the bear market/up breakout category. Thus, the morning star is not as robust a performer as other candle types. Based on the performance rank, the pattern does best after a downward breakout, not an upward one. A downward breakout would mean a continuation of the downward price trend.

Table 69.3 shows height statistics.

Candle height. Tall candles outperform. To determine whether the candle is short or tall, compute its height from highest high to lowest low price in the candle pattern and divide by the breakout price. If the result is higher than the median, then you have a tall candle; otherwise it's short.

Table 69.3
Height Statistics

Description	Bull Market, Up Breakout	Bear Market, Up Breakout	Bull Market, Down Breakout	Bear Market, Down Breakout
Median candle height as a percentage of breakout price	5.67%	8.13%	5.53%	9.31%
Short candle, performance	4.78%	6.16%	−4.23%	−9.52%
Tall candle, performance	10.25%	13.02%	−8.51%	−15.09%
Percentage meeting price target (measure rule)	48%	49%	35%	42%
Median upper shadow as a percentage of breakout price	0.36%	0.60%	0.44%	0.68%
Short upper shadow, performance	6.24%	7.15%	−4.99%	−13.85%
Tall upper shadow, performance	7.96%	11.71%	−6.83%	−9.87%
Median lower shadow as a percentage of breakout price	0.31%	0.32%	0.36%	0.50%
Short lower shadow, performance	6.05%	8.56%	−5.47%	−9.36%
Tall lower shadow, performance	8.46%	10.42%	−6.33%	−14.87%

For example, suppose Susan finds a morning star with a high price of 37 and a low of 34. Is the candle short or tall? The height is 37 – 34, or 3, so the measure for a bull market/up breakout would be 3/37, or 8.10%, making this a tall candle (but in a bear market it would be short).

Measure rule. Use the measure rule to help predict how far price will rise or fall. Compute the height of the candle pattern and multiply it by the appropriate percentage shown in the table; then apply it to the breakout price.

What are Susan's price targets? The upward breakout target would be (3 × 48%) + 37, or 38.44, and the downward breakout target would be 34 – (3 × 35%), or 32.95.

Notice that the measure rule percentages are all less than 50%. That means price has difficulty moving too far beyond the breakout.

Shadows. The table's results pertain to the last candle line in the pattern. To determine whether the shadow is short or tall, compute the height of the shadow and divide by the breakout price. Compare the result to the median in the table. Tall shadows have a percentage higher than the median.

Upper shadow performance. Tall upper shadows result in the best performance in all cases except for bear market/down breakouts. Those do better with short shadows.

Lower shadow performance. Tall lower shadows result in the best performance under all market conditions and breakout directions.

Table 69.4 shows volume statistics.

Candle volume trend. Rising candle volume works best for bull markets, and falling candle volume leads to better performance in bear markets.

Average candle volume. Heavy volume in the candle means better post-breakout performance across the board.

Breakout volume. Heavy breakout volume also suggests good post-breakout performance in all categories except for bear market/down breakouts.

Table 69.4
Volume Statistics

Description	Bull Market, Up Breakout	Bear Market, Up Breakout	Bull Market, Down Breakout	Bear Market, Down Breakout
Rising candle volume, performance	7.43%	9.15%	−6.45%	−10.53%
Falling candle volume, performance	6.53%	9.89%	−5.35%	−12.85%
Above-average candle volume, performance	7.29%	9.62%	−6.90%	−12.04%
Below-average candle volume, performance	6.79%	9.20%	−4.86%	−11.67%
Heavy breakout volume, performance	7.81%	10.05%	−6.55%	−11.43%
Light breakout volume, performance	6.27%	8.90%	−4.87%	−12.84%

Figure 69.2 A morning star appears at the end of a retracement of an upward trend.

Trading Tactics

Figure 69.2 shows the ideal trading setup for the morning star candle. Look for the primary price trend to be upward; then price retraces a portion of the prior rise. Search for a retracement of 38%, 50%, or 62% before a morning star appears. If it does appear at one of those retracement values, then a reversal is more likely. Other underlying support might also lead to a price rebound, so be sure to check for prior peaks, valleys, or other excuses near the bottom of the morning star that might cause price to reverse.

If price is in one of the rise-retrace patterns but breaks out downward, then there's a decent chance that it will rebound within a week. If it doesn't, then close out your position; or if the down move is strong, then exit quickly.

Avoid depending on morning star candles to reverse a primary downtrend. They usually don't, and you'll get burned hoping they will. Price may break out upward, but the move higher is likely to be short-lived.

I split trading tactics into two basic studies, one concerning reversal rates and the other concerning performance. Of the two, reversal rates are more important, because it's better to trade in the direction of the trend and let price run as far as it can.

Table 69.5
Reversal Rates

Description	Bull Market	Bear Market
Closing price confirmation reversal rate	92%	92%
Candle color confirmation reversal rate	91%	86%
Opening gap confirmation reversal rate	85%	75%
Reversal: trend down, breakout up	78%	66%
Continuation: trend down, breakout down	22%	34%
Percentage of reversals (R)/continuations (C) for each 12-month low (L), middle (M), or high (H)	L 70% R/30% C, M 70% R/30% C, H 85% R/15% C	L 56% R/44% C, M 67% R/33% C, H 81% R/19% C

Table 69.5 gives tips to find the trend direction.

Confirmation reversal rates. Waiting for price to close higher the day after the morning star boosts the reversal rate to over 90%. That's not saying much, though, because price is so close to the top of the candle anyway that with only a little shove it closes above the top of the candle, resulting in a confirmed reversal. Delaying buying by a day can be costly. With a 75% reversal rate, find a rise-retrace setup as described earlier in the Trading Tactics section and consider buying in without waiting for a confirming close. It is more risky than waiting for confirmation, but it will get you in sooner and that tends to boost profits.

Reversal, continuation rates. Upward breakouts rule.

Yearly range reversals. Price reverses most often when the breakout is within a third of the yearly high.

Table 69.6 shows performance indicators that can give hints as to how your stock will behave after the breakout from this candle pattern.

Confirmation, performance. The opening gap method leads to the best performance. That means buying the stock only if price gaps open higher the next day.

Moving average. Candles with breakouts below the 50-day moving average tend to perform better after the breakout.

Closing position. Few morning stars have closes near the intraday low on the last line of the candle. When price closes within a third of the intraday high, price tends to perform better. The lone exception to this is from candles in the bear market/down breakout category. Those do best when the close is in the middle of the day's trading range.

Sample Trade

Susan was shopping for candle patterns and found a morning star on the chart shown in Figure 69.3. Price had been trending downward for three and a

Table 69.6
Performance Indicators

Description	Bull Market, Up Breakout	Bear Market, Up Breakout	Bull Market, Down Breakout	Bear Market, Down Breakout
Closing price confirmation, performance	6.49%	8.19%	N/A	N/A
Candle color confirmation, performance	6.28%	8.95%	N/A	N/A
Opening gap confirmation, performance	7.06%	12.16%	N/A	N/A
Breakout above 50-day moving average, performance	6.85%	7.06%	−5.27%	−9.51%*
Breakout below 50-day moving average, performance	7.43%	11.78%	−6.09%	−12.03%
Last candle: close in highest third, performance	7.42%	9.63%	−6.14%	−11.77%
Last candle: close in middle third, performance	4.25%	8.68%	−4.68%	−12.91%
Last candle: close in lowest third, performance	4.52%*	0.00%	0.00%	0.00%

N/A means not applicable.
*Fewer than 30 samples.

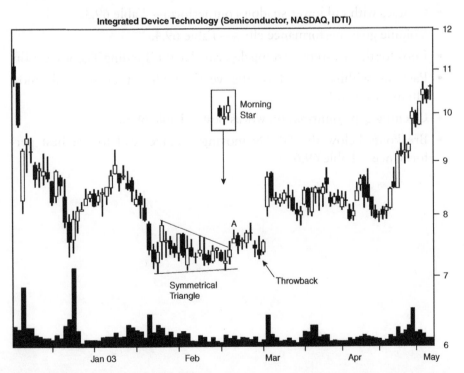

Figure 69.3 A morning star combined with a symmetrical triangle leads to a profitable trade.

half months from a high of 13 (a portion of the decline appears in the chart). Contemplating trading a morning star in a primary downtrend like this one is a risky endeavor, but she saw a unique setup.

When she first spotted the symmetrical triangle, her heart beat as it does when her new boyfriend calls. As price developed, she saw the morning star appear. She didn't wait for a higher close. Instead, she bought at the open the next day (A).

Price threw back (as it does 37% of the time for symmetrical triangle bottoms) before gapping upward. Then price moved horizontally from March to mid-April as if gathering strength for the next push up.

For Best Performance

The following list offers tips and observations to help choose candles that perform well. Consult the associated table for more information.

- Use the identification guidelines to help select the pattern—Table 69.1.
- Candles within a third of the yearly low perform best—Table 69.2.
- Select tall candles—Table 69.3.
- Use the measure rule to predict a price target—Table 69.3.
- Candles with tall lower shadows outperform—Table 69.3.
- Volume gives performance clues—Table 69.4.
- Look for the rise-retrace setup described in the Trading Tactics section.
- Patterns within a third of the yearly high act as reversals most often—Table 69.5.
- Opening gap confirmation works best—Table 69.6.
- Breakouts below the 50-day moving average lead to the best performance—Table 69.6.

70

On Neck

Behavior and Rank

Theoretical: Bearish continuation.

Actual bull market: Bearish continuation 56% of the time (ranking 29).

Actual bear market: Bearish continuation 58% of the time (ranking 25).

Frequency: 70th out of 103.

Overall performance over time: 33rd out of 103.

The on neck pattern is a continuation pattern but just barely—56% of the time it acts that way. If price closes above the top of this candle pattern, then close out any short position.

The pattern is somewhat rare, with a frequency rank of 70 out of 103 candles, where 1 is best. The overall performance is quite good, at 33. Much of that success comes after an upward breakout, meaning the candle acts as a reversal.

The psychology behind the pattern starts with the downward price trend leading to the candle. Bears force price lower, eventually forming a tall black candle. The next day price gaps lower still, and the bears are overjoyed, but the celebrations come too soon. By day's end, the stock closes at the price of the prior low. Despite the bullish enthusiasm shown by the white candle, the bulls are supposed to be disappointed because they didn't force a higher close. I'm not sure that's adequate justification for price continuing downward in the coming days, but that's what one source said. That tepid explanation mirrors the weak performance of the candle.

Identification Guidelines

Figure 70.1 shows what an on neck candle pattern looks like. Price forms a second peak on May 31 that is not far above the prior one. Failure of the stock to continue trending higher is bearish in many cases, including this one. Price tumbles.

During the descent, an on neck pattern appears right where you would expect to find support—at the level of the valley between the prior two peaks—accompanied by volume higher than in previous days. Support does not materialize, and the stock continues falling, eventually finding support near where it began the uphill climb.

Remember this chart, especially for climbs that are steeper (like a straight-line run-up). If price runs into trouble near the summit, it often hikes all the way back to base camp.

Table 70.1 lists identification guidelines. Look for a downward price trend leading to a tall black body. The next day, price gaps lower, forming a white candle with a close that matches the prior low.

I did not allow any variation between the closing price and the prior low, but I doubt that doing so would hurt performance much. If performance changed from dreadful to awful, would you notice?

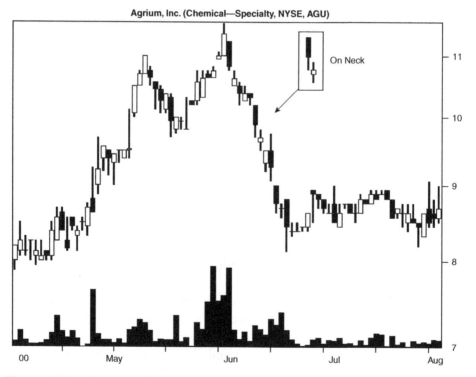

Figure 70.1   An on neck candlestick in a downward price trend leads to continued losses.

Table 70.1
Identification Guidelines

Characteristic	Discussion
Number of candle lines	Two.
Price trend	Downward leading to the start of the candle pattern.
First day	A tall black candle.
Second day	Price gaps lower but forms a white candle with a close that matches the prior low.

Statistics

Table 70.2 shows general statistics.

Number found. I found 2,881 patterns and probably should have allowed some play between the closing and the low prices shared between the two candles. That would have boosted the pattern count while still maintaining the

Table 70.2
General Statistics

Description	Bull Market, Up Breakout	Bear Market, Up Breakout	Bull Market, Down Breakout	Bear Market, Down Breakout
Number found	1,176	95	1,480	130
Reversal (R), continuation (C) performance	6.57% R	10.89% R	−6.11% C	−7.98% C
Standard & Poor's 500 change	1.69%	1.18%	−0.55%	−2.01%
Candle end to breakout (median, days)	5	6	4	4
Candle end to trend end (median, days)	9	12	6	7
Number of breakouts near the 12-month low (L), middle (M), or high (H)	L 295, M 319, H 412	L 32, M 31, H 28	L 509, M 435, H 342	L 70, M 46, H 12
Percentage move for each 12-month period	L 6.95%, M 6.60%, H 6.06%	L 12.08%, M 9.08%, H 9.56%	L −7.77%, M −5.49%, H −5.18%	L −10.04%, M −6.05%, H −7.52%
Candle end + 1 day	1.12%	2.30%	−0.74%	−0.09%
Candle end + 3 days	2.59%	3.32%	−1.67%	−0.60%
Candle end + 5 days	3.58%	5.35%	−2.00%	−2.51%
Candle end + 10 days	4.37%	8.32%	−2.25%	−2.46%
10-day performance rank	25	6	54	77

intent of the candle pattern. Nevertheless, the statistics are in their pure form, with close-low prices matching exactly.

Most on neck candles occur in a bull market.

Reversal or continuation performance. The bear market numbers show better performance than do their bull market cousins.

S&P performance. The S&P 500 index pales beside the candle's performance numbers.

Candle end to breakout. Downward breakouts take slightly less time than upward ones to reach the breakout. This is probably because of the existing downward trend. An upward breakout would be like swimming against the current—it takes longer to reach the other side of the river.

Candle end to trend end. Downward breakouts also take less time to reach the trend end, probably because the existing trend is well along. An upward breakout would *start* a new trend, placing the end that much farther away.

Yearly position, performance. The distribution of breakouts shows no consistent trend; however, those with breakouts within a third of the yearly low perform best.

Performance over time. The pattern is a reliable performer over time except for the bear market/down breakout category. In that category the period from 5 to 10 days shows weakness.

According to the performance rank, upward breakouts are what propel this candle to such a good showing. The 8.32% gain in 10 days is yummy (bear market/up breakouts).

Table 70.3 shows height statistics.

Candle height. Tall candles perform better than short ones in all cases. To determine whether the candle is short or tall, compute its height from highest high to lowest low price in the candle pattern and divide by the breakout price. If the result is higher than the median, then you have a tall candle; otherwise it's short.

For example, suppose Kirk sees an on neck candle with a high of 40 and a low of 38. Is the candle short or tall? The height is 40 − 38, or 2, so the measure would be 2/40, or 5%. In a bull market with an upward breakout, the candle is tall.

Measure rule. Use the measure rule to help predict how far price will rise or fall. Compute the height of the candle pattern and multiply it by the appropriate percentage shown in the table; then apply it to the breakout price.

What are Kirk's price targets? The upward breakout target would be $(2 \times 61\%) + 40$, or 41.22, and the downward target would be $38 − (2 \times 54\%)$, or 36.92.

Shadows. The table's results pertain to the last candle line in the pattern. To determine whether the shadow is short or tall, compute the height of the shadow and divide by the breakout price. Compare the result to the median in the table. Tall shadows have a percentage higher than the median.

Table 70.3
Height Statistics

Description	Bull Market, Up Breakout	Bear Market, Up Breakout	Bull Market, Down Breakout	Bear Market, Down Breakout
Median candle height as a percentage of breakout price	4.00%	5.92%	4.03%	5.57%
Short candle, performance	5.56%	9.21%	−5.51%	−7.60%
Tall candle, performance	8.01%	13.20%	−7.04%	−8.50%
Percentage meeting price target (measure rule)	61%	64%	54%	58%
Median upper shadow as a percentage of breakout price	0.42%	0.90%	0.52%	1.19%
Short upper shadow, performance	5.97%	8.86%	−5.60%	−8.47%
Tall upper shadow, performance	7.18%	13.46%	−6.63%	−7.51%
Median lower shadow as a percentage of breakout price	0.41%	0.68%	0.24%	0.56%
Short lower shadow, performance	5.77%	9.03%	−6.40%	−7.89%
Tall lower shadow, performance	7.32%	13.08%	−5.86%	−8.07%

Upper shadow performance. Tall upper shadows result in the best performance across the board except for bear market/down breakouts, where a short shadow does better.

Lower shadow performance. Tall lower shadows also work well in all cases except for bull market/down breakouts, where short ones perform better after the breakout.

Table 70.4 shows volume statistics.

Candle volume trend. Rising candle volume works well in a bull market, and falling volume works better in a bear market.

Average candle volume. Above-average candle volume works best when the breakout follows the market trend: bull market/up breakout and bear market/down breakout. Below-average volume works better for bear market/up breakout and bull market/down breakout conditions.

Breakout volume. Heavy breakout volume works across the board except for bear market/up breakouts, where light breakout volume means better postbreakout performance.

Trading Tactics

A review of the on neck candle pattern shows that if price closes above the candlestick's high, then a trader should cover any short position. Price is likely

Table 70.4
Volume Statistics

Description	Bull Market, Up Breakout	Bear Market, Up Breakout	Bull Market, Down Breakout	Bear Market, Down Breakout
Rising candle volume, performance	7.04%	10.68%	−6.39%	−6.78%
Falling candle volume, performance	5.96%	11.11%	−5.79%	−8.94%
Above-average candle volume, performance	6.61%	10.82%	−5.60%	−8.01%
Below-average candle volume, performance	6.54%	10.97%	−6.43%	−7.96%
Heavy breakout volume, performance	7.31%	8.14%	−6.42%	−8.22%
Light breakout volume, performance	5.86%	14.96%	−5.84%	−7.66%

to continue moving higher. Also, avoid trading the on neck pattern when the primary trend is upward. Even though price may be trending lower for a few days, the chances increase that any downward breakout will be short-lived.

I split trading tactics into two basic studies, one concerning reversal rates and the other concerning performance. Of the two, reversal rates are more important, because it's better to trade in the direction of the trend and let price run as far as it can. Table 70.5 shows reversal rates.

Reversal, continuation rates. Expect near-random performance from the on neck pattern but with a slight bias toward downward breakouts.

Yearly range reversals. Patterns that occur within a third of the yearly low act as continuations between 63% (bull market) and 69% (bear market) of the time.

Table 70.6 shows performance indicators that can give hints as to how your stock will behave after the breakout from this candle pattern.

Table 70.5
Reversal Rates

Description	Bull Market	Bear Market
Reversal: trend down, breakout up	44%	42%
Continuation: trend down, breakout down	56%	58%
Percentage of reversals (R)/continuations (C) for each 12-month low (L), middle (M), or high (H)	L 37% R/63% C, M 42% R/58% C, H 55% R/45% C	L 31% R/69% C, M 40% R/60% C, H* 70% R/30% C

*Fewer than 30 samples.

Table 70.6
Performance Indicators

Description	Bull Market, Up Breakout	Bear Market, Up Breakout	Bull Market, Down Breakout	Bear Market, Down Breakout
Closing price confirmation, performance	N/A	N/A	−6.58%	−9.57%
Candle color confirmation, performance	N/A	N/A	−6.85%	−10.20%
Opening gap confirmation, performance	N/A	N/A	−7.41%	−10.10%
Breakout above 50-day moving average, performance	6.34%	10.25%	−5.15%	−7.26%
Breakout below 50-day moving average, performance	6.65%	11.03%	−6.37%	−8.07%
Last candle: close in highest third, performance	6.68%	10.22%	−5.89%	−8.43%
Last candle: close in middle third, performance	6.65%	11.59%	−5.67%	−7.27%
Last candle: close in lowest third, performance	5.69%	11.60%*	−8.46%	−9.36%*

N/A means not applicable.
*Fewer than 30 samples.

Confirmation, performance. The opening gap method, where you wait for price to gap open lower the next day before taking a position, works well in a bull market. Bear markets do better with candle color confirmation. That's when you wait for a black candle to appear the next day before trading.

Moving average. Candles with breakouts below the 50-day moving average tend to perform better after the breakout than do those with breakouts above the average.

Closing position. Candles with the closing price near the intraday low on the last day of the candle pattern result in better performance. Since the candle is white, it must have a tall upper shadow to allow price to close within a third of the low. Anyway, this works best in all categories except bull market/up breakouts, which do better if price is near the candle's high.

Sample Trade

Kirk owns the stock shown in Figure 70.2. What should he do with it—sell, hold, or buy more?

Price finds support near 11 in mid-December and again in mid-January. A gathering of small candles—spinning tops and doji, mostly—speak of indecision as if the holiday partying has gotten carried away. Then a tall black candle

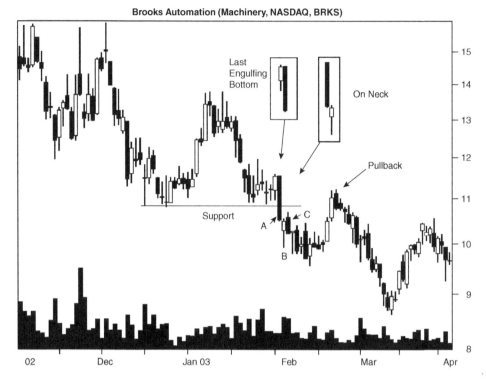

Figure 70.2 Price breaks support and forms an on neck pattern.

appears at A, piercing support. This forms what looks like a tweezers top, but the prices are uneven. It's a last engulfing bottom where the black candle body covers the white one during a downtrend, which is meager in this case.

The next day, a white candle forms (B) that closes at the prior low of candle A. This is the on neck candle, and it suggests a continuation of the downward plunge. This bearish expectation is confirmed by a lower close and a black candle the next day (C).

Price doesn't fall far over the next week, and then it recovers in a typical pullback to the support zone. This gives Kirk another opportunity to sell the stock at a decent price before the decline resumes.

Therefore, the answer to the question of sell, hold, or buy is to have a stop-loss order waiting to sell the stock if its price hits a penny below the support line. That would mean selling the stock during formation of the tall black candle at A.

For Best Performance

The following list offers tips and observations to help choose candles that perform well. Consult the associated table for more information.

- Use the identification guidelines to help select the pattern—Table 70.1.
- Candles within a third of the yearly low perform best—Table 70.2.
- Select tall candles—Table 70.3.
- Use the measure rule to predict a price target—Table 70.3.
- Many, but not all, candles with tall shadows outperform—Table 70.3.
- Volume gives performance clues—Table 70.4.
- Patterns within a third of the yearly low tend to act as continuations most often—Table 70.5.
- Opening gap confirmation works best in bull markets, and candle color excels in bear markets—Table 70.6.
- Breakouts below the 50-day moving average lead to the best performance—Table 70.6.

71

Piercing Pattern

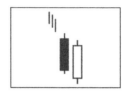

Behavior and Rank

Theoretical: Bullish reversal.

Actual bull market: Bullish reversal 64% of the time (ranking 21).

Actual bear market: Bullish reversal 60% of the time (ranking 28).

Frequency: 40th out of 103.

Overall performance over time: 13th out of 103.

Sometimes called the piercing line, I prefer piercing pattern because it is composed of two candle lines, not one. By itself, the piercing pattern does well by correctly predicting a reversal 64% of the time (bull market).

Overall performance is also exceptional: 13 out of 103 candles where 1 is best. However, downward breakouts are where this pattern shows its strength.

In the Identification Guidelines section, I describe how to recognize these candlesticks, but two of three sources I checked didn't say the first candle needed to be tall. If you require a tall black candle as the first line in the pattern, then the reversal rate climbs to 63.7% from 63%, but the number of candles that qualify drops nearly in half. Those are the combined rates for reversals in bull and bear markets.

Price trends downward leading to the start of the piercing candle, so the bears are in control. Then a black candle prints on the chart, reinforcing the bearish pressure. The next day opens with price gapping lower, below the low of yesterday's black candle. Then the bulls burst onto the scene and begin pressuring price upward. At day's end, a white candle remains and price closes above the midpoint of the prior black candle but below the top of the black candle's body. This endpoint is an arbitrary one to distinguish the piercing pattern from similar candles.

Identification Guidelines

Figure 71.1 shows one example of a piercing pattern. Price trends downward into the candle pattern and then forms a black candle followed by a white one. In this case, price continues lower after the candle ends but the breakout is still upward. A breakout occurs when price closes either above the top of the highest price in the candle formation or below the lowest low.

Table 71.1 lists identification guidelines. For a two-line formation, this is a complicated one. The guidelines are such to distinguish this from others such as the on neck, in neck, and thrusting patterns.

Look for a two-candle pattern with the first candle being a black one. I don't require a tall candle but one source I checked did and at least three sources I checked all showed a tall candle. Reversal performance is marginally better if the first candle is a tall black body.

Following the black candle is a white one. Price must open below the prior candle's low and close in the black body above the midpoint. That is,

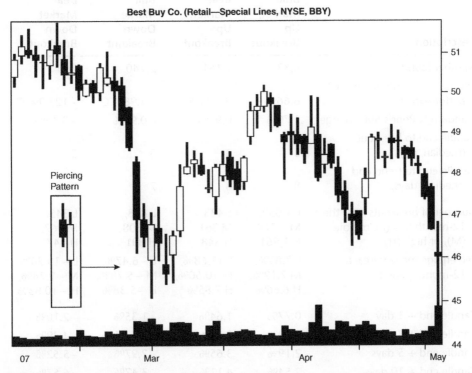

Figure 71.1   MSA piercing pattern appears near the end of a downtrend. Price reverses shortly afterward.

Table 71.1
Identification Guidelines

Characteristic	Discussion
Number of candle lines	Two.
Price trend	Downward leading to the start of the candle pattern.
First day	A black candle. Some require it to have a tall body, but I don't.
Second day	A white candle that opens below the prior candle's low and closes in the black body, between the midpoint and the open.

price must close below the black candle's open and above the black body's midpoint.

Statistics

Table 71.2 shows general statistics. I allowed both short and tall black candles as the first line of this pattern. Doing so penalized reversal performance from 63.7% to 63.0% but almost doubled the number of candles that qualified (5,390

Table 71.2
General Statistics

Description	Bull Market, Up Breakout	Bear Market, Up Breakout	Bull Market, Down Breakout	Bear Market, Down Breakout
Number found	4,831	1,151	2,740	766
Reversal (R), continuation (C) performance	6.66% R	9.88% R	−5.98% C	−12.09% C
Standard & Poor's 500 change	1.70%	0.99%	−0.94%	−3.46%
Candle end to breakout (median, days)	3	3	5	5
Candle end to trend end (median, days)	8	8	7	8
Number of breakouts near the 12-month low (L), middle (M), or high (H)	L 1,052, M 1,324, H 1,961	L 433, M 361, H 348	L 888, M 808, H 801	L 345, M 267, H 147
Percentage move for each 12-month period	L 7.83%, M 7.12%, H 6.66%	L 11.68%, M 10.50%, H 7.85%	L −6.47%, M −5.78%, H −5.38%	L −15.20%, M −9.74%, H −10.83%
Candle end + 1 day	0.77%	1.64%	−1.35%	−2.10%
Candle end + 3 days	1.70%	2.57%	−2.73%	−4.49%
Candle end + 5 days	2.19%	3.65%	−2.97%	−5.52%
Candle end + 10 days	2.54%	4.11%	−3.47%	−6.57%
10-day performance rank	66	44	28	13

changed to 9,488). I view the performance improvement as marginal, so I'm sticking with the guidelines suggested by the majority of sources I checked. Your candle may perform better or worse than those studied here. Remember that these statistics are best used to compare candle performance between themselves, not as indicators of how your candle will behave.

Number found. I found 9,488 candlestick patterns that obeyed the identification guidelines described in Table 71.1. Using a standard database to prorate the length of the bull and bear markets, this pattern appears most often in a bear market.

Reversal or continuation performance. The best performance comes from candles in a bear market, regardless of the breakout direction.

S&P performance. The piercing pattern outperforms the S&P 500 index over the same time periods.

Candle end to breakout. Upward breakouts take less time to close above the top of the pattern than downward breakouts take to close below the bottom. This makes sense because price is closer to the top of the pattern than it is to the bottom.

Candle end to trend end. The median time to the trend end is about eight days.

Yearly position, performance. Most of the time the piercing pattern appears within a third of the yearly low. The one exception occurs for patterns with upward breakouts in a bull market. They appear most often within a third of the yearly high. The best performance occurs when the candle has a breakout within a third of the yearly low.

Performance over time. The piercing pattern is a robust candle. By that, I mean performance improves over time for each of the measurement periods and in all categories. The bear market numbers beat their bull market counterparts.

The performance rank suggests that downward breakouts perform better than upward ones.

Table 71.3 shows height statistics.

Candle height. Tall candles outperform short ones. To determine whether the candle is short or tall, compute its height from highest high to lowest low price in the candle pattern and divide by the breakout price. If the result is higher than the median, then you have a tall candle; otherwise it's short.

For example, Grant sees a piercing pattern with a high at 73 and a low at 70. Is the candle short or tall? The height is 73 – 70, or 3, so the measure would be 3/73, or 4.1%. In a bull market with an upward breakout, the candle is tall.

Measure rule. Use the measure rule to help predict how far price will rise or fall. Compute the height of the candle pattern and multiply it by the appropriate percentage shown in the table; then apply it to the breakout price.

What are Grant's price targets? For upward breakouts, the target would be $(3 \times 67\%) + 73$, or 75.01, and the downward target would be $70 - (3 \times 61\%)$, or 68.17.

Table 71.3
Height Statistics

Description	Bull Market, Up Breakout	Bear Market, Up Breakout	Bull Market, Down Breakout	Bear Market, Down Breakout
Median candle height as a percentage of breakout price	3.44%	5.02%	3.35%	5.25%
Short candle, performance	5.13%	6.62%	−4.80%	−9.22%
Tall candle, performance	9.15%	13.65%	−7.62%	−15.54%
Percentage meeting price target (measure rule)	67%	64%	61%	62%
Median upper shadow as a percentage of breakout price	0.34%	0.58%	0.35%	0.66%
Short upper shadow, performance	5.64%	9.06%	−5.82%	−10.54%
Tall upper shadow, performance	7.86%	10.64%	−6.12%	−13.63%
Median lower shadow as a percentage of breakout price	0.24%	0.35%	0.11%	0.32%
Short lower shadow, performance	6.17%	8.72%	−5.72%	−10.98%
Tall lower shadow, performance	7.10%	11.10%	−6.17%	−13.16%

Shadows. The table's results pertain to the last candle line in the pattern. To determine whether the shadow is short or tall, compute the height of the shadow and divide by the breakout price. Compare the result to the median in the table. Tall shadows have a percentage higher than the median.

Candles with tall upper or lower shadows lead to better performance across the board.

Table 71.4 shows volume statistics.

Candle volume trend. Candles with a rising volume trend work well for upward breakouts. Downward breakouts do better with a falling volume trend in the two-day candle pattern.

Average candle volume. Above-average candle volume leads to the best postbreakout performance in all cases except bull market/down breakouts. Those do better with below-average volume.

Breakout volume. Heavy breakout volume leads to better performance in all categories.

Trading Tactics

If a piercing pattern occurs where the primary price trend is downward, then don't expect price to make a lasting reversal. Price might break out upward, but the forces pushing price lower over the longer term will tend to keep the rise short.

Table 71.4
Volume Statistics

Description	Bull Market, Up Breakout	Bear Market, Up Breakout	Bull Market, Down Breakout	Bear Market, Down Breakout
Rising candle volume, performance	7.37%	10.53%	−5.96%	−10.89%
Falling candle volume, performance	6.96%	8.81%	−6.00%	−13.69%
Above-average candle volume, performance	7.05%	10.69%	−5.67%	−13.27%
Below-average candle volume, performance	6.42%	9.19%	−6.17%	−11.08%
Heavy breakout volume, performance	7.87%	11.06%	−6.10%	−13.23%
Light breakout volume, performance	5.85%	8.85%	−5.86%	−10.70%

Many times you'll see piercing patterns occur as part of a retracement in an uptrend. Unfortunately, they sometimes appear too early in the retracement. Price breaks out upward and then tumbles, only to recover a few weeks later and then make a sustained recovery.

Look for a piercing pattern to show at 38%, 50%, or 62% retracements of the prior up move. Those points make for lasting turning points. As always, look for a support zone where the piercing pattern appears that might cause price to reverse.

I split trading tactics into two basic studies, one concerning reversal rates and the other concerning performance. Of the two, reversal rates are more important, because it's better to trade in the direction of the trend and let price run as far as it can.

Table 71.5 gives tips to find the trend direction.

Confirmation reversal rates. To confirm that a piercing pattern will act as a reversal, wait for a higher close the next day. That works between 85% and 87% of the time. The downside of waiting is you're giving up a portion of the profit. If you find a piercing pattern in a rise-retrace setup described earlier in this section (at one of the Fibonacci retracement turning points: 38%, 50%, or 62%) with underlying support, then use the opening gap method of entry. That means buying the stock if price gaps open higher the next day.

Reversal, continuation rates. Price breaks out upward most often.

Yearly range reversals. Those piercing patterns within a third of the yearly high act as reversals between 70% and 71% of the time.

Table 71.6 shows performance indicators that can give hints as to how your stock will behave after the breakout from this candle pattern.

Table 71.5
Reversal Rates

Description	Bull Market	Bear Market
Closing price confirmation reversal rate	87%	85%
Candle color confirmation reversal rate	84%	81%
Opening gap confirmation reversal rate	72%	70%
Reversal: trend down, breakout up	64%	60%
Continuation: trend down, breakout down	36%	40%
Percentage of reversals (R)/ continuations (C) for each 12-month low (L), middle (M), or high (H)	L 54% R/46% C, M 62% R/38% C, H 71% R/29% C	L 56% R/44% C, M 57% R/43% C, H 70% R/30% C

Confirmation, performance. Opening gap confirmation results in the best postbreakout performance. That means taking a position the next day only if price gaps open higher.

Moving average. Most of the time a piercing pattern with a breakout below the moving average leads to the best performance. The exception is bull market/up breakouts, which perform better when the breakout is above the moving average.

Table 71.6
Performance Indicators

Description	Bull Market, Up Breakout	Bear Market, Up Breakout	Bull Market, Down Breakout	Bear Market, Down Breakout
Closing price confirmation, performance	6.53%	10.65%	N/A	N/A
Candle color confirmation, performance	6.25%	10.56%	N/A	N/A
Opening gap confirmation, performance	7.60%	12.43%	N/A	N/A
Breakout above 50-day moving average, performance	6.92%	8.06%	−5.33%	−10.31%
Breakout below 50-day moving average, performance	6.34%	11.37%	−5.99%	−12.62%
Last candle: close in highest third, performance	6.57%	9.92%	−5.98%	−11.97%
Last candle: close in middle third, performance	7.19%	9.65%	−5.95%	−12.45%
Last candle: close in lowest third, performance	6.78%	10.37%	−6.07%	−23.58%

N/A means not applicable.
*Fewer than 30 samples.

Closing position. Piercing patterns that close in the lowest third of the last line in the candle result in the best postbreakout performance in all cases except one: bull market/up breakouts. Those do better when the close is in the middle of the intraday trading range.

Sample Trade

Figure 71.2 shows the trading setup that confronted Grant. Price reached a low at C at the end of March and then advanced to B before declining once more. He became interested in the stock when price neared the support line, shown as a horizontal line, CD.

At D, a piercing pattern appeared in the stock and that suggested price would reverse. He expected the stock to climb to the price of B. The uphill run would encompass a $10 rise, so he believed that price would have difficulty confirming a double bottom chart pattern. Thus, he decided to set a price target just below B.

The risk on the downside would be a drop below the support line, so a close below the low at C would work well. When price gapped open higher at A, he bought the stock.

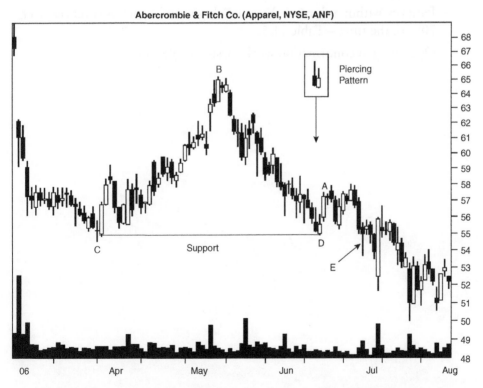

Figure 71.2 MSA piercing pattern appears in a downward price trend.

Price had difficulty sustaining the liftoff. The stock moved sideways for two weeks until hitting his stop at E, taking him out at a small loss. Sometimes stocks just don't cooperate, and you end with a losing trade, as in this case.

For Best Performance

The following list offers tips and observations to help choose candles that perform well. Consult the associated table for more information.

- Use the identification guidelines to help select the pattern—Table 71.1.
- Candles within a third of the yearly low perform best—Table 71.2.
- Select tall candles—Table 71.3.
- Use the measure rule to predict a price target—Table 71.3.
- Candles with tall shadows outperform—Table 71.3.
- Volume gives performance clues—Table 71.4.
- Avoid piercing patterns when the primary trend is downward—Trading Tactics discussion.
- Piercing patterns that form as part of a retracement in a downtrend may appear too early—Trading Tactics discussion.
- Patterns within a third of the yearly high tend to act as reversals over 70% of the time—Table 71.5.
- Opening gap confirmation works best—Table 71.6.

72

Rickshaw Man

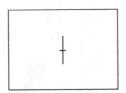

Behavior and Rank

Theoretical: Indecision.

Actual bull market: Continuation 51% of the time (ranking 47).

Actual bear market: Reversal 50% of the time (ranking 45).

Frequency: 55th out of 103.

Overall performance over time: 35th out of 103.

Yuck. Maybe a continuation rate of 51% should be expected with a doji with long shadows, but that's too close to random (50%) for my taste. That's what a rickshaw man is, a long-legged doji with a body in the middle of the candle. They say a rickshaw man is a candle speaking of indecision and they are correct. With behavior that's essentially random, why did they bother to name it? Perhaps there are tips to detect when this candle magically turns into a reversal. In that case, any pattern is worth a closer look.

The psychology behind the rickshaw man is all about where price begins and ends. Sometime during the day, bearish selling forces price down substantially but the bulls counterattack and push it back up to the open. A period of bullish enthusiasm occurs as well before being overcome by the bears. However, by the market close, the bulls and bears have called a truce. Price closes right where it began, ending near the middle of the candle. Stalemate. This candle says nothing about what's going to happen tomorrow.

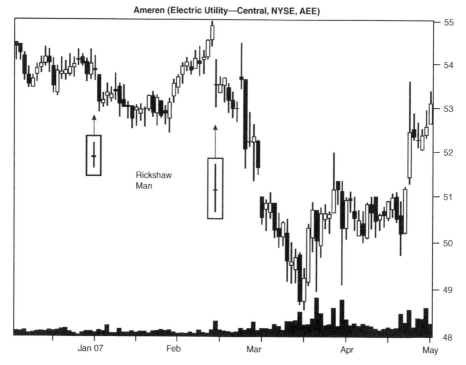

Figure 72.1 Two examples of the rickshaw man.

Identification Guidelines

Figure 72.1 shows two rickshaw man candles. The first one appears in the middle of a downward price trend. The second gaps down from price that peaks in February. Notice the body is located in the middle of a tall price line. The centering of the body is the only difference between a rickshaw man and a long-legged doji.

A rickshaw man is a long-legged doji, but a long-legged doji isn't necessarily a rickshaw man. If you understand that last sentence, then you're smarter than I am.

Table 72.1 lists identification guidelines. A doji candle is one in which the opening and closing prices are the same or nearly so. A rickshaw man is a doji

Table 72.1
Identification Guidelines

Characteristic	Discussion
Number of candle lines	One.
Configuration	A doji candle (open and close are the same price or nearly so) with the body near the middle of the candle and with exceptionally long shadows.

with exceptionally tall upper and lower shadows and with the body centered in the candle.

Statistics

Table 72.2 shows general statistics.

Number found. The rickshaw man is plentiful but not as abundant as fruit flies buzzing around an overripe banana. I uncovered 11,108 of them—rickshaw man candles, not fruit flies or bananas—most from a bull market.

Reversal or continuation performance. Reversals perform better after upward breakouts, and continuations do better after downward breakouts. The best performance comes from candles in a bear market.

S&P performance. The performance of the rickshaw man exceeds that of the S&P 500 index over the same time periods.

Candle end to breakout. It takes three or four days to break out. Bear markets take the shorter time.

Table 72.2
General Statistics

Description	Bull Market, Up Breakout	Bear Market, Up Breakout	Bull Market, Down Breakout	Bear Market, Down Breakout
Number found	5,352	394	4,963	399
Reversal (R), continuation (C) performance	6.34% C 6.93% R	8.75% C 10.28% R	−5.92% C −5.63% R	−10.14% C −9.16% R
Standard & Poor's 500 change	1.23%	0.49%	−0.56%	−2.56%
Candle end to breakout (median, days)	4	3	4	3
Candle end to trend end (median, days)	7	8	6	8
Number of breakouts near the 12-month low (L), middle (M), or high (H)	L 1,196, M 1,259, H 2,002	L 134, M 134, H 124	L 1,461, M 1,221, H 1,402	L 159, M 114, H 120
Percentage move for each 12-month period	L 8.26%, M 6.10%, H 6.12%	L 12.25%, M 9.76%, H 7.73%	L −6.93%, M −5.81%, H −4.96%	L −10.37%, M −10.90%, H −7.84%
Candle end + 1 day	1.19%	1.56%	−1.05%	−1.43%
Candle end + 3 days	2.21%	3.45%	−2.02%	−3.21%
Candle end + 5 days	2.75%	3.87%	−2.42%	−3.61%
Candle end + 10 days	3.58%	4.22%	−2.55%	−3.94%
10-day performance rank	44	43	46	52

Candle end to trend end. The median time to reach the trend end varies from six to eight days. The bull market takes less time to reach the trend end than does a bear market.

Yearly position, performance. Candles within a third of the yearly low occur most often (the lone exception: bull market/up breakouts). Performance is best near the yearly low except for candles in the middle third, which do best in bear market/down breakout conditions.

Performance over time. The rickshaw man is a robust performer over time, meaning that the returns increase over the various measurement periods. Unfortunately, the percentage change over 10 days falls far short of some candles that post 6% or higher moves. Thus, the rankings are midlevel, with 1 being the best out of 103 candles.

Table 72.3 shows height statistics.

Candle height. Tall candles outperform short ones. To determine whether the candle is short or tall, compute its height from high to low price and divide by the breakout price. If the result is higher than the median, then you have a tall candle; otherwise it's short.

For example, let's say that Melody sees a rickshaw man with a high of 30 and a low of 29. Is the candle short or tall? The height is 30 − 29, or 1, so the measure is 1/30, or 3.3%. In a bull market with an upward breakout, the candle is tall.

Table 72.3
Height Statistics

Description	Bull Market, Up Breakout	Bear Market, Up Breakout	Bull Market, Down Breakout	Bear Market, Down Breakout
Median candle height as a percentage of breakout price	3.23%	4.33%	3.32%	4.31%
Short candle, performance	5.00%	6.85%	−4.82%	−7.28%
Tall candle, performance	9.83%	13.48%	−7.71%	−13.36%
Percentage meeting price target (measure rule)	71%	71%	67%	70%
Median upper shadow as a percentage of breakout price	1.58%	2.10%	1.65%	2.17%
Short upper shadow, performance	5.04%	6.45%	−4.78%	−7.15%
Tall upper shadow, performance	9.65%	13.84%	−7.73%	−13.58%
Median lower shadow as a percentage of breakout price	1.60%	2.08%	1.60%	2.06%
Short lower shadow, performance	5.04%	6.85%	−4.77%	−7.58%
Tall lower shadow, performance	9.77%	12.99%	−7.79%	−12.82%

Table 72.4
Volume Statistics

Description	Bull Market, Up Breakout	Bear Market, Up Breakout	Bull Market, Down Breakout	Bear Market, Down Breakout
Above-average candle volume, performance	6.97%	9.94%	−5.75%	−9.46%
Below-average candle volume, performance	6.33%	9.09%	−5.80%	−9.71%
Heavy breakout volume, performance	7.74%	9.17%	−6.07%	−11.94%
Light breakout volume, performance	5.45%	9.87%	−5.54%	−7.87%

Measure rule. Use the measure rule to help predict how far price will rise or fall. Compute the height of the candle and multiply it by the appropriate percentage shown in the table; then apply it to the breakout price.

What are the price targets for Melody's candle? The upward target would be $(1 \times 71\%) + 30$, or 30.71, and the downward target would be $29 - (1 \times 67\%)$, or 28.33. Both assume a bull market.

Shadows. To determine whether the shadow is short or tall, compute the height of the shadow and divide by the breakout price. Compare the result to the median in the table. Tall shadows have a percentage higher than the median.

Candles with tall upper or lower shadows mean better postbreakout performance than short shadows.

Table 72.4 shows volume statistics.

Average candle volume. Above-average candle volume works best for upward breakouts, and below-average volume indicates better postbreakout performance after downward breakouts.

Breakout volume. Heavy breakout volume suggests good performance in all cases except bear market/up breakouts. That category does better after a breakout with light volume.

Trading Tactics

I split trading tactics into two basic studies, one concerning reversal rates and the other concerning performance. Of the two, reversal rates are more important, because it's better to trade in the direction of the trend and let price run as far as it can.

Table 72.5 gives tips to find the trend direction.

Reversal, continuation rates. Since the rickshaw man is nearly a random behavior candle, the trend leading to the candle tells little about the

Table 72.5
Reversal Rates

Description	Bull Market	Bear Market
Reversal rate: trend up, breakout down	47%	51%
Continuation rate: trend up, breakout up	53%	49%
Reversal: trend down, breakout up	51%	50%
Continuation: trend down, breakout down	49%	50%
Percentage of reversals (R)/continuations (C) for each 12-month low (L), middle (M), or high (H)	L 48% R/52% C, M 50% R/50% C, H 50% R/50% C	L 44% R/56% C, M 55% R/45% C, H 52% R/48% C
Black body reversal rate	49%	50%
White body reversal rate	48%	50%

likely breakout direction. However, I show the results in the table because you never know.

Knowing the price trend leading to the candle pattern helps determine the likely breakout direction. For example, in a bull market, if the trend is up, there's a 53% chance that price will continue rising.

Yearly range reversals. Continuations occur most often when the breakout is within a third of the yearly low, but it's close to random (50%).

Body color reversal rate. Body color has little influence on whether the candle acts as a reversal. Doji color comes from those candles in which the opening price is near, but not the same as, the closing price, which I allow.

Table 72.6 shows performance indicators that can give hints as to how your stock will behave after the breakout from this candle pattern.

Confirmation, performance. Opening gap confirmation results in the best performance. That means waiting for price to gap open the next day and trading in the direction of the gap. Assume that the breakout direction also represents the gap direction.

Moving average. Candles with breakouts below the 50-day moving average result in the best postbreakout performance.

Body color performance. The table shows performance based on body color (for a doji in which the opening and closing prices are slightly different). A black body outperforms in all cases except for bull market/up breakouts.

Sample Trade

Melody watched price unfold as shown in Figure 72.2. She connected valley A with B and extended the trendline to C, where a rickshaw man appeared. Along the tops, she drew a line from D to E and extended it to F. F was where she

Table 72.6
Performance Indicators

Description	Bull Market, Up Breakout	Bear Market, Up Breakout	Bull Market, Down Breakout	Bear Market, Down Breakout
Closing price confirmation, performance	6.50%	10.28%	−6.49%	−10.32%
Candle color confirmation, performance	6.48%	10.13%	−6.51%	−10.50%
Opening gap confirmation, performance	7.16%	11.86%	−7.04%	−10.64%
Breakout above 50-day moving average, performance	6.35%	8.10%	−5.31%	−7.67%
Breakout below 50-day moving average, performance	7.14%	12.17%	−6.14%	−11.21%
Black body, performance	6.62%	10.19%	−5.90%	−9.67%
White body, performance	6.64%	7.36%	−4.94%	−9.48%

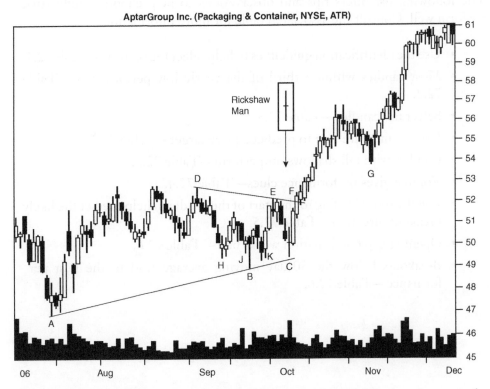

Figure 72.2 A rickshaw man appears at a support zone, leading to the start of an up move.

imagined price would be when it intersected the upper trendline, some days in the future.

The downside protection was a stop below B, comfortably below the four valleys in September (H, J, K, and C). The valleys would help support price, just as she expected it would support the rickshaw man at C.

Believing that price would reverse due to underlying support set up by the trendline and the bottoms near 49.50, Melody placed a buy order at the open the next day. That was a gutsy move, because price opened lower.

Her intuition was right. Price moved up by forming a series of white candles (forming eight new price lines candle pattern plus one extra), busting through the target at F, and continuing higher. She hung on to the stock and wasn't shaken out when it retraced to G. Rare is the stock that trends upward in a straight-line run, so retracements like G are common. Price touched a new high over 80, before adjusting for a two for one split.

For Best Performance

The following list offers tips and observations to help choose candles that perform well. Consult the associated table for more information.

- Use the identification guidelines to help select the pattern—Table 72.1.
- Most candles within a third of the yearly low perform best—Table 72.2.
- Select tall candles—Table 72.3.
- Use the measure rule to predict a price target—Table 72.3.
- Candles with tall shadows outperform—Table 72.3.
- Volume gives performance clues—Table 72.4.
- Use the trend leading to the start of the candle to help predict the likely breakout direction—Table 72.5.
- Opening gap confirmation works best—Table 72.6.
- Breakouts below the 50-day moving average lead to the best performance—Table 72.6.

73

Rising Three Methods

Behavior and Rank

Theoretical: Bullish continuation.

Actual bull market: Bullish continuation 74% of the time (ranking 5).

Actual bear market: Bullish continuation 79% of the time (ranking 2).

Frequency: 88th out of 103.

Overall performance over time: 94th out of 103.

The rising three methods candlestick is a rare pattern that functions quite well as a continuation pattern. By that I mean price continues upward 74% of the time, but there's a problem. The overall performance rank is 94 out of 103 candles where 1 is best. How can the pattern excel as a continuation but have such poor performance? Blame the few samples. The numbers suggest that although a continuation occurs often, price doesn't move far before reversing.

The rising three methods pattern is a visual representation of price taking a breather. The bulls have the ball, and they are pushing price upward leading to the start of the candlestick formation. A tall white candle prints on the chart and the bulls are ecstatic. However, the following three days have small-bodied candles that ease lower, many of them with black bodies. The bears have borrowed the ball for a while. The last day in the pattern, the bulls steal the ball back and push price upward again, printing a tall white candle on the chart.

Table 73.1
Identification Guidelines

Characteristic	Discussion
Number of candle lines	Five.
Price trend	Upward leading to the start of the candle pattern.
First day	A tall white-bodied candle.
Days 2 to 4	Small-bodied candles that trend lower and close within the high-low range of the first candle. Day 3 can be black or white, but days 2 and 4 are black candles.
Last day	A tall white candle that closes above the close of the first day.

Identification Guidelines

A rising three methods is one of the wider candles. Five days compose it, and it looks a lot like a mat hold pattern. If you don't know what a mat hold pattern looks like, then forget I mentioned it.

Table 73.1 lists identification guidelines. Once source I checked requires that the last day open within the body of the prior candle. The rising three methods shown in Figure 73.1 would not qualify, for example. I ignored that rule when collecting statistics.

Figure 73.1   MSA rising three methods candle appears in a rising price trend.

I searched for a five-candle pattern with the first and last days being tall white ones. The middle three days are small candles. The middle one can be either white or black, but days 2 and 4 must be black. The three trend downward and have closes within the high-low trading range of the first day. The final day must close above the close of the first candle. With so many conditions, it's no surprise that this candle pattern rarely appears.

Statistics

Table 73.2 shows general statistics.

Number found. I found only 102 samples, so the results are chancy at best. Based on prorated numbers from my standard database, the rising three methods candle formation appears more often in a bear market.

Reversal or continuation performance. Usually performance from a bear market beats the bull market for many candle types, but the results flip here: The bull market numbers are better.

Table 73.2
General Statistics

Description	Bull Market, Up Breakout	Bear Market, Up Breakout	Bull Market, Down Breakout	Bear Market, Down Breakout
Number found	55	22	19	6
Reversal (R), continuation (C) performance	6.86% C	3.93% C	−4.31% R	−4.10% R
Standard & Poor's 500 change	1.38%	0.61%	−1.36%	−1.59%
Candle end to breakout (median, days)	3	2	8	8
Candle end to trend end (median, days)	7	4	11	13
Number of breakouts near the 12-month low (L), middle (M), or high (H)	L 5, M 13, H 29	L 3, M 4, H 15	L 2, M 4, H 9	L 2, M 0, H 4
Percentage move for each 12-month period	L 11.92%, M 9.80%, H 4.95%	L 5.05%, M 7.58%, H 2.95%	L −11.89%, M −4.70%, H −3.11%	L −6.85%, M 0.00%, H −2.49%
Candle end + 1 day	0.84%	0.24%	−0.69%	−1.39%
Candle end + 3 days	1.63%	1.21%	−1.83%	−1.90%
Candle end + 5 days	2.49%	0.42%	−3.56%	−1.56%
Candle end + 10 days	3.96%	-2.31%	−5.10%	−4.89%
10-day performance rank	32	101	7	32

S&P performance. The rising three methods pattern works better than the S&P 500 index in all cases.

Candle end to breakout. Upward breakouts take less time to occur than downward ones. This is because price closes near the top of the candle.

Candle end to trend end. Upward breakouts, being well on their way to the trend end, take less time to complete the move than downward breakouts.

Yearly position, performance. Most patterns appear within a third of the yearly high. Performance is often best when the breakout is within a third of the yearly low. The lone exception is bear market/up breakouts, which do better when the breakout is in the middle third of the yearly price range.

Performance over time. I find the results disappointing. The bear market numbers show weakness after three days. Performance is very good for bull market/down breakouts and very bad for bear market/up breakouts.

Table 73.3 shows height statistics.

Candle height. Tall candles perform better than short ones. To determine whether the candle is short or tall, compute its height from highest high to lowest low price in the candle pattern and divide by the breakout price. If the result is higher than the median, then you have a tall candle; otherwise it's short.

Table 73.3
Height Statistics

Description	Bull Market, Up Breakout	Bear Market, Up Breakout*	Bull Market, Down Breakout*	Bear Market, Down Breakout*
Median candle height as a percentage of breakout price	4.92%	7.39%	6.04%	5.17%
Short candle, performance	5.24%*	2.73%	−3.13%	−2.46%
Tall candle, performance	9.33%*	6.31%	−6.13%	−6.30%
Percentage meeting price target (measure rule)	60%	23%	21%	33%
Median upper shadow as a percentage of breakout price	0.20%	0.44%	0.45%	0.47%
Short upper shadow, performance	6.31%*	3.47%	−5.20%	−5.00%
Tall upper shadow, performance	7.49%*	4.47%	−3.48%	−3.10%
Median lower shadow as a percentage of breakout price	0.20%	0.38%	0.35%	0.07%
Short lower shadow, performance	6.21%*	2.87%	−2.77%	−0.87%
Tall lower shadow, performance	7.62%*	5.37%	−5.97%	−6.87%

*Fewer than 30 samples.

For example, Jeb sees a rising three methods candle formation with a high of 62 and a low of 58. The height is 62 – 58, or 4, so the measure is 4/62, or 6.5% (assume bull market/up breakout). The candle is tall.

Measure rule. Use the measure rule to help predict how far price will rise or fall. Compute the height of the candle pattern and multiply it by the appropriate percentage shown in the table; then apply it to the breakout price.

What are the price targets for Jeb's candle? The upward target would be (4 × 60%) + 62, or 64.40, and the downward target would be 58 – (4 × 21%), or 57.16.

Since many of the hit rates are quite low, it suggests poor performance for the stock after the breakout. Of course, the low sample count may be the reason, but trade this pattern with caution.

Shadows. The table's results pertain to the last candle line in the pattern. To determine whether the shadow is short or tall, compute the height of the shadow and divide by the breakout price. Compare the result to the median in the table. Tall shadows have a percentage higher than the median.

Upper shadow performance. Tall upper shadows result in the best performance after upward breakouts, and short shadows do well after downward breakouts.

Lower shadow performance. Tall lower shadows suggest better post-breakout performance across the board.

Table 73.4 shows volume statistics.

Candle volume trend. Upward breakouts perform better when the candle shows rising volume. Downward breakouts do better after a falling volume trend.

Table 73.4
Volume Statistics

Description	Bull Market, Up Breakout	Bear Market, Up Breakout*	Bull Market, Down Breakout*	Bear Market, Down Breakout*
Rising candle volume, performance	8.78%*	4.93%	−3.71%	−0.77%
Falling candle volume, performance	6.16%	3.24%	−4.58%	−5.62%
Above-average candle volume, performance	7.37%*	3.72%	−3.49%	−3.91%
Below-average candle volume, performance	6.49%*	4.10%	−5.33%	−4.23%
Heavy breakout volume, performance	6.84%	4.39%	−4.97%	−2.94%
Light breakout volume, performance	6.87%*	3.61%	−3.43%	−4.96%

*Fewer than 30 samples.

Average candle volume. Below-average volume results in the best post-breakout performance in all cases except for bull market/up breakouts.

Breakout volume. Light breakout volume works well for bull market/up breakouts and bear market/down breakouts. Heavy volume works better for the inner two columns, bear market/up breakouts and bull market/down breakouts. Most candle types work best with heavy breakout volume, so blame the low sample counts.

Trading Tactics

If you are going to rely on this candle pattern, then make sure it appears in a primary uptrend. Betting that price will continue up when the pattern appears as part of an upward retracement in a downtrend is asking for trouble—and a loss.

I split trading tactics into two basic studies, one concerning reversal rates and the other concerning performance. Of the two, reversal rates are more important, because it's better to trade in the direction of the trend and let price run as far as it can.

Table 73.5 gives tips to find the trend direction.

Confirmation reversal rates. Waiting for a lower close the next day results in a downward breakout between 35% (bear market) and 43% (bull market) of the time. I would not depend on a reversal happening. Instead, bank on price continuing to rise.

Reversal, continuation rates. The numbers show that price breaks out upward most often.

Yearly range reversals. All of the numbers have few samples, but continuations happen most often when price is away from the yearly low.

Table 73.5
Reversal Rates

Description	Bull Market	Bear Market*
Closing price confirmation reversal rate	43%*	35%
Candle color confirmation reversal rate	33%*	28%
Opening gap confirmation reversal rate	35%*	33%
Reversal rate: trend up, breakout down	26%	21%
Continuation rate: trend up, breakout up	74%	79%
Percentage of reversals (R)/continuations (C) for each 12-month low (L), middle (M), or high (H)	L* 29% R/71% C, M* 24% R/76% C, H* 24% R/76% C	L 40% R/60% C, M 0% R/100% C, H 21% R/79% C

*Fewer than 30 samples.

Table 73.6
Performance Indicators

Description	Bull Market, Up Breakout	Bear Market, Up Breakout*	Bull Market, Down Breakout*	Bear Market, Down Breakout*
Closing price confirmation, performance	6.33%	3.29%	N/A	N/A
Candle color confirmation, performance	6.38%	2.87%	N/A	N/A
Opening gap confirmation, performance	7.78%	5.89%	N/A	N/A
Breakout above 50-day moving average, performance	6.49%	3.70%	−4.86%	−3.91%
Breakout below 50-day moving average, performance	11.60%*	5.05%	−2.89%	−4.51%
Last candle: close in highest third, performance	6.90%	4.22%	−4.41%	−5.62%
Last candle: close in middle third, performance	4.17%*	1.75%	−3.83%	−0.77%
Last candle: close in lowest third, performance	0.00%*	0.00%	0.00%	0.00%

N/A means not applicable.
*Fewer than 30 samples.

Table 73.6 shows performance indicators that can give hints as to how your stock will behave after the breakout from this candle pattern.

Confirmation, performance. Opening gap confirmation results in the best postbreakout performance. That means trading only if price gaps open higher the next day.

Moving average. When the breakout from the candle is below the 50-day moving average, price tends to perform well. The one exception is bull market/down breakouts, which do better when the breakout is above the moving average.

Closing position. The best performance comes when the last candle line of the pattern closes near the intraday high.

Sample Trade

Figure 73.2 shows a situation that Jeb faced. He owned the stock and was concerned about price stalling out or reversing when it reached overhead resistance set up by the peak at A. Should he sell his stock when price reaches that level?

Since we can look into the future and see that price trends higher, the answer is obviously no. He should hold on to his stock. However, what clue

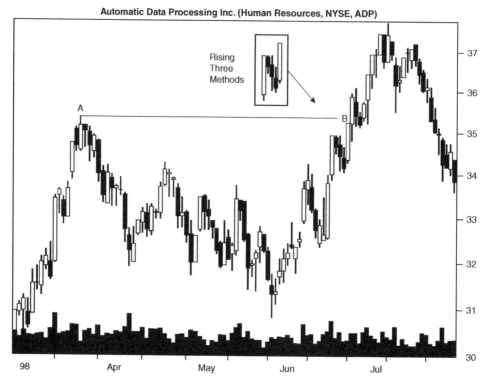

Figure 73.2   MSA rising three methods candle formation appears at overhead resistance.

suggests a continuation of the uptrend? The answer is the rising three methods candle. It appears at B, right where price is expected to pause or reverse. The candle suggests a continuation of the upward trend.

The next day, price forms another white candle, closing higher and confirming the upward trend.

I consider the behavior of this stock to be unusual. My guess would be that price would reverse after the rising three methods pattern, but that didn't happen. Some might say that this is an example of the 38% Fibonacci extension of the move from the May low to B, continuing upward.

For Best Performance

The following list offers tips and observations to help choose candles that perform well. Consult the associated table for more information.

- Use the identification guidelines to help select the pattern—Table 73.1.
- Candles within a third of the yearly low perform best in most, but not all, cases—Table 73.2.

- Select tall candles—Table 73.3.
- Use the measure rule to predict a price target—Table 73.3.
- Candles with tall lower shadows on the last candle line outperform—Table 73.3.
- Volume gives performance clues—Table 73.4.
- Rely on this pattern only when the primary price trend is up—Trading Tactics discussion.
- Price frequently breaks out upward—Table 73.5.
- Patterns well above the yearly low tend to act as continuations most often—Table 73.5.
- Opening gap confirmation works best—Table 73.6.

74

Separating Lines, Bearish

Behavior and Rank

Theoretical: Bearish continuation.

Actual bull market: Bearish continuation 63% of the time (ranking 17).

Actual bear market: Bearish continuation 76% of the time (ranking 3).

Frequency: 82nd out of 103.

Overall performance over time: 40th out of 103.

Separating lines are also called dividing lines. These candle patterns tend to disappear in a bear market like hummingbirds in the northern states during winter. You can find them in zoos then, but few other places (hummingbirds, that is, not separating lines).

As a continuation pattern they rank well, especially in a bear market: 3 out of 103 where 1 is best. Sporting a frequency rank of 82, the pattern is rare. Overall, the performance rank is 40, which I consider respectable.

As for pattern psychology, selling pressure forces price lower, but then a tall white candle appears, giving bulls hope that a reversal is at hand. However, the next day price opens where it opened the prior day, meaning that those holding the stock just visited the woodshed for punishment. The bears are at it again, selling the stock and forming a tall black candle as price drops. In the coming days, selling pressure will override buying demand and price will continue dropping, in theory.

Identification Guidelines

I made a change to the candle pattern identification. I originally did research with *matching* opening prices and found a continuation rate of 69.5%. Then I changed the pattern so prices *near* the opening qualified. In other words, if the opening prices were two or three cents apart, the two lines qualified. The continuation rate dropped to 64.1% but the number of samples doubled. I decided to stick with the uneven combination because the additional samples improved the validity of the statistics. You can use the statistics as guidance and then find separating lines with matching opening prices if you prefer.

Figure 74.1 shows the bearish separating lines candle pattern in the middle of a downward price trend. The stock forms an uneven double top chart pattern at peaks A and B, and a trader knowledgeable about such things knows the chart pattern doesn't become official until price closes below the confirmation line. That is a line starting at the lowest price below the two peaks. Most of the time, price does not drop far enough to confirm the pattern, so you end with just squiggles on the chart and not a double top.

Figure 74.1 A bearish separating lines formation indicates more downward movement ahead.

Table 74.1
Identification Guidelines

Characteristic	Discussion
Number of candle lines	Two.
Price trend	Downward leading to the start of the candle pattern.
First day	A tall white candle.
Second day	A tall black candle that opens at or near the same price as the prior candle opened.

In the situation shown in the figure, a trader would expect price to continue lower because that's what the separating lines hint. Price does move down for another day before finding support and bouncing. The rally is short-lived, though, and price eases lower to the confirmation line. There the support zone set up by prior valleys (at C and before) makes price pause. In fact, the February low marks the turning point for the stock.

Table 74.1 lists identification guidelines. Look for a tall white candle followed by a tall black one. The opening prices should be the same or nearly so. Look for matching opening prices if you want to boost continuation performance.

Statistics

Table 74.2 shows general statistics.

Number found. I found 2,572 patterns, most from a bull market. In fact, this pattern is rarely found in a bear market.

Reversal or continuation performance. Separating lines in a bear market outperform those in a bull market. This result agrees with other candle pattern types.

S&P performance. Separating lines outperform the S&P 500 index across all categories.

Candle end to breakout. It takes between three and six days for price to break out. Downward breakouts take less time because the closing price is near the pattern's low.

Candle end to trend end. Since the downtrend is already underway, the trend end is closer than for upward breakouts.

Yearly position, performance. The pattern occurs most often within a third of the yearly low, and that also results in the best performance. The one exception is for bear market/down breakouts. Those do better when the breakout is in the middle of the yearly price range.

Performance over time. This pattern shows solid performance across the periods studied, with the exception of bear market/down breakouts. Despite

Table 74.2
General Statistics

Description	Bull Market, Up Breakout	Bear Market, Up Breakout	Bull Market, Down Breakout	Bear Market, Down Breakout
Number found	891	32	1,546	103
Reversal (R), continuation (C) performance	6.31% R	7.13% R	−6.09% C	−10.84% C
Standard & Poor's 500 change	1.43%	0.75%	−0.29%	−2.26%
Candle end to breakout (median, days)	6	6	3	4
Candle end to trend end (median, days)	8	8	5	6
Number of breakouts near the 12-month low (L), middle (M), or high (H)	L 270, M 172, H 235	L 12, M 10, H 9	L 503, M 395, H 299	L 56, M 30, H 15
Percentage move for each 12-month period	L 6.73%, M 6.38%, H 5.30%	L 9.08%, M 6.73%, H 6.43%	L −7.00%, M −5.63%, H −5.40%	L −11.74%, M −11.90%, H −7.16%
Candle end + 1 day	1.52%	2.69%	−0.73%	0.87%
Candle end + 3 days	3.16%	3.94%	−1.49%	0.45%
Candle end + 5 days	3.91%	5.97%	−1.62%	−2.48%
Candle end + 10 days	4.93%	8.36%	−1.85%	−1.33%
10-day performance rank	11	5	67	94

a downward breakout, price rises for up to five days before showing a lower average close. By day 10, some of the patterns have higher prices because the average climbs (meaning it's less negative).

Based on the performance rank, upward breakouts are where this pattern does best. Of course, that means it acts as a reversal of the downtrend, not as a continuation pattern.

Table 74.3 shows height statistics.

Candle height. Tall candles perform better than short ones. To determine whether the candle is short or tall, compute its height from highest high to lowest low price in the candle pattern and divide by the breakout price. If the result is higher than the median, then you have a tall candle; otherwise it's short.

Kent sees separating lines with a high of 97 and a low of 93. Is the candlestick short or tall? The height is 97 − 93, or 4, so the measure would be 4/97, or 4.1% (assume bull market/up breakout). The candle is tall.

Measure rule. Use the measure rule to help predict how far price will rise or fall. Compute the height of the candle pattern and multiply it by the appropriate percentage shown in the table; then apply it to the breakout price.

Table 74.3
Height Statistics

Description	Bull Market, Up Breakout	Bear Market, Up Breakout*	Bull Market, Down Breakout	Bear Market, Down Breakout
Median candle height as a percentage of breakout price	3.75%	4.79%	3.90%	7.50%
Short candle, performance	5.33%	5.09%	−4.89%	−7.51%
Tall candle, performance	7.77%	10.50%	−7.76%	−13.58%
Percentage meeting price target (measure rule)	67%	63%	62%	56%
Median upper shadow as a percentage of breakout price	0.00%	0.26%	0.00%	0.28%
Short upper shadow, performance	6.51%	6.62%	−6.31%	−8.00%
Tall upper shadow, performance	6.09%	7.58%	−5.90%	−12.18%
Median lower shadow as a percentage of breakout price	0.00%	0.16%	0.00%	0.35%
Short lower shadow, performance	6.66%	4.95%	−6.06%	−13.54%
Tall lower shadow, performance	5.94%	9.11%	−6.12%	−8.95%

*Fewer than 30 samples.

What are the targets for Kent's candle? The upward target would be $(4 \times 67\%) + 97$, or 99.68. The downward target would be $93 − (4 \times 62\%)$, or 90.52.

Shadows. The table's results pertain to the last candle line in the pattern. To determine whether the shadow is short or tall, compute the height of the shadow and divide by the breakout price. Compare the result to the median in the table. Tall shadows have a percentage higher than the median.

Upper shadow performance. A zero median means separating lines have a number of candles with no shadow. In many candlestick types, tall shadows outperform. In this situation, though, short shadows work best in bull markets and tall shadows work best in bear markets.

Lower shadow performance. Short lower shadows give the best post-breakout performance under the conditions of bull market/up breakout and bear market/down breakout. Tall lower shadows do well for bear market/up breakouts and bull market/down breakouts.

Table 74.4 shows volume statistics.

Candle volume trend. Falling candle volume results in the best post-breakout performance in all categories except bull market/down breakout. That category does better for candles showing rising volume.

Average candle volume. Below-average candle volume works across the board with one exception: bear market/up breakout, but the samples are few.

Table 74.4
Volume Statistics

Description	Bull Market, Up Breakout	Bear Market, Up Breakout*	Bull Market, Down Breakout	Bear Market, Down Breakout
Rising candle volume, performance	5.88%	6.82%	−6.38%	−8.35%
Falling candle volume, performance	7.02%	7.94%	−5.62%	−17.88%
Above-average candle volume, performance	6.17%	9.13%	−5.96%	−8.44%
Below-average candle volume, performance	6.39%	6.01%	−6.18%	−14.30%
Heavy breakout volume, performance	7.15%	6.53%	−6.62%	−12.63%
Light breakout volume, performance	5.22%	7.56%	−5.58%	−8.14%

*Fewer than 30 samples.

Breakout volume. Heavy breakout volume works best as shown in all columns except bear market/up breakout.

Trading Tactics

Avoid trading bearish separating lines when they appear as downward retracements in an uptrend. The tendency is for price to either break out upward or turn up after a short decline.

I split trading tactics into two basic studies, one concerning reversal rates and the other concerning performance. Of the two, reversal rates are more important, because it's better to trade in the direction of the trend and let price run as far as it can.

Table 74.5 gives tips to find the trend direction.

Confirmation reversal rates. If you want to hunt for a reversal among bearish separating lines, then wait for price to close higher after the pattern ends. That works 61% of the time in a bull market.

Reversal, continuation rates. Bearish separating lines break out downward most often.

Yearly range reversals. In a bull market, the middle of the yearly price range shows the most continuation patterns, 70%. In a bear market, separating lines within a third of the yearly low act as continuations most often—82% of the time.

Table 74.6 shows performance indicators that can give hints as to how your stock will behave after the breakout from this candle pattern.

Table 74.5
Reversal Rates

Description	Bull Market	Bear Market*
Closing price confirmation reversal rate	61%	38%
Candle color confirmation reversal rate	60%	37%
Opening gap confirmation reversal rate	47%	28%
Reversal: trend down, breakout up	37%	24%
Continuation: trend down, breakout down	63%	76%
Percentage of reversals (R)/continuations (C) for each 12-month low (L), middle (M), or high (H)	L 35% R/65% C, M 30% R/70% C, H 44% R/56% C	L 18% R/82% C, M 25% R/75% C, H 38% R/62% C

*Fewer than 30 samples.

Confirmation, performance. Opening gap confirmation gives the best performance in a bull market. That's when you wait for price to gap open lower the next day. Candle color works better in a bear market. That's when you trade only if another black candle appears the next day.

Moving average. Separating lines below the 50-day moving average outperform except for bear market/up breakout. Those also have few samples,

Table 74.6
Performance Indicators

Description	Bull Market, Up Breakout	Bear Market, Up Breakout*	Bull Market, Down Breakout	Bear Market, Down Breakout
Closing price confirmation, performance	N/A	N/A	−5.42%	−8.04%
Candle color confirmation, performance	N/A	N/A	−5.85%	−9.36%
Opening gap confirmation, performance	N/A	N/A	−6.29%	−8.33%
Breakout above 50-day moving average, performance	6.22%	8.33%	−5.34%	−7.23%*
Breakout below 50-day moving average, performance	6.29%	4.32%	−6.16%	−11.40%
Last candle: close in highest third, performance	4.19%*	0%*	−7.67%*	−5.01%*
Last candle: close in middle third, performance	6.24%	10.48%	−6.01%	−10.94%*
Last candle: close in lowest third, performance	6.34%	6.51%	−6.08%	−10.89%

N/A means not applicable.
*Fewer than 30 samples.

and most other candle types work best when the breakout is below the moving average.

Closing position. Where price closes in the last line shows no consistent performance advantage.

Sample Trade

Figure 74.2 shows the losing trade that occupied Kent's attention when he was a novice trader. He bought the stock on the way up from D. Price peaked at A and then dropped to C before recovering to B.

At B, he had a potential double bottom (assume that price was higher to the left of D), provided that price closed above A. It didn't. As the chart shows, price started a long slide down to E. If price closed below C, then it would confirm a double top and that would be a sell signal.

Kent didn't know any of this. He was sure price would rebound; he just had to give it time. Price dropped through the confirmation line (the horizontal line starting at C, the lowest low between peaks A and B) and formed bearish separating lines at E, suggesting price would continue lower.

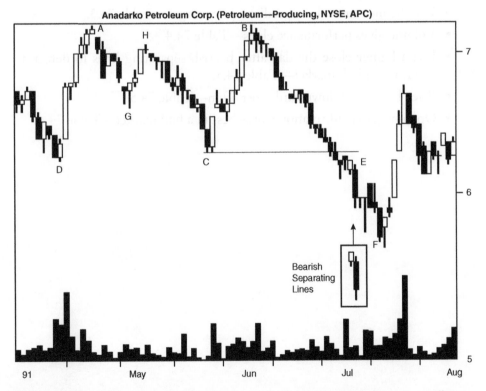

Figure 74.2 A bearish separating lines candle formation suggests price will continue lower.

As price dropped, Kent became more and more upset. Eventually, he was so distressed at seeing a profitable trade turn into a massive loss that he sold the stock at F, a day before price reached the low.

I'm sure many of us have made the same mistake. A correctly placed stop-loss order would have gotten him out of the trade near breakeven. For example, the retracement to G was normal in that price did not drop below 62% of the DA move. The failure of price to reach a new high at H was one sell signal. Another sell signal occurred when price closed below G, and a third was when price closed below C (near E).

For Best Performance

The following list offers tips and observations to help choose candles that perform well. Consult the associated table for more information.

- Use the identification guidelines to help select the pattern—Table 74.1.
- Most candles within a third of the yearly low perform best—Table 74.2.
- Select tall candles—Table 74.3.
- Use the measure rule to predict a price target—Table 74.3.
- Volume gives performance clues—Table 74.4.
- Use a higher close the day after bearish separating lines to detect a reversal in a bull market—Table 74.5.
- Price breaks out downward most often—Table 74.5.
- Opening gap confirmation works best in a bull market—Table 74.6.

75

Separating Lines, Bullish

Behavior and Rank

Theoretical: Bullish continuation.
Actual bull market: Bullish continuation 72% of the time (ranking 6).
Actual bear market: Bullish continuation 69% of the time (ranking 10).
Frequency: 76th out of 103.
Overall performance over time: 36th out of 103.

The bullish separating lines candle is a continuation pattern that works well under many circumstances. In researching this pattern, I found that it often appears as a breakout pattern from a congestion region.

The continuation ranks of 6 and 10 are almost at the top of the list: 1 is best out of 103. However, the frequency rank is 76 and that means the pattern is somewhat rare. When you do find them, they perform well, with an overall performance rank of 36.

The psychology behind the pattern has the bulls forcing price upward in a buying spree leading to the start of the candle. Price gaps open much higher but closes well below the open, printing a tall black candle on the chart. The bulls are upset at seeing such a giveback in profits so the next day, before the open, they huddle and decide what to do. When the market opens, buying demand causes price to gap up to meet the prior opening price. By the close, price prints a tall white candle on the chart. The bulls rejoice at their good fortune and look forward to continued upward momentum in the coming days.

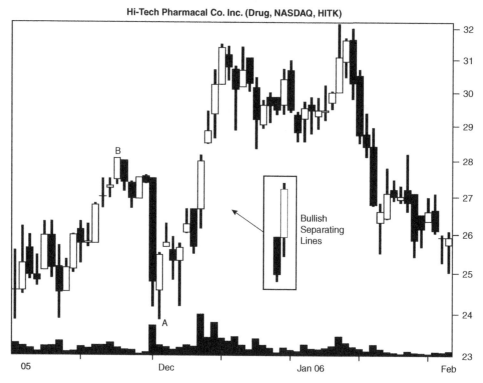

Figure 75.1 A bullish separating lines pattern appears in an uptrend.

Identification Guidelines

Figure 75.1 shows what bullish separating lines look like. Price forms a new high at B and then drops to A, where underlying support causes it to rebound. One would expect price to pause or even reverse when it reaches the price level of B, but it doesn't. The bullish separating lines candle formation appears with a very tall white body as the second line in the pattern. Price gaps higher a day later, speaking to the upward momentum created by buying demand.

Table 75.1 lists identification guidelines. The candlestick pattern is a two-day affair, with the first line black and the second one white. They share

Table 75.1
Identification Guidelines

Characteristic	Discussion
Number of candle lines	Two.
Price trend	Upward leading to the start of the candle pattern.
First day	A tall black candle.
Second day	A tall white candle that opens at or near the prior day's open.

a common opening price. That's the theory, but two candles having the same opening price is rare, especially in a bear market. Therefore, I allow price to open *near* to each other, usually just a few cents apart. That boosted the sample count and gave more solid statistics. Read the statistical results and then select candles with matching opening prices if you like.

Statistics

Table 75.2 shows general statistics.

Number found. I found only 2,842 patterns, many from a bull market. In fact, this pattern is quite rare in a bear market.

Reversal or continuation performance. The bear market gives the best results for this pattern.

S&P performance. Separating lines outperform the S&P 500 index over the same holding period.

Candle end to breakout. Upward breakouts take less time to reach the breakout than downward ones. This is because price is near the pattern's high.

Table 75.2
General Statistics

Description	Bull Market, Up Breakout	Bear Market, Up Breakout	Bull Market, Down Breakout	Bear Market, Down Breakout
Number found	1,946	93	761	42
Reversal (R), continuation (C) performance	6.50% C	7.88% C	−4.91% R	−11.64% R
Standard & Poor's 500 change	0.88%	0.30%	−0.56%	−2.76%
Candle end to breakout (median, days)	3	3	6	6
Candle end to trend end (median, days)	5	5	7	12
Number of breakouts near the 12-month low (L), middle (M), or high (H)	L 271, M 326, H 927	L 21, M 26, H 41	L 167, M 165, H 259	L 13, M 13, H 15
Percentage move for each 12-month period	L 7.87%, M 6.38%, H 5.87%	L 6.60%, M 8.61%, H 7.45%	L −6.22%, M −4.91%, H −4.03%	L −12.16%, M −10.13%, H −9.79%
Candle end + 1 day	0.70%	1.27%	−1.88%	−1.72%
Candle end + 3 days	1.49%	0.91%	−3.16%	−2.90%
Candle end + 5 days	2.05%	1.38%	−4.01%	−4.52%
Candle end + 10 days	2.52%	2.43%	−3.95%	−8.05%
10-day performance rank	67	66	15	4

Candle end to trend end. Upward breakouts take less time to reach the trend end than do downward breakouts. This is because bullish separating lines occur in an uptrend, so the trend end is often closer than for downward breakouts, which start a new trend.

Yearly position, performance. Most patterns occur within a third of the yearly high. However, performance is best when price is within a third of the yearly low. The exception is bear market/up breakouts. Those perform better when the breakout is in the middle of the yearly price range.

Performance over time. Performance over time is weak. In bear market/up breakouts, performance suffers between one and three days after the pattern ends. Bull market/down breakouts also have trouble between days 5 and 10. A robust candle performer would have price posting higher numbers over each measurement period.

The performance rank shows how the pattern stacks up against others. It shows that downward breakouts perform better than upward ones. Thus, when the pattern acts as a reversal, price tends to travel farther.

Table 75.3 shows height statistics.

Candle height. Tall candles work better in all cases except for bear market/down breakouts. Those have low samples, so the results are likely to change.

Table 75.3
Height Statistics

Description	Bull Market, Up Breakout	Bear Market, Up Breakout	Bull Market, Down Breakout	Bear Market, Down Breakout
Median candle height as a percentage of breakout price	3.81%	7.04%	3.78%	6.17%
Short candle, performance	4.96%	6.57%	−3.88%	−14.50%*
Tall candle, performance	8.44%	10.06%	−6.20%	−8.64%*
Percentage meeting price target (measure rule)	63%	49%	56%	52%
Median upper shadow as a percentage of breakout price	0.00%	0.53%	0.00%	0.46%
Short upper shadow, performance	6.42%	6.60%	−5.26%	−13.80%*
Tall upper shadow, performance	6.56%	8.86%	−4.58%	−9.57%*
Median lower shadow as a percentage of breakout price	0.00%	0.21%	0.00%	0.44%
Short lower shadow, performance	6.15%	6.02%	−4.84%	−15.82%*
Tall lower shadow, performance	6.71%	9.32%	−4.95%	−9.22%*

*Fewer than 30 samples.

To determine whether the candle is short or tall, compute its height from highest high to lowest low price in the candle pattern and divide by the breakout price. If the result is higher than the median, then you have a tall candle; otherwise it's short.

For example, let's say Andy sees separating lines with a high price of 40 and a low of 36. Is the pattern short or tall? The height is 40 – 36, or 4, so the measure for an upward breakout in a bull market would be 4/40, or 10%. That's a tall candle.

Measure rule. Use the measure rule to help predict how far price will rise or fall. Compute the height of the candle and multiply it by the appropriate percentage shown in the table; then apply it to the breakout price.

What are the price targets for Andy's candle? The upward target would be (4 × 63%) + 40, or 42.52. The downward target would be 36 – (4 × 56%), or 33.76.

Shadows. The table's results pertain to the last candle line in the pattern. To determine whether the shadow is short or tall, compute the height of the shadow and divide by the breakout price. Compare the result to the median in the table. Tall shadows have a percentage higher than the median.

Upper shadow performance. Don't be alarmed by a 0.00% median. That just means the candle has a number of patterns in which the last candle line doesn't have a shadow. Tall upper shadows work best for upward breakouts, and short shadows lead to better performance for downward breakouts.

Lower shadow performance. Tall lower shadows result in better post-breakout performance in all cases except for the low-sample-count bear market/down breakout category.

Table 75.4 shows volume statistics.

Table 75.4
Volume Statistics

Description	Bull Market, Up Breakout	Bear Market, Up Breakout	Bull Market, Down Breakout	Bear Market, Down Breakout*
Rising candle volume, performance	6.82%	7.79%	−4.92%	−12.98%
Falling candle volume, performance	5.66%	8.22%*	−4.90%	−7.86%
Above-average candle volume, performance	6.87%	7.83%	−4.10%	−4.52%
Below-average candle volume, performance	6.12%	7.95%	−5.43%	−18.77%
Heavy breakout volume, performance	8.12%	8.61%	−4.75%	−6.57%
Light breakout volume, performance	4.57%	6.51%	−5.01%	−14.72%

*Fewer than 30 samples.

Candle volume trend. A rising volume trend leads to the best breakout performance except for bear market/up breakouts. Those perform better if the candle shows falling volume.

Average candle volume. Candles with below-average volume lead to better postbreakout performance in all cases except for bull market/up breakouts. Those do better with above-average volume.

Breakout volume. Heavy breakout volume works best for upward breakouts, and light breakout volume scores for downward breakouts. The results are somewhat unusual, because heavy breakout volume usually works best in all cases.

Trading Tactics

In reviewing the behavior of these patterns, I found a number of them breaking out of a congestion region. It's as if price is a coiled spring waiting to explode and the separating lines candle is the antimatter that triggers the release. The Sample Trade section shows an example of this setup.

I split trading tactics into two basic studies, one concerning reversal rates and the other concerning performance. Of the two, reversal rates are more important, because it's better to trade in the direction of the trend and let price run as far as it can.

Table 75.5 gives tips to find the trend direction.

Confirmation reversal rates. To help determine whether a reversal will occur, look for price to close lower the day after the bullish separating lines ends. In a bull market, the method works 48% of the time, but it's slightly higher in a bear market: 52%.

Reversal, continuation rates. Price breaks out upward most often.

Yearly range reversals. If the breakout from bullish separating lines occurs within a third of the yearly high, the chances are 78% in a bull market

Table 75.5
Reversal Rates

Description	Bull Market	Bear Market
Closing price confirmation reversal rate	48%	52%
Candle color confirmation reversal rate	47%	50%*
Opening gap confirmation reversal rate	40%	47%*
Reversal rate: trend up, breakout down	28%	31%
Continuation rate: trend up, breakout up	72%	69%
Percentage of reversals (R)/continuations (C) for each 12-month low (L), middle (M), or high (H)	L 38% R/62% C, M 34% R/66% C, H 22% R/78% C	L* 38% R/62% C, M* 33% R/67% C, H* 27% R/73% C

*Fewer than 30 samples.

Table 75.6
Performance Indicators

Description	Bull Market, Up Breakout	Bear Market, Up Breakout	Bull Market, Down Breakout	Bear Market, Down Breakout*
Closing price confirmation, performance	5.80%	8.45%	N/A	N/A
Candle color confirmation, performance	6.13%	8.42%	N/A	N/A
Opening gap confirmation, performance	6.86%	10.81%	N/A	N/A
Breakout above 50-day moving average, performance	6.51%	8.15%	−4.88%	−7.21%
Breakout below 50-day moving average, performance	6.48%	6.64%*	−4.96%	−13.90%
Last candle: close in highest third, performance	6.76%	8.56%	−4.98%	−12.43%
Last candle: close in middle third, performance	5.30%	5.52%*	−4.74%	−9.57%
Last candle: close in lowest third, performance	4.06%*	7.29%*	−2.01%*	−20.78%

N/A means not applicable.
*Fewer than 30 samples.

that the pattern will act as a continuation pattern. That may not mean much, though, because price is near the high of the candle and all it has to do is close above the highest price in the candle to be labeled a reversal.

Table 75.6 shows performance indicators that can give hints as to how your stock will behave after the breakout from this candle pattern.

Confirmation, performance. Opening gap confirmation is the best method as an entry signal the next day. That means buy the stock if price gaps open higher.

Moving average. Upward breakouts above the moving average tend to outperform after the breakout. Downward breakouts do better if the breakout price is below the moving average. The results are at odds with other candle types. They usually perform better when the breakout is below the moving average.

Closing position. When price closes within a third of the intraday high in the last candle line of the pattern, postbreakout performance is better in all cases except for bear market/down breakouts. Those do best if price is near the intraday low.

Sample Trade

Figure 75.2 shows the trade that Andy made. Price formed a high at A and then fell off a cliff before finding support at the April valley. Price recovered

Figure 75.2   Bullish separating lines break out of a congestion region.

more slowly than the cliff dive, but that's typical. Downward moves often have higher velocity than upward ones.

Price reached overhead resistance at B, set up by the peak at A and surrounding congestion. On the bottom, price found support at C (the flat line).

The bullish separating lines candle pattern poked through the top of overhead resistance, and that was the buy signal Andy was waiting for. He pounced on the stock, and his buying helped price rise even higher.

This scenario, a congestion region (BC) followed by bullish separating lines, often leads to a good price move. In fact, the appearance of separating lines as price breaks out of congestion occurs frequently.

For Best Performance

The following list offers tips and observations to help choose candles that perform well. Consult the associated table for more information.

- Use the identification guidelines to help select the pattern—Table 75.1.
- Candles within a third of the yearly low perform best most often (except for bear market/up breakouts)—Table 75.2.

- Select tall candles (except for bear market/down breakouts)—Table 75.3.
- Use the measure rule to predict a price target—Table 75.3.
- Candles with tall lower shadows outperform in many (but not all) cases—Table 75.3.
- Volume gives performance clues—Table 75.4.
- The breakout is upward most often—Table 75.5.
- Patterns within a third of the yearly high tend to act as continuations most often—Table 75.5.
- Opening gap confirmation works best—Table 75.6.

76

Shooting Star, One-Candle

Behavior and Rank

Theoretical: Bearish reversal.

Actual bull market: Bearish reversal 59% of the time (ranking 33).

Actual bear market: Bearish reversal 60% of the time (ranking 27).

Frequency: 37th out of 103.

Overall performance over time: 55th out of 103.

From a candle recognition perspective, the shooting star is a huge pain. Each of the sources I looked at had its own interpretation of what one should look like. Some required a gap and some didn't. Some said the upper shadow should be at least twice the body height and some said three times. Some said a shooting star is a two-candle pattern while the others said it's a single candle line.

I therefore split the shooting star into two chapters. This chapter discusses the single-line version.

The shooting star functions as a bearish reversal of the uptrend 59% of the time in a bull market. It occurs frequently (rank 37 out of 103 candles where 1 is best) and the performance is middle-of-the-road 55.

The psychology behind the pattern is one of exhausted bulls attempting to push price higher. At the end of an uptrend, price soars to a new high but then the bears come in and knock price down, leaving a tall upper shadow and

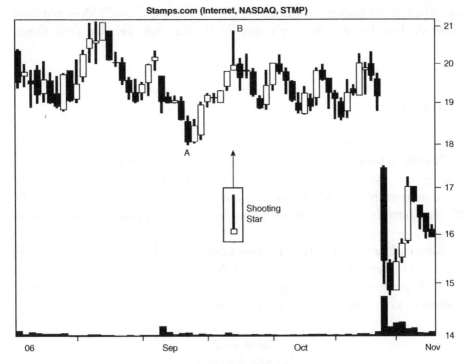

Stamps.com (Internet, NASDAQ, STMP)

Figure 76.1   A shooting star marks the end of an uptrend.

a small body behind. The coming days will tell what direction price will travel, because the outcome is almost random (58.8% reverse).

Identification Guidelines

Figure 76.1 shows what a shooting star looks like. This one tops out at B from an upward price trend that begins at A. The candle pattern shows how the bulls tried to hold on to a new high, but the bears hammered price down to near where it opened. What remains is a distinctive candle easily spotted.

Table 76.1 lists identification guidelines. Price forms a long upper shadow that is at least twice as tall as the body. The small body can be any color, and

Table 76.1
Identification Guidelines

Characteristic	Discussion
Number of candle lines	One.
Price trend	Upward leading to the start of the candle pattern.
Configuration	Look for a tall upper shadow at least twice the body height above a small body. The body should be at or near the candle's low, with no lower shadow (or a very small one).

it's perched at the bottom of the candle. Most times the candle does not have a lower shadow, but if it does, it's very small, like a whisker that your shaver missed.

Statistics

Table 76.2 shows general statistics.

Number found. My search of over 4.7 million candles found 15,917 shooting stars, but that doesn't count the ones you'll see in August during the Perseid meteor shower. Most shooting stars appear in a bull market, especially if it's dark outside with few clouds. (That latter part is a joke, in case you were dozing.)

Reversal or continuation performance. Shooting stars perform best in a bear market, regardless of the breakout direction.

S&P performance. The performance of the S&P 500 index pales in comparison to the shooting star over the same period.

Table 76.2
General Statistics

Description	Bull Market, Up Breakout	Bear Market, Up Breakout	Bull Market, Down Breakout	Bear Market, Down Breakout
Number found	5,453	1,098	7,698	1,668
Reversal (R), continuation (C) performance	6.22% C	8.20% C	−6.39% R	−11.15% R
Standard & Poor's 500 change	1.41%	0.61%	−0.61%	−2.64%
Candle end to breakout (median, days)	3	3	2	2
Candle end to trend end (median, days)	6	6	9	10
Number of breakouts near the 12-month low (L), middle (M), or high (H)	L 750, M 1,185, H 2,816	L 245, M 350, H 485	L 1,211, M 1,806, H 3,684	L 426, M 580, H 639
Percentage move for each 12-month period	L 8.63%, M 6.33%, H 5.64%	L 10.05%, M 8.92%, H 7.08%	L −7.53%, M −6.79%, H −5.99%	L −12.38%, M −11.42%, H −10.22%
Candle end + 1 day	1.65%	2.56%	−0.76%	−1.11%
Candle end + 3 days	2.73%	3.64%	−1.37%	−2.35%
Candle end + 5 days	3.03%	3.74%	−1.41%	−2.99%
Candle end + 10 days	3.34%	3.86%	−1.34%	−3.57%
10-day performance rank	46	47	84	60

Candle end to breakout. Upward breakouts take longer to occur, and that makes sense because price should be nearer to the intraday low than the high. A breakout occurs when price closes either above the top or below the bottom of the candle.

Candle end to trend end. Upward breakouts take less time to reach the trend end than downward breakouts. This is probably due to the upward trend leading to the candle. The shooting star forms toward the end of the upward trend. A downward breakout would start a new trend, and that would take longer to complete.

Yearly position, performance. Shooting stars occur most often when price is within a third of the yearly high. However, the best performance comes from stars within a third of the yearly low.

Performance over time. Shooting stars show respectable performance over time. The one fault is with bull market/down breakouts between 5 and 10 days. Performance suffers over that time.

The performance rank is nothing exciting, with the best performance coming after an upward breakout when compared to other candle types. A rank of 1 is best out of 103 candles, by the way.

Table 76.3 shows height statistics.

Candle height. Tall patterns outperform. To determine whether the candle is short or tall, compute its height from high to low price and divide by the breakout price. If the result is higher than the median, then you have a tall candle; otherwise it's short.

For example, Rich sees a shooting star with a high of 40 and a low of 39. Is the candle short or tall? The height is 40 − 39, or 1, so the measure would be 1/40, or 2.5%, for upward breakouts in a bull market. The candle is tall.

Table 76.3
Height Statistics

Description	Bull Market, Up Breakout	Bear Market, Up Breakout	Bull Market, Down Breakout	Bear Market, Down Breakout
Median candle height as a percentage of breakout price	2.03%	2.88%	2.14%	3.14%
Short candle, performance	5.15%	6.46%	−5.13%	−8.94%
Tall candle, performance	7.72%	10.43%	−8.37%	−13.82%
Percentage meeting price target (measure rule)	81%	79%	82%	84%
Median upper shadow as a percentage of breakout price	1.57%	2.23%	1.66%	2.50%
Short upper shadow, performance	5.19%	6.54%	−5.18%	−9.13%
Tall upper shadow, performance	7.57%	10.27%	−8.20%	−13.49%

Table 76.4
Volume Statistics

Description	Bull Market, Up Breakout	Bear Market, Up Breakout	Bull Market, Down Breakout	Bear Market, Down Breakout
Above-average candle volume, performance	6.29%	8.18%	−6.58%	−10.96%
Below-average candle volume, performance	6.15%	8.21%	−6.23%	−11.30%
Heavy breakout volume, performance	7.02%	9.15%	−6.76%	−11.02%
Light breakout volume, performance	5.37%	7.18%	−6.21%	−11.23%

Measure rule. Use the measure rule to help predict how far price will rise or fall. Compute the height of the candle and multiply it by the appropriate percentage shown in the table; then apply it to the breakout price.

What are Rich's price targets? The upward target would be $(1 \times 81\%) + 40$, or 40.81. The downward target would be $39 - (1 \times 82\%)$, or 38.18.

Upper shadow performance. To determine whether the shadow is short or tall, compute the height of the shadow and divide by the breakout price. Compare the result to the median in the table. Tall shadows have a percentage higher than the median, and they suggest good postbreakout performance across the board.

Table 76.4 shows volume statistics.

Average candle volume. Candles in bull markets perform better with above-average volume. Bear market candles do better if the candle has below-average volume.

Breakout volume. Heavy breakout volume leads to better performance in all cases except for bear market/down breakouts. Those do better after light breakout volume.

Trading Tactics

The best performance from a shooting star is obtained by trading it as part of an upward retracement in a downward price trend. That way the downward breakout joins with the primary price trend to carry the stock lower. In an uptrend, the breakout is downward, too, but it's not likely to last long. Price often forms an inverted and ascending scallop chart pattern.

I split trading tactics into two basic studies, one concerning reversal rates and the other concerning performance. Of the two, reversal rates are more

Table 76.5
Reversal Rates

Description	Bull Market	Bear Market
Closing price confirmation reversal rate	93%	94%
Candle color confirmation reversal rate	84%	84%
Opening gap confirmation reversal rate	74%	73%
Reversal rate: trend up, breakout down	59%	60%
Continuation rate: trend up, breakout up	41%	40%
Percentage of reversals (R)/continuations (C) for each 12-month low (L), middle (M), or high (H)	L 62% R/38% C, M 60% R/40% C, H 57% R/43% C	L 63% R/37% C, M 62% R/38% C, H 57% R/43% C
Black body reversal rate	62%	65%
White body reversal rate	58%	59%

important, because it's better to trade in the direction of the trend and let price run as far as it can.

Table 76.5 gives tips to find the trend direction.

Confirmation reversal rates. To verify that a shooting star will work as a reversal, wait for price to close lower the next day. If that happens, the chances are 93% in a bull market that price will reverse. That may sound good, but it's not that big a deal. Price is already near the candle's low, so another day might cause a downward breakout and that would label the shooting star as a reversal.

Reversal, continuation rates. A slight majority break out downward.

Yearly range reversals. Reversals are most likely to happen when the breakout is within a third of the yearly low.

Body color reversal rate. Candle color has little influence on reversal rate. However, black bodies tend to reverse slightly more often than white ones.

Table 76.6 shows performance indicators that can give hints as to how your stock will behave after the breakout from this candle pattern.

Confirmation, performance. Use opening gap confirmation to enter the trade quickly and make a bundle. That means if price gaps open lower the next day, consider shorting the stock or selling an existing holding.

Moving average. Breakouts below the 50-day moving average tend to perform better than those above the moving average.

Closing position. With the body sited at the bottom of the candle, price doesn't close in the highest third. The close in the middle third of the candle results in the best postbreakout performance.

Body color performance. A black-bodied shooting star shows better performance in all cases except for bull market/up breakouts. Those do better with white candles.

Table 76.6
Performance Indicators

Description	Bull Market, Up Breakout	Bear Market, Up Breakout	Bull Market, Down Breakout	Bear Market, Down Breakout
Closing price confirmation, performance	N/A	N/A	−6.15%	−9.85%
Candle color confirmation, performance	N/A	N/A	−6.35%	−10.07%
Opening gap confirmation, performance	N/A	N/A	−6.83%	−10.74%
Breakout above 50-day moving average, performance	6.03%	7.86%	−6.37%	−10.60%
Breakout below 50-day moving average, performance	7.21%	9.57%	−7.09%	−12.16%
Last candle: close in highest third, performance	0.00%	0.00%	0.00%	0.00%
Last candle: close in middle third, performance	7.34%	8.76%	−8.86%	−14.40%
Last candle: close in lowest third, performance	6.20%	8.19%	−6.37%	−11.07%
Black body, performance	6.12%	8.74%	−6.89%	−11.16%
White body, performance	6.24%	8.10%	−6.27%	−11.15%

N/A means not applicable.

Sample Trade

Figure 76.2 shows a trade that Rich found upsetting. Price made a substantial rise to A and then plummeted to C, a 16-point drop in just two days. That massive decline in such a short time suggested inherent weakness in the stock. Therefore, when the shooting star at B appeared, Rich decided to short the stock at the open the next day.

Price cooperated by opening lower, confirming the candle as a reversal. Would price drop to C and confirm a double top as Rich hoped? Only time would tell. However, a tall black body, such as candle A, often acts as a support zone. In this case, two days after B price found support just below A's midpoint. Then the stock staged a recovery. When it closed above peak B at D, Rich closed out his trade for a loss. Then, however, price made the move he had been hoping for, eventually bottoming at 37 and change (not shown). Rich's instincts were right, but his timing wasn't.

For Best Performance

The following list offers tips and observations to help choose candles that perform well. Consult the associated table for more information.

Figure 76.2 A shooting star leads to a reversal but not a substantial one.

- Use the identification guidelines to help select the pattern—Table 76.1.
- Candles within a third of the yearly low perform best—Table 76.2.
- Select tall candles—Table 76.3.
- Use the measure rule to predict a price target—Table 76.3.
- Candles with tall upper shadows outperform—Table 76.3.
- Volume gives performance clues—Table 76.4.
- Select candles as part of an upward retracement in a downward price trend—Trading Tactics discussion.
- Closing price confirmation can help determine whether the candle will break out downward in a reversal of the uptrend—Table 76.5.
- Patterns within a third of the yearly low tend to act as reversals most often—Table 76.5.
- Opening gap confirmation works best—Table 76.6.
- Breakouts below the 50-day moving average lead to the best performance—Table 76.6.

77

Shooting Star, Two-Candle

Behavior and Rank

Theoretical: Bearish reversal.

Actual bull market: Bullish continuation 61% of the time (ranking 20).

Actual bear market: Bullish continuation 58% of the time (ranking 24).

Frequency: 51st out of 103.

Overall performance over time: 52nd out of 103.

The shooting star comes in two varieties. This version is a two-candle line pattern. The other version is covered in the prior chapter. The differences between the two versions extend beyond their shape. The two-candle version acts as a continuation pattern 61% of the time, but the single-line version is a reversal 59% of the time (bull market). The reason for this behavior change is that a reversal has to close below the candle's low. With a two-line pattern that's harder to do. If price rises above the top of the candle first, then it's a continuation pattern. In a single-line candle with price closing near the low, a downward breakout (and thus a reversal) is easier to achieve.

As a continuation, performance is quite good, ranking 20 in a bull market out of 103 candles, where 1 is best. The frequency rank of 51 also means it appears often enough to be worth the chase. However, with an overall performance rank of 52, it's a midlist performer. In an upward price trend and an upward breakout, price tends to move horizontally for about a week in many cases.

The psychology behind the pattern starts with an upward trend leading to a white candle. The white candle means buying demand is helping price rise. The next day price gaps open upward and races to a new high, but then it closes much lower, near the day's low. The tall upper shadow means the rally could not be maintained and a downward turn might follow. In many cases, a downturn *does* occur but it's not deep enough to cause price to reverse (meaning it fails to close below the first candle's low). Price often resumes the uptrend before that happens.

Identification Guidelines

Figure 77.1 shows a two-candle shooting star acting as a continuation pattern. The uptrend begins at A and rises to C where the shooting star ends. Since C is close to the level of B and price at B turned because of overhead resistance, I would expect price to reverse at C. It doesn't. Price gaps open higher and forms a tall white candle followed by another high two days later. A shooting star is supposed to act as a reversal, but it doesn't in this case and in the majority of cases I looked at.

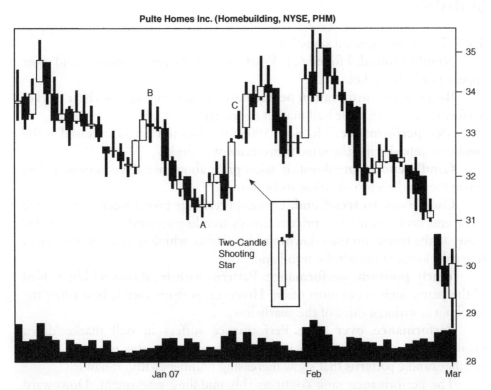

Figure 77.1 A two-candle shooting star should reverse the price trend but doesn't.

Table 77.1
Identification Guidelines

Characteristic	Discussion
Number of candle lines	Two.
Price trend	Upward leading to the start of the candle pattern.
First day	A white candle.
Second day	A candle with an upper shadow at least three times the height of the body. The small body is at the bottom end of the candle and the candle has no lower shadow or a very small one. The body gaps above the prior day's body.

Table 77.1 lists identification guidelines. In this two-candle version, look for a white candle that forms in an upward price trend. Price gaps higher the next day (a higher body—ignore the shadows) and forms a candle with an upper shadow at least three times as tall as the body. The body is a small one that resides at the low end of the candle. The candle has no lower shadow (or if it does, it's very small).

Statistics

Table 77.2 shows general statistics.

Number found. I found 6,434 patterns out of over 4.7 million, and most appear in a bull market.

Reversal or continuation performance. Shooting stars in a bear market perform better than their bull market counterparts.

S&P performance. The S&P 500 index does not perform as well as the candle despite sharing the same measurement periods.

Candle end to breakout. It takes price about five days to close either above the candle's top or below its bottom.

Candle end to trend end. Upward breakouts take a week to reach the trend end, probably because price is already trending upward. This places price closer to the trend end than downward breakouts, which start a new trend and thus take longer to reach the trend end.

Yearly position, performance. Patterns with breakouts within a third of the yearly high occur most often. However, performance is best when the breakout is within a third of the yearly low.

Performance over time. Performance suffers in bull market/down breakouts between days 5 and 10. Thus, the shooting star is not as robust as other candle patterns that show increasing numbers without flaws.

The performance rank confirms this middling assessment. Downward breakouts show a slight performance lead over upward breakouts when compared to other candle types.

Table 77.2
General Statistics

Description	Bull Market, Up Breakout	Bear Market, Up Breakout	Bull Market, Down Breakout	Bear Market, Down Breakout
Number found	3,355	515	2,188	376
Reversal (R), continuation (C) performance	6.01% C	7.15% C	−4.84% R	−9.01% R
Standard & Poor's 500 change	1.29%	0.27%	−0.85%	−2.54%
Candle end to breakout (median, days)	5	5	6	5
Candle end to trend end (median, days)	7	7	10	10
Number of breakouts near the 12-month low (L), middle (M), or high (H)	L 347, M 687, H 1,748	L 108, M 164, H 237	L 351, M 489, H 1,010	L 112, M 120, H 141
Percentage move for each 12-month period	L 7.53%, M 5.78%, H 5.52%	L 9.87%, M 8.46%, H 5.66%	L −6.69%, M −5.50%, H −5.00%	L −10.67%, M −9.87%, H −7.56%
Candle end + 1 day	1.08%	1.79%	−0.69%	−0.82%
Candle end + 3 days	1.93%	2.91%	−1.85%	−2.73%
Candle end + 5 days	2.41%	3.22%	−2.55%	−4.18%
Candle end + 10 days	3.27%	3.70%	−2.48%	−4.93%
10-day performance rank	51	48	47	31

Table 77.3 shows height statistics.

Candle height. Tall candles outperform. To determine whether the candle is short or tall, compute its height from highest high to lowest low price in the candle pattern and divide by the breakout price. If the result is higher than the median, then you have a tall candle; otherwise it's short.

Lou sees a shooting star with a high price of 89 and a low of 84. Is the candle short or tall? The height is 89 − 84, or 5, so the measure is 5/89, or 5.6% in a bull market/up breakout scenario. The candle is tall.

Measure rule. Use the measure rule to help predict how far price will rise or fall. Compute the height of the candle pattern and multiply it by the appropriate percentage shown in the table; then apply it to the breakout price.

What are the price targets for Lou's candle? The upward target would be $(5 \times 52\%) + 89$, or 91.60, and the downward target would be $89 - (5 \times 48\%)$, or 86.60. This assumes a bull market.

Upper shadow performance. The table's results pertain to the last candle line in the pattern. To determine whether the shadow is short or tall,

Table 77.3
Height Statistics

Description	Bull Market, Up Breakout	Bear Market, Up Breakout	Bull Market, Down Breakout	Bear Market, Down Breakout
Median candle height as a percentage of breakout price	4.26%	6.39%	4.47%	6.72%
Short candle, performance	4.86%	6.38%	−4.08%	−7.14%
Tall candle, performance	7.64%	8.10%	−6.40%	−11.33%
Percentage meeting price target (measure rule)	52%	48%	48%	49%
Median upper shadow as a percentage of breakout price	1.64%	2.76%	1.73%	2.89%
Short upper shadow, performance	5.11%	6.30%	−4.17%	−6.51%
Tall upper shadow, performance	7.07%	8.18%	−6.00%	−11.68%

compute the height of the shadow and divide by the breakout price. Compare the result to the median in the table. Tall shadows have a percentage higher than the median. Candles with tall upper shadows result in the best performance.

Table 77.4 shows volume statistics.

Candle volume trend. A rising volume trend works best most often. The exception is bear market/up breakouts. Those do better if the candle shows falling volume.

Table 77.4
Volume Statistics

Description	Bull Market, Up Breakout	Bear Market, Up Breakout	Bull Market, Down Breakout	Bear Market, Down Breakout
Rising candle volume, performance	6.11%	7.00%	−5.56%	−9.04%
Falling candle volume, performance	5.89%	7.34%	−5.26%	−9.03%
Above-average candle volume, performance	6.16%	6.89%	−5.26%	−9.40%
Below-average candle volume, performance	5.82%	7.42%	−4.51%	−8.67%
Heavy breakout volume, performance	6.72%	8.00%	−5.87%	−10.20%
Light breakout volume, performance	5.17%	6.28%	−4.24%	−7.89%

Average candle volume. Candles with above-average volume do better after the breakout. The one exception comes from upward breakouts in a bear market. Those do better if volume is below average.

Breakout volume. Heavy breakout volume results in the best performance across the board.

Trading Tactics

When the trend is upward in the very short term (but the primary price trend is downward), the two-candle shooting star acts as a reversal, taking price lower. If the primary price trend is upward, then expect any reversal of the uptrend to be short-lived unless it appears after a long, straight-line run-up.

As mentioned earlier in the Behavior and Rank section of this chapter, price tends to move horizontally for about a week or so in a primary uptrend after an upward breakout from this candle.

I split trading tactics into two basic studies, one concerning reversal rates and the other concerning performance. Of the two, reversal rates are more important, because it's better to trade in the direction of the trend and let price run as far as it can.

Table 77.5 gives tips to find the trend direction.

Confirmation reversal rates. If you want to hunt for a shooting star that acts as a reversal, wait for price to close lower the next day. That works 65% of the time.

Reversal, continuation rates. Price breaks out upward most often.

Yearly range reversals. Breakouts within a third of the yearly high result in continuation patterns 63% of the time.

Table 77.6 shows performance indicators that can give hints as to how your stock will behave after the breakout from this candle pattern.

Confirmation, performance. In a bull market, the opening gap method of confirmation works best. That means waiting for price to gap open lower the

Table 77.5
Reversal Rates

Description	Bull Market	Bear Market
Closing price confirmation reversal rate	65%	65%
Candle color confirmation reversal rate	58%	61%
Opening gap confirmation reversal rate	56%	54%
Reversal rate: trend up, breakout down	39%	42%
Continuation rate: trend up, breakout up	61%	58%
Percentage of reversals (R)/continuations (C) for each 12-month low (L), middle (M), or high (H)	L 50% R/50% C, M 42% R/58% C, H 37% R/63% C	L 51% R/49% C, M 42% R/58% C, H 37% R/63% C

Table 77.6
Performance Indicators

Description	Bull Market, Up Breakout	Bear Market, Up Breakout	Bull Market, Down Breakout	Bear Market, Down Breakout
Closing price confirmation, performance	N/A	N/A	−7.91%	−9.90%
Candle color confirmation, performance	N/A	N/A	−6.83%	−10.85%
Opening gap confirmation, performance	N/A	N/A	−8.31%	−9.32%
Breakout above 50-day moving average, performance	5.95%	6.96%	−4.98%	−7.90%
Breakout below 50-day moving average, performance	6.58%	8.76%	−4.56%	−11.40%

N/A means not applicable.

next day to confirm a reversal. In a bear market, use candle color as confirmation of a reversal. That means waiting for a black candle the next day before taking a position.

Moving average. Candles with breakouts below the 50-day moving average tend to outperform. The one exception is bull market/down breakouts, which do better when the breakout is above the moving average.

Sample Trade

Lou liked the oilfield services stock pictured in Figure 77.2, so he bought it after it formed an ugly double bottom at C. That's when price forms two uneven bottoms with a tall peak between them.

As price climbed, he became more nervous, wondering when the good times would end. When price climbed to B and formed a two-candle shooting star, he felt relieved. The two-candle version of the shooting star acts as a continuation pattern most often and that would mean more upside to follow. Additionally, it was within a third of the yearly high, and that suggested a continuation pattern 63% of the time (see Table 77.5).

Then he saw that price at B matched the high at A. Prior peaks and valleys are known points of support and resistance, so this made him feel nervous again. He decided to wait and see which way price broke out of the pattern.

A black candle formed a day after B, followed by a tall black candle that confirmed a downward breakout and a reversal of the uptrend. He sold the stock a day later.

For Best Performance

The following list offers tips and observations to help choose candles that perform well. Consult the associated table for more information.

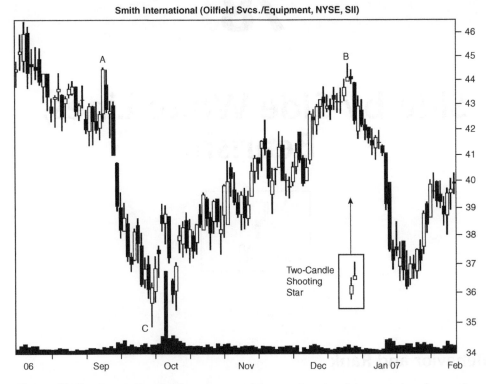

Figure 77.2 A two-candle shooting star hits overhead resistance set up by a prior peak, and price reverses direction.

- Use the identification guidelines to help select the pattern—Table 77.1.
- Candles within a third of the yearly low perform best—Table 77.2.
- Select tall candles—Table 77.3.
- Use the measure rule to predict a price target—Table 77.3.
- Candles with tall upper shadows outperform—Table 77.3.
- Volume gives performance clues—Table 77.4.
- To help detect a reversal, look for a lower close the next day—Table 77.5.
- Patterns within a third of the yearly high tend to act as continuations most often—Table 77.5.
- Opening gap confirmation of a reversal works best in a bull market—Table 77.6.
- Breakouts below the 50-day moving average lead to the best performance most of the time (the exception: bull market/down breakouts)—Table 77.6.

78

Side-by-Side White Lines, Bearish

Behavior and Rank

Theoretical: Bearish continuation.

Actual bull market: Bearish continuation 56% of the time (ranking 27).

Actual bear market: Bearish continuation 57% of the time (ranking 27).

Frequency: 86th out of 103.

Overall performance over time: 29th out of 103.

I found the side-by-side white lines pattern to be confusing. The descriptions from multiple sources said that the opening price of the last two candle lines should be similar, and yet it's the closing price that appears the same in their pictures. I took them at their word and coded for a similar open, and that's what the statistics reflect. I'll discuss identification guidelines in a moment.

The continuation ranks are quite good at 27 out of 103 candles, with 1 being the best. However, the pattern is rare, ranking 86, so you might never see it. If you do, the performance rank is very good at 29.

The psychology behind the pattern also has a bit of a twist. This pattern is supposed to act as a continuation, and testing reveals that it does. Price trends lower as the bears are on the hunt for nervous bulls. A tall black candle appears, confirming the dearth of buying demand. Price gaps lower the next day, but here comes the twist. The covering of short selling over the next two days helps two bullish white candles print on the chart. Once the short covering is done, however, price is free to resume its downward move.

Whether short covering or buying demand spurred by a cheap price is the reason for the two white candles is anyone's guess. However, price does then move down 56% of the time. That's not much above random, so I wouldn't trust this pattern. Since it's scarce, I might not see it again in my lifetime, anyway.

Identification Guidelines

Figure 78.1 shows what the side-by-side white lines pattern looks like. This one appears in a downward price trend, as all of them should, and price breaks out downward, as expected. Just three days later, though, price stages a recovery. Based on this one chart, it appears that the decline after the pattern ends is not a lasting one.

Table 78.1 lists identification guidelines. Price forms a black candle in a downward price trend. It need not be a tall candle. The next day, price gaps lower but forms a white candle whose close remains below the prior close, thereby leaving the gap intact. The final day shows another white candle similar in size to the prior candle with similar opening prices and a closing price that remains below the black candle's close. Again, the body gap between the black candle and the two white ones remains intact.

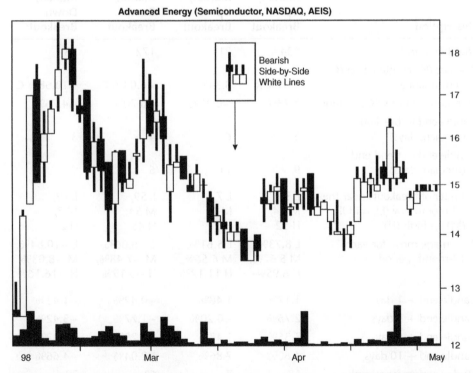

Figure 78.1 Side-by-side white lines appear in a downtrend just before price reverses four days later.

Table 78.1
Identification Guidelines

Characteristic	Discussion
Number of candle lines	Three.
Price trend	Downward leading to the start of the candle pattern.
First day	A black candle.
Days 2 and 3	White candles with bodies about the same size and opening prices near the same value. The closing prices in both candles remain below the body of the black candle.

Statistics

Table 78.2 shows general statistics. The sample counts are few for this candle pattern, so the results and conclusions are likely to change.

Number found. I found 355 patterns out of over 4.7 million candle lines. Most patterns appeared in a bull market.

Table 78.2
General Statistics

Description	Bull Market, Up Breakout	Bear Market, Up Breakout*	Bull Market, Down Breakout	Bear Market, Down Breakout*
Number found	134	21	172	28
Reversal (R), continuation (C) performance	7.01% R	8.34% R	−6.04% C	−10.68% C
Standard & Poor's 500 change	1.73%	−0.25%	−0.70%	−4.76%
Candle end to breakout (median, days)	5	6	4	3
Candle end to trend end (median, days)	9	11	6	9
Number of breakouts near the 12-month low (L), middle (M), or high (H)	L 35, M 34, H 52	L 7, M 7, H 7	L 59, M 54, H 45	L 19, M 7, H 2
Percentage move for each 12-month period	L 8.73%, M 5.67%, H 6.95%	L 5.61%, M 6.56%, H 11.12%	L −6.06%, M −7.48%, H −5.19%	L −10.84%, M −8.03%, H −16.16%
Candle end + 1 day	1.17%	1.48%	−0.42%	−1.43%
Candle end + 3 days	2.76%	−0.20%	−1.77%	−3.42%
Candle end + 5 days	3.35%	1.48%	−2.28%	−5.32%
Candle end + 10 days	4.60%	7.86%	−2.04%	−4.66%
10-day performance rank	18	7	63	38

*Fewer than 30 samples.

Reversal or continuation performance. The best performance comes from patterns in a bear market, and that result agrees with what we've seen for other candle types.

S&P performance. The candle pattern beats the S&P 500 index in all conditions.

Candle end to breakout. Price takes between three and six days to break out. Downward breakouts take less time because price is already trending downward and the close is nearer the pattern's low than the high.

Candle end to trend end. Downward breakouts also take less time to the trend end than upward breakouts. Again, this is due to price being closer to the end of the trend for downward breakouts. Upward breakouts would begin a new trend, so that would take longer to complete than one midway along.

Yearly position, performance. The candle pattern appears most often within a third of the yearly low for downward breakouts. The best performance occurs when the breakout is within a third of the yearly high in a bear market. Bull market performance shows no consistent trend.

Performance over time. In three out of the four columns, performance decreases from one period to the next at least once instead of increasing. In a robust candle, the numbers would climb over time. The candle may not be worth relying on, but additional samples might turn the tide.

Upward breakouts show better performance ranks than downward breakouts. That's evident in the percentage change after 10 days. With 1 being the best rank out of 103 candles, the candle performs better when it acts as a reversal of the downtrend.

Table 78.3 shows height statistics.

Candle height. Tall candles outperform. To determine whether the candle is short or tall, compute its height from highest high to lowest low price in the candle pattern and divide by the breakout price. If the result is higher than the median, then you have a tall candle; otherwise it's short.

For example, Sandy has a side-by-side white lines candle formation with a high of 40 and a low of 38. Is the candle tall or short? The height is 40 – 38, or 2, so the measure would be 2/40, or 5%. In a bull market with an upward breakout, the candle would be tall.

Measure rule. Use the measure rule to help predict how far price will rise or fall. Compute the height of the candle pattern and multiply it by the appropriate percentage shown in the table; then apply it to the breakout price.

What are the price targets for Sandy's candle? The upward target would be $(2 \times 65\%) + 40$, or 41.30, and the downward target would be $38 - (2 \times 52\%)$, or 36.96. Both assume a bull market.

Shadows. The table's results pertain to the last candle line in the pattern. To determine whether the shadow is short or tall, compute the height of the shadow and divide by the breakout price. Compare the result to the median in the table. Tall shadows have a percentage higher than the median.

Table 78.3
Height Statistics

Description	Bull Market, Up Breakout	Bear Market, Up Breakout*	Bull Market, Down Breakout	Bear Market, Down Breakout*
Median candle height as a percentage of breakout price	4.02%	6.06%	4.37%	5.37%
Short candle, performance	5.59%	4.56%	−4.61%	−7.94%
Tall candle, performance	9.24%	11.31%	−8.11%	−14.32%
Percentage meeting price target (measure rule)	65%	38%	52%	71%
Median upper shadow as a percentage of breakout price	0.86%	1.96%	0.66%	1.26%
Short upper shadow, performance	6.47%	6.44%	−4.94%	−8.62%
Tall upper shadow, performance	7.68%	9.70%	−7.13%	−13.53%
Median lower shadow as a percentage of breakout price	0.35%	1.22%	0.28%	0.89%
Short lower shadow, performance	6.68%	8.30%	−6.62%	−15.50%
Tall lower shadow, performance	7.30%	8.41%	−5.60%	−8.13%

*Fewer than 30 samples.

Upper shadow performance. Tall upper shadows outperform short ones in all cases.

Lower shadow performance. Tall lower shadows work better for upward breakouts, and short shadows work better for downward breakouts.

Table 78.4 shows volume statistics.

Table 78.4
Volume Statistics

Description	Bull Market, Up Breakout	Bear Market, Up Breakout*	Bull Market, Down Breakout	Bear Market, Down Breakout*
Rising candle volume, performance	8.76%	6.77%	−7.06%	−7.47%
Falling candle volume, performance	5.97%	9.61%	−5.33%	−13.98%
Above-average candle volume, performance	7.79%	10.29%	−7.02%	−14.25%
Below-average candle volume, performance	6.25%	4.68%	−5.29%	−8.82%
Heavy breakout volume, performance	7.20%	9.52%	−6.42%	−8.18%
Light breakout volume, performance	6.72%	6.25%	−5.74%	−12.89%

*Fewer than 30 samples.

Candle volume trend. A rising volume trend works best for candles in a bull market, and falling volume leads to better postbreakout performance in a bear market.

Average candle volume. Above-average candle volume suggests good performance in every situation.

Breakout volume. Heavy breakout volume means better postbreakout performance in all cases except for bear market/down breakouts. Those do better with light breakout volume. That's unusual, because most chart pattern types do best after heavy breakout volume.

Trading Tactics

In an upward price trend, you often see side-by-side white lines forming at the end of the downward retracement, perhaps when price declines to 38%, 50%, or 62% of the prior up move. Those act as reversals of the small downtrend.

If the candle has a downward breakout in the same rise-retrace price movement, then it's probably because price has not retraced far enough (to one of the 38%, 50%, or 62% Fibonacci retracement levels).

Side-by-side white lines candlestick patterns, when the primary price trend is downward, often break out downward, continuing the trend. Those that break out upward may find that price stops rising soon after the breakout (a week or two).

I split trading tactics into two basic studies, one concerning reversal rates and the other concerning performance. Of the two, reversal rates are more important, because it's better to trade in the direction of the trend and let price run as far as it can.

Table 78.5 gives tips to find the trend direction.

Table 78.5
Reversal Rates

Description	Bull Market	Bear Market*
Closing price confirmation reversal rate	67%	73%
Candle color confirmation reversal rate	63%	68%
Opening gap confirmation reversal rate	48%	38%
Reversal: trend down, breakout up	44%	43%
Continuation: trend down, breakout down	56%	57%
Percentage of reversals (R)/continuations (C) for each 12-month low (L), middle (M), or high (H)	L 37% R/63% C, M 39% R/61% C, H 54% R/46% C	L 27% R/73% C, M 50% R/50% C, H 78% R/22% C

*Fewer than 30 samples.

Table 78.6
Performance Indicators

Description	Bull Market, Up Breakout	Bear Market, Up Breakout*	Bull Market, Down Breakout	Bear Market, Down Breakout*
Closing price confirmation, performance	N/A	N/A	−6.01%	−15.67%
Candle color confirmation, performance	N/A	N/A	−6.97%	−15.28%
Opening gap confirmation, performance	N/A	N/A	−7.28%	−10.15%
Breakout above 50-day moving average, performance	6.65%	10.24%	−5.25%	−6.76%
Breakout below 50-day moving average, performance	7.29%	5.05%	−6.44%	−11.40%
Last candle: close in highest third, performance	6.79%	7.10%	−5.87%	−7.72%
Last candle: close in middle third, performance	7.42%	5.07%	−4.56%	−12.60%
Last candle: close in lowest third, performance	6.37%*	12.26%	−10.13%	−14.21%

N/A means not applicable.
*Fewer than 30 samples.

Confirmation reversal rates. The best method of detecting a reversal is to wait for price to close higher the next day. That works between 67% and 73% of the time.

Reversal, continuation rates. As the table shows, the breakout direction is often downward but it's close to random (50%).

Yearly range reversals. Patterns with breakouts within a third of the yearly low often lead to continuations of the price trend—63% of the time in a bull market and 73% of the time in a bear market.

Table 78.6 shows performance indicators that can give hints as to how your stock will behave after the breakout from this candle pattern.

Confirmation, performance. Opening gap confirmation in a bull market gives the best performance. That's when you wait for price to gap open lower before trading the stock. Bear markets do better with closing price confirmation. That's when you wait for a lower close the next day before trading.

Moving average. Candles with breakouts below the 50-day moving average tend to perform well after the breakout. The lone exception is bear market/up breakouts, which do better when the breakout is above the moving average.

Closing position. A close in the lowest third of the last candle line suggests good performance post breakout. However, bull market/up breakouts do better when the price is in the middle third of the candle high-low range.

Sample Trade

Sandy has been swing trading the stock shown in Figure 78.2 for years, so she knows it well. She draws a horizontal support line connecting the valleys at B and C and extends it to A. Along the top, she connects peaks D and E with another trendline and extends it forward to F. F is the intended price target.

The result of her artwork is a descending triangle in which price trends downward along the peaks and remains horizontal along the bottom. Descending triangles predict downward breakouts 64% of the time.

When price forms the side-by-side white lines at A, her instinct says that price will reverse instead of continuing down. However, she waits for the open the next day for confirmation. Price cooperates by gapping higher, so she buys the stock.

Price moves up in rapid fashion like a climber on a cliff wall facing inclement weather in two days. At G, three white soldiers are a bullish candle signal. The stock has already closed above the down-sloping trendline and her target price, F. Therefore, Sandy decides to hold on, hoping for a sustained breakout trend.

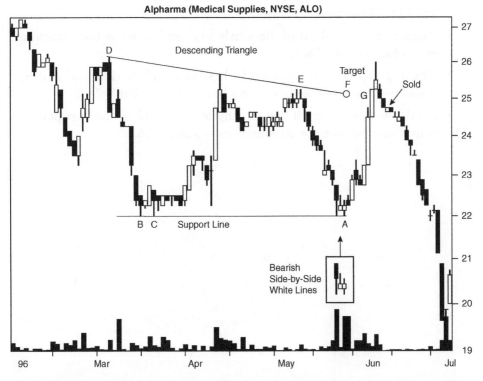

Figure 78.2 A swing trade after a side-by-side white lines candle pattern results in a profit.

The next day price moves up and forms a shooting star type of pattern but one with an upper shadow too short to qualify. Still, it looks bearish to Sandy. When price drops below the top trendline, she can tell the up move is over and sells the stock.

For Best Performance

The following list offers tips and observations to help choose candles that perform well. Consult the associated table for more information.

- Use the identification guidelines to help select the pattern—Table 78.1.
- Candles within a third of the yearly low in a bull market and upward breakout perform best—Table 78.2.
- Select tall candles—Table 78.3.
- Use the measure rule to predict a price target—Table 78.3.
- Candles with tall upper shadows outperform—Table 78.3.
- Volume gives performance clues—Table 78.4.
- To help detect a reversal, use the closing price the day after the side-by-side white lines candle formation ends. That works between 67% and 73% of the time—Table 78.5.
- Patterns within a third of the yearly low tend to act as continuations most often—Table 78.5.
- Opening gap confirmation works best in a bull market, and closing price confirmation does better in a bear market—Table 78.6.
- Breakouts below the 50-day moving average lead to the best performance in most, but not all, situations—Table 78.6.

79

Side-by-Side White Lines, Bullish

Behavior and Rank

Theoretical: Bullish continuation.

Actual bull market: Bullish continuation 66% of the time (ranking 12).

Actual bear market: Bullish continuation 64% of the time (ranking 18).

Frequency: 73rd out of 103.

Overall performance over time: 46th out of 103.

The sources I checked were right after all. The bullish variety of side-by-side white lines appears more often than the bearish one, by a ratio of 3 to 1. The bullish one also works much better. Two out of three act as continuation patterns in a bull market, ranking 12 out of 103 candles, where 1 is best. The pattern's performance is mediocre, though. Thus, you may get a continuation but price may not climb far.

The psychology behind the pattern has the bulls in control, pushing price upward to the start of the candle pattern. Price moves up in a white candle, reflecting buying demand. The next day, price gaps up and forms another white candle. The bears jump into the ring and go another round with the bulls the next day by forcing price to open lower, but by day's end the stock has formed a third white candle, suggesting the uptrend is intact.

Figure 79.1 Bullish side-by-side white lines appear near the end of the up-trend.

Identification Guidelines

Figure 79.1 shows what a bullish side-by-side white lines pattern looks like. Price trends higher and then forms three white candles. The last two have bodies of similar shape and open near the same price. In this example, price breaks out downward in a black candle the next day, but that's unusual. Normally, the candlestick acts as a continuation pattern 65% of the time.

Table 79.1 lists identification guidelines. This candle pattern uses three lines. It's trickier than many other candles because the opening prices during

Table 79.1
Identification Guidelines

Characteristic	Discussion
Number of candle lines	Three.
Price trend	Upward leading to the start of the candle pattern.
First day	A white candle.
Days 2 and 3	Two white candles with bodies of similar size and opening prices near each other. The bodies of both candles remain above the body of the first white candle, leaving a gap.

days 2 and 3 are similar, as are the bodies of the two candles. In addition, the opening price in the last two days gaps above the close of the first day.

Statistics

Table 79.2 shows general statistics.

Number found. This candle pattern is rare. Out of over 4.7 million candle lines, I found just 984, many from a bull market.

Reversal or continuation performance. Patterns in a bear market outperform those from the bull market.

S&P performance. The candlestick beats the performance of the S&P 500 index over the same periods.

Candle end to breakout. It takes price between three and six days to break out. A breakout occurs when price closes either above the top of the candle or below the bottom.

Candle end to trend end. Upward breakouts take about a week to reach the trend end, a slightly shorter time than downward breakouts. This makes

Table 79.2
General Statistics

Description	Bull Market, Up Breakout	Bear Market, Up Breakout	Bull Market, Down Breakout	Bear Market, Down Breakout
Number found	541	101	285	57
Reversal (R), continuation (C) performance	5.28% C	6.91% C	−5.09% R	−9.32% R
Standard & Poor's 500 change	1.05%	0.51%	−1.12%	−2.95%
Candle end to breakout (median, days)	4	3	6	4
Candle end to trend end (median, days)	7	7	8	11
Number of breakouts near the 12-month low (L), middle (M), or high (H)	L 56, M 112, H 327	L 22, M 31, H 47	L 51, M 66, H 144	L 12, M 19, H 22
Percentage move for each 12-month period	L 5.53%, M 5.31%, H 5.27%	L 7.86%, M 8.84%, H 5.79%	L −5.39%, M −4.94%, H −4.99%	L −10.56%, M −10.02%, H −7.78%
Candle end + 1 day	0.49%	1.03%	−1.18%	−1.95%
Candle end + 3 days	1.08%	1.94%	−2.69%	−4.08%
Candle end + 5 days	1.52%	2.76%	−3.34%	−4.68%
Candle end + 10 days	2.02%	3.34%	−3.58%	−6.07%
10-day performance rank	88	53	24	17

sense because price closes near the top of the candle in an uptrend, so it's closer to the trend end. A downward breakout would start a new trend. Price in the middle of a trend will take less time to reach the trend end than one starting out.

Yearly position, performance. The pattern occurs most often within a third of the yearly high, but performance is best within a third of the yearly low. The one exception comes from candles in the middle of the range in bear market/up breakouts.

Performance over time. This candle pattern is a robust performer. I reserve that term for candles that show better performance over every time period and in all categories, as this one does.

The performance rank, which compares this candle with the performance of others, shows that downward breakouts perform better than upward ones. A rank of 1 is best out of 103 candles.

Table 79.3 shows height statistics.

Candle height. Tall candles outperform. To determine whether the candle is short or tall, compute its height from highest high to lowest low price in the candle pattern and divide by the breakout price. If the result is higher than the median, then you have a tall candle; otherwise it's short.

Frank sees a bullish side-by-side white lines candle pattern with a high of 69 and a low of 64. Is the candle short or tall? The height is 69 – 64, or 5, so

Table 79.3
Height Statistics

Description	Bull Market, Up Breakout	Bear Market, Up Breakout	Bull Market, Down Breakout	Bear Market, Down Breakout
Median candle height as a percentage of breakout price	3.79%	5.13%	4.18%	5.48%
Short candle, performance	3.91%	4.67%	−4.46%	−8.51%
Tall candle, performance	7.13%	9.60%	−6.04%	−10.28%
Percentage meeting price target (measure rule)	50%	54%	48%	61%
Median upper shadow as a percentage of breakout price	0.50%	0.98%	0.55%	1.23%
Short upper shadow, performance	4.16%	5.63%	−5.31%	−8.18%*
Tall upper shadow, performance	6.43%	8.17%	−4.91%	−11.04%*
Median lower shadow as a percentage of breakout price	0.43%	1.03%	0.53%	0.65%
Short lower shadow, performance	4.83%	6.00%	−4.45%	−10.32%*
Tall lower shadow, performance	5.70%	7.77%	−5.68%	−8.50%*

*Fewer than 30 samples.

the measure would be 5/69, or 7.2%. For an upward breakout in a bull market, the candle is tall. Frank's thinking of celebrating the news.

Measure rule. Use the measure rule to help predict how far price will rise or fall. Compute the height of the candle pattern and multiply it by the appropriate percentage shown in the table; then apply it to the breakout price.

What are the price targets for Frank's candle? The upward target would be $(5 \times 50\%) + 69$, or 71.50, and the downward target would be $64 - (5 \times 48\%)$, or 61.60.

Shadows. The table's results pertain to the last candle line in the pattern. To determine whether the shadow is short or tall, compute the height of the shadow and divide by the breakout price. Compare the result to the median in the table. Tall shadows have a percentage higher than the median.

Upper shadow performance. Tall upper shadows mean better performance after the breakout in all cases except for bull market/down breakouts.

Lower shadow performance. Tall lower shadows suggest good post-breakout performance in all categories except for bear market/down breakouts, which do better with short shadows. That's at odds with other chart pattern types, which indicate longer shadows mean better performance in all categories. Perhaps the low sample count is to blame.

Table 79.4 shows volume statistics.

Candle volume trend. A rising volume trend works best for candles in the conditions of bull market/up breakouts and bear market/down breakouts. Falling volume works best in the other two categories: bear market/up breakouts and bull market/down breakouts.

Average candle volume. Average candle volume works similarly to volume trend, with below-average volume working well in bull markets with upward breakouts and bear markets with downward breakouts. The inner two columns work better with above-average candle volume.

Table 79.4
Volume Statistics

Description	Bull Market, Up Breakout	Bear Market, Up Breakout	Bull Market, Down Breakout	Bear Market, Down Breakout
Rising candle volume, performance	5.79%	5.60%	−4.47%	−9.58%*
Falling candle volume, performance	4.96%	7.77%	−5.51%	−9.18%
Above-average candle volume, performance	5.11%	7.13%	−5.25%	−8.83%*
Below-average candle volume, performance	5.40%	6.73%	−4.95%	−9.73%
Heavy breakout volume, performance	5.88%	9.00%	−4.53%	−9.94%*
Light breakout volume, performance	4.77%	5.39%	−5.58%	−8.66%*

*Fewer than 30 samples.

Breakout volume. Heavy breakout volume means better postbreakout performance in all cases except for bull market/down breakouts.

Trading Tactics

Trade this pattern when the primary trend is upward. Should price close below the bottom of the pattern, then close out a long trade.

When the primary trend is downward, watch for a reversal if the trend is a straight-line run of a few weeks' duration. The white lines could signal an end to the trend and a quick but substantial upward retracement. Again, a downward breakout from the candle pattern will signal a warning.

I split trading tactics into two basic studies, one concerning reversal rates and the other concerning performance. Of the two, reversal rates are more important, because it's better to trade in the direction of the trend and let price run as far as it can.

Table 79.5 gives tips to find the trend direction.

Confirmation reversal rates. Waiting for price to close lower the day after the candle pattern ends results in a confirmed reversal between 54% (bull market) and 61% (bear market) of the time. I don't consider those numbers very exciting, but I guess they are better than hitting yourself on the head with a board.

Reversal, continuation rates. Most bullish side-by-side white lines candles break out upward.

Yearly range reversals. The best performance comes from patterns within a third of the yearly high. They tend to break out upward 68% to 69% of the time (continuing the uptrend).

Table 79.6 shows performance indicators that can give hints as to how your stock will behave after the breakout from this candle pattern.

Table 79.5
Reversal Rates

Description	Bull Market	Bear Market
Closing price confirmation reversal rate	54%	61%
Candle color confirmation reversal rate	53%	58%
Opening gap confirmation reversal rate	43%	46%
Reversal rate: trend up, breakout down	35%	36%
Continuation rate: trend up, breakout up	65%	64%
Percentage of reversals (R)/continuations (C) for each 12-month low (L), middle (M), or high (H)	L 48% R/52% C, M 37% R/63% C, H 31% R/69% C	L 35% R/65% C, M 38% R/62% C, H 32% R/68% C

Table 79.6
Performance Indicators

Description	Bull Market, Up Breakout	Bear Market, Up Breakout	Bull Market, Down Breakout	Bear Market, Down Breakout
Closing price confirmation, performance	4.99%	7.73%	N/A	N/A
Candle color confirmation, performance	5.04%	7.54%	N/A	N/A
Opening gap confirmation, performance	5.94%	9.53%	N/A	N/A
Breakout above 50-day moving average, performance	5.27%	6.99%	−5.19%	−6.94%
Breakout below 50-day moving average, performance	5.29%	6.21%	−4.91%	−13.24%*
Last candle: close in highest third, performance	4.67%	7.99%	−5.90%	−8.06%*
Last candle: close in middle third, performance	5.92%	6.63%	−4.51%	−10.00%*
Last candle: close in lowest third, performance	5.62%	4.84%*	−4.28%	−10.30%*

N/A means not applicable.
*Fewer than 30 samples.

Confirmation, performance. Opening gap confirmation works best with this candlestick pattern. That means trading only if price gaps open higher after the side-by-side white lines candle formation ends.

Moving average. Most candle types do best when the breakout is below the moving average. That's the case here only when price follows the market trend—upward in bull markets and downward in bear markets. The countertrend markets (bear/up and bull/down) do better when the breakout is above the moving average.

Closing position. Where price closes shows no consistent trend.

Sample Trade

Frank made the trade shown in Figure 79.2, so let me tell you about it. Price trended down at A and formed a head-and-shoulders bottom chart pattern (LS means left shoulder, and RS means right shoulder) in February and March. When price pierced the line connecting the armpits, he already had a buy order in place that was triggered. Price made lower lows for two days but moved upward with force on the second day.

When price reached B, it paused at overhead resistance set up by peak A. Price dropped and formed what look like a handle to a cup. This was not a true

Figure 79.2   A bullish side-by-side white lines candle formation suggests an upward breakout.

cup with handle pattern, though, because price didn't rise by more than 30% leading to A, the start of the cup.

When price made the bullish side-by-side white lines candlestick formation at C, Frank believed that price would break out upward, and he was right. He added to his position the next day.

Price threw back to D, but that was normal behavior so Frank didn't panic. Price recovered to make a new high.

For Best Performance

The following list offers tips and observations to help choose candles that perform well. Consult the associated table for more information.

- Use the identification guidelines to help select the pattern—Table 79.1.
- Candles within a third of the yearly low perform best most of the time—Table 79.2.
- Select tall candles—Table 79.3.

- Use the measure rule to predict a price target—Table 79.3.
- Volume gives performance clues—Table 79.4.
- Trade this pattern in a primary uptrend—Trading Tactics discussion.
- Expect an upward breakout—Table 79.5.
- Patterns within a third of the yearly high tend to act as continuations most often—Table 79.5.
- Opening gap confirmation works best—Table 79.6.

80

Spinning Top, Black

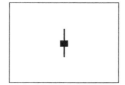

Behavior and Rank

Theoretical: Indecision.

Actual bull market: Reversal 51% of the time (ranking 49).

Actual bear market: Reversal 52% of the time (ranking 38).

Frequency: 1st out of 103.

Overall performance over time: 73rd out of 103.

Black spinning tops are ants at a picnic, having the highest frequency rank of any candle. The candles are everywhere, and they don't mean much when they do appear. As the 51% (bull market) reversal rate attests, you won't be able to glean any significant direction information from these candles. The overall performance rank is 73, which is well down the list from 1 (best) out of 103 candles.

The psychology behind the pattern is what occurs on any given day. Price opens and the bulls and the bears begin fighting immediately, sending price higher and lower during the day, in this case ending with the bears on top, proclaiming victory. What remains is a small black candle with shadows taller than the body.

Identification Guidelines

Figure 80.1 shows several black spinning tops. Marked by arrows, the first two appear in a downtrend and the last two occur in an uptrend. The middle two in June are nothing special. Notice the tall shadows of the candles when compared

Figure 80.1   A number of black spinning tops appear (arrows), with two high-lighted.

to the small bodies. The shadow length is what separates a spinning top from a short black candle. The small but nonzero body height is what differentiates the spinner from a doji.

Table 80.1 lists identification guidelines, and this candle is an easy one to spot. Look for a black day that has a small body and upper and lower shadows that are each taller than the body.

Statistics

Table 80.2 shows general statistics.

Number found. I dug up 71,826 black spinning tops, and that was from just one of four databases I used to hunt for candles. I limited the samples to

Table 80.1
Identification Guidelines

Characteristic	Discussion
Number of candle lines	One.
Configuration	A small black body with shadows longer than the body.

Table 80.2
General Statistics

Description	Bull Market, Up Breakout	Bear Market, Up Breakout	Bull Market, Down Breakout	Bear Market, Down Breakout
Number found	6,809	2,674	7,313	3,204
Reversal (R), continuation (C) performance	6.55% C 7.02% R	7.00% C 9.69% R	−5.74% C −5.91% R	−10.46% C −10.13% R
Standard & Poor's 500 change	1.62%	1.04%	−0.95%	−2.54%
Candle end to breakout (median, days)	2	2	2	2
Candle end to trend end (median, days)	8	7	6	7
Number of breakouts near the 12-month low (L), middle (M), or high (H)	L 1,271, M 1,819, H 3,719	L 800, M 881, H 993	L 1,687, M 2,141, H 3,485	L 1,100, M 1,021, H 1,083
Percentage move for each 12-month period	L 8.55%, M 6.49%, H 6.50%	L 11.83%, M 8.02%, H 6.66%	L −6.22%, M −5.75%, H −5.75%	L −12.41%, M −9.54%, H −9.40%
Candle end + 1 day	1.32%	2.04%	−1.07%	−1.80%
Candle end + 3 days	2.17%	3.13%	−1.73%	−3.01%
Candle end + 5 days	2.48%	2.95%	−1.70%	−3.12%
Candle end + 10 days	2.74%	2.12%	−1.22%	−3.36%
10-day performance rank	58	69	87	65

20,000. If you look at the standard database and prorate the numbers, you'll find this pattern occurs more frequently in a bear market.

Reversal or continuation performance. The bear market results are better than the bull market ones. Reversals also tend to perform better than continuations, but not in every case.

S&P performance. The black spinning top leads to performance that is better than that of the S&P 500 index.

Candle end to breakout. It takes a median of two days for price to close either above the top or below the bottom of the candle.

Candle end to trend end. Upward breakouts take slightly longer to reach the trend end than downward breakouts. This may be an example of downward trends falling faster than upward ones can rise (which I tested and found to be true for price trends).

Yearly position, performance. In three of four cases, these candles appear most often within a third of the yearly high. The exception, bear market/down breakouts, appear slightly more often within a third of the yearly low. In all cases, performance is best when the candle has a breakout in the lowest third of the yearly trading range.

Table 80.3
Height Statistics

Description	Bull Market, Up Breakout	Bear Market, Up Breakout	Bull Market, Down Breakout	Bear Market, Down Breakout
Median candle height as a percentage of breakout price	2.01%	2.96%	2.03%	3.00%
Short candle, performance	5.29%	6.13%	−4.61%	−8.29%
Tall candle, performance	8.76%	11.04%	−7.47%	−12.64%
Percentage meeting price target (measure rule)	83%	80%	79%	81%
Median upper shadow as a percentage of breakout price	0.79%	1.12%	0.86%	1.27%
Short upper shadow, performance	5.54%	6.47%	−4.84%	−8.66%
Tall upper shadow, performance	8.27%	10.46%	−7.01%	−12.13%
Median lower shadow as a percentage of breakout price	0.82%	1.25%	0.75%	1.15%
Short lower shadow, performance	5.54%	6.65%	−4.80%	−8.70%
Tall lower shadow, performance	8.34%	10.32%	−7.12%	−12.06%

Performance over time. The results of this candle I consider poor because in the middle two columns, bear market/up breakouts and bull market/down breakouts, performance decreases after three days.

The performance rank, when compared to other candles, leaves little to write home about. The numbers are not exciting. For reference, a rank of 1 is best out of 103 candles.

Table 80.3 shows height statistics.

Candle height. Tall candles perform better than short ones. To determine whether the candle is short or tall, compute its height from high to low price and divide by the breakout price. If the result is higher than the median, then you have a tall candle; otherwise it's short.

Joe has a black spinning top with a high of 80 and a low of 79. In a bull market with an upward breakout, is the candle tall or short? The height is 80 − 79, or 1, so the measure would be 1/80, or 1.3%. Thus, the candle is short.

Measure rule. Use the measure rule to help predict how far price will rise or fall. Compute the height of the candle and multiply it by the appropriate percentage shown in the table; then apply it to the breakout price.

What are the price targets for Joe's candle? The upward target would be $(1 \times 83\%) + 80$, or 80.83, and the downward target would be $79 − (1 \times 79\%)$, or 78.21.

Shadows. To determine whether the shadow is short or tall, compute the height of the shadow and divide by the breakout price. Compare the result

Table 80.4
Volume Statistics

Description	Bull Market, Up Breakout	Bear Market, Up Breakout	Bull Market, Down Breakout	Bear Market, Down Breakout
Above-average candle volume, performance	6.83%	8.90%	−5.74%	−10.46%
Below-average candle volume, performance	6.75%	8.10%	−5.88%	−10.18%
Heavy breakout volume, performance	7.43%	9.11%	−6.14%	−11.06%
Light breakout volume, performance	6.28%	7.84%	−5.62%	−9.69%

to the median in the table. Tall shadows have a percentage higher than the median.

Candles with tall upper or lower shadows perform better after the breakouts than do those with short shadows.

Table 80.4 shows volume statistics.

Average candle volume. Candle volume that's above average leads to better performance after the breakout in all cases except for bull market/down breakouts.

Breakout volume. Heavy breakout volume results in the best performance across the board.

Trading Tactics

I split trading tactics into two basic studies, one concerning reversal rates and the other concerning performance. Of the two, reversal rates are more important, because it's better to trade in the direction of the trend and let price run as far as it can.

Table 80.5 gives tips to find the trend direction.

Table 80.5
Reversal Rates

Description	Bull Market	Bear Market
Reversal rate: trend up, breakout down	53%	57%
Continuation rate: trend up, breakout up	47%	43%
Reversal: trend down, breakout up	49%	48%
Continuation: trend down, breakout down	51%	52%
Percentage of reversals (R)/continuations (C) for each 12-month low (L), middle (M), or high (H)	L 49% R/51% C, M 51% R/49% C, H 52% R/48% C	L 50% R/50% C, M 53% R/47% C, H 53% R/47% C

Table 80.6
Performance Indicators

Description	Bull Market, Up Breakout	Bear Market, Up Breakout	Bull Market, Down Breakout	Bear Market, Down Breakout
Closing price confirmation, performance	6.44%	8.78%	−5.81%	−9.50%
Candle color confirmation, performance	6.39%	8.82%	−5.91%	−9.47%
Opening gap confirmation, performance	7.10%	10.43%	−6.78%	−10.58%
Breakout above 50-day moving average, performance	6.57%	7.22%	−5.84%	−8.97%
Breakout below 50-day moving average, performance	7.20%	10.00%	−5.82%	−11.53%
Last candle: close in highest third, performance	7.88%	7.86%	−5.77%	−9.45%
Last candle: close in middle third, performance	8.59%	8.51%	−5.82%	−10.46%
Last candle: close in lowest third, performance	6.83%	8.35%	−5.86%	−10.17%

Reversal, continuation rates. Since the results hover around 50% (random), using the prevailing price trend to determine the breakout direction is unreliable.

Yearly range reversals. Sorting the reversal or continuation behavior into where the breakout occurs in the yearly price range, the results show no meaningful trend.

Table 80.6 shows performance indicators that can give hints as to how your stock will behave after the breakout from this candle pattern.

Confirmation, performance. Use opening gap confirmation to trade, because it gets you in early and results in the best performance. That means waiting for price to gap open the next day and then considering trading in the direction of the gap—go long for gaps up and go short for downward price gaps.

Moving average. Breakouts below the 50-day moving average tend to outperform in all cases except for bull market/down breakouts.

Closing position. Closes in the middle third of the candle's high-low range result in slightly better postbreakout performance in all cases except for bull market/down breakouts, which do better when the close is near the candle's low.

Sample Trade

Joe held the stock shown in Figure 80.2 and was considering selling it as price developed over time. The uptrend leading to the main consolidation zone in

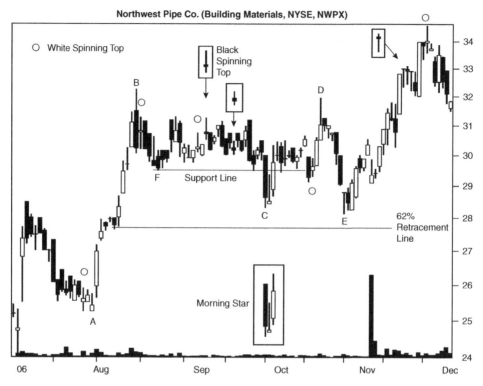

Figure 80.2 The circles mark white spinning tops and the rectangles highlight black spinning tops.

the center of the chart began at A, shortly after a white spinning top appeared (marked with the first circle).

Price climbed to B and then started moving sideways. The circles mark white spinning tops and the rectangles highlight the black ones. Price formed a bottom held up by the support line at F, generally touching the price lows.

At C a bullish morning star appeared, but that only pushed price back into the trading range. Peaks B and D did not form a double top because price didn't close below the lowest valley (C) between the peaks.

Joe decided that if price closed below the 62% retracement of the move from A to B, then he would sell. As the chart shows, price never closed below that line, so he held on to the stock.

Notice how the black and white spinning tops appeared like pepper lightly sprinkled on a pizza. The B to D congestion region showed many small-bodied candles, speaking of indecision among traders as to the trend direction.

For Best Performance

The following list offers tips and observations to help choose candles that perform well. Consult the associated table for more information.

- Use the identification guidelines to help select the pattern—Table 80.1.
- Candles within a third of the yearly low perform best—Table 80.2.
- Select tall candles—Table 80.3.
- Use the measure rule to predict a price target—Table 80.3.
- Candles with tall shadows outperform—Table 80.3.
- Volume gives performance clues—Table 80.4.
- Opening gap confirmation works best—Table 80.6.
- Breakouts below the 50-day moving average lead to the best performance except for bull market/down breakouts.—Table 80.6.

81

Spinning Top, White

Behavior and Rank

Theoretical: Indecision.
Actual bull market: Reversal 50% of the time (ranking 53).
Actual bear market: Reversal 52% of the time (ranking 37).
Frequency: 2nd out of 103.
Overall performance over time: 69th out of 103.

The white spinning top is a random pattern, with a reversal rate of 50%. Sources I checked said that if it appears after a long trend, when price is looking tired, a spinning top might suggest a trend change. It *does* act as a reversal but not by any amount that you would be able to detect in the field.

The frequency rank is 2 out of 103, where 1 is best. That means it occurs often. The overall performance rank is about what you would expect: 69. That means there is nothing earthshaking here.

From a psychological point of view, the bulls push price up and the bears take it back down—or the reverse happens—but price ends slightly higher than where it began the day. That leaves a small white body with tall shadows. By itself, the white candle is bullish; but the tall shadows and small body suggest indecision, as if the bulls and bears decided to call a truce for the day. What will happen tomorrow is anyone's guess.

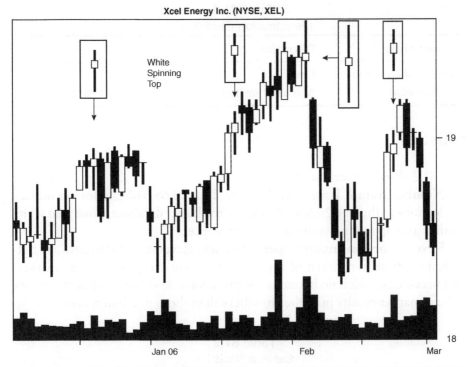

Figure 81.1   Multiple white spinning tops appear, most buried in existing trends.

Identification Guidelines

Figure 81.1 shows what a white spinning top looks like. The first one that is highlighted appears near the end of an uptrend, when price moves horizontally before tumbling. This spinning top makes sense to me. Price is undecided so it moves sideways, waiting to determine a trend.

The second spinner appears in mid-January in the midst of an uptrend. It is supposed to represent indecision, but the upward trend doesn't slow at all until two days later when it stumbles and then recovers.

The third spinner acts as a reversal, and it has unusually long shadows. Clearly, both the bulls and the bears have made up their minds about the trend direction. Price gaps lower, falling off a cliff.

The last spinning top looks like the second one, but this one appears near the end of the trend. Price hesitates for two days before sinking.

Table 81.1 lists identification guidelines. This is an easy candle to spot. It has long upper and lower shadows—at least as long as the body—and the body is a small white one. At least one source I checked didn't require shadows, just a small body. The high wave, short black, and short white candles are similarly shaped candles that I discuss in their own chapters.

Table 81.1
Identification Guidelines

Characteristic	Discussion
Number of candle lines	One.
Configuration	A small white body with shadows longer than the body.

Statistics

Table 81.2 shows general statistics.

Number found. Using one database, I found 68,630 candles but limited my selections to the first 20,000. Prorating the larger database shows that white spinning tops appear most often in a bear market.

Reversal or continuation performance. Reversals tend to perform better than continuations most of the time. The one exception is bear market/down breakouts, which do better as continuations. Also note that performance in a bear market results in higher numbers than those in a bull market.

Table 81.2
General Statistics

Description	Bull Market, Up Breakout	Bear Market, Up Breakout	Bull Market, Down Breakout	Bear Market, Down Breakout
Number found	7,502	3,234	6,373	2,891
Reversal (R), continuation (C) performance	6.37% C 7.26% R	7.24% C 9.27% R	−5.87% C −5.88% R	−10.89% C −9.82% R
Standard & Poor's 500 change	1.50%	0.98%	−1.07%	−2.70%
Candle end to breakout (median, days)	2	2	2	2
Candle end to trend end (median, days)	7	7	7	7
Number of breakouts near the 12-month low (L), middle (M), or high (H)	L 1,346, M 1,992, H 4,164	L 971, M 1,059, H 1,204	L 1,421, M 1,848, H 3,104	L 970, M 955, H 966
Percentage move for each 12-month period	L 8.42%, M 6.43%, H 6.53%	L 10.93%, M 7.94%, H 6.88%	L −6.63%, M −5.77%, H −5.69%	L −12.28%, M −9.91%, H −9.23%
Candle end + 1 day	1.16%	1.83%	−1.18%	−1.91%
Candle end + 3 days	2.03%	2.64%	−1.94%	−3.32%
Candle end + 5 days	2.30%	2.62%	−1.96%	−3.57%
Candle end + 10 days	2.43%	2.33%	−1.69%	−3.63%
10-day performance rank	72	67	74	58

S&P performance. The candle pattern outperforms the S&P 500 index over the same time periods.

Candle end to breakout. It takes two days for price to close either above the top or below the bottom of the candle. This suggests the body is centered in the high-low range.

Candle end to trend end. It takes a week for price to reach the trend end.

Yearly position, performance. Most white spinning tops appear within a third of the yearly high. The one exception is bear market/down breakouts. A slight majority of them appear near the yearly low. Performance is best, across the board, when the candle appears within a third of the yearly low.

Performance over time. The candle is not a robust performer, because in two columns the numbers decrease over time at least once. This happens in bear market/up breakouts after three days and bull market/down breakouts after five days. A well-behaved price trend would show higher numbers in all periods.

The performance ranks, which compare the percentage change with other candle types, show midlist performance.

Table 81.3 shows height statistics.

Candle height. Tall candles outperform. To determine whether the candle is short or tall, compute its height from high to low price and divide by

Table 81.3
Height Statistics

Description	Bull Market, Up Breakout	Bear Market, Up Breakout	Bull Market, Down Breakout	Bear Market, Down Breakout
Median candle height as a percentage of breakout price	2.03%	2.90%	1.97%	2.93%
Short candle, performance	5.22%	5.99%	−4.73%	−8.06%
Tall candle, performance	8.72%	10.84%	−7.41%	−12.85%
Percentage meeting price target (measure rule)	83%	81%	80%	82%
Median upper shadow as a percentage of breakout price	0.80%	1.11%	0.86%	1.28%
Short upper shadow, performance	5.59%	6.39%	−4.91%	−8.22%
Tall upper shadow, performance	8.14%	10.24%	−7.00%	−12.58%
Median lower shadow as a percentage of breakout price	0.82%	1.22%	0.73%	1.09%
Short lower shadow, performance	5.47%	6.43%	−4.95%	−8.41%
Tall lower shadow, performance	8.35%	10.24%	−7.08%	−12.34%

Table 81.4
Volume Statistics

Description	Bull Market, Up Breakout	Bear Market, Up Breakout	Bull Market, Down Breakout	Bear Market, Down Breakout
Above-average candle volume, performance	6.90%	8.91%	−6.04%	−10.46%
Below-average candle volume, performance	6.68%	7.85%	−5.79%	−10.19%
Heavy breakout volume, performance	7.56%	9.26%	−6.35%	−11.16%
Light breakout volume, performance	6.11%	7.49%	−5.54%	−9.62%

the breakout price. If the result is higher than the median, then you have a tall candle; otherwise it's short.

If Gina has a white spinning top with a high of 99 and a low of 97, is the candle short or tall? The height is 99 − 97, or 2, so the measure is 2/99, or 2.0%. Assuming a bull market with an upward breakout, it's a short candle.

Measure rule. Use the measure rule to help predict how far price will rise or fall. Compute the height of the candle and multiply it by the appropriate percentage shown in the table; then apply it to the breakout price.

What are Gina's price targets? The upward target would be (2 × 83%) + 99, or 100.66, and the downward target would be 97 − (2 × 80%), or 95.40.

Shadows. To determine whether the shadow is short or tall, compute the height of the shadow and divide by the breakout price. Compare the result to the median in the table. Tall shadows have a percentage higher than the median.

Tall upper or lower shadows suggest better performance after the breakout.

Table 81.4 shows volume statistics.

Average candle volume. Candles with above-average volume tend to do better after the breakout.

Breakout volume. Heavy breakout volume also suggests better post-breakout performance.

Trading Tactics

I split trading tactics into two basic studies, one concerning reversal rates and the other concerning performance. Of the two, reversal rates are more important, because it's better to trade in the direction of the trend and let price run as far as it can.

Table 81.5 gives tips to find the trend direction.

Table 81.5
Reversal Rates

Description	Bull Market	Bear Market
Reversal rate: trend up, breakout down	47%	49%
Continuation rate: trend up, breakout up	53%	51%
Reversal: trend down, breakout up	55%	55%
Continuation: trend down, breakout down	45%	45%
Percentage of reversals (R)/continuations (C) for each 12-month low (L), middle (M), or high (H)	L 51% R/49% C, M 50% R/50% C, H 50% R/50% C	L 51% R/49% C, M 53% R/47% C, H 52% R/48% C

Reversal, continuation rates. The trend leading to the white spinning top is not a good predictor of the breakout direction. The numbers are too close to random, 50%.

Yearly range reversals. Where the white spinning top appears in the yearly price range is also not a good predictor of where price is likely to reverse.

Table 81.6 shows performance indicators that can give hints as to how your stock will behave after the breakout from this candle pattern.

Confirmation, performance. Use the opening gap method to confirm the price trend. That method works in all cases because it gets you into the

Table 81.6
Performance Indicators

Description	Bull Market, Up Breakout	Bear Market, Up Breakout	Bull Market, Down Breakout	Bear Market, Down Breakout
Closing price confirmation, performance	6.22%	7.96%	−6.19%	−9.95%
Candle color confirmation, performance	6.24%	7.86%	−6.19%	−10.02%
Opening gap confirmation, performance	7.04%	9.40%	−6.94%	−10.38%
Breakout above 50-day moving average, performance	6.42%	7.22%	−5.78%	−8.76%
Breakout below 50-day moving average, performance	7.50%	9.77%	−6.00%	−11.72%
Last candle: close in highest third, performance	6.85%	8.04%	−5.84%	−9.47%
Last candle: close in middle third, performance	6.77%	8.40%	−5.87%	−10.60%
Last candle: close in lowest third, performance	6.39%	7.80%	−5.95%	−10.37%

trade soonest. Trade in the direction of the opening price gap the day after the spinning top.

Moving average. Candles with breakouts below the moving average tend to do well after the breakout.

Closing position. Where price closes shows no consistent trend.

Sample Trade

Figure 81.2 shows a trade Gina made. Price trended up to B and then moved sideways. A trendline drawn along peaks B and C and extended to A looked like the flight deck of an aircraft carrier. Along the bottom of the chart pattern, she connected valleys D and E. That trendline sloped up, and the combination took on the shape of an ascending triangle chart pattern.

Gina's experience with ascending triangles was mixed, because price after the breakout has a tendency to rise 10% or so and then die. Therefore, she used candles to improve her timing and selection.

In the situation shown in the chart, a plethora of candles after E with small bodies and a slight upward price trend told of buyers quietly accumulating the

Figure 81.2 An ascending triangle with white spinning tops (marked with circles) results in a profitable trade.

stock. Volume trended lower as it does in many ascending triangles, falling to low levels just before the breakout.

She placed a buy order a penny above the price level of C, just to get in at the start of the breakout. When price shot out of the consolidation region ending with the white spinning top the day before A, her buy order was triggered and she grabbed the stock.

Since buying, price has climbed 13% but now shows spinning tops and generally small-bodied candles. That's a warning of a potential trend change. She's undecided about selling or not, and will base her decision on whether price breaks out downward. If price does drop, then she'll sell; otherwise she'll hold on.

For Best Performance

The following list offers tips and observations to help choose candles that perform well. Consult the associated table for more information.

- Use the identification guidelines to help select the pattern—Table 81.1.
- Candles within a third of the yearly low perform best—Table 81.2.
- Select tall candles—Table 81.3.
- Use the measure rule to predict a price target—Table 81.3.
- Candles with tall shadows outperform—Table 81.3.
- Volume gives performance clues—Table 81.4.
- Opening gap confirmation works best—Table 81.6.
- Breakouts below the 50-day moving average lead to the best performance—Table 81.6.

82

Stick Sandwich

Behavior and Rank

Theoretical: Bullish reversal.

Actual bull market: Bearish continuation 62% of the time (ranking 18).

Actual bear market: Bearish continuation 63% of the time (ranking 19).

Frequency: 59th out of 103.

Overall performance over time: 14th out of 103.

I was hot for the stick sandwich. Maybe the descriptive name attracted me to the candle pattern, but after testing it, I found that price continues lower 62% of the time in a bull market. That's good for a continuation pattern because it ranks 18 out of 103 candles, with 1 being the best. The frequency rank is midrange at 59, so this candle isn't as plentiful as clouds during a storm but it's close. The overall performance rank is 14, which I consider excellent.

The psychology behind the pattern begins with the bears in control, forcing price down by their selling pressure. A black candle prints on the chart, indicating that the bulls have been scared off. However, the next day price gaps open higher and even closes higher, making a white candle. This could be short covering or the bulls counterattacking, signaling that the downtrend is over.

Unfortunately, the next day price closes much lower, about equal to where it was two days before. Many will say that since price has matched the previous close then it's a support level. That's certainly true, but I don't believe it's strong enough to reverse the downtrend. Price continues lower in most cases.

Procter & Gamble Co. (Household Products, NYSE, PG)

Figure 82.1 A stick sandwich fails to reverse the downtrend.

Identification Guidelines

Figure 82.1 shows a typical example of a stick sandwich. The candle pattern appears in a downward price trend that stretches from A to B without much of a pause along the way.

The bottoms of the candle bodies of the first and third days are supposed to act as a support region, according to many. In this example, it's more of a resistance zone because price bumps up against it twice (the horizontal line shows the region) in the coming days.

Table 82.1 lists identification guidelines. I changed the guidelines so that the closes of the first and third days need not match exactly. If they are off by

Table 82.1
Identification Guidelines

Characteristic	Discussion
Number of candle lines	Three.
Price trend	Downward leading to the start of the candle pattern.
First day	A black candle.
Second day	A white candle that trades above the close of the first day.
Third day	A black candle that closes at or near the close of the first day.

a few cents, that's hunky-dory with me. Allowing slightly mismatched closes also boosts the sample count for this rare pattern.

Look for the candle in a downward price trend. Price should form a black-white-black sandwich. The white candle should trade higher than the first day's close, and the first and last days should match or nearly match closing prices. Ignore the shadows in this pattern, and the candles can be any height. Thus, you can find some weird-looking, but valid, stick sandwiches.

Statistics

Table 82.2 shows general statistics.

Number found. Out of over 4.7 million candle lines, I uncovered 3,402 of these patterns, making the stick sandwich a rare candle. Most appear in a bull market, even when you prorate the standard database numbers.

Reversal or continuation performance. Performance is best in a bear market, and reversals outperform continuations.

Table 82.2
General Statistics

Description	Bull Market, Up Breakout	Bear Market, Up Breakout	Bull Market, Down Breakout	Bear Market, Down Breakout
Number found	1,091	193	1,795	323
Reversal (R), continuation (C) performance	6.70% R	9.48% R	−5.66% C	−9.36% C
Standard & Poor's 500 change	1.93%	1.05%	−0.77%	−1.86%
Candle end to breakout (median, days)	5	5	3	3
Candle end to trend end (median, days)	9	10	6	6
Number of breakouts near the 12-month low (L), middle (M), or high (H)	L 253, M 266, H 439	L 80, M 61, H 48	L 535, M 512, H 520	L 142, M 104, H 74
Percentage move for each 12-month period	L 7.11%, M 6.44%, H 6.51%	L 9.86%, M 10.19%, H 8.41%	L −7.04%, M −4.94%, H −5.08%	L −11.26%, M −9.24%, H −7.47%
Candle end + 1 day	1.25%	2.66%	−0.70%	−1.22%
Candle end + 3 days	2.97%	5.44%	−1.32%	−1.39%
Candle end + 5 days	3.73%	6.37%	−1.49%	−3.07%
Candle end + 10 days	4.69%	7.43%	−1.48%	−2.99%
10-day performance rank	16	11	80	72

S&P performance. The performance of the S&P 500 index over the same period is inferior to the performance of the candle pattern.

Candle end to breakout. It takes between three and five days for price to close either above the highest high in the stick sandwich or below the lowest low. Since price in the last candle is near the low, downward breakouts should take less time, and that's what we see.

Candle end to trend end. The time from the candle end to the trend end ranges from 6 to 10 days. Again, downward breakouts take less time because the downward trend is already under way. An upward turn would start a new trend that would likely take longer than one approaching the trend end.

Yearly position, performance. Most patterns (three out of four categories) appear within a third of the yearly low, and that's also where you find the best performance. The exception to performance comes from candles in bear market/up breakouts, which do better in the middle of the yearly price range.

Performance over time. This pattern is a poor performer where downward breakouts are concerned. Both show trend weakness from 5 to 10 days. The performance rank agrees with that assessment. Upward breakouts are where this candle shines. Thus, when it acts as a reversal, the move should be a good one.

Table 82.3 shows height statistics.

Table 82.3
Height Statistics

Description	Bull Market, Up Breakout	Bear Market, Up Breakout	Bull Market, Down Breakout	Bear Market, Down Breakout
Median candle height as a percentage of breakout price	3.51%	5.15%	3.58%	5.68%
Short candle, performance	5.62%	7.57%	−4.64%	−7.67%
Tall candle, performance	8.20%	11.38%	−7.03%	−11.19%
Percentage meeting price target (measure rule)	67%	65%	56%	56%
Median upper shadow as a percentage of breakout price	0.20%	0.43%	0.23%	0.40%
Short upper shadow, performance	6.82%	9.53%	−5.71%	−9.19%
Tall upper shadow, performance	6.60%	9.44%	−5.61%	−9.51%
Median lower shadow as a percentage of breakout price	0.29%	0.48%	0.31%	0.58%
Short lower shadow, performance	6.00%	9.61%	−5.40%	−9.10%
Tall lower shadow, performance	7.32%	9.37%	−5.91%	−9.67%

Candle height. Tall candles outperform. To determine whether the candle is short or tall, compute its height from highest high to lowest low price in the candle pattern and divide by the breakout price. If the result is higher than the median, then you have a tall candle; otherwise it's short.

If Janice sees a stick sandwich with a high price of 80 and a low of 78, how full will she be if the stick sandwich is short? First, determine if the candle is short or tall by finding the height (80 – 78, or 2) and then finishing the computation for bull market/up breakout category (for example): 2/80, or 2.5%. The candle is short. If she's used to eating tall candles, then she might still be hungry. She should look for another pattern to trade.

Measure rule. Use the measure rule to help predict how far price will rise or fall. Compute the height of the candle pattern and multiply it by the appropriate percentage shown in the table; then apply it to the breakout price.

In Janice's situation, what are the price targets? The upward target would be $(2 \times 67\%) + 80$, or 81.34. The downward target would be $78 - (2 \times 56\%)$, or 76.88.

Shadows. The table's results pertain to the last candle line in the pattern. To determine whether the shadow is short or tall, compute the height of the shadow and divide by the breakout price. Compare the result to the median in the table. Tall shadows have a percentage higher than the median.

Upper shadow performance. Short upper shadows perform best in all cases except for bear market/down breakouts, which do better with tall shadows.

The results are somewhat unusual, because tall upper shadows often lead to better postbreakout performance. However, they are not as reliable as the results from lower shadows.

Lower shadow performance. Tall lower shadows suggest better post-breakout performance in all cases except for bear market/up breakouts.

Table 82.4 shows volume statistics.

Table 82.4
Volume Statistics

Description	Bull Market, Up Breakout	Bear Market, Up Breakout	Bull Market, Down Breakout	Bear Market, Down Breakout
Rising candle volume, performance	6.82%	8.33%	−5.74%	−8.31%
Falling candle volume, performance	6.60%	10.19%	−5.51%	−10.18%
Above-average candle volume, performance	7.03%	8.55%	−5.56%	−8.47%
Below-average candle volume, performance	6.49%	10.61%	−5.73%	−10.23%
Heavy breakout volume, performance	7.34%	10.52%	−6.32%	−9.43%
Light breakout volume, performance	6.02%	8.39%	−5.03%	−9.28%

Candle volume trend. Performance from the volume trend tracks the market condition. That means bull markets do better after rising candle volume and bear markets do better after falling volume.

Average candle volume. Most categories show better performance when volume in the candle is below average. The exception: bull market/up break-outs, which do better after above-average volume appears in the candle.

Breakout volume. Heavy breakout volume suggests good performance across the board.

Trading Tactics

A review of the stick sandwich in many stocks shows that the best performance comes from buying a sandwich when the candle appears as part of a downward retracement in an upward price trend. Figure 82.2 shows an example of this configuration.

This rise-retrace setup works best if the sandwich appears near the end of the retracement, not near the start as in this chart. If price closes below the candle's low (the lowest of the three candle lines), then it's best to close out the long position.

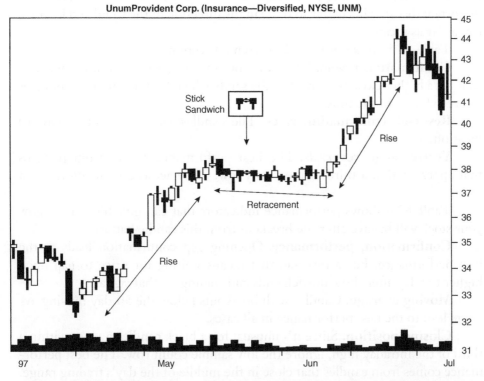

Figure 82.2 A small stick sandwich appears in a rise-retrace configuration.

Table 82.5
Reversal Rates

Description	Bull Market	Bear Market
Closing price confirmation reversal rate	62%	62%
Candle color confirmation reversal rate	61%	58%
Opening gap confirmation reversal rate	45%	44%
Reversal: trend down, breakout up	38%	37%
Continuation: trend down, breakout down	62%	63%
Percentage of reversals (R)/continuations (C) for each 12-month low (L), middle (M), or high (H)	L 32% R/68% C, M 34% R/66% C, H 46% R/54% C	L 36% R/64% C, M 37% R/63% C, H 39% R/61% C

Avoid trading this candlestick when the primary trend is downward and you expect a reversal (price to begin trending upward). The breakout may be upward, but it's not likely to last long. Again, if price closes below the candle's low, then exit the long trade.

If you are expecting a downward breakout, then trade only those stocks that show a downward primary trend.

I split trading tactics into two basic studies, one concerning reversal rates and the other concerning performance. Of the two, reversal rates are more important, because it's better to trade in the direction of the trend and let price run as far as it can.

Table 82.5 gives tips to find the trend direction.

Confirmation reversal rates. If you want to go reversal hunting, then wait for a higher close the day after the sandwich ends. That method confirms a reversal 62% of the time.

Reversal, continuation rates. The candlestick breaks out downward most often.

Yearly range reversals. The best performance comes from patterns that appear within a third of the yearly low. They act as continuations most often.

Table 82.6 shows performance indicators that can give hints as to how your stock will behave after the breakout from this candle pattern.

Confirmation, performance. Opening gap confirmation leads to the best performance. For a reversal, that means waiting for price to gap open higher the day after the sandwich ends and trading on that signal.

Moving average. Candles with breakouts below the 50-day moving average lead to the best performance in all cases.

Closing position. Since it's unusual for a black candle to close within a third of the intraday high, ignore the low sample count row. The best performance comes from candles that close in the middle of the day's trading range.

Table 82.6
Performance Indicators

Description	Bull Market, Up Breakout	Bear Market, Up Breakout	Bull Market, Down Breakout	Bear Market, Down Breakout
Closing price confirmation, performance	7.60%	11.77%	N/A	N/A
Candle color confirmation, performance	7.44%	11.17%	N/A	N/A
Opening gap confirmation, performance	7.86%	12.39%	N/A	N/A
Breakout above 50-day moving average, performance	6.44%	8.20%	−5.07%	−6.87%
Breakout below 50-day moving average, performance	7.07%	10.50%	−5.84%	−10.18%
Last candle: close in highest third, performance	5.96%*	8.74%*	−5.85%*	−16.83%*
Last candle: close in middle third, performance	6.99%	10.95%	−5.74%	−7.20%
Last candle: close in lowest third, performance	6.63%	9.05%	−5.64%	−9.63%

N/A means not applicable.
*Fewer than 30 samples.

The one exception is bear market/down breakouts, which do better when the close is near the candle's low.

Sample Trade

Figure 82.3 shows the stock that Janice held. She drew a horizontal trendline starting at A and slicing through B and C and extending to the right. Along the peaks, she drew another trendline, this one sloping downward, connecting F and G. The combination outlined a descending triangle chart pattern. Those break out downward 64% of the time, so she was worried about her long position.

At C, a stick sandwich formed right at the support shown as the horizontal trendline. This suggested the pattern would act as a reversal, and it did, too, until price returned to the support line and closed below it at D.

When price closed below the trendline, or even below the lowest low in the descending triangle chart pattern, that was the sell signal. Janice missed it. She held on to the stock but recognized her mistake. When price pulled back up to the bottom of the descending triangle at E and completed a tweezers top, she sold at the open the next day. The bearish tweezers top must have been pulling her leg, though, because price moved even higher during the next two days.

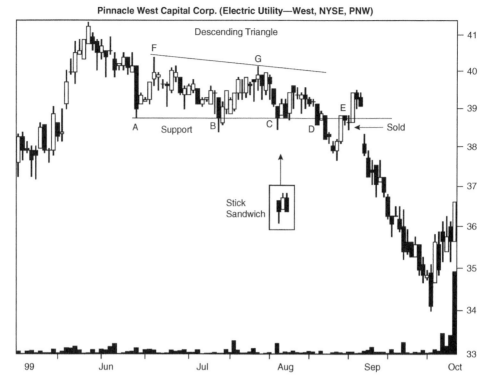

Figure 82.3   The stick sandwich forms at the support created by a descending triangle.

She should have sold when price closed below the descending triangle, but played her hand as well as expected during the pullback.

For Best Performance

The following list offers tips and observations to help choose candles that perform well. Consult the associated table for more information.

- Use the identification guidelines to help select the pattern—Table 82.1.
- Candles within a third of the yearly low perform best except for bear market/up breakouts—Table 82.2.
- Select tall candles—Table 82.3.
- Use the measure rule to predict a price target—Table 82.3.
- Volume gives performance clues—Table 82.4.
- See Trading Tactics discussion for buying candles during a retracement of the uptrend. Avoid buying candles when the primary trend is downward.

- The closing price helps detect reversals of the downtrend—Table 82.5.
- Patterns within a third of the yearly low tend to act as continuations most often—Table 82.5.
- Opening gap confirmation works best for reversals—Table 82.6.
- Breakouts below the 50-day moving average lead to the best performance—Table 82.6.

83

Takuri Line

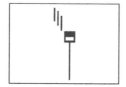

Behavior and Rank

Theoretical: Bullish reversal.

Actual bull market: Bullish reversal 66% of the time (ranking 18).

Actual bear market: Bullish reversal 63% of the time (ranking 21).

Frequency: 28th out of 103.

Overall performance over time: 47th out of 103.

As I was researching the hammer candle, I discovered the Takuri line. It's a hammer with a longer lower shadow. If that doesn't help, then think of a lollipop with a long stick in a downward price trend. That's a Takuri line.

The reversal rate is a strong 66%, meaning it ranks 18 in a bull market out of 103 candles, with 1 being the best. The frequency rank is 28, which says the candle is also plentiful. However, the overall performance rank is just so-so at 47, but that covers both bull and bear markets, up and down breakouts.

The psychology behind the pattern starts with the downward price trend. The bears are pushing price lower and then the Takuri line forms. Price opens near the high for the day and the bears pounce. They force price down, way down, until the bulls not only think but know the selling is overdone. They buy and their gobbling up shares forces price back up near the high. At day's end, what remains is a small candle body with a long lower shadow.

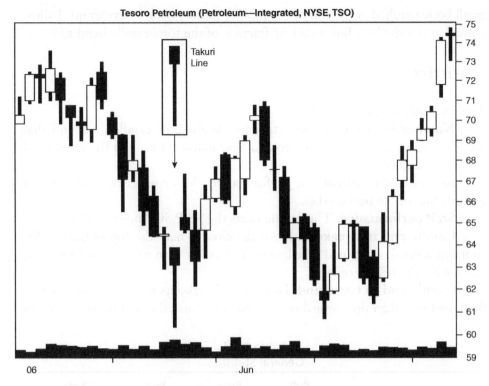

Figure 83.1   A Takuri line appears at a turning point in the downtrend.

Identification Guidelines

Figure 83.1 shows a perfect example of a Takuri line. Price trends lower leading to the candle. Then a small body, either black or white, appears along with a shadow at least three times the height of the body. In this example, price reverses by closing above the top of the candle the next day, confirming the reversal.

Table 83.1 lists identification guidelines. Look for a candle with an exceedingly long lower shadow—at least three times the body height—and a

Table 83.1
Identification Guidelines

Characteristic	Discussion
Number of candle lines	One.
Price trend	Downward leading to the start of the candle pattern.
Configuration	A small candle body with no upper shadow, or a very small one, and a lower shadow at least three times the height of the body.

small body perched at the top of the candle. Candle color is irrelevant. I allow a small upper shadow, but it's a tiny fraction of the total candle height.

Statistics

Table 83.2 shows general statistics.

Number found. Using my standard database of candles, I found that the Takuri line appears most often in a bear market. I limited the number of samples to 20,000.

Reversal or continuation performance. Performance in a bear market exceeds that of the bull market.

S&P performance. The candle beats the S&P 500 index in all cases.

Candle end to breakout. Since the close is near the top of the candle, an upward breakout should take less time to occur than a downward one, and that's what the results reflect.

Candle end to trend end. Downward breakouts take less time to reach the trend end than do upward ones. That's because this candle occurs in an

Table 83.2
General Statistics

Description	Bull Market, Up Breakout	Bear Market, Up Breakout	Bull Market, Down Breakout	Bear Market, Down Breakout
Number found	9,995	3,006	5,260	1,739
Reversal (R), continuation (C) performance	7.90% R	10.31% R	−6.30% C	−10.35% C
Standard & Poor's 500 change	1.54%	0.91%	−1.01%	−2.77%
Candle end to breakout (median, days)	2	2	3	3
Candle end to trend end (median, days)	9	9	6	7
Number of breakouts near the 12-month low (L), middle (M), or high (H)	L 2,482, M 3,054, H 4,459	L 1,018, M 1,041, H 947	L 1,709, M 1,693, H 1,858	L 747, M 614, H 378
Percentage move for each 12-month period	L 9.04%, M 8.06%, H 7.34%	L 13.20%, M 10.06%, H 8.28%	L −7.09%, M −6.44%, H −5.69%	L −12.73%, M −9.55%, H −8.09%
Candle end + 1 day	0.87%	1.26%	−1.77%	−2.50%
Candle end + 3 days	1.67%	2.29%	−2.95%	−4.36%
Candle end + 5 days	1.89%	2.46%	−3.13%	−4.90%
Candle end + 10 days	2.03%	2.54%	−2.66%	−4.45%
10-day performance rank	86	62	39	40

Table 83.3
Height Statistics

Description	Bull Market, Up Breakout	Bear Market, Up Breakout	Bull Market, Down Breakout	Bear Market, Down Breakout
Median candle height as a percentage of breakout price	2.43%	3.33%	2.34%	3.31%
Short candle, performance	6.11%	7.38%	−5.25%	−8.06%
Tall candle, performance	10.55%	13.96%	−7.83%	−13.48%
Percentage meeting price target (measure rule)	82%	80%	78%	79%
Median lower shadow as a percentage of breakout price	1.97%	2.74%	1.88%	2.69%
Short lower shadow, performance	6.13%	7.44%	−5.26%	−8.11%
Tall lower shadow, performance	10.50%	13.80%	−7.80%	−13.37%

existing downtrend. Upward breakouts start a new trend, so they take longer than a trend already under way.

Yearly position, performance. Where the candle appears in the yearly price range shows no consistent trend (the high scores best, twice), but those candles with breakouts within a third of the yearly low outperform.

Performance over time. The Takuri line is not a robust performer. Downward breakouts show weakness between days 5 and 10. A robust candle shows performance that increases over all time periods, regardless of market conditions and breakout directions.

The performance rank, which compares the performance of this candle with 102 others, shows that downward breakouts are where this pattern does best.

Table 83.3 shows height statistics.

Candle height. Tall candles show significantly better performance in all cases. To determine whether the candle is short or tall, compute its height from high to low price and divide by the breakout price. If the result is higher than the median, then you have a tall candle; otherwise it's short.

If Pamela sees a Takuri line with a high of 57 and a low of 56, is the candle short or tall? The height is 57 − 56, or 1, so the measure would be 1/57, or 1.8% in a bull market with an upward breakout. The candle is short.

Measure rule. Use the measure rule to help predict how far price will rise or fall. Compute the height of the candle and multiply it by the appropriate percentage shown in the table; then apply it to the breakout price.

What are Pamela's price targets? The upward target would be (1 × 82%) + 57, or 57.82, and the downward target would be 56 − (1 × 78%), or 55.22.

Table 83.4
Volume Statistics

Description	Bull Market, Up Breakout	Bear Market, Up Breakout	Bull Market, Down Breakout	Bear Market, Down Breakout
Above-average candle volume, performance	8.02%	10.94%	−6.36%	−10.20%
Below-average candle volume, performance	7.81%	9.82%	−6.27%	−10.46%
Heavy breakout volume, performance	8.44%	11.64%	−6.54%	−10.90%
Light breakout volume, performance	7.54%	9.40%	−6.10%	−9.83%

Lower shadow performance. Tall lower shadows suggest better post-breakout performance. To determine whether the shadow is short or tall, compute the height of the shadow and divide by the breakout price. Compare the result to the median in the table. Tall shadows have a percentage higher than the median.

Table 83.4 shows volume statistics.

Average candle volume. Above-average candle volume means better postbreakout performance in all categories except for bear market/down breakouts. That category does better after below-average candle volume.

Breakout volume. Heavy breakout volume results in better postbreakout performance across the board.

Trading Tactics

If the candle appears in a primary downtrend, do not depend on it showing a reversal. If price does break out upward, the chances are that it will begin heading back down in a week or two.

This candle pattern appears to do best as part of a downward retracement of a primary uptrend. In other words, you'll see Takuri lines form when the stock takes a breather from a long uptrend. The breather is in the form of a slight move down, retracing a portion of the prior uptrend. Look for the candle to appear at 38%, 50%, or 62% retracements of the uptrend. If the candle appears outside of those retracement values, then more of a decline might be in store. The sample trade shows this rise-retrace pattern.

I split trading tactics into two basic studies, one concerning reversal rates and the other concerning performance. Of the two, reversal rates are more important, because it's better to trade in the direction of the trend and let price run as far as it can.

Table 83.5 gives tips to find the trend direction.

Confirmation reversal rates. To confirm that a reversal has occurred, wait for price to close the next day. If the close is higher, then there is a 95%

Table 83.5
Reversal Rates

Description	Bull Market	Bear Market
Closing price confirmation reversal rate	96%	95%
Candle color confirmation reversal rate	91%	90%
Opening gap confirmation reversal rate	76%	75%
Reversal: trend down, breakout up	66%	63%
Continuation: trend down, breakout down	34%	37%
Percentage of reversals (R)/continuations (C) for each 12-month low (L), middle (M), or high (H)	L 59% R/41% C, M 64% R/36% C, H 71% R/29% C	L 58% R/42% C, M 63% R/37% C, H 71% R/29% C
Black body reversal rate	62%	61%
White body reversal rate	70%	66%

to 96% chance that price has reversed the downtrend. That's not really saying much, though, because all price has to do is close above the top of the candle. Since price is near the top of the candle to begin with, it makes a reversal more likely.

Reversal, continuation rates. Price frequently breaks out upward.

Yearly range reversals. Reversals occur most often when the breakout price is within a third of the yearly high.

Body color reversal rate. Look for the candle to have a white body to increase your chances of having a reversal. A reversal means a close above the top of the candle, and that is more likely to happen in a white candle than a black one (because the closing price is higher in a white candle than in a black one).

Table 83.6 shows performance indicators that can give hints as to how your stock will behave after the breakout from this candle pattern.

Confirmation, performance. Use the opening gap method for early entry in a reversal candle. That means if price gaps open higher the day after a Takuri line, buy the stock.

Moving average. When the breakout is below the 50-day moving average, performance tends to improve.

Body color performance. Candles with black bodies perform slightly better than white ones. That's true in all cases except for bull market/up breakouts, which do better with white candles.

Sample Trade

Figure 83.2 shows the rise-retrace pattern that often occurs in an upward price trend. Pamela recognized this pattern and waited for the stars to align.

Table 83.6
Performance Indicators

Description	Bull Market, Up Breakout	Bear Market, Up Breakout	Bull Market, Down Breakout	Bear Market, Down Breakout
Closing price confirmation, performance	6.56%	8.46%	N/A	N/A
Candle color confirmation, performance	6.68%	8.77%	N/A	N/A
Opening gap confirmation, performance	7.61%	10.74%	N/A	N/A
Breakout above 50-day moving average, performance	7.53%	8.59%	−5.94%	−8.39%
Breakout below 50-day moving average, performance	8.24%	11.60%	−6.47%	−11.05%
Black body, performance	7.72%	10.54%	−6.38%	−10.37%
White body, performance	8.16%	10.00%	−6.16%	−10.33%

N/A means not applicable.

Figure 83.2   Two Takuri lines appear in downward retracements of the upward trend.

Price began the uptrend at A and climbed to B. Then it eased lower to the first Takuri line at D. This coincided with a 38% retracement of the AB move. However, since price often drops to 62% of the prior up move, she decided to wait instead of buying the stock.

During the next two weeks, price formed a support zone delineated by D, E, and C on the bottom. At C was another Takuri line. When she saw it, she decided that it was a bullish reversal candle because price had held the support line to that point. The next day, when price gapped open higher, she bought the stock.

She held on to the stock as price climbed. She compared the retracement from G to the horizontal line at F versus the rise from C to G and saw that it was also 38%. This time, though, price continued lower, and when it closed below the 38% support line, she sold (not shown).

For Best Performance

The following list offers tips and observations to help choose candles that perform well. Consult the associated table for more information.

- Use the identification guidelines to help select the pattern—Table 83.1.
- Candles within a third of the yearly low perform best—Table 83.2.
- Select tall candles—Table 83.3.
- Use the measure rule to predict a price target—Table 83.3.
- Candles with tall lower shadows outperform—Table 83.3.
- Volume gives performance clues—Table 83.4.
- Look for Takuri lines as part of a downward retracement of the primary uptrend—Trading Tactics discussion.
- To confirm the candle as a reversal, wait for price to close higher the next day—Table 83.5.
- Patterns within a third of the yearly high tend to act as reversals most often—Table 83.5.
- Opening gap confirmation works best—Table 83.6.
- Breakouts below the 50-day moving average lead to the best performance—Table 83.6.

84

Three Black Crows

Behavior and Rank

Theoretical: Bearish reversal.

Actual bull market: Bearish reversal 78% of the time (ranking 7).

Actual bear market: Bearish reversal 79% of the time (ranking 6).

Frequency: 60th out of 103.

Overall performance over time: 3rd out of 103.

On the surface, three black crows is a remarkable candle pattern because it reverses the uptrend 78% of the time (bull market). However, since the pattern is so tall, it establishes its own trend, pulling price lower. By the time you recognize the candle pattern, the trend may be near its end. The chance of price tumbling the height of the three black crows post breakout is just 33%, and that's in a bear market.

The performance rank is near the top of the list, ranking 3 out of 103 candles where 1 is best. Coupled with a reversal rank of 6 to 7, this candle is worth exploring.

This pattern works best when the primary trend is downward. You get an upward retracement and then the black crows form and a good decline usually results. When the primary price trend is upward, the three black crows often mark the end of the retracement and a resumption of the uptrend within days of the crows completing.

If the breakout is upward from a three black crows pattern, then consider buying the stock, especially if the primary price trend is also upward. That setup usually leads to lasting up moves. We'll see later that the performance rank for such a setup is 2, regardless of a bull or bear market.

The psychology behind the pattern is all about the black candles. The bulls have control of the market leading to the start of this pattern. They push price upward and then the bears take over. Each day a new black candle prints, and each day the bears force price a bit lower. By the time the third black candle appears, the bulls have tired of fighting a losing battle. However, if price gets cheap enough, the bulls will start bottom-fishing, and their buying will send the bears scurrying for cover.

Identification Guidelines

Figure 84.1 shows a good example of price reversing the uptrend but not making a lasting move. The three black crows appear when the primary price trend is upward. Price moves lower in the crows pattern, drops one more day, and then begins a recovery. A resumption of the uptrend follows.

The candle formation may look like the *identical* three crows pattern, and indeed it might qualify as one if there is only a small overlap between the

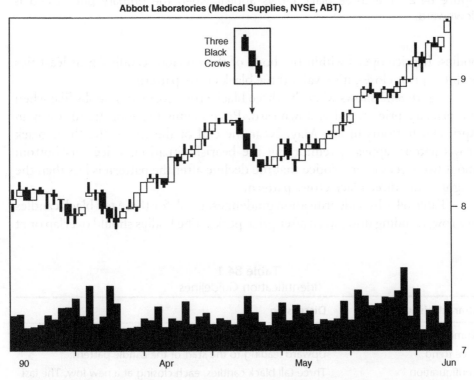

Figure 84.1   Three black crows appear and take price lower, but not far.

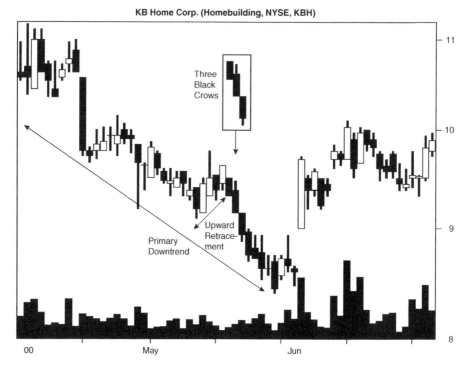

Figure 84.2 The three black crows appear when the primary price trend is downward.

bodies. If price opens within the body of the previous candle (or at least ties with the prior close), it's a valid three black crows pattern.

Figure 84.2 shows what the three black crows formation looks like when the primary price trend is downward. Price begins the long trend lower in April and bottoms in late May. Near the end of the trend, the three black crows pattern appears, reinforcing the bearish situation. Price hits bottom about two weeks later. Notice that the decline after the pattern is less than the height of the three black crows pattern.

Table 84.1 lists identification guidelines. Look for three tall black candles in a row, trending downward after price peaks. The bodies should overlap or at

Table 84.1
Identification Guidelines

Characteristic	Discussion
Number of candle lines	Three.
Price trend	Upward leading to the start of the candle pattern.
Configuration	Three tall black candles, each closing at a new low. The last two candles open within the body of the previous candle. All should close at or near their lows.

least tie with the closing price of the prior candle but make a new low. Lower shadows, if any, should be short, meaning the body should close near the low.

Statistics

Table 84.2 shows general statistics.

Number found. Out of over 4.7 million candle lines, I found just 2,660 of the crows. Most came from a bull market even after prorating the standard database.

Reversal or continuation performance. The three black crows perform better in a bear market than in a bull market, and that's typical for many candle types.

S&P performance. The crows pattern beats the performance of the S&P 500 index over the same time periods.

Candle end to breakout. Price breaks out downward quickly because it is near the low, while upward breakouts take longer to climb their way out of the candle pattern.

Table 84.2
General Statistics

Description	Bull Market, Up Breakout	Bear Market, Up Breakout	Bull Market, Down Breakout	Bear Market, Down Breakout
Number found	524	66	1,828	242
Reversal (R), continuation (C) performance	5.52% C	8.28% C	−5.19% R	−9.75% R
Standard & Poor's 500 change	2.23%	1.59%	−0.41%	−2.35%
Candle end to breakout (median, days)	10	10	3	3
Candle end to trend end (median, days)	12	14	5	5
Number of breakouts near the 12-month low (L), middle (M), or high (H)	L 75, M 102, H 278	L 15, M 19, H 30	L 441, M 540, H 631	L 100, M 54, H 84
Percentage move for each 12-month period	L 8.36%, M 5.87%, H 4.91%	L 12.55%, M 9.62%, H 6.11%	L −5.97%, M −5.32%, H −4.74%	L −10.52%, M −10.73%, H −8.92%
Candle end + 1 day	1.89%	3.60%	−0.39%	−0.95%
Candle end + 3 days	3.73%	7.67%	−0.75%	−1.40%
Candle end + 5 days	5.31%	9.62%	−0.75%	−1.59%
Candle end + 10 days	6.95%	13.31%	−0.51%	−1.41%
10-day performance rank	2	2	102	91

Candle end to trend end. A downward move in an existing downtrend reaches the trend end sooner than when price turns up and starts a new trend.

Yearly position, performance. In three out of four categories, the three black crows appear most often within a third of the yearly high (the exception being bear market/down breakouts). Performance is best when the breakout is within a third of the yearly low except for bear market/down breakouts. Those perform slightly better when the breakout is in the middle of the yearly price range.

Performance over time. Price struggles after a downward breakout between 5 and 10 days. Robust performers show higher numbers over time and in every category, so this candle pattern's performance is inferior.

Look at the size of the numbers for upward breakouts compared to downward ones. The results suggest trading when price breaks out upward after three black crows. The performance rank confirms this assessment with a rank of 2 out of 103 candles where 1 is best. Downward breakouts show lousy performance when compared to other candle types.

Table 84.3 shows height statistics.

Candle height. Tall candles outperform. To determine whether the candle is short or tall, compute its height from highest high to lowest low in the candle pattern and divide by the breakout price. If the result is higher than the median, then you have a tall candle; otherwise it's short.

Table 84.3
Height Statistics

Description	Bull Market, Up Breakout	Bear Market, Up Breakout	Bull Market, Down Breakout	Bear Market, Down Breakout
Median candle height as a percentage of breakout price	6.38%	10.30%	6.67%	10.95%
Short candle, performance	4.54%	6.00%	−4.30%	−8.16%
Tall candle, performance	7.09%	10.86%	−6.54%	−11.95%
Percentage meeting price target (measure rule)	33%	36%	29%	33%
Median upper shadow as a percentage of breakout price	0.19%	0.28%	0.09%	0.31%
Short upper shadow, performance	5.50%	5.84%	−5.25%	−9.55%
Tall upper shadow, performance	5.54%	10.14%	−5.15%	−9.93%
Median lower shadow as a percentage of breakout price	0.18%	0.46%	0.12%	0.42%
Short lower shadow, performance	5.42%	5.11%	−4.76%	−9.17%
Tall lower shadow, performance	5.62%	11.68%	−5.54%	−10.45%

Martin sees three black crows with a high of 77 and a low of 70. Is the pattern short or tall? The height is 77 – 70, or 7, so in a bull market with a downward breakout, the measure would be 7/70, or 10%. The candle is tall.

Measure rule. Use the measure rule to help predict how far price will rise or fall. Compute the height of the candle pattern and multiply it by the appropriate percentage shown in the table; then apply it to the breakout price.

What are the price targets for Martin's candle? The upward target would be (7 × 33%) + 77, or 79.31, and the downward target would be 70 – (7 × 29%), or 67.97.

Shadows. The table's results pertain to the last candle line in the pattern. To determine whether the shadow is short or tall, compute the height of the shadow and divide by the breakout price. Compare the result to the median in the table. Tall shadows have a percentage higher than the median.

Upper shadow performance. Tall upper shadows suggest good performance in all cases except for bull market/down breakouts. Those do slightly better if the upper shadow is short.

Lower shadow performance. Tall lower shadows suggest better post-breakout performance across the board.

Table 84.4 shows volume statistics.

Candle volume trend. Falling candle volume works better in bull markets, and rising candle volume suggests better performance in bear markets.

Average candle volume. Candles with above-average volume work best in bull markets, and candles with below-average volume work better in bear markets.

Breakout volume. Heavy breakout volume often leads to better post-breakout performance when compared to candles with light breakout volume.

Table 84.4
Volume Statistics

Description	Bull Market, Up Breakout	Bear Market, Up Breakout	Bull Market, Down Breakout	Bear Market, Down Breakout
Rising candle volume, performance	5.16%	10.37%	−4.95%	−9.94%
Falling candle volume, performance	6.00%	4.74%*	−5.59%	−9.55%
Above-average candle volume, performance	5.62%	6.33%	−5.41%	−9.67%
Below-average candle volume, performance	5.44%	9.41%	−5.00%	−9.82%
Heavy breakout volume, performance	6.13%	9.45%	−5.30%	−10.72%
Light breakout volume, performance	4.66%	5.31%*	−5.05%	−7.81%

*Fewer than 30 samples.

Trading Tactics

If price breaks out upward (meaning price closes above the highest high in the three black crows pattern), especially if the primary trend is upward, consider buying the stock. That setup often leads to additional gains.

I split trading tactics into two basic studies, one concerning reversal rates and the other concerning performance. Of the two, reversal rates are more important, because it's better to trade in the direction of the trend and let price run as far as it can.

Table 84.5 gives tips to find the trend direction.

Confirmation reversal rates. If you wait a day for price to close lower, it confirms a reversal has occurred 97% of the time. That's not saying much, though, because a reversal happens when price closes below the lowest low in the candle, and with price near the low at candle's end it doesn't take much of a decline to confirm the reversal. As Table 84.2 showed (performance over time), the decline after a downward breakout is often meager.

Reversal, continuation rates. Price breaks out downward most often.

Yearly range reversals. Most reversals occur within a third of the yearly low. In a bear market, that doesn't happen often (meaning samples are few).

Table 84.6 shows performance indicators that can give hints as to how your stock will behave after the breakout from this candle pattern.

Confirmation, performance. If price gaps open lower the next day, it confirms the candle and leads to better performance than the other confirmation methods.

Moving average. Candles with breakouts below the 50-trading-day moving average tend to perform better than do those above the average. The one exception is in bull market/up breakouts, which do better when the breakout is above the moving average. I consider that unusual since most candle types outperform when the breakout is below the moving average.

Table 84.5
Reversal Rates

Description	Bull Market	Bear Market
Closing price confirmation reversal rate	97%	97%
Candle color confirmation reversal rate	92%	90%
Opening gap confirmation reversal rate	89%	93%
Reversal rate: trend up, breakout down	78%	79%
Continuation rate: trend up, breakout up	22%	21%
Percentage of reversals (R)/continuations (C) for each 12-month low (L), middle (M), or high (H)	L 85% R/15% C, M 84% R/16% C, H 69% R/31% C	L* 87% R/13% C, M* 74% R/26% C, H 74% R/26% C

*Fewer than 30 samples.

Table 84.6
Performance Indicators

Description	Bull Market, Up Breakout	Bear Market, Up Breakout	Bull Market, Down Breakout	Bear Market, Down Breakout
Closing price confirmation, performance	N/A	N/A	−4.65%	−8.26%
Candle color confirmation, performance	N/A	N/A	−5.08%	−9.00%
Opening gap confirmation, performance	N/A	N/A	−5.66%	−11.51%
Breakout above 50-day moving average, performance	5.59%	8.08%	−5.06%	−7.08%
Breakout below 50-day moving average, performance	5.46%	9.89%*	−5.26%	−10.71%

N/A means not applicable.
*Fewer than 30 samples.

Sample Trade

Figure 84.3 shows a situation that confronted Martin. He owned the stock, but should he sell at B?

The setup that Martin faced is one that happens to traders and investors frequently. Price formed a high at A, retraced to C, and then climbed to B.

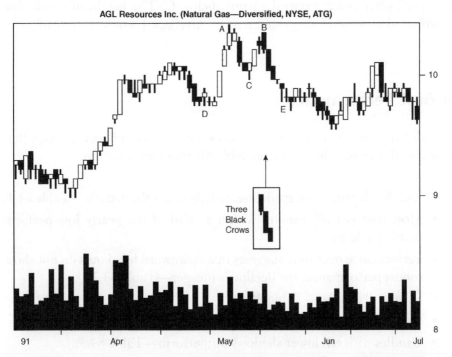

Figure 84.3 Price forms a double top, and three black crows lead the way lower.

Statistics on double tops (peaks A and B) say that price will fail to confirm the double top 65% of the time. That means price will not close below the low at C before first closing above the higher of peaks A and B. As you can see, price *did* close below C, confirming the small double top pattern.

Martin approached the setup this way. He asked how far price was likely to drop. He saw the support zone at D and thought price would stall or even reverse there. D was also located near a peak that occurred in February (not shown), and that helped bolster the support zone.

Below that, price could tumble to the next support area at around 9.25, which had been about five months long. He thought it unlikely that price would drop that far—but if it did, that would probably be as far as it was going.

He checked the price of natural gas and prices of other stocks in the industry, just to get a feel for how the natural gas sector was doing. Right or wrong, he decided to hold on to the stock because he thought it held more upside potential despite any near-term weakness.

Price formed the three black crows pattern and then dropped, confirming the double top at E and finding support at the price level of D, just as Martin had predicted.

After about two weeks at that level, price dropped lower before recovering and moving horizontally again. It took price until late August (not shown) before it climbed above A.

Martin's method of looking for underlying support to gauge whether to sell is a good one, provided you make the right choice. If this were my stock, I would sell when price dropped a penny below C. The height of the double top projected downward suggested a profit giveback I would be unwilling to tolerate.

For Best Performance

The following list offers tips and observations to help choose candles that perform well. Consult the associated table for more information.

- Use the identification guidelines to help select the pattern—Table 84.1.
- Most (but not all) candles within a third of the yearly low perform best—Table 84.2.
- Performance over time suggests that downward breakouts do not show robust performance; the decline is meager—Table 84.2.
- Select tall candles—Table 84.3.
- Use the measure rule to predict a price target—Table 84.3.
- Candles with tall lower shadows outperform—Table 84.3.
- Volume gives performance clues—Table 84.4.

- If price breaks out upward from the three black crows, consider buying—Trading Tactics discussion.
- A lower close the day after the candle ends confirms a reversal 97% of the time—Table 84.5.
- Patterns within a third of the yearly low tend to act as reversals most often—Table 84.5.
- Opening gap confirmation works best—Table 84.6.

85

Three Inside Down

Behavior and Rank

Theoretical: Bearish reversal.

Actual bull market: Bearish reversal 60% of the time (ranking 29).

Actual bear market: Bearish reversal 63% of the time (ranking 22).

Frequency: 33rd out of 103.

Overall performance over time: 56th out of 103.

The three inside down candle pattern was developed by Gregory Morris as confirmation of the bearish harami. The pattern is a harami with one additional candle line that must close lower.

The pattern shows a good reversal rate and ranking of 29 (bull market) where 1 is best out of 103 candles. Frequency rank is also good, so this pattern is as plentiful as fruit flies in the orchard at harvest time. The overall rank of 56 is midrange, comparing performance in bull and bear markets, up and down breakouts with other candles.

Pattern psychology: The bulls are in control and pushing price higher leading to the start of this candle pattern. A tall white candle prints on the chart, confirming the bullish buying pressure. Then a small black candle appears, and it's the first sign of weakness. The bears are battling with the bulls now, and winning. If the next day shows a lower close, then the bears have wrested control from the bulls, and the belief is that price will continue lower. It does, but only 61% of the time.

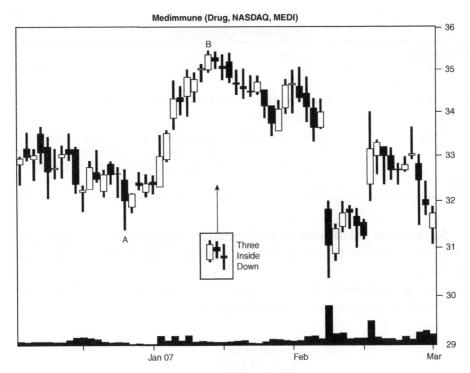

Figure 85.1   A three inside down candle formation appears at the end of an uptrend.

Identification Guidelines

Figure 85.1 shows an example of a three inside down candle. Price begins trending upward at A and peaks at B. A bearish harami candle forms where a black candle appears inside the open and close range (the body) of the prior white candle (B). When price closes lower the next day, the combination turns this candle into a three inside down pattern. Price cooperates in this example by trending lower thereafter.

Table 85.1 lists identification guidelines. If you can recognize a bearish harami, then you're two-thirds of the way home. Look for a tall white candle followed by a small black candle that fits inside the body of the first day. The last day in the pattern must close lower and it's usually black.

Statistics

Table 85.2 shows general statistics.

Number found. I found plenty of these candles, so I limited the number to 20,000. Prorating the standard database shows that this candle appears most often in a bear market.

Table 85.1
Identification Guidelines

Characteristic	Discussion
Number of candle lines	Three.
Price trend	Upward leading to the start of the candle pattern.
First day	A tall white candle.
Second day	A small black candle. The open and close must be within the body of the first day, but ignore the shadows. Either the tops or the bottoms of the bodies can be equal, but not both.
Third day	Price must close lower.

Reversal or continuation performance. The three inside down pattern performs better in a bear market, and reversals perform better than continuations.

S&P performance. The candle pattern beats the S&P 500 index regardless of market condition or breakout direction.

Table 85.2
General Statistics

Description	Bull Market, Up Breakout	Bear Market, Up Breakout	Bull Market, Down Breakout	Bear Market, Down Breakout
Number found	6,876	1,006	10,416	1,702
Reversal (R), continuation (C) performance	5.85% C	8.27% C	−5.89% R	−9.60% R
Standard & Poor's 500 change	1.31%	0.74%	−0.54%	−2.12%
Candle end to breakout (median, days)	5	5	3	3
Candle end to trend end (median, days)	8	9	6	7
Number of breakouts near the 12-month low (L), middle (M), or high (H)	L 1,002, M 1,693, H 4,181	L 199, M 329, H 478	L 2,211, M 2,949, H 5,256	L 500, M 567, H 635
Percentage move for each 12-month period	L 7.07%, M 5.91%, H 5.63%	L 13.75%, M 7.64%, H 7.10%	L −6.33%, M −6.30%, H −5.58%	L −11.27%, M −9.22%, H −9.02%
Candle end + 1 day	1.17%	1.78%	−0.69%	−0.97%
Candle end + 3 days	2.46%	3.40%	−1.42%	−2.21%
Candle end + 5 days	3.04%	4.24%	−1.76%	−2.48%
Candle end + 10 days	3.83%	4.93%	−1.78%	−3.15%
10-day performance rank	38	30	70	69

Candle end to breakout. Downward breakouts take less time than upward breakouts. This is because the closing price is closer to the bottom of the candle than the top of it.

Candle end to trend end. The time to the trend end ranges from six to nine days. Downward breakouts take slightly less time because price in the candle has been trending lower for a few days. An upward breakout would require a reversal—a start of a new trend—and that would take longer than one already underway.

Yearly position, performance. Most three inside down formations appear within a third of the yearly high, but the best performance comes from patterns within a third of the yearly low.

Performance over time. This candle pattern is a robust performer. Price over time posts larger numbers in all columns. If there's a chink in the armor, it's that the numbers aren't very high. For a $10 stock, as an example, that means a gain of less than 50 cents in two weeks. And that's for the best average performance. For downward breakouts, the worst case is a drop of less than 32 cents over two weeks. (Of course, a million shares times 32 cents turns into real money.)

The performance rank confirms this assessment. Upward breakouts perform better than many other candle types, but downward breakouts are on the losing end.

Table 85.3 shows height statistics.

Table 85.3
Height Statistics

Description	Bull Market, Up Breakout	Bear Market, Up Breakout	Bull Market, Down Breakout	Bear Market, Down Breakout
Median candle height as a percentage of breakout price	3.62%	5.21%	3.84%	5.88%
Short candle, performance	4.65%	6.48%	−4.81%	−7.52%
Tall candle, performance	7.51%	10.43%	−7.36%	−12.10%
Percentage meeting price target (measure rule)	58%	55%	56%	52%
Median upper shadow as a percentage of breakout price	0.25%	0.40%	0.17%	0.43%
Short upper shadow, performance	5.65%	7.72%	−5.80%	−8.36%
Tall upper shadow, performance	6.02%	8.84%	−5.97%	−10.76%
Median lower shadow as a percentage of breakout price	0.37%	0.76%	0.32%	0.63%
Short lower shadow, performance	5.40%	7.54%	−5.26%	−9.39%
Tall lower shadow, performance	6.24%	8.98%	−6.44%	−9.79%

Candle height. Tall candles outperform. To determine whether the candle is short or tall, compute its height from highest high to lowest low price in the candle pattern and divide by the breakout price. If the result is higher than the median, then you have a tall candle; otherwise it's short.

Ed has a three inside down candle with a high of 50 and a low of 47. Is the candle short or tall? The height is 50 – 47, or 3, so the measure would be 3/47, or 6.4%. In a bull market with a downward breakout, that means it's a tall candle.

Measure rule. Use the measure rule to help predict how far price will rise or fall. Compute the height of the candle and multiply it by the appropriate percentage shown in the table; then apply it to the breakout price.

What are Ed's price targets? The upward target would be (3 × 58%) + 50, or 51.74, and the downward target would be 47 − (3 × 56%), or 45.32.

Shadows. The table's results pertain to the last candle line in the pattern. To determine whether the shadow is short or tall, compute the height of the shadow and divide by the breakout price. Compare the result to the median in the table. Tall shadows have a percentage higher than the median. Tall upper or lower shadows suggest good postbreakout performance in all cases.

Table 85.4 shows volume statistics.

Candle volume trend. A falling volume trend suggests better performance across the board.

Average candle volume. Candles with below-average volume perform better than do those with above-average volume, except for bear market/down breakouts.

Table 85.4
Volume Statistics

Description	Bull Market, Up Breakout	Bear Market, Up Breakout	Bull Market, Down Breakout	Bear Market, Down Breakout
Rising candle volume, performance	5.78%	7.81%	−5.67%	−9.31%
Falling candle volume, performance	5.87%	8.47%	−6.01%	−9.76%
Above-average candle volume, performance	5.82%	7.54%	−5.75%	−9.93%
Below-average candle volume, performance	5.87%	8.79%	−5.99%	−9.35%
Heavy breakout volume, performance	6.53%	8.45%	−6.36%	−10.03%
Light breakout volume, performance	5.05%	8.05%	−5.58%	−9.28%

Breakout volume. Heavy breakout volume suggests better postbreakout performance in all cases.

Trading Tactics

Avoid depending on this candle pattern if the primary price trend is upward. In such a case, there is a high tendency for price to break out upward, resuming the upward trend. Save this candle for downward price trends where a short upward retracement forms the three inside down candle. Those are more likely to break out downward and result in a lasting decline.

Swing traders can trade this candle pattern if it appears near the top of a trend channel. Price will drop to the lower end of the channel and then rebound.

I split trading tactics into two basic studies, one concerning reversal rates and the other concerning performance. Of the two, reversal rates are more important, because it's better to trade in the direction of the trend and let price run as far as it can.

Table 85.5 gives tips to find the trend direction.

Confirmation reversal rates. Since a lower close confirms the bearish harami and forms a three inside down candle, you might feel there is no need to confirm it a second time. However, you can boost the reversal rate from 61% to 84% (bull market) by waiting for a lower close after the three inside down candle completes. Waiting also means you'll probably make less, though.

Reversal, continuation rates. Price breaks out downward 60% of the time (bull market), but this may be a function of how low the close is to the bottom of the candle.

Yearly range reversals. The band with the highest reversal rate comes from candles with breakouts within a third of the yearly low. They reverse more often than candles in the other two ranges.

Table 85.5
Reversal Rates

Description	Bull Market	Bear Market
Closing price confirmation reversal rate	84%	83%
Candle color confirmation reversal rate	81%	81%
Opening gap confirmation reversal rate	70%	69%
Reversal rate: trend up, breakout down	60%	63%
Continuation rate: trend up, breakout up	40%	37%
Percentage of reversals (R)/continuations (C) for each 12-month low (L), middle (M), or high (H)	L 69% R/31% C, M 64% R/36% C, H 56% R/44% C	L 72% R/28% C, M 63% R/37% C, H 57% R/43% C

Table 85.6
Performance Indicators

Description	Bull Market, Up Breakout	Bear Market, Up Breakout	Bull Market, Down Breakout	Bear Market, Down Breakout
Closing price confirmation, performance	N/A	N/A	−6.20%	−9.77%
Candle color confirmation, performance	N/A	N/A	−6.29%	−10.46%
Opening gap confirmation, performance	N/A	N/A	−6.82%	−10.66%
Breakout above 50-day moving average, performance	5.80%	7.71%	−5.71%	−8.63%
Breakout below 50-day moving average, performance	6.19%	11.45%	−6.26%	−11.14%
Last candle: close in highest third, performance	5.47%	7.15%	−5.80%	−8.12%
Last candle: close in middle third, performance	5.61%	8.08%	−5.94%	−8.19%
Last candle: close in lowest third, performance	6.08%	8.69%	−5.89%	−10.43%

N/A means not applicable.

Table 85.6 shows performance indicators that can give hints as to how your stock will behave after the breakout from this candle pattern.

Confirmation, performance. Use the opening gap method to confirm this candle and as a buy signal. That means waiting for price to gap open lower the day after the three inside down ends and then trading the stock.

Moving average. Candles below the 50-day moving average tend to perform better than do those above the moving average.

Closing position. A close in the lowest third of the last candle suggests good postbreakout performance in all cases except for bull market/down breakouts. That column does better if the last line closes in the middle third of the candle.

Sample Trade

Figure 85.2 shows a three inside down candle that concerned Ed. Price began the trend up at A, sloping higher at a good, sustainable rate, and then took off at D. The rise turned almost vertical, and he knew that it could not continue

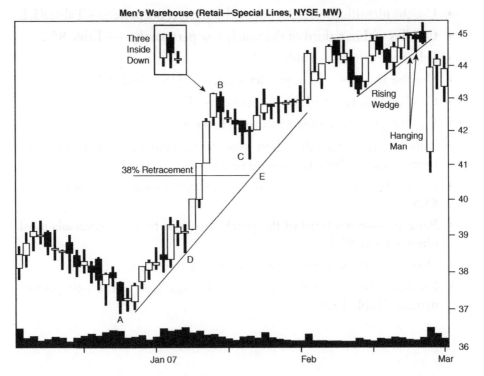

Figure 85.2 A three inside down candle pattern appears in an uptrend.

for long at that rate. Then the three inside down appeared. Was this the time to take profits in the stock?

Ed measured the rise from A to B and assumed that price would retrace at least 38% (based on a Fibonacci retracement value) of the prior rise, perhaps as much as 62%. He then drew a trendline from A to D and extended it upward. The line intersected the 38% retracement line at E. If price closed below that intersection, he decided, he would sell.

As the chart shows, price turned lower and dropped only to C before staging a recovery. Price resumed following the trendline upward until it started forming a rising wedge. That's a chart pattern in which both trendlines slope upward but they converge. A downward breakout from the rising wedge usually takes price down to at least the low of the wedge (about 43 in this case).

The rising wedge chart pattern worried Ed because it is a bearish pattern. When the two hanging man candles appeared, he didn't want to be left hanging on to a loss, so he sold a day before the tall white candle.

For Best Performance

The following list offers tips and observations to help choose candles that perform well. Consult the associated table for more information.

- Use the identification guidelines to help select the pattern—Table 85.1.
- Candles within a third of the yearly low perform best—Table 85.2.
- Select tall candles—Table 85.3.
- Use the measure rule to predict a price target—Table 85.3.
- Candles with tall shadows outperform—Table 85.3.
- Volume gives performance clues—Table 85.4.
- This candle pattern does best as a retracement in a downward price trend—see Trading Tactics discussion.
- Use confirmation to increase your chances of a successful trade—Table 85.5.
- Patterns within a third of the yearly low tend to act as reversals most often—Table 85.5.
- Opening gap confirmation works best—Table 85.6.
- Breakouts below the 50-day moving average lead to the best performance—Table 85.6.

86

Three Inside Up

Behavior and Rank

Theoretical: Bullish reversal.

Actual bull market: Bullish reversal 65% of the time (ranking 20).

Actual bear market: Bullish reversal 63% of the time (ranking 23).

Frequency: 31st out of 103.

Overall performance over time: 20th out of 103.

Three inside up is a confirmed bullish harami pattern. What does that mean? Think of an inside day or a harami with a third candle that closes higher than the prior day. The candle pattern was developed by Gregory Morris to improve the performance of the harami candlestick.

A bullish reversal ranking of 20, where 1 is best out of 103, I consider very good. The frequency rank (31) means the pattern occurs often, and the overall performance rank (20) is excellent.

The psychology behind the pattern starts with a downward price trend. The bears have the ball and they are not giving it up easily. Price prints a tall black candle, showing the determination of bears to push price lower. The bulls then steal the ball, but the bears fight to get it back. A small white candle develops. The next day another white candle appears, confirming that the bulls still have control of the ball and they won't make the mistake of letting the bears steal it back anytime soon. The white candle confirms that the trend has reversed from down to up.

Lincoln National Corp. (Insurance—Life, NYSE, LNC)

Figure 86.1 The three inside up candle accurately predicts a reversal of the downtrend.

Identification Guidelines

Figure 86.1 shows an example of the three inside up candle formation. The downtrend leading to the candle pattern is short because it begins at A. The middle candle line of the three-day pattern is at B. Price at B nears the low at C, which is a support zone. Thus, underlying support coupled with the bullish reversal candle sends price higher.

Table 86.1 lists identification guidelines. If you know what a bullish harami candle looks like, then add another line that closes higher. If you don't know what a bullish harami is, then never mind.

Table 86.1
Identification Guidelines

Characteristic	Discussion
Number of candle lines	Three.
Price trend	Downward leading to the start of the candle pattern.
First day	A tall black candle.
Second day	A small-bodied white candle. The body must be within the prior candle's body. The tops or bottoms of the two bodies can be the same price but not both.
Third day	A white candle that closes above the prior day's close.

Look for a tall black candle followed by two white ones. The first white candle is a short one whose body nestles inside the body of the prior black candle. The last white candle in the pattern confirms the bullish harami by closing above the prior close.

Statistics

Table 86.2 shows general statistics.

Number found. The candle is plentiful, so I limited selections to the first 20,000 patterns. Prorating the standard database shows that three inside up appears most often in a bear market.

Reversal or continuation performance. Performance from the candle is best in a bear market.

S&P performance. The candle pattern beats the performance of the S&P 500 index over the same time periods.

Candle end to breakout. Upward breakouts take less time to break out than downward ones because price closes near the high of the candle. A

Table 86.2
General Statistics

Description	Bull Market, Up Breakout	Bear Market, Up Breakout	Bull Market, Down Breakout	Bear Market, Down Breakout
Number found	11,090	1,783	6,069	1,058
Reversal (R), continuation (C) performance	6.73% R	9.47% R	−5.76% C	−10.63% C
Standard & Poor's 500 change	1.28%	0.88%	−0.81%	−2.62%
Candle end to breakout (median, days)	3	3	5	5
Candle end to trend end (median, days)	7	7	7	8
Number of breakouts near the 12-month low (L), middle (M), or high (H)	L 2,946, M 3,307, H 4,837	L 649, M 581, H 553	L 2,298, M 2,041, H 1,730	L 530, M 324, H 204
Percentage move for each 12-month period	L 7.93%, M 6.67%, H 6.03%	L 12.51%, M 9.17%, H 7.41%	L −6.14%, M −5.83%, H −5.43%	L −13.36%, M −9.06%, H −8.79%
Candle end + 1 day	0.76%	0.96%	−1.17%	−1.98%
Candle end + 3 days	1.68%	2.62%	−2.60%	−4.20%
Candle end + 5 days	2.15%	2.89%	−3.29%	−5.56%
Candle end + 10 days	2.61%	2.84%	−3.44%	−7.00%
10-day performance rank	63	58	29	9

breakout occurs when price closes either above the highest high in the candle pattern or below the lowest low.

Candle end to trend end. It takes about a week for price to reach the trend end.

Yearly position, performance. In three of four categories, the candle appears most often within a third of the yearly low. Performance is best when the candle is within a third of the yearly low, too, regardless of the breakout direction or market condition.

Performance over time. Performance is respectable over time but not exceptional. In a robust candle all periods should show increasing performance, but this one doesn't between 5 and 10 days during bear market/up breakouts.

The performance rank, when compared to other candle types, shows that downward breakouts from this candle are where you'll get the best performance.

Table 86.3 shows height statistics.

Candle height. Tall candles perform better than short ones in all cases. To determine whether the candle pattern is short or tall, compute its height from highest high to lowest low price in the candle pattern and divide by the breakout price. If the result is higher than the median, then you have a tall candle; otherwise it's short.

Table 86.3
Height Statistics

Description	Bull Market, Up Breakout	Bear Market, Up Breakout	Bull Market, Down Breakout	Bear Market, Down Breakout
Median candle height as a percentage of breakout price	4.04%	6.51%	4.02%	6.45%
Short candle, performance	5.31%	7.02%	−4.71%	−7.62%
Tall candle, performance	8.57%	12.21%	−7.19%	−14.36%
Percentage meeting price target (measure rule)	60%	55%	54%	57%
Median upper shadow as a percentage of breakout price	0.35%	0.72%	0.41%	0.87%
Short upper shadow, performance	6.25%	8.03%	−5.32%	−8.97%
Tall upper shadow, performance	7.13%	10.85%	−6.16%	−12.18%
Median lower shadow as a percentage of breakout price	0.29%	0.54%	0.34%	0.57%
Short lower shadow, performance	6.21%	8.32%	−5.43%	−9.79%
Tall lower shadow, performance	7.21%	10.63%	−6.12%	−11.53%

Andy sees a three inside up candle with a high price of 87 and a low of 85. Is the candle short or tall? The height is 87 – 85, or 2, so the measure in a bull market with an upward breakout would be 2/87, or 2.3%. It's a short candle.

Measure rule. Use the measure rule to help predict how far price will rise or fall. Compute the height of the candle pattern and multiply it by the appropriate percentage shown in the table; then apply it to the breakout price.

What are the price targets for Andy's candle? The upward target would be (2 × 60%) + 87, or 88.20, and the downward target would be 85 – (2 × 54%), or 83.92.

Shadows. The table's results pertain to the last candle line in the pattern. To determine whether the shadow is short or tall, compute the height of the shadow and divide by the breakout price. Compare the result to the median in the table. Tall shadows have a percentage higher than the median.

Tall upper or lower shadows on the last candle line suggest better performance.

Table 86.4 shows volume statistics.

Candle volume trend. Candles with a rising volume trend work best in bull market/up breakouts and bear market/down breakouts. Falling volume leads to better performance for the inner two columns: bear market/up breakouts and bull market/down breakouts.

Average candle volume. Candles with above-average volume tend to perform better than those with below-average volume.

Breakout volume. Heavy breakout volume leads to better performance than does light breakout volume.

Table 86.4
Volume Statistics

Description	Bull Market, Up Breakout	Bear Market, Up Breakout	Bull Market, Down Breakout	Bear Market, Down Breakout
Rising candle volume, performance	6.76%	8.99%	−5.73%	−10.93%
Falling candle volume, performance	6.71%	9.79%	−5.82%	−10.45%
Above-average candle volume, performance	6.94%	9.77%	−5.85%	−11.25%
Below-average candle volume, performance	6.56%	9.19%	−5.74%	−10.07%
Heavy breakout volume, performance	7.68%	10.20%	−6.38%	−11.69%
Light breakout volume, performance	5.80%	8.80%	−5.17%	−9.33%

Trading Tactics

This candle pattern works best when it appears as a reversal of the downward price trend in an upward primary trend. That means price trends higher over time, but when it takes a rest and declines for a few days or weeks, the three inside up candle appears and signals a resumption of the uptrend.

Measure the extent of the retracement compared to the prior rise and see if it's close to the Fibonacci numbers of 38%, 50%, or 62%. If it is, then the chances of a reversal improve. If it's not, then price might ease lower for another week or two before staging a lasting reversal.

Avoid expecting a trend change if the primary trend is downward. The breakout may be upward but it usually doesn't last long before price resumes the downward trend. Of course, every situation differs, but look for underlying support that might help a reversal of the downtrend stick.

I split trading tactics into two basic studies, one concerning reversal rates and the other concerning performance. Of the two, reversal rates are more important, because it's better to trade in the direction of the trend and let price run as far as it can.

Table 86.5 gives tips to find the trend direction.

Confirmation reversal rates. The three inside up was designed as confirmation of a bullish harami candle, so it doesn't need another confirmation candle. However, if you use one and wait for a higher close after the candle ends, it confirms a reversal 87% of the time in a bull market.

That may sound good, but a reversal occurs when price closes above the highest high in the candle. With two days of higher closes, it's no wonder the reversal rate is high. The performance over time rows in Table 86.2 (upward breakouts) show comparatively low numbers, so be cautious if you expect price to stage a major recovery.

Reversal, continuation rates. Price breaks out upward most often. This is likely due to the candle having a closing price near the top of the pattern.

Table 86.5
Reversal Rates

Description	Bull Market	Bear Market
Closing price confirmation reversal rate	87%	85%
Candle color confirmation reversal rate	85%	84%
Opening gap confirmation reversal rate	73%	69%
Reversal: trend down, breakout up	65%	63%
Continuation: trend down, breakout down	35%	37%
Percentage of reversals (R)/continuations (C) for each 12-month low (L), middle (M), or high (H)	L 56% R/44% C, M 62% R/38% C, H 74% R/26% C	L 55% R/45% C, M 64% R/36% C, H 73% R/27% C

Table 86.6
Performance Indicators

Description	Bull Market, Up Breakout	Bear Market, Up Breakout	Bull Market, Down Breakout	Bear Market, Down Breakout
Closing price confirmation, performance	6.48%	9.85%	N/A	N/A
Candle color confirmation, performance	6.40%	9.68%	N/A	N/A
Opening gap confirmation, performance	7.49%	12.00%	N/A	N/A
Breakout above 50-day moving average, performance	6.51%	8.23%	−5.10%	−8.61%
Breakout below 50-day moving average, performance	7.02%	10.73%	−6.00%	−11.26%
Last candle: close in highest third, performance	6.85%	9.22%	−5.81%	−11.27%
Last candle: close in middle third, performance	6.72%	9.80%	−5.78%	−10.37%
Last candle: close in lowest third, performance	6.07%	9.97%	−5.69%	−9.27%

N/A means not applicable.

Yearly range reversals. Most reversals appear within a third of the yearly high.

Table 86.6 shows performance indicators that can give hints as to how your stock will behave after the breakout from this candle pattern.

Confirmation, performance. Waiting for price to gap open higher a day after the candle pattern ends leads to the best performance.

Moving average. Candles with breakouts below the 50-day moving average perform better.

Closing position. A close in the highest third works best in all cases except for bear market/up breakouts, which do better when price closes in the lowest third of the last candle line.

Sample Trade

Figure 86.2 shows a trade Andy considered making. From the high at D, price fell off a cliff and hit bottom at A; it bounced to B, and then the climbers still alive made their way up a new mountain to E. The peak at E was slightly below the price of D. When price declined to C, Andy drew in the trendlines connecting valleys A, B, and C along with peaks D and E, forming a symmetrical triangle chart pattern.

Figure 86.2   A three inside up candle points the way out of a symmetrical triangle chart pattern.

Using the difference between the two trendlines at C, he considered making a trade starting at the opening price a day after C and selling if and when price reversed at the top trendline. With luck, price would break out upward, but he wouldn't depend on that.

He used the high at candle C, 28.34, and the projected target price of 29.57 as the potential profit. If he traded it perfectly, without commissions or other charges, he could make $1.23 per share. His risk would be if price broke out downward from the triangle. That would mean a close below C, at 27.85. The difference there would be 49 cents. Thus, the risk/reward profile would be over 2:1 in his favor.

The next day, he bought the stock when price gapped open higher, confirming the harami candle. A day later, the stock shot through his price target and closed above the top of the symmetrical triangle. This meant more upside would likely follow, but the tall white candle also warned that a minor high was likely within a day (plus or minus). That's what happened the next day.

Since the white candle was so tall, he thought it would support price midway down its body and decided to hold on to the stock. Price eased lower during the next three days (to F) before resuming the uptrend, finding support near the midpoint of the candle just as he had predicted.

He drew a trendline connecting valleys C and F and extended it upward. When price closed below that trendline, coupled with ominous-looking tall black candles, he decided to sell. He timed the exit at G and sold near the intraday high.

For Best Performance

The following list offers tips and observations to help choose candles that perform well. Consult the associated table for more information.

- Use the identification guidelines to help select the pattern—Table 86.1.
- Candles within a third of the yearly low perform best—Table 86.2.
- Select tall candles—Table 86.3.
- Use the measure rule to predict a price target—Table 86.3.
- Candles with tall shadows outperform—Table 86.3.
- Volume gives performance clues—Table 86.4.
- Trade this candle during a downward retracement of the primary uptrend. Avoid expecting a reversal when the primary price trend is downward. See Trading Tactics discussion.
- The candle breaks out upward most often—Table 86.5.
- Patterns within a third of the yearly high tend to act as reversals most often—Table 86.5.
- Opening gap confirmation works best—Table 86.6.
- Breakouts below the 50-day moving average lead to the best performance—Table 86.6.

87

Three-Line Strike, Bearish

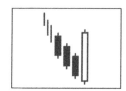

Behavior and Rank

Theoretical: Bearish continuation.

Actual bull market: Bullish reversal 84% of the time (ranking 2).

Actual bear market: Bullish reversal 77% of the time (ranking 7).

Frequency: 94th out of 103.

Overall performance over time: 1st out of 103.

I found the bearish three-line strike candle to be a surprise. It's supposed to be a bearish continuation pattern, but my testing found that it's a bullish reversal 84% of the time in a bull market. Of course, that's because price is near the top of the pattern and all it has to do is close above the highest high to confirm a bullish reversal. That's easy. However, a visual inspection confirms that this pattern acts as a bullish reversal.

The rankings are some of the best numbers we've seen. The reversal rank is 2 where 1 is best out of 103. The frequency rank of 94 means you won't find this anytime soon in the grocery store aisles. The overall performance rank is 1, but that's because the samples are so few. With more samples, I'm confident that performance would worsen.

The psychology behind the pattern begins with price trending lower as bears sell the stock or sell it short. Three black candles print on the chart, each closing lower, energizing the bears. Then they decide to cover their short positions, and this brings in the bulls. They are happy to gather some profits. Unless the downward price trend is a strong one, the tall white candle that prints on the chart is the beginning of an upward price trend. The next few

756

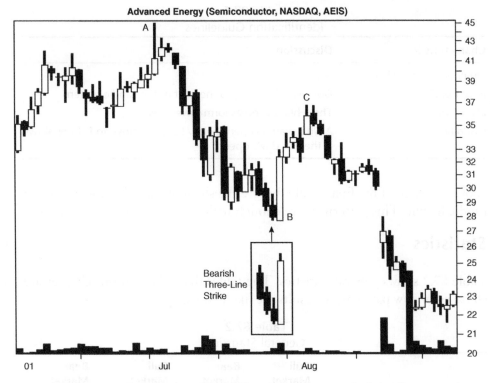

Figure 87.1   A bearish three-line strike acts as a reversal of the downtrend.

days may post lower closes, but make no mistake—the trend has probably changed from down to up, at least in the short term, especially if the primary trend was upward, too.

Identification Guidelines

Figure 87.1 shows the typical behavior of the bearish three-line strike. Price trends down from peak A and bottoms at B where the candle pattern ends. Three black candles, each closing lower, appear, followed by a tall white candle at B. This bullish buying sets a new tone and reverses the downward momentum. In the next week, the buying enthusiasm continues and price coasts higher, peaking at C. Then the primary downward price trend resumes and carries price lower . . . much lower.

Table 87.1 lists identification guidelines. Some will say this candle is three black crows followed by a confirming white candle. Actually, there are some differences. In the bearish three-line strike candle, the black candles need not be tall ones and they appear in an established downtrend. Both of those features are different from the three black crows pattern.

In the three-line strike pattern, the last white candle is usually a tall one to engulf the bodies of the prior three black candles. It opens lower and closes

Table 87.1
Identification Guidelines

Characteristic	Discussion
Number of candle lines	Four.
Price trend	Downward leading to the start of the candle pattern.
Days 1 to 3	Three black candles form lower closes.
Last day	A white candle opens below the prior close and closes above the first day's open.

above the open of the first candle. Ignore the shadows, and don't worry about candle height. This pattern is rare enough without requiring those features.

Statistics

Table 87.2 shows general statistics. The tables that follow in this chapter are all based on few patterns, so results are likely to change.

Table 87.2
General Statistics

Description	Bull Market, Up Breakout	Bear Market, Up Breakout*	Bull Market, Down Breakout*	Bear Market, Down Breakout*
Number found	53	17	10	5
Reversal (R), continuation (C) performance	5.45% R	15.62% R	−8.60% C	−8.57% C
Standard & Poor's 500 change	1.22%	2.58%	−1.15%	0.27%
Candle end to breakout (median, days)	3	3	8	5
Candle end to trend end (median, days)	7	5	13	8
Number of breakouts near the 12-month low (L), middle (M), or high (H)	L 14, M 14, H 18	L 7, M 7, H 3	L 6, M 2, H 1	L 2, M 2, H 1
Percentage move for each 12-month period	L 7.37%, M 3.68%, H 4.46%	L 26.30%, M 8.15%, H 9.44%	L −10.85%, M −8.97%, H −4.99%	L −11.62%, M −8.14%, H −3.06%
Candle end + 1 day	0.82%	1.42%	−1.46%	−2.50%
Candle end + 3 days	1.19%	4.30%	−2.42%	−9.95%
Candle end + 5 days	1.94%	6.01%	−6.13%	−3.61%
Candle end + 10 days	2.47%	7.53%	−8.81%	−6.82%
10-day performance rank	70	10	1	11

*Fewer than 30 samples.

Number found. Out of over 4.7 million candle lines, I found 85 bearish three-line strike patterns. Prorating the results reveals that this pattern appears most often in a bear market.

Reversal or continuation performance. Usually, patterns in a bear market outperform their bull market counterparts, but that's not always the case here.

S&P performance. The candle pattern beats the performance of the S&P 500 index in all columns.

Candle end to breakout. It takes between three and eight days to break out. Upward breakouts take less time because the closing price in the last candle is near the pattern's high, so all it takes is a close above the high to break out upward.

Candle end to trend end. The median time to the trend end ranges between 5 and 13 days. Upward breakouts take less time than downward ones. The last candle in the pattern makes it appear like the prior three candles never existed. Thus, an upward move would be closer to the trend end since a bullish candle has already printed on the chart. A downward move would begin a new trend and would thus take longer than one already on its way.

Yearly position, performance. The best performance comes from candles with breakouts within a third of the yearly low. Where the candles appear most often is near the yearly low except for bull market/up breakouts where the highest third scores the most patterns.

Performance over time. This candle posts very good numbers except for the bear market/down breakout column, in which the low sample count (five samples) is probably responsible for the inconsistent trend over time.

Downward breakouts appear to do better than upward ones, and the ranks of 1 and 11 confirm that assessment. You will notice that the highest sample count (53 in bull market/up breakouts) also has the worst rank. Thus, my guess is that additional samples in the other columns would show deteriorating performance.

Table 87.3 shows height statistics.

Candle height. Tall candles outperform. To determine whether the candle is short or tall, compute its height from highest high to lowest low price in the candle pattern and divide by the breakout price. If the result is higher than the median, then you have a tall candle; otherwise it's short.

Clark sees a three-line strike candle with a high of 63 and a low of 60. Is the candle short or tall? The height is 63 − 60, or 3, so the measure for an upward breakout in a bull market would be 3/63, or 4.8%. The candle is short.

Measure rule. Use the measure rule to help predict how far price will rise or fall. Compute the height of the candle pattern and multiply it by the appropriate percentage shown in the table; then apply it to the breakout price.

What are Clark's price targets for his candle? The upward target would be (3 × 40%) + 63, or 64.20, and the downward target would be 60 − (3 × 80%), or 57.60.

Table 87.3
Height Statistics*

Description	Bull Market, Up Breakout	Bear Market, Up Breakout	Bull Market, Down Breakout	Bear Market, Down Breakout
Median candle height as a percentage of breakout price	5.69%	10.91%	6.01%	6.93%
Short candle, performance	4.01%	7.75%	−8.37%	−8.03%
Tall candle, performance	6.91%	22.28%	−8.71%	−9.43%
Percentage meeting price target (measure rule)	40%	41%	80%	60%
Median upper shadow as a percentage of breakout price	0.29%	0.45%	0.58%	0.55%
Short upper shadow, performance	5.71%	8.19%	−6.93%	−8.03%
Tall upper shadow, performance	5.25%	22.29%	−10.65%	−9.43%
Median lower shadow as a percentage of breakout price	0.13%	0.34%	0.29%	0.00%
Short lower shadow, performance	4.79%	7.04%	−9.73%	−7.71%
Tall lower shadow, performance	6.36%	24.68%	−8.06%	−10.65%

*Fewer than 30 samples.

Shadows. The table's results pertain to the last candle line in the pattern. To determine whether the shadow is short or tall, compute the height of the shadow and divide by the breakout price. Compare the result to the median in the table. Tall shadows have a percentage higher than the median.

Upper shadow performance. A tall upper shadow results in the best performance in all cases except for bull market/up breakouts. Those do better when the shadow is short.

Lower shadow performance. Tall lower shadows also suggest better postbreakout performance, except for bull market/down breakouts. Those do better after a short shadow appears. Incidentally, a 0.00% median length says that over half of the candles had no lower shadow.

Table 87.4 shows volume statistics.

Candle volume trend. A rising volume trend suggests better postbreakout performance in all cases except for bull market/down breakouts. Those do better after the candle shows a falling volume trend.

Average candle volume. Upward breakouts do better post breakout if candle volume is below average, and downward breakouts do better after above-average candle volume.

Breakout volume. Light breakout volume suggests better postbreakout performance in all cases except for bull market/down breakouts. Heavy

Table 87.4
Volume Statistics*

Description	Bull Market, Up Breakout	Bear Market, Up Breakout	Bull Market, Down Breakout	Bear Market, Down Breakout
Rising candle volume, performance	5.95%	19.46%	−8.23%	−10.14%
Falling candle volume, performance	2.81%	5.61%	−9.84%	−7.08%
Above-average candle volume, performance	4.83%	13.88%	−8.80%	−9.36%
Below-average candle volume, performance	5.75%	18.41%	−8.17%	−8.38%
Heavy breakout volume, performance	5.05%	13.76%	−8.89%	−7.56%
Light breakout volume, performance	5.75%	18.63%	−6.48%	−13.20%

*Fewer than 30 samples.

breakout volume usually leads to the best performance in other candle types, so I distrust the results shown in the table.

Trading Tactics

The bearish three-line strike candle isn't bearish at all. As a bullish reversal, it works best if it appears as part of a downward retracement in a primary uptrend. That means price over the longer term trends upward except for a brief drop when the candle appears.

Avoid expecting a lasting reversal (upward breakout) when the primary trend is downward. Figure 87.1 shows an example of this. An upward breakout is usually short-lived unless accompanied by underlying support.

I split trading tactics into two basic studies, one concerning reversal rates and the other concerning performance. Of the two, reversal rates are more important, because it's better to trade in the direction of the trend and let price run as far as it can.

Table 87.5 gives tips to find the trend direction.

Confirmation reversal rates. If you wait for price to close higher the day after the candlestick ends, the reversal rate climbs to 97% in a bull market.

Reversal, continuation rates. Price breaks out upward most often.

Yearly range reversals. Most reversals occur when the breakout is within a third of the yearly high in a bull market. The bear market is more evenly split.

Table 87.5
Reversal Rates*

Description	Bull Market	Bear Market
Closing price confirmation reversal rate	97%	92%
Candle color confirmation reversal rate	97%	92%
Opening gap confirmation reversal rate	77%	67%
Reversal: trend down, breakout up	84%	77%
Continuation: trend down, breakout down	16%	23%
Percentage of reversals (R)/continuations (C) for each 12-month low (L), middle (M), or high (H)	L 70% R/30% C, M 88% R/12% C, H 95% R/5% C	L 78% R/22% C, M 78% R/22% C, H 75% R/25% C

*Fewer than 30 samples.

Table 87.6 shows performance indicators that can give hints as to how your stock will behave after the breakout from this candle pattern.

Confirmation, performance. Waiting for a black candle to appear the next day leads to better downward breakout performance in a bull market. In a bear market, waiting for price to gap open lower leads to better performance.

Moving average. Breakouts below the 50-day moving average suggest better postbreakout performance.

Sample Trade

Figure 87.2 shows a trade that involved Clark. Price bottomed at A after trending lower for about a month and then moved horizontally until forming

Table 87.6
Performance Indicators*

Description	Bull Market, Up Breakout	Bear Market, Up Breakout	Bull Market, Down Breakout	Bear Market, Down Breakout
Closing price confirmation, performance	N/A	N/A	−8.52%	−14.07%
Candle color confirmation, performance	N/A	N/A	−8.74%	−14.07%
Opening gap confirmation, performance	N/A	N/A	−6.95%	−17.47%
Breakout above 50-day moving average, performance	4.79%	8.55%	−3.90%	−3.06%
Breakout below 50-day moving average, performance	6.07%	17.83%	−9.11%	−10.30%

N/A means not applicable.
*Fewer than 30 samples.

Figure 87.2 A three-line strike candle formation appears just before price rises.

a second bottom at B. The tall white candle at B completed a three-line strike pattern.

Since price found support at A and since B bottomed near that, Clark bought the stock when price gapped open higher the next day, at C. He placed a stop a few pennies below B.

Two days later, price almost hit his stop when it gapped open lower at D but formed a tall white candle. After that, it was clear sailing. He drew an up-sloping trendline starting at E along price bottoms and sold the stock a day after price pierced the trendline in mid-January (not shown).

For Best Performance

The following list offers tips and observations to help choose candles that perform well. Consult the associated table for more information.

- Use the identification guidelines to help select the pattern—Table 87.1.
- Candles within a third of the yearly low perform best—Table 87.2.
- Select tall candles—Table 87.3.
- Use the measure rule to predict a price target—Table 87.3.

- Volume gives performance clues—Table 87.4.
- Trade the candle as a bullish reversal when it appears in a downward retracement of an upward price trend—see Trading Tactics discussion.
- Price breaks out upward most often—Table 87.5.
- Patterns within a third of the yearly high tend to act as reversals most often—Table 87.5.
- Breakouts below the 50-day moving average lead to the best performance—Table 87.6.

88

Three-Line Strike, Bullish

Behavior and Rank

Theoretical: Bullish continuation.

Actual bull market: Bearish reversal 65% of the time (ranking 19).

Actual bear market: Bearish reversal 83% of the time (ranking 4).

Frequency: 95th out of 103.

Overall performance over time: 2nd out of 103.

I dislike patterns like this one that almost never appear. Out of over 4.7 million candle lines, I found just 69 of these. When you split them into bull and bear markets, up and down breakouts, there's not enough left to warrant being placed on the endangered species list. Let's put this another way: If you updated quotes for 100 stocks every trading day, you'd find one bullish three-line strike candle every two and a half years. If you looked at just one stock per day, you'd likely find only one of these candlestick patterns in your lifetime.

As a bearish reversal, the stock ranks 19 out of 103, where 1 is best. This is quite good. The overall performance ranks 2, probably because of the few samples. My guess is additional samples will degrade the performance.

Candle psychology begins with the bulls pushing price up by buying the stock and scared bears covering their short positions. Three white candles print on the chart, and that's good news. It adds to the party atmosphere the bulls have created.

The next day, however, the smart money sells the stock and down it goes. The bears pile on and the bulls run for cover, perhaps selling their holdings. The one-day decline erases all the work of the prior three days, closing below the opening of the first candle in the pattern. Such a decline is often viewed as temporary profit taking, and that might be right. When the primary price trend is upward and the three-line strike pattern breaks out downward, price often rebounds in three days or less. More about that in the Trading Tactics section.

Identification Guidelines

Figure 88.1 shows an example of a bullish three-line strike formation in an uptrend. Price forms the tall black candle at B but then doesn't do much for about a week. Then a closing white marubozu candle at C appears. That's a bullish candle, in theory, but you can see how well that theory works. Price drops after attempting a new high and confirms the three-line strike candle when it closes below the low of the candle pattern at A. From there, the climbers don't just descend the mountain; they fall off it in an avalanche of tumbling prices.

Table 88.1 lists identification guidelines. Look for a four-line pattern composed of three white lines and one black one. The white candles come first and they close at successively higher prices. The last day forms a black candle that engulfs the prior three. It opens above the prior close but closes below the open of the first day.

Figure 88.1   A bullish three-line strike sees price tumble after a delay.

Table 88.1
Identification Guidelines

Characteristic	Discussion
Number of candle lines	Four.
Price trend	Upward leading to the start of the candle pattern.
Days 1 to 3	Three white candles, each with a higher close.
Last day	A black candle that opens higher but closes below the open of the first candle.

Statistics

Table 88.2 shows general statistics. The statistics in this chapter are based on too few samples to make me comfortable (meaning far less than 20,000). The conclusions presented will likely be wrong or at least subject to change.

Number found. I found 69 patterns, most from the bull market.

Table 88.2
General Statistics

Description	Bull Market, Up Breakout	Bear Market, Up Breakout	Bull Market, Down Breakout	Bear Market, Down Breakout
Number found	20	2	37	10
Reversal (R), continuation (C) performance	4.60% C	12.71% C	−7.86% R	−4.06% R
Standard & Poor's 500 change	1.99%	−0.27%	−0.71%	−0.53%
Candle end to breakout (median, days)	5	15	2	5
Candle end to trend end (median, days)	9	16	7	4
Number of breakouts near the 12-month low (L), middle (M), or high (H)	L 1, M 5, H 13	L 0, M 0, H 2	L 6, M 12, H 19	L 1, M 2, H 7
Percentage move for each 12-month period	L 4.15%, M 4.45%, H 4.68%	L 0.00%, M 0.00%, H 12.71%	L −4.20%, M −6.22%, H −10.14%	L −4.29%, M −10.98%, H −1.87%
Candle end + 1 day	1.77%	6.75%	−0.82%	0.27%
Candle end + 3 days	2.99%	8.96%	−1.93%	−0.10%
Candle end + 5 days	4.45%	12.00%	−3.25%	1.61%
Candle end + 10 days	4.25%	16.91%	−4.23%	1.30%
10-day performance rank	28	1	13	103

Reversal or continuation performance. Usually, candle patterns work better in a bear market, but this one shows no consistent trend.

S&P performance. The candle pattern beats the performance of the S&P 500 index over the same periods.

Candle end to breakout. It takes between 2 and 15 days for price to close either above the top of the candle or below the bottom. Since price is near the bottom of the candle, the downward breakout numbers are expected to be less than the upward breakout ones.

Candle end to trend end. Downward breakouts reach the trend end sooner than upward breakouts. That's because a downward move has already begun so it's closer to the trend end.

Yearly position, performance. Most candles appear within a third of the yearly high. In almost all other candle types, the best performers are those that appear within a third of the yearly low. This candle shows those near the yearly high doing best in three out of four categories. The one exception, bear market/down breakout, does better when the breakout is in the middle of the yearly price range.

Performance over time. This candle is an uneven performer at best. Good, robust performers show increasing numbers over each time period and in all categories. This one is weak from days 5 to 10 in bull market/up breakouts, and performance stumbles like a drunk in bear market/down breakouts.

The performance rank ranges from red hot (1, best) to ice cold (103, worst). If the sample numbers were increased, the performance would likely even out across the various categories. Do not depend on this candle performing up to expectations.

Table 88.3 shows height statistics.

Candle height. Almost without exception, tall candles work better than short ones. With this candle, however, the results are mixed. Upward breakouts do better with short candles, whereas downward breakouts do better with tall ones.

To determine whether the candle is short or tall, compute its height from highest high to lowest low price in the candle pattern and divide by the breakout price. If the result is higher than the median, then you have a tall candle; otherwise it's short.

For example, let's say Scotty has a bullish three-line strike with a high of 43 and a low of 39. Is the candle short or tall (assume bull market, up breakout)? The height is 43 − 39, or 4, so the measure would be 4/43, or 9.3%. That's a tall candle.

Measure rule. Use the measure rule to help predict how far price will rise or fall. Compute the height of the candle pattern and multiply it by the appropriate percentage shown in the table; then apply it to the breakout price.

Table 88.3
Height Statistics*

Description	Bull Market, Up Breakout	Bear Market, Up Breakout	Bull Market, Down Breakout	Bear Market, Down Breakout
Median candle height as a percentage of breakout price	3.39%	9.84%	4.92%	6.41%
Short candle, performance	4.80%	16.17%	−6.00%	−2.75%
Tall candle, performance	4.37%	1.59%	−11.48%	−6.96%
Percentage meeting price target (measure rule)	45%	50%	46%	30%
Median upper shadow as a percentage of breakout price	0.18%	1.21%	0.00%	0.14%
Short upper shadow, performance	3.58%	16.17%	−6.73%	−4.37%
Tall upper shadow, performance	5.65%	1.59%	−9.26%	−3.77%
Median lower shadow as a percentage of breakout price	0.26%	2.17%	0.27%	0.14%
Short lower shadow, performance	4.95%	16.17%	−8.56%	−5.96%
Tall lower shadow, performance	4.29%	1.59%	−6.91%	−3.12%

*Fewer than 30 samples.

What are Scotty's price targets? The upward target would be (4 × 45%) + 43, or 44.80, and the downward target would be 39 − (4 × 46%), or 37.16.

Shadows. The table's results pertain to the last candle line in the pattern. To determine whether the shadow is short or tall, compute the height of the shadow and divide by the breakout price. Compare the result to the median in the table. Tall shadows have a percentage higher than the median.

Upper shadow performance. Bullish three-line strikes in bull markets do better with tall upper shadows, and those in bear markets do better with short shadows.

Lower shadow performance. Short lower shadows suggest better post-breakout performance across the board. I find that suspicious, because tall lower shadows usually mean better performance for other candle types.

Table 88.4 shows volume statistics.

Candle volume trend. Patterns in bull markets do better with rising candle volume, and those in bear markets outperform on falling volume.

Average candle volume. Below-average candle volume works best for bullish three-line strike patterns in all categories.

Breakout volume. Heavy breakout volume suggests better postbreakout performance across the board.

Table 88.4
Volume Statistics*

Description	Bull Market, Up Breakout	Bear Market, Up Breakout	Bull Market, Down Breakout	Bear Market, Down Breakout
Rising candle volume, performance	5.47%	1.59%	−8.63%	−2.93%
Falling candle volume, performance	3.17%	16.17%	−5.94%	−6.01%
Above-average candle volume, performance	4.38%	0.00%	−6.07%	−1.35%
Below-average candle volume, performance	4.81%	12.71%	−10.14%	−5.39%
Heavy breakout volume, performance	5.45%	16.17%	−8.23%	−4.89%
Light breakout volume, performance	3.68%	1.59%	−7.14%	−2.73%

*Fewer than 30 samples.

Trading Tactics

If price is trending upward and you see a bullish three-line strike pattern with a downward breakout, wait for three days. If price continues lower after three days, then sell a holding or consider shorting the stock. The chances are, however, that price will make a new low within three days before starting to rebound. In other words, when the primary price trend is upward, a downward breakout tends to be short-lived.

I split trading tactics into two basic studies, one concerning reversal rates and the other concerning performance. Of the two, reversal rates are more important, because it's better to trade in the direction of the trend and let price run as far as it can.

Table 88.5 gives tips to find the trend direction.

Table 88.5
Reversal Rates*

Description	Bull Market	Bear Market
Closing price confirmation reversal rate	92%	100%
Candle color confirmation reversal rate	85%	100%
Opening gap confirmation reversal rate	71%	100%
Reversal rate: trend up, breakout down	65%	83%
Continuation rate: trend up, breakout up	35%	17%
Percentage of reversals (R)/continuations (C) for each 12-month low (L), middle (M), or high (H)	L 86% R/14% C, M 71% R/29% C, H 59% R/41% C	L 100% R/0% C, M 100% R/0% C, H 78% R/22% C

*Fewer than 30 samples.

Table 88.6
Performance Indicators*

Description	Bull Market, Up Breakout	Bear Market, Up Breakout	Bull Market, Down Breakout	Bear Market, Down Breakout
Closing price confirmation, performance	6.63%	9.49%	N/A	N/A
Candle color confirmation, performance	7.27%	10.02%	N/A	N/A
Opening gap confirmation, performance	7.56%	7.83%	N/A	N/A
Breakout above 50-day moving average, performance	4.73%	12.71%	−6.50%	−3.84%
Breakout below 50-day moving average, performance	2.38%	0.00%	−9.24%	−7.88%

N/A means not applicable.
*Fewer than 30 samples.

Confirmation reversal rates. Waiting the next day for price to close lower means there's a 92% chance of the pattern acting as a reversal. That really doesn't say much, though, because all price has to do is close below the pattern. With price already near the bottom, a lower close might seal its fate.

Reversal, continuation rates. Price breaks out downward most often.

Yearly range reversals. Reversals occur most frequently when the breakout is within a third of the yearly low (bull market).

Table 88.6 shows performance indicators that can give hints as to how your stock will behave after the breakout from this candle pattern.

Confirmation, performance. Patterns in bull markets perform best when the opening gap method is used to trade. That means waiting for price to gap open higher the day after the bullish three-line strike candle ends. For bear markets, candle color (wait for a white candle) works best.

Moving average. In most other candle types, breakouts below the moving average show better postbreakout performance. With this candle, that's true only for downward breakouts. Upward breakouts do better when they occur above the 50-day moving average.

Sample Trade

Scotty has a position in the stock shown in Figure 88.2. He bought the stock just after it bottomed at E and is loath to give back his profits.

Price at A formed a new high, but as price climbed, so did his worries. How much longer would the uptrend last?

The stock dropped to C and that's when he almost sold. However, he hung on by telling himself that tops take longer to form and that there is usually a try at a higher high before price tumbles. Of course, he's describing a double top chart pattern.

Allstate Corp. (Insurance—Prop./Casualty, NYSE, ALL)

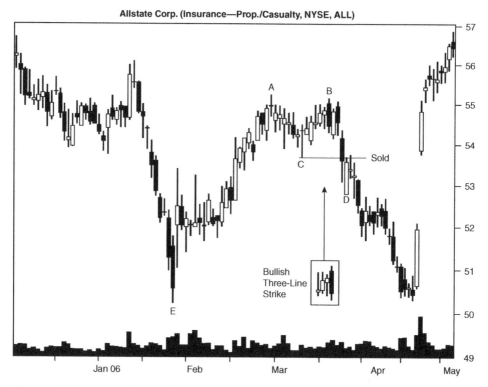

Figure 88.2   Price after a three-line strike candle fails to make a new high, and price tumbles.

Price climbs to B and that's when he sees the bullish three-line strike candle. Since price has tried to make a new high at B, it confirms his suspicions about the inherent weakness in the stock.

Price forms a white candle and then a black one before tumbling to the level of C and closing below the lowest low between the two peaks. That's where he has a stop-loss order already placed with his broker. The close confirms the double top and also means he is able to protect at least a portion of his profits.

For Best Performance

The following list offers tips and observations to help choose candles that perform well. Consult the associated table for more information.

- Use the identification guidelines to help select the pattern—Table 88.1.
- The candle works best when it appears within a third of the yearly high except for bear market/down breakouts—Table 88.2.
- Select tall candles in a bear market—Table 88.3.
- Use the measure rule to predict a price target—Table 88.3.

- Candles with short lower shadows outperform—Table 88.3.
- Volume gives performance clues—Table 88.4.
- In a primary price uptrend with a downward breakout from a three-line strike pattern, consider waiting for three days before selling—Trading Tactics discussion.
- Price breaks out downward most often—Table 88.5.
- Patterns within a third of the yearly low tend to act as reversals—Table 88.5.
- Opening gap confirmation works best in a bull market—Table 88.6.

89

Three Outside Down

Behavior and Rank

Theoretical: Bearish reversal.

Actual bull market: Bearish reversal 69% of the time (ranking 15).

Actual bear market: Bearish reversal 70% of the time (ranking 16).

Frequency: 21st out of 103.

Overall performance over time: 39th out of 103.

The three outside down pattern was developed by Gregory Morris to confirm a bearish engulfing candle. An engulfing candle is a candle whose body covers the prior day's body. Morris requires the following candle to close lower to confirm the pattern.

The performance rank in a bull market is very good, 15, when 1 is best out of 103 candles. However, just because price reverses doesn't mean it moves far. That's where the overall rank of 39 comes into play. This is a gauge of how the pattern stacks up against other candle types, based on the percentage change over time in bull and bear markets, up and down breakouts. A rank of 39 is decent—not exceptional, mind you, but decent.

The psychology behind the pattern starts with an upward price trend. The bulls are in control, buying everything in sight, pushing price upward, and leaving a white candle on the chart. The next day, price opens higher but closes lower, disappointing the bulls. That's when the bears take over the party and tell everyone to go home. The next trading day confirms their authority when price closes lower.

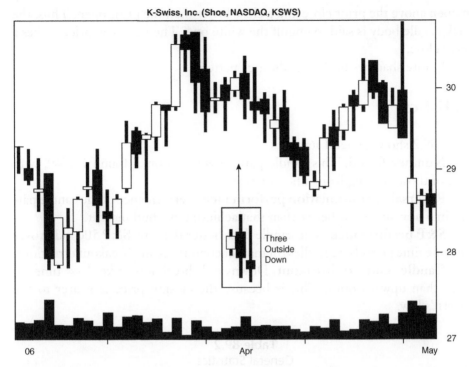

K-Swiss, Inc. (Shoe, NASDAQ, KSWS)

Three
Outside
Down

Figure 89.1   A three outside down candle appears after a slight uptrend, and price reverses.

Identification Guidelines

Figure 89.1 shows an example of the three outside down candle. Price trends upward for a few days leading to the start of the candle. When the pattern completes, price trends downward for about two weeks before recovering.

Table 89.1 lists identification guidelines. The three outside down candle is a bearish engulfing candle followed by a lower close. That means price forms a white candle on day one and a black candle the next day. The black candle has

Table 89.1
Identification Guidelines

Characteristic	Discussion
Number of candle lines	Three.
Price trend	Upward leading to the start of the candle pattern.
First day	A white candle.
Second day	A black candle opens higher and closes lower than the prior candle's body, engulfing it.
Last day	A candle with a lower close.

an open above the prior close and a close lower than the prior open. Thus, the black candle body is said to engulf the white one. The next day, price makes a lower close.

Ignore shadows in this candlestick pattern.

Statistics

Table 89.2 shows general statistics.

Number found. This candle pattern is common. I found 17,569, with most of those coming from a bull market.

Reversal or continuation performance. Performance of the candle pattern in a bear market is better than that achieved in a bull market.

S&P performance. The candle does better than the S&P 500 index over the same time periods, regardless of market conditions and breakout directions.

Candle end to breakout. Downward breakouts take less time to occur than upward ones. This is because the closing price is nearer to the pattern's low.

Table 89.2
General Statistics

Description	Bull Market, Up Breakout	Bear Market, Up Breakout	Bull Market, Down Breakout	Bear Market, Down Breakout
Number found	4,069	1,332	9,059	3,109
Reversal (R), continuation (C) performance	6.26% C	6.83% C	−5.41% R	−9.38% R
Standard & Poor's 500 change	2.14%	1.26%	−0.77%	−2.21%
Candle end to breakout (median, days)	6	6	3	3
Candle end to trend end (median, days)	11	10	6	7
Number of breakouts near the 12-month low (L), middle (M), or high (H)	L 454, M 844, H 2,226	L 272, M 386, H 658	L 1,709, M 2,257, H 4,126	L 939, M 983, H 1,157
Percentage move for each 12-month period	L 7.87%, M 5.87%, H 6.14%	L 9.21%, M 7.28%, H 5.86%	L −5.96%, M −5.53%, H −5.22%	L −11.24%, M −9.32%, H −8.19%
Candle end + 1 day	1.47%	1.99%	−0.56%	−0.88%
Candle end + 3 days	3.11%	4.22%	−1.13%	−1.86%
Candle end + 5 days	3.94%	5.33%	−1.29%	−2.22%
Candle end + 10 days	4.84%	6.30%	−1.11%	−2.57%
10-day performance rank	13	18	92	76

Candle end to trend end. Downward breakouts also take less time to reach the trend end. This is a function of a downward trend already under way (two black candles suggests a declining price trend). Thus, a trend already under way is closer to the end than one just starting. An upward move would indeed start a new trend.

Yearly position, performance. Most three outside down patterns appear within a third of the yearly high, but performance is best when they appear within a third of the yearly low.

Performance over time. This candle pattern is not a strong performer. Weakness occurs during days 5 to 10 in bull market/down breakouts. A robust performer would show increasing numbers in all columns and over all time periods.

Based on a comparison with other candle types, this pattern excels during an upward breakout, meaning a continuation of the uptrend. Ranks of 13 and 18 are very good, whereas the 92 and 76 ranks for a downward breakout are very poor.

Table 89.3 shows height statistics.

Candle height. Tall candles perform better than short ones. To determine whether the candle is short or tall, compute its height from highest high to lowest low price in the candle pattern and divide by the breakout price. If the result is higher than the median, then you have a tall candle; otherwise it's short.

Table 89.3
Height Statistics

Description	Bull Market, Up Breakout	Bear Market, Up Breakout	Bull Market, Down Breakout	Bear Market, Down Breakout
Median candle height as a percentage of breakout price	4.08%	5.61%	4.59%	6.38%
Short candle, performance	4.89%	5.86%	−4.30%	−7.50%
Tall candle, performance	8.02%	7.85%	−6.86%	−11.49%
Percentage meeting price target (measure rule)	55%	48%	44%	47%
Median upper shadow as a percentage of breakout price	0.43%	0.50%	0.39%	0.56%
Short upper shadow, performance	5.50%	6.03%	−5.10%	−8.54%
Tall upper shadow, performance	7.06%	7.66%	−5.74%	−10.24%
Median lower shadow as a percentage of breakout price	0.53%	0.81%	0.46%	0.70%
Short lower shadow, performance	5.34%	6.46%	−4.86%	−8.90%
Tall lower shadow, performance	7.32%	7.20%	−6.04%	−9.88%

Table 89.4
Volume Statistics

Description	Bull Market, Up Breakout	Bear Market, Up Breakout	Bull Market, Down Breakout	Bear Market, Down Breakout
Rising candle volume, performance	5.89%	6.70%	−5.32%	−9.70%
Falling candle volume, performance	6.64%	6.96%	−5.51%	−9.02%
Above-average candle volume, performance	6.06%	6.32%	−5.38%	−9.15%
Below-average candle volume, performance	6.36%	7.09%	−5.43%	−9.53%
Heavy breakout volume, performance	6.82%	7.33%	−5.79%	−10.81%
Light breakout volume, performance	5.54%	6.26%	−5.06%	−7.98%

Cary sees a three outside down with a high of 53 and a low of 49. Is the candle short or tall? The height is 53 − 49, or 4. In a bull market with an upward breakout, the measure would be 4/53, or 7.5%. It's a tall candle.

Measure rule. Use the measure rule to help predict how far price will rise or fall. Compute the height of the candle pattern and multiply it by the appropriate percentage shown in the table; then apply it to the breakout price.

What are the price targets for Cary's candle? The upward target would be (4 × 55%) + 53, or 55.20, and the downward target would be 49 − (4 × 44%), or 47.24.

Shadows. The table's results pertain to the last candle line in the pattern. To determine whether the shadow is short or tall, compute the height of the shadow and divide by the breakout price. Compare the result to the median in the table. Tall shadows have a percentage higher than the median.

Tall upper or lower shadows result in better performance than short ones, in all cases.

Table 89.4 shows volume statistics.

Candle volume trend. A falling volume trend works best in all cases except for bear market/down breakouts. Those do better after rising candle volume.

Average candle volume. Below-average volume inside the candle pattern suggests better postbreakout performance.

Breakout volume. Candles with heavy breakout volume perform better than do those with light breakout volume.

Trading Tactics

The three outside down pattern works best when the primary price trend is downward and a short-term upward retracement occurs. When the three

Table 89.5
Reversal Rates

Description	Bull Market	Bear Market
Closing price confirmation reversal rate	91%	90%
Candle color confirmation reversal rate	87%	88%
Opening gap confirmation reversal rate	78%	78%
Reversal rate: trend up, breakout down	69%	70%
Continuation rate: trend up, breakout up	31%	30%
Percentage of reversals (R)/continuations (C) for each 12-month low (L), middle (M), or high (H)	L 79% R/21% C, M 73% R/27% C, H 65% R/35% C	L 78% R/22% C, M 72% R/28% C, H 64% R/36% C

outside down candle occurs, price reverses the uptrend and is then free to resume the primary downtrend.

I split trading tactics into two basic studies, one concerning reversal rates and the other concerning performance. Of the two, reversal rates are more important, because it's better to trade in the direction of the trend and let price run as far as it can.

Table 89.5 gives tips to find the trend direction.

Confirmation reversal rates. Waiting for price to close lower the next day boosts the reversal rate to 90% or more.

Reversal, continuation rates. Most three outside down patterns break out downward.

Yearly range reversals. Most reversals appear within a third of the yearly low.

Table 89.6 shows performance indicators that can give hints as to how your stock will behave after the breakout from this candle pattern.

Confirmation, performance. Waiting for price to gap open lower the next day leads to better performance. Consider using that as the buy signal.

Moving average. Candles with breakouts below the 50-day moving average result in better postbreakout performance in all categories.

Closing position. In bull markets, a closing price in the middle of the last candle line leads to better performance. For bear markets, a close in the lowest third of the candle works best.

Sample Trade

Cary held the stock shown in Figure 89.2. Price gapped up to A on volume that dwarfed any other day on the chart. As is usual with such moves, price retraced a portion of the rise. In this case, the stock dropped to D before beginning another attempt at a new high.

Table 89.6
Performance Indicators

Description	Bull Market, Up Breakout	Bear Market, Up Breakout	Bull Market, Down Breakout	Bear Market, Down Breakout
Closing price confirmation, performance	N/A	N/A	−5.40%	−9.38%
Candle color confirmation, performance	N/A	N/A	−5.70%	−9.57%
Opening gap confirmation, performance	N/A	N/A	−6.33%	−10.84%
Breakout above 50-day moving average, performance	6.23%	6.51%	−5.18%	−7.92%
Breakout below 50-day moving average, performance	6.34%	8.21%	−5.73%	−10.66%
Last candle: close in highest third, performance	5.73%	5.61%	−5.07%	−8.13%
Last candle: close in middle third, performance	6.68%	6.78%	−5.44%	−8.73%
Last candle: close in lowest third, performance	6.10%	7.13%	−5.43%	−9.82%

N/A means not applicable.

Figure 89.2 A three outside down candle hits overhead resistance and price reverses.

At B, price tried to make a new high but failed. The failure was confirmed two days later when the three outside down pattern completed. Cary saw this failure and considered selling, but he wanted to be sure that price was headed lower. Often, it will drop some before resuming the uptrend. He didn't want to sell if price would continue higher, preferring to trade only if it changed trend from up to down for the long term.

He drew an up-sloping trendline along the valleys in October. When the stock dropped and closed below the line at C, it represented a tentative sell signal. A stronger signal occurred at E when price closed below the level of D, the valley between the two peaks A and B. That move confirmed the double top chart pattern, so he sold the stock.

For Best Performance

The following list offers tips and observations to help choose candles that perform well. Consult the associated table for more information.

- Use the identification guidelines to help select the pattern—Table 89.1.
- Candles within a third of the yearly low perform best—Table 89.2.
- Select tall candles—Table 89.3.
- Use the measure rule to predict a price target—Table 89.3.
- Candles with tall upper and lower shadows outperform—Table 89.3.
- Volume gives performance clues—Table 89.4.
- Select three outside down candles in an upward retracement of the downward primary trend—Trading Tactics discussion.
- Closing price confirmation boosts the reversal rate to 90%—Table 89.5.
- Most three outside down candles break out downward—Table 89.5.
- Opening gap confirmation works best—Table 89.6.
- Breakouts below the 50-day moving average lead to the best performance—Table 89.6.

90

Three Outside Up

Behavior and Rank

Theoretical: Bullish reversal.
Actual bull market: Bullish reversal 75% of the time (ranking 9).
Actual bear market: Bullish reversal 74% of the time (ranking 8).
Frequency: 24th out of 103.
Overall performance over time: 34th out of 103.

Gregory Morris added a candle line to a bullish engulfing pattern and called it a three outside up candle. His intent was to change a yucky performing candle into one much better. The reversal rate of 75% in a bull market ranks 9 out of 103 candles, where 1 is best. It's a good score. With a high frequency, meaning the pattern appears often, the number should withstand rigorous testing. The overall performance is 34, and it's as good as it is because of the excellent performance of candles with downward breakouts, but is pulled down by the lousy performance of those with upward breakouts.

The psychology behind the pattern begins with a downward price trend and the bears in control. They dribble the ball and pass it often, but they can't score. Then the bulls grab the ball on the rebound: Price opens lower the next day but closes higher, high enough that the white body of the candle engulfs the prior black body. The bulls press their advantage, and the next day price posts a higher close. What happens in the game after that is anyone's guess, but price usually continues higher.

National Semiconductor Corp. (Semiconductor, NYSE, NSM)

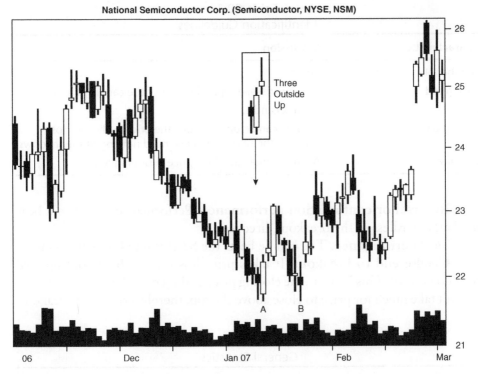

Figure 90.1   The first bottom of a double bottom chart pattern begins with the three outside up candle pattern.

Identification Guidelines

Figure 90.1 shows an example of a three outside up candle pattern. Price trends downward from the high in November and stops at A. That candle line is in the middle of the three outside up candle formation. The white line at A engulfs the body of the prior candle, and the next candle, another white one, confirms the bullish engulfing pattern with a higher close.

Table 90.1 lists identification guidelines. Look for a bullish engulfing candle. That pattern begins with a black candle followed by a taller white candle. By *taller*, I mean that price opens lower than the prior close and closes higher than the prior open, engulfing the body of the black candle. The next day closes higher, forming a white candle.

Statistics

Table 90.2 shows general statistics.

Number found. I found a bunch of these candles, so I limited selections to the first 20,000. Prorating the standard database means the candle appears most often in a bear market.

Table 90.1
Identification Guidelines

Characteristic	Discussion
Number of candle lines	Three.
Price trend	Downward leading to the start of the candle pattern.
First day	A black candle.
Second day	A white candle opens below the prior body and closes above the body, too. Price need not engulf the shadows.
Last day	A white candle in which price closes higher.

Reversal or continuation performance. Performance is best in a bear market, regardless of the breakout direction.

S&P performance. The candle beats the S&P 500 index in all columns.

Candle end to breakout. It takes price less time to break out upward than downward. This is due to the closing price ending near the candle's high. It doesn't take much for price to close above the top, thereby creating a breakout.

Table 90.2
General Statistics

Description	Bull Market, Up Breakout	Bear Market, Up Breakout	Bull Market, Down Breakout	Bear Market, Down Breakout
Number found	12,214	2,726	4,121	939
Reversal (R), continuation (C) performance	6.25% R	7.24% R	−5.51% C	−8.88% C
Standard & Poor's 500 change	1.39%	0.71%	−1.25%	−3.42%
Candle end to breakout (median, days)	3	3	7	6
Candle end to trend end (median, days)	7	7	10	10
Number of breakouts near the 12-month low (L), middle (M), or high (H)	L 2,116, M 2,791, H 5,273	L 754, M 810, H 1,128	L 1,110, M 1,157, H 1,221	L 338, M 313, H 276
Percentage move for each 12-month period	L 7.24%, M 5.79%, H 5.90%	L 9.39%, M 7.17%, H 6.11%	L −6.15%, M −5.65%, H −4.95%	L −10.67%, M −8.35%, H −7.53%
Candle end + 1 day	0.56%	0.51%	−1.36%	−2.04%
Candle end + 3 days	1.25%	1.30%	−2.96%	−4.54%
Candle end + 5 days	1.69%	1.71%	−3.84%	−5.92%
Candle end + 10 days	2.13%	1.68%	−4.50%	−7.14%
10-day performance rank	78	78	10	7

Candle end to trend end. Upward breakouts are closer to the trend end because price has been rising for a couple of days in the candle pattern. Downward breakouts would start a new trend, and that would take longer to reach the trend end than one midway along.

Yearly position, performance. Most three outside up candles appear within a third of the yearly high. The one exception is bear market/down breakouts, which appear most often near the yearly low. The yearly low is also where the candle performs best.

Performance over time. This candle pattern is not a top performer. In a bear market/up breakout scenario, performance weakens between 5 and 10 days. The upward breakout numbers must be considered poor because they are so low. Thus, if the breakout is upward, don't expect price to rise much.

Based on the performance of the candle against other candle types, downward breakouts show excellent ranks: 7 and 10. Upward breakouts are a pathetic lot.

Table 90.3 shows height statistics.

Candle height. Tall candles outperform. To determine whether the candle is short or tall, compute its height from highest high to lowest low price in the candle pattern and divide by the breakout price. If the result is higher than the median, then you have a tall candle; otherwise it's short.

Table 90.3
Height Statistics

Description	Bull Market, Up Breakout	Bear Market, Up Breakout	Bull Market, Down Breakout	Bear Market, Down Breakout
Median candle height as a percentage of breakout price	5.05%	6.56%	4.87%	6.58%
Short candle, performance	5.01%	5.70%	−4.57%	−7.30%
Tall candle, performance	7.99%	8.92%	−6.92%	−10.74%
Percentage meeting price target (measure rule)	47%	42%	44%	46%
Median upper shadow as a percentage of breakout price	0.45%	0.72%	0.57%	0.86%
Short upper shadow, performance	5.64%	6.08%	−5.08%	−7.95%
Tall upper shadow, performance	6.90%	8.45%	−5.98%	−9.93%
Median lower shadow as a percentage of breakout price	0.36%	0.53%	0.40%	0.61%
Short lower shadow, performance	5.69%	6.44%	−5.04%	−8.32%
Tall lower shadow, performance	6.84%	8.05%	−6.01%	−9.55%

Table 90.4
Volume Statistics

Description	Bull Market, Up Breakout	Bear Market, Up Breakout	Bull Market, Down Breakout	Bear Market, Down Breakout
Rising candle volume, performance	6.38%	7.14%	−5.55%	−8.61%
Falling candle volume, performance	6.07%	7.35%	−5.45%	−9.20%
Above-average candle volume, performance	6.34%	7.75%	−5.59%	−9.02%
Below-average candle volume, performance	6.17%	6.82%	−5.45%	−8.79%
Heavy breakout volume, performance	6.79%	7.70%	−6.05%	−9.78%
Light breakout volume, performance	5.68%	6.84%	−4.91%	−7.66%

If Robert sees a three outside up candle with a high of 56 and a low of 51, is the candle tall? The height is 56 − 51, or 5, so the measure would be 5/56, or 8.9% in a bull market with an upward breakout. The candle is tall.

Measure rule. Use the measure rule to help predict how far price will rise or fall. Compute the height of the candle pattern and multiply it by the appropriate percentage shown in the table; then apply it to the breakout price.

What are Robert's price targets for his candle? The upward target would be (5 × 47%) + 56, or 58.35, and the downward target would be 51 − (5 × 44%), or 48.80.

Shadows. The table's results pertain to the last candle line in the pattern. To determine whether the shadow is short or tall, compute the height of the shadow and divide by the breakout price. Compare the result to the median in the table. Tall shadows have a percentage higher than the median.

Candles with tall upper or lower shadows perform better than candles with short shadows.

Table 90.4 shows volume statistics.

Candle volume trend. Rising candle volume in a bull market leads to better performance. In a bear market, falling volume leads to good performance.

Average candle volume. Candles with above-average volume perform better than do those with below-average volume.

Breakout volume. Look for candles with heavy breakout volume, because they tend to do well.

Trading Tactics

This pattern does well when the primary price trend is upward. Price retraces a portion of the up move until the three outside up candle appears, and then the downtrend ends with price climbing away. You will want to either avoid this candle pattern altogether in a primary downtrend or trade it cautiously.

Table 90.5
Reversal Rates

Description	Bull Market	Bear Market
Closing price confirmation reversal rate	93%	91%
Candle color confirmation reversal rate	91%	90%
Opening gap confirmation reversal rate	81%	80%
Reversal: trend down, breakout up	75%	74%
Continuation: trend down, breakout down	25%	26%
Percentage of reversals (R)/continuations (C) for each 12-month low (L), middle (M), or high (H)	L 66% R/34% C, M 71% R/29% C, H 81% R/19% C	L 69% R/31% C, M 72% R/28% C, H 80% R/20% C

Even if it appears after a long downtrend, price might bounce around while trying to find a bottom.

I split trading tactics into two basic studies, one concerning reversal rates and the other concerning performance. Of the two, reversal rates are more important, because it's better to trade in the direction of the trend and let price run as far as it can.

Table 90.5 gives tips to find the trend direction.

Confirmation reversal rates. If price closes higher after the three outside up, the chance is 93% that a reversal will occur (bull market). That's not saying much, though, because price is near the high of the pattern and all it has to do is close above the top to stage a reversal.

Reversal, continuation rates. Price breaks out upward most often.

Yearly range reversals. The highest third of the yearly price range shows the most reversals.

Table 90.6 shows performance indicators that can give hints as to how your stock will behave after the breakout from this candle pattern.

Confirmation, performance. Use the opening gap method as a trading signal. That means buy the stock if price gaps open higher a day after the candlestick ends.

Moving average. Candles with breakouts below the 50-day moving average tend to outperform.

Closing position. Patterns in a bull market with a close in the middle third of the intraday trading range (in the last candle line) tend to perform slightly better than the other two ranges. In a bear market, the lowest third works best.

Sample Trade

Figure 90.2 shows a trade that Robert made. Price moved up in a smart advance from A to B and then retraced to C. The retracement ended at the

Table 90.6
Performance Indicators

Description	Bull Market, Up Breakout	Bear Market, Up Breakout	Bull Market, Down Breakout	Bear Market, Down Breakout
Closing price confirmation, performance	5.80%	7.28%	N/A	N/A
Candle color confirmation, performance	5.90%	7.42%	N/A	N/A
Opening gap confirmation, performance	6.86%	9.09%	N/A	N/A
Breakout above 50-day moving average, performance	6.14%	6.67%	−4.89%	−6.78%
Breakout below 50-day moving average, performance	6.33%	8.28%	−5.77%	−9.69%
Last candle: close in highest third, performance	6.20%	7.08%	−5.38%	−8.28%
Last candle: close in middle third, performance	6.33%	7.35%	−5.87%	−8.91%
Last candle: close in lowest third, performance	6.32%	8.07%	−5.05%	−11.90%

N/A means not applicable.

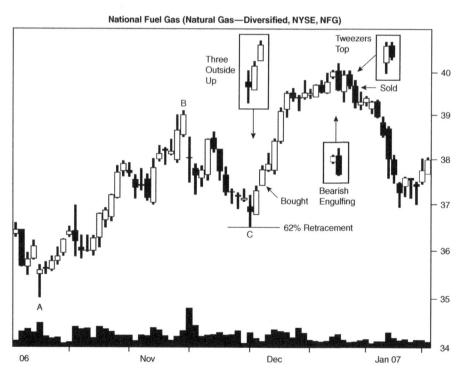

Figure 90.2   Price finds support at the 62% retracement of the prior up move, and then a three outside up candle pattern forms.

62% Fibonacci retracement level. That's when Robert became interested in the stock.

The small-bodied candle at C along with the prior few candles suggested indecision among traders about the stock. Since the candles were mostly black, the bias was downward. However, the 62% retracement level is often a strong support area, one that Robert has had success trading in the past.

He waited a day for price to signal a direction. That occurred with the white candle, which turned out to be part of a three outside up formation. The next day, he bought at the opening price, and the three outside up completed.

The stock cooperated by moving higher in a series of white candles, but then upward momentum slowed. Short candles with short shadows appeared as if the bulls and bears were waiting for the fundamentals to catch up.

Robert saw the bearish engulfing pattern appear, followed by a tweezers top. Because both candle patterns were bearish, he decided to sell the stock. He didn't want to ride price back down and risk giving away his profits in the process. The stock looked "tired," as he put it. He sold at the opening price after the tweezers top.

For Best Performance

The following list offers tips and observations to help choose candles that perform well. Consult the associated table for more information.

- Use the identification guidelines to help select the pattern—Table 90.1.
- Candles within a third of the yearly low perform best—Table 90.2.
- Select tall candles—Table 90.3.
- Use the measure rule to predict a price target—Table 90.3.
- Candles with tall upper and lower shadows outperform—Table 90.3.
- Volume gives performance clues—Table 90.4.
- Look for the pattern to appear as part of a downward retracement in an upward price trend—Trading Tactics discussion.
- Price breaks out upward most often—Table 90.5.
- Patterns within a third of the yearly high frequently act as reversals—Table 90.5.
- Opening gap confirmation works best—Table 90.6.
- Breakouts below the 50-day moving average lead to the best performance—Table 90.6.

91

Three Stars in the South

Behavior and Rank

Theoretical: Bullish reversal.
Actual bull market: Bullish reversal 86% of the time (ranking 1).
Actual bear market: Bullish reversal 100% of the time (ranking 1).
Frequency: 99th out of 103.
Overall performance over time: 103rd out of 103.

Out of over 4.7 million candle lines, I found just nine examples of the three stars in the South pattern. That is well short of the minimum number for a good statistical analysis, so this chapter is an abbreviated one.

The reversal rates of 86% and 100% are due to the small sample count. Even so, they placed first out of 103 candles. Overall performance, however, was in last place. Why? Again, it's because of the few samples available. Those that I looked at almost always reversed but didn't move far after that, so performance over time (the rank) suffered.

Pattern psychology beings this way: Bearish selling pressure forces price lower moving into the pattern. A tall black candle prints on the chart with a long lower shadow. The lower shadow suggests the bulls are becoming more active in trying to wrest control from the bears. However, the candle remains a black one and that says the bears won the round.

The next day, a similar but smaller candle appears. This candle's low is above the prior low. The bulls try for a second time to stage a coup but fail to oust the regime. The last day is a black marubozu candle that fits inside the previous day's trading range. It says that the bears still maintain power, but the day's outcome was dicey. The coming days will likely see the end of the bear administration when the bulls take over.

Identification Guidelines

Figure 91.1 shows an example of this candle pattern in a rise-retrace pattern that is often lucrative for bullish reversals. Price begins to rise from A and peaks at B; it then retraces to C. Retracements often drift down 38%, 50%, or 62% before finding support and recovering. In this case, the three stars in the South formation stops the short-term decline. After that, price moves horizontally, forming a small symmetrical triangle (it's not a pennant, because there is no flagpole). Price eases out from the end of the triangle and trends higher.

Table 91.1 lists the identification guidelines. The three stars in the South candle pattern looks deceptively simple, but the identification requirements narrow the list of candidates to almost zero.

Looking for the pattern in a downward price trend, first find a tall black candle. The candle should have a long lower shadow. The next day is a repeat

Figure 91.1 A three stars in the South candle formation appears as a reversal in a short-term downtrend.

Table 91.1
Identification Guidelines

Characteristic	Discussion
Number of candle lines	Three.
Price trend	Downward leading to the start of the candle.
First day	A tall black candle with a long lower shadow.
Second day	Similar to the first day but smaller and with a low above the previous day's low.
Last day	A black marubozu type candle fits inside the high-low trading range of the prior day.

of the prior one but smaller in size with the low price remaining above the prior low. The final day is a black marubozu candle that fits inside the high-low trading range of the prior candle. A black marubozu is one that doesn't have shadows, but in this case the candle need not be a tall one.

Figure 91.2 shows another example of the three stars in the South candle pattern. This one forms in a longer-term downtrend that lasts about two

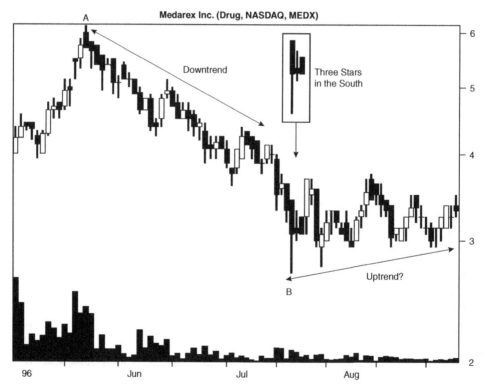

Figure 91.2 A three stars in the South candle pattern reverses the downtrend.

months (the move from A to B). Price bottoms at B where the three stars in the South candle appears, and then price moves horizontally with a slight upward tilt. The pattern acts as a reversal of the downtrend, and if you could look to the right, you would see price moving up.

How you trade this candle I leave up to you. With the candle so rare, at least in stocks, you may never see it twice in a lifetime.

92

Three White Soldiers

Behavior and Rank

Theoretical: Bullish reversal.

Actual bull market: Bullish reversal 82% of the time (ranking 3).

Actual bear market: Bullish reversal 84% of the time (ranking 3).

Frequency: 67th out of 103.

Overall performance over time: 32nd out of 103.

Three white soldiers is a bullish reversal candle that appears in a downward price trend. The high reversal rate in a bull market, 82%, is possible because price closes near the top of the candle pattern. Another price bar, one that closes above the top, confirms the pattern as a reversal. That's much easier to do than price backtracking all the way down and closing below the candle's low.

Even so, the pattern ranks 3 for bullish reversals, where 1 is best out of 103 candles. The overall performance is 32, suggesting that the move after the reversal may not be as delicious as you hope.

The psychology behind the pattern is all about the bulls taking control of the stock. In a downward price trend with the bears forcing price lower, the bulls are police with batons at the ready, halting a riot. Day after day, price closes higher as the bulls push the bears back until there are few bears left in the march. The candle series is tall enough that its upward price movement creates its own bullish excitement, a microclimate that feeds on itself. The performance numbers suggest that price will continue higher after the candle pattern ends.

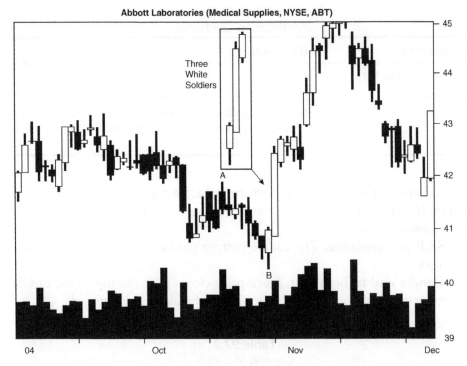

Figure 92.1 Three white soldiers appear at the end of a downward move.

Identification Guidelines

Figure 92.1 shows an example of three white soldiers converting a downward price trend into an upward one. The short-term trend begins either at A in October or back in mid-September, depending on your perspective and whether you're using reading glasses. It ends at B. Bullish buying grips the stock where the smart money knows the price is oversold. Their buying pressure is a rocket propelling the stock higher. Three white candles post higher closes; then price pauses for several days before the climb resumes.

Table 92.1 lists identification guidelines. The guidelines limit the number of candles that you'll find in the bush. Look for three tall white candles. Each should open within the body of the prior candle (except the first one) and close higher, near the top of the candle.

Statistics

Table 92.2 shows general statistics.

Number found. Three white soldiers are somewhat rare. I found 3,333, and if you prorate their numbers from the standard database, you find that they occur more often in a bear market.

Table 92.1
Identification Guidelines

Characteristic	Discussion
Number of candle lines	Three.
Price trend	Downward leading to the start of the candle pattern.
Three days	Tall white candles with higher closes and price that opens within the previous body. Price should close near the high each day.

Reversal or continuation performance. Performance is best in a bear market. If you ignore the breakout direction, reversals tend to perform better than continuations.

S&P performance. The candle pattern performs better than the S&P 500 index.

Candle end to breakout. Since price closes near the top of the candle pattern, price breaks out upward faster than it breaks out downward.

Table 92.2
General Statistics

Description	Bull Market, Up Breakout	Bear Market, Up Breakout	Bull Market, Down Breakout	Bear Market, Down Breakout
Number found	2,435	305	537	56
Reversal (R), continuation (C) performance	5.88% R	7.47% R	−5.35% C	−7.26% C
Standard & Poor's 500 change	0.90%	0.39%	−0.85%	−2.04%
Candle end to breakout (median, days)	3	3	11	13
Candle end to trend end (median, days)	5	6	11	14
Number of breakouts near the 12-month low (L), middle (M), or high (H)	L 364, M 515, H 1,076	L 63, M 102, H 133	L 142, M 147, H 153	L 24, M 17, H 15
Percentage move for each 12-month period	L 7.79%, M 6.06%, H 5.13%	L 9.23%, M 7.72%, H 6.65%	L −4.88%, M −5.67%, H −5.18%	L −7.81%, M −6.52%, H −7.43%
Candle end + 1 day	0.30%	0.67%	−2.00%	−1.95%
Candle end + 3 days	0.64%	0.95%	−3.98%	−3.28%
Candle end + 5 days	1.12%	0.94%	−5.15%	−5.21%
Candle end + 10 days	1.49%	1.90%	−6.41%	−7.66%
10-day performance rank	96	74	4	6

Candle end to trend end. With price already trending upward, it takes less time for upward breakouts to reach the trend end than downward moves.

Yearly position, performance. Most three white soldiers formations occur within a third of the yearly high (bear market/down breakouts are the exception), but the yearly low is where you'll find the best performance in most cases. The middle third works best for bull market/down breakouts.

Performance over time. This candle does not knock the ball out of the park for upward breakouts. By that, I mean the percentage gain over 10 days is small. In addition, the candle has a difficult time between days 3 and 5, when performance drops slightly in bear market/up breakouts.

The performance ranks agree, with upward breakouts having a difficult time. Downward breakouts are near the top of the list, ranking 4 and 6 for performance where 1 is best out of 103.

Table 92.3 shows height statistics.

Candle height. Tall candles outperform in all cases except for bear market/down breakouts. The instigator is probably the low sample count. Since most candles work best if they are taller than the median, I'm sure the result will flip with additional samples.

To determine whether the candle is short or tall, compute its height from highest high to lowest low price in the candle pattern and divide by the

Table 92.3
Height Statistics

Description	Bull Market, Up Breakout	Bear Market, Up Breakout	Bull Market, Down Breakout	Bear Market, Down Breakout
Median candle height as a percentage of breakout price	6.97%	9.17%	7.20%	9.94%
Short candle, performance	4.96%	6.38%	−4.92%	−7.53%*
Tall candle, performance	7.16%	8.77%	−6.05%	−6.94%*
Percentage meeting price target (measure rule)	34%	33%	32%	30%*
Median upper shadow as a percentage of breakout price	0.00%	0.25%	0.00%	0.36%
Short upper shadow, performance	5.48%	7.67%	−5.60%	−9.11%*
Tall upper shadow, performance	6.20%	7.29%	−5.12%	−5.54%*
Median lower shadow as a percentage of breakout price	0.00%	0.29%	0.00%	0.36%
Short lower shadow, performance	6.11%	7.68%	−6.44%	−6.19%*
Tall lower shadow, performance	5.59%	7.28%	−3.95%	−8.36%*

*Fewer than 30 samples.

breakout price. If the result is higher than the median, then you have a tall candle; otherwise it's short.

Ashley sees a three white soldiers candle formation with a high of 63 and a low of 58. Is the candle short or tall? The height is 63 – 58, or 5, so the measure would be 5/63, or 7.9%, assuming a bull market/up breakout. The candle is tall.

Measure rule. Use the measure rule to help predict how far price will rise or fall. Compute the height of the candle pattern and multiply it by the appropriate percentage shown in the table; then apply it to the breakout price.

What are Ashley's price targets? The upward target would be (5 × 34%) + 63, or 64.70, and the downward target would be 58 – (5 × 32%), or 56.40.

Shadows. The table's results pertain to the last candle line in the pattern. To determine whether the shadow is short or tall, compute the height of the shadow and divide by the breakout price. Compare the result to the median in the table. Tall shadows have a percentage higher than the median.

Don't be alarmed by a 0.00% median. That just means a large number of candles didn't have shadows.

Upper shadow performance. Short upper shadows mean better performance in all cases except bull market/up breakouts. Those do better with tall shadows.

Lower shadow performance. Short lower shadows also mean better performance in all cases except one category: bear market/down breakouts. The low sample counts may be to blame for the odd results: Long upper and lower shadows work best for most other candle types.

Table 92.4 shows volume statistics.

Candle volume trend. Candles with falling volume perform better than do those with rising volume in bull markets. In bear markets candles do better with rising volume, but the samples are few for bear markets/down breakouts.

Table 92.4
Volume Statistics

Description	Bull Market, Up Breakout	Bear Market, Up Breakout	Bull Market, Down Breakout	Bear Market, Down Breakout
Rising candle volume, performance	5.78%	7.84%	−5.01%	−7.50%
Falling candle volume, performance	6.07%	6.90%	−5.87%	−7.00%*
Above-average candle volume, performance	6.06%	7.23%	−4.40%	−7.76%
Below-average candle volume, performance	5.67%	7.67%	−6.29%	−6.08%*
Heavy breakout volume, performance	6.30%	8.61%	−5.90%	−9.24%
Light breakout volume, performance	5.32%	6.18%	−4.68%	−5.01%*

*Fewer than 30 samples.

Average candle volume. Candles with above-average volume lead to better performance in bull market/up breakouts and bear market/down breakouts. The other two columns, bear market/up breakouts and bull market/down breakouts, do better with below-average volume.

Breakout volume. Heavy breakout volume works best under all conditions.

Trading Tactics

The best-performing patterns are those that appear as the candle reverses the short-term downtrend in a primary up move. This is especially effective if price bottoms near one of the Fibonacci retracement values: 38%, 50%, or 62%. If price does not break out upward the next day, then be on guard for a possible reversal of the primary uptrend. If price closes below the bottom of the candlestick, then exit any long position.

Although this technique may sound like a contradiction of the results shown in Table 92.3 (performance over time), it's not. The table shows performance over 10 days. I'm talking about a longer holding period.

If the primary price trend is downward, then expect an upward breakout to end quickly and the downtrend to resume. If price breaks out downward, then expect the stock to continue lower. The setup might make for a trade on the short side.

I split trading tactics into two basic studies, one concerning reversal rates and the other concerning performance. Of the two, reversal rates are more important, because it's better to trade in the direction of the trend and let price run as far as it can.

Table 92.5 gives tips to find the trend direction.

Confirmation reversal rates. If you wait for price to close upward the next day, then the resulting move confirms the reversal 98% of the time. Since

Table 92.5
Reversal Rates

Description	Bull Market	Bear Market
Closing price confirmation reversal rate	98%	98%
Candle color confirmation reversal rate	91%	94%
Opening gap confirmation reversal rate	90%	91%
Reversal: trend down, breakout up	82%	84%
Continuation: trend down, breakout down	18%	16%
Percentage of reversals (R)/continuations (C) for each 12-month low (L), middle (M), or high (H)	L 72% R/28% C, M 78% R/22% C, H 88% R/12% C	L 72% R/28% C, M 86% R/14% C, H 90% R/10% C

Table 92.6
Performance Indicators

Description	Bull Market, Up Breakout	Bear Market, Up Breakout	Bull Market, Down Breakout	Bear Market, Down Breakout
Closing price confirmation, performance	4.88%	6.32%	N/A	N/A
Candle color confirmation, performance	6.07%	6.73%	N/A	N/A
Opening gap confirmation, performance	5.56%	7.87%	N/A	N/A
Breakout above 50-day moving average, performance	5.76%	7.70%	−6.31%	−5.32%*
Breakout below 50-day moving average, performance	6.29%	6.60%	−4.85%	−7.81%

N/A means not applicable.
*Fewer than 30 samples.

price is near the top of the candle, that really doesn't mean much because it should take little for price to close above the candle top versus below the bottom of the candle pattern.

Reversal, continuation rates. Price breaks out upward most often.

Yearly range reversals. Reversals occur frequently when the breakout price is within a third of the yearly high.

Table 92.6 shows performance indicators that can give hints as to how your stock will behave after the breakout from this candle pattern.

Confirmation, performance. In a bull market, candle color confirmation works best. That means waiting for a white candle to appear the next day (after the three white soldiers candle ends) before taking a position in the stock.

For a bear market, the opening gap method works best as a trading signal. That means waiting for price to gap open higher the next day.

Moving average. In most candlestick types, breakouts below the 50-day moving average work best. In this candle pattern, breakouts below the moving average work best only for bull market/up breakouts and bear market/down breakouts.

Sample Trade

Figure 92.2 shows another example of the three white soldiers candle, this one central to a trade that Ashley made.

Price broke out of a long congestion region with an uptrend beginning at A and rising quickly to B. It then retraced a good portion of the climb by falling to C. That point was at the bottom of the tall white candle, which is a

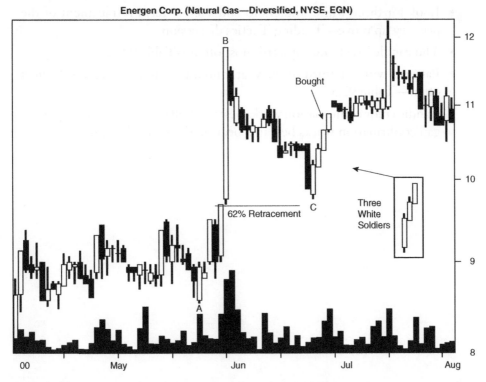

Figure 92.2 Three white soldiers appear at the 62% Fibonacci retracement value.

common support region (as is anywhere within an unusually tall white body). It was also the point of a 62% Fibonacci retracement of the AB rise.

Ashley waited for price to recover from this drop. When the three white soldiers completed, that was the buy signal she was waiting for. She bought the stock the next day at the open.

For Best Performance

The following list offers tips and observations to help choose candles that perform well. Consult the associated table for more information.

- Use the identification guidelines to help select the pattern—Table 92.1.
- Many, but not all, candles within a third of the yearly low perform best—Table 92.2.
- Select tall candles—Table 92.3.
- Use the measure rule to predict a price target—Table 92.3.
- Volume gives performance clues—Table 92.4.

- Look for three white soldiers to end a short-term retracement of the primary up move—Trading Tactics discussion.
- The candle breaks out upward most often—Table 92.5.
- Patterns within a third of the yearly high tend to act as reversals most often—Table 92.5.
- Candle color confirmation works best in a bull market, whereas opening gap confirmation works best in a bear market—Table 92.6.

93

Thrusting

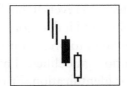

Behavior and Rank

Theoretical: Bearish continuation.
Actual bull market: Bullish reversal 57% of the time (ranking 35).
Actual bear market: Bullish reversal 57% of the time (ranking 33).
Frequency: 56th out of 103.
Overall performance over time: 15th out of 103.

Based on the identification guidelines, this is one strange candlestick. It's supposed to be a bearish continuation pattern, meaning price should break out lower, but that happens only 43% of the time. I found this pattern acted as a bullish reversal most often.

Once price finished with the candle pattern, it trended and scored a very good rank of 15 for overall performance, where 1 is best out of 103. The frequency rank is almost high enough that you might actually find this pattern during a full moon.

The psychology behind the pattern supports the reversal theory from my vantage point. Price trends lower with the bears selling the stock each time the bulls try to grab a foothold. A black day forms, meaning that the bears maintain control of the stock.

The next day is the key to the pattern. Price gaps open lower, below the prior low, but by day's end price closes near (but still below) the midpoint of the first candle. This is a bullish sign, even if it's caused by short covering. A higher close the next day in a bull market will signal that the trend has reversed 82% of the time.

Identification Guidelines

Figure 93.1 shows two thrusting patterns. The first one, at B, forms the second bottom of what I call an ugly double bottom chart pattern. An ugly double bottom is similar to a regular double bottom, but the second bottom is much higher than the first. The pattern confirms when price closes above the high between the two bottoms (C). In this example, the thrusting pattern is the reversal that creates the second bottom.

The August thrusting pattern is a reversal that fails to reverse. Price should find support at the price level of C, and it does for several days surrounding the thrusting pattern, but it isn't enough to prevent price from continuing lower.

Table 93.1 lists identification guidelines. This two-candle combination is rare because of strict rules for identification. Price forms a black candle and then a white one. The white candle has to open below the prior low and close near but below the middle of the black body.

If the close ties the prior low, then you have an on neck candle. If the closing price is a bit higher, above but near the prior close, then you have an in neck candle. If price closes above the midpoint, then you have a piercing pattern. These different combinations are why the identification guidelines are so strict.

Figure 93.1   Two thrusting patterns appear in downtrends. The first acts as a reversal and the second as a continuation.

Table 93.1
Identification Guidelines

Characteristic	Discussion
Number of candle lines	Two.
Price trend	Downward leading to the start of the candle pattern.
First day	A black candle.
Second day	A white candle opens below the prior low and closes near but below the midpoint of the prior body.

Statistics

Table 93.2 shows general statistics.

Number found. The thrusting candle is a rare one, rarer than I expected. I found 4,596 of them; prorating the standard database, it occurs most often in a bear market.

Table 93.2
General Statistics

Description	Bull Market, Up Breakout	Bear Market, Up Breakout	Bull Market, Down Breakout	Bear Market, Down Breakout
Number found	2,120	502	1,592	382
Reversal (R), continuation (C) performance	6.71% R	9.67% R	−5.50% C	−11.95% C
Standard & Poor's 500 change	1.74%	0.99%	−0.87%	−2.66%
Candle end to breakout (median, days)	4	3	4	4
Candle end to trend end (median, days)	9	10	7	8
Number of breakouts near the 12-month low (L), middle (M), or high (H)	L 469, M 571, H 862	L 181, M 169, H 149	L 479, M 499, H 455	L 188, M 118, H 71
Percentage move for each 12-month period	L 7.68%, M 6.59%, H 6.31%	L 11.44%, M 8.60%, H 8.62%	L −6.23%, M −5.72%, H −4.89%	L −14.72%, M −11.96%, H −7.18%
Candle end + 1 day	1.07%	1.95%	−1.05%	−1.71%
Candle end + 3 days	2.20%	3.28%	−2.26%	−4.03%
Candle end + 5 days	2.91%	3.65%	−2.44%	−5.32%
Candle end + 10 days	3.34%	4.40%	−2.57%	−5.92%
10-day performance rank	47	42	44	20

Reversal or continuation performance. The best performance comes from thrusting candles in a bear market.

S&P performance. The thrusting candle beats the performance of the S&P 500 index over the same periods.

Candle end to breakout. It takes about four days for price to break out.

Candle end to trend end. Downward breakouts take slightly less time to reach the trend end than upward breakouts. Upward breakouts would signal a reversal and the start of a new trend, whereas downward breakouts are in the middle of an existing trend.

Yearly position, performance. Bear market thrusting patterns occur most often within a third of the yearly low. Bull market results show no consistent trend. Performance is best across the board when the candle appears within a third of the yearly low.

Performance over time. The thrusting candle is one of the few robust performers that I have seen. Performance improves during each measurement period and in all market conditions and breakout directions.

The performance rank tells a slightly different tale, considering 1 is the best rank out of 103 candles. I compared the performance over the 10 days for each category with other candles to create the rank. This candlestick is a midlist performer, and that is because the percentage change after 10 days is as exciting as being told by your mom to brush your teeth.

Table 93.3 shows height statistics.

Table 93.3
Height Statistics

Description	Bull Market, Up Breakout	Bear Market, Up Breakout	Bull Market, Down Breakout	Bear Market, Down Breakout
Median candle height as a percentage of breakout price	3.61%	5.78%	3.52%	5.92%
Short candle, performance	5.56%	6.63%	−4.58%	−7.97%
Tall candle, performance	8.26%	12.62%	−6.71%	−17.16%
Percentage meeting price target (measure rule)	65%	58%	54%	60%
Median upper shadow as a percentage of breakout price	0.41%	0.73%	0.44%	0.89%
Short upper shadow, performance	6.09%	7.18%	−4.84%	−11.24%
Tall upper shadow, performance	7.34%	11.79%	−6.18%	−12.76%
Median lower shadow as a percentage of breakout price	0.26%	0.42%	0.16%	0.39%
Short lower shadow, performance	6.42%	8.15%	−5.40%	−10.77%
Tall lower shadow, performance	6.99%	11.05%	−5.59%	−13.19%

Candle height. Tall candles outperform. To determine whether the candle is short or tall, compute its height from highest high to lowest low price in the candle pattern and divide by the breakout price. If the result is higher than the median, then you have a tall candle; otherwise it's short.

Rudy sees a thrusting candle with a high of 51 and a low of 47. Is the candle short or tall? The height is 51 − 47, or 4, so the measure would be (assume up breakout/bull market) 4/51, or 7.8%. The candle is tall.

Measure rule. Use the measure rule to help predict how far price will rise or fall. Compute the height of the candle pattern and multiply it by the appropriate percentage shown in the table; then apply it to the breakout price.

What are the price targets for Rudy's candle? The upward target would be (4 × 65%) + 51, or 53.60, and the downward target would be 47 − (4 × 54%), or 44.84.

Shadows. The table's results pertain to the last candle line in the pattern. To determine whether the shadow is short or tall, compute the height of the shadow and divide by the breakout price. Compare the result to the median in the table. Tall shadows have a percentage higher than the median.

Candles with tall upper or lower shadows result in performance better than those with short shadows.

Table 93.4 shows volume statistics.

Candle volume trend. Candles with falling volume tend to perform better than do those with rising volume. The one exception occurs in bear market/up breakouts, which do best with rising volume.

Average candle volume. Candles with below-average volume tend to do better in a bull market. Those with above-average volume perform better, post breakout, in a bear market.

Table 93.4
Volume Statistics

Description	Bull Market, Up Breakout	Bear Market, Up Breakout	Bull Market, Down Breakout	Bear Market, Down Breakout
Rising candle volume, performance	6.53%	10.12%	−5.32%	−11.55%
Falling candle volume, performance	6.98%	8.93%	−5.72%	−12.50%
Above-average candle volume, performance	6.65%	11.11%	−5.26%	−15.30%
Below-average candle volume, performance	6.76%	8.28%	−5.66%	−9.60%
Heavy breakout volume, performance	7.30%	10.76%	−6.09%	−14.37%
Light breakout volume, performance	6.18%	8.48%	−4.91%	−9.02%

Breakout volume. Candles with heavy breakout volume perform best in all conditions.

Trading Tactics

If the primary (longer-term) trend is downward, then avoid trading this as a reversal. The breakout may be upward, but it probably won't last long before the downtrend resumes.

The best performers come from thrusting candles when the primary trend is upward (although a very short trend takes price lower into the thrusting candle). Price breaks out upward and rejoins the primary trend to continue higher.

I split trading tactics into two basic studies, one concerning reversal rates and the other concerning performance. Of the two, reversal rates are more important, because it's better to trade in the direction of the trend and let price run as far as it can.

Table 93.5 gives tips to find the trend direction.

Confirmation reversal rates. If you wait for price to close higher the next day, you increase your chances of finding a reversal to 82% in a bull market.

Reversal, continuation rates. Candles break out upward most often.

Yearly range reversals. Most reversals occur when the breakout is within a third of the yearly high.

Table 93.6 shows performance indicators that can give hints as to how your stock will behave after the breakout from this candle pattern.

Confirmation, performance. If you wait for price to gap open lower the next day, performance improves. That is, the opening gap confirmation method results in the best trading signal.

Table 93.5
Reversal Rates

Description	Bull Market	Bear Market
Closing price confirmation reversal rate	82%	78%
Candle color confirmation reversal rate	79%	76%
Opening gap confirmation reversal rate	66%	65%
Reversal: trend down, breakout up	57%	57%
Continuation: trend down, breakout down	43%	43%
Percentage of reversals (R)/continuations (C) for each 12-month low (L), middle (M), or high (H)	L 49% R/51% C, M 53% R/47% C, H 65% R/35% C	L 49% R/51% C, M 59% R/41% C, H 68% R/32% C

Table 93.6
Performance Indicators

Description	Bull Market, Up Breakout	Bear Market, Up Breakout	Bull Market, Down Breakout	Bear Market, Down Breakout
Closing price confirmation, performance	N/A	N/A	−7.07%	−13.03%
Candle color confirmation, performance	N/A	N/A	−7.05%	−13.37%
Opening gap confirmation, performance	N/A	N/A	−7.29%	−13.41%
Breakout above 50-day moving average, performance	6.32%	8.91%	−5.04%	−7.95%
Breakout below 50-day moving average, performance	7.10%	10.28%	−5.66%	−13.05%
Last candle: close in highest third, performance	6.72%	9.81%	−5.52%	−13.46%
Last candle: close in middle third, performance	6.62%	9.25%	−5.29%	−9.09%
Last candle: close in lowest third, performance	7.92%*	12.76%*	−9.21%*	−7.82%*

N/A means not applicable.
*Fewer than 30 samples.

Moving average. Candles with breakouts below the 50-day moving average tend to perform better than do those with breakouts above the moving average.

Closing position. Ignore the lowest third because of the low sample count. Candles with closing prices in the highest third of the last line in the candle pattern tend to perform slightly better than do those with the closing price in the middle of the candle.

Sample Trade

Figure 93.2 shows the sample trade that Rudy made. Price formed a valley at A and another at B. He drew a trendline connecting them and extended it to C. That's where a thrusting candle appeared.

Since the thrusting candle was near support (the trendline), and since it was slightly below the peak at D, he was prepared to wait a day before entering a trade. When price gapped open higher at E, he went ahead and bought the stock. The bullish gap was a signal he didn't want to miss.

He placed his stop a few pennies below the low at C, just in case. Three days later, an opening black marubozu formed and price hit his stop. It took him out of the trade just before the climbing team set out for an attempt at the summit.

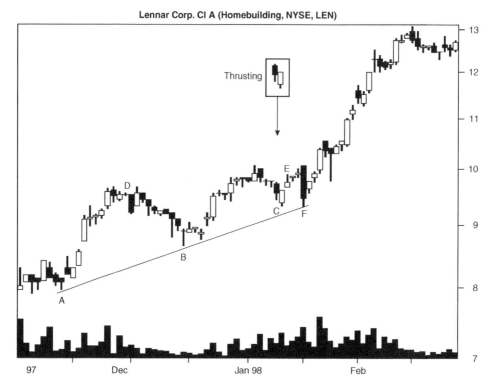

Figure 93.2   A thrusting candle near a trendline suggests price will reverse.

What did he do wrong? Clearly, he placed his stop too close. How could he have prevented this? If he placed his stop below the trendline or used a volatility stop, he would have been safe. See my web site, ThePatternSite.com, for more details on a volatility stop.

For Best Performance

The following list offers tips and observations to help choose candles that perform well. Consult the associated table for more information.

- Use the identification guidelines to help select the pattern—Table 93.1.
- Candles within a third of the yearly low perform best—Table 93.2.
- Select tall candles—Table 93.3.
- Use the measure rule to predict a price target—Table 93.3.
- Candles with tall upper or lower shadows outperform—Table 93.3.
- Volume gives performance clues—Table 93.4.

- Avoid trading this candle as a reversal of the primary downtrend. This works better in uptrends—Trading Tactics discussion.
- The candle breaks out upward most often—Table 93.5.
- Patterns within a third of the yearly high tend to act as reversals most often—Table 93.5.
- Opening gap confirmation works best—Table 93.6.
- Breakouts below the 50-day moving average lead to the best performance—Table 93.6.

94

Tri-Star, Bearish

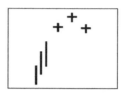

Behavior and Rank

Theoretical: Bearish reversal.
Actual bull market: Bearish reversal 52% of the time (ranking 46).
Actual bear market: Bearish reversal 61% of the time (ranking 26).
Frequency: 77th out of 103.
Overall performance over time: 76th out of 103.

Steve Nison developed the bearish tri-star candle pattern. I had high hopes that this candle pattern, consisting of three doji, would perform remarkably well; but its bull market reversal rate is about random: 52%. I might be able to do better tossing coins, especially with some of the dinged-up pennies I have.

The reversal rank is decidedly mediocre at 46, where 1 is best out of 103 candles. The overall performance rank is even worse: 76. The candle pattern has its moments, but only if you trade with the trend (upward breakout in a bull market or downward breakout in a bear market).

As for pattern psychology, a doji is a small candle that suggests indecision, a stalemate between the bulls and the bears. When three of them occur, one after the other, what can you say about the trading environment? Maybe the bulls and bears went on vacation. That reminds me of a joke: "A firm day of decisions! Or is it?" Perhaps that sums up the doji candle.

The only hint about this pattern comes from the layout of the three doji. The middle one is above the others, and that suggests that the price trend may have turned from bullish to bearish.

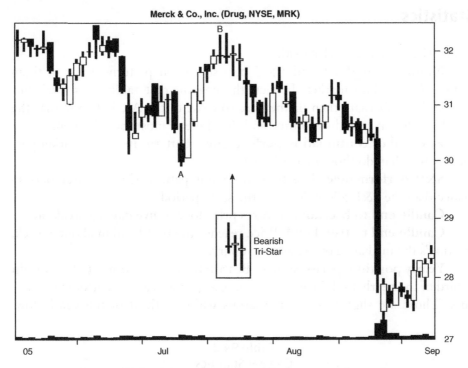

Figure 94.1   A bearish tri-star calls the reversal exactly.

Identification Guidelines

Figure 94.1 shows an example of the bearish tri-star pattern. Price trends upward from A and then peaks at B, a doji. Three more doji follow the first one, and those three create the tri-star pattern. Notice that the middle doji has a body above the other two. That's the combination you look for, a higher center doji in an uptrend. In this example, price continues lower.

In case you are wondering, the large decline in late August occurred when the company lost a Vioxx trial, potentially costing over $250 million.

Table 94.1 lists identification guidelines. A doji has the opening and closing price the same or nearly so. The middle one of the three doji should have a body above the other two, and the pattern should begin in an uptrend.

Table 94.1
Identification Guidelines

Characteristic	Discussion
Number of candle lines	Three.
Price trend	Upward leading to the start of the candle pattern.
Configuration	Look for three doji, the middle one has a body above the other two.

Statistics

Table 94.2 shows general statistics.

Number found. I found 5,555 bearish tri-star patterns, most of them coming from a bull market. In fact, the bear market rarely sees a tri-star. Maybe they hibernate then or they are so close to the Arctic Circle that the sun shines for six months at a time and they hide as most stars do then.

Reversal or continuation performance. Patterns in a bear market perform better than do those in a bull market.

S&P performance. The bearish tri-star pattern shows better performance than the S&P 500 index over the same periods.

Candle end to breakout. It takes price four or five days to break out.

Candle end to trend end. Price reaches the trend end in about a week, but that's the median. Your results may vary.

Yearly position, performance. Bearish tri-stars occur most often within a third of the yearly high in all categories except for bear market/down breakouts. Those are slightly more numerous within a third of the yearly low.

Table 94.2
General Statistics

Description	Bull Market, Up Breakout	Bear Market, Up Breakout	Bull Market, Down Breakout	Bear Market, Down Breakout
Number found	2,595	52	2,825	83
Reversal (R), continuation (C) performance	6.70% C	7.04% C	−4.99% R	−8.67% R
Standard & Poor's 500 change	1.15%	0.01%	−0.47%	−1.34%
Candle end to breakout (median, days)	5	4	5	4
Candle end to trend end (median, days)	7	6	6	7
Number of breakouts near the 12-month low (L), middle (M), or high (H)	L 293, M 410, H 1,268	L 12, M 19, H 20	L 445, M 559, H 1,143	L 28, M 27, H 26
Percentage move for each 12-month period	L 10.34%, M 6.54%, H 5.94%	L 20.42%, M 5.47%, H 5.59%	L −5.87%, M −4.51%, H −4.70%	L −13.08%, M −8.50%, H −7.22%
Candle end + 1 day	0.96%	1.03%	−0.84%	−1.35%
Candle end + 3 days	2.19%	2.82%	−1.61%	−2.16%
Candle end + 5 days	2.90%	3.02%	−1.72%	−2.98%
Candle end + 10 days	3.78%	2.06%	−1.46%	−4.29%
10-day performance rank	41	71	81	45

Table 94.3
Height Statistics

Description	Bull Market, Up Breakout	Bear Market, Up Breakout	Bull Market, Down Breakout	Bear Market, Down Breakout
Median candle height as a percentage of breakout price	3.42%	3.53%	3.47%	4.17%
Short candle, performance	5.69%	4.62%*	−4.19%	−8.12%
Tall candle, performance	9.82%	16.73%*	−7.31%	−10.41%
Percentage meeting price target (measure rule)	68%	69%	63%	72%
Median upper shadow as a percentage of breakout price	0.20%	0.63%	0.21%	0.44%
Short upper shadow, performance	5.87%	5.69%*	−4.76%	−6.97%
Tall upper shadow, performance	7.22%	8.23%*	−5.12%	−10.51%
Median lower shadow as a percentage of breakout price	0.11%	0.64%	0.25%	0.41%
Short lower shadow, performance	5.63%	4.95%*	−4.78%	−7.02%
Tall lower shadow, performance	7.43%	9.76%*	−5.15%	−9.97%

*Fewer than 30 samples.

Regardless of market conditions or breakout directions, the best performance comes from patterns within a third of the yearly low.

Performance over time. In the bear market/up breakout and bull market/down breakout columns, performance stumbles from days 5 to 10. Coupled with a poor showing over the 10 days, what results is a lousy performance rank. By comparison, the best rank is 1 out of 103 candles.

Table 94.3 shows height statistics.

Candle height. Tall candles outperform. To determine whether the candle is short or tall, compute its height from highest high to lowest low price in the candle pattern and divide by the breakout price. If the result is higher than the median, then you have a tall candle; otherwise it's short.

Joel sees a bearish tri-star pattern with a high of 16 and a low of 15. Is the candle pattern short or tall? The height is 16 − 15, or 1, so the measure in a bull market with an upward breakout would be 1/16, or 6.3%. It's a tall candle.

Measure rule. Use the measure rule to help predict how far price will rise or fall. Compute the height of the candle pattern and multiply it by the appropriate percentage shown in the table; then apply it to the breakout price.

What are the price targets for Joel's candle? The upward target would be $(1 \times 68\%) + 16$, or 16.68, and the downward target would be $15 - (1 \times 63\%)$, or 14.37.

Table 94.4
Volume Statistics

Description	Bull Market, Up Breakout	Bear Market, Up Breakout*	Bull Market, Down Breakout	Bear Market, Down Breakout
Rising candle volume, performance	6.62%	5.89%	−5.01%	−9.67%
Falling candle volume, performance	6.79%	7.94%	−4.97%	−7.44%
Above-average candle volume, performance	6.72%	3.45%	−5.01%	−7.34%*
Below-average candle volume, performance	6.69%	8.24%	−4.98%	−9.74%
Heavy breakout volume, performance	7.80%	7.79%	−5.23%	−7.52%*
Light breakout volume, performance	5.70%	6.51%	−4.81%	−9.30%

*Fewer than 30 samples.

Shadows. The table's results pertain to the last candle line in the pattern. To determine whether the shadow is short or tall, compute the height of the shadow and divide by the breakout price. Compare the result to the median in the table. Tall shadows have a percentage higher than the median.

Patterns with tall upper or lower shadows perform better than do those with short ones.

Table 94.4 shows volume statistics.

Candle volume trend. Candles with falling volume perform better after breaking out upward, and those with rising volume do better after a downward breakout.

Average candle volume. Candles with above-average volume show a slight tendency toward better performance in a bull market. Those with below-average volume do better in a bear market.

Breakout volume. Usually high breakout volume suggests better post-breakout performance in many candle types. That's true for this candle, too, except in bear market/down breakouts (where there is a low sample count).

Trading Tactics

The bearish tri-star candle appears most often in thinly traded stocks. You'll sometimes see them appear at the *start* of a retracement in a primary upward price trend. Thus, the decline usually doesn't carry far. Figure 94.1 shows an example of this, but it's when the primary trend is downward. Those (bearish tri-star candles when the primary trend is downward) can lead to profitable moves.

I split trading tactics into two basic studies, one concerning reversal rates and the other concerning performance. Of the two, reversal rates are more

Table 94.5
Reversal Rates

Description	Bull Market	Bear Market
Closing price confirmation reversal rate	80%	88%
Candle color confirmation reversal rate	77%	87%
Opening gap confirmation reversal rate	67%	71%
Reversal rate: trend up, breakout down	52%	61%
Continuation rate: trend up, breakout up	48%	39%
Percentage of reversals (R)/continuations (C) for each 12-month low (L), middle (M), or high (H)	L 60% R/40% C, M 58% R/42% C, H 47% R/53% C	L* 70% R/30% C, M* 59% R/41% C, H* 57% R/43% C

*Fewer than 30 samples.

important, because it's better to trade in the direction of the trend and let price run as far as it can.

Table 94.5 gives tips to find the trend direction.

Confirmation reversal rates. To confirm that price has reversed trend, wait for a lower close the next day. That method works at least 80% of the time.

Reversal, continuation rates. Price breaks out downward 52% of the time in bull markets. That's not much above random (50%). The poor performance suggests you wait for confirmation (a lower close).

Yearly range reversals. More reversals occur within a third of the yearly low than in the other two ranges.

Table 94.6 shows performance indicators that can give hints as to how your stock will behave after the breakout from this candle pattern.

Confirmation, performance. The opening gap method of confirmation works well in a bull market. That trading signal occurs when price gaps open lower the day after the pattern ends.

You'll do better with candle color confirmation in a bear market. Trade only if the next day shows a black candle.

Moving average. Candles with breakouts below the 50-day moving average tend to outperform.

Closing position. Where price closes in the doji shows no consistent trend that would suggest better performance.

Sample Trade

Joel owned the stock shown in Figure 94.2. He bought it as a long-term holding before the time period covered in the chart. Price made valleys at A and B, which he connected with a trendline, and he extended the line as price climbed higher.

Table 94.6
Performance Indicators

Description	Bull Market, Up Breakout	Bear Market, Up Breakout	Bull Market, Down Breakout	Bear Market, Down Breakout
Closing price confirmation, performance	N/A	N/A	−5.37%	−8.55%
Candle color confirmation, performance	N/A	N/A	−5.60%	−9.15%
Opening gap confirmation, performance	N/A	N/A	−5.98%	−7.97%
Breakout above 50-day moving average, performance	6.57%	5.65%	−4.92%	−7.60%
Breakout below 50-day moving average, performance	7.16%	20.09%*	−5.17%	−11.59%
Last candle: close in highest third, performance	7.60%	3.46%*	−4.85%	−6.07%*
Last candle: close in middle third, performance	6.93%	7.80%*	−5.03%	−10.67%
Last candle: close in lowest third, performance	6.18%	8.94%*	−5.01%	−8.44%

N/A means not applicable.
*Fewer than 30 samples.

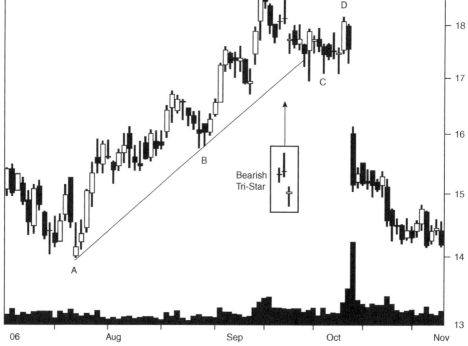

Figure 94.2 A bearish tri-star candle suggests a downturn ahead.

Price peaked at E and then formed three doji, a tri-star pattern. During the prior few days price had trended downward into the tri-star so it's not strictly a bearish tri-star pattern according to the price trend criterion. However, the candle police are nowhere in sight, so I think we're okay.

The bearish tri-star candle was a warning of a trend change, one that Joel missed. When the candle closed below the up-sloping trendline at C, he still wasn't worried. Based on classic candle analysis, the last engulfing bottom (twice), homing pigeon, and southern doji that appeared after the bearish tri star but before D all suggested a bullish turn. Even the long lower shadows suggested price should at least climb stairs like a 90-year-old and return to the high at E.

Price tried. If you extend the trendline to D, you'll see that price pulled back to the trendline now acting as overhead resistance instead of support, and it would likely turn price lower. That's what happened when traders pulled the rug out from under the stock. Price gapped lower on an earnings release.

I asked Joel why he didn't sell. "Oops" was his reply. The moral of the story is: Don't ignore long-term holdings.

For Best Performance

The following list offers tips and observations to help choose candles that perform well. Consult the associated table for more information.

- Use the identification guidelines to help select the pattern—Table 94.1.
- Candles within a third of the yearly low perform best—Table 94.2.
- Select tall candles—Table 94.3.
- Use the measure rule to predict a price target—Table 94.3.
- Candles with tall shadows outperform—Table 94.3.
- Volume gives performance clues—Table 94.4.
- Trade this one during an upward retrace of a downward primary price trend—Trading Tactics discussion.
- Use the closing price a day after the bearish tri-star to confirm a reversal—Table 94.5.
- Patterns within a third of the yearly low tend to act as reversals most often—Table 94.5.
- Opening gap confirmation works best in a bull market; candle color confirmation excels in a bear market—Table 94.6.
- Breakouts below the 50-day moving average lead to the best performance—Table 94.6.

95

Tri-Star, Bullish

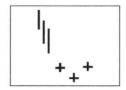

Behavior and Rank

Theoretical: Bullish reversal.

Actual bull market: Bullish reversal 60% of the time (ranking 30).

Actual bear market: Bullish reversal 55% of the time (ranking 35).

Frequency: 79th out of 103.

Overall performance over time: 28th out of 103.

Steve Nison developed the bullish tri-star candle pattern, and it's a rare pattern that shows a reversal rate of 60% in a bull market. A check of the pattern in its native environment shows that it appears most often in thinly traded stocks, and many times it doesn't work well when it does occur. In a longer-term downtrend, it's almost dangerous. Price may break out upward, but the move often isn't a lasting one. Even in a retracement of an uptrend where many reversal candles excel, this one is prone to premature breakouts. The stock tries to move up but stalls and then drops to form a stronger base upon which to launch a new up move.

However, the flip side is reassuring. When price moves horizontally (or even trends downward), a tri-star may signal the start of a wonderful up move. Sometimes it's a month or so premature, but other times its timing is precise.

The psychology behind the pattern is unrevealing. The bears have control by pushing price lower leading to the start of the bullish tri-star. Then three doji print on the chart. Each says that the bulls and bears are undecided about the direction the stock should take. The only clue is that the middle doji is lower than the adjacent ones. This suggests a turn from bearish to bullish.

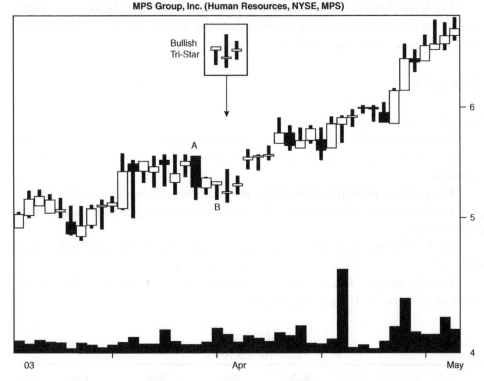

MPS Group, Inc. (Human Resources, NYSE, MPS)

Figure 95.1 A bullish tri-star when the primary trend is upward leads to a good gain.

Identification Guidelines

Figure 95.1 shows a good example of a bullish tri-star pattern when the primary price trend is upward. A short downtrend begins at A, and the tri-star forms at B. The three doji signal a reversal when the middle body hides below the adjacent ones. A day after the pattern completes, price gaps open higher and off price goes, moving higher like a child's helium balloon set free.

Table 95.1 lists identification guidelines. This is an easy pattern to spot if you don't need to wear reading glasses and can ignore overwhelming shadows that sometimes obscure the pattern like a leopard in tall grass.

Table 95.1
Identification Guidelines

Characteristic	Discussion
Number of candle lines	Three.
Price trend	Downward leading to the start of the candle pattern.
Configuration	Three doji. The middle one has a body below the other two.

Look for three doji with the middle one having a body below the other two. A doji has the opening and closing prices the same or nearly so. On a price chart, that makes the body look like a horizontal line.

Statistics

Table 95.2 shows general statistics.

Number found. The bullish tri-star pattern appears most often in a bull market. I found 5,105 out of over 4.7 million candle lines, so the tri-star's a rare bird.

Reversal or continuation performance. Patterns in a bear market outperform those from a bull market. In addition, reversals perform better than continuations.

S&P performance. The bullish tri-star pattern beats the S&P 500 index under all market conditions and breakout directions.

Candle end to breakout. Price takes about four days to either close above or close below the candle pattern.

Table 95.2
General Statistics

Description	Bull Market, Up Breakout	Bear Market, Up Breakout	Bull Market, Down Breakout	Bear Market, Down Breakout
Number found	2,924	114	1,972	95
Reversal (R), continuation (C) performance	7.30% R	11.84% R	−5.59% C	−9.71% C
Standard & Poor's 500 change	1.29%	0.70%	−0.56%	−1.45%
Candle end to breakout (median, days)	4	4	5	4
Candle end to trend end (median, days)	7	7	6	8
Number of breakouts near the 12-month low (L), middle (M), or high (H)	L 683, M 590, H 921	L 61, M 33, H 19	L 615, M 459, H 446	L 54, M 29, H 12
Percentage move for each 12-month period	L 10.29%, M 6.79%, H 5.97%	L 18.23%, M 10.06%, H 5.35%	L −6.96%, M −4.94%, H −4.78%	L −9.58%, M −10.88%, H −6.70%
Candle end + 1 day	0.86%	1.67%	−1.03%	−1.34%
Candle end + 3 days	1.92%	3.48%	−2.01%	−3.08%
Candle end + 5 days	2.62%	4.88%	−2.30%	−3.62%
Candle end + 10 days	3.63%	5.11%	−2.28%	−4.02%
10-day performance rank	42	26	52	49

Candle end to trend end. From the end of the candle to the trend end takes between six and eight days.

Yearly position, performance. Most of the columns show breakouts from the bullish tri-star pattern appearing within a third of the yearly low. The one exception is from patterns in a bull market with upward breakouts. Those appear most often near the yearly high.

The pattern performs best when the breakout is within a third of the yearly low except for bear market/down breakouts. Those do better when the breakout is in the middle of the yearly range.

Performance over time. The tri-star is a weak performer, because price fails to continue posting higher numbers over time. I cite the bull market/down breakout during days 5 and 10. If not for that tiny slip, the results would be admirable.

When compared to other candles, however, the performance rank looks undistinguished. The range is 1 out of 103, where 1 is best, and this candle peaks at 26.

Table 95.3 shows height statistics.

Candle height. Tall candles perform better than short ones. To determine whether the candle is short or tall, compute its height from highest high to lowest low price in the candle pattern and divide by the breakout price. If the result is higher than the median, then you have a tall candle; otherwise it's short.

Table 95.3
Height Statistics

Description	Bull Market, Up Breakout	Bear Market, Up Breakout	Bull Market, Down Breakout	Bear Market, Down Breakout
Median candle height as a percentage of breakout price	3.53%	4.06%	3.40%	5.07%
Short candle, performance	5.96%	9.51%	−4.76%	−8.79%
Tall candle, performance	11.04%	18.77%	−8.08%	−12.45%
Percentage meeting price target (measure rule)	73%	77%	65%	72%
Median upper shadow as a percentage of breakout price	0.11%	0.56%	0.10%	0.85%
Short upper shadow, performance	7.27%	10.85%	−5.89%	−6.89%
Tall upper shadow, performance	7.32%	12.54%	−5.41%	−13.36%
Median lower shadow as a percentage of breakout price	0.25%	0.69%	0.32%	0.86%
Short lower shadow, performance	6.83%	11.01%	−5.25%	−6.02%
Tall lower shadow, performance	7.59%	12.64%	−5.81%	−16.10%

Rodney sees a bullish tri-star with a high of 67 and a low of 65. Is the candle short or tall? The height would be 67 − 65, or 2, so the measure in a bull market with an upward breakout would be 2/67, or 3%. The candle is short.

Measure rule. Use the measure rule to help predict how far price will rise or fall. Compute the height of the candle pattern and multiply it by the appropriate percentage shown in the table; then apply it to the breakout price.

What are Rodney's price targets? The upward target would be (2 × 73%) + 67, or 68.46, and the downward target would be 65 − (2 × 65%), or 63.70.

Shadows. The table's results pertain to the last candle line in the pattern. To determine whether the shadow is short or tall, compute the height of the shadow and divide by the breakout price. Compare the result to the median in the table. Tall shadows have a percentage higher than the median.

Upper shadow performance. Candles with tall upper shadows perform better than do those with short shadows in all cases except for bull market/down breakouts. Those do better with short shadows.

Lower shadow performance. Tall lower shadows suggested better post-breakout performance across the board.

Table 95.4 shows volume statistics.

Candle volume trend. Candles with rising volume generally perform better than do those with falling volume. In one column, however, candles with falling volume do better: bull market/down breakouts.

Average candle volume. The performance of candles with average volume tracks the market trend: Bull market/up breakouts and bear market/down breakouts do best when volume in the candle is below average. The other two situations, bear market/up breakouts and bull market/down breakouts, perform best post breakout with above-average volume.

Breakout volume. Candles experiencing heavy breakout volume tend to perform better than do those with light breakout volume. The lone exception

Table 95.4
Volume Statistics

Description	Bull Market, Up Breakout	Bear Market, Up Breakout	Bull Market, Down Breakout	Bear Market, Down Breakout
Rising candle volume, performance	7.51%	13.13%	−5.42%	−12.27%
Falling candle volume, performance	7.12%	10.21%	−5.77%	−7.92%
Above-average candle volume, performance	7.17%	15.74%	−5.74%	−6.28%
Below-average candle volume, performance	7.37%	9.86%	−5.54%	−11.37%
Heavy breakout volume, performance	8.55%	13.23%	−5.70%	−9.60%
Light breakout volume, performance	6.23%	10.67%	−5.50%	−9.79%

comes from candles in a bear market with downward breakouts. Those do best after a light-volume breakout.

Trading Tactics

Avoid depending on the bullish tri-star as a reversal of the primary down trend. Often it fails miserably. The breakout is upward, but price buckles under the stress of bears trying to force price lower. Use additional tools to verify that the trend has changed.

The bullish tri-star does well when the primary price trend is upward. These splash-and-dash weather systems appear when price takes a momentary breather in the uptrend. The tri-star appears and then price continues on its merry way upward. However, take care in that rise-retrace setup. Often the candle pattern appears too early in the retracement. Price breaks out upward for a week or so and then drops down to rebuild a stronger foundation before making a lasting up move out of the decline.

I split trading tactics into two basic studies, one concerning reversal rates and the other concerning performance. Of the two, reversal rates are more important, because it's better to trade in the direction of the trend and let price run as far as it can.

Table 95.5 gives tips to find the trend direction.

Confirmation reversal rates. The reversal rate climbs from 60% to 85% (bull market) if you wait for price to close higher a day after the bullish tri-star pattern ends before trading.

Reversal, continuation rates. Most bullish tri-star candles break out upward.

Yearly range reversals. The highest proportion of reversals occurs when the breakout is within a third of the yearly high.

Table 95.5
Reversal Rates

Description	Bull Market	Bear Market
Closing price confirmation reversal rate	85%	74%
Candle color confirmation reversal rate	83%	72%
Opening gap confirmation reversal rate	71%	63%
Reversal: trend down, breakout up	60%	55%
Continuation: trend down, breakout down	40%	45%
Percentage of reversals (R)/continuations (C) for each 12-month low (L), middle (M), or high (H)	L 53% R/47% C, M 55% R/44% C, H 67% R/33% C	L 53% R/47% C, M* 53% R/47% C, H* 61% R/39% C

*Fewer than 30 samples.

Table 95.6
Performance Indicators

Description	Bull Market, Up Breakout	Bear Market, Up Breakout	Bull Market, Down Breakout	Bear Market, Down Breakout
Closing price confirmation, performance	6.72%	11.28%	N/A	N/A
Candle color confirmation, performance	6.87%	11.48%	N/A	N/A
Opening gap confirmation, performance	7.19%	14.55%	N/A	N/A
Breakout above 50-day moving average, performance	6.63%	9.05%	−4.59%	−7.82%*
Breakout below 50-day moving average, performance	8.10%	13.57%	−5.96%	−10.56%
Last candle: close in highest third, performance	7.49%	11.13%	−5.81%	−7.45%
Last candle: close in middle third, performance	7.48%	11.95%	−5.50%	−13.25%
Last candle: close in lowest third, performance	6.49%	12.53%*	−5.23%	−7.54%*

N/A means not applicable.
*Fewer than 30 samples.

Table 95.6 shows performance indicators that can give hints as to how your stock will behave after the breakout from this candle pattern.

Confirmation, performance. The opening gap method of confirmation gets you into a trade sooner than the other methods and results in the best performance. Wait for price to gap open higher a day after the bullish tri-star ends.

Moving average. Bullish tri-star candles with breakouts below the 50-day moving average perform better than do those with breakouts above the average.

Closing position. Where price closes in the last doji shows no consistent trend that might lead to better performance.

Sample Trade

Figure 95.2 shows a trade Rodney made. Price formed three lower lows, at A, B, and C. He drew a trendline connecting those valleys. Along the top, he connected D and F and then extended the trendline lower. He didn't mind slicing the tall upper shadow off at E because, well, this is a fictitious trade and he doesn't care about such things. Some traders cut off the tops of the trees like this trendline does to highlight what the majority of traders are doing. They even have a name for it: internal trendline. Shall I hum a few bars?

Figure 95.2 A falling wedge chart pattern coupled with a bullish tri-star lead to a successful entry.

Price a day after C formed a bullish tri-star pattern, and Rodney considered buying the next day when price gapped open higher. He held back to be sure price pierced the upper trendline. When that happened at G, he bought the stock intraday and held on for a huge gain.

For Best Performance

The following list offers tips and observations to help choose candles that perform well. Consult the associated table for more information.

- Use the identification guidelines to help select the pattern—Table 95.1.
- Most, but not all, candles within a third of the yearly low perform best—Table 95.2.
- Select tall candles—Table 95.3.
- Use the measure rule to predict a price target—Table 95.3.
- Candles with tall lower shadows outperform—Table 95.3.
- Volume gives performance clues—Table 95.4.

- Find this candle in a small retracement of a primary upward price trend—Trading Tactics discussion.
- The candle breaks out upward most often—Table 95.5.
- Patterns within a third of the yearly high tend to act as reversals most often—Table 95.5.
- Opening gap confirmation works best—Table 95.6.
- Breakouts below the 50-day moving average lead to the best performance—Table 95.6.

96

Tweezers Bottom

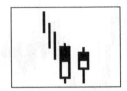

Behavior and Rank

Theoretical: Bullish reversal.
Actual bull market: Bearish continuation 52% of the time (ranking 40).
Actual bear market: Bearish continuation 56% of the time (ranking 30).
Frequency: 39th out of 103.
Overall performance over time: 44th out of 103.

Imagine that the bears have pushed price lower for the past week and two candles form. Both of those candles reach exactly the same low price. The twin lows form a small support zone, an indication that price will reverse in the coming days.

That's the psychology behind the tweezers bottom pattern. What happens after the twin lows? Price continues lower, of course. That may shock many candle players, but that's what I found. The continuation rate is slight, 52% in a bull market, which is just an ant's height above random (50%).

That places the continuation rank at 40 in a bull market out of 103 candles where 1 is best, so as a continuation pattern, it's not good and not bad. Overall performance is also midrange, at 44.

Identification Guidelines

Figure 96.1 shows a good example of how this candlestick pattern behaves. Price climbs to a new high at A and then falls. A series of black candles prints on the chart, and at C the tweezers bottom appears. The two lows are at the

Figure 96.1 A tweezers bottom appears in the middle of a sell-off.

same price, and then what looks like a shooting star appears. It's not a shooting star because price trends downward, but it has a long upper shadow. That's not good news for anyone who bought the tweezers bottom.

Why? Because the selling at D meant that the bulls could not hold on to the stock when the bears came along and pushed price lower. Additional selling would likely force price down still more. That's what happens at B when price makes a new low, but after that, price stages a nice recovery.

Table 96.1 lists identification guidelines. This candle pattern is simplicity itself. Look for two candles in a downward price trend that share the same low price. Sometimes the candle pair will form recognizable patterns such as a harami, piercing pattern, a pair of doji or hammers, lions, tigers, and bears. Oh my! Upper shadows and candle color do not matter in this pattern.

Table 96.1
Identification Guidelines

Characteristic	Discussion
Number of candle lines	Two.
Price trend	Downward leading to the start of the candle pattern.
Configuration	Two candles (any color) that share the same low price.

Statistics

Table 96.2 shows general statistics.

Number found. This candle pattern is as plentiful as mosquitoes on a late spring morning. I found a gazillion of them, so I limited selections to the first 20,000. Most appear in a bull market and comparatively few happen in a bear market.

Reversal or continuation performance. Tweezers bottoms in a bear market perform better than do those in a bull market.

S&P performance. The S&P 500 index fails to beat the tweezers bottom, regardless of the market conditions or breakout directions.

Candle end to breakout. It takes about four days for price to reach the breakout. A breakout occurs when price closes either above the highest high or below the lowest low in the candlestick pattern.

Candle end to trend end. The median time to the trend end varies from six to nine days. Downward breakouts take less time to reach the trend end. This makes sense when coupled with a downward trend already in existence.

Table 96.2
General Statistics

Description	Bull Market, Up Breakout	Bear Market, Up Breakout	Bull Market, Down Breakout	Bear Market, Down Breakout
Number found	8,968	497	9,899	636
Reversal (R), continuation (C) performance	6.98% R	9.22% R	−6.04% C	−9.77% C
Standard & Poor's 500 change	1.22%	0.63%	−0.40%	−1.49%
Candle end to breakout (median, days)	4	4	4	3
Candle end to trend end (median, days)	7	9	6	6
Number of breakouts near the 12-month low (L), middle (M), or high (H)	L 3,092, M 2,634, H 3,242	L 240, M 138, H 119	L 4,429, M 3,036, H 2,434	L 364, M 176, H 96
Percentage move for each 12-month period	L 8.09%, M 6.66%, H 6.49%	L 10.95%, M 9.05%, H 7.49%	L −6.66%, M −6.21%, H −5.12%	L −11.63%, M −9.75%, H −6.44%
Candle end + 1 day	1.17%	1.59%	−0.91%	−1.72%
Candle end + 3 days	2.43%	3.22%	−1.79%	−2.96%
Candle end + 5 days	3.00%	4.08%	−2.04%	−3.35%
Candle end + 10 days	3.62%	4.95%	−2.09%	−3.32%
10-day performance rank	43	29	58	66

A trend well along toward the trend end would take less time than one just starting out (as in the case of price moving up).

Yearly position, performance. Most tweezers bottoms form within a third of the yearly low except in bull market/up breakouts. Those appear slightly more often near the yearly high. Performance is best when the breakout is within a third of the yearly low.

Performance over time. This candle would be a robust performer except for one flaw. In bear market/down breakouts, performance weakens from days 5 to 10. Also, the numbers posted over time are not as high as they could be (6% or higher is very good).

When compared to other candles, the performance rank is about what you would expect. Upward breakouts show a higher rank than downward breakouts. A rank of 1 is best out of 103 candles.

Table 96.3 shows height statistics.

Candle height. Tall candles perform better than short ones. To determine whether the candle is short or tall, compute its height from highest high to lowest low price in the candle pattern and divide by the breakout price. If the result is higher than the median, then you have a tall candle; otherwise it's short.

Steve sees a tweezers bottom with a high of 69 and a low of 68. Is the candle short or tall? The height is 69 – 68, or 1, so the measure would be 1/69, or 1.4% (assume bull market/up breakout). The candle is short.

Table 96.3
Height Statistics

Description	Bull Market, Up Breakout	Bear Market, Up Breakout	Bull Market, Down Breakout	Bear Market, Down Breakout
Median candle height as a percentage of breakout price	3.17%	4.51%	3.35%	4.83%
Short candle, performance	5.54%	8.07%	−5.00%	−7.63%
Tall candle, performance	9.23%	10.77%	−7.73%	−12.70%
Percentage meeting price target (measure rule)	71%	69%	65%	65%
Median upper shadow as a percentage of breakout price	0.27%	0.68%	0.38%	0.74%
Short upper shadow, performance	6.78%	8.58%	−5.69%	−9.09%
Tall upper shadow, performance	7.15%	9.79%	−6.38%	−10.34%
Median lower shadow as a percentage of breakout price	0.00%	0.34%	0.00%	0.41%
Short lower shadow, performance	6.75%	8.30%	−6.01%	−8.02%
Tall lower shadow, performance	7.18%	10.04%	−6.07%	−11.20%

Table 96.4

Volume Statistics

Description	Bull Market, Up Breakout	Bear Market, Up Breakout	Bull Market, Down Breakout	Bear Market, Down Breakout
Rising candle volume, performance	7.16%	8.19%	−6.04%	−9.52%
Falling candle volume, performance	6.83%	10.08%	−6.03%	−9.95%
Above-average candle volume, performance	6.97%	9.10%	−5.96%	−9.09%
Below-average candle volume, performance	6.99%	9.32%	−6.10%	−10.28%
Heavy breakout volume, performance	7.87%	10.49%	−6.45%	−10.67%
Light breakout volume, performance	6.11%	7.99%	−5.73%	−8.78%

Measure rule. Use the measure rule to help predict how far price will rise or fall. Compute the height of the candle pattern and multiply it by the appropriate percentage shown in the table; then apply it to the breakout price.

What are the price targets for Steve's candle? The upward target would be 69 + (1 × 71%), or 69.71, and the downward target would be 68 − (1 × 65%), or 67.35.

Shadows. The table's results pertain to the last candle line in the pattern. To determine whether the shadow is short or tall, compute the height of the shadow and divide by the breakout price. Compare the result to the median in the table. Tall shadows have a percentage higher than the median.

Candles with tall upper or lower shadows show the best postbreakout performance in all categories. They perform better than tweezers bottoms with short shadows. Don't worry about a 0.00% median. That just means a number of candles had no lower shadow.

Table 96.4 shows volume statistics.

Candle volume trend. Candles with rising volume do best in bull markets, and those with falling volume do best in bear markets.

Average candle volume. Candles with below-average volume perform best in all categories.

Breakout volume. Heavy breakout volume suggests good postbreakout performance regardless of the market conditions and breakout directions.

Trading Tactics

If the primary price trend is upward and a tweezers bottom occurs, consider buying the stock. The tweezers should form at the bottom of a small retracement of the uptrend, offering a low-risk, high-reward setup.

If the primary trend is downward, price may break out upward but the tendency is for price to rise little before collapsing. If price breaks out downward, then expect the decline to continue.

Table 96.5
Reversal Rates

Description	Bull Market	Bear Market
Closing price confirmation reversal rate	72%	69%
Candle color confirmation reversal rate	70%	68%
Opening gap confirmation reversal rate	55%	51%
Reversal: trend down, breakout up	48%	44%
Continuation: trend down, breakout down	52%	56%
Percentage of reversals (R)/continuations (C) for each 12-month low (L), middle (M), or high (H)	L 41% R/59% C, M 46% R/54% C, H 57% R/43% C	L 40% R/60% C, M 44% R/56% C, H 55% R/45% C

I split trading tactics into two basic studies, one concerning reversal rates and the other concerning performance. Of the two, reversal rates are more important, because it's better to trade in the direction of the trend and let price run as far as it can.

Table 96.5 gives tips to find the trend direction.

Confirmation reversal rates. To help detect a reversal of the downtrend, wait for price to close higher the next day. That method works 72% of the time in a bull market.

Reversal, continuation rates. Price breaks out downward slightly more often than upward.

Yearly range reversals. Tweezers bottoms within a third of the yearly high tend to act as reversals more often than do those that appear in the other two ranges. Patterns acting as continuations occur most often near the yearly low. That means price continues to drop, and that's why it's difficult to bottom-fish—price just keeps on tumbling.

Table 96.6 shows performance indicators that can give hints as to how your stock will behave after the breakout from this candle pattern.

Confirmation, performance. Opening gap confirmation results in the best performance of the methods of entry. That means waiting for price to gap open upward the day after the tweezers bottom.

Moving average. Tweezers bottoms with breakouts below the 50-day moving average perform better than do those above the moving average.

Closing position. Where price closes in the last candle line shows no consistent performance trend.

Sample Trade

Steve thought he had discovered sunken treasure when he looked at the stock pictured in Figure 96.2. Price made a large move up from A to B on news that

Table 96.6
Performance Indicators

Description	Bull Market, Up Breakout	Bear Market, Up Breakout	Bull Market, Down Breakout	Bear Market, Down Breakout
Closing price confirmation, performance	7.04%	10.05%	N/A	N/A
Candle color confirmation, performance	6.97%	10.07%	N/A	N/A
Opening gap confirmation, performance	7.67%	11.05%	N/A	N/A
Breakout above 50-day moving average, performance	6.63%	8.03%	−5.44%	−7.69%
Breakout below 50-day moving average, performance	7.31%	10.44%	−6.22%	−10.33%
Last candle: close in highest third, performance	7.02%	8.30%	−5.99%	−10.46%
Last candle: close in middle third, performance	6.85%	10.54%	−5.97%	−10.10%
Last candle: close in lowest third, performance	7.04%	9.43%	−6.15%	−8.51%

N/A means not applicable.

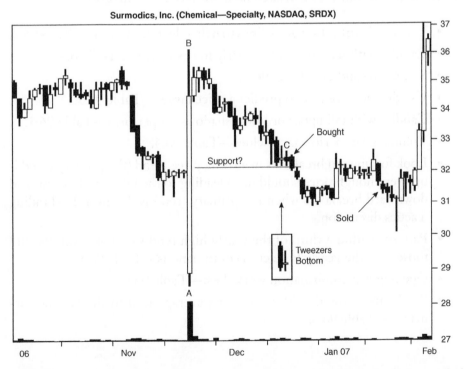

Figure 96.2 A tall white candle was supposed to act as support when coupled with the tweezers bottom. It didn't.

Johnson & Johnson was buying a company that had a deal with Surmodics. The thinking was that the larger distribution channel of J&J would help boost sales of Surmodics goods, too. Traders were skeptical at first (the stock gapped open much lower) but then loved the idea.

Steve noticed the tweezers bottom at C, and he saw the tall white candle AB. Half of that candle body was a point near where price was trading. Tall candles often show support zones. Coupled with the tweezers bottom as another support zone along with a Fibonacci retracement of 50% of the prior AB move up, the indications were that he had the makings of a killer trade.

When price gapped open higher the next day, he bought the stock. The butterflies nesting in his stomach started acting up almost immediately, especially as price dropped. About two weeks later, the stock recovered in a tall white candle, moved horizontally for another two weeks, and then turned back down. After a tall black candle appeared, he decided to sell the stock. About a week later, price took off, resuming the uptrend he originally expected but was now no longer a part of.

For Best Performance

The following list offers tips and observations to help choose candles that perform well. Consult the associated table for more information.

- Use the identification guidelines to help select the pattern—Table 96.1.
- Candles within a third of the yearly low perform best—Table 96.2.
- Select tall candles—Table 96.3.
- Use the measure rule to predict a price target—Table 96.3.
- Candles with tall upper or lower shadows outperform—Table 96.3.
- Volume gives performance clues—Table 96.4.
- Look for upward breakouts in a rising price trend (the primary trend is up even though price should drop leading to the tweezers bottom) and downward breakouts when the primary trend is downward—Trading Tactics discussion.
- Patterns within a third of the yearly high tend to act as reversals, and those near the yearly low act as continuations—Table 96.5.
- Opening gap confirmation works best—Table 96.6.
- Breakouts below the 50-day moving average lead to the best performance—Table 96.6.

97

Tweezers Top

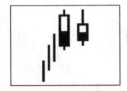

Behavior and Rank

Theoretical: Bearish reversal.

Actual bull market: Bullish continuation 56% of the time (ranking 28).

Actual bear market: Bullish continuation 55% of the time (ranking 34).

Frequency: 35th out of 103.

Overall performance over time: 81st out of 103.

The tweezers top is supposed to be a bearish reversal pattern, but my testing shows that it actually performs as a bullish continuation pattern 56% of the time. The rank in a bull market shows how it stacks up against other candle types.

The frequency rank at 35, where 1 is best out of 103 candles, means that you should be able to find the candle easily enough. However, the performance rank of 81 suggests it's a poor performer over time (when compared to other candles, that is).

As far as psychology is concerned, there's not much to talk about. The bulls force price to the same high two times in a row. This sets up overhead resistance or it highlights an existing resistance zone that the bulls are not allowed to cross. Whether that remains true depends on what price does next. My testing shows the bullies cross the line drawn in the sand slightly more often than not.

Johnson & Johnson (Medical Supplies, NYSE, JNJ)

Figure 97.1   A tweezers top acts as a continuation pattern, not a reversal.

Identification Guidelines

Figure 97.1 shows an example of when a tweezers top should act as a reversal but doesn't. Price climbs a mountain of worry through May and June to peak A. Then price gaps down when a firm downgrades the stock. The price climbers do not admit defeat, though, and set out from base camp to attempt the summit once more. They climb to B, the site of the old high.

At that point, price should hit overhead resistance set up by peak A and turn down, especially when twin candles C arrive. Coupled with candle B, the triplet marks three lines within a penny of the high price. The tweezers top (C) highlights overhead resistance and price should tumble, but what happens? With hardly a missed beat, price advances to a new high, ignoring both the potential double top and the overhead resistance highlighted by the tweezers top and the candle at B.

Table 97.1 lists identification guidelines. For a tweezers top, look for any two candle lines that share the same high price. The candles can be any length, any color, and any combination you can think of, just as long as the high price remains the same for two consecutive days.

Table 97.1
Identification Guidelines

Characteristic	Discussion
Number of candle lines	Two.
Price trend	Upward leading to the start of the candle pattern.
Configuration	Two adjacent candle lines (any color) share the same high price.

Statistics

Table 97.2 shows general statistics.

Number found. I found tens of thousands of tweezers tops, so I limited them to the first 20,000 patterns. Most came from a bull market.

Reversal or continuation performance. Tweezers tops in a bear market perform better than do those in a bull market.

Table 97.2
General Statistics

Description	Bull Market, Up Breakout	Bear Market, Up Breakout	Bull Market, Down Breakout	Bear Market, Down Breakout
Number found	10,215	974	8,008	803
Reversal (R), continuation (C) performance	5.79% C	7.05% C	−5.70% R	−7.86% R
Standard & Poor's 500 change	1.01%	0.08%	−0.57%	−2.10%
Candle end to breakout (median, days)	4	3	4	4
Candle end to trend end (median, days)	6	7	7	8
Number of breakouts near the 12-month low (L), middle (M), or high (H)	L 1,644, M 2,607, H 5,964	L 214, M 297, H 463	L 1,907, M 2,183, H 3,918	L 246, M 263, H 294
Percentage move for each 12-month period	L 7.17%, M 5.87%, H 5.52%	L 9.16%, M 7.12%, H 6.43%	L −6.40%, M −6.30%, H −5.19%	L −9.06%, M −7.55%, H −7.54%
Candle end + 1 day	0.81%	0.97%	−0.97%	−1.18%
Candle end + 3 days	1.70%	2.22%	−1.96%	−2.37%
Candle end + 5 days	2.09%	2.27%	−2.37%	−2.92%
Candle end + 10 days	2.45%	2.79%	−2.59%	−3.21%
10-day performance rank	71	59	42	67

S&P performance. The tweezers top performs better than the S&P 500 index over the same holding time.

Candle end to breakout. It takes about four days for price to break out. A breakout occurs when price closes either above the highest high or below the lowest low in the candle pattern.

Candle end to trend end. Downward breakouts take slightly longer to reach the trend end than do upward ones. This is due to the uptrend already underway. A reversal (downward breakout) would be like swimming against the current. You may still make it to the other bank, but it will take longer, especially if you are run over by a boat.

Yearly position, performance. Most tweezers tops appear within a third of the yearly high. However, performance is best when they appear within a third of the yearly low.

Performance over time. Tweezers tops are robust performers. That means performance improves during each period, regardless of market conditions and breakout directions. The only scuff on the polished armor is that the percentage change after 10 days isn't huge (over 5% or 6% would be a good move).

The performance rank confirms the dismal performance when compared to other candle patterns. Tweezers tops are midlist performers, like lukewarm water: not too hot and not too cold.

Table 97.3 shows height statistics.

Table 97.3
Height Statistics

Description	Bull Market, Up Breakout	Bear Market, Up Breakout	Bull Market, Down Breakout	Bear Market, Down Breakout
Median candle height as a percentage of breakout price	3.02%	4.11%	3.18%	4.17%
Short candle, performance	4.68%	6.11%	−4.65%	−6.99%
Tall candle, performance	7.44%	8.33%	−7.34%	−9.10%
Percentage meeting price target (measure rule)	65%	65%	64%	65%
Median upper shadow as a percentage of breakout price	0.00%	0.28%	0.00%	0.27%
Short upper shadow, performance	5.67%	6.34%	−5.58%	−7.26%
Tall upper shadow, performance	5.90%	7.74%	−5.80%	−8.43%
Median lower shadow as a percentage of breakout price	0.47%	0.77%	0.41%	0.67%
Short lower shadow, performance	5.34%	6.87%	−5.26%	−7.78%
Tall lower shadow, performance	6.22%	7.21%	−6.10%	−7.95%

Candle height. Tall candles perform better than short ones. To determine whether the candle is short or tall, compute its height from highest high to lowest low price in the candle pattern and divide by the breakout price. If the result is higher than the median, then you have a tall candle; otherwise it's short.

Larry sees a tweezers top with a high of 51 and a low of 49. Is the candle short or tall? The height is 51 − 49, or 2, so the measure would be 2/51, or 3.9%. Assume an upward breakout in a bull market, and the candle is tall.

Measure rule. Use the measure rule to help predict how far price will rise or fall. Compute the height of the candle pattern and multiply it by the appropriate percentage shown in the table; then apply it to the breakout price.

What are Larry's price targets? The upward target would be (2 × 65%) + 51, or 52.30, and the downward target would be 49 − (2 × 64%), or 47.72.

Shadows. The table's results pertain to the last candle line in the pattern. To determine whether the shadow is short or tall, compute the height of the shadow and divide by the breakout price. Compare the result to the median in the table. Tall shadows have a percentage higher than the median.

A zero median means a large number of candles have no shadow. Candles with tall upper or lower shadows perform better than short shadows after the breakout.

Table 97.4 shows volume statistics.

Candle volume trend. Falling candle volume works best in all cases except for bear market/down breakouts. Those show better performance after rising candle volume.

Average candle volume. Candles with above-average volume lead to better performance after the breakout. This is true in all cases except for bear market/up breakouts. In that situation, price performs better if the candle showed below-average volume.

Breakout volume. Heavy breakout volume suggests better performance after the breakout than those candles showing light breakout volume. Many

Table 97.4
Volume Statistics

Description	Bull Market, Up Breakout	Bear Market, Up Breakout	Bull Market, Down Breakout	Bear Market, Down Breakout
Rising candle volume, performance	5.63%	7.03%	−5.58%	−8.03%
Falling candle volume, performance	5.88%	7.05%	−5.76%	−7.78%
Above-average candle volume, performance	5.90%	6.99%	−5.87%	−7.87%
Below-average candle volume, performance	5.71%	7.10%	−5.57%	−7.86%
Heavy breakout volume, performance	6.55%	7.38%	−5.85%	−8.21%
Light breakout volume, performance	5.04%	6.75%	−5.60%	−7.63%

of the numbers (in each column), are comparatively far apart, so it might be worth your while to look for heavy breakout volume.

Trading Tactics

For trading, I would treat this candle as a noncandle. By that, I mean just trade with the primary trend and don't worry about the tweezers top. Price may rise in a downtrend or fall in an uptrend for a week or so, but it should turn and align itself with the primary (longer-term) trend soon after.

I split trading tactics into two basic studies, one concerning reversal rates and the other concerning performance. Of the two, reversal rates are more important, because it's better to trade in the direction of the trend and let price run as far as it can.

Table 97.5 gives tips to find the trend direction.

Confirmation reversal rates. If you wait for price to close lower the day after a tweezers top, you increase your chances of finding a reversal to 66% (bull market).

Reversal, continuation rates. Price breaks out upward most often.

Yearly range reversals. The continuation rate is highest for those tweezers tops with breakouts within a third of the yearly high.

Table 97.6 shows performance indicators that can give hints as to how your stock will behave after the breakout from this candle pattern.

Confirmation, performance. Opening gap confirmation results in the best performance. That means waiting for price to gap open lower the next day before trading. This assumes you're looking for a reversal of the uptrend.

Moving average. Tweezers with breakouts below the 50-day moving average tend to perform better than do those above the moving average.

Closing position. Candles with closes in the lowest third of the last candle line suggest better performance in all categories except for bear market/ down breakouts. Those do better if the close is near the candle's high.

Table 97.5
Reversal Rates

Description	Bull Market	Bear Market
Closing price confirmation reversal rate	66%	68%
Candle color confirmation reversal rate	65%	66%
Opening gap confirmation reversal rate	52%	49%
Reversal rate: trend up, breakout down	44%	45%
Continuation rate: trend up, breakout up	56%	55%
Percentage of reversals (R)/continuations (C) for each 12-month low (L), middle (M), or high (H)	L 54% R/46% C, M 46% R/54% C, H 40% R/60% C	L 53% R/47% C, M 47% R/53% C, H 39% R/61% C

Table 97.6
Performance Indicators

Description	Bull Market, Up Breakout	Bear Market, Up Breakout	Bull Market, Down Breakout	Bear Market, Down Breakout
Closing price confirmation, performance	N/A	N/A	−6.42%	−8.79%
Candle color confirmation, performance	N/A	N/A	−6.36%	−8.65%
Opening gap confirmation, performance	N/A	N/A	−6.94%	−9.22%
Breakout above 50-day moving average, performance	5.76%	6.81%	−5.44%	−7.25%
Breakout below 50-day moving average, performance	6.00%	8.90%	−6.25%	−9.37%
Last candle: close in highest third, performance	5.70%	6.96%	−5.53%	−8.64%
Last candle: close in middle third, performance	5.78%	6.96%	−5.45%	−6.59%
Last candle: close in lowest third, performance	5.89%	7.24%	−5.91%	−8.35%

N/A means not applicable.

Sample Trade

Figure 97.2 shows a mistake that Larry made in one of his trades. Price climbed to a congestion area marked by peak A, then retraced and climbed back up to B. Over a month later, price again reached the AB level, shown here as C. He drew a trendline connecting points A, B, and C.

The chart pattern formed by the top trendline and another connecting the valleys (not shown) was a right-angled and descending broadening top. I have found that they don't work well as a tradable chart pattern, but I digress.

Larry saw the resistance line ABC and believed that price would turn lower. He didn't want to take the chance of giving back most of his profit, so he sold the stock a day after the tweezers top completed. Price gapped open higher and he was glad to exit on an up note.

At D, price closed above the ABC trendline, confirming an upward breakout to the chart pattern and an upward breakout of the tweezers top. Price climbed after that. Larry missed an opportunity to increase his gains by exiting before price confirmed the breakout direction.

For Best Performance

The following list offers tips and observations to help choose candles that perform well. Consult the associated table for more information.

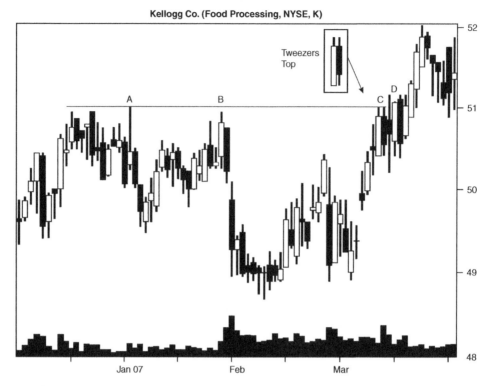

Figure 97.2 Price is expected to reverse at the tweezers top but doesn't.

- Use the identification guidelines to help select the pattern—Table 97.1.
- Candles within a third of the yearly low perform best—Table 97.2.
- Select tall candles—Table 97.3.
- Use the measure rule to predict a price target—Table 97.3.
- Candles with tall upper and lower shadows outperform—Table 97.3.
- Volume gives performance clues—Table 97.4.
- Trade in the direction of the primary trend—Trading Tactics discussion.
- The candle breaks out upward most often—Table 97.5.
- Patterns within a third of the yearly high tend to act as continuations most often—Table 97.5.
- Opening gap confirmation works best—Table 97.6.
- Breakouts below the 50-day moving average lead to the best performance—Table 97.6.

98

Two Black
Gapping Candles

Behavior and Rank

Theoretical: Bearish continuation.

Actual bull market: Bearish continuation 68% of the time (ranking 10).

Actual bear market: Bearish continuation 69% of the time (ranking 9).

Frequency: 29th out of 103.

Overall performance over time: 10th out of 103.

Every time I see a continuation pattern, I wonder why anyone would hunt for one of those. The answer is clear: If I knew that price would continue trending downward tomorrow, then that's worth money.

A rank of 10 for the bull market continuation is close to the best, 1 out of 103 candles. The pattern occurs often (29 rank) and performance is stellar (10 rank) when compared to other candles. The performance over time suggests that upward breakouts are the direction in which to place your money. Of course, that would mean trading this candle pattern as a bullish reversal, not a bearish continuation pattern.

The psychology behind the two black gapping candles is a study in over-head resistance and downward momentum. In a falling price trend, the bears are strong enough to force price lower at the open the next day and keep the high price from closing the gap. That creates a falling window, or resistance against an up move. That day and the next, the bears continue forcing price lower, creating black candles. That completes the two black gapping

Figure 98.1   A two black gapping candles pattern sees price move lower, eventually.

candles pattern. What happens next is that price breaks out downward 68% of the time.

Identification Guidelines

Figure 98.1 shows an example of the two black gapping candles. Price gaps below candle A and then forms two black candles. After that, price recovers for a few days before the downtrend resumes. Even though a tall white candle closes higher than the prior candle after the candle pattern ends, the breakout is still downward because price first closed below the bottom of the entire pattern and not above the top.

Table 98.1 lists identification guidelines. I found only one source describing this candle, Nison's *Beyond Candlesticks* (John Wiley & Sons, 1994), and details were sketchy. Look for two black candles after price gaps lower. I require that the second candle have a lower high than the first one. That means price leaves the gap open. The black candles can be any size and the shadows any length, provided they are not tall enough to close the falling window (gap).

Table 98.1
Identification Guidelines

Characteristic	Discussion
Number of candle lines	Two.
Price trend	Downward leading to the start of the candle pattern.
First day	Price gaps lower from the prior day and forms a black candle.
Second day	A lower high forms on the second black candle.

Statistics

Table 98.2 shows general statistics.

Number found. Two black gapping candles happen a lot. I discovered 18,264 of them in two of the four databases I used, and if you prorate the standard database numbers, you'll find that they occur more often in a bear market.

Reversal or continuation performance. The candle pattern in a bear market performs better than it does in a bull market.

Table 98.2
General Statistics

Description	Bull Market, Up Breakout	Bear Market, Up Breakout	Bull Market, Down Breakout	Bear Market, Down Breakout
Number found	4,533	1,328	9,459	2,944
Reversal (R), continuation (C) performance	6.97% R	9.27% R	−6.09% C	−11.49% C
Standard & Poor's 500 change	2.28%	2.01%	−0.76%	−2.41%
Candle end to breakout (median, days)	5	5	3	3
Candle end to trend end (median, days)	11	11	6	6
Number of breakouts near the 12-month low (L), middle (M), or high (H)	L 1,010, M 1,265, H 1,905	L 468, M 468, H 377	L 3,076, M 3,046, H 2,571	L 1,495, M 944, H 452
Percentage move for each 12-month period	L 7.95%, M 6.61%, H 6.69%	L 11.73%, M 8.56%, H 7.75%	L −6.76%, M −6.03%, H −5.39%	L −13.08%, M −10.53%, H −9.22%
Candle end + 1 day	1.62%	2.58%	−0.79%	−1.09%
Candle end + 3 days	3.19%	5.34%	−1.43%	−2.61%
Candle end + 5 days	3.90%	6.85%	−1.67%	−2.54%
Candle end + 10 days	4.83%	6.45%	−1.64%	−3.11%
10-day performance rank	14	15	76	71

S&P performance. The S&P 500 index puts up good numbers, but the gapping candle puts up better ones.

Candle end to breakout. Downward moves take less time to break out than upward ones. This makes sense since the closing price is nearer the bottom of the candle than the top.

Candle end to trend end. Price takes less time to reach the trend end during downward breakouts than upward ones. That's because the downtrend is already well along the way to the end, whereas upward breakouts would start a new trend.

Yearly position, performance. Most candles appear within a third of the yearly low except in bull market/up breakouts. Those appear within a third of the yearly high most often. Performance is best when the candle is within a third of the yearly low.

Performance over time. Two black gapping candles are poor performers over time. I see weakness during days 5 to 10 in the middle two columns (bear market/up breakouts and bull market/down breakouts) and between days 3 and 5 in the last column (bear market/down breakouts).

When compared to other candle patterns, the performance is quite good after an upward breakout. That appears to be the direction to trade with this candle. Downward breakouts show that the percentage change over 10 days is unexciting, and that's why the ranks are so poor (76 and 71, where 1 is best out of 103 candles).

Table 98.3 shows height statistics.

Candle height. Tall candles outperform. To determine whether the candle is short or tall, compute its height from highest high to lowest low price in the candle pattern and divide by the breakout price. Do not include the gap in the computation. If the result is higher than the median, then you have a tall candle; otherwise it's short.

If Rusty sees two black gapping candles with a high of 87 and a low of 84, is the candle short or tall? The height is 87 − 84, or 3, so the measure in a bull market with a downward breakout would be 3/84, or 3.6%. That's a short candle.

Measure rule. Use the measure rule to help predict how far price will rise or fall. Compute the height of the candle pattern and multiply it by the appropriate percentage shown in the table; then apply it to the breakout price.

What are Rusty's price targets? The upward target would be $(3 \times 61\%) + 87$, or 88.83, and the downward target would be $84 − (3 \times 49\%)$, or 82.53.

Shadows. The table's results pertain to the last candle line in the pattern. To determine whether the shadow is short or tall, compute the height of the shadow and divide by the breakout price. Compare the result to the median in the table. Tall shadows have a percentage higher than the median.

Candles with tall upper or lower shadows perform better than do those with short shadows.

Table 98.3
Height Statistics

Description	Bull Market, Up Breakout	Bear Market, Up Breakout	Bull Market, Down Breakout	Bear Market, Down Breakout
Median candle height as a percentage of breakout price	4.16%	6.72%	4.57%	7.30%
Short candle, performance	5.73%	7.34%	−4.68%	−9.21%
Tall candle, performance	8.54%	11.27%	−7.76%	−14.06%
Percentage meeting price target (measure rule)	61%	55%	49%	53%
Median upper shadow as a percentage of breakout price	0.29%	0.44%	0.27%	0.52%
Short upper shadow, performance	6.50%	8.31%	−5.91%	−10.54%
Tall upper shadow, performance	7.37%	10.14%	−6.23%	−12.45%
Median lower shadow as a percentage of breakout price	0.62%	1.14%	0.49%	0.92%
Short lower shadow, performance	6.16%	7.97%	−5.30%	−11.35%
Tall lower shadow, performance	7.84%	10.55%	−6.86%	−11.64%

Table 98.4 shows volume statistics.

Candle volume trend. Patterns in a bull market perform better with rising candle volume, and those in a bear market do better after the candle shows falling volume.

Average candle volume. Candles with below-average volume tend to perform better than do those with above-average volume.

Breakout volume. Heavy breakout volume suggests better performance in all cases.

Table 98.4
Volume Statistics

Description	Bull Market, Up Breakout	Bear Market, Up Breakout	Bull Market, Down Breakout	Bear Market, Down Breakout
Rising candle volume, performance	7.47%	9.17%	−6.31%	−11.43%
Falling candle volume, performance	6.61%	9.35%	−5.94%	−11.54%
Above-average candle volume, performance	6.70%	9.22%	−5.95%	−11.48%
Below-average candle volume, performance	7.48%	9.35%	−6.36%	−11.53%
Heavy breakout volume, performance	7.38%	10.00%	−6.27%	−12.01%
Light breakout volume, performance	6.46%	8.43%	−5.81%	−10.52%

Trading Tactics

For downward breakouts, trade this candle when the primary price trend is also downward. That setup often leads to good moves. Avoid trading the pattern when the primary trend is upward and the gapping candlestick appears as a downward retracement.

I split trading tactics into two basic studies, one concerning reversal rates and the other concerning performance. Of the two, reversal rates are more important, because it's better to trade in the direction of the trend and let price run as far as it can.

Table 98.5 gives tips to find the trend direction.

Confirmation reversal rates. To help separate a potential reversal from a continuation pattern, wait for price to close higher the next day. If that happens, a reversal occurs 55% of the time in a bull market. Since random is 50%, waiting for a higher close is not much help.

Reversal, continuation rates. Price breaks out downward most often.

Yearly range reversals. Continuations occur frequently when price breaks out within a third of the yearly low.

Table 98.6 shows performance indicators that can give hints as to how your stock will behave after the breakout from this candle pattern.

Confirmation, performance. Use the opening gap confirmation method to trade this candle. That means waiting for price to gap open lower the next day before taking a position in the stock.

Moving average. Candles with breakouts below the 50-day moving average work better than do those with breakouts above the moving average.

Closing position. The best performance comes from candles when the closing price is within a third of the low, and it works in all cases except bull market/up breakouts. Those do better when the close is in the middle of the candle. For this measure, use only the last candle line in the pattern and separate the line into thirds.

Table 98.5
Reversal Rates

Description	Bull Market	Bear Market
Closing price confirmation reversal rate	55%	52%
Candle color confirmation reversal rate	54%	51%
Opening gap confirmation reversal rate	41%	36%
Reversal: trend down, breakout up	32%	31%
Continuation: trend down, breakout down	68%	69%
Percentage of reversals (R)/continuations (C) for each 12-month low (L), middle (M), or high (H)	L 25% R/75% C, M 29% R/71% C, H 43% R/57% C	L 24% R/76% C, M 33% R/67% C, H 45% R/55% C

Table 98.6
Performance Indicators

Description	Bull Market, Up Breakout	Bear Market, Up Breakout	Bull Market, Down Breakout	Bear Market, Down Breakout
Closing price confirmation, performance	N/A	N/A	−5.95%	−10.89%
Candle color confirmation, performance	N/A	N/A	−6.31%	−11.44%
Opening gap confirmation, performance	N/A	N/A	−7.15%	−12.58%
Breakout above 50-day moving average, performance	6.84%	8.05%	−5.64%	−9.33%
Breakout below 50-day moving average, performance	7.04%	10.19%	−6.21%	−11.87%
Last candle: close in highest third, performance	6.85%	9.33%	−5.83%	−7.58%
Last candle: close in middle third, performance	7.34%	8.93%	−6.05%	−10.57%
Last candle: close in lowest third, performance	6.77%	9.50%	−6.12%	−12.27%

N/A means not applicable.

Sample Trade

Figure 98.2 shows a trade that Rusty made. Price formed a double top created by the long peak at A and the sharper one at B. You could also call this a triple top, but Rusty didn't see it that way at first.

Along the bottom, he drew a neckline CD and extended it to E. A neckline is used most often for head-and-shoulders patterns, but in this case, it had absolutely no benefit over traditional methods. Go figure. The traditional method would be to sell once price closed below the lowest low in the double or triple top. Theoretically, the up-sloping neckline could get you out sooner, but the price difference between the two methods is negligible here.

Price formed two black gapping candles that ended at E. This told him that price was likely to continue lower, so the next day he sold his holdings in the stock at the open. As the chart shows, selling then was a timely move.

For Best Performance

The following list offers tips and observations to help choose candles that perform well. Consult the associated table for more information.

Figure 98.2 Two black gapping candles lead to a timely sale.

- Use the identification guidelines to help select the pattern—Table 98.1.
- Candles within a third of the yearly low perform best—Table 98.2.
- Select tall candles—Table 98.3.
- Use the measure rule to predict a price target—Table 98.3.
- Candles with tall upper or lower shadows outperform—Table 98.3.
- Volume gives performance clues—Table 98.4.
- Trade this candle pattern when the primary price trend is downward; avoid trading it in an uptrend—Trading Tactics discussion.
- The candle frequently breaks out downward—Table 98.5.
- Patterns within a third of the yearly low tend to act as continuations most often—Table 98.5.
- Opening gap confirmation works best—Table 98.6.
- Breakouts below the 50-day moving average lead to the best performance—Table 98.6.

99

Two Crows

Behavior and Rank

Theoretical: Bearish reversal.

Actual bull market: Bearish reversal 54% of the time (ranking 40).

Actual bear market: Bearish reversal 58% of the time (ranking 31).

Frequency: 64th out of 103.

Overall performance over time: 61st out of 103.

Two crows is an interesting name for a *three*-candle pattern. Of course, when you consider candle color, then it all makes sense (or cents). Looking for this candle pattern, I sometimes found it perched atop a minor high, waiting for price to drop. The decline after those tops was breathtaking; just don't assume it will occur every time—it won't. In fact, price reverses just 54% of the time in a bull market. That ranks 40, where 1 is best out of 103 candles. Overall performance is 61, meaning it's a mediocre performer.

Pattern psychology begins with the bulls staging an advance. A tall white candle is not a flag of surrender, but it turns out that way. Price gaps higher the next day; however, the bears appear and force price to print a black candle. They accept the surrender of the bulls and the next day the bears are at it again, slowly at first when price opens little changed from the prior day, but more aggressively as time passes. They push price down into the body of the first candle. What remains at the close is a rainbow reversal from white to black and up to down.

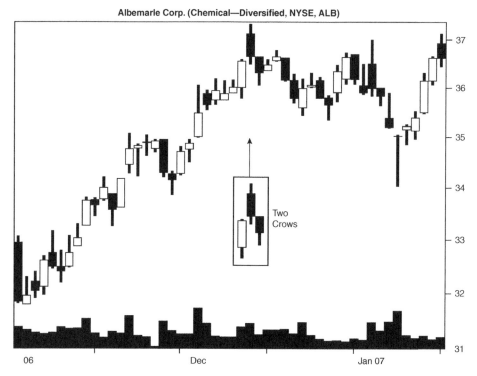

Figure 99.1 Two crows forms a minor high that sees price tumble.

Identification Guidelines

Figure 99.1 shows an example of the two crows pattern. Price forms a tall white candle at the start of the pattern and after a price advance. Then price gaps higher and forms a black candle. The next day, another black candle forms and it's supposed to straddle the prior two candles, closing the gap. This one does, but it would look nicer if its price opened a bit higher into the middle candle instead of where it does. It opens at the prior close and that's fine—it's just not a perfect example.

Table 99.1 lists identification guidelines. Look for a tall white candle in an upward price trend. Following that, price jumps upward, leaving a gap between the two bodies. Don't worry about overlapping shadows. The next day, another black candle covers the gap by opening within the body of the first black candle and closing within the body of the white candle.

Statistics

Table 99.2 shows general statistics.

Number found. Two crows are rare. I found 1,534 hiding in the trees during a search of over 4.7 million candles, and most came from a bull market.

Table 99.1
Identification Guidelines

Characteristic	Discussion
Number of candle lines	Three.
Price trend	Upward leading to the start of the candle pattern.
First day	A tall white candle.
Second day	A black candle with a body that gaps above the prior body.
Third day	A black candle that opens within the prior body and closes within the white candle's body (first day).

Reversal or continuation performance. Performance is best in a bear market. You might think it's because of the low sample count, but other candle types show similar results.

S&P performance. The candle beats the S&P 500 index in all market conditions and breakout directions.

Table 99.2
General Statistics

Description	Bull Market, Up Breakout	Bear Market, Up Breakout	Bull Market, Down Breakout	Bear Market, Down Breakout
Number found	593	100	705	136
Reversal (R), continuation (C) performance	6.39% C	6.58% C	−6.29% R	−9.19% R
Standard & Poor's 500 change	1.53%	0.73%	−0.67%	−1.85%
Candle end to breakout (median, days)	6	4	4	4
Candle end to trend end (median, days)	8	7	8	11
Number of breakouts near the 12-month low (L), middle (M), or high (H)	L 76, M 134, H 315	L 26, M 19, H 55	L 135, M 178, H 326	L 52, M 37, H 46
Percentage move for each 12-month period	L 6.81%, M 6.66%, H 6.04%	L 7.21%, M 5.57%, H 6.66%	L −7.03%, M −5.46%, H −6.84%	L −10.95%, M −7.86%, H −8.76%
Candle end + 1 day	0.99%	1.76%	−0.87%	−1.16%
Candle end + 3 days	2.52%	2.85%	−2.15%	−2.33%
Candle end + 5 days	3.28%	2.06%	−2.51%	−3.12%
Candle end + 10 days	4.30%	1.37%	−2.57%	−4.84%
10-day performance rank	26	87	43	34

Candle end to breakout. It takes about four days for price to reach the breakout. Upward breakouts take slightly longer because they have to climb up the candle before breaking out.

Candle end to trend end. It takes between 7 and 11 days to reach the trend end.

Yearly position, performance. Separating the candles into where they occur in the yearly price range shows that many occur within a third of the yearly high. Bear markets with downward breakouts are the one exception. Those occur more frequently near the yearly low, and that's also where you'll find the best performance.

Performance over time. The two crows candle pattern is not a robust performer. After three days in a bear market with an upward breakout, performance begins to deteriorate. A robust candle would show increasing numbers in all categories.

The performance rank confirms this analysis when compared to the performance of other candles. A rank of 1 is best out of 103 candles.

Table 99.3 shows height statistics.

Candle height. Tall candles outperform. To determine whether the candle is short or tall, compute its height from highest high to lowest low price in the candle pattern and divide by the breakout price. If the result is higher than the median, then you have a tall candle; otherwise it's short.

Table 99.3
Height Statistics

Description	Bull Market, Up Breakout	Bear Market, Up Breakout	Bull Market, Down Breakout	Bear Market, Down Breakout
Median candle height as a percentage of breakout price	5.10%	6.06%	5.02%	6.45%
Short candle, performance	5.01%	5.87%	−4.80%	−7.43%
Tall candle, performance	8.57%	7.26%	−8.55%	−11.31%
Percentage meeting price target (measure rule)	47%	49%	44%	54%
Median upper shadow as a percentage of breakout price	0.20%	0.30%	0.16%	0.13%
Short upper shadow, performance	5.59%	6.59%	−5.52%	−8.59%
Tall upper shadow, performance	7.11%	6.56%	−6.94%	−9.67%
Median lower shadow as a percentage of breakout price	0.52%	0.52%	0.47%	0.64%
Short lower shadow, performance	5.57%	5.96%	−5.35%	−8.22%
Tall lower shadow, performance	7.24%	7.14%	−7.37%	−10.20%

Glen sees a two crows pattern with a high of 97 and a low of 94. Is the candle short or tall? The height is 97 – 94, or 3, so the measure would be 3/97, or 3.1%. If the breakout is upward in a bull market, the candle is short. In fact, it's short under any conditions.

Measure rule. Use the measure rule to help predict how far price will rise or fall. Compute the height of the candle pattern and multiply it by the appropriate percentage shown in the table; then apply it to the breakout price.

What are the price targets for Glen's candle? The upward target would be (3 × 47%) + 97, or 98.41, and the downward target would be 94 – (3 × 44%), or 92.68. This assumes a bull market.

Shadows. The table's results pertain to the last candle line in the pattern. To determine whether the shadow is short or tall, compute the height of the shadow and divide by the breakout price. Compare the result to the median in the table. Tall shadows have a percentage higher than the median.

Upper shadow performance. Tall upper shadows mean better performance in all cases except for bear market/up breakouts, but even there the numbers are close.

Lower shadow performance. Tall lower shadows suggest better postbreakout performance across the board.

Table 99.4 shows volume statistics.

Candle volume trend. Candles with falling volume work best in all categories except bull market/down breakouts. Those do better with rising volume.

Average candle volume. Candles with below-average volume tend to outperform in bull markets, and those with above-average volume do best in bear markets.

Breakout volume. Heavy breakout volume suggests better postbreakout performance in every category.

Table 99.4
Volume Statistics

Description	Bull Market, Up Breakout	Bear Market, Up Breakout	Bull Market, Down Breakout	Bear Market, Down Breakout
Rising candle volume, performance	6.05%	5.98%	−7.34%	−6.74%
Falling candle volume, performance	6.53%	6.83%	−5.78%	−10.17%
Above-average candle volume, performance	6.03%	6.73%	−5.94%	−9.44%
Below-average candle volume, performance	6.79%	6.40%	−6.60%	−8.92%
Heavy breakout volume, performance	6.88%	7.18%	−6.77%	−9.39%
Light breakout volume, performance	5.70%	5.98%	−5.94%	−9.04%

Trading Tactics

For the largest decline, trade this candle pattern when the primary price trend is downward. The two crows will appear as a minor high—an upward retracement—in the downtrend. Avoid depending on this reversing the primary uptrend, especially if the breakout is upward. In all circumstances, close out a short position after an upward breakout.

I split trading tactics into two basic studies, one concerning reversal rates and the other concerning performance. Of the two, reversal rates are more important, because it's better to trade in the direction of the trend and let price run as far as it can.

Table 99.5 gives tips to find the trend direction.

Confirmation reversal rates. To help verify that price has reversed, wait for a lower close the next day. That boosts the reversal rate to at least 73%.

Reversal, continuation rates. Two crows break out downward most often.

Yearly range reversals. Candles with breakouts within a third of the yearly low tend to act as reversals most often.

Table 99.6 shows performance indicators that can give hints as to how your stock will behave after the breakout from this candle pattern.

Confirmation, performance. In a bull market, the opening gap method results in the best performance. That means trading the candle if price gaps open lower a day after the candle ends. In a bear market, candle color works best. In that setup, you wait for a black candle to appear the next day and then trade.

Moving average. Candles with breakouts above the 50-day moving average work better than do those below the moving average. This is opposite

Table 99.5
Reversal Rates

Description	Bull Market	Bear Market
Closing price confirmation reversal rate	73%	81%
Candle color confirmation reversal rate	70%	79%
Opening gap confirmation reversal rate	63%	67%
Reversal rate: trend up, breakout down	54%	58%
Continuation rate: trend up, breakout up	46%	42%
Percentage of reversals (R)/continuations (C) for each 12-month low (L), middle (M), or high (H)	L 64% R/36% C, M 57% R/43% C, H 51% R/49% C	L* 67% R/33% C, M* 66% R/34% C, H 46% R/54% C

*Fewer than 30 samples.

Table 99.6
Performance Indicators

Description	Bull Market, Up Breakout	Bear Market, Up Breakout	Bull Market, Down Breakout	Bear Market, Down Breakout
Closing price confirmation, performance	N/A	N/A	−7.20%	−10.92%
Candle color confirmation, performance	N/A	N/A	−7.76%	−11.49%
Opening gap confirmation, performance	N/A	N/A	−7.86%	−10.14%
Breakout above 50-day moving average, performance	6.42%	6.99%	−6.57%	−9.67%
Breakout below 50-day moving average, performance	6.33%	3.65%*	−5.87%	−8.14%
Last candle: close in highest third, performance	3.90%*	5.38%*	−3.72%*	−3.38%*
Last candle: close in middle third, performance	6.66%	5.93%	−7.18%	−7.67%
Last candle: close in lowest third, performance	6.38%	6.95%	−6.00%	−9.99%

N/A means not applicable.
*Fewer than 30 samples.

to what we see for other candle types, so I would be cautious about believing the results.

Closing position. The last candle with a close in the middle third of the price bar gives better performance in bull markets. Bear markets do better if the close is near the candle's low.

Sample Trade

Glen owned the stock shown in Figure 99.2. The stock started an advance at A. As price climbed, so did his nervousness. When should he sell? That was a question he thought about each night.

The high at B came and went, and the drop down from that high increased his apprehension. He vowed to leave the highway at the first exit. When the two crows appeared at C, he knew it was time to sell. Price nearly matched the high at B and with a bearish reversal showing, the up move was over. Or so he believed.

When the stock opened slightly higher the next day, he sold the stock. Not only did this cure his anxiety, but he also sold near the top. In this case, that turned out to be the smart play because price dropped to 84 and change within the next two months, as the chart shows.

Boeing Company (Aerospace/Defense, NYSE, BA)

Figure 99.2 Two crows signal a trend change.

For Best Performance

The following list offers tips and observations to help choose candles that perform well. Consult the associated table for more information.

- Use the identification guidelines to help select the pattern—Table 99.1.
- Candles within a third of the yearly low perform best—Table 99.2.
- Select tall candles—Table 99.3.
- Use the measure rule to predict a price target—Table 99.3.
- Candles with tall lower shadows outperform—Table 99.3.
- Volume gives performance clues—Table 99.4.
- Trade this candle when the primary trend is downward—Trading Tactics discussion.
- The candle breaks out downward most often—Table 99.5.
- Patterns within a third of the yearly low frequently act as reversals—Table 99.5.
- Opening gap confirmation works best in a bull market—Table 99.6.

100

Unique Three-River Bottom

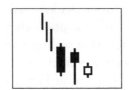

Behavior and Rank

Theoretical: Bullish reversal.
Actual bull market: Bearish continuation 60% of the time (ranking 22).
Actual bear market: Bearish continuation 57% of the time (ranking 28).
Frequency: 89th out of 103.
Overall performance over time: 60th out of 103.

The unique three-river bottom didn't seem like a candle pattern with a lot of rules that would limit its appearance, but I was wrong. It is rare, as the sample count suggests. I found 80 examples out of over 4.7 million candle lines.

The ranking shows that it acts as a bearish continuation pattern more often instead of the theoretical bullish reversal. When compared to other candles in a bull market, it ranks 22 out of 103, with 1 being best. Overall performance is a dismal 60. There's nothing exciting here, especially since it's so rare.

The psychology behind development of the pattern begins with the bears in control of a falling market. Price makes a tall black candle and the bulls scatter. The next day sees price forced down by additional selling pressure, but by day's end price has risen to close well above the low. The bears are scratching their heads, wondering if this is the start of a new bullish attack.

The next day, a small white candle prints on the chart. The bulls have returned to the markets and have successfully fought off the bears. The theory for the pattern says that if price rises another day, then a trend reversal has arrived. The statistics confirm that, but the reversal rate rises to just 57% in a bull market. That doesn't sound like much to get excited about.

Identification Guidelines

Figure 100.1 shows how the unique three-river bottom is supposed to work. Price turns downward at A and bottoms at B. The day before B, the unique three-river bottom starts with a tall black candle followed by a small black body with a long lower shadow. The lower shadow makes a new low. The next day sees the first hint of a reversal with a white body printing on the chart. After that, price zips higher like Spider-Man scaling a skyscraper.

Table 100.1 lists identification guidelines. For a three-day candle, this one is complicated. It begins in a downward price trend that forms a tall black candle. The next day is also a black day, but the body is nestled inside the price range of the prior black body. Except for the body color, it's a harami configuration. The low of the second black candle is below the low of the first black candle. The last day is a short white candle with a body below the body

Figure 100.1 A unique three-river bottom candlestick formation appears at a turning point.

Table 100.1
Identification Guidelines

Characteristic	Discussion
Number of candle lines	Three.
Price trend	Downward leading to the start of the candle pattern.
First day	A tall-bodied black candle.
Second day	The black body is inside the prior body, but the low price (long lower shadow) is below the prior day's low.
Third day	A short-bodied white candle, which is below the body of the prior day.

of the second day. If these rules make little sense, don't worry about it. You probably won't see this pattern many times during your life.

Statistics

The sample size for this candle pattern is very small, so any conclusions are likely to change.

Table 100.2 shows general statistics.

Number found. The unique three-river bottom appears most often in a bear market, according to my standard database. I found 80 of them.

Reversal or continuation performance. Patterns in a bear market perform better than do those in a bull market. Also, reversals outperform continuation patterns.

S&P performance. The unique three-river bottom beats the performance of the S&P 500 index in all categories.

Candle end to breakout. It takes between three and seven days for price to reach the breakout. The breakout is a close either above the top of the pattern or below the bottom.

Candle end to trend end. Most times, it takes about a week to reach the trend end. Bull market/up breakouts take longer: 11 days.

Yearly position, performance. Most often (except for bull market/up breakouts), the candle forms near the yearly low. However, the location of the best performance is mixed. Bear market/up breakouts and bull market/down breakouts do best when the breakout is within a third of the yearly low. Bull market/up breakouts and bear market/down breakouts show the best candle performance when the patterns are in the middle of the yearly price range. (Most other candle types show the best performance when the breakout is near the yearly low.)

Performance over time. The performance of price over time after a unique three-river bottom is weak. Bear market/up breakouts run into trouble

Table 100.2
General Statistics

Description	Bull Market, Up Breakout	Bear Market, Up Breakout*	Bull Market, Down Breakout	Bear Market, Down Breakout*
Number found	23	10	34	13
Reversal (R), continuation (C) performance	6.94% R	8.08% R	−5.45% C	−7.57% C
Standard & Poor's 500 change	1.50%	1.31%	−1.42%	−3.09%
Candle end to breakout (median, days)	7	3	5	4
Candle end to trend end (median, days)	11	6	6	7
Number of breakouts near the 12-month low (L), middle (M), or high (H)	L 7, M 9, H 7	L 4, M 4, H 2	L 14, M 9, H 10	L 7, M 3, H 3
Percentage move for each 12-month period	L 7.88%, M 9.03%, H 2.16%	L 12.60%, M 7.45%, H 5.09%	L −6.25%, M −5.78%, H −4.73%	L −7.68%, M −11.63%, H −3.78%
Candle end + 1 day	1.39%	2.46%	−0.45%	−2.95%
Candle end + 3 days	2.21%	3.93%	−0.57%	−3.40%
Candle end + 5 days	2.56%	3.14%	−1.64%	−1.55%
Candle end + 10 days	3.22%	1.59%	−2.13%	−5.60%
10-day performance rank	52	81	57	25

*Fewer than 30 samples.

after three days, and bear market/down breakouts suffer from days 3 to 5 before recovering.

When compared to other candles, the performance ranges from a very good rank of 25 to a lousy 81. A rank of 1 is best out of 103 candles.

Table 100.3 shows height statistics.

Candle height. Tall candles outperform. To determine whether the candle is short or tall, compute its height from highest high to lowest low price in the candle pattern and divide by the breakout price. If the result is higher than the median, then you have a tall candle; otherwise it's short.

Gwen sees a unique three-river bottom with a high of 76 and a low of 75. Is the candle short or tall? The candle height is 76 − 75, or 1. In a bull market with a downward breakout, the measure would be 1/75, or 1.3%, which means the candle is short.

Measure rule. Use the measure rule to help predict how far price will rise or fall. Compute the height of the candle pattern and multiply it by the appropriate percentage shown in the table; then apply it to the breakout price.

Table 100.3
Height Statistics*

Description	Bull Market, Up Breakout	Bear Market, Up Breakout	Bull Market, Down Breakout	Bear Market, Down Breakout
Median candle height as a percentage of breakout price	3.56%	5.38%	4.12%	6.52%
Short candle, performance	6.72%	6.27%	−3.89%	−7.02%
Tall candle, performance	7.75%	9.54%	−8.46%	−8.38%
Percentage meeting price target (measure rule)	52%	50%	41%	38%
Median upper shadow as a percentage of breakout price	1.19%	1.18%	1.01%	1.94%
Short upper shadow, performance	6.83%	7.56%	−4.73%	−7.36%
Tall upper shadow, performance	7.28%	8.49%	−6.51%	−7.82%
Median lower shadow as a percentage of breakout price	0.36%	0.37%	0.32%	0.56%
Short lower shadow, performance	8.57%	8.21%	−5.72%	−10.15%
Tall lower shadow, performance	3.31%	7.99%	−5.16%	−4.66%

*Fewer than 30 samples.

What are the price targets for Gwen's candle? The upward target would be (1 × 52%) + 76, or 76.52, and the downward target would be 75 − (1 × 41%), or 74.59.

Shadows. The table's results pertain to the last candle line in the pattern. To determine whether the shadow is short or tall, compute the height of the shadow and divide by the breakout price. Compare the result to the median in the table. Tall shadows have a percentage higher than the median.

Upper shadow performance. Candles with tall upper shadows perform better than do those with short shadows.

Lower shadow performance. Candles with short lower shadows work better, and that's odd. Usually tall lower shadows lead to better performance for most candle types.

Table 100.4 shows volume statistics.

Candle volume trend. Candles with falling volume perform better than do those with rising volume except for candles in bear markets with downward breakouts. Those do better with rising volume.

Average candle volume. Candles in a bull market do better with below-average candle volume, and those in a bear market do better with above-average volume.

Breakout volume. Heavy breakout volume suggests better postbreakout performance in all cases.

Table 100.4
Volume Statistics*

Description	Bull Market, Up Breakout	Bear Market, Up Breakout	Bull Market, Down Breakout	Bear Market, Down Breakout
Rising candle volume, performance	4.67%	7.85%	−5.28%	−11.81%
Falling candle volume, performance	7.59%	8.30%	−5.64%	−6.07%
Above-average candle volume, performance	4.25%	9.54%	−5.43%	−7.75%
Below-average candle volume, performance	8.06%	6.27%	−5.46%	−7.50%
Heavy breakout volume, performance	10.82%	10.59%	−6.03%	−9.49%
Light breakout volume, performance	6.19%	3.41%	−4.91%	−6.98%

*Fewer than 30 samples.

Trading Tactics

If you expect price to break out downward, then trade this one when the primary trend is also downward. A breakout upward might lead to a lasting reversal, but those are rare. Most unique three-river bottoms break out downward and lead to an extended decline.

I split trading tactics into two basic studies, one concerning reversal rates and the other concerning performance. Of the two, reversal rates are more important, because it's better to trade in the direction of the trend and let price run as far as it can.

Table 100.5 gives tips to find the trend direction.

Confirmation reversal rates. To help verify an upward breakout or reversal, wait for a higher close the day after the candle pattern. That works 57% of the time in a bull market.

Table 100.5
Reversal Rates*

Description	Bull Market	Bear Market
Closing price confirmation reversal rate	57%	89%
Candle color confirmation reversal rate	57%	73%
Opening gap confirmation reversal rate	47%	38%
Reversal: trend down, breakout up	40%	43%
Continuation: trend down, breakout down	60%	57%
Percentage of reversals (R)/continuations (C) for each 12-month low (L), middle (M), or high (H)	L 33% R/67% C, M 50% R/50% C, H 41% R/59% C	L 36% R/64% C, M 57% R/43% C, H 40% R/60% C

*Fewer than 30 samples.

Table 100.6
Performance Indicators*

Description	Bull Market, Up Breakout	Bear Market, Up Breakout	Bull Market, Down Breakout	Bear Market, Down Breakout
Closing price confirmation, performance	8.06%	8.56%	N/A	N/A
Candle color confirmation, performance	7.95%	7.62%	N/A	N/A
Opening gap confirmation, performance	8.21%	10.63%	N/A	N/A
Breakout above 50-day moving average, performance	3.36%	6.80%	−5.81%	−4.65%
Breakout below 50-day moving average, performance	8.20%	9.60%	−5.31%	−8.27%
Last candle: close in highest third, performance	0.00%	4.66%	−8.40%	−3.87%
Last candle: close in middle third, performance	4.30%	8.76%	−4.33%	−10.21%
Last candle: close in lowest third, performance	8.43%	4.37%	−6.73%	−2.89%

N/A means not applicable.
*Fewer than 30 samples.

Reversal, continuation rates. The candle breaks out downward 60% of the time in a bull market.

Yearly range reversals. Continuations occur most often when the breakout is within a third of the yearly low.

Table 100.6 shows performance indicators that can give hints as to how your stock will behave after the breakout from this candle pattern.

Confirmation, performance. Use the opening gap confirmation method as a trading signal for the best performance. That means waiting for price to gap higher the day after the candle ends before trading.

Moving average. Candle patterns with breakouts below the 50-day moving average work best under most conditions except for bull market/down breakouts. Those do better if the breakout is above the moving average.

Closing position. The closing price shows no consistent trend to help improve performance. None of the 23 samples found in a bull market with an upward breakout had price close in the upper third of the last candle line.

Sample Trade

Gwen wanted to own stock in the utility shown in Figure 100.2. She watched price rise from the low at A to the high at B and then begin a slow decline. As price declined each day, she asked herself if today price would bottom.

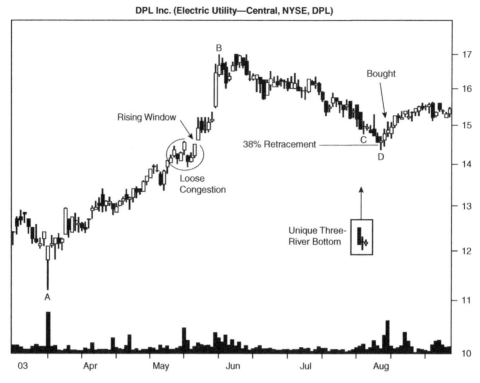

DPL Inc. (Electric Utility—Central, NYSE, DPL)

Figure 100.2   A unique three-river bottom suggests waiting to buy the stock.

When the unique three-river bottom appeared (surrounding C), she was sure that price had more digging to do. Why? Because the candle pattern acts as a continuation more often than a reversal. She decided not to buy yet, and price reinforced her decision the next day when it gapped open lower.

At D, she wondered if price was going to change trend. It wasn't a southern doji because the opening and closing prices were four cents apart, but it sure looked like one. When price formed a white candle the next day, she grew more confident. Looking to the left of D, she saw the rising window supported by a loose price congestion area (circled).

She drew the 38% Fibonacci retracement of the AB move on the chart and saw that price touched the line at D. The retracement line is often a support zone, so that was the last piece of the puzzle she needed to form a buy opinion. At the open the next day, she bought the stock.

For Best Performance

The following list offers tips and observations to help choose candles that perform well. Consult the associated table for more information.

- Use the identification guidelines to help select the pattern—Table 100.1.
- Candles within a third of the yearly low perform best in a bull market after a downward breakout—Table 100.2.
- Select tall candles—Table 100.3.
- Use the measure rule to predict a price target—Table 100.3.
- Candles with tall upper shadows outperform—Table 100.3.
- Volume gives performance clues—Table 100.4.
- If expecting a downward breakout, then trade this candle pattern in a primary downtrend—Trading Tactics discussion.
- The candle breaks out downward most often—Table 100.5.
- Patterns within a third of the yearly low frequently act as continuations—Table 100.5.
- Opening gap confirmation works best—Table 100.6.

101

Upside Gap
Three Methods

Behavior and Rank

Theoretical: Bullish continuation.

Actual bull market: Bearish reversal 59% of the time (ranking 32).

Actual bear market: Bearish reversal 72% of the time (ranking 9).

Frequency: 85th out of 103.

Overall performance over time: 27th out of 103.

I'm scratching my head over this candlestick pattern. It's supposed to act as a continuation pattern—and it does, but only 41% of the time in a bull market. My tests show that its primary function is as a reversal. If the primary price trend is upward, then don't expect price to drop far after the upside gap three methods completes.

A ranking of 32 shows how this candle stacks up with others as a bearish reversal in a bull market. A rank of 1 is best out of 103 candles. The frequency rank of 85 means this candle is rare, and that may account for the difference of opinion on its behavior. An overall performance rank of 27 suggests good performance when compared to other candles.

If the primary trend is downward, then the candle pattern appears as part of an upward retracement. Those don't happen that often, though. If price then breaks out upward from the candle pattern, then it might be a lasting move. That's the time to consider going long.

The psychology behind the pattern begins with bullish buying demand that forces price higher. Two tall white candles appear with a gap between them as if saying, "Sell me everything you have!" and "When can I buy more?" That's when the bears show up at the counter with a dozen 18-wheelers full of shares to sell. Price drops the next day and forms a black candle. The downtrend will continue until the big rigs are empty.

Identification Guidelines

Figure 101.1 shows a downward primary price trend. At A, the secondary trend reverses and leads to the three methods candle. Price confirms the candle pattern as a reversal when it closes below the lowest low in the pattern. That happens at C, below the horizontal line marking the lowest low. After that, price resumes the decline, finally bottoming at 21 about two months later (not shown).

Table 101.1 lists identification guidelines. In an uptrend, look for two tall white candles and a gap between them. The shadows should not overlap and

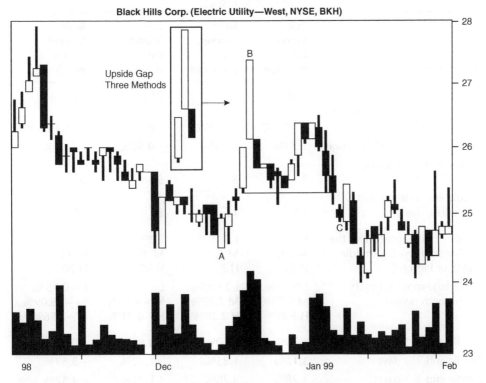

Figure 101.1 An upside gap three methods candle formation shows a downward breakout.

Table 101.1
Identification Guidelines

Characteristic	Discussion
Number of candle lines	Three.
Price trend	Upward leading to the start of the candle pattern.
Days 1 and 2	Two tall white candles with a gap between them, even between the shadows.
Last day	A black candle fills the gap.

fill the gap. The next day, a black candle opens within the body of the prior white candle and closes within the body of the first white candle. This closes the gap between the first two candles.

Statistics

Table 101.2 shows general statistics.

Table 101.2
General Statistics

Description	Bull Market, Up Breakout	Bear Market, Up Breakout*	Bull Market, Down Breakout	Bear Market, Down Breakout
Number found	148	17	215	44
Reversal (R), continuation (C) performance	6.46% C	5.62% C	−6.04% R	−11.14% R
Standard & Poor's 500 change	1.73%	0.75%	−0.58%	−2.61%
Candle end to breakout (median, days)	8	8	5	5
Candle end to trend end (median, days)	12	11	8	10
Number of breakouts near the 12-month low (L), middle (M), or high (H)	L 14, M 29, H 80	L 2, M 6, H 8	L 39, M 40, H 90	L 12, M 11, H 20
Percentage move for each 12-month period	L 9.71%, M 6.75%, H 5.97%	L 15.85%, M 7.22%, H 3.20%	L −5.91%, M −4.35%, H −6.41%	L −9.15%, M −18.09%, H −7.56%
Candle end + 1 day	1.38%	1.00%	−0.86%	−0.88%
Candle end + 3 days	3.17%	1.85%	−1.70%	−3.89%
Candle end + 5 days	3.28%	3.28%	−1.71%	−4.52%
Candle end + 10 days	4.92%	4.68%	−2.57%	−4.18%
10-day performance rank	12	36	45	47

*Fewer than 30 samples.

Number found. This candle pattern is rare. Out of over 4.7 million, I found just 424. Prorating the standard database means this pattern appears most often in a bear market.

Reversal or continuation performance. This candle pattern is one in which the bull market performance beats at least one of the bear market numbers. You can blame the low sample count, but I prefer to blame my next-door neighbor.

S&P performance. The upside gap three methods pattern beats the S&P 500 index in all categories.

Candle end to breakout. A breakout occurs when price closes either above the top of the candle pattern or below the bottom.

Downward breakouts take less time to occur than upward ones. This makes sense because the closing price is nearer the bottom of the candle than the top.

Candle end to trend end. Upward breakouts take longer to reach the trend end than downward breakouts. This is probably due to the downtrend already in progress. An upward breakout would start a new trend, which would take longer to reach the trend end.

Yearly position, performance. Upside gap three methods formations appear most often within a third of the yearly high. However, performance is best for upward breakouts when they occur within a third of the yearly low. Downward breakouts show mixed performance locations.

Performance over time. Houston, we have a problem and it appears in the last column, bear market/down breakout, from days 5 to 10. Performance decreases over that period. Other than that, the results are quite good.

According to the performance rank, where 1 is best out of 103 candles, upward breakouts do better than downward ones. The rank is a comparison of performance over time to other candle types, by the way.

Table 101.3 shows height statistics.

Candle height. Tall candles outperform. To determine whether the candle is short or tall, compute its height from highest high to lowest low price in the candle pattern and divide by the breakout price. If the result is higher than the median, then you have a tall candle; otherwise it's short.

Arthur sees an upside gap three methods candle with a high of 84 and a low of 80. Is the candle short or tall? The height is 84 – 80, or 4, so the measure in a bull market with a downward breakout would be 4/80, or 5%. The candle is short.

Measure rule. Use the measure rule to help predict how far price will rise or fall. Compute the height of the candle pattern and multiply it by the appropriate percentage shown in the table; then apply it to the breakout price.

What are Arthur's price targets for his candle? The upward target would be (4 × 39%) + 84, or 85.56, and the downward target would be 80 – (4 × 34%), or 78.64.

Table 101.3
Height Statistics

Description	Bull Market, Up Breakout	Bear Market, Up Breakout*	Bull Market, Down Breakout	Bear Market, Down Breakout
Median candle height as a percentage of breakout price	6.14%	4.94%	5.73%	8.63%
Short candle, performance	4.96%	2.76%	−4.86%	−8.02%
Tall candle, performance	8.22%	8.70%	−7.94%	−13.73%
Percentage meeting price target (measure rule)	39%	35%	34%	32%
Median upper shadow as a percentage of breakout price	0.00%	0.27%	0.02%	0.19%
Short upper shadow, performance	5.34%	7.11%	−5.77%	−8.07%
Tall upper shadow, performance	7.51%	4.48%	−6.30%	−13.27%
Median lower shadow as a percentage of breakout price	0.27%	0.32%	0.20%	0.49%
Short lower shadow, performance	6.28%	3.07%	−5.59%	−8.95%
Tall lower shadow, performance	6.58%	9.27%	−6.48%	−12.75%

*Fewer than 30 samples.

Shadows. The table's results pertain to the last candle line in the pattern. To determine whether the shadow is short or tall, compute the height of the shadow and divide by the breakout price. Compare the result to the median in the table. Tall shadows have a percentage higher than the median.

Upper shadow performance. A zero median just means that many candles do not have upper shadows.

Tall upper shadows mean better performance in all cases except bear market/up breakouts. Those perform better with short shadows, but that result may be due to the low sample count.

Lower shadow performance. Candles with tall lower shadows perform better than do those with short shadows.

Table 101.4 shows volume statistics.

Candle volume trend. Candles with a rising volume trend perform better than do those with a falling trend in all cases except for bear market/up breakouts.

Average candle volume. Candles with upward breakouts perform best with below-average candle volume, and those with downward breakouts do better when the upside gap three methods pattern has above-average volume.

Breakout volume. Heavy breakout volume results in the best postbreakout performance in all situations except for bear market/down breakouts.

Table 101.4
Volume Statistics

Description	Bull Market, Up Breakout	Bear Market, Up Breakout*	Bull Market, Down Breakout	Bear Market, Down Breakout
Rising candle volume, performance	7.12%	4.13%	−6.10%	−12.04%
Falling candle volume, performance	5.79%	6.52%	−6.00%	−9.30%
Above-average candle volume, performance	5.98%	4.96%	−6.77%	−13.29%
Below-average candle volume, performance	7.18%	6.25%	−4.95%	−6.38%
Heavy breakout volume, performance	7.36%	7.40%	−6.82%	−9.96%
Light breakout volume, performance	4.95%	3.50%	−5.16%	−12.32%

*Fewer than 30 samples.

Those do better with light breakout volume, but it's probably due to the low sample count. Why do I say that? Because most other candle types show the best performance after heavy breakout volume.

Trading Tactics

If the three methods pattern appears in a primary uptrend, then expect the decline from a downward breakout to be short-lived.

I split trading tactics into two basic studies, one concerning reversal rates and the other concerning performance. Of the two, reversal rates are more important, because it's better to trade in the direction of the trend and let price run as far as it can.

Table 101.5 gives tips to find the trend direction.

Table 101.5
Reversal Rates

Description	Bull Market	Bear Market*
Closing price confirmation reversal rate	81%	94%
Candle color confirmation reversal rate	78%	88%
Opening gap confirmation reversal rate	70%	86%
Reversal rate: trend up, breakout down	59%	72%
Continuation rate: trend up, breakout up	41%	28%
Percentage of reversals (R)/continuations (C) for each 12-month low (L), middle (M), or high (H)	L 74% R/26% C, M 58% R/42% C, H 53% R/47% C	L 86% R/14% C, M 65% R/35% C, H 71% R/29% C

*Fewer than 30 samples.

Table 101.6
Performance Indicators

Description	Bull Market, Up Breakout	Bear Market, Up Breakout*	Bull Market, Down Breakout	Bear Market, Down Breakout
Closing price confirmation, performance	9.48%	13.32%	N/A	N/A
Candle color confirmation, performance	8.54%	18.12%	N/A	N/A
Opening gap confirmation, performance	8.68%	13.04%	N/A	N/A
Breakout above 50-day moving average, performance	6.37%	5.67%	−5.91%	−8.11%*
Breakout below 50-day moving average, performance	6.69%	2.13%	−6.34%	−15.03%*
Last candle: close in highest third, performance	0.00%	0.00%	0.00%	0.00%
Last candle: close in middle third, performance	5.49%*	0.00%	−4.24%*	−0.14%*
Last candle: close in lowest third, performance	6.58%	5.62%	−6.21%	−11.32%

N/A means not applicable.
*Fewer than 30 samples.

Confirmation reversal rates. If you wait for price to close lower the day after the upside gap three methods formation ends, then the candle acts as a trend reversal 81% of the time in a bull market.

Reversal, continuation rates. Price breaks out downward most often.

Yearly range reversals. Reversals occur frequently when the breakout is within a third of the yearly low.

Table 101.6 shows performance indicators that can give hints as to how your stock will behave after the breakout from this candle pattern.

Confirmation, performance. In a bull market, waiting for price to close upward the day after the upside gap three methods ends results in the best performance. In a bear market, waiting for a white candle the next day leads to better performance.

Moving average. Candles with breakouts below the 50-day moving average tend to reward candle players with better performance in all cases except for bear market/up breakouts.

Closing position. Since we are dealing with a black candle and few samples, the results are unreliable.

Sample Trade

Figure 101.2 shows the situation that confronted Arthur. Price made a smart move up from the September lows and peaked at A. At B, price attempted to

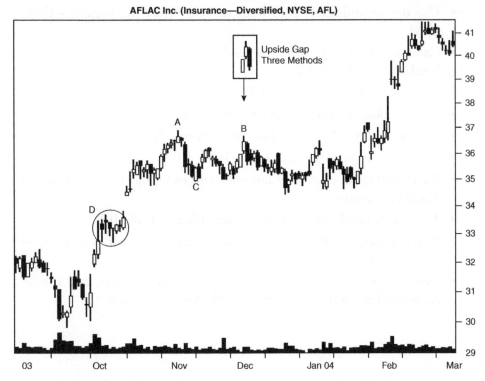

AFLAC Inc. (Insurance—Diversified, NYSE, AFL)

Figure 101.2 An upside gap three methods formation with a downward breakout does not lead to a large decline.

make a new high but failed. That was when Arthur noticed the upside gap three methods pattern. Three days later, price broke out downward from the pattern. The uptrend had reversed.

How far would price drop? If price closed below C (the lowest low between peaks A and B), then it would confirm a double top and price would likely plummet. The measure rule for the double top is the height subtracted from the lowest low in the chart pattern. To put numbers to it, that meant a decline to about 33.

The congestion zone circled near D would act as support, and that was also near 33. From the high at B, that meant a decline of 10%. Arthur decided to hold on to the stock and ride out the potential decline.

Price didn't drop to 33 as he had feared. Instead, it dropped only as low as 34.44 before rebounding. In this case, he had made the right choice to hold on to the stock.

For Best Performance

The following list offers tips and observations to help choose candles that perform well. Consult the associated table for more information.

- Use the identification guidelines to help select the pattern—Table 101.1.
- Candles within a third of the yearly low perform best after upward breakouts—Table 101.2.
- Select tall candles—Table 101.3.
- Use the measure rule to predict a price target—Table 101.3.
- Candles with tall lower shadows outperform—Table 101.3.
- Volume gives performance clues—Table 101.4.
- Price declines in a primary uptrend tend to be short-lived—Trading Tactics discussion.
- The candle breaks out downward most often—Table 101.5.
- Patterns within a third of the yearly low frequently act as reversals—Table 101.5.
- Closing price confirmation works best in bull markets, and candle color confirmation excels in bear markets—Table 101.6.

102

Upside Gap Two Crows

Behavior and Rank

Theoretical: Bearish reversal.

Actual bull market: Bullish continuation 60% of the time (ranking 21).

Actual bear market: Bullish continuation 53% of the time (ranking 41).

Frequency: 75th out of 103.

Overall performance over time: 74th out of 103.

This is another candle pattern that works as a bearish reversal in theory but performs differently in the real world. I found that the pattern behaves as a bullish continuation 60% of the time in a bull market. That places its rank at 21 out of 103 candles, where 1 is best. Unfortunately, the overall performance after the candle ends falls well short of its promise, ranking 74. Performance is best after a downward breakout, according to the comparison with other candles.

The psychology behind the pattern begins with buying demand pushing price upward. A tall white candle prints on the chart, and that's like a dog marking its territory: The bulls will defend their ground. The next day continues the uptrend, at least for a while, as price gaps upward at the open. However, by day's end, a black candle remains hovering like a storm cloud above the tall white candle.

The next day, a wider trading range develops as the bulls and bears fight for position. The action is more violent, encompassing the body of the prior day; but when trading ceases at the close of the market, a black candle remains. This candle also hovers above the body of the first day, suggesting that the bears—while wonderful at forming black candles—have not succeeded in driving price much lower from the day before. However, if the bears can force price to close lower the next day, then the candle pattern will likely be a reversal 56% of the time in a bull market.

Identification Guidelines

Figure 102.1 shows an example of the upside gap two crows pattern acting as a continuation pattern. Price trends upward starting at A and reaches the start of the candle formation two days before B (B signals the end of the candle formation). Price eventually breaks out upward at C before quickly heading back down.

You could say that since price trended upward into the pattern and left it moving horizontally, then the pattern acted as a reversal. That's true, but it's also not how I measure things. If you bought the stock based on the candle formation, then price moving horizontally means nothing to your bank account. It's only when price trends up or down that matters. Therefore, I count this candlestick example as a continuation pattern because price closes

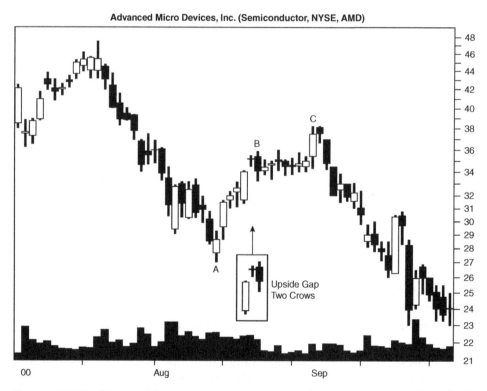

Figure 102.1   The upside gap two crows pattern changes an uptrend into horizontal price movement until a short-lived breakout appears about two weeks later.

Table 102.1
Identification Guidelines

Characteristic	Discussion
Number of candle lines	Three.
Price trend	Upward leading to the start of the candle pattern.
First day	A tall white candle.
Second day	A black candle with a body gapping above the prior candle's body.
Third day	A black candle that engulfs the body of the prior day. The close remains above the close of the first day.

above the top of the candle (breaking out upward), resuming the move upward from A, albeit briefly.

Table 102.1 lists identification guidelines. Look for a three-candle pattern in an uptrend. The first day is a tall white candle, and a black candle follows. I require that the bodies of the two candles show a gap between them, but the shadows can overlap. Allowing the shadow overlap means a significant increase in samples and more reliable results.

The last black candle engulfs the body of the prior black candle. That means the last day has a higher open but a lower close. The close must not drop below the close of the white candle, though. In other words, the gap between the black and white bodies remains intact.

Statistics

Table 102.2 shows general statistics.

Number found. I used four databases, and after a search of over 4.7 million candle lines, I found 757 upside gap two crows patterns. Most came from a bull market.

Reversal or continuation performance. Crows in a bear market perform better than do those from a bull market.

S&P performance. The upside gap two crows pattern beats the S&P 500 index over the same time periods.

Candle end to breakout. It takes between five and seven days for price to reach the breakout. A breakout occurs when price closes either above the top or below the bottom of the candle pattern.

Candle end to trend end. Measuring from the end of the candle formation to the end of the trend shows that it takes price a median of 7 to 10 days to complete the journey.

Yearly position, performance. Most candles appear within a third of the yearly high, the exception being bear market/down breakouts, but the numbers are close. Performance is best when the breakout is within a third of the yearly

Table 102.2
General Statistics

Description	Bull Market, Up Breakout	Bear Market, Up Breakout	Bull Market, Down Breakout	Bear Market, Down Breakout
Number found	386	63	253	55
Reversal (R), continuation (C) performance	6.60% C	7.63% C	−5.83% R	−8.27% R
Standard & Poor's 500 change	1.31%	0.30%	−0.85%	−2.74%
Candle end to breakout (median, days)	5	6	7	5
Candle end to trend end (median, days)	9	7	10	8
Number of breakouts near the 12-month low (L), middle (M), or high (H)	L 58, M 86, H 223	L 11, M 18, H 32	L 44, M 70, H 123	L 15, M 20, H 19
Percentage move for each 12-month period	L 7.60%, M 5.35%, H 6.73%	L 7.43%, M 8.55%, H 7.26%	L −6.20%, M −4.88%, H −6.14%	L −17.26%, M −7.11%, H −6.21%
Candle end + 1 day	0.75%	0.95%	−1.01%	−1.28%
Candle end + 3 days	1.67%	2.17%	−1.28%	−3.19%
Candle end + 5 days	2.26%	0.17%	−3.16%	−4.79%
Candle end + 10 days	2.94%	0.82%	−3.64%	−5.50%
10-day performance rank	56	93	22	26

low except in the case of bear market/up breakouts. Those do best when the breakout is in the middle of the yearly trading range.

Performance over time. Robust-performing candles show improving performance over time and under all conditions, but this one is not robust. The pattern stumbles badly from three to five days in bear market/up breakouts.

The performance rank concurs with that assessment. In fact, downward breakouts show better performance and rank than upward ones. A rank of 1 is best out of 103 candles.

Table 102.3 shows height statistics.

Candle height. Tall candles outperform. To determine whether the candle is short or tall, compute its height from highest high to lowest low price in the candle pattern and divide by the breakout price. If the result is higher than the median, then you have a tall candle; otherwise it's short.

Kevin sees an upside gap two crows pattern with a high of 40 and a low of 36. Is the candle short or tall? The height is 40 – 36, or 4, so the measure for bull market/up breakouts would be 4/40, or 10%. That represents a tall candle.

Table 102.3
Height Statistics

Description	Bull Market, Up Breakout	Bear Market, Up Breakout	Bull Market, Down Breakout	Bear Market, Down Breakout*
Median candle height as a percentage of breakout price	5.36%	7.64%	5.49%	7.45%
Short candle, performance	4.66%	6.02%	−4.53%	−6.45%
Tall candle, performance	9.79%	8.81%	−8.01%	−12.47%
Percentage meeting price target (measure rule)	45%	41%	38%	45%
Median upper shadow as a percentage of breakout price	0.27%	0.45%	0.20%	0.48%
Short upper shadow, performance	5.57%	7.82%	−4.79%	−8.02%
Tall upper shadow, performance	7.56%	7.45%	−6.76%	−8.67%
Median lower shadow as a percentage of breakout price	0.46%	0.67%	0.51%	0.91%
Short lower shadow, performance	5.17%	7.62%	−5.16%	−7.58%
Tall lower shadow, performance	8.30%	7.65%	−6.73%	−8.99%

*Fewer than 30 samples.

Measure rule. Use the measure rule to help predict how far price will rise or fall. Compute the height of the candle pattern and multiply it by the appropriate percentage shown in the table; then apply it to the breakout price.

What are Kevin's price targets for his candle? The upward target would be (4 × 45%) + 40, or 41.80, and the downward target would be 36 − (4 × 38%), or 34.48.

Shadows. The table's results pertain to the last candle line in the pattern. To determine whether the shadow is short or tall, compute the height of the shadow and divide by the breakout price. Compare the result to the median in the table. Tall shadows have a percentage higher than the median.

Upper shadow performance. Tall upper shadows perform better than short ones in all cases except bear market/up breakouts. Those do better with short shadows.

Lower shadow performance. Candles with tall lower shadows perform better than do those with short shadows.

Table 102.4 shows volume statistics.

Candle volume trend. Candles with a falling volume trend outperform those with a rising trend in all cases.

Average candle volume. Above-average volume works best for candles in the bear market/up breakout category. Below-average volume works best for the other three categories.

Table 102.4
Volume Statistics

Description	Bull Market, Up Breakout	Bear Market, Up Breakout	Bull Market, Down Breakout	Bear Market, Down Breakout
Rising candle volume, performance	5.79%	6.06%*	−5.78%	−7.39%*
Falling candle volume, performance	6.86%	8.19%	−5.85%	−8.39%
Above-average candle volume, performance	6.45%	7.66%	−5.38%	−7.85%
Below-average candle volume, performance	6.77%	7.58%*	−6.33%	−9.03%*
Heavy breakout volume, performance	6.71%	8.52%*	−6.82%	−7.57%*
Light breakout volume, performance	6.50%	7.03%	−4.92%	−8.97%

*Fewer than 30 samples.

Breakout volume. Candles with heavy breakout volume perform best post breakout in all cases except for bear market/down breakouts.

Trading Tactics

If the primary price trend is upward, then expect an upward breakout to carry price much higher. If the breakout is downward, then the decline is likely to be shallow.

If the primary trend is downward and price breaks out downward, then expect a long decline. Any adverse breakout from the intended direction should result in your closing out the trade quickly or suffering the consequences as price moves against your position. For the most profitable trades, trade in the direction of the prevailing, primary trend.

I split trading tactics into two basic studies, one concerning reversal rates and the other concerning performance. Of the two, reversal rates are more important, because it's better to trade in the direction of the trend and let price run as far as it can.

Table 102.5 gives tips to find the trend direction.

Confirmation reversal rates. To confirm that a reversal is under way, wait for a lower close the day after the upside gap two crows candle. That works 56% of the time in a bull market. That may not sound like much, but the candle acts as a *continuation* pattern 60% of the time, not as a reversal.

Reversal, continuation rates. Price breaks out upward most often.

Yearly range reversals. Candles within a third of the yearly high tend to act as continuation patterns most often.

Table 102.6 shows performance indicators that can give hints as to how your stock will behave after the breakout from this candle pattern.

Table 102.5
Reversal Rates

Description	Bull Market	Bear Market
Closing price confirmation reversal rate	56%	59%
Candle color confirmation reversal rate	51%	59%
Opening gap confirmation reversal rate	49%	51%
Reversal rate: trend up, breakout down	40%	47%
Continuation rate: trend up, breakout up	60%	53%
Percentage of reversals (R)/continuations (C) for each 12-month low (L), middle (M), or high (H)	L 43% R/57% C, M 45% R/55% C, H 36% R/64% C	L* 58% R/42% C, M* 53% R/47% C, H* 37% R/63% C

*Fewer than 30 samples.

Confirmation, performance. Use the opening gap confirmation method to increase your chances of a profitable trade. That means taking a position in the stock if price gaps open lower the next day (assuming you want to trade a reversal).

Moving average. Crows with breakouts below the 50-day moving average tend to perform better than do those above the average in all cases except for bear market/up breakouts.

Table 102.6
Performance Indicators

Description	Bull Market, Up Breakout	Bear Market, Up Breakout	Bull Market, Down Breakout	Bear Market, Down Breakout
Closing price confirmation, performance	N/A	N/A	−9.54%	−12.11%
Candle color confirmation, performance	N/A	N/A	−7.92%	−11.78%
Opening gap confirmation, performance	N/A	N/A	−9.97%	−12.83%
Breakout above 50-day moving average, performance	6.47%	7.73%	−5.56%	−6.72%
Breakout below 50-day moving average, performance	8.56%	5.84%*	−6.29%	−12.70%*
Last candle: close in highest third, performance	5.77%*	5.95%*	−8.99%*	−4.79%*
Last candle: close in middle third, performance	6.64%	8.27%*	−5.85%	−7.75%*
Last candle: close in lowest third, performance	6.63%	7.35%	−5.70%	−9.20%

N/A means not applicable.
*Fewer than 30 samples.

Closing position. The sample counts are too few to make the results reliable, and there's no consistent trend anyway.

Sample Trade

Figure 102.2 shows the situation that confronted Kevin. He owned the stock and when price started trending upward at A, he became excited. The one question nagging him was "When should I take profits?"

The stock formed a series of white candles, not an eight new price lines candle series as I define it, but a strong, straight-line uptrend anyway. When the upside gap two crows appeared at B, he suspected that the uptrend had ended. Price confirmed his suspicion when it closed lower the next day. Remember that a lower close suggests that price will reverse (from trending up to trending down) 56% of the time in a bull market.

He drew a trendline up from A toward B, skirting the bottoms of the candles along the way. When price closed below the trendline, he decided to sell the stock. That occurred the next day, at C. Combining the upside gap two crows candle as a reversal with the piercing of the trendline allowed him to keep more of the profit (exit sooner) than using other exit methods.

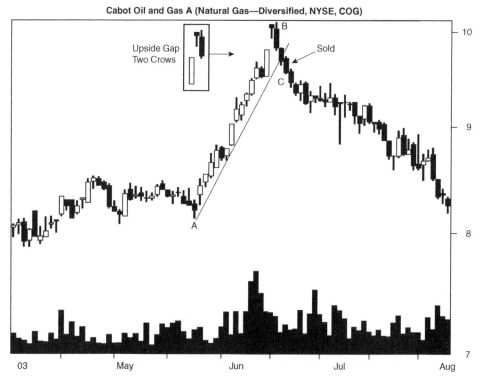

Figure 102.2   An upside gap two crows pattern acts as a reversal of the uptrend.

For Best Performance

The following list offers tips and observations to help choose candles that perform well. Consult the associated table for more information.

- Use the identification guidelines to help select the pattern—Table 102.1.
- Candles within a third of the yearly low perform best under most, but not all, conditions—Table 102.2.
- Select tall candles—Table 102.3.
- Use the measure rule to predict a price target—Table 102.3.
- Candles with tall lower shadows outperform—Table 102.3.
- Volume gives performance clues—Table 102.4.
- Trade breakouts in the direction of the primary trend—Trading Tactics discussion.
- The candle breaks out upward most often—Table 102.5.
- Patterns within a third of the yearly high tend to act as continuations most often—Table 102.5.
- Opening gap confirmation works best—Table 102.6.

103

Upside Tasuki Gap

Behavior and Rank

Theoretical: Bullish continuation.

Actual bull market: Bullish continuation 57% of the time (ranking 26).

Actual bear market: Bullish continuation 53% of the time (ranking 42).

Frequency: 74th out of 103.

Overall performance over time: 5th out of 103.

While researching this candle pattern, I discovered that after a downward breakout price often returns to the launch price. Sometimes it stops above the launch price and sometimes it continues lower, but the finding serves as a good benchmark. I discuss this more in detail in the Trading Tactics section of this chapter.

The bullish continuation rank of 26, where 1 is best out of 103, is quite good. The overall performance is even better: 5. Oddly, the best performance comes from downward breakouts in a bear market, so the candle acts as a reversal under those circumstances. That dovetails with what I said about price returning to the launch price.

The psychology behind the upside Tasuki gap pattern begins with the pattern appearing in an uptrend, when the bulls are in control. A white candle prints on the chart followed by a second white candle. The second one gaps above the first one, signaling unbounded enthusiasm, like children opening presents on Christmas day.

The next day sees price open down and close even lower, a signifi-cant change from the prior days. Maybe the bulls were hung over from the

Christmas party? Whatever the reason, the bears stir up trouble—but not enough to close the window left open by the first two candles.

However, many times the bears succeed in pushing price down to close the gap but not far enough to close below the lowest low in the candle pattern (which would be a downward breakout). The bulls return from sick leave and put the bears in their place by forcing price to new highs (an upward breakout). That may take a week or two of fighting but that's what usually happens.

Identification Guidelines

Figure 103.1 shows what the candle pattern looks like. Price begins the uptrend at A, and two days later the upside Tasuki gap begins. A tall white candle forms, followed by a second white candle that gaps higher. The gap is between the shadows, so there is no overlap. The next day, price closes lower and forms a black candle, but the black candle does not close the gap.

From the peak at B to the bottom at C, the retracement can carry price much lower but usually doesn't. You can use a Fibonacci retracement (38%, 50%, or 62%) of the up move to help determine the extent of the retracement.

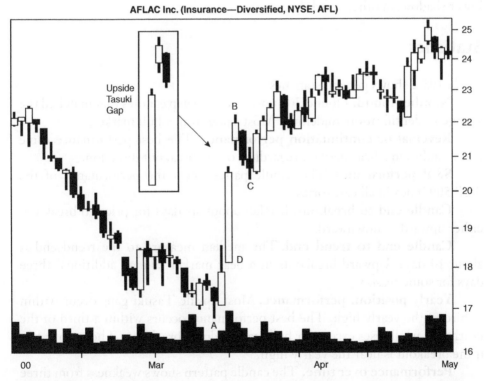

AFLAC Inc. (Insurance—Diversified, NYSE, AFL)

Figure 103.1 A tall upside Tasuki gap sees price retrace for two days before resuming the uptrend.

Table 103.1
Identification Guidelines

Characteristic	Discussion
Number of candle lines	Three.
Price trend	Upward leading to the start of the candle pattern.
First day	A white candle.
Second day	A white candle. Price gaps higher, including the shadows, leaving a rising window between the two candles.
Third day	A black candle opens in the body of the prior candle and closes within the gap. The gap remains open if you ignore the lower shadow.

It usually takes about a week or so for price to climb back above the top of the candle pattern and for patience to be rewarded.

Table 103.1 lists identification guidelines. Look for the upside Tasuki gap candle formation in an upward price trend. The bodies of the candles need not be tall ones. In my testing, I didn't allow the shadows to fill the gap between the first two candles because the sources I checked were unclear on this point. The last day also sees the close remain above the high of the first candle but below the low of the second candle. The gap remains open if you ignore the lower shadow, in other words.

Statistics

Table 103.2 shows general statistics.

Number found. I found 704 upside Tasuki gap candles that matched the stringent identification guidelines. Most came from a bull market.

Reversal or continuation performance. The best performance came from candles in a bear market, regardless of the breakout direction.

S&P performance. The candle pattern beat the performance of the S&P 500 index in all categories.

Candle end to breakout. It takes about six days for price to break out either upward or downward.

Candle end to trend end. The median measure to the trend end is about 10 days. Upward breakouts in a bear market take an additional three days for some reason.

Yearly position, performance. Most upside Tasuki gaps occur within a third of the yearly high. The best performance occurs within a third of the yearly low in all cases except for bull market/down breakouts. Those do better if the breakout is near the yearly high.

Performance over time. The candle pattern shows weakness from three to five days in bear market/up breakouts. This means it is not as reliable as some other candle types.

Table 103.2
General Statistics

Description	Bull Market, Up Breakout	Bear Market, Up Breakout	Bull Market, Down Breakout	Bear Market, Down Breakout
Number found	334	61	225	54
Reversal (R), continuation (C) performance	6.62% C	7.35% C	−5.72% R	−12.10% R
Standard & Poor's 500 change	1.76%	0.23%	−0.69%	−4.19%
Candle end to breakout (median, days)	6	7	6	6
Candle end to trend end (median, days)	10	13	10	10
Number of breakouts near the 12-month low (L), middle (M), or high (H)	L 38, M 62, H 197	L 8, M 19, H 34	L 35, M 68, H 109	L 17, M 15, H 22
Percentage move for each 12-month period	L 12.90%, M 6.57%, H 6.13%	L 10.56%, M 7.13%, H 6.77%	L −5.83%, M −4.52%, H −6.62%	L −19.20%, M −8.75%, H −9.11%
Candle end + 1 day	1.18%	1.61%	−0.89%	−1.53%
Candle end + 3 days	2.47%	3.11%	−1.98%	−4.30%
Candle end + 5 days	3.39%	2.84%	−2.55%	−6.96%
Candle end + 10 days	4.49%	4.70%	−3.24%	−9.20%
10-day performance rank	22	34	30	2

The performance rank compares the performance over time with that posted by other candle types. A rank of 1 is best out of 103 candles. The table shows that downward breakouts in a bear market have the best rank: 2. The large percentage change over the 10 days is the reason. My guess is that additional samples would degrade performance.

Table 103.3 shows height statistics.

Candle height. Tall patterns outperform in all cases except for bear market/up breakouts. To determine whether the candle is short or tall, compute its height from highest high to lowest low price in the candle pattern and divide by the breakout price. If the result is higher than the median, then you have a tall candle; otherwise it's short.

If Gina sees an upside Tasuki gap with a high of 63 and a low of 60, is the pattern short or tall? The height is 63 − 60, or 3, so the measure would be 3/63, or 4.8%. In a bull market with an upward breakout, that's a short candle. In fact, it's a short candle regardless of the market condition or breakout direction.

Measure rule. Use the measure rule to help predict how far price will rise or fall. Compute the height of the candle pattern and multiply it by

Table 103.3
Height Statistics

Description	Bull Market, Up Breakout	Bear Market, Up Breakout	Bull Market, Down Breakout	Bear Market, Down Breakout
Median candle height as a percentage of breakout price	6.57%	7.54%	6.49%	9.62%
Short candle, performance	4.97%	7.86%	−4.64%	−6.21%*
Tall candle, performance	8.71%	6.76%	−6.87%	−17.13%*
Percentage meeting price target (measure rule)	37%	38%	36%	35%
Median upper shadow as a percentage of breakout price	0.24%	0.60%	0.25%	0.47%
Short upper shadow, performance	6.44%	6.58%	−5.77%	−9.94%*
Tall upper shadow, performance	6.79%	8.16%	−5.68%	−13.97%*
Median lower shadow as a percentage of breakout price	0.46%	0.54%	0.40%	0.93%
Short lower shadow, performance	5.70%	4.96%	−5.07%	−6.51%*
Tall lower shadow, performance	7.57%	10.16%	−6.29%	−16.51%*

*Fewer than 30 samples.

the appropriate percentage shown in the table; then apply it to the breakout price.

What are the price targets for Gina's candle? The upward target would be $(3 \times 37\%) + 63$, or 64.11, and the downward target would be $60 - (3 \times 36\%)$, or 58.92.

Shadows. The table's results pertain to the last candle line in the pattern. To determine whether the shadow is short or tall, compute the height of the shadow and divide by the breakout price. Compare the result to the median in the table. Tall shadows have a percentage higher than the median.

Upper shadow performance. Candles with tall upper shadows result in better performance than do those with short shadows except in bull market/down breakouts.

Lower shadow performance. Upside Tasuki gap patterns with tall lower shadows outperform their short brothers.

Table 103.4 shows volume statistics.

Candle volume trend. Candles with a rising volume trend tend to outperform in all conditions except for bull market/up breakouts.

Average candle volume. Candles with below-average volume perform best except in bull market/down breakouts. Those do better if the candle shows above-average volume.

Table 103.4
Volume Statistics

Description	Bull Market, Up Breakout	Bear Market, Up Breakout	Bull Market, Down Breakout	Bear Market, Down Breakout
Rising candle volume, performance	5.50%	8.29%*	−6.09%	−16.58%*
Falling candle volume, performance	7.76%	6.60%	−5.20%	−8.57%
Above-average candle volume, performance	6.54%	5.68%	−5.85%	−9.83%
Below-average candle volume, performance	6.75%	10.25%*	−5.45%	−16.32%*
Heavy breakout volume, performance	7.25%	8.69%	−6.22%	−9.33%
Light breakout volume, performance	5.73%	5.96%*	−5.13%	−15.97%*

*Fewer than 30 samples.

Breakout volume. Heavy breakout volume suggests better postbreak-out performance in all cases except for bear market/down breakouts. Those have a low sample count, but they perform better after a breakout on light volume.

Trading Tactics

Often this candle pattern is a tall one, so price will retrace a portion of the rise. Do not be alarmed. If the primary trend is upward, the rise should resume after several days. However, if price closes below the first candle, then exit any long position.

If the primary trend is downward, then don't expect an upward breakout to carry price far.

This doesn't always work, but if price breaks out downward, then expect the decline to halt near (usually slightly above) the price of the prior minor low. Figure 103.2 shows an example. The launch price is at A (the prior minor low), and the stock climbs to the upside Tasuki gap. Then price slides lower, breaking out downward at C and continuing on to B. In this example, the decline to B is nearly the same as the prior minor low, A.

I split trading tactics into two basic studies, one concerning reversal rates and the other concerning performance. Of the two, reversal rates are more important, because it's better to trade in the direction of the trend and let price run as far as it can.

Table 103.5 gives tips to find the trend direction.

Confirmation reversal rates. To help confirm a reversal, wait for price to close lower the day after the Tasuki gap ends. That works 61% of the time in a bull market.

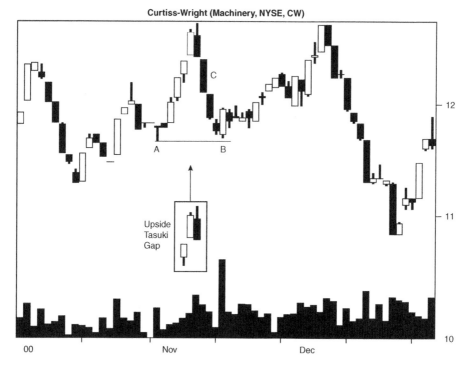

Figure 103.2 After a downward breakout from an upside Tasuki gap, the stock returns to the launch price.

Reversal, continuation rates. The breakout is upward 57% of the time in a bull market.

Yearly range reversals. The largest concentration of continuation patterns occurs when the breakout is within a third of the yearly high.

Table 103.6 shows performance indicators that can give hints as to how your stock will behave after the breakout from this candle pattern.

Table 103.5
Reversal Rates

Description	Bull Market	Bear Market
Closing price confirmation reversal rate	61%	69%
Candle color confirmation reversal rate	59%	65%
Opening gap confirmation reversal rate	52%	53%*
Reversal rate: trend up, breakout down	43%	47%
Continuation rate: trend up, breakout up	57%	53%
Percentage of reversals (R)/continuations (C) for each 12-month low (L), middle (M), or high (H)	L 48% R/52% C, M 52% R/48% C, H 36% R/64% C	L* 68% R/32% C, M* 44% R/56% C, H* 39% R/61% C

*Fewer than 30 samples.

Table 103.6
Performance Indicators

Description	Bull Market, Up Breakout	Bear Market, Up Breakout	Bull Market, Down Breakout	Bear Market, Down Breakout
Closing price confirmation, performance	8.19%	11.24%	N/A	N/A
Candle color confirmation, performance	8.43%	11.44%	N/A	N/A
Opening gap confirmation, performance	8.97%	14.01%	N/A	N/A
Breakout above 50-day moving average, performance	6.44%	7.25%	−6.08%	−8.06%*
Breakout below 50-day moving average, performance	10.09%*	8.34%*	−4.88%	−16.21%*
Last candle: close in highest third, performance	4.60%*	1.29%*	−6.40%*	0.00%
Last candle: close in middle third, performance	8.17%	8.32%*	−6.92%	−7.63%*
Last candle: close in lowest third, performance	6.16%	7.25%	−5.39%	−13.02%

N/A means not applicable.
*Fewer than 30 samples.

Confirmation, performance. Use opening gap confirmation to improve performance. That means waiting for price to gap open higher the next day before taking a position in the stock.

Moving average. Candles with breakouts below the 50-day moving average tend to perform better than do those with breakouts above the moving average. The one exception comes from downward breakouts in a bull market.

Closing position. Candles with a close in the middle of the last candle line tend to perform better than closes in the other two thirds of the candle. The lone exception to this is in bear market/down breakouts, which do best when the close is near the day's low.

Sample Trade

Figure 103.3 shows a stock Gina owned. Price peaked at A and then retraced before moving horizontally for about a month to C. At C, price gapped up to B and then moved down one day to create the upside Tasuki gap.

The price at A had set a new yearly high. According to Table 103.5, breakouts near the yearly high tend to act as continuations. This information, coupled with knowing that the upside Tasuki gap candle pattern acts as a continuation slightly more often than a reversal (57% of the time), led Gina

Figure 103.3   An upside Tasuki gap acts as a reversal.

to decide to hold on to the stock. If it closed below the start of the candle, C, then she would be wrong and a stop placed there would take her out.

Price gapped open lower the next day after the upside Tasuki gap and closed lower still, warning of a reversal. When price closes lower the day after the pattern ends, it tends to reverse 61% of the time (from Table 103.5).

"I had a stop in place," she said and shrugged. "Let price do what it will." Sometimes price needs room to work before it resumes trending.

Anyway, the gambit worked. Price formed a minor low and then climbed to rise slightly above B. The upward breakout was a good sign. She was home free, or so she thought.

But then price moved lower, easing down over the next week before taking two deep plunges and piercing Gina's stop order. She was out of the game about two weeks before price resumed the uptrend.

That's how trades go sometimes. If this were my trade and the stock made a new high after B, I would raise the stop based on volatility. That would have narrowed the loss to just over 4%.

What do I mean by volatility? Measure the intraday high-low range for each day over the prior 22 price bars (about one month) and average the result. Multiply it by 2 and then subtract it from the current low. Place a stop no closer than the result or you risk being stopped out by normal price action.

For Best Performance

The following list offers tips and observations to help choose candles that perform well. Consult the associated table for more information.

- Use the identification guidelines to help select the pattern—Table 103.1.
- Candles within a third of the yearly low perform best in most, but not all, markets—Table 103.2.
- Select tall candles except for bear market/up breakouts—Table 103.3.
- Use the measure rule to predict a price target—Table 103.3.
- Candles with tall lower shadows outperform—Table 103.3.
- Volume gives performance clues—Table 103.4.
- If the breakout is downward, price sometimes returns to near the launch price—Trading Tactics discussion and Figure 103.2.
- The candle breaks out upward most often—Table 103.5.
- Patterns within a third of the yearly high tend to act as continuations most often—Table 103.5.
- Opening gap confirmation works best—Table 103.6.

104

Window, Falling

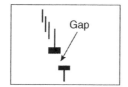

Behavior and Rank

Theoretical: Bearish continuation.

Actual bull market: Bearish continuation 67% of the time (ranking 11).

Actual bear market: Bearish continuation 73% of the time (ranking 6).

Frequency: 23rd out of 103.

Overall performance over time: 7th out of 103.

A falling window is a gap between two candles. How do you measure whether it acts as a reversal or continuation? You do that by including the two adjacent price bars. That's the approach I took.

As a continuation pattern, falling windows work well, ranking 11 in a bull market out of 103 candles, where 1 is best. Overall performance is also top-notch, ranking 7.

The psychology begins with the bears pushing price down. They do this with excessive selling pressure that overwhelms buying demand. At the open, this pressure is large enough that price gaps lower, leaving a falling window on the chart. Buying demand set up by hungry bulls is still no match for the selling pressure throughout the day. At day's end, if the bears have their way, the trading range of price throughout the day is not high enough to reach the prior day's low price. The falling window remains intact and appears as a space on the chart.

OGE Energy Corp. (Electric Utility—Central, NYSE, OGE)

Figure 104.1 A falling window appears in a declining price trend.

Identification Guidelines

Figure 104.1 shows an example of a falling window. Price at A forms a tall black candle. The next day, another black candle forms but this one (B) drops below the low of the prior candle, leaving a gap on the chart. In other words, the high at B is below the low at A.

Notice about a month later at D that price hesitates in its climb. About a quarter of the time the level of the falling window (the gap) offers resistance to future price movement. In this case, the stock pauses in its uphill run at D but is able to soldier on after a day's rest.

Another falling window occurs a month later at C. There price breaks away from congestion set up by short candles with long lower shadows in the week leading to the falling window. The long lower shadows are supposed to be a bullish omen, and price does make a strong advance but can't hold it. The candle above C sports a long upper shadow (bearish) and a small body with a small lower wick. It's a bearish sign, and price gaps lower the next day.

Table 104.1 lists identification guidelines. A falling window refers to the gap left on the chart, so the pattern does not include any candle lines. What's

Table 104.1
Identification Guidelines

Characteristic	Discussion
Number of candle lines	None.
Price trend	Downward leading to the start of the candle pattern.
Configuration	The high today is below the low of the prior day, leaving a gap on the chart.

important is that price gaps lower. That means today's high remains below the prior candle's low, leaving a gap on the chart.

Statistics

The statistics in the falling and rising windows chapters are different from others in this book due to the nature of the patterns. The most important questions that traders want answers to are: Does the gap act as a resistance zone? What happens to price over time? I answer those questions in the following paragraphs.

Table 104.2 shows general statistics for the falling window.

Number found. I looked at 13,997 candles from the standard database, and that was enough to get a good idea of how well falling windows acted as resistance zones.

Stopped in gap. This is the number of times a minor high appeared within the gap before price closed the gap. By *close the gap*, I mean price had to approach from below and *close* above the top of the gap before the end of data. This is also the same as how often a gap worked as a resistance zone to an upward price move.

I found all the minor highs from the day after the gap until price closed the gap (or end of data). Since this was a falling window, only minor highs

Table 104.2
General Statistics

Description	Bull Market	Bear Market
Number found	9,374	4,623
Stopped in gap	25%	33%
Average time to gap closed	55 days	86 days
Median time to gap closed	9 days	11 days
Number not closed	3%	2%
Average gap size	$0.30	$0.52
Median gap size	$0.12	$0.19

mattered. I counted the number of times that the upper shadow of a candle stopped within the gap and the number of times price moved above the gap but didn't close it. In other words, the upper shadow of a candle was tall enough to span the gap but the candle closed below the top of the gap. The day when it closed the gap, assuming it did before end of data, counted as the gap not showing overhead resistance.

In a bull market, 25% of the time the gap worked as overhead resistance to an upward price move.

Average/median time to gap closed. These are the average time and the median time it took for price to close above the top of the gap after approaching from below. The wide difference between the average and the median is due to several samples having large values, which tend to pull up the average but do not affect the median.

Number not closed. This is the percentage of gaps remaining open during the period of the study.

Average/median gap size. These measure from the top of the gap to the bottom of it. Again, the average is pulled up by large values.

Table 104.3 shows what happens to price over time after the gap ends. Gap+1 means the day after the gap completes; that is, if price gaps lower on Monday, then Gap+1 would be Tuesday. The table shows what happens to the closing price for two weeks after the gap.

To create the table, I found all gaps in stocks priced over $5 per share with an average daily volume over the prior 100 days of at least 250,000 shares. In other words, I wanted to eliminate thinly traded stocks. I found 12,706 samples that qualified.

In a bull market, price is 1.9% lower as measured from the high price the day the gap occurred (i.e., Monday's high price, continuing the analogy) to

Table 104.3
Price over Time Statistics

Description	Bull Market	Bear Market
Gap+1	−1.9%	−3.3%
Gap+2	−1.8%	−3.3%
Gap+3	−1.7%	−3.5%
Gap+4	−1.6%	−3.5%
Gap+5	−1.5%	−3.3%
Gap+6	−1.5%	−3.1%
Gap+7	−1.3%	−3.5%
Gap+8	−1.3%	−3.3%
Gap+9	−1.2%	−3.1%
Gap+10	−1.2%	−3.4%

the following day's close (Tuesday's close). A day later, price has closed higher slightly, on average, to 1.8% below the gap. Two weeks later (Gap+10), price has narrowed the difference to 1.2% below the gap.

To be succinct, after a falling window, price in a bull market tends to rise during the next two weeks but not close the gap. In a bear market, price remains essentially constant.

105

Window, Rising

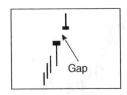

Behavior and Rank

Theoretical: Bullish continuation.

Actual bull market: Bullish continuation 75% of the time (ranking 4).

Actual bear market: Bullish continuation 72% of the time (ranking 7).

Frequency: 20th out of 103.

Overall performance over time: 42nd out of 103.

Now that I have completed researching rising and falling windows, I can see why stock traders don't put much emphasis on them. I certainly don't. A rising window will support price just 20% of the time in a bull market. That's once out of every five trades. Yuck. Maybe this works better in markets other than stocks.

The rank shows that a rising window acts as a bullish continuation 75% of the time, ranking 4 where 1 is best out of 103 candles. The overall performance is 42, a midlist rank.

The psychology begins with a rising price trend and bullish buying demand sending price higher. Before the open, the demand is so high that price gaps open and doesn't return to close the gap throughout the day. At day's end, price may have narrowed the gap but not closed it. What remains is a space on the chart, a rising window.

The theory behind a rising window is that it will act as a support zone. As we will see in the statistics section, that theory doesn't work well in the stock market on the daily scale.

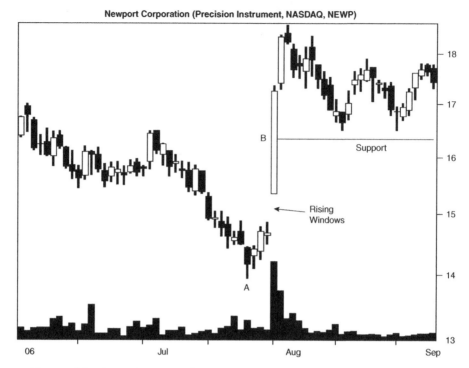

Figure 105.1 A rising window appears days after price changed trend.

Identification Guidelines

Figure 105.1 shows what a rising window looks like. This gap is an unusually tall one. Notice the tall white candle at B. Midway down the candle body is a support zone. I am more inclined to believe that a tall candle will support price midway down its body than I am that a rising window will support price. Just a few days ago, I placed an order to buy midway down a tall white candle. When price reached the midpoint, my order filled, and price climbed after that. It's a wonderful feeling when theory works in practice. Before I return to the rising window, research discussed in this book says that the mid-candle support or resistance area is a myth. Price is no more likely to find support or resistance there than anywhere else on a tall candle.

Table 105.1 lists identification guidelines. Rising windows appear in uptrends when price gaps higher. That means today's low price is above the prior high, leaving white space on the chart between the two price bars. A rising window is a gap and so it includes no candle lines.

Statistics

The statistics in the falling and rising windows chapters are different from others in this book due to the nature of the patterns.

Table 105.1
Identification Guidelines

Characteristic	Discussion
Number of candle lines	None.
Price trend	Upward leading to the start of the candle pattern.
Configuration	The low today is above the high of the prior day, leaving a gap on the chart.

Table 105.2 shows general statistics for the rising window.

Number found. I found 18,229 rising windows in my standard database.

Stopped in gap. This tells how often price stopped within a gap. I used minor lows and compared the low price with the gap. If price entered the gap but didn't drop below the far side, then the gap acted as support (success). If the low price did drop below the far side, then that counted as a failure. The gap closed and the analysis ended when price closed below the high price the day before the gap.

I found that just 20% of the time price found support within the gap. The other 80% saw price continuing lower.

Average/median time to gap closed. The average and the median are two ways to look at the same data. The average can be swayed by several large values, as the results show. The median is just the midrange value in a sorted list of numbers. The median time to close the gap is 10 or 11 days. The average is much higher because some stocks had gaps that remained open for years.

Number not closed. This is the percentage of gaps that never closed by the end of data.

Average/median gap size. These show how tall the gap is using both the average and the median measures. I counted gaps as small as a penny in the analysis.

Table 105.3 shows what happens to price over time after the gap ends. Gap+1 means that if price gaps higher on Monday, then Gap+1 would be

Table 105.2
General Statistics

Description	Bull Market	Bear Market
Number found	14,224	5,089
Stopped in gap	20%	16%
Average time to gap closed	79 days	49 days
Median time to gap closed	11 days	10 days
Number not closed	9%	1%
Average gap size	$0.27	$0.33
Median gap size	$0.12	$0.15

Table 105.3
Price over Time Statistics

Description	Bull Market	Bear Market
Gap+1	1.8%	2.4%
Gap+2	1.9%	2.2%
Gap+3	2.0%	1.9%
Gap+4	2.1%	1.5%
Gap+5	2.0%	1.4%
Gap+6	2.1%	1.2%
Gap+7	2.1%	1.3%
Gap+8	2.1%	1.1%
Gap+9	2.2%	1.2%
Gap+10	2.2%	1.1%

Tuesday. The table shows what happens to the closing price for two weeks after the gap as measured from the top of the gap (i.e., Monday's low price, to continue the analogy).

To create the table, I found all gaps in stocks priced more than $5 per share with an average daily volume of at least 250,000 shares over the prior 100 days. In other words, I wanted to eliminate thinly traded stocks. I found 16,415 samples that qualified in the standard database.

Another research team found that upward gaps (rising windows) showed price trending lower over one day, two days, and a week later, but they did not separate bull and bear market data. I sorted the data by market condition and found that in a bull market, price coasted higher after the gap. In a bear market, the gap tended to narrow considerably (more than half) during the next two weeks.

Bibliography

In researching candle patterns for this book, I used several sources that appear here and cross referenced them with an Internet search to assure reliability. Every attempt was made to identify the creator of a candlestick. I do not claim to have discovered any of the patterns in this book; rather, it was my intention to test them.

Anderson, Chip. *Candlestick Pattern Dictionary*. StockCharts.com. http://stockcharts. com/school/doku.php?id=chart_school:chart_analysis:candlestick_pattern.

Bigalow, Stephen W. *Profitable Candlestick Trading: Pinpointing Market Opportunities to Maximize Profits*, Hoboken, NJ: John Wiley & Sons, 2002.

Bristol International, Inc. "Candlestick Pattern Glossary." http://www.vss2000. com/support/iChartPROc.asp?rf=.

CandlestickChart.com. "Glossary of Candlestick Indicators." Lit Wick Co., LLC, http://www.candlestickchart.com/glossary.html.

Candlesticker by Americanbulls.com. Japanese Candlesticks. http://www.candle sticker.com/Default.asp.

Candlestick Trading Forum. "Major Candlestick Signals." http://candlestickforum. com/PPF/Parameters/16_332_/candlestick.asp.

Daytrader's Bulletin. "Candlestick Patterns: An Overview." http://www.daytraders bulletin.com/html/cs1.html.

FXtrek.com. "Inverted Hammer and Shooting Star." http://www.fxtrek.com/glos sary/.

HotCandlestick.com. Candlestick Charting Frequently Asked Questions. http://www. hotcandlestick.com/faq.htm.

Investopedia.com. "Homing pigeon." Answers Corporation. http://www.answers. com/homing+pigeon?cat=biz-fin.

Morris, Gregory L. *Candlestick Charting Explained*, New York: McGraw-Hill, 1995.

Nison, Steve. *Beyond Candlesticks: New Japanese Charting Techniques Revealed*. New York: John Wiley & Sons, 1994.

Nison, Steve. *The Candlestick Course*. Hoboken, NJ: John Wiley & Sons, 2003.

Renegade Solutions Inc. "Inverted Hammer Bull Candlestick Chart Indicator." The Renegade. http://www.renegadesolutions.net/tc2000_candlesticks/bull/invert ed_hammer.shtml.

Rightline Charts. Rightline Power Trading. http://rightline.iqchart.com/partner/ rightline/education/candle.asp.

Steve Nison's MarketScan. "Candlestick Patterns." www.nisonmarketscan.com/ Out/HelpCandleStickPatterns.aspx.

Glossary and Methodology

Here are the statistics tables with a brief explanation of what each entry means. A glossary of selected terminology follows.

Behavior and Rank

Theoretical: This is the behavior (bullish, bearish, reversal, continuation, or indecision) according to published sources.

Actual bull market: I found this behavior through testing. The percentage represents a tally of the candlestick patterns acting as continuations or reversals as a percentage of all candles of the same type in a bull market. The ranking is how the percentage ranked among 103 candle types, where 1 is best.

Actual bear market: Same as bull market but it applies to a bear market.

Frequency: The frequency rank—how often a candle appears in the standard database.

Overall performance over time: A rank of the sum of performance over time in all categories. See *overall rank* in the glossary for a definition.

Statistics

Table 2

General Statistics

Description	Explanation
Number found	A count of the number of candlestick patterns used in the statistics.
Reversal (R), continuation (C) performance	Shows the average rise or decline of reversals and continuations from breakout to trend end.

(Continued)

Table 2
(Continued)

Description	Explanation
Standard & Poor's 500 change	The average change in the S&P 500 index from the day of the candle pattern end to the day price reached the trend end.
Candle end to breakout (median, days)	The median number of days between the candle pattern end and breakout.
Candle end to trend end (median, days)	The median number of days between the candle pattern end and trend end.
Number of breakouts near the 12-month low (L), middle (M), or high (H)	A count of the number of candle patterns that break out within a third of the yearly low, middle, or high.
Percentage move for each 12-month period	The average performance from candle patterns with breakouts within a third of the yearly low, middle, or high.
Candle end + 1–10 days	The average move from the closing price the day the candle pattern ends to the close 1, 3, 5, or 10 trading days later.
10-day performance rank	A rank of the sum of the percentage changes over 1, 3, 5, and 10 trading days for each category (bull market/up breakout, e.g.) compared to the other candle types (103 total).

Table 3
Height Statistics

Description	Explanation
Median candle height as a percentage of breakout price	The median of the height from highest high to lowest low in the candle pattern divided by the breakout price, expressed as a percentage.
Short candle, performance	The average rise/decline for patterns equal to or shorter than the median, expressed as a percentage.
Tall candle, performance	The average rise/decline for patterns taller than the median, expressed as a percentage.
Percentage meeting price target (measure rule)	The measure rule price target is the candle pattern's height added to the pattern's highest high or subtracted from the pattern's lowest low, depending on the breakout direction. The result is the percentage of candle patterns in which price reaches or exceeds the predicted target price after the breakout. For exceptionally tall candles (8, 10, 12, and 13 new price lines, e.g.), the height is adjusted.
Median upper shadow as a percentage of breakout price	The median height of the upper shadow as a percentage of the breakout price.

(Continued)

222

Table 3
(*Continued*)

Description	Explanation
Short upper shadow, performance	The average performance for patterns with upper shadows less than or equal to the median.
Tall upper shadow, performance	The average performance for patterns with upper shadows greater than the median.
Median lower shadow as a percentage of breakout price	The median height of the lower shadow as a percentage of the breakout price.
Short lower shadow, performance	The average performance for patterns with lower shadows less than or equal to the median.
Tall lower shadow, performance	The average performance for patterns with lower shadows greater than the median.

Table 4
Volume Statistics

Description	Explanation
Rising/falling candle volume, performance	The average performance sorted by the volume trend (rising or falling volume) from the start to end of the candle pattern, expressed as a percentage. Does not apply to single candle lines.
Above/below-average candle volume, performance	The average performance using a comparison of the average volume in the candle pattern (from start to end) with the prior 21-trading-day average volume, sorted into above-average and below-average categories.
Heavy/light breakout volume, performance	The average performance using a comparison of the average breakout-day volume with the average volume leading to the candle pattern, sorted into above-average (heavy) and average or below-average (light) categories.

Trading Tactics

Table 5
Reversal Rates

Description	Explanation
Closing price confirmation reversal rate	Whichever direction represents a reversal of the price trend leading to the candle pattern, look for a higher/lower close the day after the candle pattern ends. For example, if price trends up leading to the pattern and you expect a reversal, look for a lower close the next day. If that occurs, it confirms the candle as a valid reversal. The percentage tells how often the method worked. May not apply to continuation patterns.

(*Continued*)

Table 5
(Continued)

Description	Explanation
Candle color confirmation reversal rate	Whichever direction represents a reversal of the price trend leading to the candle pattern, look for a black (downtrend)/white (uptrend) candle the day after the candle pattern ends. For example, if price trends up leading to the candle pattern and you expect a reversal, look for a black candle the day after the pattern ends. If it occurs, it confirms the candle pattern as a valid reversal. The percentage tells how often the method worked. May not apply to continuation patterns.
Opening gap confirmation reversal rate	Whichever direction represents a reversal of the price trend leading to the candle pattern, look for price to gap open higher/lower the day after the candle pattern ends (using the daily chart, not intraday). For example, if price trends up leading to the candle pattern and you expect a reversal, look for price to gap open lower the day after the pattern ends. If it occurs, it confirms the candle pattern as a valid reversal. The percentage tells how often the method worked. May not apply to continuation patterns.
Reversal/continuation rate: trend up/down, breakout up/down	The percentage of candle patterns with price trending up/down leading to the candle pattern and breaking out up/down. Use this to help determine the likely breakout direction based on the trend leading to the candle pattern. This also tells how often a candle pattern breaks out in a given direction.
Percentage of reversals (R)/ continuations (C) for each 12-month low (L), middle (M), or high (H)	A frequency distribution of the breakout price over the yearly price range for patterns acting as reversals or continuations. High numbers might indicate behavior. For example, if a candle pattern shows that it acts as a reversal 80% of the time within a third of the yearly low, then expect a reversal if your candle appears near the yearly low.
Black/white body reversal rate	For single line candles where the body can be any color. This shows how often the candle acted as a reversal, sorted by body color. For example, if a black candle line acts as a reversal 80% of the time and you see a black candle line, then expect a reversal.

Table 6
Performance Indicators

Description	Explanation
Closing price confirmation, performance	The closing price (a higher/lower close) the day after the candle pattern completes determines the breakout direction and confirmation as a valid candle pattern. In the case of an unchanged close, the search continues until the closing price changes or data ends. If price confirms the candle pattern, then the average of the new closing price to the trend high/low determines performance. Applies only to the direction representing a reversal, otherwise N/A (not applicable).

(Continued)

Table 6
(*Continued*)

Description	Explanation
Candle color confirmation, performance	If a candle pattern is bullish, then a white candle the next day (after the candle pattern ends) will confirm the candle pattern. For a bearish candle pattern, a black candle the next day (after the candle pattern ends) will confirm the candle pattern. Confirming candles with opposite color (e.g., a black candle for a bullish candle pattern) mean the candle pattern is not confirmed and the result is not used. The close of the confirming (colored) candle represents the breakout price. If the candle shows no color (like a doji), then following days are used until a color change occurs. If color confirms the candle pattern, then the average of the confirming candle's closing price to the trend end determines performance. Applies only to the direction representing a reversal, otherwise N/A (not applicable).
Opening gap confirmation, performance	If price opens higher/lower than the prior close, then the opening price determines the breakout direction and breakout price. If price confirms the candle pattern, then the average of the opening price to the trend end determines performance. Applies only to the direction representing a reversal, otherwise N/A (not applicable).
Breakout above/below 50-day moving average, performance	A 50-trading day (not calendar) exponential moving average of price was compared to the breakout price of each candle pattern, then sorted by whether the breakout price was above or below the moving average. The average gain/loss from the breakout to trend end for each category is shown.
Last candle: close in highest/middle/lowest third, performance	The last candle line in the pattern was split into thirds and it was determined into which third price closed. Similar thirds were grouped together (all of the upper thirds, e.g.) to determine average performance from breakout to trend end.
Black/white body, performance	For single-line candles only where the body can be any color. This is the average performance from breakout to trend end, sorted by candle color.

Terminology

Average   The sum of scores divided by the number of scores.

Average performance   The rise from the breakout price to the trend high, or the decline from the breakout price to the trend low, is determined for each occurrence of the candle pattern; then the average is computed.

Average volume   When it pertains to the volume leading to the candlestick pattern, this is an average of volume during the prior 21 trading days (approximately 30 calendar days) ending the day before the candle pattern starts.

Bear market   The decline in the Standard & Poor's 500 index from March 24, 2000, to the low on October 10, 2002.

Body   The area between the opening and closing price on a candle line. Often called a real body. Makes you wonder what an unreal body would look like, doesn't it?

Breakout   A close above the highest high (upward breakout) or below the lowest low (downward breakout) in the candle pattern. For very tall candles, such as the various new price lines patterns, the breakout price may be different.

Breakout price   The price at which the stock broke out. Usually either the highest high or lowest low in the candle pattern, depending on the breakout direction. For very tall candles, such as the various new price lines patterns, the breakout price may be different.

Breakout volume   The volume level on the breakout day. The breakout day's volume is compared to the average volume over the prior 21 trading days (about a month, not including the breakout day).

Bull market   Every trading day outside of the bear market from March 24, 2000, to October 10, 2002, as posted by the Standard & Poor's 500 index.

Candle, candlestick, or candle pattern   A method of displaying open, high, low, and close price data. See Figure G.1. In some cases, candle, candlestick, and candle pattern refer to the entire series of price lines that compose a pattern.

Candle height   The difference between the highest high and lowest low in the candle pattern.

Candle line   *See* Line.

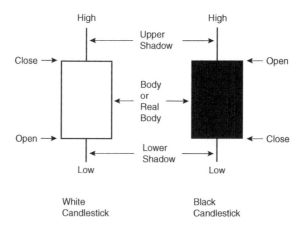

Figure G.1   A candlestick displays the open, high, low, and close, with the body of the candle (white or black) indicating whether price closed higher or lower than the opening price, not whether price closed higher or lower than the day before.

Candle volume   Comes in three flavors: trend, average, and breakout. Table 4 in the Statistics section of each candle chapter discusses volume. The volume trend is whether volume is rising or falling from candle pattern start to end. Above- or below-average volume compares the volume within the candle (from candle pattern start to end) with volume during the prior 21 trading days. Breakout volume is a measure of whether volume on the breakout day is above (heavy) or below (light) the prior 21-trading-day average.

Confirmation   Occurs when price validates the predicted breakout direction. If a reversal of an uptrend is expected, for example, and price gaps lower the next day, then the opening gap confirms the candle pattern. For an explanation of the various types, see the associated table entries in Tables 5 and 6 at the start of this chapter.

Continuation   Price breaks out in the same direction as it was trending leading to the candle pattern.

Continuation rank   *See* Rank; Reversal/continuation rank.

Data   To construct the frequency rank, the database consisted of 500 stocks from the Standard & Poor's 500 index as of August 2006. The period studied ranged from August 1, 1996, to August 25, 2006, but not all stocks covered the entire range. The total number of days (price bars or candle lines) examined was 1,204,083. Each of the candle patterns used the same database to establish how often a particular candle pattern appeared.

    For candle statistics, three additional databases were used to boost the sample count when necessary. The number of candles examined varied because I included current data as the book progressed. The total candle (price bars) count is 4,711,362.

Frequency distribution   A method to assign data to one of several nonoverlapping intervals. A frequency distribution shows how often values occur.

Frequency rank   A ranking of the number of candle patterns found in the standard database. Any ties were resolved by using the number of samples from all databases, so no ties were allowed. A rank of 1 is best out of 103 candlesticks. This is the frequency rank that appears near the start of each chapter.

Line or candle line   A one-day price bar.

Linear regression   Fits a straight line to a series of numbers; the slope of the resulting line gives the trend. Used to find whether volume within a candle pattern (from start to end) is trending upward or downward.

Measure rule   The candle pattern's height (the lowest low subtracted from the highest high in a single-bar or multiple-bar candle pattern) is multiplied by the measure rule percentage (success rate or hit rate), then added to (upward breakouts) or subtracted from (downward breakouts) the breakout price. Sometimes, as with tall candles like eight new price lines, a different method is used. See the individual chapters for details.

For example, suppose a candle pattern has a high of 87 and a low of 83. In a bull market, using the full height will result in success 60% of the time for upward breakouts and 53% of the time for downward breakouts. What are the price targets using the 60% and 53% hit rates to adjust the height? The height is 87 − 83, or 4, so the upward target would be (4 × 60%) + 87, or 89.40, and the downward target would be 83 − (4 × 53%), or 80.88.

Median   The middle value in a sorted list such that half the values are below the median and half above. (If no middle value exists, the average of the two closest values is used.) For example, in the list 10, 15, 30, 41, and 52, the median is 30 because there are two values on either side of it.

Minor high   A price peak usually separated from other peaks by at least a week.

Minor low   A price valley usually separated from other valleys by at least a week.

Overall rank   A ranked sum of the percentage price changes (close-to-close price change) during days 1, 3, 5, and 10 trading days after the candle ends for *all* four categories (bull market/up breakouts, bull market/down breakouts, and so on). The thinking here is that the best-performing candle should do well over time and in all market conditions (bull or bear) and breakout directions (up or down).

Downward breakout performance was multiplied by −1 (so any rise in price after a downward breakout would detract from the rank and any drop would improve the rank). Any ties were resolved by looking at frequency. In a tie, candles appearing more often were given a better rank. A rank of 1 is best out of 103 candlesticks.

Percentage meeting price target (measure rule)   How often price reaches or exceeds the price target found using the measure rule. For a more accurate measure, adjust the height by the measure rule success rate and then apply it to the breakout direction. *See* Measure rule.

Performance rank   The "10-day performance rank" that appears in the Statistics section of each chapter, Table 2. The thinking here is that the best-performing candle should do well over time within the selected market condition (bull or bear) and breakout direction (up or down). For each category (such as bull market/up breakouts) the percentage price change over 1, 3, 5, and 10 days was summed and then ranked. Downward breakout performance was multiplied by −1 (so any rise in price after a downward breakout would detract from the rank and any drop would improve the rank). Any ties were resolved by looking at frequency. In a tie, candles appearing more often were given a better rank. A rank of 1 is best out of 103 candlesticks. For additional details, *see* Rank.

Postbreakout performance   The performance from breakout to trend high/low, expressed as an average.

Price trend   Refers to the rising or falling price pattern in the days leading to the start of a candle pattern. The price trend can be as short as one day but is usually longer (typically three to seven days).

Primary trend   The major or longer-term trend before the start of the candle pattern. It is usually several months long. For example, if price climbs for three months and then drops for a month leading to a doji, the primary trend is still considered to be upward.

Rank   There are three types of rank, with 1 being the best out of 103 candles. No ties allowed.

> **Frequency rank** is a numerical display of how often a candle pattern appears in the standard database. The better the rank, the more often the candle pattern appears in the database.

> The **performance rank** sorts candle pattern performance, and a low number means better performance than a high one.

> The **reversal rank** or **continuation rank** shows how well a pattern reverses or continues the trend. A low number means a better-performing reversal or continuation.

> *See also* Frequency rank; Performance rank; Reversal/continuation rank.

Reversal   Price trends into and breaks out of the candle pattern on the same side (both up or both down).

Reversal/continuation performance   The average move from the breakout to the trend high/low after sorting the candle patterns into reversals or continuations.

Reversal/continuation rank   The rank for actual bull market or bear market that appears near the start of each candle chapter. It describes how many times a candle pattern acted as a reversal or continuation in a bull or bear market for up or down breakouts. For example, "Actual bull market: Bearish continuation 55% of the time (ranking 32)" means that when it occurred during a downtrend in a bull market, the candle continued that downtrend 55% of the time. That performance ranked 32nd where 1 is best out of 103 candle types. *See* Rank.

Shadow, lower   The difference between the intraday low and the opening (white candle) or closing (black candle) price. Appears as a line below the body. Sometimes called a wick.

Shadow, upper   The difference between the intraday high and the opening (black candle) or closing (white candle) price. Appears as a line above the body. Sometimes called a wick.

Shadow height   The average height of the candle shadows (or wicks) for each stock. Testing revealed that the average of the prior six price bars (leading to but not including the candle) gave the best results for computing the average shadow height.

Short   *See* Tall or short patterns.

Standard database   The database consists of data from 500 stocks in the Standard & Poor's 500 index from August 1, 1996, to August 25, 2006. I used this database to determine the candle frequency (how often a candle pattern appeared) for both bull and bear markets. Since the database included a bear market and the database's duration and composition were fixed, I prorated any bear market candle patterns to determine if they appeared more often in a bear market than a bull market. That information appears in the Statistics section of each chapter, Table 2, under "Number found."

Standard & Poor's 500 change   The date of the candle pattern's breakout to the date of the trend high or low applied to the price change in the S&P 500 index between those two dates. The comparison I make with candle pattern performance in this book is unfair because the candle pattern has a given breakout direction (up, e.g.), but the S&P can move either up or down over the periods chosen. I think it's like an Olympic downhill skier comparing his time to yours and then saying, "I beat you." No kidding.

Tall or short patterns   The difference between the highest high and the lowest low in the candle pattern, divided by the breakout price to get a percentage of height to price. The median value determines whether a candle pattern is tall or short.

For example, if a candle pattern has a high of 30 and a low of 25, the height would be 30 – 25, or 5. For an upward breakout, the measure would be 5/30, or 16.6%. For a downward breakout, the measure would be 5/25, or 20%. Tall candle patterns have percentages higher than the median, and short candle patterns have percentages lower than the median.

Trend end   A minor high or minor low where the short-term trend reverses. Sometimes called a swing high or swing low.

Trend high   A swing high point, usually ending in a minor high.

Trend low   A swing low point, usually ending in a minor low.

Volume trend   The slope of a line found using linear regression on volume data to determine the trend. A rising volume trend means volume generally increases over time; a falling volume trend is one that recedes over time.

Visual Index

This index separates candles patterns by how many lines compose them and then alphabetically within each category.

One-Line Candles

Belt Hold, Bearish, page 118

Belt Hold, Bullish, page 127

Candle, Black, page 146

Candle, Short Black, page 154

Candle, Short White, page 162

Candle, White, page 170

Doji, Dragonfly, page 202

Doji, Gapping Down, page 211

Doji, Gapping Up, page 221

Doji, Gravestone, page 230

Doji, Long-Legged, page 239

Doji, Northern, page 248

Doji, Southern, page 257

Hammer, page 348

Hanging Man, page 365

High Wave, page 409

Long Black Day, page 488

Long White Day, page 496

Marubozu, Black, page 504

Marubozu, Closing Black, page 512

Marubozu, Closing White, page 520

Marubozu, Opening Black, page 528

Marubozu, Opening White, page 536

Marubozu, White, page 544

Rickshaw Man, page 625

Shooting Star, One-Candle,
page 660

Spinning Top, Black, page 694

Spinning Top, White, page 702

Takuri Line, page 720

Two-Line Candles

Above the Stomach, page 89

Below the Stomach, page 108

Dark Cloud Cover, page 182

Doji Star, Bearish, page 266

Doji Star, Bullish, page 276

Engulfing, Bearish, page 308

Three-Line Candles

Abandoned Baby, Bearish, page 70

Abandoned Baby, Bullish, page 80

Advance Block, page 98

Deliberation, page 191

Doji Star, Collapsing, page 285

Downside Gap Three Methods, page 289

Downside Tasuki Gap, page 299

Evening Doji Star, page 326

Evening Star, page 335

Identical Three Crows, page 427

Morning Doji Star, page 588

Morning Star, page 598

Side-by-Side White Lines, Bearish, page 676

Side-by-Side White Lines, Bullish, page 685

Stick Sandwich, page 710

Three Black Crows, page 728

Three Inside Down, page 738

Three Inside Up, page 747

Three Outside Down, page 774

Three Outside Up, page 782

Three Stars in the South, page 790

Three White Soldiers, page 794

Tri-Star, Bearish, page 812

Tri-Star, Bullish, page 820

Two Crows, page 853

Unique Three-River Bottom, page 861

Upside Gap Two Crows, page 879

Upside Gap Three Methods, page 870

Upside Tasuki Gap, page 888

Four-Line Candles

Concealing Baby Swallow, page 178

Three-Line Strike, Bullish, page 765

Three-Line Strike, Bearish, page 756

Five-Line (or More) Candles

8 New Price Lines, page 27

10 New Price Lines, page 38

Subject Index

Page numbers in **bold** refer to chapters; numbers in *italics* refer to illustrations.

929

top-performing, statistics summary, 20–26

trade bearish, 15–16

trade bullish, 15, *16*

unusually tall, 9–10, *10*, 11

yearly price range and, 18–19

Candlestick Charting Explained (Morris), 137

Candle volume, 17–18, 915

CCI (Commodity Channel Index), 2–3

Channel lines, gravestone doji and, 236–237, *237*

Closing black marubozu, **512**, *513*, *518*, *920*

Closing price confirmation:
  performance, definition of, 912
  reversal rate, definition of, 911

Closing white marubozu, **520**, *521*, *526*, *766*, *920*

Collapsing doji star, **285**, *286*, *287*

Color of candles, 537

Commodity Channel Index (CCI), 2–3

Common gap, downside gap three methods and, 289

Concealing baby swallow, **178**, *179*, *180*, *181*, *926*

Confirmation line:
  bearish separating lines and, *643*, *649*
  definition of, 915
  identical three crows and, 434, *434*

Confirming bearish engulfing candle, 774

Congestion area:
  bearish harami cross and, *399*
  bullish doji star and, *281*
  bullish separating lines and, 656, *658*
  deliberation and, *199*, 200
  gapping-up doji and, *222*, *228*
  gravestone doji and, 234–235
  inverted hammer and, *357*
  price breaking out of support zone and, 123
  thirteen new price lines and, *68*
  unique three-river bottom and, *868*
  upside gap three methods and, *877*

Continuation, definition of, 915

Continuation pattern:
  bearish meeting lines and, 571, *571*
  bear market, 23–24

bull market, 22

candles post breakout and, 5–6

exhaustion gap and, 216

falling window as, 898

importance of, 845

last engulfing bottom and, 470, *471*

last engulfing top and, 479, *480*

reversal compared to, 18

stick sandwich as, 710

tweezers top as, 837, *838*

two-candle shooting star as, 669, 674

upside gap two crows as, *880*, 880–881

Continuation performance, definition of, 917

Continuation rank, definition of, 917

Counterattack lines, *see* Meeting lines

Cup with handle, 691–692, *692*

Curving trendline, evening doji star and, *333*

D

Dark cloud cover, **182**, *183*, *187*, *189*, *921*

Data, definition of, 915

Database, standard, 4–5

Deliberation:
  black marubozu and, 509, *510*
  description of, **191**
  examples of, *192*, *193*, *197*, *199*, *924*
  as investment grade candle, 9
  short white candle and, 162–163, *163*

Descending scallop, below the stomach and, *109*

Descending triangle:
  bearish side-by-side white lines and, 683, *683*
  closing black marubozu and, 518, *518*
  deliberation and, *197*
  description of, 1
  example of, *2*
  gapping-down doji and, 219
  gravestone doji and, *231*
  hanging man and, *372*
  short black candle and, 159, *160*
  stick sandwich and, 717, *718*

Diamond bottom, inverted hammer and, *357*

Dividing lines, *see* Separating lines

Tri-star:
  bearish, **812**, *813*, *818*, *925*
  bullish, **820**, *821*, *827*, *925*
Tweezers bottom, **829**, *830*, *835*,
    923
Tweezers top:
  bearish, 517, *518*
  description of, **837**
  examples of, *838*, *844*, *923*
  ladder bottom and, 467, *468*
  stick sandwich and, 717, *718*
  thirteen new price lines and, *68*
  three outside up and, *788*, 789
Twelve new price lines, **49**, *50*, *55*, *57*,
    927
2B pattern, 77
Two black gapping candles, 9, **845**, *846*,
    852, *923*
Two-candle patterns, *921–923*
Two crows:
  bearish meeting lines and, *571*
  description of, **853**
  examples of, *854*, *860*, *925*
  upside gap, **879**, *880*, *886*, *926*

U
Unique three-river bottom, **861**, *862*,
    868, *926*
Unusually tall candles, 9–10, *10*, 11
Upper shadow, 4, *4*
Upside gap three methods, **870**, *871*,
    877, *926*
Upside gap two crows, **879**, *880*, *886*,
    926
Upside Tasuki gap, **888**, *889*, *894*, *896*,
    926
Uptrend:
  bearish belt hold and, *119*
  bearish harami and, 374, *375*
  bearish harami cross and, 392
  bearish separating lines and,
    647
  bearish side-by-side white lines and,
    681
  bearish three-line strike and, 761
  bearish tri-star and, 813, 816
  bullish belt hold and, 132–133
  bullish breakaway and, *144*
  bullish engulfing and, *324*

  bullish side-by-side white lines and,
    686, 690
  bullish three-line strike and, 766, *766*,
    770
  bullish tri-star and, *821*, 825
  deliberation and, 200
  exhaustion gap and, 216
  hanging man and, *366*, 369
  identical three crows and, 427, 432
  inverted hammer and, 361
  ladder bottom and, 465, *465*
  last engulfing bottom and, 475
  long white day and, 500
  matching low and, 565–566
  morning doji star and, 593
  morning star and, 603
  on neck and, 612
  northern doji and, 248–249
  opening black marubozu and, 529
  opening white marubozu and, 537
  rising three methods and, *634*, 638
  short white candle and, 167, *168*
  stick sandwich and, 715, *715*
  Takuri line and, 724, *726*
  three black crows and, 728, 729, 734
  three inside down and, 743, *745*
  three outside up and, 786
  thrusting and, 808
  tweezers bottom and, 833
  two black gapping candles and, 850
  two-candle shooting star and, 673
  upside gap three methods and, 875
  upside Tasuki gap and, 890, 893
Upward breakout:
  bearish meeting lines and, 575, 577,
    578
  bullish side-by-side white lines and,
    692
  candle performance and, 11
  concealing baby swallow and, *181*
  definition of, 5
  doji star and, 271
  eight new price lines, 32, *33*
  hanging man and, 371
  identical three crows and, 427
  inverted hammer and, 357
  last engulfing bottom and, 475
  long white day and, 497
  mat hold and, 558

Printed and bound by CPI Group (UK) Ltd, Croydon, CR0 4YY

31/03/2025

14650511-0001